This is the story of Jane and Chuck, five years married and actors by profession, who give up their happy life in Hollywood to serve their country during World War II.

Chuck joins the Navy, and becomes the gunnery officer on a small minelayer stationed in the Pacific, seeing action in the Solomon Islands, Augusta Bay, Bougainville Strait, and finally Iwo Jima, where his ship is hit.

Jane joins the USO and is sent on a tour of the Pacific, in a troupe headed by the Shakespearean actor, Maurice Evans. Jane is given the lead in the play, *Personal Appearance* and is advised by Evans to bleach her hair platinum to bring out the "blonde personality" of the character. The effect is striking, and Jane creates a sensation everywhere she goes. It's a heady atmosphere, with the five girls constantly surrounded by adoring men. Chuck begins to worry, and cautions her. Jane takes offense.

After playing in the military theatres around Oahu, and doing a variety show in the hospitals, Jane's troupe is sent island hopping throughout the central and south Pacific. The girls are treated as celebrities and invited to meet the other celebrities who are passing through, such as Bob Hope, Dean Martin, and Frank Capra. They also spent time with professional baseball players, such as Joe DiMaggio, who are now enlisted men, getting ready to play in the "mini-world series" Army-Navy game.

As part of their job, the girls are required to talk to the men and socialize with the officers, some of whom try and make Jane forget she's married. Sometimes, she does.

The USO tour concluded after six months, with Jane and Chuck almost, but never quite, meeting until they both returned to San Francisco within a week of each other. Fireworks ensue, with Jane declaring, at the end of one awful evening, that she had enjoyed her illicit love life. Chuck changes tactics, forgiving her and charming her back. He is successful, and subsequently teases Jane about the letters she is receiving from all parts of the Pacific, from men who read more into their evening together at the Officers club than she meant them to. She tries to let them down gently.

Chuck ships out again, and in February, 1945, is involved in the assault on Iwo Jima. His ship is hit, but not sunk, and is towed to Saipan, where Chuck and his fellow officers spend the next several months as the conflict pushes on to Okinawa. They go spear fishing, and souvenir hunting in areas they belatedly find out are still dangerous, and rig up the plumbing system on their damaged ship so they can once again have showers on board. In May, the *Gamble* is towed to Guam to be evaluated. The Navy decides the ship is not worth saving, which upsets Chuck, but the next day he is reassigned to gunnery school in Washington, D.C.

After Jane returns to California, she signs up for another USO tour, of all the Army and Navy hospitals in the United States. This trip has none of the excitement of the first tour, but more of the tragedy. The girls joke with and cheer up ward after ward of enlisted who are burned, blind or amputees, who are doing their best to be brave. The tour has almost reached its ultimate destination, New York, when the narrative ends. The final entry is Chuck's telegram to Jane father, asking him to tell her he's coming.

The letters included convey all of the charm and intimacy of Jane and Chuck's relationship and of the World War II era. To allow the reader to enjoy them as written, the wording and spelling of the original letters are presented intact.

LETTERS
★ FROM THE ★
PACIFIC

A WORLD WAR II ROMANCE
AS TOLD THROUGH
THE LETTERS OF JANE AND CHUCK FLYNN

COMPILED BY KATHY FLYNN DE GAXIOLA
WITH LUZ GAXIOLA FLYNN AND MICA GAXIOLA FLYNN

Published in the USA by:
BearManor Media
PO Box 1129
Duncan, Oklahoma 73534-1129
www.bearmanormedia.com

ISBN 978-1-59393-690-7

Printed in the United States of America.
Book design by Brian Pearce | Red Jacket Press.

TABLE OF
★ CONTENTS ★

For Jane, Chuck, Elizabeth, and Mike.
With thanks to Micaela, Luz, Charles, Hector, Marcia, and Joby.

PRE-WAR
AND
★1941★

[Gran Hotel Alhambra] Malaga
March 23rd 1936

Dear Aunt Gen:

Boy you are one brick! I'll never forget you for this and I mean never! About the dough. Of course it's a loan and I will repay you next summer when I return.

Now about the reason, well let's blame it on the Irish in me. To shorten a long sad story I was walking down a street in Alicante, Spain, wearing my German leather short trousers (they are really very nifty!) Now I've become immune to hoots, giggles, and Bronx cheers after having worn them for 2 months all through Sicily & N. Africa. But on the fateful morning, this man (about 28) got up from the sidewalk cafe where he was sitting and running out to me, grabbed me by the arm and began feeling of the trousers, well I've even had that happen before, but soon he began hanging on to me, and making loud remarks for the for the benefit of his companion who obviously thought him a great wit. I stood all I could, I even counted ten, then I punched him in the chest and he went over backwards on top of a marble topped table loaded with drinks. It fell and broke all the glasses and the table and he came back at me with fight in his eye. He was pretty big and looked tough, but he forgot to keep his chin covered, I put all I had into a smack that hit him on the button. He went down and out. Feeling I'd done a good morning's work when three, not one or two, but three Gendarmes leapt on me. Well they'd seen it all, it later turned out, all, that is, from where I pushed him in the chest. To continue — I was yanked to the city gaol where the intelligent officials spoke neither French, German, or English. In fact before I was through I was surprised they even spoke Spanish!!

The nearest American Consul was 300 miles away. So I wired you. I couldn't ask Dad as he had just cabled me an allowance 10 days before and wouldn't' be able to figure it out, and probably not able to raise the dough.

I guess I hit the guy pretty hard, anyway it broke his lower jaw bone. That cost $50. The restaurant man demanded $12. Well I couldn't do anything but pay. Or spend six weeks in the jail. That seemed liked quite a while to me.

Your money hadn't arrived on Tues noon. (I learned this A.M. It went to N.Y., Madrid, Alicante) so the boy I'm with had a hundred from which he lent me the $62 and we got out of town. If the money from you wasn't here this morning we would have both begun slaving. But Gote si dank you sent it. Boy you're my favorite aunt!!

The trip goes on well. I'm seeing all the great galleries and Operas and such. And I'll be so cultured when I come home you won't know me. We just finished 2000 kms on the bikes yesterday (1,250 miles) through N. Africa, Sicily, and Spain. I'll probably do another 4,000 before I get home.

I will drop you cards along the way (and without requests for money!) If you have time to bang out a letter on the L. C. Smith my address is Charles Flynn Am Express Co Munich, Germany

So again a million thanks, and I think you could tell dad but not mother. She'd worry for months.

Love, Charles

1937

Dear Jane:

I am writing this down, because I doubt if I will be able to tell you tonight exactly what I mean. Oh course I am going out with you, but that will probably upset me being such a rare and undeserved occasion, but I will try to bear up, and not trip over my feet.

Obviously that won't be what I try to tell you, but this is. Once in a while you meet someone, with whom you agree in such entirety that it makes you gasp when you realize it. I was pretty sure that I had met such a person last Sunday when we went swimming, but it wasn't till the other night when Minch and that other drone and myself all called on you, that the full force of the truth laid about my ears like a club. For I found you lovely. Not only to look at, but to talk to, and not only do you talk well, but intelligently, a rarity in these days.

What I am trying to say can be summed up in this. I realized the other night that I am going to like you a lot. If I have ever felt the first quick spark of love, I have felt it with you. Probably nothing will come of it, but on the other hand, something might, and if the advance notices are any indications of the merit of the show, may I go on record as saying it will be a smash hit, if and when it is produced in this town.

So now that you have read this, forget it. No maybe not forget it, but just remember a little of it.

I will tell you what makes me wonder. First I get such a hell of a kick out of just seeing you. Second I like to call you. Third I am looking forward so much to seeing you in a few minutes.

God I am a simple ass — Chas

JANE (True-blue) PATTON.

Honey:

Despite my ripping you apart when we work together, I still think you have millions to offer, or I wouldn't bother to work with you. You have perception & fire and naiveté & youth & sex (yes sex, darling!!!) So you enter the lists well armed!

Remember that Max is only human and his job consists of finding kids like you, who can put guts into it so talk up, made him read the full cue and think please whilst you're a' doin it. Please and let the chips fall where they may. In the old B. H. I am holding that thought, honey!

Love, Chas

2/27/38
Charles Flynn c/o Mountain Inn Kernville California]

Dearest Chuck:

I am sitting here alone, and it is such a marvelous nite. Jerry is gone and I have just come in from my cousin's in Glendale. For some reason the sounds from the boulevard are clearer than I ever heard them before.

So very much has happened since you left, and it seems such a long time. Thousands of ideas for our one-acts have come up, and we have a director — a Mr. Price who is one of the directors of "Gone with the Wind," and what do you think — we are planning to do "Coriolanus" like Orson Wells is doing — "Caesar" and have the adaptation practically all planned. Last nite was a late session here with Chet & Bob & Jerry & Doug and I arguing about Fascism and the play's message — and feverishly reading speeches. We are also looking at Restoration comedies and at E. Rice's "Not for Children." Mr. Price thought Chet's was a fine play. Also "Mr. Rosy" and "Literature." If you were only here, they would probably do "Bavarian Idyll." Mr. Price has thousands of marvelous ideas, and now we are beginning to really have something.

But most important to you is the fact that your mother & father went as planned on Friday morning. They were over for a long visit Thursday evening, and I did so hate to see them go. They were a bit perturbed about a man who saw me in the Biltmore found out where I lived and was there when I came. He wanted to introduce me to Sid Grauman, Archie Mayo, etc., because he "was attracted by my appearance." He was a bit "shifty-eyed" though, so I "called the whole thing off" (an oil salesman). They left your things here with lots of messages, and some cookies for you - anyway half of them for you. We talked and talked & talked, and they are going to go see my mother.

Sophie's letter came — you will read it when you return, but no recommendations for one acts except "Bury the Dead" and "Waiting for Lefty" — She wants to know about the "75 a week." Also there are two letters for you — one from Parker Williams and one from Europe - I hesitate to send them with this because this probably won't reach you.

It will probably rain here tomorrow.

Darling, I have just been reading your letter, and I can really say that it is the most wonderful one I have ever received - everything about it. So if you go to N.Y., and when you do, that will be some help.

Our store in the bank was still there today, although it is beginning to look bigger & bigger as my $4.99 deposit looms before my eyes. It is mostly yours now.

Please, Dear, have a good time & do as much work as you can for them, think about me once in a while and I'll see you next week.

My love — Jane

P.S. We have enough wine bottles for two qts., so when you come back we can have a celebration. Your mother brought me so many good things. She said you liked the Worcestershire sauce. They were so nice and they went off holding hands.

Goodnite dear,

Jane

March 24, 1938
Mrs. E. M. Flynn 1321 Grand Ave Everett, WA

Dear Mother:

All set? All right, here goes. Jane and I are married! Now that you have recovered from the shock a little, I will go into more detail.

This all happened two weeks ago, on the eighth of March as a matter of fact. We had been to a rehearsal of our one acts and had stopped for a glass of beer at the Hof Brau Garden. With us was Chet Huntley and wife, Bill Bryan and wife. Chet is one of our group, and went to school at Washington as did his wife. I knew them both up there, and they are grand people, Chet is an announcer at KFI as is Bill. Well we were talking about this and that and Chet said "Why don't you kids get married?" We said oh no, we were waiting, and then they went to work on us. Well they didn't go to work till the next day at four so we piled into Chet's new car and drove down to Mexico and got married. Ten thirty in the morning with the four of them as witnesses.

I have done a lot of things in my life that takes guts, but I don't think I was ever so scared as I was as that morning after we went through San Diego!!! Boy Jane and I were both a mass of jitters. But Ingrid, Chet's wife, lent us her ring for the ceremony, and it was really something to remember. Nuts I know, but different, and cheaper than something like Peter went through with.

Well we came back home, and Jerry moved over to her girlfriend's house for a couple of days, but the second night just as we were about ready for bed comes a knock on the door, and it was Janie's mother and father, they had never seen me before in their lives, so you can imagine. Mr. Patten was absolutely swell, just took it all in his stride, Mrs. Patten kinda went to pieces, but she is all right now, and all for me. The old man liked me right from the word go though. In order to make it seem a little more planned, he has told everybody up north that we are engaged and Mrs. Patten is staying down another week, and when she goes home she will announce us married. Seems kinda silly to Jane and me but whatever they want is jake with me.

I know what you are thinking, that we should have waited. But why mother? Jane and I are both capable of earning money, and we spend a lot more living apart than we ever would together. We can get along just fine, there may be times when we could use a little more money, but every young couple has a struggle for a while. And together it doesn't make any difference. Our love goes bigger and deeper every day. And it's going to keep on doing that.

I would have told you a long time ago, but we were trying to keep it secret, until it was all established. Now that it is all settled with the Pattens, I told Jane last night that I was going to write and tell you today, "Give her my love, and tell her we are sorry if she feels that we should have waited" Jane said. Please understand, Mommy, and give us the well-known blessing.

I know how you feel losing your only son, but there was never a sweeter nor nicer girl in the world than Jane , and you know yourself that I will be a lot more steadied down and responsible as a result of this.

Have you sold the old car yet? And if not, could we have it? I don't know how we will get it here exactly but there is still a lot of automobile in that Studie and Mrs. Flynn and I could sure use it. Mrs. Charles Flynn. That was the first thing I said after we were married. In fact I said it twice, I liked the sound of it so well.

And another thing, fellows. It cost twenty-five bucks to get married down there. I know it's scandalous, but after we went that far to get married, we had to go through with it. Consequently I am a little low, and as Jane and I want to move into the apartment she and Jerry are living in now on the first of the month: Well what I am hinting at amounts to this. If you could send me fifty bucks as a wedding present, it would sure smooth out a lot of rocks, but now don't think you are going to be responsible for us, oh no, we are standing on our two feet, and taking on all comers!!! I have a job lined up to work a few hours a night in a gas station at the corner of Franklin and Highland, this would leave my days free for acting, that is if nothing big breaks in the next few days. Jane worked yesterday, and made eleven bucks, what a wife!!! So if I can get the rent paid $32.50 and buy a little food, we are all set. We have decided to use Jane's money for a while, but as soon as we can get by on what I earn, we are going to put Jane's earning in a special savings account. So when we are both stars, we will already have a slug in the bank.

Besides acting in two of the one acts, I am also directing a third, and as I called a rehearsal for one o'clock, and it is now 12:20 I have to close and take my shower and catch some lunch.

I am sending this air mail-special so you will be sure to get it tomorrow, so sit down and answer it when you have cooled off a little, and tell me about the car and stuff.

I feel like a tramp doing this to you mother, but after all, you knew it was coming before you left for home so it is not quite such as shock as it was to Mrs. Patten. I really have to go now, but forgive me mammy and pappy, but I love the gal-

All my love to you both,

Charles

P.S. Don't tell anyone 'till I give the word — O.K.?

P.P.S. I sure beat Park and Dave and Eddie, huh? Ha ha!!!

March 30, 1938

Dear Daddy;

I remember getting out of the car two weeks ago Wednesday morning - telling you that I was going to try to put all my thanks and appreciation to you in a letter. Truly, there are very few people lucky enough to have a father who would have acted as you did in such a situation. No person has ever aroused so great a respect in me for them, and I'm certainly glad it was you. Don't think I fail to realize how difficult it must have been for you. Such calmness and analysis and impartiality was — well I can only say it was overwhelming, and that I only hope I can follow your example in the difficulties of my life. Please don't think I am gushing or insincere — I am trying my best to express my feelings to you.

Now, as to the development of the present situation Mother has probably told you all about it. For reasons which I have discussed with her, I would much prefer not having a second marriage. She seems to agree with me. So, to make appearances reasonable, we secured a license and will tell everyone we married on Friday. There don't seem to be any loopholes in this arrangement, because the licenses are published in the paper but the marriages are not.

There were many reasons for coming to a definite decision right at this time. In the first place it was necessary to preserve the - shall we say, happiness of this. A much longer delay would have spoiled everything. Besides, we now have enough money to get started and a little coming in all the time, so we will be able to get along pretty well. In the second place, some decision had to be made about our place by the first of the month. Rent has to be paid in advance on the first and some arrangement had to be made in regard to Jerry, etc. As the situation stands now, Jerry will stay here for a week or longer with Mother and they can keep the place as long as they like. If you and Mary come down spring vacation, which I am ardently hoping you will, then you can stay here because Jerry is going to Balboa for eleven days...so please do come...I am longing to see Mary...I think it would be marvelous. Mother and I have just been talking about it. Perhaps you could drive Chuck's car down. Staying here would make it very inexpensive. Mother is wondering when spring vacation starts. Mother must have told you about the little house we found today. It is a perfect dream. I have described it quite fully to Ma Wee and you will probably see it soon.

I made $16.50 yesterday at Warner Brothers, so that helps. A few more of those and I will be pretty well set.

I am glad you talked to the Flynns and liked them. They were perfectly wonderful about it all.

This may all seem terribly hasty to you, Daddy, but I realize how important it is to get started on an "open" basis as soon as possible if everything is not going to be spoiled. I am very happy about it and so is Chuck, and I am sure that with cooperation and hard work and scraping we can make it work and get a long way.

Daddy, for everything I thank you again and again and again.

All my love, Jane

Mr. and Mrs. J. P. Paten 3854 42nd N.E. Seattle, Washington
Friday, October tenth 1941
Beachwood Studio

Dearest Mother and Daddy;

It seems that I am carrying on most of my correspondence from this theatre. Last night during rehearsal, I wrote Mary a letter and tonight I am writing you one. But I have had to spend so much time here lately, a great deal of the time doing nothing, that it seems the logical thing to do.

I can't tell you my emotions on opening that envelope and finding that present from you. My first impulse was surprise and the second joy and the third to send it back. I honestly don't think much of myself that I didn't. I should have but I yielded to my weaker impulses. I can't tell you how very very much I appreciated it but I really do feel guilty for accepting it. I never would have kept it if Aunty Nell hadn't told me about a timber deal. It shouldn't have swayed me but it did ease my conscience a bit, I must confess, although it shouldn't have. I am going on at a great rate here, am I not. What I am trying to say is that I love you for sending it and it supplied a great deal of throat ease...really it did...it paid for it...and thank you so terribly much but I shouldn't have kept it and I do feel guilty about it. But I won't say that I couldn't use it. I certainly could. That's where the temptation came in. Throat ease really does come high. It was of awfully good use. Thanks a million. I was so surprised. Manna from heaven.

Chuck and I went on a very fine interview yesterday. Buck arranged it for us. It seems that at Paramount they are going to do a movie of the play "Out of the Frying Pan" that ran on Broadway last year. It is the story of a bunch of young actors and actresses living together...on a very high moral plane...and the troubles they go through trying to get jobs. The director, Mr. Griffiths, is going to do it. Well he is looking for some unknown young people. Naturally they will want to look at the people at Paramount first but after that, they will go outside the studio and Buck suggested us...told them that we were naturals for it. So we went to see Mr. Griffith's assistant and he seemed to be very enthusiastic about us. Of course they won't really get on it for about a month, but cross your fingers. It would really be a good deal to even get some interest about it. He simply raved about our pictures-said we were real life models of what they were looking for. I hope he is not a kidder.

I wrote a letter to Mary last night trying to persuade her to come down here as soon as possible. We are really terribly anxious to have her, I can't tell you how very anxious we are. We talk about it all the time so please put the deal over for her to come. If she wants to get a job here, it could be easily accomplished. The place is booming and they are really to be very easily had. I hope I conveyed to her how really anxious we were to see her. Let me know as soon as possible when we can expect her so that I can fix things up for her. Now I will be terribly unhappy if she doesn't come. Bear that in mind.

This part of the letter is for Mary. Johnny is with us now. We think he is simply swell-such a nice boy. He called last night as I said, and Chuck picked him up this morning and brought him out. We didn't do anything exciting, but he seems to be having a good time. Chuck had to work on flats for the play this afternoon so we came over to the theatre a little while and then drove around and went home. We had to be at rehearsal at six so we had an early dinner and came over here. He said he would love to see the rehearsal when we asked him so he is here too and watching them work on the third act. He is going to spend the night with us...on the studio couch. Bob Marinaro found it comfortable for two weeks, so I dare say he will like it alright. We took the wooden back off it so it is really better now than when Bobby Patten slept on it. He is staying way out in Huntington Park so we thought that was too far for him to go tonight and we like him so well that we would love to have him with us. He doesn't seem a bit shy. He thinks Mary has the most wonderful disposition of anyone he has ever met. In fact, he thinks she's "a queen of a girl."

[CHANGES TO HANDWRITTEN]

Well, I am really feeling better now. (I gave up the typewriter because Margaret Douglas wanted to use the typewriter to type her part) That sulfanilamide really turned the trick. I am feeling quite fine but don't have much ambition. That medicine takes it out of you. I am trying to take it as easy as possible however because I don't want to run another week. I am afraid that everyone is going to think I'm lazy.

You will be awfully happy to hear that last week we got rid of all our cats but Tuffy — Shakespeare and Rosiland are gone. The

Humane Society, upon receipt of fifty cents for each cat, found homes for them. It's a great relief and a great saving, I must admit.

I would love to write more, but I have to go into the rehearsal now and I would like to get this mailed tonite, so I'll have to give you my love and thanks. And if I have a chance, I'll write some more.

So much love, Jane

I got a lovely letter form Ma Wee yesterday which I'll answer tomorrow nite.

Love, Jane and Chuck

★1942-1943★

Monday afternoon

Honey

Just time to write a line to you to let you know that I am thinking of you, and missing you like hell. It seems impossible to realize
that you have only been gone since Friday, seems like it has been
at least a month. I am glad you remembered to write me from the
city, just got it this afternoon. I suppose you had some fun at the
fair, can't say as I blame you. As you might have expected, I have
been a thoroughly bad boy ever since you left. Friday night Jim,
Buck, Chet, Frank Graham, and a boy named Jack La Fonda, or
some such, all went out together. Out to the S.S. Rex. I only had
a dollar, and I lost that. Buck didn't go out there with us, but the
rest of us had a lot of fun, and temporarily won a lot of dough, but
of course we lost it all back. We got in the habit of saying "on the
beam," you know, the expression that Phil Harris corns up. Well
everything was "on the beam," are you still "on the beam." We have
really worked it to death. Chet stayed out all night with us, and I
guess mammy was plenty peeved. The next night was Sat. and Jim
and I tried to find something to do, but no one seemed to be home,
we tried Jack Brander, and Will's and all around, so I took him
home at ten. As I was driving back, I went by the Wilshire Ebell
and as it was an Intermission I went in. I saw Soph, and stayed and
saw the rest of the play. Then afterward I went backstage and saw
the kids, and Nina Gabrowlitch, you know Mark Twain's grand-
daughter invited me up to a party at her apt. Mary and Jack and
Jena Douglas and some Russians and some others, and we drank
and listened to records and stayed 'till the manager threw us out.
So that was Sat. But yesterday I was the worst of all. Jim and I
took two Girls to a movie, and fed them a hamburger afterward, I
know I am a devil, but I didn't have any fun at all, and I was Not
a bad boy in any sense of the word. You don't need to worry about
me darling and stay as long as you like, that is, not over five or

six days. Honey I do miss you so terribly, please let's not ever get separated again, I feel like something is wrong with me, like I just lost half of my mind, or I only have one leg or something.

It isn't that I miss you, it just is that I am not really alive while you are gone. I love you my little perisphere, and until you get back, I will be "on the beam" with Marc, and Narcissa, and "Try-lon" later. If you know what I mean. I realize it wasn't good so don't read it. Thanks. love — love — love — love —

Chas

To: Mrs. Jane Flynn
The Challenger
2041 Ivan Ave
Los Angeles Hollywood, California
Dec. 29, 1942
Tues nite

Dearest Honey:

Well here I am about to come into Salt Lake City — and every mile is one farther away from you — God Damn It!

I was so proud of you at the station last night so beautiful and so brave, you've got the stuff kid!

I know you were sharing thoughts with me last night — I felt it as I lay awake in my berth — and the last thing I did was to say "Goodnight Honey" "I love you."

Whoever wrote that bilge about "Parting being such sweet sorrow" must have been a real Jerk! It's just an aching tearing pain — isn't it?

Now that I've probably made you cry, I'll try not ever to go on in this vein again. The die is cast so let's tough it through.

The kids all seem like very nice boys and we have some pretty good discussions — Albert & Jones and a couple of others. So we will live.

The scenery has been beautiful today — the sun is just going down now, but across the valley behind Salt Lake huge recumbent mountains laden with snow look almost complacent in their quiet repose — I image they are 60-80 miles away, but the air is so clear over here that fairly loom up.

The food is excellent, we eat first of anyone at 6:45!! Sausage, eggs, potatoes, rolls and fries for breakfast, roast veal & choc pudding for lunch, and Swiss Steak & ice cream for dinner — with all trimmings.

We are now going around the lake and I want to look at what little I can see as the sun is just dipping out of sight. — I'll write every day — at least a card — and I love you honey — Bless you!

Goodnight Honey Chas

P.S. Say hello to Giddy, Kathy & Toughie Two!

[To: Mrs. Jane Flynn
Physicians & Surgeons Hospital Glendale, California
Original address: 2041 Ivan Ave. Letter re-routed to hospital]

Dearest Honey:

Well here we are in old, cold, windy Chicago. To tell the truth it isn't so cold as I thought it would be, but not quite as warm as South Cal by about 60°.

While this hasn't been a bad trip — food good, nice kids etc., still it is long and boring and wearisome.

We lost half of our boys here this morning — they go to U. Western, & 14 of us go on to Cornell! About six of us stuck together after lunch and I know I amazed them by suggesting the Chicago Art Museum. They all came, however, but I feel some of them suffered their first encounter with Kultur!

A couple of them really seemed to like it, and I of course loved it. They had some remarkably good Impressionists, and I did so enjoy it. I picked up a couple of cards I thought you might enjoy — hope you do.

We are here for an eight hour stop — over, so I guess we will go to a flicker when I finish this. I really haven't much to tell except as you see we are writing this from the Palmer House and some delightful string music is welling up from the main dining room — Strauss yetz!

I hope you haven't been too lonesome, but hold tight and Mary will be down soon. I will write when I get to Cornell tomorrow and air-mail address.

all my love Honey...Chas

P.S. Pull for U.C.L.A. tomorrow! I will be too

Monday nite.

Dearest Honey:

Oh God honey I wish I had the time to really write you and tell you in detail how much I love & miss and need you! I think about you all the time, and I have been getting so many wonderful letters from you, it just makes me eager to get home to read them they really do help a lot, so keep them coming honey — I sure need them.

I hope the wire didn't scare you, but I got a swell letter from you yesterday, with all those letters from Mom & Dad & Bob and another letter to me here. I just reveled in them. I thought that letter from my family to you was one of the sweetest I had ever read. They are really top-drawer. I got another letter from you today and also one from Mom and she said you had written her the nicest letter back. That's swell honey & keep it up.

To get back to you — Don't you ever think I am not missing you — I get so lonesome for you at times — God! I am glad for that reason they pile the work — it doesn't give me time to think.

I have exactly 2 1/2 hours to study now and here is what: 100 pages of Naval Customs, traditions, & Usages. — 10 trig problems — 100 navy terms to look up — the names of all parts of a cruiser — 30 pages of Navy Regulations (dry as dust!) and a test on local rules for the running of this station 60 page booklet.

All that for tomorrow — to do it right it's about ten hours work, at least 3 for the Math alone!

Friday I signed a lot of stuff in my file, and I saw my commission signed by Knox. Guess when I got it! Nov. 19th. That's something of a record as I sent in the papers on Nov. 3rd — only two days over 2 weeks ago!!

Well in two weeks I'll be beautiful in my new gimp! I wish you could be here to see me get it — oh honey — do I!

Well honey the grind goes on and I must get to study — damn it! But keep up the letters and the chin. Try to find out how soon you could fly back here. One of the other boy's wife is coming and we thought maybe we could get a furnished house for both families company for you both during the week and a better deal on rent than an apt. they run from $60-120 a month furnished for a single, but a nice big house for about $80. What do you think? All my love darling honey — Chas X XXX XXX

P.S. I am thrilled about Kathie, tell her to be a good girl for me!
P.P.S. All my love to Hazel!!!

Mrs. Charles Flynn 3854 42nd Ave. N.E. Seattle, Wash.
Letter number three
June 16, 1943

Darling;

I have felt so badly all day because I skipped writing you yesterday. I hope the two parts of the letter I wrote you the day before
will make up for it a little. It wasn't that I wasn't thinking of you,
but it was such a day. I got up early, scrubbed all the floors and
quite a job it was, and then took the laundry down and went up
to Pat's and left the slip and the money and then carried the beer
bottles up to Ollie's...I did it all in one trip, too. Then I finished
packing the bags and returned things and had a sandwich with
her and got dressed and went down and found a cab and loaded
the bags in and went down to that awful baggage room in the
Ferry building and checked the ones that were to go to Seattle. I
was there way over an hour just waiting and nearly going crazy.
Finally I begged one of the men to wait on me so that I wouldn't
miss the train to Monterey and he condescended to do it. Then I
took the two bags to go to Monterey and the typewriter and got
another cab and I really got stuck because it was one of those
darned limousines. I went over to the other station and had a boy
put the bags on the train for me because they wouldn't check them,
having no baggage car. Then I bought a ticket and got on the train
and just absolutely collapsed! Add to all that, we are having a
recurrence of that hot weather of a few weeks ago and I was just
sopping wet. Then the train was a close rival of the Lehigh valley
line. Well, I finally got to Betty's and naturally wasn't good for
anything. We had dinner and a few drinks and rather sat around
talking 'til about midnight.

This morning I got up at eight o'clock and helped with Mickey
and did this and that, and then we went for lunch and the afternoon to a friend of Betty's who lives out of town a little way. Her
husband is a lieutenant-colonel stationed at Fort Ord. They have
a lovely rambling house and around a hundred and seventy-five

acres with goats and horses and chickens and a big garden and a complete dog kennel which is a joy to behold.

Anyway it was very nice if a little more quiet and interior decoraty than I am accustomed to. I bought two newspapers just now so I could read the news of the world because nobody down here seems to pay much attention to it. The funniest thing is that Charlie Chaplin has eloped with Eugene O'Neill's daughter. I bought one paper just to read that article. The other was the Chronicle with the really important news in it.

Betty is terribly excited tonight because Mike is coming home in a little while. He called last night and said he might be able to get up here. He couldn't stay but a day, but that is something. She is constantly looking out of the windows and worrying that they were driving too fast or something. However, he should be here in a few minutes.

Mickey is just as cute as ever and he can stand up by himself now. Today I taught him to do a little trick we call "round and round." He is supposed to make his hands go in circles but I guess that requires too much coordination from a baby so he just makes his arms go up and down. I have been trying to teach him to say Jane but he doesn't seem to be able to quite manage it. I have thought of his saying Chuck but hesitated to try for fear that it would have scandalous results if you know what I mean.

I believe I told you that I would be in Seattle next Sunday afternoon. I disregarded your injunctions and took the sit — up train because I saved eleven dollars in one night and it did seem worth it considering their state of finances. Besides it won't be so bad and I'd feel guilty if I didn't, so I beg your pardon for disobeying you. I know you probably must have more important things on your mind than the type of my railroad ticket, but these are the things I am doing and I want to tell you about them.

Mike came home and what a reception he got. It made me feel pretty envious. I hope it won't be too long, darling, before I can kiss you hello. I just live for that day.

Honey, that is all the news. I just can't tell you how much I miss you and love you. I'm afraid it would make you feel bad instead of good, but if you want to feel good that I love you so much, you can... because I just can't imagine anybody loving anybody more than I do you. All my love darling and goodnight until tomorrow.

Love, love, love, love, love, love, love...Jane

Mrs. Charles Flynn 3854 42nd Ave. N.E. Seattle, Wash.
June 19, 1943
Letter number four

Darling;

Well here I am on my way north from San Francisco. We passed all the places that I wanted you to look at when you wanted to play rummy just a bit ago. It gives me an awful pang when I think we were coming the opposite way and so hoping that we would have a few days together. Now it is all over and I'm on my way home. But it won't be long again before we are going someplace wonderful together. Even on trains we have fun which is really saying something.

Well, honey, Monterey was grand. I am so happy and grateful to you for insisting that I go. I was busy every moment of the time what with the things that Betty had arranged and with helping her with Mickey and painting. I must admit I am ready to die from sheer fatigue, now but it certainly did keep me busy. Last night I painted a desk for her with Fuller soft lite paint. It had been quite a day. In the morning I helped around and then went shopping for a tie for Daddy and something for a house gift. I got Mickey some beads and a little T shirt and Betty, Mike, and Matt each one of those little cigarette lighters that work in the wind built on the same principal as a Zippo. I don't know why I didn't get myself one while I was about it. I was awfully worried when Mike came home about my being there — that they wouldn't have a chance to be alone. Matt realized the situation so he took me to dinner at Del Monte Thursday night which was very considerate of him. So they had dinner "en famille" and that evening had people in, serving sherry just like we do. It was a wondrous and delightful gathering — one of everything and they were all simply fascinated with each other. There were that crazy artist Yonka Varda, and his wife. He is really terribly interesting because he has an amazing interest in everyone else. Also a Lieutenant Colonel Adams and his wife — friends of Izzy's, incidentally. Then that Polly who runs the Mexican Idol shop and another artist. It was really something. Yesterday I saw a bunch of their Italian fisherman friends who are pretty dull but very sweet. "in their own vulgar way," as Betty says, so I am not being catty.

Honey, you have no idea what a help it all was. What with being determined not to be emotional and being so busy, the week has gone by pretty well. Yesterday afternoon though, it just came over me with a bang that you weren't there, so I had to go out and pace up and down in the garden trying not to let anybody see or myself get weepy over how terribly I love you and miss you.

I have finished your sweater, darling, and shall mail it Monday morning. The yarn is all ready to go for the next one.

This car is really the best I have ever been on. Set-up or no. I think they must have taken it off the Daylight. I am going to change my dress for the night, relax, and enjoy myself. I had a 5 hour stopover today and spent it at Pat's. Before she got home I locked myself out of her house and had to borrow a ladder from Ollie to get over the fence!! I think of you and love you all the time, darling. We will see each other soon. All the love there is to you, honey,

Jane

Thurs Night 7:00

Dear Honey:

This is Just going to be a line as I have Watch duty tonight from 10-12 and 3 tests tomorrow.

I was of course awfully upset and unhappy when I talked to Hazel last night. I had tried to call you Tues. but got no answer so I imagined you were out to dinner with some of our friends.

Hazel said everything will be okay if you take it easy — I hope and pray so honey, but if the worst should happen it would be awfully unfortunate but nothing that time and another chance couldn't remedy. There will always be a tomorrow and it will be bright — believe me so whatever way it turns out know that I am with you a thousand percent and what will be will be.

Gad, I sound like Cotton Mather on the pulpit. Well now to cheer you up — so far I have kept up on my math assignments don't ask me how, I've covered two years of algebra in two day! And we have spent 2 days on logarithms & square roots of logs. And I didn't even know what the word meant until yesterday! We have the test tomorrow and I think I have a chance to pass it. If I can get through math I will be a deck officer of the line instead of Armed Guards so I am breaking my back.

Oh, also today I was appointed platoon leader of my platoon. About 60-65 men. I march them to class, fall them in, etc. There are only 2 student platoon leaders & a company commander out of 175 men, so I am one of the 3 — not bad, huh!

I really know my stuff in marching men, and I got along fine today, even drew a word of faint praise from our instructor officer. "That's the way to sing out a command, Flynn" says he.

Well chicken, back to the grind. I hope you are home tonight and all okay — and tell Hazel how wonderful she is to rally `round like she did — what a mom! I trust the animals haven't ruined the house and are still eating. Give them my love'& try and send the things I asked for as soon as possible.

If you have an extra $5 or so (Izzy?) you might send it — I have had to buy so much stuff I have only 32 cents left. God honey I love you — Good luck — Chas

Cornell, Ithaca, N.Y. Wednesday
1:00. 1/29/43

Dearest Honey: —

Well we just finished lunch and stood a formation that was supposed to take us to our one o'clock class, which is drill. But for some reason it is called off, so we have an extra hour to study, so I will snitch a few minutes, but only a few to write to you.

Am I amazed! My grades last Friday were 3 in number, 2 of them finals for the courses. In one I got 3.3 in the other 3.55 — But then in math they decided all above 1.0 was passing and I got 2.6!! Don't ask me how, I am not sure myself as it was advanced Geom and Trig., but there it is. Out of my class of 63, over 20 got less than 1.0 and only 12 of us were over 2.0, so I guess the lad can apply himself when the chips are down.

Although the scuttle-butt (rumor) has it that a large percentage will go in as Armed Guard — there will be a percentage of us who will become officers on regular naval vessels. That is what I am working so hard on. But as I say — it's all rumor — maybe we all go to Armed Guard — maybe none of us, but if grades have any bearing, I am going to see that mine are high enough to get the best deal.

Yesterday in 3 quizzes (all of which count in courses) I got 3.5, 3.6 and 4.0, so you see I am working hard. I hope all this grade talk isn't boring to you, as it is the most important thing in our lives here — work — study — drill — take tests — and then wait for the grades to be posted! I am well in the top 10% now — maybe even in the top 5% — See!!

The weather here has been atrocious. Sunday it was about 35 and thawed and then rained, but from 5:00 Sunday night on the rain froze — so when we arose at 5:50 Monday there was 1/2 of solid ice over everything. It must have been laughable seeing us trying to get up the hills to our classes! Of course they cindered all roads & walks later in the morning so it wasn't bad. Then yesterday it rose to about 40° and everything melted. About 5:00, just before chow last night it started to blow clear. The wind is still blowing very hard and the temp at noon was 10° above — at formation this morning it was 5° below — brother is this a cold spot — "High above Cayuga' s waters" Nuts! Give me S. Cal...any time. Paper says colder tonight and tomorrow — it ain't possible!!

One note of humor, one of our instructors yesterday (a regular old Navy man) with lots of combat service in this and the last war bemoaning his fate in class yesterday. "How will I explain to my grandchildren," says he, "that I spent most of this war attached to the 'Lake Cayuga Task Force!' " He got a big laugh.

The classes usually, however, are devoid of any humor, and the prime objective of all instructors seems to be to cram as much useless, dry and outdated crap pertaining to the Navy down your throats in their 50 minutes per day as they can. I doubt, for instance, that the fact that the "Constitution" carried 55 guns; carronades & long guns combined against the British " Guerriere's" 49 guns (primarily carronades) is going to help me a hell of a lot when I am trying to line up a "3" deck rifle on a Fokke — Nulfe that is trying to lift me out of the water! But then it's the Navy way.

There is a popular saying here — "There are two ways to do a thing, the right way, and the Navy way!" Don't get me wrong, Honey, I like it even though it's hard to find time to light a cig. I suppose I was just letting off steam because of the fact that our math instructor this morning took 11 minutes to explain spherical triangles. They involve Geom, Trig (of the highest order) and the Logarithmic interpretation & interpolation of sides and angles!! In college they take a year to teach it — we cover it in 11 minutes by the clock! We don't waste much time here.

I had no letters from either you or Mom yesterday and none this A.M. Perhaps one will come this aft. I hope so. I am wondering if you are up today — this was to be it wasn't it? I am hoping so, darling. When I think that you have been in bed almost 3 weeks my heart aches for you. I must admit to a tinge of envy however. Gad, imagine being able to sleep in the mornings!

I just wish I could see you for a few minutes, Darling. I am so lonesome for the sight of you! Are you as pretty as the girl I say "Good night, Honey. I love you" to every night? Better keep your hair combed & your snappers shined up as that girl is completely out of this world!!

Honey, I do love you so much — never forget those last 5 years however the cards turn up — as far as I'm concerned, it was 5 years of holding a straight flush! Royal, too!!!

Well, Baby Girl, I hope all is well with you, and that you are up. This note I was going to dash off has used up nearly all of my extra study hour. But I couldn't have spent it better.

Will Hazel stay on for a while after Mary arrives? Tell her how wonderful I think she is, and that all the interior decor sounds wonderful!

All my love, Honey XXX Chas

Sunday night, June 13, 1943
Letter one

My Darling:

Well, sweetheart, it's the end of the first day and I can't say that it's been very short or very joyful. But it's one of the days over with and I can feel a little better with every one that passes because I know you'll be back that much sooner. It's the darndest thing how empty everything is...but enough of that...I can't go on crying to you about how much I miss you...you aren't on a vacation cruise yourself and it won't improve matters much to have me weeping about how much I miss you.

I have worked pretty hard today which was good. But I fell and hurt my back so it has been a bit of a struggle. I am much afraid that old tail-bone...better known by coccyx or something of the sort is cracked again...however if it is, it just means some adhesive tape from here to there. If it isn't better in the morning, I'll go find out. First, however, I will laboriously hoist myself in a hot tub and see if that will help matters. Now I am all packed and if things go as planned, I will take the four o'clock train to Monterey tomorrow and leave there Friday morning to get into Seattle on Saturday night...if it can be done.

I kept in touch with Pat last night but didn't go up there. She was pretty tired and wanted to go to bed and the Commander and Sue seemed to want to buy us drinks. I just couldn't believe that you wouldn't be back...after I walked away from there, I would have given anything in the world for just one more look at you. It was just awful. Anyway, Vivian stayed here last night but she didn't feel very well this morning and went back to her room to have a nap and get things packed. I will meet her in the morning. I went up to Pat's late this afternoon and started a new sleeve for you...if I mail it in the next few days, it will get there almost as quickly as you do. I ate with them and sat and listened to the radio.

Darling, we've had so much fun the last month that it is just wonderful to look back on it and that is what I try to keep thinking about. But I want to be sure to get out of Number one, August Alley tomorrow because everything here reminds me of you and that is definitely not good. I talked to Daddy this morning and he is sending me some money. Buddy was home but is going right back. I know this letter and its news will be pretty ancient by the time you get it, but, honey, I'll just write it as if you would get it the next day. You take care of yourself, darling. The day you come home will be the happiest of all the five years we've had. I love you with all my heart. Now I will hie myself to a hot bath and bed but I'll have no shoulder to sleep on...not even your pillow. I'll write again tomorrow honey...it will take you hours to read the letters you will have waiting for you. I love you so much, darling...be good...I have no pen so I have to type my name.

Love, love, love

Jane

Mrs. Charles Flynn
3854 42nd Ave. N.E. Seattle, Washington
June 14, 1943
Letter Two

Darling;

Well, this is the end of the second day and it has been a wee bit better...I am getting a little more numb at the edges and can at least smile at a good joke now. Yesterday was ghastly but I'll learn and practice. Today was at least a little bit adventuresome. I went to Treasure Island all on my own...got a pass and everything. When I went I wasn't so happy about it, but I could appreciate the sights on leaving in my relief. Remember I told you I fell yesterday. Anyway, it was a lot worse this morning and I really thought I'd better take advantage of that medical service offered. I got up very early thinking that if everything was alright, I would be able to arrange about my ticket to Seattle, check the bags and take the train to Monterey after I finished with the Navy. Well I got into the doctor very soon only to have him tell me after feeling around that my coccyx bone was all twisted and he thought it was fractured and he was pretty sure I had fractured the fifth lumbar vertebra or something of the sort...and that I should get over to Treasure Island immediately and get an X-ray because it might be very serious if I let it go. Well, that threw me into a panic. I could just see myself in a cast and of course it began to hurt worse. By the time I got over there at one o'clock, I was practically a hospital case. That was just the crowning touch. Well; they took them and finally at two — thirty they informed me that nothing was broken...two were out of place and they pushed them back in and recommended hot baths. What a relief. That Navy medical business is just wonderful. They gave me medicine and sleeping tablets all for nothing and those terribly expensive X-rays. Anyway, it's beginning to feel just fine and I'm so relieved that it makes it feel that much better. You might know that as soon as you get out of town, I would fall. You had been threatening me with it for days.

Well, by the time that was all over, it was three o'clock and I couldn't possibly get things done to go today so I am going tomorrow. I went up in that awful bedlam and got a ticket to Seattle. I had planned on Friday, but the earliest thing I could get was Saturday which will put me there on my birthday and Father's Day, which is a good time to get anyplace. Vivian can't go to Monterey and I'm awfully sorry. It seems that she either had to wait two weeks for a reservation or take the train tomorrow morning on a cancellation. Those were the only two possibilities. So she is going at six-thirty in the morning. I have just bade her goodbye. We bought a little gift for Pat and Annie and signed all four of our names to it...I thought you would be glad to know. It was a glass brick vase with a frog shaped like two lily leaves and is very attractive.

It looks around here just like it did when we came, only cleaner. All the bags are piled in the middle of the floor...everything I want I have to fetch out of a suitcase and put back in when I finish. I thought it would just kill me to be here this long, but it isn't so bad because This is continued to part two...

Love, Jane

Letter two, part two
June 14, 1943

Honey...I will just continue from the last part...because I can just look around here and think of all the happy times we have had. It almost makes it seem as if you were just up at Ollie's getting the beer. If only you were...but you were for a whole month and that is what I'll remember.

Vivian had dinner with Sue and the Commander tonight and I ate with Pat. We had steak! I suppose you will be having very good meat now if the stories we have heard are true.

I hope you don't get tired of hearing my daily doings because you will probably have plenty of these things waiting for you when you get there. But it is a good substitute for talking to you. You can sort them out and read one after the other and it will be just like a diary.

I suppose you have discovered by this time that we forgot to put in the sock forms complete with socks. I am going to mail them with your sweater. It is half done...the sleeve I mean...it should be finished in a couple of days so will get there almost as soon as you will. I bought some gorgeous blue yarn for you today. However, it will probably never be cold in the South Pacific. Still they are a token of my esteem and you can just know that a lot of love went into each stitch even if they are useless to you.

Tell Roy that that little girl Pat from Ithaca who lives up the hill wanted to write his wife a note so I gave her her address. She had forgotten to ask him. It seems she met her up there.

Honey darling, I will say goodnight now because nothing much else happened today that is interesting and I can't go on about how much I love you and miss you...that would be too demoralizing. I'll write you again tomorrow night when I get to Monterey.

I love you darling with all my heart.

All my love,

Jane

I thought you would be amused to know that Izz and Jintz called Pat at one-thirty last night absolutely polluted...they were having a party and wanted to ask us all down to another one. Pat said she couldn't understand ten words they said but they were terribly sorry to hear that you had gone???. Remember the night they kept calling and finally you threw the pillow at the telephone and we could still hear them talking. Pat has found out that Hal will be home about the first of July and will have two weeks leave. So she is all excited and happy again.

All the love there is darling...

Jane XXXXX

Mrs. Charles Flynn 3854 42nd Ave. N.E. Seattle, Wash.
June 20, 1943
Letter five

Hello Darling;

Well congratulations. It is my 25th birthday and I have long passed the stage of being a child bride. I arrived in Seattle today — the train late as usual. Mary, Bobby, Mother and Daddy met me. Great complications about baggage. Then we stopped off to see Ma Wee and then came home. I wasn't as tired as I thought I'd be because, with the exception of the time I wrote you yesterday evening, and ate dinner and breakfast, I slept straight through from Portland to Oakland — rather backwards.

I kept pretending you were sitting beside me in the train. I'd look over and smile at you in my heart. That is when I missed you most of all. I just caught myself pretending that you were in the bedroom waiting for me to finish writing this letter and reading Colliers. I shouldn't do those things because then you aren't — and it's a great disappointment. It's fun at the time though. I can make everything seem just like it should be — and shall be again soon.

I called your mother as soon as I got in. She hadn't received my letter, which I can't understand, but probably will tomorrow. I am going to try to get up to see her in the next few days as I know she is pretty lonesome.

The family is fine. Buddy will be home next weekend and I have two inches done on your blue sweater.

All the love I have honey and all you can possibly imagine. I love you, Jane

Mrs. Charles Flynn 3854 42nd Ave. N.E. Seattle, Wash.
June 21, 1943
Letter number five

Honey Darling;

Your sweater is finished at last. It is lying here in front of me on the dining room table all knitted, pressed, and sewn...it is a thing of beauty and it is so warm that you will never be able to wear it. But I shall send it tomorrow anyway, and just keep it around even if you can't wear it because to me it shows a little bit how much I love you. I have started the blue one which I am sure will be much more useful to you.

Gideon is lying here beside me. I was so hurt yesterday because he made no great fuss at all about my arrival. I was completely crushed. However now he is following me around again and seems to know who I am, so I have forgiven him. And after all I have done for him, I keep telling him. He recognized you after all that time.

Well, I have completed my first day in Seattle, and quite a hard working one it was, too, what with unpacking bags, and washing clothes, and ironing and all such guck, besides the housework I did. It is pretty lonesome around here in the daytimes, which would be one reason why I wouldn't stay permanently. We have been bustling around for so long that it's quite a letdown. However, I am glad to be here to help out. Mother and I had a nice talk this evening, although we were the only ones here. Bobby is in a play at the Penthouse, Mary works at night, and Daddy had to go to Tacoma. I think I will call Billie Barnes in a couple of days, though, when I get organized. I would love to see her husband of the legends. And maybe Jean Douglas and Charlotte Field and M. E. Groff. Then that will probably relieve the lonesomeness which was pretty acute today. I have always been so tied up in you and people have always come to us, and it is a bit hard for me to get used to that if I want to see anyone, I'll have to let them know I'm around. We have always been such sociable people that although I enjoy knitting and reading and working around, I couldn't stand the solitary life without friends for long. Of course when I get back to Los Angeles, I will spend all my time trying to get jobs and that will do the trick. It is almost the first of July now, so I think I will stay here until early in August. That will give me time to satisfy a few bills and start out in good shape. And by the way, honey, I hate to be practical when I love you so much, but I just thought I'd remind you not to forget what extra money you have, because what with Pat and the uniform payment and all, I could still use it. I hate to sound wifey, but I hope you haven't forgotten the non-playing of poker deal. So when you get there, don't forget.

I am going to write your mother a letter when I finish this. I will get up there to see her in a few days and stay overnight. I know I really should go tomorrow, but I keep delaying any definite action on anything until I get myself and my mind in order. Oh, honey, I love you so much and I think about you all the time. What a terrific thrill it will be the day the first letter. comes from you, I will just die of excitement and happiness. With every day that goes by it gets closer. Goodnight, Darling.

All my love,
Jane

3854 42nd Ave. N.E. Seattle, Wash.
June 22, 1943
Letter Number six

Good evening, Darling;

This is my customary time of the day for writing you so I can tell you all the happenings of the day, if any...just before I go to bed. Did I tell you that night before last I had every nightmare in the book. Most people just content themselves with saying that they had a terrible nightmare...I had ten of them...each more gory than the last. I was actually screaming all night. Finally the family congregated to see what was the matter with me, and when I told them the succession of things I had been going through — they all burst into laughter. I had all my money stolen, I was in a terrible wreck, I misplaced a car that somebody had loaned me, I met a magician and he made me drop through a trapdoor and I was chased by ghosts, I was in a bombing...well there was even more than that and all in one night.

Let me see, what did happen today...nothing at all exciting or worth recording in the slightest degree. I went to the doctor. I am such an old hypo and I get so tired of coughing up those little specks that I thought I might as well relieve my mind and find out that nothing was the matter with me. They really have a wonderful set — up here...all consolidated and really nice. When I described my symptoms, the doctor said, "I bet you thought you had T.B."...I confessed that some such silly fear had been lurking in the back of my mind..."Well," he said..."I don't think you have. I see no sign of it." But here is the pay-off, he said he was sure that I had had whooping cough and didn't know it, and was over it now, but some of the irritation hung on. Well, if I did, you did, too. Isn't that funny. They were quite indignant about not having come to a doctor, saying that that was what they were there for. Anyway, I think it is very amusing. He gave me some stuff and said to come back in a week.

When I finished there, I had a little time to kill so I dropped into the Bon Marche and saw Charlotte Field. She seemed simply delighted and wanted to be remembered to you. She has a very good job in the display department and controls what the mannequins... the ones in the windows...will wear. She loves it. She looks just the same as ever...trying her best, but not quite succeeding in hiding her good looks.

I am sitting here with a glass of beer in front of me...I know you will simply die with envy, but it is the first I have had in days and days. There hasn't been any car around here for two days and it is too close to the campus to buy any around here. I didn't know that there was some silly law about not being able to buy it within a mile of the campus, but it seems there is. I was really guessing about the whole situation...I said, "It is too much...having Chuck go away and not even having a glass of beer for comfort and to remind me of him." I swear this Seattle is without doubt the most awful town I have ever seen in my life. Nobody is smiling or friendly. You would think you were on the east coast. There is none of that wonderful vigor and humor freshness that is all over San Francisco. There is...

[REST OF LETTER IS MISSING]

2854 42nd Ave. N.E. Seattle, Wash. June 23, 1943
Letter Number seven

Darling;

Another evening's letter to you and with each one that is written, another day is gone. As time goes by, that is the only good part. Tonight, honey, you are probably still in the middle of the ocean...it is hard to imagine it and what you are doing. I wonder if you are studying as you had planned, and if you have had any big arguments with Fry and what you do all day...it seems like such a lifetime you have been gone and you are probably just started. Well, I read in Life that it was not a good thing to ruin a person's morale by telling them how much you miss them and how empty everything seems without them, so I'm skating on thin ice and I'll stop it and tell you some amusing gossip. Only I can't think of any, but I can tell you what happened today.

I had the car, so I spent the afternoon with Ma Wee. It was quite a struggle to get up as after I wrote you last night, Mary and Bobby came in and, much to Mother's horror, we sat up a couple of hours talking. There was great excitement in the household because Mary got a letter from Johnny yesterday. I told her about it over the telephone and she actually broke a date so she could get home sooner to read it. But I did have a little fun out of the treasure hunt I made out of it...I put little progressive notes all around and of course the letter was in the last one...a towel that she has been embroidering for us...very cute too...well, you should have seen her dashing from place to place. My opinion from what she told me of the letter is that Johnny is making tentative attempts to get back into the fold. He is an Air Cadet now someplace in South Carolina...she is getting some sense, though, as she didn't sit down immediately to answer it. Mother stayed home from work this morning and we cleaned up the house and went marketing...then I went over and spent the afternoon with Ma Wee and Billy, me armed with my knitting. She still looks far from well, but is so much better than when we were here last time.

Lee, I think has the bug. He and some other little boys under his supervision, had constructed a puppet theatre out of some boxes and were using the Christmas tree lights for special effects... they all stood around admiring the lights and using clothespins for puppets until they could beg, borrow, or steal some. Lee was in the midst of writing a play about a fairy that gave a king three wishes, and his language wasn't bad. He stood solemnly in the middle of the kitchen floor and read the script for me. It seems that I am looked on as quite an authority, having been in pictures. They were consulting me as to the length of time required to make a movie, as one of them was under the illusion that it took two days. They intend to have the script written, memorized, and the puppets made by tomorrow so they can give a performance. Billy said they had to clear up the basement first, though, so the audience could get in.

We had a letter from Buddy yesterday saying that by the first or on the first of July, they were all going into the regular army...I guess as Air Cadets, but when he graduates, I guess he will be in the regular army but still in the Ferry Command instead of as a Combat pilot. He is taking eye exercises like mad though in the hope that he can still get his eyes good enough as they aren't much off. He is such a hard worker. Bobby has now decided that he will go into the air corps. They have started a new reserve for boys seventeen and he doesn't go into training until he is eighteen, so he will be able to get in one more quarter of college and take some math. Mary is seriously thinking of getting into this Red Cross overseas service. The only thing that. is holding her back is that she is still hoping that they will "unground" the plane and she can get enough hours to get into the Ferry Command. She is trying to do something about it. All these air-minded people around me, and I have never even set foot in a plane. I feel like a slacker, although only Buddy is really doing anything...Sometimes I feel as if it's enough just to have you gone, but I do have to do something useful. But definitely not in Seattle. I just couldn't get stuck here. I have given up the school idea, as it is too late in the quarter. I shall just buzz down to L.A. around the first of August and get going.

I'll bet not one of my letters is ever censored. I never mention anything except personal affairs...But after all, you surely hear the news on the short wave as much as I do on the radio, and I know we are together on what we think about things, and we can't have our good discussions and arguments because this present conversation is wholly one-sided as far as I am concerned. For me, the best and most satisfactory letter would be just single-spaced "I love you" for pages and pages and pages.

Honey, I tried to send your sock forms today and they wouldn't take them. They were too long. That thirty — six inch thing works very peculiarly. Maybe you could have some made. The sweater is on its way, though.

That is everything that happened today, sweetheart...I love you so terribly much and I know that you'll be home soon. All my love, Jane

3854 42nd Ave. N.E. Seattle, Wash. June 24, 1943
Letter number eight

Honey Darling;

I just talked to your mother and I am going up there tomorrow and stay overnight. I would stay longer, but we think Buddy is coming home this weekend after all, so I shall go up and see her again next week. She sounded grand and cheerful. Your aunt was up there a couple of days this week so that took away from the lonesomeness. I offered to give her a driving lesson but nobody has any faith in me anyway...I mean as far as driving is concerned. I shall tell her about everything we did in San Francisco — slightly abridged, of course, and she will be so happy to hear all about you.

I have had a long busy day...not that I have done anything worth mentioning...housework and washing and shopping and cooking and knitting and writing letters. You were right about the housework, but I am glad to do what I can to help out while I am here. I tried my first application of your gift of leg makeup today and it wasn't a failure...thank heavens...although I did spend hours getting it on.

I sat myself down tonight and said that I was going to answer some of the millions of letters we owe...but you know how I am about writing letters...I expand and not many get done. I did write, though, to Pat and Buck and Izz and Jintz. But the ones to the Cornell people are still waiting and I don't think I'll get those done tonight. I gave them all your address and commanded them to write to you immediately so you will have something else coming in besides my daily diary.

A man from across the street who is a big real estate broker came up today and asked if I would consider showing Gideon in show early in July. I told him that I would think it over. I really don't know whether he has ever been registered, though. He wanted to know if I would mind if some man from the Times that is an expert on such things came out and met him because he admired him so. It might be kind of fun if it weren't for the horrible clip, and of course I would have to find out from Tom if he is registered. Besides, I think his pedigree is in our official papers at home. Furthermore, I don't think he'd stand up for the judging. I just know he'd roll over on his back and want to be petted...which would be exceedingly embarrassing. I got him some new kind of meat today, which is actually made of ground up turkey heads of all things...but it looks and smells delicious and I understand that that pulverized bone is very good for them. Besides, you just can't get anything here. I wanted to make some spaghetti tonight, but couldn't get any ground beef in town...pork is going to get a little dull...but don't misunderstand me, I'm not complaining.

Honey, I've violated one of the most sacred rules of letter writing. Practically every paragraph starts with an I. But I guess the books didn't make provision for writing all the letters at one time and getting all the answers in a bunch at a much later date. With every day that passes, the day of the letters is closer.

I almost had kittens today when they said over the radio that several small Navy warships had been attacked off Savu Island. Of course I had no idea where Savu Island was, but it was somewhere in the Pacific so I was immediately scared to death...but then they said that there were patrol boats and there weren't any casualties, so then I felt fine. You have no idea what awful fears come to your mind every time you turn on the radio. A place they mention in the Pacific may be six thousand miles from wherever you may be, but I immediately think of it as a menace...but then I don't know where you are, although you must still be steaming along...so how can I tell that it isn't.

I don't like to sound as if I were reduced to talking about the weather, but a great thing happened today...the sun came out...I

too, a few minutes and I went out and to sleep on the grass. Actually, I think the Japanese have done something to whatever stream
is supposed to make this place warm. It is even worse than last
summer...I could say the same thing as you said about Ithaca. But
today it was really lovely...for which I am duly grateful.

Honey baby, that is all to tell today...just jillions of love to you
from me...that is my main subject of thought, anyway. Before too
long, I will have dozens of interesting happenings in the workaday
world to talk to you about...I have some pictures for you which I
will send as soon as they are enlarged...

I love you, darling, with all my heart, so goodnight for now,
honey...soon I will kiss you goodnight.

All my love,

3854 42nd Ave. N.E.
Seattle, Wash.
June 26, 1943
Letter number nine

Hello Darling, and a very good evening to you;

I neglected you last night honey because I was up at your mother's
and we talked until after eleven, and then I knew if I stayed up
later and wrote to you that it would disturb her, so I decided to
wait and consolidate the two letters tonight. She seemed so happy
to see me that I was sorry I couldn't stay longer, but we expected
Buddy home. So far, he hasn't come, so I am feeling kind of bad
about leaving so soon. However I would hate to miss him and I can
go up there again next week, as I plan to do.

Today has been one of the bad days — I don't know whether I
should say that, but it certainly couldn't hurt a person's morale to
have their wife tell them how much they miss them. I suppose I'll
get used to your being away, darling, but I do wish I would hurry
up and get numb. I've just seen too much of you the last five years —
that's all. A good hunk of my spirit is waiting until you get back — I
wish I could find something that to me was just as important,
regardless of your presence. But everything seems terribly trivial
that people think or talk about when held up to the fact that you
are gone. But enough of that stuff. It is acting like a conceited ass

to attach that much importance to your own feelings. After all, it is true that we are what we give and not what we manage to get out of things. After all, who are we that we expect everyone else to do things for our benefit. I know we have to have a hand in it. It's just that I miss you.

Yesterday I thought your mother looked better than I had ever seen her. I was supposed to go up there on the four o'clock bus, but I was packing a hand bag that was very heavy and thought what I had to do could wait until Monday, so I caught the three o'clock and arrived an hour early. Your mother met me as I walked up the alley. She really did look fine and was so cheerful and dying to hear about everything that was done by us.

Today she sort of slipped a little, but was still fine. If only she would get her courage in her hands and drive the car.

Honey...this is Sunday afternoon. I stopped writing last night when I went to sleep in the chair when I finished that last sentence. And when I was too sleepy to write your letter, that was really extreme. Today has been very nice and we've done a lot of housework. It seems that stuff never ends. I called M.E. Groff and she asked me to dinner Wednesday night to meet her new husband. And that is really the gist of the news of today.

I was telling you about your mother. In the afternoon yesterday we took the car out and I drove her to the cemetery. The muffler was gone, which made her pretty nervous. I did think it was something very simple but she was scared to death. I suppose that is one reason why she can't drive the car. I'm sure she will force herself to eventually, but I don't know. It's a shame because it would be such a pleasure.

I took the four o'clock bus from there yesterday afternoon and Daddy picked me up at the station on his way home from the office. I should have stayed longer because we haven't heard from Buddy yet, so I don't imagine he will get here...it is about seven in the evening now.

Uncle Milt and Edna called last night and asked if I wanted to go with them over to see some friends of theirs...I was very happy to go of course...not terribly interesting as they were all awfully sweet. We had a couple of drinks...whiskey and water, but all they did was make me sleepy. It was a good thing I have a strong stomach because the hostess followed that up with strawberries, ice cream, and meringue...But I have had no ill effects...it's a wonder. They had a lovely house on the lake...we watched the searchlights after it was dark...The living and dining rooms had rugs the like of which I have never seen in my life. I believe they are called Kartoum rugs... the one in the living room was twenty-nine by eighteen...imagine that...of course crystal and silver and massive mirrors sitting all around. They say he is making more money than he can count out of owning the buses which take the soldiers back and forth from Fort Lewis...that does seem kind of terrible...I think he would have a guilty conscience as I understand he charges a pretty good price.

I got home about midnight and sat down to write you and, as I said, went to sleep. I give you my word, darling,...there is nothing else to talk about...I love the family, but I begin to think I will be awfully happy to get back to Hollywood. I am doing housework and alone most of the time, and when Mary and Bobby are here, they are just dashing in and out between plans and I am getting darned sick of hearing about Mary's boy friends and all such stuff. However, I shouldn't complain...I'm just used to being in a hustle and bustle and can't get used to the quiet life...it isn't the quiet life, though — It's just no companions at all...however, this will probably drive me out upon the world and give me a lot of ambition. Honey, it will be wonderful when you come home.

So many many millions of love to you, darling, from me, and I think about you all the time...so be good and I'll see you soon. Just think, I may hear from you soon...

All my love,

Jane

When you write me, put Seattle 5, Washington as they have divided this place up into zones. Love love love love love love

3854 42nd Ave. N.E. Seattle 5, Washington June 28, 1943
Letter number ten

Darling;

You will have to bear with my handwriting for a few days because I took the typewriter up to the book store to be cleaned and oiled. It was getting pretty stiff and it's such a valuable piece of property right now that I thought maybe I'd better get it fixed. They tried to persuade me to have the $7.50 job, but I said there wasn't that much the matter with it. So I got the $1.50 plus $1.00 for some new part.

About two hours has elapsed, darling...since I wrote that last paragraph. I was just getting all set to talk to you when the phone rang and it was a woman "answering my message about clipping the dog." I informed her I didn't know what she was talking about...well it seemed that Mr. Ewing, the man across the street, had called...he's the one who wants him to be in the show. He adores Gideon and wants to take his little grandson. Well, I went across the street to talk to him and he was suffering from the gout. He informed me that drinking made it worse. He must have been on quite a binge because his foot was swollen to about twice its size. He said tomorrow he'd be able to get in his slipper and, if so, he'd drive Gid to be clipped. Also the entrance has closed, but they are holding it until tomorrow morning for me to make up my mind. I have to decide by 8:30 in the morning. I don't know what to do. He'd have to be bathed, clipped, all by the Fourth of July. Besides, I don't have a decent brush or a show leash...not to mention his lack of training. I started to work on him tonight, using Friskies as a reward, and I will say, he learns fast. He would still have to be in the novice class, though. It might be kind of fun, but he'd probably lie down in the middle of the ring and want to be petted.

Well, I got back from visiting him and who should walk in but Buddy, looking more than ever like Richard Ney. He may be home any day from two days to two months. Then he is going into the army and he has had such success with his eye exercises, which he takes religiously, that he thinks he will get into regular air force instead of as an instructor or Ferry Pilot. He certainly is ardent about it. He looks marvelous and he is the sweetest thing. We went up to the University District and got Mary, and since then they've all been gathered around talking.

[INCOMPLETE]

3854 42nd Ave. N.E. Seattle 5, Washington June 29, 1943
Letter number eleven

Honey Darling;
    It seems like every night I have so much to write to you, but it is almost like talking...of course not quite, but it's some good.

Today has been one of those hot, muggy Seattle days...it is midnight and I've been sitting out on the steps until this very minute
talking with Daddy and Phil Helditch. I called to tell him you got
off alright and he came over after his Coast Guard meeting and saw
the pictures of us all on the lawn that day. We had a big political
discussion...no arguments. Daddy is surprisingly well informed on
most anything you could mention. So now I am inside carrying on
my little evening conversation with you. I gave Phil your address
and he is going to write you.

I hit the ceiling today and spent an hour or writing a couple of
very impassioned letters. It seems that Beverly wrote to tell me
they had had a great "stroke of luck." Some friends of theirs had
given them some furniture and they had got some of their own, and
so they could stop "renting" ours and put ours in storage...that our
six months deal would be up in July. Well...I wrote them immediately saying that there had been a ghastly misunderstanding ...
that in the first place, our agreement was for eight months, in the
second place that the only reason I had rented the apartment to
them in that way was so I could keep it...that I considered them
such good friends that I had felt that a verbal agreement was all
that was necessary. That we considered that our home and please
not to try to take it away from us, etc. I told them I had wanted
the apartment back before that, but had planned to wait until the
time was up so as not in inconvenience them...That if they would
find another place for our furniture, I would take up the rent. Then
I wrote Don and explained the whole situation and asked him to
help us. I hope and am sure he will. I was a fool not to get it down
on paper, but I didn't think it was necessary. But I won't let them
do it. So don't worry.

I decided not to show Gideon because I felt it would be an unwise
investment. The cost of clipping, entrance fees, show leash, etc.,
mount up, and I don't have his papers here so he'd have to be
entered in the open class, and even if he did win he couldn't be
used if I couldn't remember the name of his parents. It's silly to go
off half-cocked like that.

The rest of the day I talked to Buddy and went downtown and
did housework. Tomorrow M.E. Groff asked me to dinner. So things
aren't so bad.

Just think, darling, this letter will probably reach you after
you get there. It is has been so long now. I just can't believe that

it hasn't been three weeks yet. I will be interested to know if you get quite a few letters in a bunch.

I will say goodnight now, honey...sleep tight and I'll see you soon.

All my love to you, Jane

3854 42nd Ave. N.E. Seattle, 5, Washington July 1, 1943
Letter eleven

Honey Darling;

I didn't write you last night because I wasn't at home. But I did think an awful lot of you. I went over to M. E. Groff's for dinner and stayed all night...her husband...his name is Wayne Wright, went to work at Boeing late in the evening...the swing shift, and she begged me to stay, and so I did and we talked until about four this morning and slept until noon and I got home about five o'clock. It was really fun, but I guess I just can't take it...I was simply exhausted this evening. I lay down after dinner until I had to get dressed to go up and see Bobby act and could just barely make it. I am losing my youth. We really recalled all the old college people like mad...people that I had forgotten existed. I was delighted to see that M. E. had changed as much as I had, and in the same way, so we were still good friends.

As you know, Bobby is playing Charley in Charley's Aunt and he is really awfully cute and awfully good. This was about the last chance to see him, as the play closes Saturday night. He insists he is going to California after that with a couple of boys. He really has the wanderlust, and maybe it is just as well because he will only have a little time more before he is eighteen. He seems to have definitely decided to go into that Air Corps Reserve right away and I am sure he can make it. Then you go to school until you are eighteen before you can go into training. That is only one more quarter, but he will have a chance to get in a little more math.

Buddy has now decided to go back to Spokane next week so he can get his eye exercises. That poor boy is so anxious to get his eyes perfect and he has almost brought them up so he can get in the combat part. I guess it's wonderful what the exercises can do.

M. E. and her husband live in a penthouse apartment which is up on Bellevue North and looks all over Lake Union and the harbor.

It isn't as grand as it sounds...it is just a little place on the roof, but the view is wonderful. Last night it was terribly hot, so we sat out in their deck chairs and talked. I told them it was the closest thing I had seen next to San Francisco yet, which from me was really a compliment. It was something on the order of Number One August Alley, only larger and not half as cute...much more conventional, but definitely with a little bit of the Bohemian, anyway.

I am waiting with baited breath because I should hear from Beverly tomorrow. I hope and pray that there won't be any trouble from them. If there is, I would be sorely tempted to pick up and go down and settle the thing, but I guess that Don will be able to take care of it for us if they happen to feel objectionable. I could sue them for moving the furniture without authorization, we shall see what happens. I am sure there won't be any unpleasantness.

I was going to take Gideon over to be clipped tomorrow, but Daddy is in Tacoma with the car so I guess the poor dog will have to suffer one more day. He nearly knocked himself out when I came home today. In the evening he likes to sit out on the front porch and wait for everyone to get in.

Honey, that is all the news from here. I am just waiting the most patient I can, which isn't very, to hear of your news. Just think, before too long, some letters should arrive. I hope that you have been writing from day to day so I will know what has been going on with you. I think about you all the time and you are a most familiar character to everyone I meet because I talk about you so much.

I love you, honey, so goodnight and sleep tight...All my love, Jane

3854 42nd Ave. N.E. Seattle 5, Washington July 2, 1943
Letter no 13

Honey. Darling;

I have been numbering all these letters so faithfully, although last night I got the number wrong and had to correct it on the envelope. Mother just told me the army doesn't allow numbered letters. I don't think the navy is the same because I think Pat and Hal number theirs.

At last I have done it...actually cut out that muslin for the dress after all these months. I don't see how I'll get a chance to work on it this weekend because Ma Wee is coming over and I suppose that will keep me pretty busy. I have to go over and get her in the morning. I had planned to have Giddy clipped, too, but maybe if I get up early, I can get them both in. Here is what the dress is like.

[DRAWING]

Those circles are the apples. If you don't think that was a job — getting the pattern in the right places. I had a yard more of material than the pattern called for, but just barely got it out. I'm sure this must be very dull for you — this talk of dresses — but you always liked the material so well. I hope it will be still new when you come home.

Well the President had a little victory today after the humiliation of the anti — strike bill. He vetoed the anti — subsidy bill and the House just barely didn't pass it. I just can't figure those subsidies — but enough of politics. I imagine you hear the news on the radio. I meant that I couldn't decide whether they were a good idea or not. But under the present set — up it does look like the best thing.

Today I went down to the Navy doctor again. I told you he was an old beau of Mother's. As a matter of fact, don't you know him Parke Willis. That just occurred to me. I know he knows the Lathams. He waxed quite sentimental over my being Mother's daughter. Calls me Jane. And I didn't have to wait. He met me in the hall and took me in before a whole roomful of people. Of course my visit was just to ascertain the results of a blood test. My cough got worse. I told you that. Well they wanted to determine whether it was my chest or my nose, so they took a blood test to see if I showed any signs of chest trouble. It was my nose. So I have some drops to use night and morning. They taste like garlic and are marvelous. When I remember to use them, I don't cough all day. He said I was very wise to come in because I could very possibly have been something else. He hadn't been sure himself — and I wasn't a hypochondriac. So there. It's a great relief.

I sat down last night and wrote you and then a letter to the Jaegers and one to Viv. I gave the J's your address and told them to write, so maybe you'll be hearing from them — if they get my letter. I hadn't heard a word from Viv since she left, so I was kind of wondering if she got home in good shape.

Did I tell you I lost that match folder with the address of Chuck Meyer's girl on it. It just makes me sick, but in the tension of the moment I don't even know whether I put it back in my purse.

Just think, honey, tomorrow it will be three weeks, twenty-one days since I kissed you goodbye. It seems to take everyone 21 days to get any place in the South Pacific. Maybe you are even there by now. Happy landing, darling. I hope it has been a safe and uneventful trip.

I am going to bed now. It is midnight and seven thirty comes too soon. If I make it at that time, it will be the second time in ages. The first was when you had to get down to the Federal building at nine o'clock Saturday morning three weeks ago. I was so unhappy and trying not to show it and I had the cold shower and was shaking like mad. You said I would surely fall and you were right. The next day I did. You see I even need and love you for holding me up. I love you, honey. Sleep tight and I'll see you soon.

All the love there is, Jane

Soon I'll deliver them in person!!

3854 42nd Ave. N.E. Seattle 5, Washington July 3, 1943
Letter number fourteen

Sweetheart;

It was getting kind of late and I'd been sewing all evening, and I was debating whether or not to write you twice as long letter tomorrow, when they played Moonlight Bay on the radio — your favorite. I'd never really noticed the words much before but this time I listened intently to them. Remember, "There's a harbor of dream boats anchored on Moonlight Bay, waiting to sail again some sunny day." How true. It's my favorite now, too. Not even a sunny day is required.

It is midnight. I've just finished putting together the blouse of my dress and a good job it is, too. I haven't sat down really before this since eight-thirty this morning when I rose sleepy eyed from my hot little bed. Mary, the miniature heating system slept with me last night. I rushed through housework, fetched Ma Wee for the weekend, fixed her up, washed the breakfast dishes, made lunch, washed dishes, ironed, picked up Giddy from his clip. I had dropped him off about ten, bought groceries, picked up Mother, helped with dinner and the dishes. Then I sewed quite a day. You were so right about the housework. It seems the least I can do, but I'll have to get better organized so I will have time for the things I want to do. I had planned my little campaign of self-improvement but for the first time in my life, I haven't even had time for a shower today and that — being as it is right here, is positively low. I don't know what I'm going to do, but it will have to be something — maybe not be so conscientious. That conscience is the curse of my life.

I got my allotment today — which was a very pleasant surprise. I had never really expected it to be on time. Again honey, I hate to sound wifey but don't forget the you know what — something like $30.00 for Pat. Without it, my financial basis is shaky — being as I have obligations.

Buddy is going up to Mount Rainier to work for a couple of weeks. He is so miserable with his hay fever here and it is pretty lonesome for him here with all his friends away — poor kid. There's nobody left for him here and he has six weeks between courses.

The sweetest letter from Buckley came today. He said he was writing one to you at the same time, so I imagine you have all news of him. I'm so happy that he got in the O.W.I. It is perfect for him in view of everything and he'll get to do something pretty important. I'll enclose the letter tomorrow after I've answered it. I have been madly trying to catch up on letters we owe and his was one of the first I wrote.

Haven't heard from Beverly yet, but fully expect to on Monday. If not, I'll write her again — but in any case, I should hear from Don.

Well darling, my head is about to drop into the paper. Did I ever thank you for being so wonderful that I could love you so much. A million million kisses to you, honey — take care of yourself. I hope you have no fireworks tomorrow.

All my love to you, darling,
Jane XXXXXXXXXXXXXXXXXXXXX

3854 42nd Ave. N.E. Seattle 5, Washington July 4, 1943
Letter number 15

Hello Darling;
This is the last day — no, next to last that you will be subjected to my handwriting. The typewriter will be finished Tuesday.

This has certainly been a unique Fourth of July — as you know, this is Mother's day off (Sunday) and she was seized with a streak of ambition this morning. As a matter of fact, I was too — for while she cleaned the upstairs and the attic of the accumulation of years, I re — clipped, combed, bathed, and brushed Gideon. What brought all my energy about, I don't know, because the task on Gideon, while a major one, was definitely extra-curricular and only done after much downstairs cleaning. I set up a table in the backyard and really did improve that sloppy 3 dollar job of yesterday. I am definitely learning, because he is certainly on the chic side now. The two combings were really something, as he is filled with mats. I had half a notion to give him a modified Dutch boy clip and just cut them out, but decided against it. His mustache had already been cut off. He looks fine on top now, but I never did get the underneath mats out. I brushed him so long after his bath that he finally rebelled and refused to stay any longer, which is definitely unusual for him.

I told you that Ma Wee was here. She is so much better. Gets up to meals and around most of the day. She recalls the past so much — her memory is remarkable. As you know, she loves to talk but most of it is very interesting. She said to send you her love. I had planned to go up to see your mother on Tuesday, but I think Ma Wee is going to be here a few more days and if she is, of course I can't leave but I will go later in the week.

Today was quite a day of unusual baseball scores. Seattle took two from L.A., Portland two from San Francisco, and St. Louis beat the Dodgers twice. I'm enclosing some clippings I thought you might like.

I have become a strategist. Of course I listen to news broadcasts avidly all day and I've developed from the little bits of information dropped here and there, a new theory about the war. If true, it would certainly be surprising. But it's interesting to speculate and just for fun, I'll write it all down — it has to happen in the next month if it does. So then I'll tell you if I'm right. It might be the big surprise Churchill just spoke of. We'll see.

I'm anxious to hear from Pat and Jerry about the safe arrival of the baby. You know that if it's a boy they are going to name it Charlie. So I expect it will be soon.

Mary just walked in with a few friends of hers and caught me with my robe on. I've been making small talk with them. I'll never get over her putting the cream in Johnny's coffee and generally waiting on him. I tell her it's a great mistake to wait on a man like that. She eventually loses every one of them. So after all my advice, our boy wants a drink of water and instead of just giving him one, she goes out in the kitchen for ten minutes and makes a great ceremony out of chopping ice like mad. The poor boy was probably dying of thirst in the meantime. She just broke up with this very cute boy in the Navy and I'm firmly convinced that it was because she kept feeding him and waiting on him and being possessive. It's enough to scare a guy to death.

I have traded Mary for my blue denim suit (which is too big for me) and my yellow coat (which is too short) the loveliest covert cloth suit with long jacket and pleated skirt. It is really quite an addition and the other things fit her, and this, me. It has really never been worn. Also she presented me with a pair of new white shoes which fit around the ankles, because they were too narrow for her and she couldn't return. My muslin apple dress is well along now. I'm gathering together a few more clothes for when I get down to L.A. So far, very good.

Oh, honey, I'm keeping busy as a bird dog because it is a good idea. It's getting easier now, though, because I keep thinking every day you'll be home that much sooner. So until tomorrow, darling, goodnight and all my love to you.

Love Love Love

Jane

Monday, July 5, 1943 3854 52nd Ave. N.E. Seattle 5, Washington
Letter number sixteen

Honey Darling;

You are speaking to a sad, bedraggled character tonight — one who is having hot and cold chills and all from sunburn. It all started when Phil Helditch called about noon and asked if I wanted to go sailing. Well, it was a lovely day and Mary was here to look out for Ma Wee, so I said yes. It was a lovely boat — you remember those two pictures Phil had of it. It belongs to a friend of his named Anchor Jennsen!! Imagine. Well he was nice and the other girl was nice and it really was much fun. It was calm and hot all afternoon, so I rolled up my slacks and my sleeves and exposed them to old Sol.

A nice little breeze came up about five, so we came back like mad. I must say I'm only a passenger as I've never been sailing, much but I did, at least, keep out of the way at the right times. I kept thinking of how much you would have loved it.

When Phil brought me home, Mother gave him some dinner and then he proposed we go see Action in the North Atlantic. I remembered you had worked in it, so I was naturally anxious to see it. But you had all been cut out. I caught one glimpse of you though, and was no good for the rest of the picture. Maybe it isn't a good idea just to see you standing there for a second and then to have you gone. It's too nerve-wracking. Not that it isn't wonderful at the time but when it's gone you feel worse. I suppose the picture was very fine, but much too realistic for me at the moment.

I came home and talked to Mother awhile and then Mary and Bobby came in. We had a sandwich and now I'm talking to you. Mother has the moving bug again. It seems the owners want to sell this house. Well they can't if Mother and Daddy can't find anything else, because the only reason he wants to sell is because he can't raise the rent. However, Mother would like to find another place if possible, so I suppose I'll be looking for that, maybe.

Honey darling, I'm going to say goodnight now. I hope to hear from you soon. I miss you so much, darling.

All my love,
Jane

3854 42nd Ave. N.E. Seattle 5, Washington July 6, 1943
Letter number 17

Hello Darling;

I'm afraid I've got most horribly mixed up on the numbers of these letters. Yesterday's (July 5), should have been sixteen and I think I marked it fifteen. At any rate, this is seventeen and I will try to keep better track after this. I probably got off someplace before that, but now I am writing them down instead of trusting to memory, so from now on it will be right. I'm not using our typewriter yet, as you see, because I had too much to do today to go up and get it. Tomorrow, however, I am going to go up to the University District and cash my check and get the typewriter and get you a birthday present...that gives it almost five weeks to get there, but it will probably be late. However, you will still need what it is going to be. I have given your mother a couple of pertinent suggestions, too.

I had to call your mother today and tell her that I couldn't come up this afternoon. Ma Wee is still here and of course I couldn't leave because there would be no one to stay with her during the daytime. Now Daddy is going to Morton tomorrow and there is no way to get her home, and she wants to stay here a few days longer, anyway, until some sort of a gathering that Billy is having is over. I told your mother I would be up on Thursday, too. Mother suggested tonight that I call your mother in the morning and ask her to come down here Thursday and stay overnight. I think that is a darned good suggestion and I do hope she will do it. I think it will be awfully good for her and I shall certainly do my best to persuade her.

I had a big day today...I washed my hair, which is always a major event and talked about for days before it takes place...then I sat in the sun and improved my tan. When you come home and catch a glimpse of me you'll feel just like you were back in the south seas again... tomorrow I am going to work on the strong sun lamp. On second thought, maybe it would be better to stay lily white and not remind you. Then too, Ma Wee had a bath which is a major achievement, too. I am going to invent a bathtub with some sort of steps for old people. I was frightened all the time that she would slip and hurt herself.

Mother received a letter from Junie today. He is the most bitter boy. You remember seeing the letter when he said he couldn't understand why Mary and I were writing to him...did we think there was some sort of a bequest for us in his will. Well, that kind of hurt me. Honey, I hope you don't ever get like that. Just remember that there's me who loves you terribly much and never means or thinks anything that could be misconstrued no matter how much effort... about you. Anyway I love you like hell.

I really think I am about to get my teeth fixed, and high time. Uncle Milt has no appointments open for several weeks, but has promised me the first cancellation and he says there are a lot of them right now, what with vacations and all.

Just think, honey, I really think I should hear from you in about nine days if my amateur calculations are correct. Oh, I hope so. That will definitely be a big day. Honey, I will say good night now and hold the thought that I will hear from you soon.

All my love, Jane

3854 42nd Ave. N.E. Seattle 5, Washington July 8, 1943
Letter number eighteen

Hello my Darling;

It's well past the shank of the evening, as it usually is when I sit down to write to you, because then everything during the day has happened and I am sitting here by myself, which is the best way to write to you. May I be permitted to say that I would love to see you. Permission or no, it is most achingly true. Also, allow me to say that I love you.

Well, your mother did come and was delighted with the invitation. And I know it has been good for her, in spite of the fact that it has been very quiet. Mother and I have been trying to persuade her to stay tomorrow night too, but I'm afraid she feels she has to go home. We couldn't go out to dinner or anything because of Ma Wee being here, but it did rain terribly hard today anyway so home was really the most comfortable place. I met her downtown at the bus station about ten minutes to three, and we went to Frederick's and the Bon Marche and looked the stores over. I had planned to buy your birthday present today, but...great tragedy, the postmaster at Everett told her that you positively couldn't send things unless they were requested. I was sure it was untrue because I sent the sweater and all and the thing from the Fleet Post Office said there were no limitations, but she was so positive I began to doubt my own convictions and decided to go home and look. Well, it was a gross untruth — those regulations only applied to the army and they have now been withdrawn...so I will get it tomorrow. But we both consider it her patriotic duty to correct the Postmaster at Everett and to tell a few of those poor people who probably had been under the misconception all the time that they couldn't send packages. After all, that is quite a large town and you would think a man in his position would keep up with regulations. All this fuss about your birthday present when birthdays are something you now want to forget. Don't worry, honey, I won't even acknowledge your advanced age.

To continue, a great find was made in the shape of an all — leather purse which she immediately bought. It is fun to watch her being so thrilled over it. Then we traipsed out in the rain and caught the bus for home and actually got seats, which is a great surprise around here. Ma Wee has been deliriously happy all evening with the presence of somebody new to talk to. Reading and conversation are her two favorite occupations and she indulges both of them to the full. She was telling me today how much she longs for political conversations and talk about books. She tried to draw Daddy out on the political situation the other night, but he just answered that we might all be dead by the next Presidential convention, so that was no success. Anyway she just talked an ear off us all evening and, surprising enough, it was thoroughly enjoyable. Your mother saw my sewing projects and immediately started to work on them. I almost swooned with gratitude, especially when she gathered the skirt of the big apple dress for me and joined it to the top and put the zipper in. Then she told me how to fix another skirt and ripped up a sports jacket. She seemed to enjoy it, but I don't want her to think I was trying to make her work.

Did I say solitary evening?...it was a mistake...Mary came in about an hour ago and has been talking ever since about Beverly, Helen, Don McKean, and doings in Hollywood. Then Bobby came in just five minutes ago. It seems they have a melodrama at the repertory which he attended for free tonight, and one of the soloists involved a magician who needed a member of the audience. So Bobby was involved immediately. Anyway...after all the tricks, he put a pair of handcuffs on him, probably just to get him out of the way because the only way he could get it open was with the key. Anyway, Bobby sat down on the side of the stage and, while the magician was talking, he managed to get his foot through the handcuffs and got it caught and had to be pulled off the stage because his foot was in the way of the key. He stole the show, as you can well imagine. I no sooner got rid of Mary by commanding her to go fix her hair, that Bobby walked in. Sometime tonight I will finish this letter.

Yesterday I had a big official day. I put the check in the bank and sent the money to Pat and to the Lathams...an installment on that. I picked up the typewriter and did a lot of other little errands...it was shot as the dickens and when I got home, they had done something to the typewriter so it wouldn't work — the roller wouldn't go around and the space bar was stuck. I had to cart it all the way back on the bus, and they had washed the roller with alcohol and put it back before it was dry and it got stuck. On top of my fury over that, I got a letter from Beverly yesterday which left me in a blind fury. It was the quintessence of everything mean and untrue. She informs me that our furniture isn't worth anything, and she won't pay any more, and that I had taken advantage of her and they have no intention of moving until you come home. I shouldn't even tell you this. Thank goodness, I restrained myself until Mother got home and took her advice to write a nice restrained letter so she couldn't gossip about me to the neighbors, which it is quite obvious she is in the habit of doing. I told them that to me, the quite obvious issue was that we made an agreement and asked them if they had forgotten it or if they intended to break it. And more of that...I will let you know the next thing that happens. I can't imagine why I haven't heard from Don yet, but am sure I will tomorrow. I'm sure that by hook or crook it will come out alright. The more she loses her temper, the more she puts herself in the wrong. I shall endeavor to remain calm and I think we can pull through.

It is two in the morning and this crazy family is being crazier than ever...Mary is washing in the machine and Bobby has just caught an enormous and ghastly moth in the glass bulb. They should both be in bed and I'm scared to death they are keeping your mother awake, but I can't help laughing at them.

Honey darling, I'll write you again tomorrow and it will be a good letter — I'm about to drop...maybe you get the dregs of my mentality in the evening. Oh darling, I do hope it is soon I hear from you. Take care of yourself.

All my love, Jane

3854 42nd Ave. N.E. Seattle 5, Washington July 9, 1943
Letter number nineteen

Good evening, Sweetheart;

Again it is morning...at least just the start of it. I had a big evening tonight. I went out with Bobby. To the Showboat to see "Cradle Song." He is quite the young man around there, so we went backstage and really had a fine time. He is certainly not bothered by any lack of self-confidence. Then we went up and ate with the people and they were a scream...so conscious of the fact that they are in the drama department and trying so hard to uphold the reputation, and being awfully brittle and Bohemian and so young. Were the good old days really like that? I hope not. It looks so ridiculous. Then Bobby and I caught the bus home after refusing an invitation to a party, and Mary was here. Mother had gone to bed but Mary is in high disfavor because she went out with Freddy this evening. It seems that she told him to go out and about his business when we were first here, and now the boy has been suffering from hallucinations that he has broken her heart. I think she disillusioned him convincingly enough. This family is really something. Mary has just come in and thanked me for my advice to her on how to treat men. As if I should know anything about it! Anyway, she finally tried it on Freddy tonight and had him eating out of her hand by the end of the evening. He even skipped the "I Am" meeting, which is definitely a victory. It merely consists of not letting them get the idea that you like them...I mean not waiting on them really, and acting possessive. Of course, that doesn't apply after you're married, so I don't have to use it.

Well, your mother has probably written you by this time of her visit here. I tried to make her stay overnight tonight, but she had to get home to see a man about some lots in the morning. We went shopping today and she found innumerable things she had been looking for in vain in Everett. But my shopping trip was a complete failure. I trudged the streets of Seattle...everyone and from one end to the other. I was looking for what I have my heart set on to give you for your birthday and it was not to be found. There is one store which thinks they are getting some in on Monday, so I finally left it at that. So if your present is late, honey, know that it wasn't for lack of trying. I did get you one thing which is just for sometime, which I think you'll enjoy, and I'll send it to you as soon as I've looked it over myself.

Here are some more baseball scores. I have completely lost touch with it myself now that I don't have you around to refresh me on it. I will try after this to read the sports page, though, for your sake. Also a picture of a certain person that I thought you might get a kick out of.

I had a letter from Viv today in reply to the one I wrote her last week...saying she longed for California weather...it was so darned hot back there. She has gone to work already with a very good job and makes me feel quite guilty. However, by the time you get this letter, Fry will probably have told you all news of her.

[INCOMPLETE LETTER]

3854 42nd Ave. N.E. Seattle 5, Washington July 10, 1943
Letter number twenty

Hello Darling;

Gideon now has a Dutch boy clip. I did it myself with the able assistance of Bobby. My right thumb is still numb from holding the scissors. It really isn't so bad and the poor dog has a new lease on life. I'm afraid I didn't realize how hot he was. He has been romping like Kathie ever since he got off the surgical table. Of course, I don't like it as well as the other, but it had to be done. Those mats were even worse than I thought and right down to the skin...so many of them, too. The only thing to do was to cut them out. I do think, though, that tomorrow I better trim his head and legs a little more. The contrast is too great. A typical barber I... don't know when to stop. Of course this precludes all possibility of showing him until he grows back, but his coat could never have been brushed out with those mats.

What a workaday world this is and what a glutton for punishment I am. It is no use for me to complain about the work I do because I am always making up things to keep myself occupied. Besides that major task today, I washed, ironed, mangled, and the routine duty of cleaning house. I helped with dinner, washed dishes, and, this evening while the Rosses were here, I knitted. I am just the busy one, that's all, and I have no one but myself to blame. Mother said I should get to bed earlier and I answered what is the use? I have things I want to do to myself and the only time I can get them done is in the late evening, because if I have more daytime as a result of going to bed earlier, I will just invent tasks that I think need doing right up until dinner time anyway. I do think I'll go have a manicure, though. I need it.

I saw Poppy Agnew last night with Bobby and asked her where Georgia was. She saw Georgia today and she called me. You knew, of course, that she was married. She actually met the boy through Cy's brother in Pasadena. She remet him while she was up here and he was waiting for a ship to take him to Alaska. They fell in love, were married, had three weeks, and now he has been up there for nine months. She said the time seemed interminable and I know what she means after one minus two days. I am to meet her for lunch on Monday and we will probably talk each other hoarse.

Mother wants to go up to Hood's Canal tomorrow to see Aunty Nell if it is a nice day. I don't know as I'm particularly enthusiastic about going, but it will probably be my only chance. I think she wants to stay overnight. In that case, I would have to postpone seeing Georgia until the next day. But all this is very trivial... however it seems that so is everything I do lately. I am trying to get myself prepared to do something big, but I really don't know whether I will get that done here.

I have finished my muslin dress, though, and it is a knockout. I will send you a picture of it and me in it.

The Rosses dropped in tonight with a great deal of interesting conversation of what they had heard about Guadalcanal and the South Pacific and all...I am so happy you are in the Navy, honey, and safer from all those bugs and malaria. Mrs. R. just doesn't like Margaret Latham and I don't know why. She thinks she is terribly selfish and I don't quite get that. The only thing I ever got a little mad at her about was the housework. However, I didn't give her any ammunition. When she asked me if I liked her, I said what good friends they had been and how wonderful they had been to Kathie. Now that I remember, Margaret said Mrs. Ross was a gossip. Maybe the lack of regard is mutual. She was also telling me that Phil Hilditch was in love with Peggy Hilen and that Wylie Hemphill was being more successful in that little rivalry. I don't know if you knew Wylie...he was in the same class I was and I once got scolded by the history teacher in high school for passing notes to him while she was lecturing. I thought he was fascinating at the time and he never gave me a tumble. He wasn't really, now that I think about it. I can't understand why I thought so, but extreme youth has many peculiar ideas. Mother asked her what had happened to Phil's parents...it seemed the Rosses had been very good friends or theirs. I didn't know that they had died while he was in high school. He always kept worrying whether there was something the matter with him mentally because his father had committed suicide and his doctor asked Mr. Ross to help make him feel better. It is too bad...to say the least. Also it seems that after his mother died and before his father killed himself, he used to see Mrs. Bradner quite a lot...the father I mean. She had just got her divorce and they tried to console each other. But then he thought he had cancer so he shot himself. Mrs. Bradner was quite broken up about it because I guess she had developed quite an affection for him. Wouldn't it have been funny to think of Phil and Jack Brandar as brothers? I asked Mrs. Ross if Jack had gone back to his wife...remember the last time we saw him, they were separated? Anyway, they are together and very happy and Jack is doing very well in his defense job. I guess Mrs. R. is a gossip...she deems to know everything about everybody but not maliciously. Betty and Pat's mother was a sorority sister of hers and she knows them well. I showed them the pictures of Ithaca and you and they thought you looked very handsome. So do I.

Well, what do you think of the invasion of Sicily. Of course it wasn't any particular surprise. In lieu of actual news, which they haven't seemed to be able to get today, the commentators have indulged in all sorts of wild speculation about the possibilities of other invasions at other points and have even dragged in some sort of Spanish naval expert whom nobody ever heard of before to corroborate their opinion and add a fillip. That seemed to be going a little too far. But if they can't get the news, I suppose they have to start talking a little more in the form of conjectures. Everyone seems to think that Sicily is about the size of Pantelleria and as soon as they get someplace good, it will be all over. But from what I remember you said about the terrain of the place, it will take a good long time. But people want to be optimistic now and the President said it was the beginning of the end, so they are taking that statement for more than it is worth in the way of time, even if it is true, which of course, it is. I hate to think of all those poor boys, though.

Here it is after one o'clock, darling, and I am still going strong. Just to think that just before dinner, after the Gideon episode. But I am going to have a good hot bath (Hope there is no reason for that to make you envious) and throw myself into bed and sleep late in the morning. I have had hay fever the last few days...this damned Seattle...all it reminds me of, actually, is not Mount Rainier over the lake, but nose trouble.

Remember the day I wrote that note for you and Fry for the uniform installment? Well, I guess they thought that we were all one big happy family because today I received his official papers...I got yours the other day...I shall send them to Viv in the morning. All sorts of addressed envelopes and the copy of the contract and really...they have taken out a policy on your lives so they will be sure to get their payments...can you imagine that! I suppose the best thing to do is to see the funny side of things like that. Did I tell you that I got a letter from them the other day telling me that I was two months ahead on the payments and thanking me very much. I thought the things started on the fifteenth of April, and they started the sixth of June. Of course that is wonderful, but it tickled me to think that I'd been under a misconception like that all the time. I won't disillusion them, though. They thanked me for being so business like, and there are very few people who would pay me that compliment. I need a good kick in the teeth and other places for not being more so and neglecting to get a written agreement from the Moretons.

I am going to bed now, darling. It is terribly lonesome without you and our little goodnight talk. But I guess that will just have to be stood until you get home. So until then, honey, I'll bid you goodnight by letter.

All my love to you forever and ever, Jane

3854 42nd Ave. N.E. Seattle 5, Washington July 11, 1943
Letter number twenty-one

My Honey Darling;

I have just written a letter to Pat with check enclosed, one to Viv with uniform papers enclosed, and answered Buckley's so I can send it on to you. Now I am at the most important letter of the evening and then I am going to get to bed at a decent hour for a change... at least a little more decent than I am accustomed to.

It will be one month tomorrow since you left...I won't say it has been very short...sometimes it has seemed interminable. In fact, most of the time has dragged. But it's just one month sooner that you'll be home and this is the way to think about it. I think the twelfth of June, 1943 will be engraved on my memory forever. What a day of trying to be cheerful and wanting to beat your head against the wall, and having so much to say and do before you left and not being able to say much at all..I remember every minute of it. I would like to have stood there all evening and watched you if we couldn't even say anything to each other, but I know it was best to go. It was hard enough, knowing you were still there and I couldn't see you. Honey, I love you very much and I'll see you soon.

I am sitting here at one end of the dining room table typing like mad on the rejuvenated machine, and Daddy is at the other, figuring on one of his innumerable logging maps. Mother is asleep and Bobby got in a little while ago, very early, but he is taking his physical for the Air Corps this week and wants to be in top shape. Mary is out with the young man across the street. She says she doesn't like him but is having quite a time with him. This is the sixth time he has asked her, but the first time she has gone. He is a well established character, which is something of a change for her.

I did give Gideon the Dutch boy...I told you about that last night... pardon me for repeating it.

Ma Wee went home today. We were going to take her, but when Daddy took some things down to the car, he discovered that the springs were broken in two places and said it wouldn't be safe to drive it. So Billy, in spite of very little gas, came over to get her. I was sorry to see her go. Mother and I drove over to the University district with them, had a Chinese dinner and went to see "Keeper of the Flame" with Spencer Tracy and Katherine Hepburn. It was an immensely interesting picture...the only bad thing about it was that the pace was terribly slow. It was a wonder they were able to hold your interest.

I will talk to you again tomorrow, darling. In the meantime, be good and I love you and sleep tight even if it is daytime there now.

So much love I just can't tell you, Jane

July 11, 1943

Dear Honey,

I just finished a lunch of steak, potatoes, peas, pineapple juice, lettuce and tomatoes, sliced peaches, petit fours and coffee — all this ten-thousand feet in the air.

I told you in some earlier letters that I was...but I think you'll get this before those.

I am flying over to the...got it? There I hope to catch up to my ship, because from there...for some new stuff — the dope I got is that we will be there a couple of months — and after that who knows — maybe even the states. When you get this figured out, would you call mother and tell her? I can't explain it...that language.

The boys came down to the Navy landing to see me off last nite. I had...overnite as we shoved off early. It was right touchin'to say goodbye to those yokels after six and a half months.

Fry went aboard yesterday on his little pip — squeak and he is the Exec! What a laugh! His boat shoved out this a.m. and I saw it creeping along from the air.

I am really quite proud of myself — I got the dope my ship had left 4 hours before I was assigned to her — but in all probability I would have sat on my can...three months — well I...up and meaningful a...priority on a seat on the...did it in few hours...Most everybody gets 3...I just peeked out the window and the home of the Caribbean band is coming. into sight! It really has been a break to get this trip.

That's about all I have time for, honey — call Mom please and close your fingers on that bare chance I might see you in a couple

All me, love, Chas

Use the new address!

3854 42nd Ave. N.E. Seattle 5, Washington July 13, 1943
Letter twenty-two

My Darling;

For the first time since you left, I am not writing you late at night...it is the middle of today...Tuesday afternoon and I am sitting out in the back yard in shorts. trying to get a good dose of this temperamental Seattle sun. Unfortunately the terrain slants more than slightly and, since I must have my face to the sun, the typewriter is considerably below me.

I didn't write to you yesterday, but I sent your birthday present. It is a real good one, so I hope you don't have one already. It is from Hazel, too...it cost more than I thought it would so she said she had wanted to send you something too, but had no time for shopping and didn't know what to send, so she would like to go in on this with me, so she wanted to give the additional so she would be giving you something, too. It will probably be late. We had a heck of a time trying to make the size fit the postal regulations, but finally got it under the line.

I think the question of the Moretons and the apartment has resolved itself, thanks to Don...if not terribly pleasantly, at least partly satisfactorily. I had a letter from him yesterday saying that they were finding another place to put their furniture and would get out by October. That is, at least something. As to the question of the money which Beverly refused to pay, I don't know yet. I am waiting for a well — considered answer from them on that point. I was a little hurt by the implied criticism of me in the letter from Don...he evidently thought I was being a little unreasonable. However, you can't blame him as he told me what Beverly had told him that she told me. It wasn't true. I wrote him a letter back saying that I had always valued his opinion of me very highly...that I was afraid he was under the wrong impression, that while I didn't wish to quarrel with anyone, much less the Moretons, I did feel obligated to defend myself. I enclosed the two letters which Beverly had written me and which speak for themselves. From those, he will be able to see that she wasn't telling the truth. I asked him not to say that I had sent them because this was a private matter between ourselves. I hope I did the right thing. Mother thought so. It is astonishing to discover that people whom you liked and admired could be so untrustworthy and malicious. When this difficulty is resolved, I will probably continue to be friends with them, but never on a basis of confidence or trust. But so it goes, and you might as well find it out now or later. Anyway, I'm sure it will turn out all right. If they were to apologize, it would make me very happy because then I could trust them again but I'm afraid they won't.

I really had a pretty nice day yesterday, all things considered. I met Georgia for lunch and afterwards we went up to the Olympic Grill and talked all afternoon over a glass of beer. She had a lot of news about different people. Bob Skiles seems to be in Africa and Ken Annenson has his commission in the Signal Corps now... she had letters from both of them. I was awfully disturbed when she said that she had read a couple of months ago that a Tom Potts from Tacoma (where he did originally live) had been killed in action. Life for this week has a list of the casualties and I looked at it immediately, and she must have made a mistake because he is not there. Bobby told me last night that his mother lives at the College Inn, so I shall call her and try to get their address. I don't know why I say try...I mean...get it. It's funny how we completely lost track of them., I was commenting to Georgia yesterday that it is really wonderful that practically everyone we know, with the exception of Jack Finch who turned down an opportunity, who has gone into any branch of the service, has a commission. It makes you awfully proud of them all.

After dinner, I went up to see Mother Patten for a few minutes and then over to M. E. Groff's. Her husband was still asleep as he works at night and he had to stay up all that morning. He works at night so he can study for his Masters in the daytime...Quite a schedule. Anyway, we had a cuba libre and sat out on her roof overlooking the whole of Seattle...while watching .the sun go down. The sky was full of pink horses tails and it cast a pink reflection on Lake Union.

My plans grow a little more vague by the day. This desultory life is not for me. I am anxious to be up and doing something useful, but as you know, I definitely don't want to get a job in Seattle. I had planned to leave here the early part of August. But in order to do that, I have to plan on my railroad fare and have enough money left to live a month down there. I have no real expenses for living this month, but what with the extra bills such as Pat, etc., that must be paid, I don't see how I'm going to save any money to apply on next month. Of course, when the money arrives from you, that may make it a different story. I haven't put it all down on paper yet. I would hate to stay here another month as I am feeling terribly guilty about not being up and at it. But if I can't figure it out right, I may have to. We'll see, but I'm awful anxious to get out and do something useful as soon as possible.

Honey, I've heard vague rumors from different people that I shouldn't number these letters...for fear they would think it was some kind of a code. I suppose they could just cut it out and not hold it against us, but let me know when you write if they come through all right. I did get terribly mixed up on them in the first, but now I write them all down so I am straight.

That is all the news, my darling. Soon now, I hope, I will hear from you. I send you all my love and hope I will soon be able to present it in person...

Love, love, love,

Jane

July 14th, 1943

Dear Mom and Jane:

Well I finally laid my hands on a typewriter, as you see, and I thought I could kill two birds with one stone by using a carbon for the part of both letters that will have to be the same, as it is news in general of what I have been doing.

I missed my ship at the old fraternity homeland and they flew me on up here, a considerable ways farther, and now I am waiting for her to get here so I can report aboard. As you gather I have seen a awful lot of Pacific Ocean in the last few weeks. I will probably be here for a couple of months, the way it looks now. I am attached in an office here pending the ship's arrival, hence the use of the typewriter. I am sorry I can't be more specific, but you know why.

The plane ride was really something, but it was inclined to get a bit monotonous after a while, as there is an awful lot of salt water out in these parts. Knowing how much you have always wanted to fly, Jane, I can fairly. see you burning up with envy. As for you, Mom, I am not so sure I get the same picture. But it was a marvelous adventure and I wouldn't miss it for worlds.

I still can't get over how much mail I had waiting for me when I got down there, you were both wonderful to write so much, and did they sound good, and read better. -------------- brother!!!! (I am not quite used to this machine as you can see) Of course I haven't had any mail from you since I left and won't get any until the ship gets here, as I had all my mail forwarded to her, however, I will continue to write, and wait for the big gob that will be mine when she gets in.

This war news is really encouraging isn't it? If we keep up the good work as we are doing now, it won't be long before it will all be over, or am I being too much of an optimist? That Sicily deal really surprised me. I had a hunch they were going to try on the other end around Palermo and Trapani; apparently that is what the Duce's boys thought, too, because they seem to have been caught with their pants in you know what position. I wonder how long it is going to take to clean up the whole island; at the rate they are going now, not much. However I imagine the Nazis will try a sudden smash at some place or another before they give up completely. Personally I am very happy that I am not a foot soldier slogging up and down those hills, because as I remember from bicycling over them, they are not the flattest in the world. This concludes the duplicate part of the letter:

Dearest Honey:

I hope you won't be mad at me for the two-in-one letter, but I had the same things to tell you both so that seemed the easiest way to do it. There is not much more I can tell you about where I am, but if you are as smart as I think you are, you know.

By the way, guess who I ran into the other night at one of our stops? Dave Hill! He is the asst. manager for one of Pan American bases, and he looks wonderful. We had a nice evening together. He had some beer and he got some shaved ice and a big bucket and we sat for hours dishing and drinking ice cold beer with the water running off us in streams. His family doesn't know where he is exactly, and of course I can't tell you, but it is plenty hot there, believe me. I was so surprised to see him smoking and drinking beer; all he needs was a Tondelyyo to make it complete "White Cargo." He seems to like the work well enough, although he puts in twelve hour days, but admits that he is looking forward to going home for his two months vacation that he will get in about time to make Xmas at home. Which will be nice for the family.

They have an officer's club here that I understand is very nice, although I haven't been by yet, and also free movies every night, so you know how I will spend my time. I saw a girl on the street yesterday that I thought was Valerie Ellis (Anderson) with a little boy, but when I caught up to her I saw it wasn't; I hadn't said anything so I just walked on. I felt like a fool, though, you know the way you do.

Well, when I go back to my quarters I am going to plunge into a little washing. It's hard to get done here, and takes forever. My quarters are pretty nice. I have a room to myself, and a bath adjoining with a tub and shower and hot water!!!

I miss you so much, honey, I dream about you and things we've done almost every night. The other night you were divorcing me to marry Jack Callahan, and when I tried to reason with you you told me not to be silly. Wow!!! Most of them are nice, but that one woke me up in a cold sweat. Tell me it ain't so, honey, because you know I love you.

All me, love, Chas

3854 42nd Ave. N.E. Seattle 5, Washington July 15, 1943
Letter number twenty-three

My Darling;

What a delicious, joyful surprise to have Bobby come running up the steps this morning shouting "A letter from Chuck,...a letter from Chuck." I had begun to think that you were just a wonderful figment of my imagination. You have no idea what happiness to have you restored to the world of reality. A very funny thing, though...it was a peculiar letter to be the first one I had received from you... it was marked letter number eleven, so someplace there are ten letters between here and there. How I would like to get them. This naturally started out as if it were sort of a note and you had written me the day before and I knew where you were living...U mean your quarters and who we knew that were going for a walk there. It was like picking up a correspondence in the middle without reading the first. It was the letter where you described the natives and said the countryside reminded you of San Clemente and Southern Spain and you were going to make an appointment with the dentist. Anyway it was lovely to know you are there and safe.

I won't worry so much about you now, knowing that is the name of your ship. With a name like that...just fitting you, I know that anything bad wouldn't happen. It's the luck of the Irish. It did make me laugh just as you said.

I read the letter and immediately called your mother, but she said she had already had two letters from you. I can't understand why she didn't call me as I let her know five minutes afterwards. I don't know whether she got them today or yesterday. She only said that you had had a quiet trip. I guess the telephone terrifies her. It was a good thing I got that letter today because yesterday I must admit that. I was going out of my mind — one of those moods you get in and it had been a long time and I hadn't heard a single thing and I was beginning to wonder. Suppose there will be a lot of days like that, but this had been so long and I had thought I would hear some way before. Now I can rest easy for a while, though. I certainly hope those other letters start arriving tomorrow...now I have one, I'm a glutton and want more and more. I am especially anxious to read the long one you spoke of writing on the ship. Honey, in case those don't come, will you please write me another and tell me you miss me as you must have done in one of the missing ones. It would be a great satisfaction, even if I had heard it by that time.

Today has been a day of small activity…practically none in fact, since it was one of those days. I read a Readers Digest and your letter a dozen and one times, and that is about all. Yesterday I didn't feel so good either, but I went downtown in the late afternoon and met Mother and a friend of hers and had a couple of drinks at the Washington Athletic Club. Mother was really awfully cute. She enjoyed it so and it is kind of an unusual treat for her. The cocktails I mean. Then she met some friends and went to dinner, and I met Mary and we grabbed a bite and went up to the Anderson studio where she works, and spent the whole evening until nearly midnight printing and enlarging pictures. We didn't finish all the negatives, but the ones we did, we made lots of big ones of. We did two of the scenery ones you took at Cornell and they are perfectly gorgeous… they wouldn't go any larger than about 7 by 5, but that was fine. I want to do some more of them later. One thing that bothers me, though…I can't find most of those Cornell negatives. I know they were in that big envelope with all those pictures that we fixed on the train and I know we had them up at Everett. I am wondering if we could have left them there. I will find out because there are some I would like to blow up, and naturally we want the negatives. I am sending you some pictures tonight and then I will send you some of the big ones the first chance I have to go to the post office… it will have to be day after tomorrow because Mary won't be bringing them home until tomorrow night. I made a couple real big ones that Roy was in…the ones Viv took and thought it would be nice to send them to his wife. That is really fascinating work. They, of course, have all the best equipment and I simply loved it. We are going to do it again some evening next week.

After that, some friend of Mary's who is in the Merchant Marine took us home. He seemed like sort of a diamond in the rough to me at first. That was the first time Mary ever went out with him, so I was forming judgment. He said he was getting his First Mate's papers which would make him a Lieutenant Commander. I was quite impressed until he said that he was doing it just for the money and that was all. Then I didn't like him so well. As it turned out, he was just rough and Mary didn't like him either.

Well, the war seems to be coming along in pretty good shape, thank goodness…but all the radio commentators, right along with good news, caution people a dozen times a broadcast against over-confidence. I must say, it is a fine time to have that strike people, but I guess it is...fools that they are.

There is a big article in the Reader's Digest for July about Marcus and Narcissa. Now that should provoke sort of Nation — wide interest of a sort in the subject, and I thought it might be a very good idea to write Al Kingston on the subject tonight. Maybe it won't do any good and it probably won't, but in case anybody got any ideas about doing it, it would be best to remind him about the script. And then, with it having been in there, maybe there would be current interest in the subject. So I shall do that and see if anything hap pens...I'll write him when I finish writing to my honey...mainly you...rather, namely you.

We now have a red ribbon on our typewriter and it is lovely... see...but I am afraid to use it for fear it might look like some sort of a code and I hate to have any of my deathless words omitted.

Bobby is taking his friend, Bob Anderson, up to Everett tomor-row...in the other Bob's car. It seems he has to go up there for his physical for the Air Corps...to Paine Field, and he wants Bobby to drive so he won't use his eyes. Guess there's noth-ing the matter with them, but he wants to be in perfect shape. Anyway, I thought of going up there with them because there is a six-hour wait and I could go up and see your mother. I know she will be pretty busy helping Mrs. Mitchell move, but if I didn't give her any warning, she wouldn't have to get things ready so it wouldn't be any more work for her. If things work out alright, I think that's what I'll do.

Honey, I am wondering if you sent that money order in one of the letters that haven't come yet. Let me know as soon as you can, and let me know if something happened that you don't have it, too, because I couldn't possibly go south for another month without it, so I have to know how to make plans. I will be lucky if I can with it, as a matter of fact. I hate to be a pest about this thing, but I know it is easy in the midst of all those big things to forget financial obligations and all such stuff, but I can't forget them because they are what I have to deal with all the time, and I am anxious to get down there so I can go to work and, what with Pat and the uniforms and all this month, and a few other things that you know of...I just have to know. So tell me right away. Now, don't forget, because it's really awfully important.

Speaking of Tom...I had a letter from Margaret Latham yesterday...mailed the seventh of July to San Francisco...they were really behind the times...she must have written it the day I sent her one with the money for Kathie in it...anyway she said Tom's mother had had a stroke. I am awfully sorry...she is such a young — looking woman. He didn't mention it in the letter he wrote about Gideon and his mamma and pappa, but maybe she hadn't had it yet. I must write a note immediately with my sympathy. It really must be something to see somebody you know so well way down there in a picture. Maybe you'll see me if I work hard.

Well, darling, that's thirty for tonight. All my love and lots more than that to you, my honey. Write to me often because every letter makes me so happy I can hardly stand it.

To continue on a little further...Mother was just telling me a story about Wallace's recent visit to South American that a man down at their place told them. He had lived in South America a long time and some of it came in letters to him and some was in the papers. It seemed that when Wallace announced he was going to visit President Prada, was having quite a little trouble with the people who were inclined to resent his dictatorial tendencies and inclined to resent Wallace because of the President's truck with the United States. It wasn't that they didn't like us...they didn't like the President and didn't think the United States should associate with him because he was a dictator. So they were taking to calling the new U.S. Embassy the new government building and weren't particularly happy when Wallace came. Besides they cut down a lot of trees along the golf course where he was taking the tour from the airport to the President's house. So they were a little sulky about the whole thing. Well, President Prada thought he could carry it off pretty well. in spite of the fact that the people were carrying signs about his being a dictator around in front of Wallace. But then, he thought Wallace couldn't read them so it wasn't so bad. It was suggested that Wallace address a few words to the crowd. He was expected to speak a few words of greeting in English. So Wallace stands up and begins to address the people in fluent Spanish. And of all things, he talks about the Four Freedoms. Well, one or two were all right with the President, but four!...that was just too much for him. He just couldn't bring himself to agree with all of those. But the people after two minutes threw their hats in the air and screamed and cheered and Wallace became the popular hero of the people. And on top of all that, when he left, he decided he would walk to the airport. It was quite a procession because when he walked, all the dignitaries had to walk, too, and, on top of that, six thousand people decided they would take the walk with Wallace, so there was quite a crowd. So he departed...having made himself and the U.S. most popular with the Peruvians and having embarrassed the President no end. It is sort of like a comic opera. Also I am glad to see Wallace making such a good impression. I would have loved to have seen the consternation when he started speaking Spanish.

This is really thirty for tonight, honey...I love you again .and again and again, and don't forget to write me very very often.

All my love to you, honey,

Jane

3854 42nd Ave. N.E. Seattle 5, Washington July 16, 1943
Letter twenty-three

My Darling;

Well today your letters didn't come, so maybe they will come tomorrow or Monday. I hope so. I did go up to see your mother today, honey, but didn't stay long because the friend of Bobby's had his eye test first and didn't pass it, so inside of the hour he was ready to go home, and it was his car so I had to leave. However, we had a nice little visit so it was a good thing I went.

I asked her if she had any negatives, so she gave me those of the pictures you took in Europe, many — rather most of which I have never seen. There are some really lovely ones there and I will make. them in big enlargements the next chance I get. She didn't have any of the Ithaca negatives, though, so I just can't imagine what happened to them.

Otherwise it has been a very dull day...as usual. Got back here about eleven-thirty this morning. I went over to the drugstore in the University District on the bus and then came home and did the housework and the ironing, and was still on it when the family came home. Then dinner and sat around a few minutes, and now I am writing you. If you ever have any worries about my having too good a time anyplace, save them and don't use them here. Not that I don't like it. It's just that there is nothing outside for me to do. I don't see how I can possibly leave here the first of August because of the amount of money involved, so I think I will start doing something for that extra month. I think I can get some radio work...at least I'm going to try, and I think I'll help out at the ration board during the days when I'm not busy with that. I can't do any knitting because I am already doing it. But I just have to do something if I have to stay that much longer. Then, too, I must work a little harder on getting things ready. I finished my muslin dress and it is really a knockout. I will send you a picture...of me in it, of course. The people where Mary works want to make a picture of Mary and me the first of the week, so maybe it will turn out well.

I had a lovely letter from Margaret Lathem today. She wanted advice about Joanne Desert. She has had a test and several agents are after her, and wanted to know which one was best. It seems that Levis is one of them...so he must be out of the army. I will find out. She said not to worry about Kathie...that it was the least they could do for us. She said that we took them in for two months and if it hadn't been for us, they probably would be still in Seattle at KXA. Wasn't that nice of her to be appreciative like that. They are really grand. They had been so nice to Kathie and taken her to the vet and all, so I told them they might have those chrome fog lights if they wanted to go get them. Then I thought I had better tell them a little bit about the situation with the Moretons in case the M.s said anything...not to believe them. Margaret was horrified. She said she would just like to see Chuck beat Jay up when he gets back if they persist in a dirty trick like that. I must write her and tell her that they are not moving the furniture and it looks as if they would surely be out by October. I hope so. As a postscript she added that Jimmy Hill had realized a long ambition and had taken Lena Horne out. She added that it wasn't being bruited about in his better circles, so she guessed everybody knew it. A small note of sarcasm there, if I'm not mistaken.

Your Mother looked just fine. The Mitchells moved yesterday, as she has undoubtedly told you, and the new people were moving in today. It is too bad. I know she will miss them a lot, but she will probably make friends with the new people. She doesn't have much respect for the Mitchells because it looks suspiciously as if he were doing it to get out of the draft.

I have rambled on, darling. Let me know as much as you can of what happens to you and what you are doing. I love you so much and it is so grand to know that you are there safely. Be a good boy and remember I love you.

Millions of it,

I hear that Wilbur Sparrow is a Captain! I'll try to get more details.

If you put Seattle 5, Washington — the letters will get here a day sooner.

Love, love, love, love, love, love, love, love, love, love, love...

P.S. 11:15 I just spent the rest of the evening gazing longingly and lovingly at pictures of you. Tell me if you get those I sent yesterday.

XXXXXXXXXX Jane

3854 42nd Ave. N.E. Seattle 5, Washington July 18, 1943
Letter twenty-four

Honey Darling;

Sunday evening after a really beautiful day...nice and warm and sunny, just like California. It's nine o'clock and up until now I've been sitting out in the yard reading, and up until an hour ago I was getting a sunburn. Then I laid aside my book and came in to write my honey.

Maybe you have received the first sweater I sent you by this time. Of course I haven't sent the second one yet. I was a little glad to hear that the evenings were chilly because maybe now you'll be able to wear it instead of just looking at it as a souvenir.

Nothing of any note or importance has happened since I wrote you Friday night. I haven't even had any profound thoughts. Can't even remember what happened yesterday...oh yes, I did a big washing and read a while, and in the evening I went over to see Ma Wee. It was hard getting Mary started so we didn't get there until pretty late, and then besides that, she stopped off to see some friends and they took her out to some sort of dancing place, and then she came back to meet me, so it was all very complicated, and then they wanted us to come in and I didn't get home until about two o'clock thoroughly disgusted with the whole thing which was definitely a comedy of errors. Ma Wee seemed very well. I took over all the pictures that Mary and I printed to show her, and she asked for one of you and your mother and me, which I gave her.

Mother just came home from a weekend party with a bunch of the women who work with her...much sunburned and bearing enough blackberries to make a pie. She spent the day on the beach with cool breezes and the sun, and is much refreshed for the new job which she is taking Sunday...it is head of business correspondence in the same office. She was very hesitant to take it because she doesn't know a contract from a grocery bill, but they are sure she can do it and she really has to. She can't refuse.

Jean Douglas's brother, Keith, who is a friend of Bobby's, just called to say that he was driving down to Los Angeles about the eighth of August and wanted to know if Bobby wanted to go with him. I haven't broached the subject to anyone yet, but I know somebody else who might be. That might make things work out much better than going on the train. If I figure hard, I may be able to do it...that is if he would want me to go, too. I'm having lunch with Jean Tuesday, so I'll broach the subject then. Maybe I'll talk to Bobby about it tonight. That might work out alright if I could get it all figured out.

Honey, I am the darndest letter writer tonight. I just can't get this typewriter to work and, besides, I can't think of anything to say except that I miss you terribly and I just can't keep saying that and make us both feel bad. No, it should make you feel good that I miss you...so be happy because I do an awful lot.

I met a drama boy tonight named Bill Bowles who knew the people who lived at Alta Loma Terrace after we did. It seems that Jack La Rue had it and rented the bedrooms to "young men"...from what we have heard I base that inflection — not from what he said. It is a shame, though...that lovely house. I never quite recovered from the time I went to see Mary Ellen and saw that horrible table in front of the big window and a fringed pink lamp. It was just too terrible for words to have that place desecrated so. You were there that day, too...remember. I was just trying to think why it was that we moved out into the valley — was it the money it cost, or too much company, or a combination of both. As I remember, we decided awfully quickly. Maybe we just got restless. I have the darndest memory. But I do remember all the happy times, honey, and there were an awful lot of them. I think that New York and San Francisco were the very best part of our whole married life together, don't you. Maybe it was the atmosphere of vacation and loving each other so much and appreciating every minute. It was the happiest thing of all in spite of the strain from day to day. But that just shows you how things can grow. Five years and the last was the happiest, and the next to last was the next to happiest, and the first was real good in the beginning...in spite of me throwing spoons at you...and screaming, and you the same, but that is one of the things you couldn't be without. Good love is always nurtured by a little occasional hate. That sounds awful maybe, I admit, but it's so true. Just as we have always said about the people that say they never had a cross word. They weren't worth fighting with. Or being married...or anything. My, I do get sentimental, but you're awful nice.

Ma Wee is still here...I deserted her most of today, what with going downtown and to the play this evening. I bought her copy of "The Robe" today...not a gift, an errand. She is definitely the greatest reader. I hope my eyes hold out until I'm that age and have plenty of time to read...fortune willing.

I have lost weight. Now I weight 115 with my breakfast inside of me. Three more pounds and I'll be well satisfied. The chubby person that you left is fading away. Not enough beer is the trouble.

I think I will be forced to give Gideon a modified Dutch boy clip Sunday. He is filled with terrible mats, especially around his collar. They never took it off. Of course I wouldn't shave him and I'd be very careful, but those things can never come out except by cutting. It is just impossible. They are just solid masses and if I cut him now and then, keep brushing, his coat will come out nicely again. I'm afraid I will have to do it, whether I want to or not. I had a letter from Tom Stevenson the other day saying not to forget the show blacking if I showed him, and to have him well clipped and brushed. I must tell him I decided against it because he seemed quite worried about the whole thing. He said to tell you that if you ever got to Guadalcanal...which God grant you won't...that Margaret Stevenson's son was a flyer there. You remember her... Tom' s cousin, and she is at RKO. Anyway his name is Lieutenant Terry Holburton of something called Sundown Squadron, which is a Navy fighter squadron. I don't know how he seems to think that he is there.

I am reading a book that Ma Wee brought over called "And So Victoria." Maybe you've read it. However, it is the story of the events in the royal family leading up to the succession of Victoria. What a bunch of profligates. And it is historically true in the most part. Did you know that Victoria was the thirteenth child of her father and the only legitimate one? The character the book is woven around is a boy who was the son of Princess Amelia, daughter of George III, and her brother, George's natural son, whom she married secretly without knowing the relationship. A pretty mess and, being the only nice one in the family, the shock killed her. So it seems that all the brothers who had ambitions to the throne...two of them got to be kings...used this boy for their nefarious purposes...at least they tried to, but the kind hand of Providence and a few people who weren't corrupt, saved him. It's really kind of interesting. And you know my weakness for the historical novel. The trouble is that I am always adding a little fiction to my facts...you never know the line of demarcation.

Soon, honey darling, I know I'll hear from you...very soon. The very thought gives me goose pimples of anticipation and suspense. I have taken to sleeping late in the morning so I won't have to wait as long for the mailman to come. One of these days, I won't be disappointed...soon soon soon.

Good night, honey. Sleep tight. I love you with all my heart. All my love, Jane

July 20, 1943
3854 42nd Ave. N. E. Seattle 5, Washington Letter 25

My Honey Darling;

It is the end of a hot humid day — eleven — thirty at night and all the doors still open — mosquitoes flying merrily about having a field day on my bare legs and slightly sunburned face. Everyone else is in bed except Mary who, of course, isn't home yet. She had some sort of project to go swimming off the Showboat after work, so I don't expect her for quite a while. So I'm alone with you. And I can almost make myself believe that you are really here. I am working hard on the happy faculty of remembering everything with pleasure and laughing at the things we did together. So I get happy thinking about it instead of unhappy. It's a wonderful quality to cultivate. Of course you can't always make it work, but you can a good deal of the time. We have been awfully lucky and had wonderful times, and those are the things to think about. Don't think I won't be glad to see you, though. I'll nearly die of pure ecstasy.

Well life is looking up. I have a new project — namely the building of a dress, and it makes me feel as if I were accomplishing something — which I am (also preparing myself) in my little interim. It is sort'of chartreuse and a material which looks like a lovely light weight wool only it isn't — it's called aralac, I believe, and it's made out of milk, actually. I will wear it with the silver bracelets and it will have two old silver buttons. I think it will be quite striking.

I had a letter from Don McKean tonight. He saw the light after reading the letters I sent him and has it all fixed up — with them and with his viewpoint. I still don't know about the money, but at least we have our little home with the furniture intact, and that is something.

Also, more interesting, I guess Don has actually put over the picture deal he has talked so much about for years. He has signed contracts to produce from 4 to 6 pictures a year depending on the availability of actors to start in September. He was very pointed in asking exactly when I would be down there. I wonder what he means by that. I mean is it an offer or not. I am inclined to believe that it is an offer of a job if it is possible. I wish he would be more definite, although he probably can't be yet. However, I do believe he was trying to give me an idea there is a definite possibility of something. I wonder if it is worth trying to figure out if I could go in August. I don't think that Keith Douglas — the friend of Bobby's — thing will work out.

Mother is seriously considering throwing over her job even before she gets another one. She got a kind of dirty deal down there lately. The job she had obviously been prepared for was given to somebody else — and then they turned around and offered her another one — just as responsible but with no increase in salary — head of business correspondence, as I told you — and completely out of her line. She will have to work like mad to master it and there is no great future in it anyway. She felt a great sense of loyalty toward them, but not after they pulled that. It seems that the men executives there are jealous of women.

Anyway she has an interview at Boeing in the next few days about a very big personnel job. If she got that, fortune would really be up around here. Also Daddy is working on another timber thing today, and it if all comes out he stands to make about five thousand dollars. Of course he puts that all back into capital taxes & bonds & stuff, but he says that if this and a couple more work out he's going to start logging again, which is the dream of his life.

Mary is seriously considering joining the Red Cross overseas service. She made many inquiries today and it looks good. She is a little young, but with the 3 years college and the drama training, they said they would be willing to take her. I would sort of like to do that, too — desire to be useful, but a few things should be taken care of when I get down there. I'll at least do something about the aircraft warning service. I feel like a parasite. When I get working though, I'll be doing something useful.

Buddy came home last night from Mt. Rainier all sunburned and healthy. He'll be departing for Spokane in a couple of days to continue his eye exercises. His check from the army came — 5 months retroactive so he can well afford it. He was night watchman at Paradise Inn! Loved it. He and Bobby and I were trying to sing tonight and of the three of us — Bobby was the only one who could carry even a semblance of a tune. The gods made a tragic error in this family.

I had lunch today at Fredericks. Georgia and I were the guests of Jean Douglas. She — Jean — looked perfectly gorgeous and I looked like a hag. I tried to do too much housework before I left and threw on an awful combination of clothes and left a mess. Mother was most disturbed, but I really couldn't bring myself to worry about it. It's a trivial incident today.

Aha — today we bombed the Kurilies that action in the North Pacific is just leading toward my prophecy. Maybe I'm right. So far, so good. Remember the letter where I said I'd become a prognosticator. If I'm right, I'll just take Kaltenborn's place. And it's not a wild guess. I notice little hints and facts on the radio.

I have several large pictures to send to you which I'll get off tomorrow.

Goodnight, my darling. I am praying that your letters will come tomorrow. Take care of yourself. I love you with all my heart.

Love, love, love, love…Jane

Honey, that was a heck of a letter I wrote you yesterday. I'm sorry, I shouldn't have got depressed or bored and told you about it.

It was really hot here today and, irony of all ironies — I didn't even notice it until I'd spent an hour under the sun lamp. When I finished that I cleaned house, hung out the ironing, did some errands for Mother, and went over to see Ma Wee. I could only stay there a little while as I had to pick up Mother at five. She took me to Don's Sea Food for dinner. I had fried prawns, crab cocktail, and a glass of Rainier beer. Shades of San Francisco — If only you had been there, darling — only there wasn't any lobster on the menu.

I am enclosing a letter from Dave Oswald. The envelope is a little bulky so the address is Captain David P. Oswald, 161st Infantry, APO 25, c/o Postmaster, San Francisco. I wrote him a note last night to tell him I was sending the letter on to you. I was reading it blithely to your mother when I came upon the poetic masterpiece — that called for some quick skipping.

I called and left a message for Phil tonight. I thought he might like to hear how you were as far as I knew. Besides, Mary claims he is her dream man. But I probably can't work anything out there.

I have lost two pounds and have started to religiously use the sun lamp. I might as well have a big course in self-improvement while I have the opportunity.

I met two wounded Marines today. They had been on Guadalcanal the whole time, poor kids. One was from S.F.

I have some pictures for you, honey, but am wondering whether to wait to send them until I hear from you. I'll decide tomorrow.

Did I ever tell you that I love you? I seem to remember saying something of the sort, but, just for the record, I repeat it a thousand times over.

Goodnight darling. You are probably getting up about now, but sleep tight. I hope to hear from Jerry soon, by the way. I can't remember their address so have to wait until they write me.

So terribly much love to you
honey, Jane

Chestnut St.
San Francisco, 23, Calif.
September 20, 1943 Letter one

My Darling...I was just leaning out the window watching the sunset over the towers of the Golden Gate Bridge and I thought... Chuck's ninth penny is down in there and how long will it be before he throws the tenth one in. It's all very well to keep up this big front and I flatter myself I do pretty well at it, but this business of coming home and not being able to fool myself that you'll be here tomorrow night. Honey, it's ghastly. And I rub it into myself so...I went out to buy a package of cigarettes and I saw the florist shop and thought it would be more cheerful with some flowers. So I bought some of those little pink dahlias like you brought home that day and then, when I try to put them in the vase, I can't see them for the tears in my eyes. It's awful to love anybody so much. I hated to come home tonight. I had all these big plans for improving things and having everything wonderful for you to come home to, but all the spirit has left them. But it will come back because I am just going to make myself a lot harder than I am now or I'd spend my whole time weeping.

Did you see me up on Coit tower? Of course you didn't, but I was there just the same. I couldn't just make up my mind which was you, but it was an impressive sight and I was sort of saying goodbye to you up there. Then I took the bus and went down and went to work. So tonight here I am sitting here and Heaven knows how far out you are. But I know you're doing real well and you like your job, and so that makes it better.

I went to the doctor and I thanked him for you, and he wanted to know all about you. I told him that it was absolutely the only opportunity you had had to call and that you had been so worried and he was so nice. I guess he is trying to do something about it in a hurry because he gave me a double shot today and I am to come back for another double one tomorrow morning. Also another examination tomorrow, so I will let you know what transpires. I feel lucky to have found such a human man down there. I got up there about ten minutes of eleven, which I dare say was about the same time you got to your destination. Obviously you didn't miss the ship. I half expected to hear from you all afternoon. I got up there in such a hurry because those other officers that were up there at the desk gave me a ride up to Market Street in a jeep. It was almost as bumpy as the truck. The navy evidently holds no truck with springs. Then I went up on my little pilgrimage to see you off.

Tonight I ate at that little cafeteria up the street when I got off the streetcar, and I tried to get another book by Upton Sinclair but I couldn't, so I got "After Many a Summer Dies the Swan"...I'm going to be doing a lot of reading these evenings I guess...not seeming to be especially fitted for more ambitious activities, so I will get out that letter of yours that you wrote me on the way down to Numea and see what were those books you recommended. Then I came home and did the dishes and drank a glass of beer and cleaned the place up a little bit and tried to keep from thinking about how much I missed you and just couldn't. Oh honey, we were so lucky and I know, it, and we did have such a very happy time. The only thing I could possibly have asked for were just a few of our late, slow breakfasts, but next time we'll have those. We have so many wonderful things to remember so...let's remember 'em.

I am enclosing a letter from Bob Scott which came this afternoon. Do answer it, honey, the first chance you get. He was so sweet to write and that shows you he is really a good friend. It certainly was a surprise. Nothing else came. I shall send the mail on as it does come. I have just written Maureen.

Until tomorrow, my darling...I love you so much that I couldn't even begin to say it.

All the love I have, Jane

P.S. I wrote a note to Chet, too, telling him to hurry and send to you on the Gamble. — I just drank the rest of the bourbon. I love you so much it hurts — honey darling All my love, Jane

2370 Chestnut St. San Francisco Letter two
Sept 21, 1943

Dearest Honey:

Well honey the second day — only three-hundred and sixty-three left in the year we said goodbye for. This one went pretty fast, mainly because I slept most of the day. Now I have two good books and some new knitting needles so I should keep myself fairly well occupied until I can get out in the world again. By the way, I am now in bed again just as you advised but now on orders — When I saw the doctor this morning he said I was to quit my job immediately and go home and go to bed. I pleaded, but to no avail. I will say I feel lot better. It is a relief not to run around and have your insides hurt you. If it doesn't stop by Friday, he'll give the second treatment, so in any case I'll be o.k. by the end of the week. I did hate to leave that job, though, because I really did enjoy it, and besides, it ruins all my money plans. Well, I'll just get another job in a hurry. In the meantime I'll get a good rest. I bought myself a supply of food and some beer, so I'll just hole in for a few days and wish I could see my honey darling.

The phone rang about ten-thirty last night and it was Daddy again from Portland and Mother was with him taking a three day vacation. They sounded like they were having a good time. Maybe they'll call again tonight. They were staying at the Multnomah.

Daddy wanted to know if I needed any money and I assured him I didn't. I'm not so sure now, if I have to pay some surgical expenses, but I'll cross that bridge in a day or so. The only time I hadn't been paid for was $10.69 worth.

I have been thinking about you and your two weeks solitary camping trip — if you did it for pleasure, I figure I should get some fun out of my three or four lone days. I've always thought of myself as a rather self-sufficient person, but I suppose it's because I've never had to be. Ever since I "grew up" I've had you and honey that is more than enough — something for which I couldn't be more deeply grateful. Even when I miss you so terribly you're so much a part of me that in a sense you are still here.

After getting "After Many a Summer Dies the Swan" yesterday I realized that I'd read it. I can't understand how it made so little impression on me. As it is, today I got the two books by Upton Sinclair that I wanted but I can't stop re-reading the other. It repels but at the same time interests me. Why does realism always have to be corrupt, or am I just a romanticist. It would be hard to base your social philosophy on curbs for general evil instead of on the idea that everybody would be good and kind of given freedom from want. My how I do go on, but if you do take these things seriously, it's an awful problem.

I have decided that I can't know geography well enough, so I am consulting the Atlas while the news broadcasts are on. Do you know that no map has Lae on it? I do know where it is, but it does seem peculiar.

Just think, honey, two nights ago you were here and we had our hot steak in that hot place and you mixed us some drinks and when you came in, you tried to put the bed up backwards for me. We had such a happy time, even if the axe was hanging over our heads. I can see you so clearly, too, yesterday morning leaning out of the truck waving like mad. And Burton, or whatever his name was, didn't know you were behind him so he waved like mad at me, too. It was the only funny thing in all that sadness. Now you are way out in the middle of the ocean worrying about your guns and your watch and getting those cigarettes straightened out and probably not getting enough sleep.

I love you, my darling, with all my heart — so until tomorrow — goodnight.

All. my love, Jane.

2370 Chestnut Street apartment 304
San Francisco 23, California Letter six
Sept 23

Honey Darling;

What do you think. The telephone rang a little while ago and it was Don Mckean. He said, Jane…do you want that apartment and I replied that of course I did but that Helen had already rented it. He said that he had got my letter this morning and had gone down the OPA and found out that she couldn't do that and she was just trying to bluff me, and that he would go up there in the morning and tell her that she couldn't. Well, that is fine. I thought that maybe if I had gone to the Navy Legal department or the OPA I could probably do something, too, but up here and sick, my hands were tied. Of course all sorts of problems come to my mind now… we didn't know how much rent Beverly and Jay had paid and he said he would pay the rent until the first of October if they hadn't. That means I have to pay him back and then pay the rent and then get the phone connected and all sorts of things, and I am going to be awfully strapped if I don't get a job right away, but all that would be made up by the cost of furniture storage, so it's six of one

and half dozen of the other. People do try to take advantage of me
when you are away, and it is wonderful for us to have such a good
friend as Don. To think that he took all the trouble to go down to
the OPA when I had just asked him to see that the furniture was
stored safely. I am beginning to think though that I am crazy to
tell him that I wanted to keep it. I will only have one month of hard
sledding though, and then if I get a job and you get a promotion
and I get somebody to stay with me, it will be alright. If I just hold
out a little while, all difficulties will be over.

Well, I'm afraid that unless Seattle wins both games tomorrow...in fact I know that if they don't, they are not going to win
the playoffs...they lost two to one today which gives them one and
San Francisco two...San Francisco made two runs in the fourth
inning...Seattle already had one...then Seattle did absolutely nothing
until the first half of the ninth...they had two outs and a man on
first and one on third...they both hit after the first two men went
out. It was their last chance and what did the fools do but send
the pitcher to bat, and of course, out he went. They were probably
figuring that if they went into extra innings, that they would still
want him to pitch, but it looked like throwing the game away to
me. They might have made two runs with a good hit. The pitcher's
name was Tincup...I think that is the way you spell it.

Well, the football started today. Washington is the only team
north of here that is still in the conference this year...both Oregon
and Washington State being out. Washington mowed Whitman
down by something like 36 to 0...I think that was it. I listened to
Saint Mary's and California. I imagine that one will have great
publicity in Hawaii because the one named Wedemeyer that comes
from there and plays for Saint Mary's was so good...a one man team
almost...then there is another named Fernandez, and yet another
from Hawaii. Of course they expected to be beaten by California
but they were pretty good in the first half, but then they started
that crazy Phelen stuff and practically gave California two more
touchdowns so it ended up 27 to 12. I just don't understand why
Phelen insists on passing from behind your own goal line on the
third down. Of course they did it on the five and then again on the
ten yard line so that wasn't quite so bad, but just the same, it didn't
work. It's all very well to be reckless if you know you're going to lose,
but he should know by this time that it doesn't work. Washington
lost more games that way. I'll never forget that Stanford game I

came up here to and they did that. It worked the first time so they tried it again and lost the game because of that.

It seems just impossible to believe that Russia is doing so well... now they have Smolensk. I keep thinking that they will be stopped at least for a while someplace, but no...they just keep on. Is it possible to hope that they will get into Poland. It is just hard to believe how far they have gone in the last few weeks. Just look at the distance from Stalingrad to Smolensk...of course I realize that was more than a few weeks ago, but just look at it any. They are only a hundred miles from Poland...just think of it. The radio said they were just about to take Kiev just this minute. And they say we're about to take Naples. Of course there is a long way from Naples to the Brenner Pass. Unfortunately it will be easier for the Germans to defend themselves in Italy because it is narrower. Could they have what they call a defense in depth. I suppose they could, and that is hard to crack. Oh honey, I do go on so, but just think, Don is the only person I have talked to all day today and I'm so lonesome for you. I better get out of here in a hurry or I will really start talking to myself.

The days are going, darling, and pretty soon I'll hear from you... you have been gone almost a week now...how I wish they would go a little faster so I would hear sooner...but they will...in the meantime I am absorbing a large hunk of literature and news...and loving you more every day. You will be happy to hear that the dim out is going to be modified. They don't think we're in danger any more. Isn't that nice. Goodnight, my honey darling, and all the love there is to you...Waves of love just come all over me when I think about you.
   Jane

2370 Chestnut Street
San Francisco 23 Calif.
September 23, 1943
Letter four

My darling;
   I have decided to sit and type to you tonight because it is quite obvious that there is no great point in being careful between now and tomorrow morning. Things continue on the same so he will

just have to fix it and stop relying on the shots or staying in bed. But it is nice to know that in a few days it will be over.

I have had two conversations with Howard and Maggie. They were in town last night and this morning...but so occupied with relatives that they couldn't get out. Of course they would have come if you had been here but I told them not to worry about me because I would see them in a little while anyway. They were terribly disappointed to hear that you were gone and wanted to know all about your shoulder and were so happy that it was alright.

I have a shock in store for you...personally I was shocked myself a couple of hours ago but now I've just washed my hands of the whole thing in complete disgust. It seems that Beverly and Jay left for New York last week without bothering to let us know and I got a note from Helen this afternoon saying that they thought they had better rent the apartment to somebody with more rugs because it made too much noise and the dogs would be a bother. Well, I called her up and told her the dogs weren't coming back and I was planning to get rugs and I was planning to come down there about the first of the month. She seemed genuinely sorry but she had rented it to someone else this morning. I suppose I could go to the Navy legal department and make a big fuss but it doesn't seem worth it. I guess we just aren't intended to have it. There is a certain point you reach where you just give up and no matter how hard you've fought for something, you just don't give a darn any more. That isn't the only place in town and by the time you get back, I will have found something more super...in the meantime I'll find a single with telephone service...maybe I could even get Mary Hull's if she is moving...maybe Helen will have something else soon...I have written Don McKean to ask him to take a look at our more valued things and see if they are alright. It seems they are storing them in a garage. And I will e down there soon to take them over. If I can't use them all I will store them. It looks as if I might have to store the table for a while t that won't hurt it. If I got a furnished place such as Mary's I think I would store the davenport and chairs instead of selling them because it would cost so much to replace the frames...don't you think that is the best idea. I daresay if we had gone to see Helen while we were there, this wouldn't have happened but that is all water under the bridge and I'll find something better before you get back. If I get something with phone service, then I can pay the phone co. in peace which was quite a problem. I guess it just can't be helped. Maybe it could be but I don't want to get legally involved. So that's that.

That is about all that has happened today...I have been absorbing a big bite of Upton Sinclair and two inches of Navy blue sweater besides consulting the map with every news broadcast. I got dressed and went down and mailed my letter to you and got the mail...including a letter from Mother which I shall enclose to you. Then I came back and got undressed and went to bed again...it is astonishing how you lose your strength after lying down all the time. Tomorrow or the next day I shall get this thing over with and in a few days I should hear from you. I am just counting the days my honey.

I am going to write your Mother a letter right now...

Be good my sweetheart and I love you with all my heart...don't worry about me because I'll be fine in a day or so. All the love there is to you.

Jane

Sept 27th 1943
Letter No. 1., (new series)

Dearest Honey:

Well of course this is only going to be a note because the mail is just about ready to go over and I don't want to miss it. I will write again tomorrow, and make it long, but I just wanted to tell you that I am where I can write to you again, so all is well.

Boy what a hectic time we have had. I have been going all out for days, and just now things are beginning to straighten themselves out a little. I want to tell you that my arm is almost back in shape. It is still a little sore, but I am not troubled with it too much. I know you will be glad to hear that.

Gosh, Honey, wasn't that hectic that last morning? I have been worried about you ever since. I bet your old insides were just more than jumping around. I wonder if you went to the dispensary, and, if you did, if the yeoman gave you the message. I called him and told him to tell you that all was well and that I made the ship all right. I think I will always remember you standing there in front of the ship's service building mentally wringing your hands and just knowing that I was going to miss the ship. As, it happened we fairly flew back to the base and made the ship with time to spare, I even had time to call to try and let you know.

The trip was very uneventful, not much rough weather or anything. More than that I can't say, as you know. One night

[REST OF LETTER IS MISSING]

September 28 1943
2370 Chestnut St.
Apt. 304
San Francisco 23, Calif.
Letter nine

Darling;

I am so happy because I feel so much better. When I compare the way I feel now and the way I felt last week at this time...there is just the greatest difference in the world. And it just came over me today that I felt better. I thought that the doctor was being over optimistic when he said it would clear itself perhaps but maybe he will prove to be right. When I went in this morning I said I felt better but didn't know why and after poking around, he said that I was perfectly right...I was a lot better. I think it's about to stop. I have to go back tomorrow another check...I imagine I will be going in there every day but as long as it is encouraging, that is fine. He even said that I could go out to dinner tonight...I talked my head off being so lonesome but they seemed to enjoy it and said they hadn't had a better time...that was Jean...she said she had had the best evening since she had been down here. As you may gather, I went over to the Douglas's for dinner. We had bourbon and steak and coffee royales and discussed politics and race prejudice and all sorts of interesting things for the whole evening. And they presented me with some bourbon...old Taylor. They are the perfect host and hostess...just fill you with the blarney until you believe it yourself and start expanding although it never takes much encouragement for me to do that. Honey, I do rave on but you have no idea how nice it was to see and talk to somebody...I am afraid I am definitely an extrovert.

My mother says she always thinks everything out in the bathtub and gets her best ideas there. Well, I was standing in the shower

last night and I got an idea...I don't know whether it is for a book
or a short story...I guess it couldn't be a short story because it
doesn't have any plot...I think maybe a short book...I know I will
never write it but is fun to think about it and I have written down
a partial outline for it. The trouble is that it would have to be done
immediately to be of any interest and I don't know enough even
if I could write...but it is kind of interesting in my opinion. I have
just been reading a lot of books about the events and the thinking
that led up to this war...and it seems they are all the same...there
isn't anything left to write about it that the idea I have is that
people always love to read things that are based on the future...it
is the same idea as going to fortune tellers. I thought of writing
a story now beginning with the day the war ended. It is the story
of a young couple...you and me to be exact and how they mirrored
what happens in the world at the end of the war. The gist of the
whole thing is that having thought a certain amount in a groping
he can't just resign and go back to civilian life and forget it...he
feels that peace is only the beginning of a new phase of the war
which has to be followed just as closely as the actual fighting...
so they decide to go to Europe as roving reporters sort of...just
like our idea...so they do and they wander around and see a lot
of stuff that I don't know enough to write about...you see it is a
sort of prophesy about the peace conference and the attitude of all
peoples in Europe and they know what the people in the United
States are doing and it seems that the conservative and isolationist
groups come into power again...at least they threaten to and this
young couple sees that we are failing just as we did the last time
and so they go home to enter politics...at least for him to...because
they want a hand in the continual fight...to make the whole thing
worthwhile...they might not want it but they feel they have to
take it. The whole idea is that the war is not over when the peace
is declared...we will go on fighting the war the rest of our natural
lives. Now I admit that isn't much of a plot...it is a consolidation
of the different things you have said and the ideas you have given
me...but then no books now do have a plot...It is just a sequence
of events and ideas through these two people. There are lots of
things in the idea that I can see are going to happen in this country at the end of the war...For example, when the war is over in
Europe, it won't be such a problem because they will have to start
building again and it will absorb the energies and excitement of

the people but what will happen here...nothing of ours has been ruined materially. All of a sudden the war will stop and we won't quite know what to do with this peace we have been longing for. We will want to stop our defense industries but we can't stop all of a sudden because everything will be thrown out of kilter but why would we go on...to manufacture weapons that we have no intention of using. There won't be a plan because all plans are prevented...they are nervous ones...Congress especially says don't think about them until the war is won...

Then when the men come home...everybody is terribly happy of course. But these boys have a different philosophy now...how long is it going to be before the element of the civilian population that is basically selfish will be antagonized and little their sacrifices... That is a point that if it could be written about now would prevent many people from adopting it in the future.

Then this young couple...what are they going to do...they will have such a background that they have thought of these things... In the first place, they have been married awhile...doing enough to take up their lives s after separation but still it's like an island on the lines of your palm...one line becomes two then the two divergent ones join and the other will never know completely what forces were at work while they were separated. Now with you and me, we would because we have been married long enough to understand each other and any separation is of no great importance as far as getting back together again is concerned but what of the people that have been married a little while or have been married longer and don't understand each other as well as we do. They will find they are married to different people they thought they were.

Well, I can see a lot of those things that will undoubtedly happen... but when this young couple decide not to stick to security and to go out to see what they can do about a "brave new world"...and go to Europe to look the situation over, then I am stumped because I haven't the background like you have. I've heard something about geo-politics and about the confederations of Europe and unconditional surrender and the subjugation of the Prussians and self-determination and all that but how are those things going to be solved. Well, in this I would have to arrive at the solution which might be feasible as a prophecy but I don't know enough to know what it would be... of course...the young couple has to have a baby in Europe...I forgot to mention that.

The thing is that everybody wants to read something that deals with what might happen. Remember how popular Nevil Shute's "Ordeal" was...that is a simple example...I won't go into the more far-fetched ones. Also if anyone had the power to point out in a fiction form the results of thinking now and be realistic about the whole thing, it might do a lot of good. People read novels and they base a great deal of their lives on them.

Of course I realize I could never write it especially in the time required because I've never written anything. I read descriptive passages of authors and I could never think of those things. The only way I could write is like Hemingway because I would have to be blank from necessity.

Do you get what I am aiming at. If you do, comment on the whole thing when you get this letter. It at least gives me something to toy with but I get to a certain point in my thoughts and I'm stuck. It's like Louisa May Alcott writing pot boilers about bandits...just as ludicrous. I should write little pieces about Mama wee skating in the basement and let it go at that. It's fun to think about those things though and if I were around long enough, I probably would... write something I mean...that is if there weren't so many lending libraries where you could get good things people have written who know how.

My goodness, honey, I've raved along here for an hour or so and you get probably think "My wife is drunk" but really I'm not...you just get unbalanced when you get to thinking. It's a bad idea.

Oh honey, if you were only here and we could have a drink of bourbon and talk and you could say that you didn't need to comment because you already knew what I was talking about and agreed with me because our mind worked that way. Remember the argument we had about Upton Sinclair and you wouldn't go to bed even if you did have to be up at five in the morning and neither of us knew what we were talking about because I hadn't read his early books and you hadn't read his later ones. By the way, did I ever say that I heard him talk in Seattle and was very impressed even if you do think he's nuts.

Goodnight my darling...there isn't anything that I can say that would tell you how much I love you and to what a great extent...I just do with all of me and I'll write you again tomorrow night...

All my love,
Jane

Sept 28th 1943

Dearest Honey:

Boy when the mail came aboard yesterday I had 6 letters! Four from you, one from Chet, and one from Mom! That is really service, and no kidding, I expect I'll get another letter or so today.

Honey tell me all about the operation. I was just sick when. I read about it. Honey are you sure all is well? Oh honey I love you so much, and don't let anything happen to you. You are the most wonderful gal in the world, and you represent the four freedoms as far as I am concerned. After I read that it was going to be Sat morning as our boat is due to come back and I have a million things to get squared away on the beach this aft. It's fun honey, but gad is it work! Brother!!!

Still I love it and am doing a good job I think, but boy do I have a lot to learn

Gotta Go love love Chas

Another letter tomorrow

Dear Honey:

Just time for a line before the mail boat goes over. Been making with the bang-bang practice the last two days and it went off very well, I'm proud of myself.

I will write a long letter tomorrow, but I just wanted you to know I love and miss you like hell — this is all the time there is — so — much love my darling

Chas

xxxxxx

Well honey the boat isn't quite ready to go —

I just came up to the store-keepers shack to catch the mail man, and he said I have another minute or two, as there is a typewriter here I can get a little more in this letter.

Honey I'm sorry the last one ended so abruptly, but they came down for me to go over on the beach to get some stuff, and I had to run. It isn't that I don't love you but you know when the Navy call you jump, or did you know that?

The last few days are full beyond belief, but it is kinda fun in a way, there are about ten things to be doing every minute and you never get them all done no matter how hard you try. But still that makes the time go by, not fast you understand, but at least it helps.

I now really have to sign off, they are just ready to go, so I will close with much love and write a great long one tomorrow —

All me love Chas

Sept 30th 1943 #4

Dearest Honey:

I've just had a sensational idea, get yourself a folder at a stationers that is the size for thin paper. The ship's office uses it so I can get all I want, then you keep a file of my letters just as I am keeping a file of yours. Good idea what? Be sure turn the page end for end, as that makes it easier to re-read them in the file. I'll start with this letter so you will see what I mean.

All that apt business strikes me as very funny. I am just wondering how pleasant your relations would be with Helen if you held her to it? Not very I'm afraid, however she is in the wrong and it is a lovely apt. and I know you like and it is ideally located for you. So it is your problem dear, do with it as you want. If it isn't too unpleasant, I'd like to see you take it.

I think you'd better plan to go back down to Hollywood, Honey. After all you've given up that job in S.F. and I think it is the right thing to do. I'd hoped I wouldn't have to advise you to do that, but it is the only thing to do in view of the present circumstances. I know it's tough and not what we planned, but there it is. So get all squared away with your female disorders and shove off, that's a command!

Honey, tell me the whole story on your disorder as it unfolds. It concerns me no end, so be sure and keep me posted, the Doc sounds like a very nice guy.

I got off the ship last nite at five and went in and stayed the night and had dinner with Scoop and Katie Richardson. Had a few drinks before dinner, a wonderful Swiss steak and then a nice evening with a lot of talk and a couple of drinks. Very pleasant and quiet, just the three of us.

I don't know if my mail gets to you as fast as yours comes out, but I got a letter yesterday (29th) that was postmarked S.F. 5:00 PM the 27th. That's about 36 hour service which is pretty darn good!

Well, baby, there will undoubtedly be a while go by before you get some letters. There will be a few more, then a pause, then lots!! So don't think I am just not writing, okay?

I'm sorry the way these letters always end in a rush or just chopped off, but I am so darn busy! Right now I've got to go back to my station for coming alongside dock, so I am going to have to knock off again, sorry honey.

Get one of those folders, or a filing board with rungs and keep the letters. After the war we can compare them. Goodbye for now, darling. You're the best — loved and most — missed wife in the world!

I love you so honey

Chas xxxxxxx X (Good, huh?)

[BOTTOM X IS VERY LARGE]

P.S. Enclosed is $10, I wish I could make it more, darling, but that about cleans me, and I get no more till the 10th. Chas

2370 Chestnut Street
San Francisco, 23, Calif.
September 30, 1943
Letter 11

Darling;

I got letter number one of the new series from you today and it was so wonderful...now I am hoping that number two that you were going to write the next day won't be held up. Is there any way of my knowing not to expect to hear from you? I suppose not. I just had a feeling that there would be a letter from you in the box this morning but I was so afraid of being disappointed that I didn't look until I went downtown...well, sure enough it was there and I got on the streetcar in a happy daze and sat down and read it four times. I seem to have developed a habit of anticipating pleasure. I wait just as long as I can.

I had a letter from your mother today too. I had told her that I wasn't feeling well and she got unduly disturbed about it and thought that all kinds of removal would have to take place. I don't know where she got that idea as I told her it was perfectly and easily curable. I guess it's a tendency to alarmist thinking. However I did write last night and said all was fine so maybe she won't have that idea any more. She said that she had written you four letters so you should have quite a hunk of mail waiting for you. I hope you get my latter letters before you leave there.

I will accept your advice about that job with Chet although I couldn't leave here for a while anyway so there isn't much of a question about it for a week or so anyway. But I would appreciate any advice about it because I just don't know whether to get this job here back or take that other one. Well, think about it.

Absolutely nothing has happened since yesterday that makes much difference aside from hearing from you. I ran out of cigarettes tonight though so I had to get dressed and go down and get some... it was a fool thing to forget this afternoon. That Frances Driever who lives in this apartment...remember, her husband borrowed the chairs called and asked me to drop over. I said at first I couldn't but then decided that if I were going down for the cigarettes that I could stop there on my way back so I talked to them for an hour o r so. Her husband is gone now and she lives with a girl named Betty Taylor. She is that girl that Martha Stanley promised the apartment to and she doesn't want it any more so there is no hurry for me to get out. So that is fine. They were really awfully nice.

I am reading a book called "The Senator's Last Night" by Francis Hackett. It is so erudite that I am rather hard put to follow it and have to read some things over and over to be sure what he is talking about. There is a great deal of high-flown conversation even among the servants and I really don't see the merit in being so complicated. What is the use of having good ideas if it takes a person three readings to understand it. Really though, it is very good once you get on to it. I have given up the lending library where things cost five cents a day. Up the street a few feet is one where the latest books are all ten cents.

Good heavens, the phone just rang and it was Will Price calling from Oceanside California. I was mystified. But it seemed that he had had a letter from Jim and Margaret Latham and had told him I was sick. Well, I had written the Lathams about Kathie and said I had not been able to get down and get the power of attorney and you know how these stories spread. According to Jim...through Margaret, I was nigh on to death and Will got worried that with you gone and all so he called to see if I was alright. I nearly fell over. He said not to tell Maureen that he had called...I guess she would be jealous... there was no reason though. Just the paternal attitude...actually. I told him that I had heard from you and he was so happy and would write you. I have been getting a long distance telephone call almost every night. I feel highly honored. But I shouldn't have told anyone I didn't feel well. By this time everyone probably thinks I am dead... which is very funny. Next time I'll keep my woes to myself what with having alarmed communications from both the North and the South.

Honey, I am so glad to hear that your arm is better. I was afraid I would annoy you if I inquired...because you didn't want me to talk about it...remember. But I am so happy that it is O.K. Is that little man rubbing for you every day.

That is the darndest thing about your message. You probably know by this time that I never received it. Every time I look at that yeoman up there, I think he is one of the world's sourest, most unaccommodating people but this really proves it. I never heard one word of it. The only way I knew you had caught the ship was that I didn't hear from you. I don't know whether to bawl him out or not but I really think I ought to mention it.

Gosh, darling, I wish there were more ways to say I love you. I have a feeling that all my letters have sameness to them and that I just can't make you understand how terribly much I do love you and miss you. There just isn't any other way to say it...believe me, it is so much that if there were other words, they couldn't express it either. A goodnight kiss to you my darling...I love you so much it really is just like an ache...we'll make up for it all after you get home.

All my love,
Jane
X — the biggest in the world

October 1943
Letter No. 8

Dearest Honey;

Hope you will forgive the two copies deal, but I had that much of the same to say to both of you, and it makes it a lot easier that way. This is really a spot. Tiny little island, coral of course, and they form a circular fringe around the main Island, which is itself so small that it would be very easy to go by within a few miles of it and never see it.

I haven't had any word from you for about ten days now, so I don't know what the dope is on the operation, if you had to have it or not, I would like to know, but must wait till the next part to hear.

We can get mail off here, but there is none for us. The next stop we make is where I said goodbye to Fry Couther, and Jug-head. Maybe they are still around there somewhere, I will take a good look for them you can be sure of that.

Honey I have the Mid-watch tonight, so I think I will slip into the office and write you a real mushy letter, I feel one coming on. How about that, could you stand for a lot of syrup from me. Well I'll bat out one later tonight then. I've got to close this up now, as the liberty party is due back from the beach, and I must be on hand to welcome them back, also there will be swimming call then I think I will dunk the body for a few minutes. The movie for tonight is "Mr. Lucky" I hope the name will apply to me, but why wouldn't it, after all living on the "Gamble." As one of the sailors said the other day "well Mr. Flynn, she's not much to look at but she's a home and a feeder"

Goodbye till later —

All my love —

Chuck

2370 Chestnut St.
Apt 304
San Francisco 23, California
October 2, 1943
Letter 13

Hello, Darling; I am wondering how and where you are this evening and if this letter will reach you before you go away from where you can receive it. There was no letter from you today, but I daresay that is because the mails were delayed. I was so anxious to hear from you that I just forgot that there would be times that would be very long between letters when you were someplace where there were no postboxes. I am hoping that the letters will continue to come for a few days after this at least. By the way, darling...the next time you go to sea, could you maybe grab a little while to jot down a few lines once in a while even if you couldn't mail them until later. I know there isn't much you can tell about what you are doing, but there must be some way that I could get a little more of you...I mean, how would you like me to write you such little letters. I realize you are busy, but really that busy. I get just as lonesome for you as you do for me and appreciate the mail just as much. So just once when you get the time, would you write that long letter you spoke of. Well, enough of that...you know I miss you and I just like to have you talk to me, too...So please, a little more than a note.

Jean Douglas came up to see me today and we had a long talk about Frances Farmer and various other characters that we know mutually. She stayed a couple of hours and it was really much fun for me. The Colonel brought her up and I gave them some red points I had left over as today was really the last day for them and I had bought myself more even than I needed. If I had realized before yesterday, I would have sent some to your mother. Now, though, I have only one book, so I won't have any extra.

They wanted me to go for a ride with them, Megan asked me up tonight, and the girls across the way asked me to go to a movie with them, but I declined all because the dr. said to stay in bed. It seems so silly because I look so healthy...but it will soon be fixed. I talked to the doctor this morning and informed him that the situation was still going strong, so he said that he guess that was that and I really had better go to the hospital Monday morning and he would fix it...so I will and get it over with really. Of course he had hoped it would stop and I thought it would too, but the last day it got a little worse so might as well get it fixed up. I will be awfully relieved. After all, there's nothing to it.

Good heavens, I don't know as I believe in freedom of speech the way the Republicans have been carrying on over the radio the last couple of days. They seem to have started an all-out campaign of sniping and it gets pretty disgusting to listen to. Maybe they will overstep the bounds, though. Landon talked the other night and he definitely did...I have never heard such drivel. How he did carry on! Really some people should learn to hear themselves as others hear them. With the conventions a good eight months away...we're going to have to listen to all this for a year now. And some people such as Landon are already getting so carried away that some of their statements sound more like treason than criticism. I think the English have a point...at least they don't have all this agitation at a time like this.

In "Between the Thunder and the Sun" Vincent Sheean commented on the last election and said that it was unnecessary and took up too much of the nation's energy and should be postponed... should have been, rather. I didn't agree with him when I read the book, but I am certainly inclined to now. It is a sin. They should recall Benjamin Franklin's words about hanging and stop being selfish. I think that Willkie is about the only outstanding representative of the Republicans that isn't out for personal power and using the war and criticism of the administration to gain it...and he's got himself out of such a limb that the fools will nominate Dewey instead. Well, I'll do as much as I can about it.

This book I said I was reading, "The Interpreter," is the greatest piece of back-fire anti-British propaganda I have ever read. I suppose it's because an Englishman is trying to write it .and portray Americans. Oh, what a bunch of mistakes he makes...I just feel sorry for him...What's more, it hasn't even been proofread. The man lands in New York from the Clipper after having been waiting weeks in Portugal for it, and the first thing he thinks of when he gets there is that he just left London twenty — four hours ago. This American commentator who has been in London during the blitz comes on request of the President to give a series of lectures in the United States designed to make the American people sympathetic toward the British. Well, according to the story, the President is having a devil of a time getting the American people to go the way...he is leading them to it step by step, but he brings over the commentator to facilitate matters...and has little talks with him about the problem of arousing the Americans. Well, that just makes the President out a plain liar and some people are going to take Gibbs seriously. Then the comment on the President after this Barton, the hero, meets with him, is that he has a great personality and that, not his brain, is responsible for his popularity...although he undoubtedly has a brain, too! There is a dead English wife that he mourns all the way through the book...Lady Anne. Her chief distinction is that she looked like a portrait by Romney and she really wasn't snobbish when you got to know her. He is always talking about iced drinks, which was the American predilection of the correspondent, and capitalizing such things as Coca-Cola, Grapenuts, and Camel cigarettes. That is supposed to add the American touch. The American correspondent is the most discourteous, bigoted, self-pitying character I have ever met and he excuses it all by thinking he is just a rough American and not cultured like the English. The chief protagonist of isolationism, named Val D. Turner, which sounds remarkably like Burton K. Wheeler, is characterized chiefly by the fact that he admits he is being an isolationist to get publicity, he calls dirty names on the platform, and he likes old-fashioneds at ten in the morning. Needless to say, our correspondent drinks coffee. I will say that he tries to be fair about the arguments against England — he brings them all up, but all our correspondent can think of to say is that the Cockneys were awfully brave after the bombing. I really feel sorry about the whole thing...obviously the man didn't mean that his book should create that impression. The thing shouldn't be on the market.

Well, I certainly devoted a lot of time to that...but nothing has impressed me so that I have read in a long time. My goodness, if everybody were to read that book, there would be a riot. I am seriously considering writing a letter about it

I wrote a letter. Just like you in your cupo in the Town forum in the "Citizen News."

Well, Honey Baby, that is about all for tonight...take good care of yourself and especially that arm right now, and I love you.

I am enclosing a letter from Mother...I'll send Buddy's when it comes...isn't that awful about Junie. I hope that doesn't prevent the flying. Thank goodness, you're in the Navy. I love you, Honey... goodnight, my darling.

Jane xxxxxxxxxxxxxxxxxxxxxxx

#7
Oct 4th At Sea, 1943

Dearest Honey:

Well darling it's been almost four days since I took pen in hand to write you. Not that love is lacking, or you're not being missed like hell, but duties still press. I've been working on my ship's service inventory today, and think I've got it pretty well whipped. Ship's service! Remember that last morning darling? At least it was so hectic, that no-one had time to be starry-eyed about the approaching departure. I'll always remember that view of you out up the door of the truck, all three of us waving like mad!

We did have fun being married didn't we darling? Not that I don't think we'll have fun again, but the part that has gone by was really wonderful. I can truthfully say that you are perfect, and if I had the power I would change nothing about you. Honey it's been such a wonderful, full interesting life, let's never compromise it for dull, stolid existence. It would be such a dull anti — climax to a brilliant start. Not that we can't have a little money, even some in the bank would be nice, but let's never get stuffy about it. Gloating over balances, that sort of thing.

Darling I don't know why I haven't mentioned it before, but that day we left, I was sure I saw you up at Coit tower! We got these new super glasses aboard, and I told everybody on the after dark house that my wife was up there waving goodbye to me, and oh, honey, you sweetheart, you actually were!

One other thing, it will be the 12th penny under the bridge. Remember we had a trial run one day which accounted for 9 and 10, so if you ever get a message like "reaching for 12th penny" you'll know what's up.

Also, the jacket finally caught up with me. The mail clerk brought it down yesterday and, honey, it's beautiful. Just think, only 5 more days and it would have been 2 months late! But honey I'm so glad to get it and it really is lovely. Thank you so much, darling.

Well, last night I scotch-taped up pictures of you around the room, a lot on the end of the desk by my bunk, so the last thing I see at night and the first thing in the morning is you, honey. I say hello, and goodnight to you, too — do you ever hear? Loving you so much you should be able to hear me.

Darling, that watch calls I stand 8-12 in the morning alone. Will try and write again tomorrow as we will be able to post mail in a day or two.

Goodnight my darling — All me love — Chas

...to come I know that the last thing I will do at night is to reach over for the folder and re-read some of those delightful letters. Bless you honey-child — they are wonderful.

I just lit a cigarette with "our" zippo and yep — I thought of you. I always do darling, and I smoke a couple of packs a day — so you see you come in for your share of thoughts.

What's that horrible rumor of 3 cigs a day! My God, you poor civilians. I'm not being funny either, that is terrible, why on earth is such a thing necessary? Well, as you say. it's horrible to be a hoarder, but damn if I don't think you should start buying an extra carton a week and stashing them away in a closet. I'm really serious honey. Cigs are one thing you shouldn't be forced to do without. I can think of another — can you? Brother — am I kidding!!!!!!!!

Well, darling, I wonder where you are in Hollywood, Nina's or the Highland or where, and what kind of luck you are having with the apt. hunting. As I remember, unfurnished were always easier to find. Good hunting, honey. Remember how we used to read the Citizen News every night for places, even when we had no idea of moving?

Well, my love, the watch is drawing to a close and I can go back to bed, I hope to dream about you! I'll write you again tomorrow, I think we are shoving in a couple of days-night!

All me love Chas

XXXXXXXXXXXXXXXXXXXXXXXXXXXXXX XXXXX

Look out for the wolves and woo-woo!

2370 Chestnut Street
San Francisco 23, California
October 9, 1943
Letter 17

Well, this has been a landmark of a day...it is the first day since you left that I have got up in the morning with intention of staying up all day and have done so without any bad results. I am so relieved about the whole thing and it is so wonderful. Of course I am just dead tired and will probably sleep until noon tomorrow but it's a big step in the right direction. I am wondering if you will get any place where you can write so I will hear from you by next Friday... after all that will be three weeks from the time your last letter was mailed. I would have to be Thursday though for me to get it because I made reservations for the train today for next Friday...I beg your pardon...two weeks...I had to take the San Joaquin but I am hoping that when I go to pick up the ticket on Monday that they will have something that I can change to on the Daylight. I have decided that I can't possibly stop at Monterey because I just have to get down there and do something about that furniture. Today I got a letter forwarded from the county Tax collectors that they said was the final notice of taxes before seizure and sale...well, I had never had another bill and this one was mailed on the first. I immediately sat down and wrote a check...that I thought was a final thing if there should be any trouble about that. But they should have the check on Monday morning because it has been mailed. I also mailed them a letter saying I had never relieved another bill. I can't understand why they should be so peremptory because they were the taxes for 1943 and that isn't even over yet. I didn't pay 1942 taxes until last March. It looks like a conspiracy.

I went out to dinner tonight...with Colonel Douglas of all people at Veneto's...it was a lovely dinner and he brought me a pint of bourbon and it was all very nice and It was certainly fine to not be cooking it yourself. He was very nice but you are right, he is a wolf, at least mentally...he kept it well in restraint...but it made me a little uncomfortable...he is a gentleman at the same time though because when I talked about how wonderful you were, he took it in the right spirit and didn't try to make any faux pas. So all was fine. I hope it doesn't make you uncomfortable to have me talk like this. What I mean is that if there were a pack of wolves, it wouldn't make any difference to me..I just love you so much that it is over-powering and all I can't think or talk about is you and you alone.

Honey, our life, in spite of the broke times and all has just been enchanted and I think about it all the time...it is really just like a fairy story and I just love you so much that I wish there were something I could do to express how terribly much it is and how I have loved it all. I guess just wait until after the war when we can have our happy times again.

I neglected you last night because I had so much company and they stayed so late. The three girls in the apartment came and then Annie came and she stayed until about midnight. I was worried about her going home alone so I asked her to stay the night but she wasn't afraid and she really had to get home to get ready for work this morning so she went on and phoned me when she got there. I really think she is seriously considering marrying that Johnny Wright and I think it would be a fine thing if she did. We talked about it at great length last night...and of course, I being the incurable romanticist encouraged her. He would make her a very good husband to my opinion and she certainly deserves one.

I do hope that she does marry him; evidently he's all in favor of it. No word has been heard from Pat so far by anyone. I guess she has been poured in trains all across the country at the end of visits but she should be in Washington in a day or so.

I talked to Daddy last night, he called from Portland. He sounded like he had a cold but I guess she had been smoking too much...at least, that's what he said.

I polished all the silver in the place today and washed the bathroom curtain...that at least is a little bit toward getting organized and ready to go. Now I just have to get the house cleaned and things packed and go to the doctor and the dentist and get a little sewing done and all will be fine. I am very anxious to get down there now that I have to go and get things arranged because it is getting on my mind. Thank goodness, there will be Don there to lend advice and help and he is very practical. I will have to hire somebody to pack things and move and such I am afraid because I can't lift anything and everybody that we know is working so hard that I won't be able to ask anyone to really do the heavy work. I was having a talk with the doctor about the furniture and he said it might be to our advantage if some of the stuff was missing or damaged. But I am not that much of a business person and don't want to have any legal trouble with anybody. It will all work out well though.

I am thinking of you tonight darling wherever you are and I love you like the dickens and with all my heart so take care of yourself and I'll see you soon.

All the love I have which is a lot.

Jane

XXXXXXXXXXXXXXXXXXXXXXXXXXXXXXXxx

I LOVE YOU

2370 Chestnut St., Apt. 304
San Francisco 23, Calif. October 10, 1943
Letter 18

Hello Honey Darling;

Your wife is the greatest letter writer to you...if I don't be careful, you will be saying, "Doesn't that woman ever run down or out of things to talk about. It's worse than being at home when she wouldn't let me read the newspaper at the breakfast table." Nevertheless I shall continue writing and raving over and over again about how much I love you.

I had rather an interesting evening tonight. The Douglases are being very nice to me. I went with Jean and the Colonel to the Presidio Officer's club to dinner and then to a movie at Fort Mason, and then they dropped up here for a glass of beer. It was the first time that Jean had ever seen the place with the bed up, and she was quite awed by the whole thing because it's so much nicer than their apartment. She hadn't realized it before because it had always been such an awful mess. Today though, I put the bed up and cleaned it up pretty well. It was almost like it was when you were here and made me homesick for you.

The Officer's Club at the Presidio is the oldest building in San Francisco...built in 1776. They have covered over the adobe with stucco so that unfortunately now it looks sort of fake old. It is very large, having originally been a fort and some sort of an army post for the Spaniards. They have a funny little panel in the wall and if you press a button...it slides up and a light goes on and some of the original adobe is displayed. It's rather pitiful. It looks just like those old walls in Monterey only this looks like it should have black widow spiders crawling around. They have a lovely bar and then a buffet supper and nothing but army officers and their wives were to be seen with the exception of one Admiral...poor man, he looked so out of place. One funny thing happened, I saw the man who used to be the doctor at Eatonville and a great friend of mine when I was in high school. His name is Glavotski...Russian obviously...He is a friend of all the people in the Russian ballet and I met a couple people in college through him...I mean when they had the ballet I used to see him there and he introduced me to Lichine and somebody else. He is in the dispensary at the Presidio and is a captain. It was like a bolt out of the forgotten past to see him. I knew him because he was such a good friend of a boy I used to go with that drank wood alcohol because he had to move away...you remember that. I've talked about it innumerable times.

The movie was simply wonderful. It was "Johnny Come Lately" with James Cagney. I had wanted to see it because Time gave it the best review they have ever given anything. It seems that James Cagney left Warner's and he and his brother Bill started a new producing company and this is their first picture. There is also a big article in this week's Post about it by H. Allen Smith...your pal. Of course all the big movie companies hoped that it would be a failure, but it is the best thing Cagney has ever done and the best thing Time says that has come out in a long time. It is so simply delightful and done in such wonderful. taste that it is just unbelievable. Every single bit is a jewel. If you get a chance where you are, see it. I don't know how new the movies are of course.

Mr. Maqueron came in the other day to inquire about the laundry and I had a big talk with him about politics and such stuff and he is certainly well informed. He was the head of this big French steamship line before the war and he has been all over the world. He says that to say a person is like an Australian girl is just a password for saying that they are over sexed...that they always made perfect sights of themselves on all the liners. He lays it to the fact that they eat too much meat. So if you ever get to Australia, please be careful for my sake. I never had it actually straight before as he pointed out that the reason Cornell Hull stays in the State department is that the President doesn't dare get rid of him because of the southern Democrats...he could never hope to have Congress behind him or be re-elected if he discharged him. He was meaning about Hull representing us at the coming conference... that it was just giving us a black eye because he couldn't possibly measure up to the delegates from other countries and he had no policy and he is anti-Russian. Drew Pierson was making a big fuss today because of the Russian independence day and whether we should recognize it as we did last year. It seems Hull wouldn't say yes or no and Stettinius just didn't know what to do...he is kind of a dummy. So he finally decided not to and now there is a great furor and tomorrow the President will give Stettinius a big bawling out and revoke the decision. Fine goings on when we are going to have a big conference with Russia. Then Lodge said that it was costing us a million lives not to have Russian bases which has made a great furor. Well, yesterday his colleague Senator Brewster got up and said that Lodge was a liar. It seems that Marshall told Lodge that if we got the bases, we could only hope to hold them for two weeks because we couldn't get troops there and Russia couldn't either, and Japan had them just across the border. So Marshall asked Lodge not to speak about it because it was impractical, so Lodge violated the confidence and misrepresented, and Brewster got up in the Senate and exposed him only the expose will never get into the papers. There is a big article in Colliers this week by Archbishop Spellman in which he defends Franco. I told Mr. M. about that and he said he was going home and be sick to his stomach.

It is so nice to be well again. I not only cleaned today, I washed, and then on top of that, I sewed. I decided that I wanted three-quarter sleeves on the grey velveteen, so I recut them and put tucks in the top so that it looks more sophisticated, and I got the top just perfect. I feel guilty all the time I am doing it, but I just had to get the lines the way I wanted them and I hope that your feelings won't be hurt after all the time your mother worked on it. But the way the pattern was, the sleeves had to go in sort of gathered and that didn't look good. Besides, the armholes were too small for shoulder pads, so I had to cut them out a little bit. But it will look just about the same. I feel awfully bad about it, but I just have to do it.

It was a stroke of luck that I told the Douglases that I had to take the San Joaquin because he said he thought he could get me a ticket on the Daylight tomorrow instead. That would be so much better, as you well know.

Do you know our phone bill here that I just paid was 13 dollars and there are the bills for two or three calls that haven't come in yet. I hope they don't before I go. I am afraid that we will never stop being victims of telephonitis. I come by it naturally as my family has it, but it just grew up in you. I have been reading the Navy wife and it says it is alright to get money from a bank or finance company. So I am going to get the money from the Seaboard for that telephone bill as soon as I get there, then pay it off by the month or there is going to be hell to pay. I just got a letter from Ithaca about it and time is going fast...I better hurry and pay it but immediately, and that seems the best way. I have even been thinking how I could get down there next Saturday morning to do it.

Well, that is about all the news for tonight, darling. I send all the love there is and millions more...I love you so much and miss you so much. Be good and careful, honey.

All my love,
Jane XXXXXXXXXXX
X enormous —
[HUGE X]
You better write me at the Lathams
8620 Lookout Mt. Drive, Hollywood 46, Calif. until I tell you another address.

At a lonely Island Oct 11 1943:

Dear Kids:

    I thought I would write a page of stuff to you both, and as long as it is just about where I am and what I have been doing I took the carbon in hand to save a lot of time. We have been here for a couple of days now, and will stay a few more it looks like. It is just a dot in the vast area of the Pacific. What in peace. times we would conjure up as an ideal "South sea Island" when you get right down to it though, they are pretty hot and rainy all at the same time. Yesterday we had a very good time however. (I just had to move over the other typewriter.) [THE ALIGNMENT OF THE LINE OF TEXT CHANGED NOTICEABLY WHEN HE DID.]

    The ship has a very good softball team, and the rest of us picked up a scrub nine to give them a little competition. The captain played first, Peterson, another officer played third, and I started as pitcher. I only lasted for three innings and then they got my range and shelled me out of the box. It was a lot of fun, however. The regular won 13-3 but they are playing again this afternoon. I have the deck this afternoon, so I couldn't go over, but I am going to give it another whirl tomorrow. After all, the last time I pitched a game was some twelve years ago, so there might be a little excuse for my not going the route. Then we came back to the ship and all of us went swimming over the side, it was wonderful, if anything the water was too hot, that's hard to believe I know, but it honestly was. Of course I stayed in for about an hour just swimming around, really was most refreshing. I don't know if you have the idea, but it is hotter than billy- bedamned down here. Of course that stay in S.F. with those good cold fogs didn't do much to get us acclimated to this. Actually you just sit around and sweat. Not a pretty word I know, but so help me it's the only way you can describe what we do.

    Then last night we had a very good movie aboard. "The Human Comedy." The crew of course didn't go much for it, they are very partial to musicals, and things with lots of Betty Grable's legs in it, that sort of thing, but actually I thought it was a fine picture. We have a movie every night we are in Port, and that helps pass the time pretty well. Actually we all are getting caught up on our sleep a little here, you see we were supposed to get three new officers in S.F. but we left in such a hurry that they never got aboard, well that makes only six of us to stand watches, and when you are at sea that is pretty rough going, four on eight off, and then you have to put in a full day's work in your dept. as well. Still it's all grist for the mills of the gods, and as I now know, they grind exceedingly fine.

We crossed the Equator the sixth I think it was, and brother what a field day they had on the "pollywogs." It really was rough and I am very glad I had been over once before on a ship. Berkeley, my roommate, hadn't and he is just now able to sit down' in comfort. Of course he lost most of his hair too!!!

Well kids I guess that about handles the general news, I'll add a bit for each of you and get these off in the morning. By the way, the heat may be bad, but I sure am getting my figure back, that's the only good part of the whole thing!! When you next see me I will be slim and bronzed. Woo-woo!!

2370 Chestnut Street
San Francisco 23, Calif.
October 11, 1943
Letter 19

Dearest honey darling;

Writing to you marked the end of each day and it is hard to believe that this last one has passed so quickly. It just seems a few minutes before that it was last night and I was sitting here typing. That is a welcome change because before this the time has gone so slowly. Now I am so busy that it fairly shizzes ast. It is ten in the evening and I have the satisfaction of knowing that it is nothing that a few minutes laying down won't cure. I got up at nine this morning and sewed all day and then I rested an hour and then went out and did some errands and come home and rested some more then made some dinner I spent a couple of hours ironing. I am gradually getting this place spruced up and it isn't anything like the old moldy hole that it was last week. I even washed and ironed the bathroom curtains...while ironing I kicked myself that I hadn't sent them to the laundry. I am having a drink of bourbon too which is also very fine with my sense of accomplishment.

Today is another week's anniversary...exactly three weeks since you left...it seems like a lifetime really.

Now that I am going to Los Angeles, I am anxious to get started but I do realize that I need until Friday to gradually get things ready. Today I took the lighter to the little jewelry store up the street and am having Chas put on it at last. So you see, I will think of you every time I light a cigarette...are you still doing the same with Zippo?

A letter came from Buddy today describing his first week's experiences at Fort Rearns Utah...I think it is pretty good so I will type it out and send it to you because Mother wants it back. It is the best thing about first going into the army camp that wasn't written for commercial reason and to be funny that I've ever read.

The World Series game today was just heartbreaking. It's alright if the Yankees won because they didn't last year but it should have gone on a little further and they tried so hard and had more hits than the Yankees. It was full of suspense up until the last moment and then all of sudden it was over. Maybe you heard it if you weren't busy and I hope you weren't. They said they were short-waving it.

I just had a brain wave. The big rumor tonight is that Portugal is going to declare war on Japan. Well, there doesn't seem to be all the information possible being given out. Of course we could use the Azores and then maybe capture Timor from the Japanese but what seems to me possible and something that the commentators haven't mentioned is that we might land troops there and go up through Spain and into France. Of course that is quite a way and there are Pyrenees but at the same time it would eliminate the difficulties of making a landing under fire. I just wonder if they have that idea at the back of their minds. If they have, I think they're pretty smart. Of course I realize that I haven't been any great shucks as a prognosticator. The only thing I was right about was the Aleutians and that was something I'll never forget but I just got that idea. I wonder if it is practicable.

Mr. Maqueron said he couldn't finish the article by Archbishop Spellman...that it literally did make him ill. He also heard some of the same talk by a man named Wagner over the radio yesterday and was bemoaning the whole thing. He says that the best solution would be to send the Irish Republican Army to rescue the Pope! He does have a sense of humor.

I haven't decided whether to carry the piece of the Gamble clutched in my little hand or whether to try to get it in a suitcase. At any rate it is just the most important piece of my luggage.

Ironed your pajamas tonight and all the time I was doing it I kept wondering how soon you would be home and refuse to wear them. I have quite a wardrobe of yours here...one handkerchief, one pair of shorts, one T shirt and one pair of pajamas. I just look at them every once in a while.

I just don't like all this talk about a big offensive in the Pacific. I will worry until I hear from you and then I'll start over again. However don't worry about my worrying. I shant say any more about it.

Goodnight honey. I love you.

All my love,

Jane

XXXXXXXXXXXXXXXXXXXXXXXXXXXXXXXXXXXXXXXXXXX
XXXXXXXXXXXXXXXX

October 12, 1943 In Port (of sorts)

Dearest Honey:

Well it is now one-thirty in the morning, and I am sitting here thinking very much of you. It's hard to put into words how much you love and miss a person, the emotions you try and transcribe into words never seem to come out in the re-reading the way they sounded when you heard your inner self forming them.

In a way I am very lucky. I don't mean that being away from you is good, but rather that while the fact of being away is beyond any of our control, the memories we retain, and the thoughts we have are strictly our own business. That's how I'm so lucky. I have you and our life together to think about, and to relive. To savor it and roll it around my mental tongue exactly as you do a sip of good wine, or a bite of rare steak. And the fact that there are so many and varied facets of our life together makes it an unpredictable game. Anything at all can start the wheels rolling. Take the old Packard for instance. I think of you driving it, and the time Bobby put it over the curb at Alta Vista, and the way he loved it, and the time the guy hit us, and how surprised the dog looked, and loading groceries into it at the Farmers market, and me pushing you and you steering the damn old heavy thing. Remember Honey? You never steered it the way I considered right, and I would get so furious with you because you didn't cut the wheels in time or some such silly thing. Remember the nights coming home late from some rehearsal and you would bear the agony of the split seat to sit next to me? And the way your hair smelled, and the feel of you next to me. Remember eating hemo in the kitchen and earthquakes shaking the water in the jug, and the cups jingling in the cupboard. And then we would go to bed., and I could hold you in my arms and feel all the wonderfulness of your body, and then love would come, the physical side and then we would fall asleep.

Then in the morning I'd like as not slip down the hill and spend far too much on a breakfast steak, and by the time I got my raw-fried potatoes done you would be weak from hunger, and so would I. Then we would have our cigarettes and coffee, and you'd disappear for awhile. And then we would walk out on the sundeck of the garage and the dogs would be with us, and the kittens would be playing in and out of the old torn screen door, and high up in the blue noonday sun a P-38 would go whooshing by —

See darling what I mean about memories? Anything starts them going, and once started you never know which way the road is going to turn, or what strange sights will meet your eye. I think having memories to share with you is a great and wondrous thing. Because we have such an affinity for each other. Other people get married, and have fun and friends, but they never seem to have the feeling between them that we do. Almost like we always have a little mental joke, known only to the two of us, that charms and facinates our friends, even though they will never know the joke, and probably wouldn't think it funny if it could be put into words. I don't think it is anything we have done, or something that we should take especial credit for, it just comes with our being a team, and sharing each other's lives. You know honey nights are best at sea. During the day, you are always with me, and right beside me, but I have to keep kinda putting you off because I am too busy to talk to you. Almost like I was saying "honey I have to get the guns fixed this morning and then I have the watch to stand, and to keep my ship in her station so could I talk to you a little later?" But at night. That's the time. On that long eight to twelve, when all the starts are out, and the moon is so big that it is absolutely impossible, then is when we really get together. Some night we relive months of our lives, other nights it may only be one hour, or even an episode at a party.

I know there are times when you are thinking of me, because the feeling is so strong that I can almost reach out and put my arms around you. Then when the watch is over and I come down and have a bite to eat and talk a little war, or lit. or love with Currie, I am always eager to get into bed, then I look over and there you are! At least your pictures. Altogether about eight different views of you, some with me some with other people, but always you. I look you over carefully in each then tell you "Goodnight darling, I love you with all my heart" and then I turn out the light and dream of you. In the dreams you even get aboard and come around the ship with me. Such a persistent rascal you are in those dreams.

Darling I don't know if I ought to admit how much I am yours for richer, for poorer — maybe you will get far too conceited about your charm — but even as I write the lines I don't mean them and they are cheap and not in keeping with the way I feel toward you. What I am trying to say, my darling, is that I love you, and always will. And if the Good God sees fit to bring me through this mess in safety and back to you, I shall be very grateful. But back or no, always remember my darling, that I have had more life and living with you in our five and one-half years than comes to other men in a full lifetime.

Never forget I love you, and that I plan to come back. Until then my darling, live with me mentally across all these wet miles. Knowing you are there waiting for me, makes all this somehow bearable.

It's time to close now darling — I love you — Chas

2370 Chestnut St.
San Francisco 23, Calif. October 14, 1943

Dearest Honey Darling;

Well this is the last night on Chestnut Street and it is pretty sad as far as I am concerned...thinking of all the happy times we have had here...of course it could be glad, too, thinking of the fact that we had a chance to have and did have happy times. At any rate, it was wonderful and I hate to leave it behind.

It is just midnight and everything is packed and cleaned and I am in my nightgown with my hair fixed...a ghastly sight. When I finish this letter, I shall put the strap around the typewriter. That will completely close a certain period in our lives together...but so far each one has been better than the last, even when you absolutely loved the last, so I am looking forward to the next one.

I had a lot of things to do today, but had them so well organized that I could do them in a leisurely way and enjoy myself which was very fine. I went down to the station and checked most of my baggage and with no rush about it. I went up to Penney's to see about some yarn and got involved in a big conversation with one of the sales ladies about how she didn't like grey dresses because she used to live in the Ozarks and line the coffins with gray. She was awfully good at it, she said — she could just tack as fast as they could unwind the material. The Douglases took me to dinner again and are going to take me to the train in the morning...which is a great relief...Annie and Johnnie dropped over this evening and Megan sent over the negatives from Ithaca that we had been missing.

I didn't hear from you today as I had hoped. But when I think about it, I was silly to hope that I would. There hasn't been enough time. But still I get worried and think...am I gallivanting off to Hollywood and Chuck won't know just where I am and just think where he might be and what might be happening; I just wish I were staying here so I could get the first letter in a hurry, but then I think that you told me to go and there still hasn't been enough time to hear from you and I left a lot of stamped, self addressed envelopes so I will get the letters the next day — but how wonderful it will be to hear that you are someplace and well and happy.

Well, honey, I'll write you a note on the train tomorrow. It is the Daylight, luckily. Take care of yourself and all the love there is to you...just all of it in the world...your

Jane

In case you didn't get the other letters — the Lathams' address is 620 Lookout Mt. Ave.

Hollywood 46, Calif.

I keep repeating so no slip-up in mails.

All my love X

Oct. 16th, 1943. At Sea.

Dearest Honey:

Although it has been some sixteen days, nay seventeen since I heard from you, I know that I will be getting plenty of correspondence from you tomorrow, so I thought I would have a little note ready to go over with the mail man. We are getting in in the morning, so before long I hope to have the answer to a lot of questions I have been mentally forming. Are you all right? Did you have the operation? Are you still in S.F.? Did the apt deal some all right? Are you living down there now? Do you miss your old man? All those questions and a lot more. I'll reassure you on one point, Darling, I might miss you more, but I would be a pretty horrible guy to live with if I did. We have this record player in the wardroom and we listen to records quite a lot. They remind me of many things and times and places together. Also they have a turntable in the radio shack, and they spin the platters of an evening, and it is piped all over the ship via those new speakers I showed you when you came aboard. Well, we have one in the wardroom also, and tonight at dinner they were playing "Easter Parade" and a lump the size of a California Sunkist got caught in my throat when I started thinking about us in New York last spring. Honey, those were the Golden Days weren't they. I hope when this mess gets all right again that we can have another go round at that little old city. It was fun being in the swim like that, plays and all that stuff like that there. The damn lights have gone out on our. ship, and I am sitting here in the dark making God knows how many mistakes, but I bet when the lights go back on there will be plenty. Well I am typing in the office as you can imagine, and one of the Yeoman is in here with me reading.

(Lights just came on again) He was trying to rig up a big flash light for us to work by, but now it is unnecessary. Well the mistakes weren't as bad as they could have been. The old lady is feeling her oats tonight and she is doing her thing. It doesn't bother me, but it is sometimes a question which key you are going to hit, if any!! We have been pretty lucky on weather, but of course somebody whistles, and this old tub starts leaping and gamboling.

Speaking about leaping. Up at that Island where we were for four-five days they had a bunch of PT boats. We got to know one of them pretty well. (The officers, not the boats I mean) and the day before we left I went out on one of them. They were having maneuvers with themselves, and brother!!!. What a ride. I now know why the Navy thought I was a little old for that kind of duty. We played around for a couple of hours and then they laid to and broke out all their small arms, and started firing at some drifting stuff, boxes and like that. I was sitting on one of the torpedo tubes watching a sailor fire a rifle when I glanced over the side. The water was only about five feet below me, and about two feet below the surface was a shark about 12 feet looking at me with a very speculative gleam in his eye. The guy with the rifle took a shot at him, but it didn't touch him and he very leisurely flipped his tail and swam away. The day before in the harbour I had been in swimming for a couple of hours. Look what he missed!! Nothing to worry about tho, Darling. We have

[PAGES MISSING]

8620 Lookout Mt. Ave
Hollywood 46, Calif. Oct. 18, 1943
Letter 25

Honey Darling,

I heard from you today! The two letters no 5 & 7 in the same envelope! I guess #5 was the blank piece of paper enclosed by mistake that was in the envelope dated Oct. 1. Oh honey, I was so happy and they were such wonderful letters. Honey, I love you so much it just hurts, and to get those letters made everything in the whole day happy for me. I hadn't really expected them. It was just after I finished writing to you this morning. Oh honey, how wonderful.

Everything turned out better today. I think I have made living arrangements. In the first place, I went to the Highland Hotel and they will probably have a vacancy tomorrow which I can have. So that is alright for awhile I hope. Then we finally got in touch with Nina & Pat Gleason. I've been calling her for two days and couldn't get any answer. Today I called Pat's again & Johnny Harman answered so we, Don & I, went up there & he called & called Nina 'til she answered. So Pat came down — we went up & got him & went to see the landlady at the Trend village & got her promise to disregard the working list and I could have the first vacancy. She thinks there will be one in the next week or so. I hope so because that would be the perfect place to live &.is also very cheap. Then I can see about a job. I can see about that after I get in the Highland Hotel, if I do. I haven't called Chet yet because I was waiting to get someplace fairly settled. Besides if I called him from here & got an appointment, I wouldn't have any way to get there.

Jentz Crane wants me to spend the night with her tomorrow & I may do it. Sid just left yesterday for Ventura. Of course they will have to stay here until he finds someplace for them to live. Jim Hill came over to see the Lathams tonight about selling his car. He was surprised to see me. I had been considering calling his mother & asking if Dave had seen you, but I hear that she is in Seattle. Dave is in the Fiji Islands now. I was going to wait a couple more days because I know it seemed a foolish question. And by that time, I would have been ready to grasp at anything and ask foolish questions. I talked to Lewis tonight and he was just as full of the old malarkey as ever — hasn't changed a bit. I sometimes get the feeling that these people around here are living in a dream world. I also talked to the Chamberlains. They wanted me to come to dinner but I couldn't. Maggie is in a play which is opening at the Mayan next week — something like "Sailor Beware." The first thing she asked was whether I was around a sewing machine and if I wanted to earn some money by making a wedding dress for the play. I just don't know where she got that idea. I couldn't quite get it & couldn't seem to convince her I didn't have time this week. I cut out a pair of culottes for her when you were in Florida & she has thought I was a "seamstress" ever since. I told her I'd try to find someone to do it. Everything is so different and so funny after living other places.

People have been just grand to me & its wonderful of them, but, oh darling, how happy I'll be to see you again. Nothing is as good without you. I think about you all the time — and oh honey, I love you with all my heart.

Everybody has wanted to know about your shoulder. It seems it furnished quite a subject of conversation & conjecture. All were happy to know that it was alright as they had really been worried.

I love you, I love you, I love you — my honey darling. You are the most perfect husband imaginable. Maybe it sounds silly to say things like that, but oh, honey, it's so true.

Until tomorrow darling — goodnight.

All my love,

Jane xxxxxxxxxxxxxxxxxxxx X

[HUGE ONE]

October 19th

Dearest Honey:

Just time for a line before we shove. A great disappointment no mail here. None at all! However we will probably pick up some day after tomorrow — I sure hope so. None since Sept 30th. That's too damn long.

As you see by the enclosure I found Jug-head here, might run into Fry up north Charlie says. Last night Eddie Albert and Chas and I hung on a beaut! I didn't get home till 2345! Almost midnight! Lots of laughs, and the first drink I've had since Sept 28th so I ain't exactly a rum pot yet. In the course of the evening I ran into Luta Bonynge again. Not quite as fat, but still pretty big. She has been playing up at Espirito Santos up in the Hebrides. Bout it here for mail.

Love — Chas xxx

October 20th 1943 In Port:

Dearest Honey:

Well we are still here laying around, and it is very pleasant. We are finally getting a little caught up with all the million and one things that we had to do. Of course we are not through yet, but the end is in sight in the not too far distant future.

Day before yesterday (it is now five in the morning) was my liberty day and I got over on the beach. The mine depot bunch here have a wine mess, and we were invited over. Everyone can buy a jug and they put your name on it and hold it for you until the ship gets back in here again. Best bourbon I have seen in a long time, and we all got pretty well boiled up. God how wonderful it was to wake up yesterday morning with a terrible hangover!!! The Capt. and most of the officers made the club and we really had a wonderful afternoon. It's better than the big club for officers here because that closes at a quarter to seven while this goes on as late as you want. It is just a Quonset hut with a few tables and chairs and a little bar and lots of shaved ice. It is right under a bunch of coconut palms planted in very orderly rows by the Lever Bros. And it is very pretty. The ground is all covered with green almost like lawn. Very — park-like.

Remember our fish bowl? Well, honey, all the kinds we had I have seen in the water out here, plus all their relations near and distant. Such colors and shapes you have never dreamed of. If I just had a way to ship you some I would, and you wouldn't believe them even if you actually saw them. I spend a lot of time looking over the side at them when I have the in-port watch.

I wrote a letter to Dave Oswald and also Bob Scott the other night, the same night as I last wrote you. Then last night the movie was "My Favorite Spy" and it seemed funny to see Bob and me, too in the line-up. The men on the ship really hollered when they saw me standing there. It was very funny. Speaking of Dave, I think our next call will be where we last heard of him. The secondary branch of my dept is coming in for a little do should be very interesting. I will tell you all about it when we get back here in a little while. The letters may have to stop for a few days because I think it will be tomorrow when we dust out of here. Keep your fingers crossed for us honey, we will need it.

I have some things to read before the day starts, also about fifty letters to censor, so I am going to have to knock off on this one. I might get a chance to drop another line tonight. I will if there will be a chance to mail it tomorrow, if not it will be a few days. I am enclosing another $15.00, wish it was more but I am pretty poor. I do hope you are all right; I haven't heard from you for four days now, but I imagine I will get some today. The last letter I got was the night before you were taking the Daylight down home.

Keep the letters coming, honey. God bless you darling I love you so much

All me love, Chas xxxxxxX have one on me!

October 22nd, 1943 In Port

Dearest Honey:

Darling I am so overwhelmed that I don't know how I can possibly do justice to all those letters in one answer tonight, so I will compromise and just tell you the over-all feeling I got, and then go into the details at a later date when I have had more time to assimilate them.

We got in here late last night, and early this morning the mail came aboard. I had 14 letters from you and misc. others including

Mom's that brought the grand total to twenty-two. Quite a stack
and I have had so much fun reading them. Yours are so wonderful
darling, and there is so much to comment on and discuss with you
that I have material for days of letters just by re-reading the ones I
got this morning. The last one I got was mailed the 14th; counting
the lag it is only seven days. I hope mine are getting to you that
fast. At the moment you were torn between the daylight and the
San Joquin. Or, "her Honor vs. the Col." Didn't I tell you the old goat
was a second adolescent jerk? The old fool, I should have punched
him in the nose the day I first met him when he made that crack!

I must confess that I read the last one first, as I was so damn
worried about the operation and all. I find that you did have to have
it, but so far the letters have left me in doubt. Is everything cleared
up for good and for all, and what is this business about in three
months? Honey, don't try to keep anything from me, and above all,
tell me all! I can conjure up more bad things out here just a thinkin'
than could ever possibly be true. Gosh, do you realize that it has
been well over three weeks since I heard from you, and think of all
the things that can happen in that length of time. I. was fair distraught, darling, and I do mean it. It seems all I have to do is let you
get out of my sight, and all manner of weird things happen to you.

I take it that you have given up the lovely apt., just to think
never will I see it without the cactus. Damn. I'm sure that is the
best idea however, personally if I ever lived over that Helen person
again I would deliberately drop shoes in the middle of the night. One
thing, Honey, you are so damn attractive, and Don is such a sweet
guy and so wonderful and considerate about you and us, don't ever
let him bat those sheep's eyes at you and lure you into the security
of an unwed bed. Not that I worry about you, but you know him,
and also you know drunk you can get on occasion! Save that big
drunken spree for just after the victory parade down Tokyo Blvd.

I know there is no rhyme or reason for statements like that, but
sitting way out here your damn imagination can do fearful tricks
to you. Darling I love you so much, and the thought of the life we
have had and will have together is just so wonderful to contemplate
that I find myself clutching it to my mental bosom for strength to
go on. (what a horribly mixed metaphor!) Incidentally, speaking
of the life to come, I think the idea for a book is very sound, and
interest me greatly, however I will deal with it at greater length
in another letter.

I have no business trying to write tonight, as I go on watch very soon, and I am so tired that I am falling on my face. God, I will really be glad when we get those three new ensigns aboard, it will enable us to get a nights sleep over six hours once in a while. I am just kinda standing bye tonight, but tomorrow night I have the mid watch, and as we are in port and there is not much doing at the moment, I will bang out a hell of a good letter and long, too.

I got over on the beach this afternoon for a little while, and among other things saw the theater where Lita did 'Brother Rat" with her company up here. Very nice theater for primitive and I imagine the local yokels ate it up.

Got a letter from Horne today, and should run into him up north a little further. Darling I hate to do this, but I am about to fall asleep over the machine so I'll have to close. I will get off a good one tomorrow, but in the meantime, honey, thanks so much for those wonderful letters; you don't know what they mean. It's like a breath of you, almost the touch of you in this god-dam ugly joint. Something so nice and wonderful that I am afraid to say too much or I will louse up the lovely feeling that I have. I love you, darling, and miss you more than I can say — until tomorrow then —

All me love honey — Chas

X (to grow well on!) I love you!

921 Highland Ave. Highland Hotel Hollywood, Calif.
October 23, 1943
Letter 27

Honey Darling;

Yesterday I got letter ten from you...written just six days ago. It was mailed on the 17th of October and I got it the 22nd. That is really speed. And it took a day to forward it from San Francisco. Honey, it is so wonderful to hear from you in such a hurry and to be able to visualize you in a specific place instead of looking at the map and wondering which part of that vast area you would be most likely to be on.

Well, as you can see, I am still in the Highland hotel. They moved me to a better room this morning, thank Heaven. It costs the same, but is a vast improvement. I expect in a few days if an apartment hasn't come up, to have one of their weekly rooms. It will still cost the same but have a balcony. If it weren't for the food situation, I would be very happy here, but it's rather irritating to have to go out every time you want something to eat, and not particularly good for the stomach. I guess you may as well write me here.

This is Saturday night and I have spent it very quietly and constructively. The Lathams wanted me to come up. Marg and I were going to sew all evening, but I decided not to because I had too many things that simply had to be done here. I washed my hair and am sitting here now with it in a towel. I washed clothes but, most important, I cut out your Christmas present...that is, one of them. I am going up to the Lathams' tuesday night to sew it up. I hope to get it all done then and in under the deadline of the first of November. I wrote the Stanleys about his offer of carrier of Christmas presents, but I haven't had an answer yet so I have to play safe. I had your sweater wrapped to send today, too. But of course that is not a Christmas present, in spite of the red ribbon around it. It will probably arrive about Christmas, but will be merely an extra. About the sweater...when I got it all finished, I discovered that the pattern was definitely too big, so I sewed it up the sides and cut it. It is still fine, but it means you always have to wear the ribbing turned up. You are supposed to anyway, but now you have to. I hated to do it, but it was better than having it encircle you one and a half times. I knew that you would probably want it pretty tight. Of course it is probably too hot to ever wear it, but maybe you will have a chance after you get back here.

I talked to Chet today. I decided I ought to call him because it would probably take him a time to get things set up, and I nearly fainted when he said that I had better come down Monday morning...that they had already spoken to the man about me and that they were expecting me to come in. I suppose that I won't get a job that fast. Frankly, I would rather wait a few days, but we'll see what happens. By the way, he wanted to know if you had received his letter of confirmation, and I made the mistake of telling him that you had. He has been wondering why he hasn't heard from you. I told him that you had been busy because you had been a little short of officers, but that he would probably hear from you in the next few days. So for heaven's sakes, honey, do something about that. If you can't do it, tell him, but if you can, please do it soon. There are dozens of things you could write about, even from what you have been able to tell me...the sharks, for instance, and the officer's club and all sorts of stuff...so try to do it, Honey, and keep your enthusiasm, because it is a fine thing. In any case, let him hear from you immediately.

I didn't talk to Don McKean today. I don't want to be under too great an obligation to him, but I do sort of hope that he isn't getting tired of being a good Samaritan now because I still have complications such as furniture. He has really been a real friend to both of us. Do you know that Beverly and Jay are three months behind on their payments to him? He says not to worry about it, because they are good for it, and he is going to write Jay and remind him, but it makes me feel terrible. They had plenty of money — they just forgot to pay it. I went over yesterday to see Helen Curren and got the iron and the board...the trouble is that I have no cord and don't know how I am going to get one. I left that one in San Francisco that we had, too. Maybe I shall have to write for that. Our stuff was packed very beautifully. The desk is still in the apartment, however, and I guess to get it out the door has to be taken off again. She said the people are taking very good care of it, but I don't want to leave it there too long. Gosh, I wish I could get something immediately and get this thing settled. She was very nice, and I was, too. I just can't help liking her in spite of everything. Beverly even left dirty dishes in the sink. She said she didn't know what possessed Beverly to say that. Lee had chicken pox that day, because as far as she knows he never did.

Mr. Houghton finally withdrew from the dinner at the last moment the other night. I guess he didn't feel up to it or something, so now I still don't have your stuff, but I will get it some way next week and the Hills will store it. I went anyway, however, and to Ming Howes and a very good dinner. It was Americanized Chinese food, but very delicious...really better than the genuine article. Jim was fine and works like mad — most every night, I understand. You know he's writing for Cliff Reed.

Don got me an appointment with this doctor Stevens that fixed Maureen up just to get the lowdown on this thing. I am still bothered all the time with cramps and a general lack of energy. It is for late Monday afternoon. He is a very expensive doctor but a good friend of Don's father, so he is not going to charge me much. I think it will really be worth it because I understand that if anyone can fix things in a short time, he is the one. He is an abdominal specialist and supposed to be the finest in town for women. He was the head Navy doctor for the district for a while, but slipped and hurt himself on a battleship so had to be retired from active service. I really think it will be worth it to get a complete analysis because I can't go on like this. The Navy doctors are fine, but they are so rushed that they evidently haven't gone into the situation thoroughly. I feel that, after Monday, things will definitely start improving. When this man took out Bob Hope's appendicitis, he sent him a check for five thousand dollars before he sent a bill and said that it was fine for his work and was to be used for somebody who might not be able to afford it as well as he was.

The Cranes are moving up to Ojai on Tuesday…Sid found a house in one week. It is very near Ventura, and they have a car now. Jintz is packing like mad. I would like to get down there to see them tomorrow and shall try to do it. It is something of a problem though, when you don't have a car.

Honey, I would just like to write and write and write to you, but I am so darned tired that it is an effort to sit up in the chair… and it is only ten o'clock, too. I think I will fix my hair and sleep about twelve hours.

Darling, you may say that I am the most missed wife in the world, but you are certainly the most missed husband. Nothing is the same without you. I love you to distraction and miss you to distraction, too. You are the most wonderful guy, and I love you so much that I wish I could say half as much as I mean. But I'll never be able to. Take care of yourself, Darling…don't drink quite all the liquor you can find…say hello to Fry and Roy and Chuck if you see them in your travels — and, Honey, when you think of me, know that I love you with all my heart. May God keep you safe, Darling. All the love there is…and more and more and more.

Jane

October 24th '43 In Port

Darling:

Well here it is the next day already and I am standing the 12-4 watch. It's very quiet on board, everyone is asleep, so it's a good time to write to my honey.

I got another letter from you this morning. The one you wrote the last night in old 304. I imagine it must have been tough leaving it at that. All the memories I have of it are simply wonderful. Of course I imagine being flat on your back there kinda takes some of the sweetness out of the place for you. We did have fun there though, didn't we? Remember all the cafe regular we had in the little breakfast nook and all the beer 'n brandy we consumed? It's funny, darling, but we seem to leave a little of...

[PAGES MISSING]

[NO BEGINNING, NO DATE]

...the machine guns manned, also men standing by with rifles. Just as safe as Nina's pool, almost. Being as I had the liberty the last day up there, I won't get ashore tomorrow. I hope we stay around a couple of days, as it has been a long time between drinks, almost three weeks to the day. And as you know, darling, I ain't no camel!!! I'm sure Fry and Myers are still around here; it would be fun to give them the needle about S.F. I'd like to see them, too, of course.

Well sugar, in a few minutes I have to be up on the bridge, "Giving orders," as Mom would say. So I'll have to call a whoa to this, but when I get all that mail that I expect tomorrow, I'll bang off another tomorrow night. Until then darling, you know how much I love you

It's millions worth baby

Chas

[NO BEGINNING, NO DATE]

...feel we were really getting attuned to each other's thoughts.

Words are so much pork when you are trying to put on paper a feeling that is at once as strong as a steel cable and yet has the fragility of a gossamer spider web. But you know exactly what I mean, don't you darling? And the very fact you do, is the proof of the statement, a ring-around-the-rosy way of saying it, yet it's true.

Honey, I wonder if you think of me as much as I do you. I don't mean just missing in a physical sense (on the highest plane, smarty!) but in the conversational, the intellectual side? You know we had gotten very alike in our thinking in the last year or so, and even more than that, completely aware of the other thoughts and probable reactions. To some I suppose that would mean that marriage was reaching the old shoe stage. I think it rather means reaching the marital stage that is real, and honest and completely wonderful.

God, honey, I guess every time I have the mid — watch in port you might as well get set for a letter of this kind. Damn I get so interested in loving you that I forget to write my pages right for filing! Well I'll try and remember.

I have all your letters filed away to date, not one missing up till the night before you leave for Hollywood. In the long days

[MISSING PAGES]

Highland Hotel 1921 Highland Ave.
October 26, 1943 Letter 28

Dearest Honey;

I haven't been very good about writing these last few days because I've been spending every spare minute making one of your Xmas presents...I went up to the Lathams' Sunday and spent the whole day at it. In the evening we went to a movie. Then yesterday when I got back from CBS, I did some handwork on it which took the afternoon when I should have been writing you. Then Jack is picking me up late this afternoon and Marg and I are going to sew tonight and I will spend the night with them. Then I should be finished. Then I will be a better letter writer.

I haven't heard from you since last Friday, but am hoping as usual to get a letter from my darling tomorrow. It was so wonderful to have five last week. But now I am wondering all over again where you are and if you are alright. Oh honey, I love you so much.

I got that job at CBS. Isn't that wonderful. It was just like shooting fish. Of course I realize that they probably need people pretty badly. I am to start the first of next week which is just perfect. The only thing I am worried about is that there will be some night hours... the only reason that bothers me is because of getting home without any car. I will have to do quite a bit of walking about the streets. However, I will face that situation when it comes up, and if I don't think it is good, I will just tell them that I can't do it...that is all. Everybody thinks that it is a fine job and I do, too, so all is fine.

I am in my third room in this hotel. I haven't yet graduated to one with a balcony, but this one I have now is pretty nice. It has a gas fireplace and a couple of big easy chairs and a desk and a few tables and a studio couch for the bed. It is much more human than the little holes I was in before, and I'm pretty happy with it. But I hope I can get moved into an apartment by the end of this week.

Mary Hull is sending you a Christmas present, which I thought was terribly sweet of her. She told me what it was which, of course, I won't tell you. I think you will like it, but don't use it too seriously.

I saw a movie the other night...Sunday...actually went to one. I didn't really go voluntarily because the Lathams wanted to go and I had to, but I did sort of enjoy it. It was the Fallen Sparrow with Maureen and John Garfield and, aside from being the most confusing thing I have ever seen, it was pretty good. There was a little stinker from RKO directed by Les Goodwins called "Adventure of a Rookie"...awful...just terrible, but it was so bad that it was pretty funny. The juvenile must have been trying for years and the only reason he has a job now is because he's 4F.

This is a grim day...I look out the window on Highland Avenue and one minute it's sunny and the next it's dark grey. And the awnings on the Wonder Market are blowing so hard it makes you sick to look at them. Blowing awnings has always been one of my fetishes anyway.

Did I tell you that I saw Emelia the other night and Wilbur isn't a captain at all. He's still a sergeant and still having an awful time trying to tell the officers what to do. She was just the same as ever. I don't think anyone has ever seen her ruffled or aged since you did at Palm Springs. She is working in an insurance office.

Parker is down here...Cassie told me today when I talked to her. Also Gracie. He was taking his test flights for the Ferry Command today and if he doesn't pass that, he goes straight east to some Navy school in Rhode Island. I don't know what it could be. It seems that the results are rather doubtful because he is supposed to have a thousand hours and he has had 750...he has a special letter of recommendation but doesn't know if they will let down the bars to that extent. Cassie was indignant that Helen Curren didn't call her when they rented our apartment because she had asked so many times for one in that building for Gracie. I don't know what would have happened if she had. She wanted to know all about you and how your shoulder was and everything. So I told her as much as I could, which wasn't much. Oh honey, I would just like to talk and talk and talk about you all the time. I just was looking at an Ensign walking down the street with his white cap and his blues. Gosh, I wish that were you. Hollywood is better than other places to be, but it isn't the same without you.

I love you, my darling...I really will write again tomorrow...if you can stand hearing about the sewing bee. Honey, I just wish I could tell you. There won't be a happier person in the United States than me the day you come home.

all my love,
Jane
xxx

October 27, '43 In Port

Dearest Honey:

Well I have finally finished censoring the men's mail so now I can drop a line. We are shoving off this aft so this may be the last letter I can mail for several days. Don't let the period of silence get you down and start conjuring up evil thoughts. I promise I'll have a letter ready for the mail the first port we hit again.

I haven't gotten any mail at all for several days. However there is a mail trip this aft just before we shove off. Perchance I will hit another jackpot then. The last letter I got was the night before you left so I have mentally had you riding the Daylight for several days now! I keep wondering where the new apt will be and how long it will take you to find it. One thing I am sure of, it will be unique and have the old Flynn touch. Of course I realize no car makes for a problem, but you will figure that one out.

How is the dough situation? Grim I suppose. Well I'll enclose another fiver with this. I have $12 and I'll be paid again when we get back, so don't worry about me. The only bill I owe is my mess bill of $20 for Oct, but I will pay that when I get paid. It isn't due till the first, anyway. I hope all these financial muddles get straightened out soon; they kinda worry me, honey. Of course if I am there with you no dough is no problem, but when I am away, it's different somehow. Well enough of that.

Yesterday was a pretty good day. In the morning the officers off the Breese, our sister ship and the officers off the Gamble played the officers off a new can. Soft-ball, we beat them 11-8 and it was quite a tussle. I played left field except for one inning I pitched which was pretty bad. They scored 3 runs off me, but as I had 2 errors behind me it wasn't really my fault. At the plate I popped one, got a single, a walk, and a triple. 2 for 3 or .666 not bad for an old man! But brother, do I know I played ball yesterday, today. The old joints fair creak as I lumber around. The boys yesterday said it was quite a sight to see all that beef churning around the sacks when I hit that triple. Then in the afternoon I went over to the beach and picked up my ships service stock. They have a wonderful system of warehouses here, all connected with crushed coral roads; makes you damn proud of the seebees and the armed faces in general. Of course all the streets and roads are named. One large road is "US #1" another is "US 48" then over where we played ball the boxing ring is "Madison Square Garden" and the hut that dispenses the beer to the men is "Duffy's Tavern".

The recreation field is for them (1300-1800) 3 football fields, 10 softball diamonds, 4 basketball courts, 3 tennis courts, an outdoor theater, etc. It's really damn nice. Then they get 2 beer chits and 4 soda fountain chits each day. Of course they only get liberty every 3rd day, while we get it every other day. Yesterday was my liberty day, but I didn't go in and get drunk as we were shoving off today and I wanted no hangover at sea. I had one on the way up here from my night with Eddie and Jug — head and never again. So I saw the movies and turned in at 9:00 for a good 10 hours sleep. The only thing, it's so damn hot the sleep doesn't seem to rest you much.

The movie was "Strawberry Blonde" from the play "One Sunday Afternoon" and it was quite cute. It reminded me of the show we did at the B Hills Hotel. When I was just playing a sailor, not being one.

Honey, I am enclosing a picture of the flags. It was taken before they were cut off at Hunters Point. (We have them repainted on again now) so it is the same as the hunk you have. Stick it on one corner of your bunk with scotch tape, huh?

We may have more by the time I write again, so cross your fingers for pappy — always remember, come hell or high water — I love you.

All me love —

Chas

October 29th 1943 In Port

Dearest Honey:

Well guess what? Today as we were standing into this place I saw a YMS coming in astern of us. Of course I looked to see if it was the 237, and son-of-a-gun it was!! I got over about two and stayed about two hours, and had a long chat with Fry. It was awfully good to see him, but I must say I never felt so sorry for a guy in my life. He hasn't been more than fifty miles from this place since I left him in July, practically no beer, no officers club. His ship is too small to have movie equipment, and to top it all off, last month his skipper, that he got along beautifully with, left the ship and a jerk of the first water took over. Brother, life on the Gamble may be rugged and sleep may be only a beautiful memory, but we are doing something, and we get around and manage a binge at least once in a while. I don't know if I could take that life he is leading. I am glad at any rate I don't have to make the attempt.

At least five times during the course of the two hours, right out of the blue he would say "Chas, how were the states?" It made me feel awful to think about it. I mean, remembering all the wonderful times we had there together days, and nights, too. This is perhaps the hottest place this side of eternal damnation, and I am not so sure, but perhaps this is it. Not only hot but humid, and by that I mean liquid. It makes me shudder to think of how Oswald must have felt putting the time in here that he did. Now the boy writes such pathetic letters and felt so badly about the furlough being cancelled. Brother, I would have handed in my chips and demanded a new deal.

I guess I have made it sound pretty grim haven't I? I am talking mostly about the guys on the beach, naturally, as we still have a good bed, showers, good chow, and the only bad item is the God-damn heat. I am not complaining for myself, but for a lot of kids that didn't even know these islands existed two years ago and are now expending themselves. Well, C'est la guerre, as they say in Madagascar. (Chow is on — more later)

October 30th Next Morning

Honey:

Well after I stopped last night I went up to the movies, and when I came down from our double feature it was ten thirty and, as I only had four hours sleep the night before, I had to turn in. This morning I feel fine after a lot of sleep, and as I am about to start censoring mail so I thought I would add a little to this before then, as you doff t feel much like writing after you read a lot of those. We are still laying in here and probably won't shove until tomorrow, so, as I have the 8-12 watch tonight, I will get off a little epistle to you then.

I wanted to tell you about this place a little. Yesterday we started, out in our little boat over to a repair ship, the motor stopped and we were dead in the water for about a half an hour, we drifted almost onto a coral reef. The water is crystal clear, and in looking down the bottom presented a fantasy of beautiful marine growth. Then in between all the coral and sea urchins the most wonderful little colored fish would go a swimming by. It really was beautiful. This afternoon when Burke gets off watch we are going to try and get a little boat and paddle around over the shallow water and take a real good look at them. Of course a little ship's work will probably interfere, but the idea sounds good at the moment.

The natives here have little dug-out canoes, however they do not have outriggers and as they are only about sixteen inches wide they have to balance themselves with their paddles. It's really something to see them going by. The biggest one that went by yesterday had about five men and five little children in it. They were seated alternately, and everyone had a paddle. The paddles were proportionate to their size and some of the children were not more than three or four. The funniest one that went by clearly showed the influence of the white man's navy. On the bow of it they had a little framework of canvas and on it was painted in very bad lettering "Y 0 144". wonderful.

Well, darling, I have to get to the censoring. But just let me close by saying how much I love you — Jillions!!!! All me love Chas xxxx

October 30th 1943 Nigh unto Midnight —

Dearest Honey:

This has been a hot and, with the exception of two pretty bad movies, a very uneventful night. I just finished a letter to you this a.m., but thought I would post off another line to you now before I turn in.

I just got a note from Roy — Boy (Horne) and he saw the ship today as he went out on a little run. He said that he would be back in the morning, and would try to contact me. I hope he can come aboard for lunch; I would like to see him. He is far from happy. I got a letter from him the day I saw Meyers and he was not happy up here. Of course my talk with Fry yesterday makes it very understandable. I hope he can make it over for lunch tomorrow. Well, we'll see.

We shove tomorrow, and within a few days we will be back to the port where we pick up mail, and will that be a day. I hope I get you off the Daylight soon. By the time you read this, I will be reading mail from you, so think of me as you read, I will do the same. I can't begin to tell you how I miss you, darling. I laid down for an hour this afternoon, and just before I went to sleep I thought of "Sailor Beware" and suddenly I was so mad at Don Defore that I could spit!!! I was really getting worked up and then I suddenly calmed myself down and started to laugh. I was just in that half-awake half-asleep world, and it seemed awfully real. He was kissing you and I was really going to kill him. You see darling, a mere matter of a few thousand miles won't keep me from thinking of you constantly and being insanely jealous, although I know it is completely irrational. Oh darling, I do love you so much, and spend a great deal of my time planning what our life will be like when this whole deal is over. You are undoubtedly the most wonderful wife in the world, as well as being the most beautiful, talented, and best drinking companion I could ever hope to find.

I am just trying to say how much I love you and miss you in a little different way, but it always comes out that I love you and miss you like hell. Well, if the words say what you mean, no matter how hackneyed, they are the words we must employ. Just think of all the wonderful evenings of talk we have ahead of us when I get back, and of all the wonderful years of living together facing us. Honey so help me, to get back to you faster, I personally will account for a good many of the enemy. Think of me when you read this, and know that I love you more than anything in the world.

All me love honey
Chas
X remember me?

1921 Highland Ave. Hollywood, 28, Calif.
October 31, 1943
Letter 30

My dearest Honey Darling;

It is now the night after the unnumbered, hand written letter that you may or may not receive from me first. I am home in my little room in the Highland Hotel and sitting here in my blue nightie and my peach bed jacket...a very fetching sight I assure you except for the fact that my hair is on the top of my head, which I know you don't like. It is about ten in the evening and I have left a call for eight in the morning because eleven in the morning is the time of the appointment I have finally succeeded in getting to have the pictures taken that you wanted for your Christmas present. I am afraid that that part of the present might be late, but it was the best I could do and I shall try to airmail them to you.

I went back on my decision of last night and did go out to Will and Maureen's about two o'clock today. It became obvious to me that I wasn't doing any good at the Lathams' by staying, so I thought I would go out there and see them. Maureen looked very beautiful and Willie got very drunk as usual. During the afternoon they had a Colonel and two Captains in the Marines there...in the photographic corps...I finally made myself very popular with Will, after the others had gone, by saying that it was too bad they didn't have pictures in the last war...they could have won it so much more quickly.

I give up, honey. You may as well know the truth. I have debated and debated as to whether to tell you until it was all over with, and I have fully planned not to, but the thing is that I am afraid that you will be thinking that I have been writing awfully peculiar letters lately. You will be wondering why I have been running around to people's houses and not doing anything and seemingly just having a good time lately. Well, the truth is that I am just marking time. I can do most anything within reason provided I don't be too strenuous about it until next Thursday when I go into the hospital for a big operation. But in the first place, I seem to be incapable of concealing anything from you...remember your birthday party...I know that from my letters you can probably tell that all is not normal. And in the second place, I suppose it is really better to tell you the truth than having you thinking that I am not doing what I should be doing. I mean I sound and feel as if I were just wasting my time, but there is nothing to do except sit around and wait until it is over with. I will have the operation next Friday morning unless an emergency one becomes necessary before that. As a matter of fact, I probably won't mail this letter until next Friday when I can get it off with one that will say that I am fine, but if I tell you about it now I can feel the rest of the week when I write you that I am telling the truth.

Here is the thing. It seems that Dr. Gernand in San Francisco that we thought was so wonderful didn't give me the straight dope. He told me that I would be alright and that I could leave. Well, it seemed that when I got down here I had this constant pain in my side that was driving me out of my head. Don knew that I didn't feel well and I guess we should be very grateful to him because he made me an appointment with this Doctor Stevens...he is the doctor who operated on Maureen and he has the finest reputation of any woman specialist on the coast. He is really the cream of the crop and the finest doctor that you can find. He persuaded me that I should have him examine me because it was foolish to go through all this and I finally agreed. He happened to know the doctor so he told him our circumstances and what had happened to me before. Of course he only knew that I had had a lot of trouble, but I explained it further to the doctor when I saw him. Now understand that this is the best doctor that it is possible to get and you will soon understand why I didn't go to the Navy doctors again.

It seems that I have what they call a chocolate cyst which is the type of thing that must be operated on immediately. It is very bad and in an advanced stage, and I will probably lose the right ovary because it has ruined it, he thinks, but he explained that I would be able to have all the children I wanted with one alone. It is so hard to tell this, darling, because I feel so ashamed to have so many things the matter with me all the time. He really gave me the straight goods. He explained the whole thing to me and told me that there was a five percent chance that I would be alright if not operated on within the next two weeks, but the other ninety — five percent was that it would rupture and form thousands of others and endanger my health and very probably my life. He said I could take my choice. Well, I wondered if I was worth it, but did decide that really everyone would feel quite badly if anything happened to me, even if the whole thing was awfully expensive, so I decided to have the operation. So that is the goods. I go next Thursday and have the operation Friday. I shall keep this letter until then and then I can stick another one into it telling you that all is alright so you won't worry over a period of time in case the mail is far apart. That is the reason I spoke about money last night and I am terribly sorry to worry you. I can get a job as soon as I get well. Then all will be fixed up, but I had to borrow a hundred dollars from a bank and then get a hundred from Mother and Daddy which must be paid back. Gosh, I surely am a ray of sunlight. Then I will have another hundred to pay off.

You may think it is funny that I don't go to doctors. I had planned to have the Navy doctors fix it, but it was a wonder that they hadn't killed me and that it was a very delicate thing, I decided that it was the better part of caution to have a competent man do it. You don't need to worry about my being faithful because he said it was a good thing I hadn't had any of that business because it would have ruined the whole thing and I would have been fixed definitely. That is what I meant last night when I said there was one thing I couldn't do. I hate to even talk like this, honey, but naturally I do have to tell you about it and when I am telling, there is no use not telling the whole thing because then you would just wonder. I will be in the hospital about ten days, but by the time you get this letter I will be out, and so continue to write me at the Lathams' because they have asked me to stay with them until I am well. I really feel that we owe both them and Don a vote of thanks. I would very much appreciate it if you would write them at our convenience because what they both have done for us and without and without any ulterior motive is really beyond thanks. This has been a very difficult thing to tell you because I am so ashamed of myself and my damnable insides. But I do really feel that this will be the last time and then I will be fine. I have made numerous inquiries and found that this doctor is thought by everyone to be a perfect genius and without equal. Maureen tells me that he fixed her actually a whole new set of insides with interior plastic surgery. The people at the bank said he was the finest doctor they had ever heard of. Levis said the same. There are lists of remarkable cases and I am sure we should have the utmost confidence in him. So you don't need to worry. Everything will be alright.

He is charging me a hundred and fifty dollars for the same operation approximately that he gave Maureen for twenty – five hundred. He told me that he charges the people who can pay and makes it as little as he can for those who can't. Of course that still seems like a lot of money to me, but I understand that is really Santa Claus in person with such a doctor. I am to pay part of it down and the rest in installments. It is a lot, but I suppose if it makes me well, it is worth it, and I really in all self interest don't want to go to anyone else who will botch the deal up.

Well, enough of that darling. I hope you understand. It has been very difficult to keep this thing from you and very difficult to write you about it. With my great inclination to dramatize things for a period of a few days after last Tuesday when I learned about things, I was almost desperate, but I know that was very foolish. It is simply a question of having it fixed, which is very simple if you just do it. It was just the finances because it seemed such a waste to have had all that in San Francisco. Boy, I have really given you the works in this letter but, as I say, it shall be mailed with the one after telling you that all is O.K. and now I don't feel that I am holding anything back from you. We shall still be able to have lots of little Flynns when you get home.

I talked to Mother last night and Buddy is home on a few days' leave before he goes to some place in Colorado for his basic training. His eyes are definitely alright and he is definitely in the army air corps, which I think is a remarkable thing. He is hoping to get an army plane down to here on his way and come see me. I hope that he will be able to, too.

That is all the current news for now. Did I ever tell you that I loved you so much I could hardly stand it. Well, I do. When I listen to music, all I can think of...at least all it makes me think of,...is you walking in the door. All music means that to me. I can see you in your blues and your white cap and I look at you and realize it is you, and I am so happy I can hardly stand *it, and I get* up and run to you and then...oh honey. Goodnight for now my darling, Jane

XXX...XXX

Highland Hotel Hollywood, Calif.
November 1, 1943
Letter 31

Dearest Honey Darling;

I just finished a washing that would have done credit to a laundry, and all in relays in the little undersized basin of the shared bathroom in this place that I laughingly call home. This whole room looks like a Chinese laundry with clothes draped over every unharmable piece of furniture. The ironing board alone is holding two slips, three handkerchiefs, and three white blouses. To add to the whole thing, the basin is the exact lowness to make your back ache like the dickens. Well, I can console myself with the fact that all I have to do now is to iron the stuff in the morning.

It is Monday evening and, as you can see, I am at home and being very industrious. I would really enjoy it if I just had a little radio, but the silence is rather oppressive. Today I had the pictures taken and I hope to heaven there are some good ones for you. I got up at eight and dashed around like mad getting myself fixed for the appointment at eleven and pressing dresses, etc. Well, as usual, I managed to make myself even more awful looking than usual. And of course got myself all in a tizzy. I didn't take enough dresses because I didn't dream that he would take so many pictures, and one of them wasn't right...that Irene one...I thought it would be perfect, but the shoulders hunched and I never can laugh in a picture and besides, I don't want to anyway. Well, he did sort of a draped, bare shoulder effect which might be very good. I tried to look real sexy for you, but every time I get a good expression and they scream to hold it, I freeze and lose it. But I think there were some good ones and I will try to get a present of picture to you in time for Christmas. I will have the proofs in a day or so and then it will take him a couple of weeks to make them up. It took him simply hours...by the time he finished, today was pretty well shot.

Honey, I don't want you to think I am frittering away my time and not working as I should be. I have a job and am starting as soon as it is possible. There is a very good reason why I haven't started so far and I will right away. I am slowly making arrangements about things, but it is so awful right now. It seems just impossible to get an apartment in the first place. I make inquires every day, but so far have come across absolutely nothing. It is a terrible situation.

But I do think that I have one coming up and shall be so happy to get moved and into someplace with a kitchen. I think by the end of the week, I'll be able to give you news about everything.

Well, I have been studying my military strategy like mad and I think that I have got you up to Esperitu Santos. That may be thousands of miles and probably is...that is just my logic. Maybe I should say down to there...I don't know. I sit and look at that darned map of the Pacific and wonder and wonder and guess and guess and try to figure which is the most logical.

I hope you told Lita hello for me. Will she be wherever she is for the length of the whole war? I am to take the things for you down to Dave Stanley's father's office on Thursday and he will give them to him when they get here on Friday. It won't be the whole Christmas present. ..I mean with the exception of the picture. I just wish, honey, that I could give you everything in town and then bundle myself up with the stuff and come out to see you.

I did go out to Will and Maureen's after all yesterday afternoon, but then I told you all about it in my letter of last night...I remember that now. I almost repeated myself.

Oh honey, when I looked in that garage up at Helen's and saw all that furniture that we have lived with so long and the things that meant so much to us even if they weren't all sleek and shiny... your table and the barrels and the big bed...the playground of the Pacific...and the radio and the books...all I want to do is get them in someplace for you to come home to. Each one of them is a story all its own. Remember when you made the table and everyone had to walk over it for two weeks to get in the living room or if you wanted to get close to the fire, you had to sit on it. And how Buck said you would never finish it and had to eat his words. Well, we will have those days but better soon again. If only they just had the old ads that they used to have in the Citizen News...now it's all wanted to rent columns. The landlords have it easy now. Oh honey, I love you, I love you, I love you.

Goodnight to you, my darling. I will write again tomorrow, and keep those letters coming this way, too. They are the light of my life. All my love to you honey, Jane

By the way,. continue to write me at the Lathams' as I don't think I will be here longer than a few clays„ Then I'll let you know after that. — Love, love, love, love, LOVE

xxxxxxxxxxxxxx

Highland Hotel Hollywood, California
November 2, 1943
Letter 31

My Darling;

Well, honey, today I finally succeeded in getting file for your letters and I have just been reading them over and filing them. They make quite an imposing little pile and now I can put them together in my mind so much better than I could when they were in the envelopes. There is so much that is wonderful in them, honey, and so many many things that mean the world to me. Honey, did you want me to try and get some paper that has holes in it like that, or did you want me to continue using the typing paper that I do now. The other night when I wrote you at the Lathams' I forgot to turn the sheets the right way. I am sorry.

Today has been a workaday. I ironed like mad half the day and I went down and got something for you on the boulevard. What a hellhole that is now. The people here now would make all those peculiar ones we used to talk about seem perfectly sane and normal. And then there aren't enough people in the stores and you wait hours on end. I went into the Owl drugstore and waited fifteen minutes for one simple little article that I could see right in the showcase under me. Finally I went behind the counter, got it out, put the money on the cash register, and left. They didn't seem to object and I would have been still waiting there. I was in the BarNaz cleaners today having something pressed and they wanted to know all about you and where you were, and I showed them a picture of you and they agreed with me that you were terribly handsome in your uniform. That man in the Wonder Market — the manager — the one who became such a good friend that time the bank made a mistake and our checks bounced — he wanted to know about you, too.

I have solved the question of Beth and the piano by pacifying Mrs. Hoppe. I had to expertly juggle my funds a little bit and I hope it won't strain me too much, but I know that it will. But now I can at least call her and tell her to get it and that they have taken good care of it. I knew that sooner or later she was bound to know that I was here and then it would be disastrous. So all is well, at least until the latter part of the month, on that subject, and I can assume relations with the relatives again, which is a vast relief. I had horrors of running into them on the street.

Jack Finch called a few minutes ago. He had learned from the Chamberlains that I was here, and Bob Komara was with him. It seems that he just got in today and is going to New York tomorrow. He has been out in the South Pacific someplace. They want me to go down to the Hofbrau with them for an hour or so and I know I shouldn't, but I think I will about nine-thirty. It will certainly bring back the memories of the beginning of our marriage and the start of that fabulous night. Do you realize that that man still owes us a bottle of wine? I wish I could recognize him so that I could remind him of it. That was a hectic start my darling, but how lucky I feel that it happened. I would have turned back at any time on that trip to Mexico. I know you would have too but, gosh I'm glad we didn't. It may have been a little bumpy at times but every bit was worth it. I better not keep talking like this or I will get so lonesome for you I will cry.

Honey, I was just re-reading that part about the sharks. It gives me cold chills. I suppose that makes you laugh, but don't sit out in full reach of them like that, guns or no. That and a few other things I try to keep firmly locked away in little chambers of my mind.

Dave Stanley will be in town on Friday so I am leaving some things for you down in his father's office on Friday. He says he expects to see you about the middle of September. Now remember this isn't all, as the pictures may be a little late. I do harp on that subject, don't I?

Mother and Daddy called last night and the whole family talked to me. They were all home for once and took turns in saying hello. I told you that Buddy had a few days leave didn't I, and that he was then going to Colorado. He is really and truly in the Air Corps now and his eyes are perfect.

I think I told you about Parker and that he was down here taking his tests for the Ferry Command. I talked to Cassie today and she said that he passed his tests with flying colors, and then Friday he threw his sacroiliac out of joint. They worked madly on it the whole weekend and then drove him down to Long Beach Sunday night as he had to report Monday morning in perfect physical condition. They haven't heard from him since and don't know whether he got along alright or not, as one of the things he had to do Monday morning was calisthenics. Dan said you and he were a pair. They wanted to know where you were, which I didn't know, of course, and how your shoulder was, and I was able to tell them that I thought it was alright because you hadn't mentioned it for a long time and the last time was to say that it was alright. Did you ever know that Pete Dix didn't believe you and that a couple of weeks later Jim Hill put him straight on it and that he still wasn't convinced.

That is all the news for now, my honey darling. God keep you safe and bring you back soon.

All my love, Jane xxxxxxxxxxxxxxxx X The biggest I love you!

Highland Hotel
Hollywood, California Wednesday November 3, 1943
Letter 32

Honey Darling;

Another day is gone...just think it is into the second month that you have been away. How many more to go? Not too many I do so hope. Gosh, that will be the happiest day I have ever, ever had when I see you again.

Today was mostly spent working...in fact the whole day was between sitting down periods. I am moving from here tomorrow and I was packing my stuff. Then I was wrapping your last Christmas present...and that was really a job of some little time. I seems we poor civilians can't get a box for love or money. So after much effort to acquire one someplace to put the present in, I finally hied myself over to the Wonder Market and got some sort of a cardboard thing that was awful looking. So I spent the next half hour trying to paste Christmas paper on it. It's a pretty rough job but the spirit is there, so please forgive. I am to take the stuff down to Mr. Stanley in the morning as I have to go downtown then anyway and they get in in the morning. Then Dave will bring it to you. I feel like it is just nothing, honey — but I will keep sending you more things from time to time and the pictures will come later.

I went over to the Chamberlains' for dinner tonight. We had a nice talk and poor Howard this time really received his induction notice for the nineteenth of the month. He has been having false alarms for so long that this time he can't really believe it's true. Frankly though, I think he is actually rather relieved. I hope he can get into that Helicopter thing as he wants to. Maggie is in a play down at the Mayan theatre called "Save Me a Sailor," so after dinner I went down there with her. I was terribly embarrassed because she went up to the ticket window with me and naturally I thought she was getting a comp and I'll be darned if she wasn't paying a dollar ten for the darned thing. Well, I tried to pay her and she wouldn't take it so I am going to send it to her in a letter because that is awful that she should pay for my ticket. I can't understand why she couldn't get a comp though. The house was only full in the middle. They are paying full Equity and some fool is just letting it run in the hope that it would pick up. It is not really a good show at all...in fact, it stinks. It is something on the order of Sailor Beware only the script is no good and the direction is foul. It has its funny moments though, but they are purely bad corn. It has received terrible notices. In fact, Maggie is the only one in the play who has received a good one and I guess they have really raved about her. She has only three scenes, but she is easily the outstanding person in the cast with one exception...a comedian who is really what George Yesner and Don Grusso were trying to be but couldn't.

I thought I had got over that feeling for the stage, but I'm darned if it didn't make me awfully homesick. I guess if I had my druthers I'd just be plugging away at it all my life. It just thrills me to walk into a theatre. But I guess I'll earn a little money first before I indulge myself. Though gosh it would be nice to get something like that. I went backstage with her before it started and all of a sudden someone said..."As I live and breath, Stonewall Jackson." It was Les Thomas who was the stage manager for Sailor Beware. Remember. He wanted to know all about you. Said to give you his best.

When I went over to the Chamberlains'tonight, I walked up that little alley and cut across — remember where Jerry and I lived... cut across to Hillcrest. It brought back all those hectic days. The bottle of champagne and Mother and Daddy and when we stood out in the alley and you told me that it had to be the first of April... that you were giving the orders. Well, it was, wasn't it honey. Then I looked up the hill to the honeymoon cottage. We have had an awful lot of life on that hill.

I did meet Jack and Bob last night. I had a beer at Mike Lyman's with them and then a cup of coffee at that Mayflower doughnut place on the boulevard. Bob was just in and leaving today for New York on leave...that is if he could get on the train. He spent the whole evening showing me pictures of his girls in Australia and talking about each one. They both showed a very enthusiastic and really a very sincere interest in women, so maybe that phase is over. If so, it makes me very happy. We were sitting having the coffee and Nina walked in with another one of her characters. Jack and Bob had to get back, and so Nina took me home. That way I didn't have to walk, which was a very good thing. I couldn't figure out who this new character of Nina's was, but he was long and thin and talked like he was slaphappy, although I guess he is pretty smart. She meets the darndest people. Well, honey, I should go try to wash away the smell of greasepaint and go to bed now. I love you with all of my heart. Goodnight to you my darling. Jane The last letters I had were no. 12 and 13 last Friday.

This is what you get when you get home — X

Highland Hotel Hollywood Nov. 3, 1943
Letter 33

Honey Darling;

I am putting this in with letter 30 which I wrote last Sunday night. I shall give it to Don when he takes me to the hospital tomorrow and ask him to mail it when the operation is finished with on Friday so that way when you get the letter, you will know that all is fine and not have to worry.

You will probably get these letters all in a batch anyway, so it is probably silly of me to take such precautions. I am afraid my typing wasn't so good in the other letter. In fact I just read it over and it was horrible, but it was because I was trying so hard to think of the right way to tell you and just succeeded in raving on and typing like an insane person. It did relieve my mind though, because even if I didn't mail it, I felt that I wasn't keeping anything back from you.

I have a bunch of books and some knitting, so the next ten days shouldn't be so bad. I will be relieved to have it over with and know that all is going to be well now, and me, too. The doctor said he knew I didn't have a lot of money and was acting accordingly himself, so he thought I would probably want to take a room in a ward because that would be a lot cheaper. So of course I did. I've never had one before, but it should be interesting to have all those people to talk to...You get sick of just one other person and they are usually unpleasant. I thought it would be terrible at first, but now I am really looking forward to the experience.

My goodness, it will be so nice to be well and have no troubles any more. I am actually looking forward to the whole thing, so I doff t want you to worry about it. Just be glad that everything is going to be perfect. When you get this letter, you will know that all is swell. All my love darling, Jane

November 4th 1943 At Sea

Dearest Honey:

I just have time to snatch a moment before I have to go up on watch, however we are getting in this afternoon and I know I will have some mail waiting for me from you. I have the mid-watch again so I will get off a nice long letter to you tonight.

The little do I spoke of in my last letter has been very success-fully concluded, and all is well. Of course it was far from dull, and I am no longer a virgin, if you follow me. All is well, however, and I am looking forward to a bunch of wonderful letters.

I just wanted to have a note ready to go ashore with the mailman in case this could catch an earlier plane than the letter tonight. Really nothing more to say in the time I have, so until tonight.

All me love — Chas

Nov. 4th 1943 In Port

My dearest Honey:

Oh what a bad day. We get in here filled with high hopes and the thoughts of lots of mail, and there is nothing. I'll take that back; I got a copy of the Screen Actor for August. No letters from you, or Mom, or nobody. On top of that I had the duty tonight and all the others in the off section went over to the club at the mine depot and got pleasantly potted. On top of that we are going out of here again tomorrow with another installment in my second-ary dept. and I won't even get over for a drink this time in. On top of that I have a beautiful sty starting over my left eye. Now,

if you can top that for a day that was something I had been looking forward to!

I hate to sound this way, but I thought I could put all my woes
in a lump at the first of the letter and try and salvage some of it
as I go along. First, our mail has been sent up the line and we will
pick it up in a couple of days. Second the job in my dept. is strictly
a cinceroo, should be no pain no strain, no worry connected with it.
Guarding what we got, seems to sum it up. Thirdly, the fact that
we're leaving tomorrow means although I don't get a drink, I will
get mail sooner. But fourth, that Goddamn sty is still with me; I
can't talk myself out of that. This is the first one I have ever had,
but I knew when I started feeling it coming, what it was going to
be. Well I guess they only last a couple of days, huh? I suppose
I will live through it, too. We get the same press news with our
morning coffee as you do back home, so I know we are reading the
same stuff. What do you think of this present offensive thrust in
the − − boy that is really something isn't it? It's that kind of reading that gives a man hope that we are really going to get this over
with before much longer. I will have a yarn to tell you when I see
you again. In the meantime we'll just keep slugging and plugging
and doing our damnedest.

I saw Roy-boy the other day. He *couldn't* stay but a few minutes,
but we talked loud and fast. He was so glad to see me, he greeted
me like a long lost brother. Poor guy, he is in a tough touch, same
as Fry. I have a decided edge in duty on both of them. I'll maybe see
him again in a couple of days, and I hope we can spend some time
together. He needs to talk to someone that speaks his language.

Is it possible that I have only been gone six weeks? Darling it
seems like six years. I didn't know that even loving you as much
as I do that I could miss you like this. It is a constant thing, part
of me is here, but a good part is with you. When this is over I am
never going to let you out of my sight, even overnight. If you think
that is exaggerated, wait and see. I love you so much, darling.

Well it is now almost four in the morning, and as I have to be up
at seven when we change berths, I had better get to bed. I'm sorry
that this isn't a better letter, but wait till I get those from you. I
will be positively on the top of the world and lyrical as all get out.
Oh, honey, would you do something for me? I know you can't buy
one anywhere, but would you ask all our friends and try and locate
a chromatic harmonica for me. I'm sure somebody had one kicking

around their house. You know the kind, they are pretty long and have a key you press to change scales. If you can't possibly get one of those, any real good one would be wonderful. I finally got the one Mother sent me, but it is just a little two-bitter, and you can't make much music out of it, although I try hard. See what you can find honey; put an ad in the paper if need be. Cripes what kind of a world is this when the getting of a good harmonica assumes the proportions of a major move to me.

Sorry I'm dreary tonight honey, but the eye hurts, and I am way behind in sleep. I do love you though, with all my heart. God, how I miss you, darling

All me love — Chas xXXXXX xxxxxxxxxxxxx X < — How about that one?

[NO BEGINNING, NO DATE]

Speaking of plays, maybe by the time we get where we are going Bonynge and her Red Cross unit will be up with another play. It would be kinda fun to see a play again. Ah me, the life that was passed.

I am not sure where to address this letter, Jack's or the Hotel. I guess I'll go back and re-read your letters again and then make up my mind. I have them all filed in that little folder and every other day or so I pick it up and read a few at random. Both times we have had a little my departmental do's, the last thing I did was read a few letters and kiss your picture. Does that sound silly to you? Because it was a great pleasure and comfort to me. I don't want you to think you have an old softy for a husband. But boy oh boy I sure do love you. More `n more, harder n' harder every day. Honey, won't it be wonderful when this is over and we can be together again? Wow!!!

Well darling, time for evening chow, so I'll close and go and wash up. I'll have some more letters ready when we hit port so you should get a batch at once. Do you like my letters? Boy, I should be ashamed of myself, what answer could that possibly leave you? But yours are so darn interesting and varied about people and things, and all I can write about is our relationship and how much I love you. Well I haven't exhausted the last yet, and won't ever so bear with me — God bless you, Honey —

Say, how about your physical condition? You kinda slid over that lightly with the hope that the doc could fix you up. What is it and how do you feel. Let me know at once, do you hear, at <u>once</u>! (that's from a play I was in once) But let me know sugar, cause

I'm worried about you — bye now. All me love there is — Chas

#20
Nov. 8th 1943 At Sea

Dearest Honey:

Well what a difference a couple of days can make. Here I was blue, unhappy, and feeling sorry for myself the last letter, and then I got mail! Wonderful wonderful. I got it yesterday the seventh, but was a little too busy last night to answer it then. As I said, no muss, no fuss. Very proud of myself incidentally, so that's another one. The last letter I got was dated Oct 25th; not too fast, but I am not complaining. I got a total of five from you and two from Mom.

So you are living at the Highland Hotel. Of course by the time this gets to you, you will undoubtedly be at the French Village, but my mind refuses to grasp the time lag, so I think of you where I last heard from you. And if you don't think you were on the Daylight for a long time!

I can't tell you how much your letters made me want to see you, even if only for a few minutes. All the talk of our friends and such was just wonderful, but at the same time made me miss being with you so damn much! Don is really a good friend, I am so happy he stands by like he does. Just be sure you keep him out of the sleeping quarters though. He is a veritable gremlin at slipping into people's beds, and you can read this to him so that he knows that I know what he knows. My, that's muddled isn't it? The hell it is!! I hope you get the apt. at the French Village. That would be perfect for you, as it is convenient to the town and such, and still a little ways away. What are the rents there, as I remember Pat's was incredibly low. Keep working on it honey. Turn on the old charm, and even hard-hearted landladies break down and give you what you want. Gosh you are wonderful! And I miss and love you so.

I am wondering about "Where Do We Go From Here," whether it really was sold and if so what was the price. I think I had five percent or was it two? At any rate it should mean a few bucks in the coffers which I suppose you could use. How is the money situation by the way? I have sent you every cent I could, and as soon as I get paid again I will be able to send a fairly respectable sum along. Don't feel that I am depriving myself. There is nothing to do with it out here with the exception of a few drinks once in a blue moon, so you might as well be getting some pleasure out of it. If you don't need it all (very hollow laughter at this point) you might start a savings account with it. I really should be making J.G. very soon now. The allnav that came out on the first of Oct. was three months after the last one, and still it only took up <u>one</u> month up. In other words, the July first one brought everybody up to the first of Sept. The one on the first of Oct. brought everybody up to the first of Oct. Kinda stinkin' I always say. However I think there will be one on the first of Dec., and that will be through the first of the year I feel sure. It doesn't make any particular difference to me, except the extra dough would come in handy, and to be frank I guess I would like to be a j.g., yes I really would.

I am wondering about Chet and your job. By the way, by the time I mail this I will have about ten little jobs ready to go to him. I wrote up about six the other day, but then the heat got turned on us again and I had to drop it. I don't think I will be able to mail this for two or three days, as we are on our way back down, so by then I will have it all ready to go to him, too. I am having a little trouble finding exactly the right way to put these things, and to dig up cute and interesting things, but I think that now I am beginning to get an idea, so if you talk to him, tell him that he can expect them to come in pretty regularly from now on. Also tell him that if he wants to delete, polish, change some of the wordage to make them more mike — able, to feel free to do so. After all, when I spend as much time on my feet and as little in bed as I do, some of the sparkle leaves the old speech, so explain to him will you, darling? I hope you get the job, and if you do that it is as interesting as we think it is going to be. The way the news is shaping up down in these parts right now, I would love to be on a news tables. It's really something isn't it? Boy I wish I could tell you what I know about it, but that's another story.

Speaking of plays and percentages reminded me of Wilbur, and the way he used to direct us in plays all the time, and the ones we did at the Assistance League Playhouse. Then I got to thinking about them and remembered that any exterior he always wanted quantities of some kind of a vine growing over the wall. Remember that one play that was laid in the Bahamas that Gay and I were in and we had that wall behind us, and we got all those vines from the Beverly Hills Nursery? Well all last night I tried to think of the name of it, and I still can't put my finger on it. If you remember, send it to me by mental telepathy, maybe I'll remember it too, I hope so!! Boy I'm sure getting wacky huh? As the men aboard refer to it: "Asiatic" That means off the old bean, too long out here, etc., etc.

P.S. The sty is gone, too!

St. Vincent's Hospital Nov 9, 1943
Letter 35

Dearest honey;

I haven't written you for days and days. This is Tuesday, the last letter was mailed to you Friday. But don't think I haven't been thinking about you darling. Oh honey, every minute of the time. Thursday just before I went to the hospital I got your two letters — no.'s 15 & 5 mailed the 26th and 27th of October. Those were the ones where you said not to worry if I didn't hear from you for a while. Well darling, I'm not going to start moaning about how I haven't had an easy minute, but gosh darn I'll surely be relieved when that next letter comes from you. I listen to the radio like it was a smoke — I'm almost afraid to read the newspaper. But I just know you're alright. You better be, you bum.

Well, I guess I am getting along fine although it's the most uncomfortable experience I've ever had…and my sense of humor seems to be sitting out on a limb someplace waiting for me. I am now minus a right ovary and tube and h-cyst, and have a scar the same place the same length. So now all will be fine. Honey darling, I'll write another note tomorrow. I love you with all my heart honey. Be safe darling. All my love, Jane

St. Vincent's Hospital
Nov. 10 1943
letter 36

Dearest Honey;

Halleluiah! Today I got your note — no. 18 — informing me that all was well. It has been a happy day from then on hospital or no hospital. Gosh darn it,honey, I'm so happy I could just get up out of this bed and dance. I know I could. Then on top of that, Marg phoned a message to say that there was another letter from you up there. They won't be able to bring it until morning and I can hardly wait. But it will make tomorrow a good day, too. I love you so much, honey, that you're with me every minute.

The greatest requirement from here on is patience for a couple of weeks. This is Wednesday and I think I'll be able to leave Sunday. They're taking the stitches out tomorrow. It seems pretty soon to me, but they know when they're healed enough and the better the progress, the better — the cheaper, although the whole thing couldn't by the wildest stretch of the imagination be called that.

Just as I finished that last sentence, honey, I went to sleep and when I woke up it was visiting hours. The girl next to me who, incidentally, is a good friend of Beth and Al's, I just found out, had lots of people to see her and Don came down to see me, which was very nice of him. I don't imagine anyone will come tonight as really I haven't told much of anyone except him and the Lathams that I am here. I told Maggie and Howard and they were planning to come in tomorrow night. Marv Hale and Jack Finch found out about it from somebody and they have both been down. The Lathams have been wonderful. One of them has been here every day and they brought me two beautiful bouquets and loads of fruit juice which I had put in the ice bar here and have when it gets too hot. They are really true friends. I've had two letters from your mother since I've been here and today one came from Aunt Gen. Will and M. sent me some beautiful yellow chrysanthemums, but of course haven't been here since Will isn't here and she is working. Maureen is really and truly going to have a baby. The doctor confirmed it. You see he is my doctor, too, now.

Gosh darling, I guess I don't write very interesting letters from this vantage point. All I lie here and think about is how much I love you and I don't want to burden you. I think the girl in the bed next to me knows you just about as well as I do. I have done nothing but talk about you and she is so interested and is dying to meet you. I think I have made a pretty good friend in her that I would like to know longer. Don't faint, she has had five husbands! Each one she has entered into in perfect good faith and they've all turned out to be stinkers. One couldn't practice sex, one was a drunkard, one had tantrums and hit her, one turned out to be homosexual, and they were all fine looking well educated men of good family. And she is a charming person — very fine. All this of course just kills her as she wants so badly to find someone to get on a firm basis with and have a serene life. You get to know a person pretty well in the hospital and she's really nice.

Oh honey darling, this room is just across from the elevator and I lie here and imagine how I would feel if you were one day to walk out of it and I all of a sudden saw you. I think the first time I see you I'll probably burst into tears because I cry when I think about it. But just to have that note that you were o.k. is something that makes me so happy I can hardly stand it. I hope I can sometime hear about how you're not still a "virgin". Gosh honey I was glad to hear from you. I hope it wasn't too bad honey. I know there's nothing you can tell me and I should talk not about it, but oh darling!

Good night my honey. All my love to you honey, Jane

Nov. 11th At Sea

Dearest Honey:

Well as you can see by the enclosed, I kept my word and got these ready for Chet. I am sending you this copy because I want your straight-forward criticism on them. I am aware that they are weak in spots, but point them out to me. I also think that the latter ones are better. Maybe it's just that I have to get back into the grove of writing again. I really think that has a lot to do with it.

This can't be much of a letter, but I am mailing the other long one I wrote a couple of days ago at the same time so maybe you'll forgive me. I really have spent every minute on these stories that I could to get them ready. We get in early tomorrow morning, and there is a chance that there might be some mail for me from you.

Boy I sure hope so, but I rather doubt it. I think it is going to a place farther up the line from now on. Well we will see in the morning.

I still love you beyond all belief, but honest honey I have to wind this up. I have to re — write my letter to Chet, and get everything ready to do the first thing in the morning, and I have only about half an hour before we eat, so much as I hate to do it I'll have to close. Believe me when I say I love you, cause I do!

A story is going the rounds out here about a little trouble a couple of Seamen 2nd class got into when their hip was back in the states recently. They were walking down Market Street when an Ensign hurrying by bumped into the shoulder of one of the Seamen. Without a word, he grabbed the Ensign, swung him around and hit him — a terrifying clip on the jaw. The ensign goes down but gamely gets up and comes back toward the two. Without a word the second seaman clips him and down he goes again. About this time the shore patrol arrives and takes the situation in hand.

The next day, at the court that inevitably followed for the seamen, the presiding officer, a four-striper, asked the first seaman for an explanation.

"Well, sir," he says, "when the ensign bumped into me, he hit my left arm, which is just healing from a wound, and it hurt me so that for a moment I saw red, and before I realized what I was doing, I hit the Officer, however I am very sorry, and I would like to apologize."

The four-striper thought that over for a moment and said, "Well that may be a reasonable explanation for you, but," turning to the second seaman, "what possible excuse can you offer for hitting the officer the second time?"

There followed a long pregnant silence. "Well," roared the captain. "Well, sir," said the second seaman cautiously, "when I seen my buddy Joe here swing on the officer there, I figured that the armistice had just been signed!"

The Captain is responsible for this story. As you can tell with a quick glance at the map, there are not many "Liberty Ports" in this area. Liberty Ports are places relatively untouched by the war and a good place to forget it. Well, this boat filled with men going ashore for their first real liberty in several months, passed another small boat on its way back out from the beach filled with sailors who had obviously enjoyed a wonderful time ashore.

"Hey," shouted one of the sailors in the boat going ashore, "what kind of a liberty port is this?"

"Wonderful," came back the reply. "Ice cream, beer, women, and everything!"

Well, gals, don't feel too badly. After all, out here a woman is only a memory, dimly, but lovingly remembered, but a cold bottle of beer. Brother!!!

There is a little island out here that consists of an air strip, no modern conveniences and lots of heat. It should be; it's only a skip and a jump from the equator. Not the most ideal place in the world to do a tour of duty; however, bad as any place is, I have yet to see one that gets the spirit of the men down. For example, on this island they have an outdoor theater. The seats are made of eighteen-inch high sections of coconut palms made into benches with scrap lumber from packing cases. On it is several colors. One of the men who must have had sign painting in his civilian background has created a border of in-curving palms and then in excellent lettering has written

LOEWS.

GOONA-GOONA

I contend that when there is humor like that left in men on a God-forsaken spot such as this, then there is no danger of our ever losing this, or nay other war.

Not so long ago, we were out about our business, which in this case was nocturnal. As we approached an enemy island, ghosting along at low speed and, of course, without lights, we heard the sound of an approaching plane. As we knew none of ours were out, it was simple deduction that it was one of the little enemies. "Snoopers" we call those inquisitive aircraft. Well, there was no moon up, but the stars were enormous, and as the planes kept ranging back and forth across and around us, the little exhaust flares from their motors looked almost like other stars.

They must have seen something of our wake, because they dropped several high-powered flares. They light up the scene like day, and they must have seen us. However, they didn't drop any eggs on us, and we, in turn, didn't open fire on them for the simple reason that we figured that was what they wanted so that their shore batteries, if any, could range on us, or possibly some naval units in that area. By this time the shore looked so close that you could almost throw oranges at it. Well, the flares would die away and the planes would drift in and out over us, motor flares twinkling away. We did what we set out to do and scrammed out of there, but quick.

The next morning at breakfast, many miles away, I asked one of the colored mess attendants what he thought of the Japanese planes the night before.

"I'll tell you, sir," he replied, " I watched those little flames from those planes so long and so hard that pretty soon it seemed to me that all the stars were moving around!"

He had no cause for feeling badly, however. A lot of us had much the same feeling!!

This is the straight dope. Our Captain heard it from the skipper of the LST in question. Not too long ago we were putting some men and equipment ashore on an island. The first unit off this particular LST was a SEEBEE bulldozer. He had no more than cleared the ramp when a Jap machine gun nest hidden in the shrub a couple hundred yards back from the beach cut loose on him. Thinking quicker than scat, the SEEBEE raised the blade of the bulldozer to its highest position. There it gave him a shield. He took off at a tangent, galloped through the scrub to a point behind the machine gun nest, and then, when he was almost on top of it, dropped the shield and very neatly plowed scrub, machine gun, and enemy soldiers into a nice smooth road back to the beach. Quick thinking and a lot of guts. And, by the way, if that sounds a little grim, just remember those weren't bottle corks out of a pop — gun those Japanese were spraying him with.

Censored by.
W.W. ARMSTRONG, Lt-Cdr., U.S. Navy.
Commanding.
St Vincent's Hospital Nov 11, 1943

My honey;

Today another two letters arrived from you. Jackson brought them down this morning. They were no. 10 that said you had seen Fry and the second letter you wrote Nov 4, no. 17 is missing, but I daresay it will show up. You didn't number it, but it was 19.

Oh honey — I had to stop for a few minutes there because they came in to take out my stitches, so when they finished I had to take a few minutes off to get myself together again. It isn't exactly comfortable. I kept thinking it wasn't cured enough yet, but they assured me it was. I still have a lurking fear that I am going to burst open down the middle. But they assure me that is not so. I really want somebody to rush right out and buy me a zipper.

Save all the details of your yarn, darling, to tell me when we see each other. Oh honey, if you could only tell something. I lie here and imagine the darndest things.

Poor Fry. Even after he hated to leave SF so, I hoped he would find something to do that would interest him, but I'm afraid this whole thing is going to be one long complete purgatory for him. I hope you get back to see Roy. Give them both my love when you see them again. Just then one of the sisters and a father came in to talk so we exchanged a bit of polite conversation. There is a phone in this room and it is connected, but the fools won't let you use it. I want to call Seattle collect but do you think I can get permission — hah — I've been trying for 2 days! And the brother of the girl in with me has been to the office and screamed and carried on, but no soap, Mother and Daddy have called here and the Lathams and are so worried and it would mean so much to them if I could talk to them. It makes me boil. Maureen may think this is a fine hospital, but she paid for plenty of service, but the common man is lost in the shuffle around here.

Honey I hope you had a chance to go to the doctor — have that sty fixed, but I don't suppose you did. I know how terribly they hurt. Gosh, it's nice to have heard from you.

Isn't Dave Oswald there any more? Gosh honey, the day when you get home. My mind doesn't take me any further than that. That prospect is such an enormous joyful thing that it fills my whole heart. How excited I was that day in San Francisco when you got off the cable car and I came running to meet you and you kissed me right in the middle of the street. Then we went into Ollies and he said we made him cry. The whole world was in a daze and this next time! I won't even be able to see. What a day! What a day!

Goodnight, my darling, until tomorrow. I love you with all my heart.

All my love to you,
Jane

xxxxxxxxxx

Honey, I never realized in the blur of the last few days that I hadn't thanked you for the money — I got the letter with it the day I went to the hospital. Then I was worried about you and of course I couldn't write for several days and when I did then I thought I had already thanked you. Everything was so mixed up in my mind. Honey it was a godsend. I'll probably be eating on it the last two weeks of this month and I really needed it. You couldn't have sent it at a better time! It was like a wonderful bolt from the blue. Thank you so much, darling!

Don't forget Chet because I just want to know what to say to

him. Besides, you should do it if possible for money reasons. All me love honey, Jane

Nov. 11th 1943 At Sea

Dear Chet

I am truly sorry that this first batch of material is so long in reaching you. The fact of the matter is that I have been learning a new job, and leisure time for literary meditations is at a premium. However things are working themselves around now to where I will have time to get off a few sketches to you at pretty regular intervals. Mixed in this batch are true stories, anecdotes pertaining to this area and observations.

As we agreed before I left, all material is to be undated and no names used, places or ships. In this batch I have used one name, that is of course fictitious. In regard to using my name — for the time being refer to me as "my friend Charley" and let it go at that. I hope in the near future to be able to give you permission to use my name, but until then, use the above.

As you will observe, the old head is rusty when it comes to turning neat phrases, and I am afraid. some of this stuff is long and not too good. Please feel free to edit as you see fit, and if you wish to add or delete dialogue, that's all right, too. The more of these I wrote, the easier they came, however, and I feel pretty sure that given a little time they will come to you in pretty usable form. Until then, salvage what you can, in any way you can.

As for myself, things have been far from dull, but that is a story that I will have to give you at a later date. It is an interesting life, living conditions are good, and the officers are a very swell bunch of guys. I am very happy in the set-up that is, as happy as an old home-body like me could ever be away from Jane.

The enclosed copy has been censored and approved for use only program by my commanding officer.

Well Chet, that about covers the situation. Let me know your reaction to these, and if you have any ideas on them. Give my reg to everybody, and have an extra bourbon and plain water before dinner tonight for me

Regards —

Up the line a ways there is a little island. Brother it's no bigger than a dit, but in between the scrawny growth of palm trees our SeeBees have hacked out a very nice landing strip. Of course it is crushed coral and therefore very glaring at all times. Torrential rains fall every few hours and then the sun comes out and the humidity is something out of this world. The idea I am trying to put across is that there are more desirable places in the world to live.

It is occupied by a handful of Marines, a detachment of SeeBees and a few airmen, all of whom would give their eye teeth to get other duty — any other duty! Which is the point of this tale. They swear it's true — well, make up your own mind.

Two SeeBees were sitting in their hut when one of them jumped up with

"I just figured out how I am going to get off this place." "Yeah?" says the other, disbelief in his voice, "How?"

"Well, I am going up to the Doc, ask for a medical discharge, and right in the middle of the examination"

"What are you going to do?" asks the second. "I'll tell you after I get the discharge."

And so off goes the SeeBee on the double to see the Medico.

About half an hour passes when the second sees him coming down the path, dejection in every step.

"Well, did you get it?"

"Nope."

"How come?"

"My plan didn't work."

"What was it?"

"Well right in the middle of the examination, I dropped down on my hands and knees and started barking like a dog."

"Yeah."

"Well would you believe it, the Doc drops down on his hands and knees and barks right back at me, then he said, `Don't try to pull that stuff on me son, I've been here nine months myself, and I'd like to get off too!' "

A lot has been said on this subject, but I honestly believe people still don't take it seriously enough. I refer to letters to boys you know out here. It is such a little thing to drop a line to someone you know, yet you have no conception how much it means to them. You should be aboard, when we make a port and the mail orderly comes back empty-handed! The pall of gloom is a very tangible thing. And yet when we hit a port where they have been holding our mail for us, the whole tempo of the ship changes with a very sudden and heart warming life. The effect hangs on for several days. Ship's work is done cheerfully and a great deal more quickly, and the men's attitude becomes one of "well let's get on with the war so we can get home again." It's a thrilling and very positive thing to feel and see.

So how about it, take a few minutes and bring home that much closer to some kid out here. Put in a few clippings from the home town paper, and a few snapshots, especially one of Mom and the best girl, and if she happens to be in a swimming suit or a play suit so much the better. Pictures are treasured and looked at until they are dog-eared and dull and letters are re-read until the paper gives out under the strain. Incidentally, did you gals know that your letters are referred to as "love chits" or "sugar reports" by the men?

And don't feel neglected if you don't get an answer for every one you write, remember there is not much they can say, and they have a pretty full schedule mapped out for them in winning this war. If you want an actual part in that winning, take pen in hand right now!

They've got the darndest canoes down in this part of the world. They look like you would expect an out-rigger canoe to look except they have no out-rigger. That's where the tricky part comes in. Usually every member of the crew has a paddle, and they are graduated in size in direct proportion to the size of the manipulator. As the width of even the larger ones seating six or eight doesn't exceed eighteen inches, it takes some fancy handling of the paddles to keep it in an upright condition. An eight place one went by us the other day, and there were four grown men and four tikes in it, every other one as about four or six years of age but they all had a paddle, and she was really flying along. Coming into a winding passage to an anchorage the other day I saw one with five people in it. In the bow was a large good-looking male with his arms folded across his chest. Directly behind him was his five year old son in exactly the same position. The three in the stern were brawny, buxom bare-bosomed babes who were doing all the work. I wonder what the system is he uses? Oh yes, he was nattily attired in a pair of faded blue shorts and a U.S. Navy skivy shirt — Naturally!!

The best touch of all though occurred in a rather large anchorage. There were dozens of the little craft skimming along when suddenly the silhouette of one struck me as being different. I put up my glasses and saw that up at the bow the owner had rigged a frame of cloth about a foot high by three feet long and on it was painted in very bad lettering "YO 144" Don't tell me the Navy doesn't exercise an influence!!

At one of our better established advanced bases they have a recreation center for the men. I thought I would let you know that there are some very attractive sides to this war. This recreation center consists of ten softball diamonds, four basketball courts (cement), three cement tennis courts, a boxing and wrestling arena with all the appurtenances, and outdoor theater, and area with table and benches for ship's parties and barbecues and a beer dispensary and ice cream bar.

The ships that come into the harbor buy beer chits and ice cream chits out of the ship's welfare fund and give them to the men. We generally give two beer chits and two ice cream chits to each man. They get liberty starting at one o'clock and expiring at five, so they have time to get in a game of ball and generally fool around and forget there is a war going on for an afternoon.

I thought the Moms and Dads would like to know that it is not all work. and no play for Junior out here. Of course the boxing area is labeled "Madison Square Garden" and the sign over the beer dispensary proclaims to all the world that this is "Duffy's Tavern."

I ran into a friend of mine out here a while ago who is assigned to a light mine sweeper. We know them as "Tuna Boats" but don't misunderstand me, they are doing a very important job. They are small and have a relatively small complement. As is always the case there is a great deal more freedom and lack of regs than on a larger ship.

Well, this friend of mine was on the bridge with the skipper on this particular night and they were working their way out of a small harbor. The charts showed that their present course was all clear and very safe, but my friend hanging out the side of the bridge saw a line of white foam in the bright moonlight, that always indicates a reef in these waters. Right here let me say that our charts are not always 100% accurate, as our Japanese friends have not shown the proper spirit in letting us map the islands they still retain. Well it <u>looked</u> like a reef so the friend turned to the skipper and said;

"Sir, I think we are heading for a reef, dead ahead."

The skipper looked up and then back at the chart, "The chart doesn't show any reef there."

"Aye, aye sir" replies my friend, but still he keeps watching it. It gets whiter and whiter, and you can fairly hear the water boiling over it. So again he cries, "Sir, I am sure there is a reef and on our present course we are going right over it."

The skipper takes a look and then yielding a little gives an order to the helmsman, "Right twenty degrees rudder."

"Right twenty degrees rudder, sir" the helmsman echoes. But the order came just a hair too late. The ship almost clear the extreme edge of the reef and then there is a grinding as her port screw bit into the coral. As the little ship began to shudder with the vibration that tells you you have a bent blade on a screw, the three of them stand in electrifying and stunned silence for a moment, then the friend gives out with a remark that was much more Jerry Collona- ish than he intended. "Bad Chart" he says.

St. Vincent's Hospital
Nov 15, 1943 (in hospital) Letter 38

Hello Honey Darling;

Well a couple of very uneventful days have gone by since I last heard from you — no. 1.9. But I expect that a few more will before you will have been able to mail a letter again. I enjoy your letters so honey. Don't think I don't appreciate the descriptions of the tropical fish and the coral and the people — I know you haven't much time and for you to talk to me so much — gosh, it makes me love you twice as much.

The only news as far as I am concerned is that I got up yesterday and tomorrow I can go home. I will certainly be happy to see the last of this place. This is the surgery floor and the grim example of cancers, tumors, and all the other calamities to which the human race is subject is getting pretty oppressive. I lost my roommate yesterday and with her went the atmosphere of perfumes, satin bed jackets, and femininity in which I had been living and which had made the place more a boudoir than a hospital. Not ten minutes after she left in came a Miss Larsen — a maiden lady of forty who is recovering from her second major operation since June. It seems she has been absolutely cured of cancer and feels that her obligation toward the world is to be a saint. Her teeth stick straight out, she is popeyed, lean and hunchbacked, and she simply loves everybody in her cheerful dispassionate way. She is continually giving vent to the remark that she now realizes the triviality of important things. I'd like to kick her teeth in. She may have "walked through the valley of the shadow" but that still doesn't make her god's right-hand woman. She has an insatiable interest in what goes on on this floor and is an amateur authority on all types of growths, malignant and otherwise. I now know the condition of every patient in the hall and she receives play-byplay reports on all of them. This last day is grinding exceeding slow.

Did I tell you — of course I did — that I will be staying with the Lathams? They have been so grand. They purchased a chaise lounge the other day for their living room which they assure me I will enjoy. Of course I wanted to do my part in the way of food — and knew keeping accounts would be a little difficult, so here is what I did. Don knew where to get a ham without points. Not black market; strictly legal. It seems the packers have certain hams above their quotas which they aren't allowed to sell to the butchers but can dispose of, allowed by the govt., to private parties. He knew someone who know a packer. I knew the Lathams were saving points for a ham, so I got them one as a gift for being so nice to me. It did cost quite a bit, but really nothing to equal or repay their kindness. They were very grateful and I think that does the trick as I don't want to be under too great an obligation.

The landlord at the French village says I may expect an apartment there around the first of December and, as I won't be able to do anything for two weeks anyway, that is just about perfect. I'm so happy about it because that is a place which lends itself admirably to the old Flynn "touch" and I will be able to feel that you *are* with me and the books and the pewter and the radio. And soon you will be, my darling — It will be fine to see and have some of the things that you made and that *we* packed up here and there — they will be waiting in front of the fireplace for you to come home. Me, too.

Now it is about time for me to stop writing and put on some lipstick because soon I am supposed to get up for the "great experience" of staggering across the floor to a chair and sitting down for 15 minutes. A hospital is a bad place to be. You become much too self — centered. However the doctor informed me this morning that I'd been a very good patient. Outwardly perhaps — but inwardly very rebellious.

Until tomorrow, honey — goodbye. I love you so terribly much — I can't even tell you. Be good, honey, and all my love to you — Jane

#23
Nov. 15th 1943
In Port

Dearest Honey:

Well here it is the old mid — watch and again I am writing to you. Joy of joys, I got two letters from you today. One dated Oct. 26th and the other Nov. first. However there was a gap of two letters in there, from no. 28 to 31, and in those I suppose you told me lots of things that I am trying to piece out right now.

In the first place I am terribly afraid that there is something physically wrong with you. First you said that you were going to start at CBS on Monday, then the letter on Monday said there was a very good reason why you couldn't, also that you were going to leave the Hotel and to write you at Jack's. Well, Honey, I have pieced it together and gotten you back in the hospital for a job and then convalescing at the Lathams. I suppose it is all unfounded, and I am building a horrible castle of nightmares, but please darling, don't be veiled in your allusions to yourself in the future. I have so much time on my hands to think about you out here that the thought of you not being well just drives me wild. So no matter how bad anything is that comes up, let me know the gory details, and then at least I won't let my imagination run away with me. I am not mad, just worried, and please don't let me get into this state again. Okay?

I would like to know more about the job at CBS, but I imagine reams of material on it are already en — route to me about it. Seems hard to believe that the questions I ask tonight I won't get...

[ENDS]

Nov 16th 1943 At Sea

Dear Kids.

This is going to have to be community and short. I thought we weren't getting in till about eleven and I was going to have a lot of time to write you both a nice long letter, but now we are coming in at eight-thirty, which is about ten minutes.

I haven't much news, as we haven't had any mail for about ten days, but of course I will have some this morning from you both I am sure. The only thing of major importance is that we got the three new officers the other day when we were back down the line. They are all nice kids and when they get broken in it is going to make things a lot easier. Incidentally they are all from California so now we have a majority in the wardroom from there and no one can kid us about the weather any more.

Our weather continues hot, I sometimes wonder if I will be able to stand the cold of Calif. after this tour of duty. We haven't been doing anything exciting the last few days, playing nursemaid to a bunch of liberty ships on their way up here at an excruciatingly slow rate of speed.

Just think, in a few days the old Gamble celebrates her 25th birthday, a quarter of century of service in the line of duty. We are going to organize, I mean I am going to, an amateur hour for that night, and we will make the welkin ring. As the Capt. would say, lemonade, cookies, and everything!!!

Damn, there goes the call for the boat for mail, so I have to knock this off. I will write you both tonight and tomorrow after I read the dispatches, excuse typing, and awful haste. Only reason for letter was to let you know I am alright and well

All me love —

Dearest Honey: Just time to tell you I love you. I am so eager to get the mail and find out what you are doing and all. I will really write a nice long letter tonight and really talk to you, but right now I have to run to special sea detail. God, how I
miss you, darling — Chas

#24
Nov. 17th 1943 At Sea

Dearest Baby:

Well here I am taking pen in hand again. I haven't a thing new to tell you since I wrote the other day, but I know from getting your letters how welcome they are, so I'll just shoot the breeze with you a little while. Say, I wonder if you got the allusion I made to the decorations Wilbur always had in his plays? If you didn't, call Emelia, she will remember the name if you don't. I thought it was pretty cute, but maybe I was too subtle for you, I don't really think so though.

Well as I told you we got the new officers. They are all nice as can be, if a little young, but they are going to make life a lot more pleasant, and a lot less strenuous. I got one of them as Ass. Guns, so he can take a lot of routine off my hands. Giving tests, grading them, etc. All of which is not too interesting, and takes a hell of a lot of time. Then too, in about a month when they are broken in well, we will have three sections of in port watches, instead of two, so that will mean getting to the beach little more frequently. We got a letter from the commander of a task force about starting another officers club up the line a ways. Right across from where Dave was for a while. We are spending more and more of our time there and a club would help a lot. We all are asked to put up $10.00 to get it started and then that is paid back after it gets going. By the time this war is over, they are going to have clubs all over this area. Which is all right with me. There are three things we live for, the end of the war, mail, and officers clubs. We eat sleep and talk about them in that order. Of course Sex I don't even mention, because that is in a class by itself, way out in front of them all. When I finally get home after this is over, let's plan on spending about two weeks in bed, huh? Maybe we could rig up a hot plate and an icebox beside the bed so we wouldn't even have to get up for our beer or food. Ain't I awful? But do you think I'm kidding? Hell, no!!!!'

Honey, won't it be wonderful to be back together again? Just think of all the fun we will have doing the things we like, even though they seem silly to the more refined and sensible folk, such as getting kinda boiled on sherry and not bothering about dinner 'till around ten, and sleeping in late in the morning and getting up only in time for the Broadway news, and clipping Giddy in our back yard, and eating under the sky, and being able to kiss you whenever I want. A hundred times a day if the mood moves us. Holding you so tight in my arms that you holler, and you snuggling up to me on cold nights, and the wonderful felling of oneness we have in bed, and you getting mad at me 'cause I don't want to review the day, but rather get on to the work at hand.

And then broiling steaks every night, and to hell with the vitamins having corn on the cob all the time, and always the ice box full of beer, Blue Ribbon for you and Eastside for me. And then to have people come in and get a little drunk and argue 'till far into the night. And then remember how you used to get tight sometimes at parties and act so silly, yet when I would accuse you of it how indignant you would get and deny it most vehemently? Do you remember the night I got so objectionably positive, and took the pledge for a month and stuck to it, to the amazement and consternation of our friends. And how I suffered 'cause there were all those parties that month and all that wonderful free liquor.

Best of all, honey, do you remember that the last thing we did every night, when we were both just about asleep, was to kiss each other goodnight? Does all this sound like I love you and am crazy about you? It does? Well honey darling, maybe it sounds that way because I am, could that be it?

I know you don't think this is all silly do you darling? I know you don't because you feel the same things yourself, don't you?

You remembered where you said you guessed that I was? Well you hit it right, we get in there every once in a while; as a matter of fact heading back tomorrow, and this will be mailed from there in a couple of days. The place I went first last June, we have only hit once when we came out, and that was right at first; I doubt if we get down there again for a long time. The place you guessed is our southernmost boundary now and we work up from that.

They are keeping us busier than bird dogs. If it isn't something in my dept., then it is playing nursemaid to a bunch of slowpokes. We have only had about three days in port in as many weeks. It's hard as hell on the sleeping dept., but it does pass the time rather quickly. That is as quickly as time could ever go by when I am not with you.

I did get ashore the last time we were there, four or five days ago and got over to the officers club, the Quonset hut one where you buy your own bottle. I sat and very quietly drank a quart of Shenely's reserve all by myself and then went back to the ship. A lot of tension gone out of me, and woke the next day with the most wonderful hangover!! I had almost forgotten, over three weeks without a drink of any kind. I don't think you need worry about my consumption of spirituous liquors out here darling, but baby wait till I get back!!!

I had a very pathetic letter from Dave today which I am enclosing. Drop him a line, huh? I am going to when I finish this. I am at a loss to figure out where he is. I have been as far as we have gone in this area, and have yet to find him. Isn't that terrible being in the hospital. Well at least he is getting a good rest and some decent food which is something. I wrote him about two weeks ago, just about the time he wrote that letter, so he should get that by now. I would really love to see the guy, and I'll find him yet.

Oh honey, I am just living for the day when we can pick up the loose ends of our life and start to make it tick again. This business of being away from you makes just half a man or a person out of me. It doesn't seem possible that in this enlightened day and age an otherwise somewhat sober citizen could become so involved with another person, that even his thoughts aren't his own, but shared with her. Honey I never have loved you so much, or missed you so hard. The damnable part, instead of it getting easier as the days drag by, is that it gets harder, and more impossible to reconcile myself to the fact that it may be another year or more before I see you. That may be alright for some guys that just live with their wives, but honey baby, I don't live at all when I am away from you. In the past two months I have been over ten thousand incidents in our life together, yet every day I find fresh ones to remember and mull over. I love you with all my heart honey, always remember that. We are going to have a wonderful life when this is over, but right now all I can say is I miss and love you immeasurably.

Well honey, if I am going to drop Dave a line I better get on with it. I'll have another letter ready by the time this can be mailed so you'll get at least a couple together. Goodnight my darling — All me love there is — Chas

8620 Lookout Mt. Ave Hollywood, 46, Calif.
Nov. 17, 1943
Letter 39

Honey Darling;
    It is about 5:30 in the afternoon. I am half-sitting, half lying here in the Lathams' new chaise lounge. I've had one ear cocked toward the radio, but now the important part — that about the South Pacific Offensive has been said. As you say, it's really something — but I still wish they weren't doing it right now. with you around. Sounds very much like a wife, doesn't it? But the news is so good that it is almost hard to believe that we haven't lost a single ship. It's over-whelming. I've been hungry to hear the radio since I went to the hospital — now I'll devour it. What next after Rabaul I wonder?
    I got home yesterday and what a relief it was. I was actually terribly excited. Don came down to get me and I was just shaking all over when I left the place. I'm getting awfully bored with this business of being sick. I seemed to have some sort of an idea that as soon as I got here I would be well, but walking across the floor is still a major project. I'm afraid it will be a couple of weeks. I was so tired last night that I actually went to bed at eight of my own accord. Marg said that wasn't the Jane Flynn she used to know. But in two weeks I'll be in better shape than I've been for years. Then you hurry home and I will use that one ovary I have left. It's in very good shape — thank God.
    Gee honey, there isn't anything to write about. I just sit here and knit and read a little and think about you most all of the time and wait for the passage of days. It seems an awful way to be wasting a piece of your life and I get so impatient.
    Bob Deming was here today. Jack brought him up for a little while this afternoon. He had been in Seattle last week and was on his way to Tucson where he will be stationed. He brought me 2 flat fifties and I said that, per your instructions, they would start

my hoarding. He wanted to know all about you and said to send his love.

I called Seattle last night because they had been calling here all week to find out how I was and couldn't talk to me. But nobody was home except Mary and MaWee. Mother and Daddy had gone to Morton. Too bad since they had to pay for the call. Mother has been offered a job in personnel at Boeing starting at $275 a month and the office of Censorship won't let her go. She's disgusted because this job would really have a future and the one she has now she has fully explored. I don't know what she'll do. Daddy sent me the cutest letter with a poem, of course, which I'll send tomorrow as soon as I answer it.

Oh honey, I love you so much. I laughed so when I got your letter where you were thinking about Sailor Beware and got so jealous. Now you just stop that because you don't need to be jealous of anybody in the whole world. You're for me and I just thank the lucky stars that you feel the same way. I love you so much — if you were only here I would just hug you to death even if you are 200 lbs. Take care of yourself, my honey darling — All the love there is to you, darling — Jane

8620 Lookout Mt Ave Hollywood 46, Calif.
Nov 18, 1943 Letter 40

Dearest honey;

Well today was a big day! In the first place I got two letters from you — no.'s 20 and 21 — the first was a wonderful long one and the second one was the one with the stories for Chet in it.

As it happened, Don had come up to take me to the doctor so I read him that part about the gremlin in the bed that you said to read and he laughed like the dickens and said he was going to write you a letter immediately. Actually, honey, stop worrying about him. He assumes all the ugly duties of watching out for a person and never so much as gets suggestive. And I think it's all because the first time you went away — to Ithaca — he remembers that you asked him to watch out for me. So don't worry there.

I was so happy to see that you had got the things ready for Chet. I shall call him tomorrow and see what his comments are.

In my opinion darling, they are darned interesting. As you say, the first two were a little stiff, but after that they were fascinating. The last one, about the Seabee with the tractor has already been published here. I read it someplace the other day. But I shan't say anything to Chet about it. You don't need to worry about the quality of them — they're good. The only thing I have to suggest is that you were going to write each one in letter form to add — shall we say — atmosphere. Of course he could add that, but if you could bang out each little piece like it was a letter — it might be more in keeping with your original idea. But as far as I am concerned, they are fascinating and you don't need to worry about your capacity for expression because you still have it. Tomorrow I will write you just what Chet said. That gives me a chance to hear a little bit about what you had been doing — the story of the moving stars. Gosh, honey, that. must have been awful suspense. I have been wondering if it wouldn't be interesting to write something about what a man feels like when he goes into something like that. That story in my opinion, could have been enlarged on — the story of how you all felt when the flares kept dropping. If you would have been allowed to give all details — I judge that the story of the bad chart was Fry and his new skipper. Could you have told the story of the P.J. boats and the shark. Also you wrote me some very good stuff about what I judged to be Guadalcanal that I thought would be perfect — if you had only written Chet about it. Remember to try and write like you were just writing a letter to me — minus the personal things of course, because in your descriptions to me — you really get something vital — for example the description of the coral reef and the tropical fish — while they may not seem like much to you — are terribly interesting here.

Today was also eventful day because I went to the doctor and they took. the tape off and cleaned up the scar. It — the scar I mean — is really going to be a thing of beauty because by some power of magic they took out that place where the stitches broke
before and that awful scar from that is all gone. My left side still feels like a bunch of razor blades was being constantly applied, but I can almost stand up straight now and with the tape gone, I am not so breathless as I was. When I wake up every morning, I have the wild hope that today I will feel a little more normal, but I guess it is a matter of time yet. I seem to be getting along very well though, and they complimented me on what a fine patient I

had been, which made me happy because they had made such a big concession to me on fees.

Marg had Jaunty wormed today and the poor dog is definitely on the feeble side.

I felt so much better today when I got back here because the doctor said I could have a drink if I wanted it. So on the way home I had a bourbon and soda. Life was definitely rosy on that one for a while, but now it is beginning to wear off. But tomorrow all will be fine.

Did I tell you that Maureen was actually and truly expecting. No false alarm this time — the doctor told me so. I had a long talk with her about it today. Did you ever get that picture from her?

Well it is nine, honey, and I feel time for Jane to go to bed — so I wish for sweet dreams of you — I almost wish I could stop imagining that you were going to walk in because I'm so disappointed when you don't. Oh honey — I love you like the dickens. Please take care of yourself and come home soon.

All the love in the world, Jane xxxx I'm glad the sty is gone.

8620 Lookout Mt. Ave Hollywood 46, Calif
Nov. 19, 1943 Letter 41

Dearest honey;

Well another day is waning and nothing much has happened again. Nothing from you either today or yesterday. It is just two weeks ago today that I had the operation. Time does pass, but it's been pretty darned slow. I really don't have anything to complain about and I'm very lucky, but discomfort gets annoying after a while.

I have been knitting like mad on the sweater that I am making Buddy for Christmas. I haven't been very good about it and the back isn't even finished, so I really have to get to work if I am going to make anything for anyone else. I put five inches on it today.

Haltenborn is on the radio just now and he is really speaking out against deGaulle. This Lebanon crisis is really quite disgraceful because the French won't cooperate. It is the first test of whether we will be able to enforce our principles. So we better get tough.

I was just thinking that I criticized you for not putting the thing to Chet in letter form — I happened to think that maybe he said not to in the letter he wrote you. If so, pardon me.

I haven't been able to get in touch with Ed Glover about the final result on that play business because he is in San Diego on location. I thought then that if anybody would know George Yesner would, but he is closing Shakespeare in the John Carradine Company and is in Seattle. I can't think of anyone else to ask except Johnny James and I kind of hate to call him.

I finally called Margery — she wasn't home, but will be about seven this evening. I feel rather ashamed about not having called her before, but I felt so terrible that I didn't really look anybody up. I understand though that she is leaving for S. Carolina next Monday to see Tom. Tom Devinsan called yesterday. He and Mel will probably be up some night next week. Tom has just finished 12 weeks on a picture at MGM.

I'm almost positive now that I'll have an apartment at the French village the first of December. That would be perfect and it better be true because I have to have someplace to go. And that furniture must be taken care of before the rainy season.

The Lathams are going out to dinner tonight so the great experiment of getting my own will take place. I do hope it is successful.

I had a letter from Daddy yesterday — I'll quote a paragraph. "I hope that you are feeling much better now. But be careful, get your strength back before you get frisky and ambitious. The world was not made in a day and, for that matter, neither were you. It took nine long months and a few extra days to develop our first bundle of perfection. So be careful, don't wreck the carcass. The model cannot be replaced. Our manufacturing plant is no longer functioning despite a plethora of raw materials. The industry must be rated non-essential by the War Production Board. Mamma would have a fit if she saw this last paragraph." It kills me — imagine Daddy writing something like that.

Then there's a poem.

Now I must close and get back to work.
Much churning of the windmill around here.
Lots of froth, lots of foam.
I'll make some money
And buy Giddy a bone
He likes 'em cooked. He likes "em raw.
As a final tease, he'll lift a paw
And shake your hand with solemn mien.
(As if to say) I should be heard, but never seen"

The primary purpose of the letter was to tell me that he had talked to Dr. Parton and had settled the bill with him for fifty dollars. It just makes me sick. First that he should have had to do it, second because I don't think he was entitled to that much. I talked to Daddy about it and he said he would call and offer him $25, but I guess he forgot. Then I hate to have him do so much for me and I'm so darned helpless just sitting here. Daddy said "Je 1' accuse. You have been too secretive with me. Have you other bills that are bothering you? If so, what are they? Maybe I can do something about them. Let me know Honey. This is a demand, request, order, command, and what have you." Well I wrote him right back and thanked him and said he shouldn't have done it and there weren't any other bills. I didn't say he had given him too much because he couldn't do anything about it, having already sent the check. I said we were definitely going to pay him back. Personally I don't think the man should have had any money but you have to give him some. It's not like a department store where you can take a product back if it isn't satisfactory. Ah me, such is life. Daddy writes a wonderful letter as usual.

Well, darling, tomorrow will be the two months anniversary since I waved goodbye to you galumphing away on the truck. I had such mixed feelings. I wanted you to catch the ship but I really would have been so happy if you hadn't. I went back to the apartment later that day — and you weren't there and I just couldn't bring myself to believe that you wouldn't be again. I kept pretending you were and talking to you. But you didn't answer to my questions. Well that was another little home that we moved out of. But we'll have just as happy a time in the next one. It was completely empty without you, honey. It wasn't even pretty anymore.

Honey, I have a terrible confession to make. I had the lighter engraved with "Chas" and I was so proud of it — and I lost it. I've tried so hard to get another one so you wouldn't know but I can't find one. And I miss it so because it reminded me of you This may be a fool question, but can you possibly get me one and send it to me? It would be grand if you could, but of course I don't know whether it is possible.

About your harmonica. I haven't been able to find anyone with one but my contacts have been rather limited, but as soon as I can get out, I'll really and truly get you one.

The Lathams are about to leave and they'll mail this for me so I'll stop now, honey. All my love to you darling, Jane

#25
Nov 20th 1943
At Sea

Dearest Honey,

Well here we go again. Tomorrow we should be up again to where we get mail, and I am hoping and praying that I have several letters from you and that they reassure me that you are all right. I have a feeling that I will have some, and that they will have good news in them. We didn't get any mail at the last stop where I said we might have some. I'll take that back, I got a letter from Aunt Gen, but she didn't air mail it so it came second class. No first class mail at all, so there should be a batch waiting for us up here. We got a passel of magazines though, among them LIFE for Oct 18th which had a story about an Ensign and his picture letters to his bride. He did some very interesting work I thought, and his colors were especially fine. One in particular, I think it was on page 78, the top half of some ships and greens predominated. It was very well done, get a copy of it if you haven't and take a look at it.

Well I don't know how I got off on that, but I did, oh yes mail. Well life goes on much as before. We are going on another departmental project. Never a dull moment I always say. Well it makes the time go by that much faster. It has been hotter than Billy — be — damned, but a while ago we ran into a doozy of a tropical rain squall, and it cooled the ship way down. Almost livable now, and it sure is a welcome relief. I just used the Zippo to light a cig, and as always thought of you. Ain't I the sticky sentimentalist though? I wouldn't want to be any other way, though, and you can lay to that mate!! Salty, too!

Well I am wondering if you have an apt, and does the table fit, probably not, and if you have started work and how are you feeling.

[MISSING PAGE]

...long and pretty for you when I come marching home though. Well that's about all my darling, except to say that I love *you with all my heart,* and miss you like the very devil goodness, do you know how wonderful you are?

All me love honey Chas

Nov 22nd 1943 In Port

My Dearest Honey:

Well yesterday I got about five letters from you, including delayed letter no. 30, giving me all the details of your ailing innards. Baby I am so sorry you had to go through all that again, and without me there to rally-round.

I got two letters you wrote after it was over, so that I took to be a very good sign that you were on the old recovery road. The last one was Nov. 11th just 9 days to get here (we are a day ahead of you, you know) in it you had my letter of the 3rd or fourth. That's pretty good round trip in less than 3 weeks! We will be here long enough to pick up mail again this aft. And I am praying for another letter telling me the stitches came out and without too much pain.

It seems we have had our fair share of tough luck to date, so maybe it will be all egg in our beer from here on out. Just remember to keep your chin up and stuck out. You always were a spunky little chick, maybe that's why I love you so much, (among other reasons!).

We have another departmental do coming up tomorrow and then that is the last for a quite a while — indefinitely even, so

[MISSING PAGE]

thinking and clouds your vision. But I wouldn't have it any other way, believe me darling.

Well tomorrow is Thanksgiving. It seems incongruous as hell to even think about such things when the water keeps running in little rivulets down your back and chest. It's eleven — thirty and it's still hot. However the menu reads like Thanksgiving. Turkey, oysters, all the trimmings, oh yes, ham among other things. They figured 2-1/2 lbs of turkey per man, that's for the crew I mean, so every one should do pretty well. I just asked if the captain was going to carve and he said "Hell yes, bring on the bird, I'll carve it!" He really is quite a guy, and the nice thing he wears well with age. It makes duty on here a hell of a lot nicer than it would be with some rough old ignorant jerk, as a good many of them are.

As I said before, our period of violent activity is over for a while and it looks like a spell of routine. Which is all right with us all, and you, too, I presume.

You said you pour over the maps of this area and try and visualize where I am. Someday honey we'll spread out a real chart and I'll give you a regular Baedaeker breakdown of all these islands. I'm beginning to know them pretty well, and I think before I see you again I'll know them better than the natives. I just had a thought, let's have next Thanksgiving at home, OK? I would rather have it there than out someplace. Let's have nothing fancy, just simple you know, but with some good wine and such. Maybe it isn't such a wild dream, who knows? Let's count on it anyway, okay honey?

Well, my darling, it's now 12:15 or 00:15 navy time, and the thought of all night in that old sack is getting pretty irresistible. It's not that I don't love you honey, it's just that the last couple of nights have been pretty hectic.

By the way, saw two movies tonight, "Paris Calling" Eliz. Bergner, Randolph Scott, etc., and "Slightly Dangerous" Lana Turner, Rob Young, etc. The last was quite entertaining, while the first was an awful waste of talent on a lousy script. Of course there were a couple of shots of Lana Turner slightly stripped down, and the boys went wild, but you know, honey, I caught myself comparing that body to yours, and baby, for my dough, you win in a walk!

Goodnight my gorgeous gal, drop in and see me in my dreams will you? I love you very much, darling — All me love Chas

KFI/KECA News Release Letterhead
8620 Lookout Mt. Ave. Hollywood 46, Calif.
Nov. 22, 1943
Letter 42

Dearest Honey Darling:

Blue Monday but definitely not so blue. I had two letters from you today…23 and 24,…both mailed on the eighteenth of the month. That is pretty fast service. They are here on the fifth day and I am allowing that extra day for the date line change. Oh honey, I am so happy to have you miss me, but I hate you to be unhappy about the whole thing because I know just how it is. I miss you like the dickens, too.

The name of the play was "Here Today." I am surprised that you couldn't remember it…ha ha. Yes I do remember all those vines that Wilbur insisted on having. You're pretty cute alright. I was in sort of a daze when I got the letter, but started thinking about it today and remembered the whole thing. Thank you, honey. Remember the no muss, no fuss part. I hope that is TRUE because it didn't seem like that to me.

Are you glad I have the typewriter back. I am having the darndest time trying to operate it because Linda has appointed herself my assistant...she is perfectly fascinated by the whole thing, just as the kittens were, only she is bigger and stronger and does more damage. She stands here and pulls the roller around and pushes the keys and tugs at my arm. Very cute, but a little confusing. The only thing is that I don't think I write as interesting letters when I type. This is the first attempt. I have pulled the piano bench over in front of my chaise lounge so I don't have to sit on a hard chair, as that is still a little hard on the old back.

Yesterday was a day of big adventure, too. The Lathams didn't want to cook Sunday dinner so we went to that drive-in on the corner of Laurel Canyon and Ventura. It was my first time out and I did enjoy it, but was a perfect wreck when we got home. We dropped over to see the Hills as it was right by there. It seems that Dave is in Esperito Santos...on it, rather. I thought, or rather guessed that you might be very interested in knowing that.

I had to give up the typewriter. I have made the astonishing discovery that all the movements of the body which require any effort — originate in the stomach. Besides, it's a little too much of an effort to hold the old back erect for too long. I had no sooner put the tray on my lap & was ready to go with my writing than the girl across the street came in with her little girl to see Marg, and I couldn't be discourteous, so I had to stop writing. I knitted while she was here. There was bedlam with the two babies both getting into things they shouldn't. Marg trying to make a slip cover and this other girl has never been noted for keeping quiet. She finally left & Jackson came home — after a golf game at Griffin. He said it was just as pretty as ever. So now I am finally back at talking to my honey. Marg is cooking dinner & putting Linda to bed. I feel bad about not being able to help, but I can't — I just try not to be any trouble.

I had a nice long letter from your mother today. She said she was afraid you were homesick. Gosh, if — well, I only wish that were the only thing to worry about. She has probably told you all the news of her herself. I answered a letter that Gen wrote to me the other night — now you should do the same. She said she had written to you but no answer.

I talked to Emelia today. I called her to be sure I was right about the decorations. She wanted to be remembered to you. She kept talking all about how you always used to help her. She said, "big, good-natured Chuck. I'm so fond of him." I must get Wilbur's address from her. He isn't a captain. He's still a sergeant.

Honey, I'm afraid I wasn't subtle enough for you as you pieced the whole thing together from the fact that I said to write me at the Lathams & that I wasn't taking the job or a while. I guess I shouldn't have said that about the job. It was just that I didn't want you to worry and get one letter about it and then maybe not get another for three weeks. That accounts for letter 30 being missing, because I mailed it later. I don't know where 29 could be, though. I wrote it on October 30th. [CROSSED OUT: I remember I mailed it from the Holly] no — that was another that I mailed from the Hollywood P.O., but I did write it October 30th.

It was such a nostalgic memory picture of our life together that you wrote in your letter today, Darling — with the dogs & the sherry & the sunshine and kissing each other goodnight. But I did not get drunk on parties — ever. I always acted like a perfect lady. You shouldn't even say such things. So! Of course I know that our life after the war can never be just the same as it was before. Nothing ever is. But I have a feeling it will be even better — we'll even appreciate each other more — from being apart so long. I'll never want you to be out of my sight either. Another thing, with our old life that was so wonderful — it was still kind of aimless — not that you should have a definite point in every thing you do, but you know that we both felt a little frustrated at times. If we can do this news business together, we can have a fine, good, wonderful life & still be doing something useful & interesting — really fascinating. That is, if you don't decide to stay in the Navy & have me follow you all over the world — I suppose the only merit in that would be the question of eating during the depression. However — the only thing that I'm interested in now is getting this year over with & you having a leave and maybe going to school here or something so we could be together. That is the bliss I ask at the moment.

Thanks for Lovi's letter — I feel so sorry and I shall write him one tonight. If you only knew where he was, perhaps you might see him. Keep your eye out for someplace with a big hospital.

Did I tell you I paid Mrs. Hoppe! We are now at peace with her & George says not to worry. Anyway, now Beth & Al can get their piano when they want it. I wrote them a letter about it several weeks ago — also told them I was going to the hospital & I haven't heard a word from them. It seems that Allan Hoppe is a captain & he is at Numea — in the quartermaster dept. She was very anxious that I tell you to look him up if you ever get there. I said of course I would tell you, but I imagine you could think of greater pleasures.

I hate to talk about my operation because I know that everyone looks at me kind of funny & is dying to ask if I had the whole thing out. Of course I can't say out of a clear sky, "No, only half, and they haven't been any good for years anyway." So, there are probably a few people who think the worst. Won't they be surprised sometime. In case I didn't make it very clear to you, honey, that is the case. My left side is in fine shape. The doctor said that just as he was finishing, I woke up. I asked him if he was through, and he said yes. Then I asked him if he'd had to take out the right ovary. He said yes — it was completely destroyed. Then I brightened up & asked, "Does that mean I'll only get the curse every two months?" He said no, and I protested that that wasn't fair. He got quite a kick out of that. Then he asked me if I wanted him to call Maureen & I said he might as well if he wanted to — evidently he did, because a great bunch of flowers arrived from them that afternoon.

Maureen is coming here for dinner tomorrow night. She has the laugh this time. I told you about going out there when I first got here with the Lathams. Well, Will was sitting there throwing down the bourbon in zombie glasses. Maureen has a new approach now. She says, "Will, you know how hard it is to get bourbon, and we want to save it for our friends." Nothing daunted, he pours himself another slug and says, "I'll try not to enjoy it, dear." What a horrible,. horrible husband. Will all of a sudden got a big idea for a radio program. It was for "Variety" and was to be about the latest plays & movies, but what was to distinguish it, it was to be couched in the "Variety" jargon. The New York kind that is as bad as James Joyce. He gets up & strides around the room in the throes of the thing and all of a sudden plants himself in front of poor calm Jack and snaps out, "Do you want to be the producer or the announcer?" Jack stutters in surprise & then starts to laugh, so Will is very insulted. Will, it seems, took the idea to M.C.A. the next day & they took it to Variety and V. stole it and is now going to make it, in Maureen's words, "One of the biggest radio shows in New York." She will love rubbing it in a little. Will is vindicated.

Oh, Honey, if you were only here and we could have an evening of a few drinks & a big conversation about the state of the world. These new landings on the Marshall & Gilbert islands are really something. Of course a pincers move against Truk is obvious, but the question is — will they take it or bypass & isolate is? I'm glad I don't think you're there.

Darling, I love you — so goodnight — Tomorrow perhaps there will be another letter from you. All my love, Honey — if I could only tell you in person —

Goodnight, my Darling, Jane

I had a note from Martha Stanly today & Dave is still in San Francisco. I'm scared to death your presents won't get there in time. It makes me just sick because I could have mailed them, but he said he was going right out & could take them.

So much love, Jane

This won't reach you by Thanksgiving, Darling, but I'll be thinking of you.

#27
Nov. 24th "43 At Sea.

Dearest Honey: —

I slept in all morning, and I had planned to write you. Now I must go on watch, and the mail trip (if any) will go while I still have the deck.

Just wanted you to know everything went smoothly, no pain no strain, think we are heading back down to Yam Yuen.

The old lady is jumping and quivering, hence the unreadable scrawl. Another long letter either tomorrow or in 3 days — Gotta go now, Darling

I love you All my love, Chas

8620 Lookout Mt. Ave. Hollywood 46, Calif. December 5, 1943

My Darling honey;

It is Sunday night — really very gloomy because we are having one of those infrequent and terrible rain storms...remember when we looked across Ellington and couldn't even see the streetlights... well, it is the same tonight. Margaret and Jack have gone out to dinner and to a movie. I persuaded them to do it because I thought that the house and the baby were getting Margaret down and I really wanted to stay home. So I am watching over Linda.

I have neglected you so terribly these last few days, darling...I have been living in a maze of bed jackets and sewing and knitting from the time I get up in the morning until I go to bed at night... then I had to go shopping and get the stuff to make them with and try to keep up my end of the housework and taking care of the baby and all...life has been definitely hectic. It isn't that I haven't missed you...its been harder this week than it has ever been. Maybe it's because Christmas is coming and I miss you so much and it makes me so unhappy that you won't be here. Actually I think they just ought to skip Christmas this year...and get down to business. My Christmas will be when you come home. I like to make things for people, but there isn't any joy in the whole thing without you. I will be so glad when the mail comes in the morning because then I just know there will be something from you. The last time was last Monday. I wish I would stop thinking I was intuitive because I've been afraid all week that there was something unusual or wrong. I know it is foolish of me, but I'll be so glad to hear from you. Damn it honey, I do love you so much.

Well, to be a little more cheerful. I am really making a lovely bed jacket for your mother. Now that I think about it, I am darned if I know what she will do with it...it is probably a little light for reading in bed during the winter but it's pretty. It is peach satin with a little flower pattern and I am putting cream colored lace down the front and on the collar and on the sleeves which are three-quarter length. It is really lovely. I am enchanted with it myself. It is pretty but with just the right amount of fussiness to be a little unusual for her and then not too much. It is the kind of thing that is nice to get for a present because you would never get it for yourself. I am making Hazel one, too...hers is a sort of French blue with big flowers in it and has dainty white lace. She would never get such a thing either, but she will like it. I thought they would be so simple though and they aren't. They are little things but there is so much small work to be done on them that it is just overpowering. I got some material...red...for one for Ma Wee but am just dreading making that one because I am getting sick of working on the things...but I shall probably do it. I don't have anything better to do in the next couple of days. Then everyone will be taken care of except Bobby and Daddy...they are a problem to me. For Mary I got a pair of those peasant slippers that are socks on the top. Heaven knows we can't afford all this Christmas deal, but it is something we just have to do even if it means really skimping at the end of the month because when people are so nice to you all year, the least you can do is remember them. I've managed to cut it pretty far down by a little elbow grease though. Then after that are the Lathams to whom we must give something, and Maureen and Will who should not be forgotten, and Don because he has been so nice. I'm racking my brain. Now I know what Hazel meant when she said there shouldn't be − a Christmas. That is an awful way to talk, honey, but if you were here, it would be such fun to figure and plan.

I am still in a quandary about this apartment deal. I don't have one yet and I'm going bats. I just can't stay more than a few days longer with the Lathams...they seem to like to have me, but I do interrupt their way of life. The apartment at the French village hasn't come up yet and I just don't have a glimmering of another. I haven't been able to look of course, and then they are so hard to get...it is practically an impossibility. And the furniture is still in the garage and it is raining! I have decided that I must do something about it this week by hook or crook. I had a glimmering of hope last night. Don brought me a message from Joe Hirsch... Padre you know...that Mary Ellen Pollack was back in her house and that she wanted to rent that downstairs bedroom...the one right off the living room − that sounded like an ideal solution until the apartment came up because I knew that I could make some sort of eating arrangements with her and then I could get a job...I thought I could have the radio and the books with me and put some of the stuff up in Nina's garage and the rest in storage... that I thought I wouldn't be able to use in the apartment. So I called this morning and that was all wrong. Joe got it mixed up. She merely said that she was going to rent that room...but it was to a friend of hers from Westport Connecticut...Mary Ellen has been back there and this friend is arriving next week to live with her. So that went fooey. Nina has asked me to come up there and I really think I will but I'm not sure yet. I could get a job and then move if the furniture were arranged for. I didn't want to do it that way but I can't wait too long. Besides, Helen Curren won't wait much longer. Well, I'll see how things are by Tuesday and then decide. Of course I couldn't get a job for a week or so anyway. I feel fine but get tired awfully quickly and everyone who knows keeps telling me to give myself a chance to get really well so that all this work will not have been done in vain. But in a week I think I could put in eight hours. Anyway, keep writing me here until you hear differently.

I went up to Pat's last night. I was just dying to get out and have a drink so I had three. That sounds very moderate and I am astonished by myself. But we had a lovely evening...don and Pat and I...Nine came in later...talking about philosophy and religion and the moving picture business...just like the talks we used to have at home. I was so happy there for a little while in the old atmosphere that I could hardly stand it. I think the French village is definitely the place for us...I say us because that is

like you too so much and if I were there, I would really feel that you were too. And the iron pot and the pewter and the records and the books and the lustre-ware platter would all be there in proper surrounding waiting for you, honey. I think I could feel like you were just away on location and would be back in a week or so, maybe a little longer if there was a good run. Then you would come in sunburned or with some tale or a poker game or a flight over a desert canal.

It was wonderful to be there because it was just like you. Pat had just finished painting the kitchen and had purchased a couple of prints to hang at each side of the fireplace from Sears. They were awful. He had asked me to come up — rather Nina really had in the first place...but she didn't show up...just like Nina...Don wanted to go over there and he brought a bottle of bourbon so he came up and got me, which was nice, because being way up here, I couldn't have gone otherwise. I can't get over it. I almost really thought that you were there. I cooked some hamburgers and was such a success that I am going up there soon to cook a spaghetti dinner. That should be fun because I get lonesome...the Lathams are wonderful, but I long for that old atmosphere...you know what I mean. I do dwell on how I feel, doff t I honey. It's an attack of aching homesickness for my darling.

Maggie Douglas called up today and asked me for dinner tonight. Like a fool I refused, but I had some sort of idea that I should give the Lathams a chance to get out today. I am going Wednesday night instead. Howard has been deferred for a little longer. He is getting sick of the whole thing...he wants to know if he is going or not going...he doesn't particularly care which, but the uncertainty is getting him down. It's been going on for a year now. Maggie's play closed last night — she said it was about time, but it isn't going to be so nice not having that Equity check coming in every week. She says that if Howard is drafted she is thinking of getting a job on the Graveyard shift and doing radio work in the daytime. I don't quite know if she could take it. She told me something today that I didn't know...that after you left Palm Springs and they did that play, Payment Deferred, Emery Hall had a disagreement with the theatre owner and he threatened to attach the scenery and they sneaked out with the stuff in the dead of night. She thought that Emery was right, but nevertheless they did sneak out with the sheriff at their heels. What brought that up was the fact that the sheriff was at their play last night...it seemed they hadn't paid off the director in full and he was getting the police after them...which I thought was very funny. It was such a bad play that I don't see how they kept it on as long as they did.

Well, of course I'm wondering what they decided at the conference. We're supposed to find out in the morning. I only hope that. as long as the strategy seems to be to get rid of Germany first that they got along well and decided to really do something, and in a hurry, so we can get to Japan really hard and you can come home. That's how it is...everything in the world ends up with you honey. I am wondering how Eddie Albert got on a Navy rescue crew when he was on that converted aircraft carrier. I am just wondering if that little aircraft carrier that was sunk off Gilberts wasn't his ship and he was rescued and then got to work helping in the beach. It seemed so peculiar to me.

That sweet Buddy. I believe I told you that he sent me a carton of cigarettes a week or two ago when I was sick. I wrote and thanked him and then yesterday, with no apparent reason, there came another carton. He's the nicest character, even if he is my brother.

I just did the darnedest thing...I called Seattle and nobody was home but Bobby. We have the worst time getting in touch with each other. When I called the day I got out of the hospital, nobody was home but Mary and then they called me thanksgiving and I was at the McKeans and now this time. I just wanted to say hello. It wasn't important, but they told me to call and be sure to call collect when I felt the urge. I am economical about it, but I did think this would be a good time and then only Bobby home...not that I wasn't glad to talk to him. He is going in January and thinks there is a possibility that he may be sent someplace down around here first.

If I ever get around to writing them, here is what our Christmas cards are going to be this year...I bought some Christmas stationary and some red ink and I thought I would little notes. I have to get started tomorrow at the latest, though, because I have seventy people on the list and I still keep thinking of ones I forgot. They can most of them be very short, thank goodness...I'll write you one. I was wondering in connection with that what Eddie Fahl's address was, if you have it, because I have had that picture to send to him around for months and it is a shame to lose touch when you were such good friends. Why don't you write him a note. I figured if I wrote ten a day for seven days, then I would be through.

It is now ten-thirty, honey...the Lathams should be here about midnight. I shall dash through the few dishes that there are and then I shall do a little more sewing before they get here and it is time to go to bed. So for tonight my darling, all the love in the world to you wherever you are. Goodnight my honey, Jane I love you

December 10th 1943 At Sea

Dearest Honey:

Well darling, still have had no mail from you since Thanksgiving day, and it's getting harder and harder to go on not knowing what you are doing or how you are feeling. We finally got off that Damned patrol job we were on, and are now heading down to the first place I came when I came down here last June. I don't think we will be there but a day or two, but it is a nice trip for a change. There might be a chance that we can pick up mail tomorrow, we are not supposed to stop, but the Capt. is trying to work it. I hope it goes through, because unless you have stopped writing completely, there must be a pile for me.

We haven't been paid since the fifteenth of Nov., and I think we will be paid on the fifteenth or thereabouts. I will try and send you as much of it as I can, thirty or maybe forty bucks. I wish it could be more, but at least that will help out a little, and I will send all I can to help out in the next few months. I wonder how soon you will be on your feet and able to take the job. For all I know you are probably feeling mighty fine and chipper right now. I certainly hope so, darling.

Well that is enough about that and about me. What I am really writing this for is to wish the most darling girl in the whole world merry Christmas. I haven't had time to finish your necklace so that can't get to you in time, but I trust what you did get from me met with your approval, even though it lacked the personal purchase touch that I would liked to have given it. You're so darn wonderful baby, I just hope you get the idea that I love you to distraction.

Do something for me. Do the same things we would do around Christmas, just as if I was there. Visit our friends and have drinks and talk, and know that I am vicariously enjoying them along with you. I don't mean to sound like a Pollyanna, (remember how mad I used to make you by telling you that your thinking was Pollyannish?) but I really believe it will make it an easier day for me, knowing that at least some people are enjoying the day, and acting in an intelligent and civilized manner. I know it will make it a nicer day for you, too. Most of all remember that I am always as close to you as your thoughts. I know that to be true, because you are with me constantly. Even after this long aboard you flavor all my conversations with "Jane always said, " or "my wife and I" or "Jane once said at a party" I'm beginning to think the officers here must know you better than you know yourself. It isn't my fault if they don't!!

I have just a couple of more gismoes to write up and then the next batch will be ready to send Chet. I will send you a carbon of them again, for criticism, etc. Although the last batch I sent in a month ago, I haven't heard a peep about them from anyone. of course I will if I get mail tomorrow.

Well my darling, I have to eat and go on watch. But baby, have a real Merry Merry Christmas for me, and just be sure that on that day there is a husband who will be missing you acutely, and loving you with every breath in his body. And for a Happy New Year's wish T give you the idea of the next Holiday season together, with the war behind us. Okay, so I am a Pollyanna!! I still love you to pieces. All me love Chas

[On news release letterhead for KFI, 640 on dial, NBC Red Affiliate; and KECA, 790 on the dial, Blue Network Affiliate]
2400 El Contento Drive Hollywood 28, Calif. Care of Nina Clemens December 13, 1943
Letter 48

Chuck Darling;

I made two errors in my letter of yesterday afternoon...in the first place, it was the 12th not the eleventh of December and second, Nina's address is 2400 El Contento Drive, Hollywood 28 — So that is all straightened out. I dare say that no harm has been done.

Well, I've just put the last of my stuff away and I'm moved in up here for the time being anyway. Everything worked out fine yesterday — remember I was so disturbed about Nina's not being home...well, she was and I got the stuff packed and over here about six and she was very glad to see me. This afternoon I am supposed to be down doing the rest of the moving as I planned to do, but I guess I did a little too much the last few days and my insides are a little fatigued. My plans have struck a hitch, though. I kept that chair with the green slipcover out because the Lathams wanted to use it for a while and then I thought I could probably use it in the apartment later. They were supposed to pick it up this afternoon, but Jack has to take the top of the car down to get it in there and he says that it is so hard to get it up because it has been raining and that makes it shrink. They wanted to know if Don could get it in his car and I said no because he has a rumble seat, not a turtleback. Now I don't know whether they will pick it up or not and I have to get it out of there. Oh dear. I wish I had just sent it on with the rest of the stuff. You will get so tired of hearing about this furniture deal.

I think I am going to like it here at Nina's for a little while. Life was getting a little ahead of me...always somebody at the Lathams' and much going on all day. I didn't get to write to you as much as I wanted to and I didn't keep things up as well as I should have after I could. Nina isn't here much and I can see that a little time to myself wouldn't be amiss at all. Maybe it isn't good to have too much time to think about you, but I find that I sort of lose touch with you if I am around a lot of people all the time. I don't mean lose touch...I don't know quite how to say it. I miss you just as much...even more, but I like to have time to think about what you're thinking about and doing. I have tried to follow you...I should write down my guesses and then when you come home, we can see how far wrong I am. I am waiting for that Baedaeker tour of the South Pacific.

After the moving was finished last night, five of us went out to a place called the Little Bohemia for dinner last night and had a wonderful steak. There were Nina and Jack Finch and a friend of his and Don...of course I was along, too. Honey, when you get home we are going to try a new way of frying potatoes. There they cut up little tiny green onions and fry them right in with the potatoes, and talk about wonderful. We shall have it the next time we have steak when you are home. After dinner we were sitting at the table having a bourbon and soda and a cowboy came up and wanted to *buy* our drinks...well, we hesitated and then let him buy one and then we decided that maybe we should ask him to sit down. He turned out to be that Bob Steele...of course the name was very vague to me, but you should have seen this little sailor that Jack Finch had with him...he wasn't over eighteen I'm sure, and his eyes nearly popped out. He said "Gee, wait 'til I get back to the base and tell the guys that I had drinks with Bob Steele!" He was kind of nice and very funny with his Yes Ma'am and no Ma'am and his drawl. He had his double with him who is the world's champion trick rider, but he said he was awfully worried about him...he had been trying to make the double stop working for a while and go to school because he hadn't been past the fourth grade. I said I wouldn't worry if I were he because the amount of education that he could afford to get now wouldn't do him enough good to be worth it and he was making a lot of money and happy the way he was. It's funny how worried people who haven't been to school the conventional amount are about an education. Remember Bob Oliver? The evening finally ended up with the little sailor getting awfully ill on the way home and he and Jack staying here all night. They brought me coffee and orange juice in bed this morning and left to go see Jack's aunt in Glendale. Jack thinks he is going over seas soon.

I just called Marg and there was a letter from Mother which I had her read to me. She is really going crazy, poor thing, with Christmas shopping and trying to keep up this new job and it takes a lot more time...she is still in the same place, but a different fob.

I'm afraid I just won't be able to get down to that garage today and that I'll have to do it first thing in the morning. I'll write a few Christmas cards instead. That isn't very strenuous work.

Gosh darn it honey, I love you so much. I had hoped for a letter from you today. One usually comes on Monday, but no luck. Maybe tomorrow, darling. Be good, my darling, and let me hear from you.

All the love in the world, Jane

Christmas and New Years Greetings *from the*
U.S.S. GAMBLE

As Commanding Officer and therefore a representative of the entire crew, 1 send you best wishes for the Holiday Season and for the coming year. Although your loved one. will be unable to be with you — this year, 1 know that his thoughts are of his home these days, for along with our Christmas wishes we all hold close the thoughts of our future peacetime lives.

That the day of normal livelihood will inevitably return, is evident by the work of all hands during these fighting days, I can vouch for the outstanding work of all members of this ship's company, By their excellent work they have carried the ship through crucial situations and gained for it and themselves a reputation for smartness and toughness.

You by your letter writing can keep your son, husband or brother close to his home, near to the things that are dear to home — and ready for his future normal life, therefore helping to maintain the spirit that is the very life blood of a fighting ship.

May we all look forward to the return of the days of Peace on Earth, Good Will to Man

Lieutenant Commander, U.S Navy

#37 (I think I forgot to number 36, with the stories)
December 15th 1943 At Sea

Dearest Honey:

I have about [as] much right to be writing you tonight as I have trying to fly. It is ten o'clock and I have to get up at three-fifteen to go on watch. Still and all the mail is going over very early in the morning and I wanted to have something ready to go for you, even though it may lack a little in bulk.

I also finished up your necklace today. I am sorry that it isn't strung better, but I didn't have much choice of stuff. I don't know if the clasp will hold up or not either, so in any case if you want to restring it, or have it done, don't think I will be offended. After all I did fix all the little holes, and a nice job I did, too. If I say so myself. After all, any old fool of a jeweler can string some shells, but he can't pick them up in the Islands and pick them up with the specific idea of making something for his wife out of them. So you see. I hope you can work something out with them. They are kinda pretty, I think.

Today we spent nearly all afternoon with a practice maneuvering to an imaginary dock. Simulated by a box floating in the ocean. Everyone got a crack at bringing the ship alongside. I did pretty creditably the Capt. said. But the interesting thing was that the box attracted enormous sharks, and we broke out rifles and shot at them. I know that I shot at least two hundred rounds myself, and as you may guess the old shoulder feels a little sore tonight. It was wonderful fun though and the Capt. seemed to get as big a kick out of it as anybody. This morning we had practice in my dept. The main part of my dept., and all that went very well, too. So all in all a good full day, and not without its credit.

I know you are worrying about how drunk I got the other night. Not very, back on the ship at nine thirty, but my it was fun to have a few drinks again. I ran into a couple of Cornellians, not that I knew them too well there, but we dished for a while. Then I met a simply wonderful Lt. Commander who had the god — damndest ideas for winning the war. Using mice, and microscopic cells. All manner of weird things. He was priceless, and I am going to do a little story on him for Chet, so you will see the whole thing. It was wonderful because he pretended to be dead serious about these Buck Rogers ideas. I nearly busted apart laughing, as I hope you will when you read them.

Came back to the ship and saw the last half of "In Which We Serve" and it is still a wonderful picture. What camera usage he had. Terrific.

Well, Darling, if we are here a few days I will get off another letter in a day or so; if we go out, then I'll have one waiting for the mail at the next port up. Where I should have some more mail, blessed stuff, from you. Take good care of yourself, darling, because there is a guy that loves you more than anything in the world — me! All me love. Chas

El Contento Drive Hollywood 28, California
December 16, 1943
Letter 49?

My Dearest Honey:

It is after midnight...all my resolves are crumbling...about getting to bed early, I mean. It is about one in the morning, but I figure that the thing I want to do most in the world is write a letter to my darling tonight, and so there is no sense in going to bed. I really spent most of the evening on you, honey...two letters came up to the Lathams' today...I had no way to get there all day, and I was just going crazy. Finally I called and invited myself to dinner and went out on the bus, and Marg picked me up at the bottom of the hill, and then I came in with Jackson when he had his evening program. Staying the evening was the only way I figured I could get at those letters, and they were the first thing I asked for when I came in the house. It is just like a fever when I know that there is a letter from you...I would just do anything to get at it immediately, and if I can't, I go nuts.

The last few days have been very busy, but really quite enjoyable. What with going to "Hamlet" last night and seeing "Madame Curie" tonight, and really mainly writing a screen play yesterday, and after the play maybe having an apartment coming up at the French village right away...things aren't so bad...in fact, they are looking up. The furniture isn't all moved and disposed of yet, of course, but Jackson has been too busy with his television broadcast to pick up the stuff, and so I haven't had a man. But tomorrow, I think all will get fixed. That is what I say every day, but there has to come a good one, just like your coming home...it will come, although sometimes it seems like it won't. Just think, Honey, in four days, it will be three months. That is half of half of a year... one quarter of the time I expected I would have to wait for you. It did seem a little impossible in front of the warehouse in San Francisco when I said, "I'll see you in a year or so"...I really thought that maybe you were just going out for the day, and I did expect you to come walking in the door...but it's three months, and you haven't, honey, so it's true.

I am sitting here feeling very sinful, with a tall drink of bourbon beside me. It is the only one today, though, and I probably shouldn't have had it, but it did sound so good. You see, when Jack brought me in, he let me off at Pat's. Nina was to be there, and I was to go home with her. It was a little after ten, and she wanted to know if I wanted to go see "Madame Curie"...the last show started in ten minutes. Considering that I've seen only one movie since you left, I thought it might not be a bad idea, and it was supposed to be marvelous...so we went, and it was. I have never considered Greer Garson a great actress, but if she doesn't pull down the Academy Award for this one, something is wrong...the caliber of it was so high, especially as she got older. And Walter Pidgeon, of course, in his quiet way, turned in a performance that was just as good or better. And it was so simply done...with no fanfare or guck...in other words, they didn't ruin it, which was a big surprise. The Lathams were fine...Marg was decorating the tree tonight and Jack was sitting back, commenting at times. She does get so aggravated at times, poor thing, by his inclination, or rather lack of it, to move, except under most extraordinary conditions. Poor Jackson...maybe he has just never got over being tired. They had it in the play pen on boxes so that Linda couldn't pull it down, which she would surely do if she got the chance. Just as we finished, she woke up, and so Marg went in and carried her out to see the first Christmas tree which she could remember. Her eyes were hardly open, but when she caught sight of all those lights and red balls and silver icicles, she looked as if she were in a dream. She kept pointing her hand to it and looking absolutely mystified. I imagine she will think it was really a dream until morning, that is, if she can think that well, which I seriously doubt she can yet. It is too bad it isn't next year, because Marg enjoys watching her watch the tree so, and she would enjoy it so much more next Christmas.

Do you know, last night was the first time I had ever seen a performance of Hamlet? I went with Nina and Pat, and we sat in the fourth row, and it was really quite wonderful. Mike Jeffries is the company manager and Kay Hammond plays the queen. She was really very fine. Her voice and her reading were beautiful. Then, too, George Yesner is one of the gravediggers...under the name of George Ramsey. I suppose he was happy at last, after the way he used to recite Shakespeare and Alice in Wonderland at all the parties. He played it a little too much in the traditional manner, though, I thought, because the rest of the cast was more informal. Leave it to him, though, he had a portion of his stomach sticking out, Remember Leffingwell? He was one of the players and then, too, one of the courtiers — he didn't say but one sentence, but it was delivered in his best pontifical tones, and the rest of the time he stood around looking very solemn and a little old and pathetic. In case I haven't said it before, John Carradine was, of course, the lead...Mr. Hamlet himself. I'm sure that it could never equal his performance as Jesus that you told me about, but it was good...the papers said it was one of the best thought-out performances of the part that had ever been done. You could understand the sense of every word he said, which is quite something. He was very simple and realistic, but I understand that from a little further back; his movie training showed and he didn't project. He might not have had enough fire, in my opinion, too. The use all the old furniture from the Barrymore production, and Kay wears all the queen's costumes. That is fine for the sentiment of the cast, but unfortunately the production looked pretty shabby. We met the producer in the intermission. In fact, he bought Nina and me a drink. He was very nice and a little mystified by the whole thing. He looked like a self-made man who went in for theatrical production in middle life, and he was quick to say that he didn't like Shakespeare and he never went to the show. Nina and Glen and Lou and I are going to see "Othello"...also the first time for me...on Saturday night, and then, after the show...Mike and Kay and the producer and some other people in the thing are coming up here...at least, that seems to be the current plan. Carradine was made up to look as much as possible like Barrymore...it was a little pitiful, although he succeeded pretty well, Mike said that he reserves one seat in the center of the house every night — that seat is under the name of John Barrymore.

Honey, I am going to start typing on the red part now, because the black ribbon seems to be about gone...and no wonder...I bought it in the dime store and have been using it on six months now.

It may seem to you, Honey, that I am flitting around too much socially — sometimes I think that is true myself, but when you are lonesome and people try to be nice to you, you just can't turn down invitations...you don't want to because you feel so lonesome when you are by yourself. The reason I don't have a job is that I keep thinking every day that I am going to find a place to live, and of course I can't get one until I do have one because there is just so much that I can do, and to get settled and work at the same time is impossible at the present time. I feel wonderful but still a little weak, and have to take it easy a lot of the time. Besides, I don't want to undo this operation like I evidently did the last one by being too ambitious at first, even if I do feel good. When they suspend certain things and they fall right down again, it's because you have been a little too active. This time I want to give it more time because I want it to stay where it is, because this is really the last time I can have it done. Guard my resources, as it were...I just wanted you to understand that while you're out there working so hard, I'm really not shirking my job...I mean my part of us...I just have to wait to be able to do everything the best way possible. I'm sure you know what I'm talking about.

Maybe I had a hand in a picture yesterday. Don called and said he needed somebody to type up this screen treatment that they had just finished in a story conference. They don't have their permanent offices in the studio for a few days yet, although they've been paying him all this time...so he wanted to know if I wanted to do it. He said he would hire me — well, of course I said I would be glad to do it as a favor to him, so he brought up this monstrosity. The studio had bought an idea...three different ideas, in fact, with no connection, and they were trying to put it in one picture... them, I mean. They had to have the treatment, because the agreement with the writer was that they should supply it. They have a real fine writer who is at Warners, and he is doing this on the side for below his regular price. They are so happy to get him in their little organization, that they do as he says. Well, they had the worst conglomeration that I have ever heard. It finally ended up by my asking him what it was about, and he told me, and I made a new outline for them, changing the whole thing and connecting it up, persuaded him that it was better, and I'm darned if he wasn't so enthusiastic that he called the director and told them to hold everything, that he would be in in the morning with some new material. We wrote until I went to dinner and to the play. He came along to dinner...at Musso Frank's, and then he came back here and worked until afterwards and we finished it up. I don't know how it came out, but if he calls tomorrow and says that they are going to use the way I said to do, maybe he will trust my judgment so that I can sell him one of yours for one of his later pictures. He has a contract for six with them, and if they turn out all right he has a major release. You know, Darling, I have been thinking about that script that you and Will wrote about Jonathan Hodge, and the energy drops in this Utopia in Central America, and the havoc created in New York, and every time I think about it, I think it is better. What do you think about that? It seems to me that it could be darned good. It is astonishing to me how a studio will buy something like that...not yours, Don's...and expect to make a picture out of it in the haphazard fashion that they employ. Boy, if you could just get on to the trick, with a little luck, you could make a fortune.

You asked me how Chet was. I don't know. I have only seen him once since I have been here, and the situation seems to be such now that I can't call him unless I want the job. I called him to say that I had gone to the hospital, and I called him when I got out, but I haven't heard from him at all. He's probably pretty busy.

I am going to the Lathams' Christmas morning and then up to Maggie and Howard's for dinner. The Hills asked me to go there, too, and I would really rather because it probably would be more fun. They are having several people, *but* it can't be helped because the Chamberlains asked first. We went there last year, too, and it is my tradition. The only reason I am afraid of it is that it will remind me too much of you. They had a short tonight in the movie about loved ones not being home this Christmas and showed shots of them in the Navy, etc. it was very beautiful, but sometimes, as far as I am concerned, they make me feel too bad...at times I think the less said, the better.

Oh, honey, I'm afraid the postal authorities won't take this letter. I like to write double space, but it takes up so much room, and they are a little particular about too big letters. Maybe I'd better go back to single after this.

Wherever you are tonight, Darling, I hope that you know that I love you with all my heart and miss you terrible. I had a letter from you yesterday and one today. The second letter today was the one from Captain Armstrong, the Christmas letter...it was beautifully written. I don't know if it is the custom to send those, but it was a wonderful one. I know that everyone appreciates them so terribly much. And then there was the copy of the citation, which was wonderful. Of course you weren't there then, but it *did,* as he added in a postscript, give an idea of what you were doing. He is certainly to be congratulated. Honey, your ash trays sound terribly interesting...I guess I'm a tourist at heart, too, because I'm just like you are about wanting those things...and valuing them. As I sit here, the piece of the Gamble is sitting right beside me. It is what it represents, and with that with you, you don't and can't forget. Goodnight, my darling...sleep tight...I love you,

I was not tight in the letter I wrote you Halloween Eve. It was real, pure love with no liquor at all. So there!

27 Dec. 1943 At Sea

Dear Chet:

The other day we were fortunate to be in a town that boasts an officers club. (I use that word `Town' in its limited sense!) Having put away a couple of the best, I was leaning against the bar trying in vain to get the bartender's attention when a Lt. Commander standing next to me succeeded in getting waited on. He gave his order and then as an afterthought asked me what I was drinking. I told him and he ordered for me. We fell to talking of this and that and I got the next round. Suddenly without any buildup he asked me "Are you interested in ways of shortening the war?"

I of course replied in the affirmative and for the next hour I was regaled with some of the weirdest and most wonderful schemes that man has ever heard. He must have told me twenty different ones, each a little more screwy or *inspired* than this preceding, depending on how you look at it. Later in the evening I met his commanding officer who told me that almost every day he entered the wardroom of his ship with a new idea that invariably put them in the aisles. As his commanding officer put it.

"In war zones some men go to pieces, *some* men write bad novels, some take to drink, but Commander Jones invents plans."

I strongly suspect that his reading consists largely of "Amazing Stories" or "Scientific Fiction," but that is only a guess on my part. I'd like to tell you two of the schemes that aroused the biggest laugh in me.

The first he called simply "Mice Transports." The idea being that groups of patriotic citizens back home would raise huge quantities of very sturdy mice stock. Then Higgins, the boat man, would invent a "Mice Transport," the sides of which would collapse on a signal and a vast net — work of interlocking pens would be unhinged and plunge the mice into the sea. Around the neck of each mouse would be a collar. On this collar would be a small but very powerful magnet, and a small cylinder of stainless steel filled with cyanide and coated over with an essence of cheese. The plan of attack would be first to lure the main Japanese Fleet into the open and then the Mice Transports would pass very close to them at high speed and at the nearest point dump their cargo of mice into the sea. The speed of the vessels they just left would prevent them being drawn back to their own ships so they would then be attracted to the sides of the Japanese fleet. At this point I thought I saw a flaw. "Yes, " I said, "But how could the mice" and that was as far as I got. "Oh yes, " he said. "One thing I forgot, all the mice have a stickum solution on the bottoms of their feet to enable them to climb the sides of the Japanese ships. Once they get aboard they are so exhausted by their efforts that they start to eat the cheese coated cylinders around each other's necks. Almost at the same instant their sharp little teeth puncture the thin shell of steel and the whole personnel of the main Japanese battle fleet are gassed!!! Now, if you think [that] is a wild plan, wait until you hear the other one. "'Do you know anything about Ferma-cells," he asked me. I tried to look as intelligent as possible while admitting my abysmal lack of knowledge of the Ferma-cell.

"The Ferma-cell," he went on, "is a small microscopic animal that multiplies by dividing. It can exist under many conditions, but the ideal habitat and the one conducive to the quickest multiplication of cells, is warm salt water."

I felt that some comment was needed from me at this point so I replied brilliantly "'Yes?"

"Yes indeed" he said. "Now when the Ferma-cell has reached its maximum density in a given body of water it is about the consistency of Welsh-rabbit. Now what a simple thing it would be to take a squadron of Liberators, load them up with refrigerated five gallon milk cans full of Ferma-cells and fly them up to Truk Island, where we know a large body of Japanese warships hang out. They could fly over very low late some evening, and with the temperature of the water there, by morning the whole harbor would be solid with Ferma-cells. That would successfully immobilize the fleet there, and we could finish them off at our leisure. After all, they couldn't get out of there through that stuff, now could they?"

Well I turned it over in my mind, and the more I think about it, the better I like it. Can`t you just see a good part of the Japanese battle Fleet trying in vain to steam through Welshrabbit! Gives you a wonderful mental picture doesn't it?

Well, that`s all for now, Chet. Let me know what you think of the plan. Regards

December 25, 1943
2400 El Contento Hollywood 28, Calif.
Letter 53

To you my honey it was Christmas yesterday...in fact it. is just over for you because it is shortly after midnight of Christmas morning now. It has been a very sane Christmas eve. You don't to feel sorry for me because I turned down four invitations...of them because of the Lathams' baby, but I didn't feel as if should go out on a long party and that I'm not particularly heartbroken about it.

Honey thank you so terribly much for the beautiful thing that you gave me for Christmas. I know that you don't know exactly what it is yet so I will tell you. I wore it tonight to go have dinner at the Roosevelt hotel with Nina and her mother. It was the first time and with the first opportunity I just couldn't resist it — and then with the Navy pin it was gorgeous. It is a black dress...the prettiest I have ever had. It is lovely black crepe — the really nice kind that you don't get much now and it has very square shoulders with three-quarter length sleeves and a draped skirt that is just a dream. It is really the loveliest dress I have ever had. I know you won't be angry with me honey, but I sort of caught on to what was going on about the letter and I persuaded Marg to let me pick something out myself and then she could go down and pay for it. It is from Nancy's and I won't wear it much because I want to save it for when you come home. But honey, it's so beautiful and I thank you so terribly much. I love you much much much.

I didn't finish our Christmas shopping toady because the doctor wouldn't let me go down town and shop in the crowds, so I explained to the Lathams that they would have their present on Monday. I shall tell you what it was then, as I still am not quite sure.

Nina's mother had asked me for dinner tonight and I was quite anxious to go so I decided to. She is so interesting. It was a very nice dinner and afterwards we went up to her house above the swimming pool...remember...and opened her present and Nina's. Then they gave me a gook called "Ask Me Another," which is a book of quizzes. I think I'll get one for you. Luckily I had fortified myself with a candle as per our old Christmas custom and presented it to Nina's mother. Nina was going to a party...I was asked but decided I better not go. She dropped me off at Pat's and Don was there and he took me home. There is a man named Lee Gale who is a friend of Nina's staying here...I think I told you about him last night... how he was so terribly sick with the flu and all alone in his room. We had a couple of drinks and Jackson dropped in on his way to his program and had a drink. He brought the packages to me from the family. Don went home and I decided to open the packages... there wasn't much point in not because I wouldn't have anybody to do it with in the morning. I certainly made a landslide of slips and I had really needed them. Mary gave me one and so did the Lathams, and the other day Nina had given me four of hers that she had never worn. She doesn't wear them and said it was silly of them to be lying in the drawers. Now I have nine slips, more than I have ever had in my life. There was a box of homemade candy and a pair of long black gloves...those were from Ma Wee. When Mother had asked me what I wanted for Christmas I said that was what I needed. I didn't know why then, but they just go exactly with your dress. I was appalled. One pair of gloves costing ninefifty...they left the price tag in. But they are really beautiful. Then Mother made me a cute black purse that is like a bag with handles. Also I got another dress. It was so wonderful of them, but unluckily I don't like it...it is sort [of] fuschia and I don't think that color is very becoming to me. Mother wrote that I could exchange it down here, so I think I will get a couple of sweaters and a blouse for work.

Buddy sent me three cartons of Camels! (They are very hard to get) and a set of airmail stationery. I thought his card with it was so sweet. It said, "Jane dear...The KFI KECA paper reminded me of this. Merry, merry Christmas and loads of love to my big beautiful little sister. I wish I could be with you — that Chuck could...Take awfully good care of yourself. Love, Bud." It has been a very quiet Christmas eve, honey...filled with thoughts of you.

Honey, today I got your letter with the things for Chet in it. Do not worry, I am keeping them right on file with your letters on my board. But honey, those things to Chet were terribly fine. I shall call him the first thing Monday morning and see if he has received them yet. But believe me, they were really good. I like you to do them in the letter form and they were so darned well written. I read them out loud and Don and this Lee agreed with me fully. I don't know how you could much improve on those. They were really something. Keep up that good work, honey, and they will be asking you to write a book. I honestly haven't a single criticism to make. They were that good. The writing was so smooth and expressive. I think that's some of the best writing you've ever done. I do think it would be a good idea to keep a notebook and write him one every other day as you plan. That would be easier for you and would probably help you to keep your color in them. I'll let you know Monday what Chet said.

Gosh, there still must be a bunch more letters from me someplace if you have only received eight as of the date you wrote. You probably have a lot more now as this letter took twelve days to get here.

I hope that there will be a real long letter from you in the next few days, as you said, commenting on the letters you have from me, because I like to hear what you think about things and your advice. I think that in spite of not having a place to live, I will ask Chet about the job Monday because I could walk down the hill in the morning and, if worse came to worse, I could take a cab up the hill at night for forty cents for a week or so. Nina told me that she wants me to stay as long as I like even if it should take two months to get that apartment. Of course I don't want to do that, but it is nice to know that you are welcome. I think her Mother likes having me here, too. I think she thinks I make Nina lead a more normal life.

Well, honey, I could just talk to you the whole night, but it's getting pretty late and I should go to bed because tomorrow's another day.

So much love to you, my darling. I can hardly wait to see you again.

All my love, Jane

By the way, what's this I hear about Mr. Berkely taking up all your fresh air. He is definitely not a gentleman, even by act of Congress, tell him. I know that you have to have the breezes blowing through and he should try to be a little cooperative and not use them all up. And what's this you say about his girl...I thought he was married, or is there more to this than meets the eye. What have you on your ship. I am suspending judgment until I hear more...but I don't like the sound of it. Tell him to justify himself or did you make a mistake.

Are my letters censored? If so I shan't put your middle name on the envelope. It might prejudice the censor. Do you have any [MISSING WORD] which I can't seem to find. People laugh in my face but I'll keep trying. Honey answer this — Can you play records on the ship?

Merry Xmas! Noel!

Just a memento to remind the most wonderful wife in the world that I love and miss her on this Christmas Morning:

Merry, Merry, Christmas Honey, I'll spend the next one with you. Chas

Happy New Year!

Love & Kisses!

#40!?!
Xmas Day, 1943 At Sea

Dearest Honey:

Well here it is, Christmas day, and as far as we are concerned, it's just another day, and pretty damn hot at that. However there is a silver lining to this particular dark cloud. The Exec wrote at the last port to send our mail from where they usually hold it up to meet us when we get in tomorrow. So if it gets there, and I really think it will, I'll have a good Xmas after all, that is always providing there is some mail from you. I am also hoping that those new pictures are in this batch of mail, as I am looking forward to getting them with a great deal of pleasurable anticipation. My Gawd I sound stilted don't I? Well it's not the kind of a day where all is happiness and light. As a matter of fact I wish to hell I was home with you at least for this one day. I know it's not cricket to bitch, but this is one day that has always meant a lot to me, and I had so much fun with you on this day the last few years. Well enough of that. I will try and be noble about it after all there isn't a hell of a lot else one can do is there?

We are getting back into the heat, but good, and our little breather in cooler climes makes it doubly tough to take. Two days ago I started taking half and hours exercise a day along with a little sun bathing. Already I have knocked off a little weight. Well I like to think so, at any rate. Much as I hate exercising for itself alone, you know what I mean, I am going to stick at it, and when I come marching home again, I will be the tannedest and flat belliedest guy you ever did see. I guess I am not so old yet. The sight of a pot beginning to show on me is enough to send me into a frenzy of activity doing something I don't like to do. But I want you to think I am pretty when I get back, so on with the push-ups.

In this last port they had quite a lot of stuff, souvenirs and such like that. Of course I didn't have much money, but I did get you several nice shell necklaces that I am sending by regular mail, as nothing over eight ounces can go by air. Also in the package are two ash trays made out of Japanese shells (look on the bottoms) and a small shell cut down to hold stick matches. Also a plate I got off that ship, and some little hunks of coral in various shapes. And lots of strings of beads. I hope you like them. Then also tomorrow I am mailing by air, one necklace that I kinda like, also six hand carved ivory sticks. They are for the fruit in an old-fashioned. They are pretty nice, so be careful when you unpack the box and don't throw any of them away.

Burke and I finally made a liberty together, and had a lot of fun. I am enclosing a picture of the dates we had. Nice girls and lots of fun. We found a pub that had gobs of Canadian Club for twenty cents a drink, and we didn't stint ourselves, of that you may be sure. It's all kinda a way to let off steam, but Honey even though it is fun and a change, I still get so damn lonesome for you I am about to die. When we do our travelling after the war I hope you have no idea of coming to these parts, because honey that is one area we are going to give the big go-by and in no uncertain terms. Anyplace else in the world, but as far as this is concerned, you 11 just have to take my word for it. By the way I thought that maybe Marge would like one of these necklaces, so I am sending a couple to her in a separate package. Also one to Mom. Now if you want to give any to Mary or your mom, go right ahead, but it's easier for you to send them than me. I don't know if you can even wear them except with very sport clothes, but there they are. I hope you get a little pleasure out of the box. I had a lot of fun packing it up for you, I can tell you that. Honey darling, I love you so much that I just can't tell you how much. Maybe some day when we get back together again I can show you by my exemplary conduct just how much I do love you.

Well darling, I have to put my shirt on and go on watch, but I will write again tomorrow night if we get any mail. And I am sure I will. I wonder if you have another address by this time, and how you are and oh all stuff like that. Do you miss me darling? More tomorrow.

All me love — Chas

P.S. I answered Ivan Mannings letter the other day and am enclosing it.

26, Dec. 1943 At Sea —

Dear Chet:

You know, I used to hear a lot of chatter back home about how the average guy didn't know anything about what was really going on in this war. Most people contended that the figures the Govt. issued and the actual ones were at great variance, whether it concerned casualties, planes shot down, or ships sunk. And ours or theirs made no difference; the figures were altered to look good.

Well, we get the same press news with our breakfast that you have heard late the night before, and I don't think I am tipping any mitt if I say we are often amazed at things that come out in the press. Some actual cases when we were connected with landings in one way or another, and it would just be well started when, bang, the morning press would have a write — up on it giving more details than we even knew about.

The point I am trying to make is that as far as I can see from my somewhat limited view-point, the American people are getting the news as it happens, which is the way it should be.

Take the Japanese, though. They must pass out the most horrible form of mis-information to their troops. There is a pretty well-substantiated story about a couple of English-speaking Japanese that were captured on an island down here. When some of their captors asked them how they liked the way the war was going, they shrugged their shoulders and said, "Oh, you may take an island here and there, but you will never recapture Denver or San Francisco." How about that? They must pump them full of malarkey from morning to night.

Of course, we sometimes keep our own boys in the dark about ship movements and destinations. That, of course, is the case when a large number of men are involved, and it is actually for their protection. I was talking to a Lt. Col. In the infantry the other day, and he said that the large transport that they had come down from the States on was laying off one of the islands we now hold. One of his non-coms approached the Col. as a spokesman for a group of men, and wanted to know if they were going to cross the canal in daylight!! They had themselves in the know, but just barely.

2400 El Contento Drive Hollywood, California
December 27, 1943
Letter 53

Dearest Honey;

I just don't know quite where to start to tell you how wonderful you are. I have made up my mind. The necklace came yesterday. At least the Lathams phoned me yesterday morning that it was there. So I got over there to get it, and, Honey, it is simply lovely. That clasp that you were ‾ apologizing about is simply wonderful. It is so darned artistic, actually, and it goes together wonderfully. And the shells, Honey, are so lovely and exquisite. I just don't see how you bored all those little holes. It is so lovely, Honey, and I know how terribly many hours went into making it. I shall certainly be very proud to wear it, and I thank you a million times.

Well, I called Chet today, as I said I would. And what do you think. He is using your stuff every Saturday morning at a quarter of eight...it is awfully early, but he said he would use more if you could get it there and that it has been a great success. He said that you were even beginning to get fan mail! He said to tell you to keep it up because the things were wonderful, and he could use all you sent and even more. That is really something, honey. Imagine your writing being on CBS. I shall listen next Saturday morning and report to you. Oh, Honey, I am so proud of you I am about to bust a tendon...actually. Also, last but not least, that will give us a definite little nest egg after the war. You are a success, Honey. He said he was anxious to have you start that every-other-day business and to send as much as you possibly could.

I also asked him if one of those jobs for me would be open in the near future, and he said that any day I wanted to come down, I could have it. I said that I would call him about Wednesday as soon as I really got over this flu and cold. I am over it now to all intents and purposes, but it has a reputation for attacking you when it is supposedly over, and I want to be really in good shape when I start there. It would really cook my goose if I started that thing again and got something the matter with me I am terribly enthusiastic about it, and I want to be sure that I will be able to do it well when I do it.

Well, Christmas is over, thank goodness. I still don't have the Lathams' Christmas present, as I had the well — known cramps today and didn't go downtown, but tomorrow I trust that I will have that little deal taken care of and will be able to start the New Year clean and NEW. It really wasn't a bad Christmas, considering. Howard came over for me about one in the afternoon, and, as usual, I wasn't very punctual. AS A MATTER OF FACT, I was in the shower. He patiently waited while I got dressed, and, just as I was putting on the finishing touches, two Maine lieutenants walked by the house and they invited them in for a drink. They hurdled the hedge and hopped in, so I had to sit down and be the hostess for a while, as Nina was still asleep. Then, after a drink, I departed and went over to [CUT OFF PAGE BOTTOM] sailors there from 'the USO. They were members of the amphibious landing forces and had been training at Camp Pendleton. They were pretty sure that this was their last leave. Verv sweet little characters,...18 and 19...one wanted to be an actor because he had studied drama in high school. One from Chicago and one from New York. I told them about the little kids in the back lot behind the Italian restaurant who thought you were Flash Gordon. I also read to all of them, after dinner, most of the things that you had sent the day before. They thought they were wonderful and that every word of them should be put over the air. They were really in awe of you. Remember that turkey gravy there last year, Honey, and how it was so thick and white and not enough of it? Well, I discovered why. Maggie wraps the turkey in a sock, which makes it nice and moist, but that way she never bastes it, which makes for very little juice for gravy, and then she mixes the thickening with milk instead of with water. I tried to tell her in a tactful way that I thought water was better, but the gravy was just exactly the same. That is a terrible thing to say when they were so nice, but it is what happened, and you had commented on it, so I thought I would tell you the reason. They had a Christmas stocking for me filled with this and that, including twelve bobby pins, which I was terribly happy to get, and lots of other cute little things, and then they gave me some very nice stationery. I gave Howard a carton of Camels and Maggie a manicure set...I don't mean that I did...I mean we did, and I just carried it over...then we gave them a couple of little knick-knacks with straw flowers growing out of the top that were kind of cute for a bedroom. It was an accident that we had them. I began to feel pretty rocky while I was over there and went home thinking to go to bed, but the joint was jumping, so I excused myself about eight in the evening and they all insisted that I should try the bourbon cure. Glen and Lou were here, and Pat Gleason and Don and this Lee character that has been staying here. They sat around and talked all night, and after a couple drinks, I began to feel a little better and stayed up pretty late, too. It must have worked, but what a way to cure a cold. I have felt pretty good since, though.

Well, that was Christmas. Yesterday I slept pretty late, and then Don came over, and everybody but me was asleep, so I persuaded him to take me over to the Lathams to get the package from you. Then I came home, and Nina and I cleaned house, and then she went over to Glen and Lou and I went down and ate dinner with this Lee character and then came home and went to bed. I had big ambitions for today, but the time of the month rather ruined them. We did cook a big beef stew for dinner tonight. I was right in the middle of it when Willie called to see how I felt. I told him what I was doing, and he said, and I agreed, that it was a reminder of the old days.

The Vadraegens received your Christmas letter and thought it was wonderful. I had written a little note to Gracie in case you hadn't had time to, but I was so happy that you had done it. Marjorie and the baby arrived Christmas Eve to be with Parker.

I had a note from Eddie Fahl's mother in reply to the Christmas card I sent, which I am enclosing. Why don't you write him a note. Honey, if anything unusual happened to you yesterday...it would be the 27th for you...let me know...although I did dream it this morning, so it would be the 28th. I had the most horrible dream about you. It was about four-thirty in the morning. I woke myself up screaming. Luckily, Nina was awake, so I went downstairs and talked to her. I couldn't make myself go to bed again. I suppose it is just a fabrication of the mind, but it was none the less vivid. It was such a relief to me to get a letter from you today. The Lathams brought it over this evening. It is the letter where you said that you just finished the necklace, and the necklace got here first. Did you shoot a shark. But let me know if anything unusual happened.

I called up your Mother tonight...extravagant, I know, but I thought that maybe she had been pretty lonesome over Christmas, and it was simply impossible to get through then, so I thought it would be nice to have a little talk with her. I think it made her a lot less lonesome. She is just *fine*, she said. She had heard from you the day before Christmas. I told her all about the things for Chet and thanked her for the Christmas present of ten dollars, which she sent me. It makes me sick though, because she hadn't yet received the package which I sent her. It was sent in plenty of time, too. That is really too bad. And I tried hard, too.

Honey, I am pretty sleepy, and my typing is getting pretty bad, so I guess I will stop talking for now. Just remember that there is somebody who loves you with all her heart and more than anything else in the world...me...All the love there is to you, darling, Jane X [BIG ONE] for your birthday, but you may have it in advance.

★1944★

2400 El Contento Hollywood 28, Calif.
January 2, 1944
Letter 55

Hello, Honey Darling;

Well, sweetheart, it is January the second, 1944. A new year that I hope like the dickens will bring you home and before too much of it has gone by. I wrote you a letter on New Year's Eve...just after midnight, but it was such a sentimental thing, and I was weeping over missing you, so that I decided that it would make you feel bad instead of good and that I should wait until I felt a little less self-pitying about the whole thing. Because civilians shouldn't complain too much, you know, even when they do miss their husbands like the dickens. But that was my only thought for the New Year, honey, that it would bring you home. A lot has happened in this last year. It was just one year ago today that I went to the hospital in the morning, sick, and didn't want to let you know about it. Just think, it was officially the year before that that you went to the Navy...the 28th of December, 1942...And it was the fourteenth of February that I started to Ithaca to see you. I'll never forget how excited I was. I could hardly speak intelligibly. And all those bags and Gideon down at the station...and then me starting on a trip all the way across the United States and how disappointed I was to see that practically all looked the same...at least the part I went across. And then having Pat and Ann meet me at the station and you calling...and then, at last, getting out of the cab and seeing you in your uniform, looking so wonderful that I was awed — and you kissed me, and then you saw Gideon and how crazy he went when he realized who it was. And Willard Straight and our bottle of bourbon on Saturday afternoons. Each Saturday I would get so excited because you were coming home that I just couldn't stand it. And I would clean like mad and try to have everything so well organized and the dinner almost ready, and then we would get so occupied with our own affairs that the dinner never was right, and we were usually too sleepy to enjoy it. That is, until after dinner, when you woke up and would go down to the Dutch Kitchen or out to the Country Club. And that day in the snow when I stood with Gideon outside your window, waiting and hoping that you didn't have orders for the South Pacific. And the squad or whatever you call it marched by, and I had to hold Gideon. We were standing under a tree. Then you stuck your head out of the window and said that was it. Oh, honey, that wasn't a good moment. I remember I drank a whole quart of sherry that night. But then I trained myself to think only of today and not of your going away tomorrow. And New York and how enchanting it is was. And that awful time for you in Seattle — and your father's funeral…and then, honey, we got to stay in San Francisco for a while, and that helped you. And number one August Alley and Ollie and the Rainier beer and the Iron Pot and the steaks we cooked for dinner. And then the rest of it wasn't so good after you left, but the day I got the letter to be in San Francisco changed everything back again. And you came up on the cable car, and I could hardly talk, and Ollie said we made him cry. Oh, honey, that was out of this world. And remember your birthday party that was supposed to be a surprise, but you knew all about it all the time? And our vacation down here and the people and the parties and you and your shoulder, and we almost wished we were back in San Francisco where it was quiet. And then that last morning with all of us waving like mad. And us keeping up the big grins at each other when I said…well, pal, I'll see you in about a year. Well, the time since then hasn't been too pleasant, and it seems kind of futile and wasted, but now I should really be happy that I am all well, and I'll get a job Tuesday and have a big nest egg for us when you come home. It has been a big year, darling, with all kinds of different experiences in it…especially for you. I have spoken of our times together, but there has been so much that you have done away from me that it will take weeks to tell when we see each other again. 1943 hasn't always been pleasant, but there have been times of great happiness in it, and it has certainly been interesting. Let's hope that this year we will have everything and that together.

Well, the last few days have been ones of great social activities for me. I wrote you Tuesday night…Friday morning I got up early and went to the doctor and then came home and cleaned this house but thoroughly. Nina and I had decided to have a sort of gathering for New Year's Eve, because we knew some people who wouldn't be asked anyplace else and who would be lonesome, and we thought it would be a good idea to have them up. It was certainly a conglomerate group. Nobody had really met anyone else before in the majority of the cases, but good fellowship prevailed and, contrary to all our expectations, it was a very fine party. At the New Year, everybody stood around and sang Auld Lang Syne. Myself though, when the first word came out, I retired from the scene and spent my New Year's with thoughts that I hoped reached you. It wasn't so long after that that I stayed up, because I had been invited to go to the Rose Bowl game with Bill Bowles and his family, and, oh, horrible thought, they wanted to start at ten-thirty in the morning to avoid traffic. They have the traffic so well controlled now, though, and of course there were so many less cars than in other years that there wasn't any to avoid. We had breakfast on the way... remember that sort of drive-in place with the outside umbrellas, just this side of Pasadena? We have stopped there to eat several times...I can't remember just why or when, though. The spectacle of the game was beautiful. They had about two thousand naval trainees from the U.S.C. marching in the bowl before the game, and it was wonderful. They were so perfectly drilled, and when they all saluted, and the flag was raised, and the national anthem was played, and service men all over the stadium saluted...it was very thrilling. But the game itself, oh, honey...29 to 0 for U.S.C. It was tragic and disastrous, and Washington had been the favorite! They started out beautifully. During the first quarter, they went right through U.S.C. It looked like a pushover, and then something happened to them. They seemed to be walking in a dream. Nothing they did coordinated. U.S.C. started out on passes, and just before the half, they completed one for a touchdown, and then that was all. Just passes, passes, passes, and everyone was good. I have never seen anything like it. Washington had no ability to stop them, it seemed, and when they did have the ball, their interference was so bad that it was a wonder the poor man carrying it didn't get killed. On top of everything else, we got out of the game to discover that we had a flat tire and no spare and no tools for mending. We had to get a tow car to take the car into Pasadena. We were very lucky that it was just a tack and could be mended immediately, but it did take a couple of hours to get it all fixed up. It was very irritating. The Bowles had asked me to go to the Mocambo with them that night, but I had to refuse because Jim Hill was having a party for Jack Hanover and Bobbie Gaylor, if he could get up. I had thought it was 'just to be a little gathering, but evidently it was one of the typical Hill gatherings...a little disorganized, with millions of people there. I don't know, as I never got there. I do feel terribly ashamed about it. It seems as soon as Jack Hanover got to the Hills', he said he would come pick me up so Jim wouldn't have to leave or something. So he called, and I gave him the directions. Well, it took him an age to get here because he got lost. When he got there...rather, here, there were two J.G.'s with him that he had brought along. I asked them if they wanted a drink before they started the long trek back, and they accepted with alacrity. Well, it finally came out that they didn't want to go back to the Hills'...I suggested it, but couldn't get them started. It seems that they weren't quite so used to Jim's type of hospitality and thought that they were imposing. Then, to make the situation really bad, Jack Hanover went to sleep and then I couldn't budge them. One of these characters was a terribly good friend of Phil Harris's, and he wanted to go out there to the Wilshire bowl for a few minutes, so I finally went out there for an hour with them, thinking that they would probably go to Jim's late. It was a fine time there...a good show, and Phil Harris came over to the table to talk to us and had a big conversation about his experiences in the Navy. Well, I never did get to the Hills'. Jack Hanover woke up when we got home and we talked for a time, and then Nina came in and we talked some more. Jim was really kind of hurt, and I felt terrible about it, and so did J. Hanover, but it was kind of funny...it didn't work out. He had that particular bunch of people that came in that night that we were there, honey, so I guess not a great deal was missed. So, that is what I have been doing the last couple of days. Thank goodness the holiday season is over. I am beginning to feel like Pat Zimmer must have...I don't want you to think that I am enjoying myself too much though, darling...I do these things when people want me to because, more than anything else, I dread sitting at home being lonesome for you.

I'm a little disappointed about my job. Remember the other day when I told you that Chet said I could have it back...I planned to start tomorrow. Well, it seems he called me Friday said that when I got sick they had hired another girl to take my place, and he had thought they would fire her as soon as I could take it. Well, she's not very efficient, but the powers that be are rather unwilling to fire her until she has more of a chance. Well, I certainly wouldn't want anyone to be fired for me anyway. But he says he can get me another job until there is an opening there. I wanted to see about it tomorrow, but he says that Tuesday would be better, so now I have to wait. I feel awful about it, but actually it wasn't my fault that I got sick and then that he told me that I could have it so I didn't try to find out about another. You know, Honey, though, I just can't get this Red Cross deal out of my mind. I think I am well enough now so that they would let me in, and I feel that it is the least I could do when other people are doing so much. These boys last night were telling me about disembarking the wounded from Tarawa. The civilians who were on the dock had to leave — they couldn't stand it. The only thing about it is that if you could get here, I might be someplace else, and that would never do. But, on the other hand, I might be able to arrange it to get to the South Pacific, like Leta, and I could see you a lot of the time.

Honey, I don't want you to be indignant about it, and I want to know what you think. You know how you felt when you were a civilian with all the men in uniform. I feel like a rat just sitting here. Let me know what you think if I could get in it and I could get to someplace where I wanted to.

Now, Honey, I am going to do the dishes, get dressed, and then Nina and I are going to down the hill and get something to eat, and then I'm going to bed early and do a lot of work tomorrow. Maybe I will have a letter from you tomorrow. I hope so. I am enclosing the clippings about the games in a different envelope, as this one is pretty full now. I love you with all my heart, Honey, and I hope that the New Year won't be far gone before I'll be meeting you in San Francisco. Take the best care of yourself that you possibly can. I'm thinking of you all the time. All my love to you, Jane

#43
4 Jan 1944 In Port.

Dearest Honey: —
Well, we got into port yesterday, and for the first time I didn't have a letter ready to go. But, Darling, believe me, it was not my fault. The so-called Pacific suddenly decided that her name was a misnomer and began acting up. It was pretty darn grim for a couple of days, but we all lived, and as soon as we got in and dropped the hook, the worst cases of mal-de-mer cleared up instantly. One of the new officers hadn't been able to eat anything for 2 1/2 days. He really made up for it at lunch yesterday.

Honey, the last night before we left the last port, we had a couple of movies. One of them was "The Saint in Palm Springs," and, Honey, I saw you! Had a couple of lines I heard, too. "Hello, Clarence," and, "Imagine accusing us of murder." Honey, I can't possibly describe my feelings when I saw you. It was like I was suddenly wired for sound. It was a wonderful, yet a harrowing experience. Darling, have you any idea just how much I love you?

Actually, I couldn't get to sleep for about three hours after the movie. I kept turning the light on and looking at your picture. Just like a love-struck kid. Which I guess I am, except for the kid part of it. You looked lovely, Darling, and you had that nice walk and good, erect carriage I've always admired. Oh, Honey, you certainly are a gorgeous thing. Wait until I see you again, and I'll convince you that I really mean it, too!

Well, another thing, we heard all of the Rose Bowl game, but wasn't Washington sad? It broke my heart, but thank goodness not my pocketbook. I only made one 1 dollar bet. Of course, I am broke anyway, but payday comes along in another week or 10 days again, so heigh-ho. Were you at the game? I got a great deal of pleasure out of thinking you were there, and I was listening to a broadcast from the same bowl. It made you seem ever so close to me. What did you do New Year's Eve? Somehow I pictured you and Don McKean at some people's house and then going to the game together the next day nursing tremendous hangovers. Is that the way it was? Baby, you know I want you to go out and around and have fun just like I was there, but, Honey, don't ever get to the point where you don't need me anymore. Don't get too used to doing without me, that's all I ask. Outside of that, go everywhere and do everything just as if I was there. Honey, I miss you like hell!

Well, yesterday Burke and I went ashore, and very interesting it was, too. We ran into some fraternity bros. of mine. Kinda fun. Their island has lots of Indians, complete with bullocks with tremendous horns. Usually a little kid has two of them hitched to a crooked stick for a plow. There is a little town of sorts several miles inland, and we went up there. Much to our surprise, we found an officers' lounge in the one little hotel and ran into incredibly good scotch, "King's Ransom," at 25 cents a drink, 40 cents for doubles. We didn't get bent out of shape, but we curved a little on the way home! They grow a lot of sugar cane here and have a big refinery. The ride through the countryside was fun `cause we got to peek into houses on the way by and saw women pounding meal with a mortar and pestel, that sort of thing. I guess Carpenter is right. He calls us his "tourists," but at least we get around more and see more things than anyone else I know. I'll probably do a thing for Chet on it, so I'll save some for that.

We still haven't got any mail yet and won't for a few days at least. It will be a month in six days. I don't mind telling you I am getting pretty desperate for mail. Just keep writing though, Baby, and what a day I'll have when we catch up with it. I do think it's going to be a little more regular from now on, at least it couldn't be more irregular!

I still haven't seen Dave either, but sooner or later! Well, Baby, I'll have to keep writing to Jack's until I get a letter from you.

I have to go to lunch now, Darling, but will write more tomorrow. Until then, Darling, remember I love you with all my heart.

All me love, Chas

X [BIG ONE] for '44

P. S.

There is only one thing more to say, that is I will go on loving you the rest of my life, come hell, high water, or recriminations.

It may sound silly to say, but if I could just look at you, talk to you for a few minutes, I really think I could go back to the S.P. without much trouble.

Maybe it's because I want to celebrate that 8th of March and our 6th wedding anniversary. Or perhaps it's because I love you so much that any little hurt raises a big blister. At any rate darling — I love you with all me heart.

Chas

I love you an awful lot darling! Silly, isn't it? By the way — where are my other letters?

Jan 4, 1944 In Port —

Dear Chet:

Just a line in great haste as I am trying to get this on a mail trip. I'm sorry that so long a time has slipped by since I last sent any of these on to you, but we have been busier than the proverbial cat on the tin roof. Of course, that is very good, too, as time certainly doesn't hang heavily on our hands.

I have a few more mentally written, but they need to be put on paper. I think I will have a chance to get them off within the week.

Let me have your reactions. I haven't heard from you yet; the fact that our mail is a month behind may have something to do with that.

All our previous understandings about no use of names, mine or the ship, etc., are still in effect.

I really have to sign off, Chet, or I'll miss this mail trip. Regards

Enclosed Copy Censored and Approved
W.W. Armstrong, Lt. Commander *USN Commanding.*

In Port —

Dear Chet:

Much has been written about the SEEBEES, that tough, hard-hitting outfit that can put a fighter strip or knock out a troublesome Japanese machine gun nest with equal ease and dexterity. Now what brought this little story to mind is the fact that I have read several articles lately by some of our more imaginative sob-sister feature writers. They all seemed to be convinced that there is going to be a terrific crime wave after this war. They reason something like this: men so used to killing are never going to be able to go back to the humdrum routine of civilian life. Well maybe, but let me tell you my story, and then make up your own mind.

The other day, I was over on an island that is pretty well up the line. In fact, it is now being developed as a new base of supplies. A group of the above-mentioned SEEBEES were hard at work with a drag-bucket and a few trucks, hauling coral and sand from the bottom of the bay to a new fill a few hundred yards down the beach. As I was walking toward them, it was time to knock off for the afternoon. About half of them headed for their tents, but the others ran down to where they had been dumping the stuff off the bottom and, going down to the water line, began to energetically scratch around with some little sticks.

Wondering what it was all about, I walked over. I asked the first man I came to what they were doing.

"Oh, we're getting some shells," he replied. Sure enough, that is what they were doing. A dozen great big strapping guys clad only in work shorts and heavy shoes were fastidiously culling over the crop of shells that the waves were revealing as they washed away at the new fill.

Squatting down on my haunches, I asked a few more questions, and before long I was the center of a group of bearded supermen heatedly discussing the relative merits of several families of the small multi-colored shells for making necklaces. So help me, it's the truth! These guys spend their leisure time picking up shells to make necklaces and bracelets for their mothers and girls back home.

The next time you see one of those articles foreseeing a great crime wave after the war by ruthless, trained killers, remember the picture of these SEEBEES picking up shells. Somehow I see their postwar activities as limited to sitting in their shirtsleeves at a baseball park somewhere back home, with a cold bottle of beer in one hand, and a hot dog clutched in the other, shouting, "Kill the Umpire!" "Somebody murder the Bum!" That will be the extent of their killing urge, for my dough. Regards — Chas.

At Sea —

Dear Chet:

At the risk of making this tour of duty sound like a pleasure cruise, I'd like to tell you about something that happened the other day. We were on off-shore patrol, and when you are so engaged, speed is of no great importance. Casting about for something to speed the time that was beginning to hang pretty heavily on our hands, we decided to rig a trolling line.

The line we made out of several lengths of heaving line, which is about the size of good, heavy clothesline. For a lead, we used about fifteen feet of good, heavy piano wire. We found a hook about two inches across and fastened that to a plug, which we contrived out of a section of mop handle brightly painted red and white and fringed with some hair out of a floor brush. As you can see, strictly a homemade job. I only wish I could go on and tell you that we immediately hooked a gold button Tuna, but unfortunately such was not that case. After a couple of hours of fruitless trolling, we gave up.

The next day, however, one of the men put it over the fantail and let it drag along. About ten o'clock in the morning I felt the ship shudder as we suddenly backed down on both engines. I wondered what was going on, but could see nothing that would cause us to stop. Just then, a man came running forward and said they had a big fish on. They had called the bridge and told them about hooking the fish, and the Officer of the Deck had slowed down to let them land it.

When I got back to the fantail, the fish was floating in the water at some distance from the ship, dead. He had been hauled in alongside and shot by one of the officers with a forty-five. It killed him all right, but in attempting to get him aboard, the gaff had slipped out and he was floating away from us. The Captain was back there and was giving orders to the bridge through a phone talker and was backing the ship down to pick up the fish. The easiest thing would have been to put a man over the side with a line to slip around his tail, but the Captain wouldn't let anyone go in for fear the blood in the water would attract sharks.

After a few moments of plain and fancy ship handling by the Captain, he maneuvered the ship alongside the fish and we passed a loop of line around his tail and hauled him aboard. It turned out to be a Marlin with a long bill, or do you call them swords? At any rate, he looked a good deal like a swordfish and was very beautiful. The sun on his side gave him an iridescent gleam that was something. We dragged him over to the meat scales and he weighed 93 pounds; not the biggest Marlin ever caught, but I bet none ever tasted better.

See what I mean, Chet? There are some aspects of this that make it just like a pleasure cruise, with pay! Pass the word to come on in — the water's fine!

Regards, Chas

at Sea —

Dear Chet:

I suppose being Gunnery officer on this can makes this story seem funnier to me than it really is. I still think you will get a laugh out of it. I am only sorry that it wasn't one of my boys that figures so prominently in it. But could be, could be!

As you probably don't know, the men have a term for anyone who has been out here too long. The symptoms consist of seeing enemy cruisers just coming over the horizon, hearing women's voices while far at sea — that sort of thing. It is referred to either as "going Asiatic" or, more simply, in referring to someone as "Asiatic."

Well, Gunner's Mate 1/c McKlosky, as we shall call him, was definitely "Asiatic." So much so, that in his own best interest he was granted a thirty-day leave to go back home and get a hold of himself. As the story opens, he has been back on the farm in the middle west somewhere for about a week, and the combination of peace and quiet and Mom's good home cooking have already worked wonders. This day he is sitting in the parlor, feet propped up on the fender of the old-fashioned wood stove, and the family cat is curled up in his lap, purring contentedly. Gunner's Mate McKlosky is at peace with the world and darn near asleep.

Now a short time before, his young brother had brought in a wet football and, boy-like, had chucked it behind the stove to dry out. The Gunner had a pretty good fire stoked up, and as time passed the football dried out, then the extra heat got to work on it. Finally the time *came when the* battered old pig-skin could no longer take the strain. It let go with a resounding report.

Instantly, the Gunner was on his feet. With one hand he yanked open the door to the stove, the other pitched in the family cat. He slammed the door to, locked it and stepped back a pace, at the same time shouting at the top of his voice, "Ready two!"

Well, excuse me, Chet, but I gotta go in a hurry. I just looked up and saw three Japanese cruisers coming over the horizon. In haste —Chas.

In Port —

Dear Chet:

All this morning a bunch of natives in their little dugouts have been hovering around the stern, peddling their merchandise to the sailors. You know, Chet, I am not so sure that Mr. Morganthau would be very happy if he saw the way the natives in these parts regard his medium of exchange, especially the green or folding variety. These natives may not have a formal education, but brother do they learn fast. When our forces first got down here, a couple of packs of cigarettes or a two-bit pipe and the joint was yours; anything from a cane with inlaid mother-of-pearl to a live pig was yours for the asking. Those same natives, today, have Camels running out of their ears, and ninety percent of them smoke Kaywoodie's. But to get back to Mr. Morganthau. If they are given an inspired plea by a past master in the art of pidgin English, they might consent to part with an old family heirloom, in the shape of a war club whittled out that morning, for "Two dolla, two dolla, two hundred penee." Only, of course, it has to be silver, preferably nice, new, shiny quarters. That stuff that is so near and dear to the average American, the "Long Green" is viewed with great distaste and no little lack of confidence by the boys in the dugouts.

But, now, you take canned Corned Beef. That is strictly something else again. I don't know how it started, probably some cook who was flat broke and talked a couple of natives into a swap for some little trinket. At any rate, they went for it in a big way, and the word got around about that wonderful stuff comes in cans. While it will probably make Messers Armour and Swift very happy, provide them with new and interesting advertising copy and afford them new and lucrative markets when this war is over, it makes it very tough on lads who are trying to collect a well rounded crop of souvenirs.

Well, there you have the picture. If you want hubby to bring back a coral necklace for you, send him a few cans of corned beef; could be that even corned beef hash would get by. But then, I imagine that that stuff is still rationed back home. Well, it looks like we are stymied. How about it, Mr. Morganthau? Seems to me it's definitely your move.

Regards — Chas.

At Sea —

Dear Chet:

Occasionally you get a break in this old *war*, and I would like to tell you about one that I got the other day. At the moment, the ship was engaged in a spot of off-shore patrolling along an island

that we have been in control of for some time. However, the fighting
for it had been fierce, as the presence of some Japanese transports
wrecked and beached amply testified. With the Captain's permission, as many of us as the ship's little whale-boat could hold went
over to look over one of the wrecked ships.

I may be wrong, but it looked to me like one of the large Maru
freighter-passenger line that used to bring raw silk into Seattle
in other days. If it was, this one will haul no more silk, of that you
can be sure. Apparently the skipper had realized she was mortally
wounded, and, in an effort to save the troops she was carrying, he
managed to get her to the beach. Her bow was high and dry, and
she was down by the stern with water almost up to the after part
of her superstructure.

We tied our little boat up alongside her and then proceeded to
explore what was left of her. I mean that last literally. I had no
previous first-hand acquaintance with what an H.E. aerial bomb
can do to that type of ship, but the destruction was incredible. The
thing that impressed me most was not the hits that caused her to
sink, but the appalling way her superstructure and between-deck
bulkhead were torn to pieces. There wasn't a square yard of her
above water that wasn't literally honeycombed with what must have
been fragmentation bombs. After a close view of something like
that, your admiration for the job the boys in the flying machines
are doing goes up about a thousand percent.

After we had gone over her from top to bottom carefully, we
began to look for something we could pry loose to take back with
us. The fact that a Marine encampment a few hundred yards up the
beach must have cleaned her out months ago didn't slow us down a
bit. In a few minutes, all hands were grubbing through the wreck-
age, picking up pieces of crockery, empty shell cases, parts of mess
kits, anything for a souvenir. I am happy to report that I think I
walked off with the prize of the day! A small drum gun sight off a
wrecked machine gun with actual Japanese characters on it (that,
of course, is the final criterion on a good souvenir!) The sight of all
of us scrambling for odds and ends was so much in keeping with
America and our national attitude toward such things, that I am
forced to lend a little credence to the reported remark of a Japanese
captured on an island not long ago.

"We Japanese are fighting this war for the `Eastern Asia co-
prosperity sphere,' we are fighting for our culture, our religion and

our national existence. But you Americans — you are fighting this war for one reason, and only one reason, souvenirs!"

He may have something there at that. At any rate, we are steadily increasing the stockpile of Japanese wrecks that makes for good souvenir-hunting, and incidentally wins wars at the same time! Regards — Chas.

Dear Chet:

After seeing the movies tonight, it occurred to me that you might like to hear about them, so here goes. They are the principal source of entertainment and relaxation for all hands, from the Captain on down. Due to our size, the showing of movies at sea is impossible, so we look forward with a great deal of pleasure toward spending a night in port.

Chet, you probably think you have enjoyed movies, but let me assure you that you haven't scratched the surface until you have seen one in company with a bunch of sailors that have spent several months at sea. Some of the remarks would make an old sea dog blush, but they are all very funny and very spontaneous. I am sure that most of us go as much to hear the comments as to see the film itself.

As you might suspect, the type of picture that goes over can be best described as "Girls, Girls, Girls." Lots of cute chicks running through the piece, with preferable a scantily clad chorus line coming in every reel or so is what they like. As long as the right boy gets the right girl, the piece ends happily. To hell with the subtleties of the story.

The high point of the evening comes when the hero after a long and arduous chase, finally takes the gal in his arms and administers the coup-de-grace in the form of a long kiss. The howl that goes up at that moment would make the hungriest pack of wolves on all the Russian Steppes sound like a passel of Pekes. It's terrific, believe me. Another highlight comes in every third or fourth movie we see, when the hero inadvertently expresses a wish to get away from it all to some South Sea Isle, or speculates on the wonders of a long ocean cruise. You can believe me, he is quickly and very audibly given the straight dope on both counts.

If the producers of Hollywood want to earn the undying devotion of all sailors, let them concentrate on zippy, fast moving girl shows.

Musicals are the best, but any fast action is all right, because with or without the music, you can be very sure of one thing, the sailors are going to supply the lyrics — but good!

And that's how we feel about movies — bless 'em. Regards — Chas.

2400 El Contento Drive
Hollywood 28, Calif.
January 8, 1944
Letter 56

Dearest Honey Darling;

Hold your hat, Honey, and prepare yourself to keep a secret. And I mean a secret. I know that you are going to be busting to tell somebody, but you will have to restrain yourself.

Remember the other day, when I said that I might have some news for you in the morning? Well, they lost my phone number, so I didn't get it until late afternoon, and then, when I did get it, I was so afraid that something would happen that I waited a day and a half to write you. I hate to say it out loud, but it looks pretty well set now. You are not the only one who is going to be able to do something for the war and who doesn't have to fight in the United States. Your little wife is going to Hawaii!! How's that for a bombshell. I am going to act with the Maurice Evans company, which is part of Camp Shows, Inc., and under the army, and I will be in all kinds of plays directed by him...like a stock company, and I will be paid seventy-five dollars a week and all expenses. It is wonderful, isn't it? I had even gone so far as to write to the Red Cross for an application for the overseas entertainment services when I found out about this. I will be there from three to nine months.

Oh, Honey, I do so hope that nothing happens to prevent this. I just won't be happy until that ship is on its way. Maybe I will get a chance to throw in a penny, but I don't know, of course, if that is the way. I won't be leaving for about five weeks, so that gives an awful lot of time for suspense. I'll let you know what the address is, of course, as soon as the army tells me. They have to have all that time for surveys and investigations and arrangements and such stuff.

Now, honey, I don't want you to be worried about me. Of course, we both know it is perfectly safe, so that isn't it. The thing is that this is very well organized and very well supervised, in case you were wondering. In fact, it seems to be more like a girls' school than anything else. It's the chance of a lifetime. I wanted to do something in the war so badly, and to find something that I am qualified to do and that they will let me go to do. And then, on top of everything else, when I got into the thing, I realized that it was the personal chance of a lifetime for me, too. It's really too good to be true, so I am tapping on wood and crossing my fingers and all such stuff.

The reason I asked you not to tell is because they told us that it was a military secret and that we could only tell our families until after we got there. Then, too, it might prevent me from going if they realized that you were in the South Pacific. I pointed out that there were several miles...thousands of them...of water in between the South and Central Pacific, and they saw my point but said not to mention it anyway more than necessary until I got there. I said that there wouldn't be a chance in a million years to see you. Of course, that is one happiness that I am afraid to even talk about in a letter, but just imagine what I feel about it, and imagine big, and you have it. Of course, the Gamble was in Hawaii two days or something in two years or something, and I doubt that it will ever be again...at least for another year or so. So many indescribable things have happened to us, though. Well, I'm not supposed to even admit the thought...but, Honey, it's there. But don't say anything. I love you with all my heart.

Remember that Dorothy Southworth that I was talking about in my last letter? The reason I met her was that she is going, too. She is married to the cowboy Tex Ritter — he is going on a tour, too, but I think he is going to Africa. So, she thought she would go on this while he was there. Oh, Honey, I'm so thrilled that I can just hardly stand it. I will be able to do something, too! And something that I can do well. I'd be an utter failure as a riveter, but this I can make a good contribution at.

Well, I'll have to put the rest of our stuff in storage and do something with my clothes and have a permanent...a mild one, because my hair goes straight around the salt air. And I'll have to take a few tap dancing lessons just in case I had to do a simple routine. They told me that they wouldn't waste me on dancing probably, but it would be good to be able to do a little bit in an emergency. And I have to take a couple of evening dresses. For the rest of the clothes, I think you wear uniforms in the daytime, and they take care of that. I have to be fitted for those, I guess, after the army gets busy. It will be a couple of weeks before they start the business. Jeeps, they were very impressed with my abilities as an actress!

Here is how the whole thing happened. Monday afternoon I was walking down to Zinkie's on Cahuenga to have my black plastic shoes fixed — no, it was Tuesday — after I had seen Chet. I told you about that. I ran into that actor Jack Carr...remember him, a big fat guy? I had known him off and on, and I guess you had, too, because he wanted to know how Chuck was. I told him, and he then wanted to know what I was doing, and I said that I had been away and that I was now seriously trying to get into the Red Cross overseas entertainment service. He said..."Do you want to go to Hawaii?"...well, I nearly jumped out of my skin...he said to call Jack Murton at Goldwyn...he had just got back and was organizing a group of actresses to go over for the Maurice Evans Company. I ran home and called him. He said it was pretty well set, but he liked my spirit from the way I talked, so could I come down anyway. I borrowed Nina's car and rushed down there, and I talked to him for an hour. He said for me to come over for the final selection of the girls the next evening...that he couldn't promise me anything, because he wasn't the final judge, but he would do his best. Well, when I got out of there, I called Don, who is in that same studio, and met him across the street. I told him about it, not having been told then that nobody should be told, and he said he would find out for me. Above my protests, he called this Gus Schroeder, who knows Murton very well. Well, this Mr. Schroeder came across the street to meet me. I was so excited that I thought he was just a writer, and I protested to Don that he shouldn't call him about it, and I really thought he was being kind of silly about it and perhaps ruining my chances. Well, it turned out...I found out later that he was the vice-president of Goldwyn Studios. He put in a good word for me...I don't know whether it did any good, but I guess it certainly didn't do <u>any</u> harm. Well, I went the next night — they were picking six girls out of fifteen, and I was one of the ones picked. I never thought I would be, because there were some wonderful looking girls and good actresses there. But I was. They said they would call us all the next morning with the decision. So, I went down and had dinner with Nina at Musso's...then I came home and wrote you...but I was afraid to say anything about it because I didn't know if it would turn out.

Yesterday I had to take a picture of me down to Jack Murton with my experience and the parts played written on the back of. He said I'd had a fine background. But anyway, he said...Jane, what's your husband's first name...I said Charles...and he said, my gosh, I know Charley. It seems that he had been talking to Jessie Wadsworth about me, and she said that she thought that I was your wife. He was talking about you in Lou Gherig, and he said to give you his best. So you see, you are well-remembered.

I had a letter from Fry today in answer to the Christmas letter I wrote him. It seems a shame that you have to wait so much longer for your mail. I should tell Viv what I am doing just on the chance that she will write Fry and he will see you. He said I'll probably never be able to explain my poor attitude and disposition regarding leaving. But now, despite what Chuck may think, I've become somewhat acclimatized and acclimated. Chuck is very happy, and rightfully so, with his assignment aboard the Gamble. I blew a gad bazoo about the 237 to him, not because it is so bad, but I think he appreciates the Gamble more. I've been quite fortunate, I think. I guess we can count our blessings and forget the rest...at any rate, it's much easier that way. He said to tell you that Chuck Meyers is on a tanker now...A.O. 40 Navy 131. There was some very interesting information, so I shan't send the letter back — to you, I mean. He said he'd write again in case and as soon as he dropped across the Great Irish Comic.

Levis called the other day, full of apologies. I wasn't very cruel to him but let it be understood tactfully that my feelings were hurt by his apparent indifference after all the soup we had fed him when he was sick. I really felt sorry for him because he was obviously so ashamed of himself. I've only seen him once since I've been here, and that was for a few minutes out at the Prices' before I went to the hospital.

I'm enclosing a letter from Mother. As you can read, we have a bit of scandal in the family which, if you ask me, is more than a little disgusting. That darned Tom. He has always been spoiled, but this is really inexcusable.

Will dropped up for a few minutes today. He is hoping against hope that he will be having a little change in scenery. I hope for his sake that it is true, because he is terribly anxious.

Well, Honey, it is Saturday night, and I have spent the evening giving the house a badly needed brush-up. Don was up for a little while and sat looking sleepy while I bustled around with broom and damp cloths. He departed for bed or more amusing company. I don't know. Nina is out with Glen and Lou. She said something about maybe coming back here later, but I don't think I'll stay up to find out. I want to get up early and wash my hair. I am all a hustle and a bustle of activity. It's so fine to have something wonderful to look forward to doing.

I called the family...collect...the night — no, last night...to tell them. Mother thought it was wonderful, and poor Jack said to write it down in a letter so he could really believe it. Mother will just bust not being able to tell, but she should be able to keep secrets by this time.

Oh, I had dinner with Jack Finch and Jim Hill the other night. They both called within a few minutes of each other, so I got them together because I know they amuse each other. Jim was more than his usual nuts — because he had finished a story and had imbibed rather freely the two days before. He really thinks he will be going in the army next month, but I personally don't see how, with that back. Minch is just fine — still at Santa Anita. He said to send his love to you. Everybody loves you, including Jane Fitz Randolph Patten Flynn...I had a lovely letter from your mother the other day. She is all over the flu and just fine now. I guess she told you about working at the Red Cross. I think that is fine for her.

Well, Honey, I think I'll hit the old hay before I get hungry because there isn't anything to eat in the house. Having no car, I just can't seem to get a larder laid in. There is a current shortage of butter...not even any substitutes in the market either, although I think I would rather have nothing. I got out the sandwich griller, but no butter, no fried sandwiches.

I'll write better than I have this week. It was just that I was so in suspense and couldn't say anything. I love you with all my heart, my darling. I wore the necklace you made me when I went down into Hollywood this afternoon, and the people in the shoe store thought it was lovely...Zinke's again.

Take good care of yourself, my darling. Somebody loves you with all their heart, and that's me. All my love, Jane

[Letter fragment January 1944]

evening dresses so he asked if I would model for him. He took about twenty pictures then and he is coming back Thursday night to take *some more. He* is one of those camera fanatics who when they find somebody who will model for them, just won't stop. It's a little boring for me but I will get some good pictures out of them and then I can give them to you. So I guess it is a good deal. Yesterday which was Monday I spent from nine in the morning until midnight just plain working. I cleaned the house thoroughly and sewed and washed and ironed and gave myself a pedicure and a manicure and washed my hair. At midnight I was just relaxing from my efforts and preparing to go to bed when the doorbell rang and there was Lee Gale. Incidentally in case I hadn't made it clear before, he is desperately and hopelessly in love with Nina. He was carrying a little black cocker pup six weeks old. He had bought it as a present for Nina from some friend of his who needed the money and was bringing it up after work. He was so delighted with his present. Nina was over at Pat's so I called her and told her there was a surprise here for her. She came over and she was in a mood. She took one look at the dog and said...I've told you time and again I don't like cockers...Yipe. Well, he had paid twenty-five dollars for it and she asked him how much it cost and said she wished she had the cash. It was a perfect shame because he was so hurt. Well, he loved it so that he just wanted to find a good home for it. He couldn't take it himself because he is going in the army in a couple of weeks. He gave it to Glen and Lou today and was just out twenty-five dollars and the happiness it would have given him to have given Nina a nice present. He would have given it to you and me but with going away and all, I couldn't take it. It was the sweetest little thing ever. I took it to bed with me last night because he left it here. I had said I would take care of it until he could find it a good home. So you see Lee is not a villain and neither is Don. We have his status straight anyway. So don't get such horrible thoughts. I think Nina was disappointed because she thought it seems that the surprise was Bob Skiles. He is expected out here in the next month and they have sort of a halfway marriage agreement. I hope that it works out but I'm afraid it won't.

Don't be too upset about the letter I wrote you Saturday honey. I think it all worked out alright because I was talking to Munro

Manning on the phone that evening and he sort of worked around to the subject of wouldn't it be a wonderful surprise if I were to meet my husband...I don't know whether he was pumping me or whether it was a coincidence but I played it straight and said that was out of the range of possibility. He said it would be fine with them but the War Dept mustn't think I was. I said that how when everybody knew you were so far away. and even the War Dept would realize it was a coincidence. Evans is getting very impatient and I am sure that the release will come through soon so let's just cross our fingers and try not to worry. I must say that to myself especially because with the passing of each day, I just go crazy, I get so anxious. But I mustn't get the jitters...just rely on the old Flynn luck. It just seems too good to be true that's all. But it will will will will will come true and that's all there is to it. I love you with all my heart my darling...be good and I'll be seeing you.

All my love, Jane
All for you XXXXXX

CASEY AT THE BAT

The outlook wasn't brilliant for the mudville nine that day.
The score was four to two with but one inning left to play.
And so, when Dooney died at first and Barrows did the same,
A sickly silence fell upon the patrons of the game.
A straggling few got up to go in deep despair.
The rest clung to hope which springs eternal in the human breast.
They thought, "If only Casey could but get one whack at that.
We'd put up even money now with Casey at the bat."
But Flynn preceded Casey as did also Jimmy Blake.
The former was a pudding and the latter was a cake.
So upon that stricken multitude, grim melancholy sat
For there seemed but little chance of Casey's getting to the bat.
But Flynn let drive a single to the wonderment of all
And Blake, the much-despised, tore the cover off the ball.
And when the dust had lifted and they saw what had occurred

There was Jimmy safe at second and Flynn a-huggin' third.

Then, from five thousand throats or more, there went a lusty yell.

It rumbled in the valleys and it rattled in the dell.

It knocked upon the mountain-top, recoiled upon the flat.

For Casey, mighty Casey, was advancing to the bat.

There was ease in Casey's manner as he stepped into his place.

There was pride in Casey's bearing and a smile on Casey's face.

And, when, responding to the cheers, he lightly doffed his hat,

No stranger in the crowd could doubt 'twas Casey at the bat.

Ten thousand eyes were on him as he rubbed his hands with dirt.

Five thousand tongues applauded while he wiped them on his shirt.

Then, as the writhing pitcher ground the ball into his hip,

Defiance gleamed in Casey's eye and a sneer curled Casey's lip.

And now, the leather covered sphere comes hurtling through the air.

And Casey stands a-watching it in haughty grandeur there.

Close by the sturdy batsman, the ball unheeded sped.

"That ain't me style" said Casey. "Strike one!" the umpire said.

From the benches, black with people, there went up a muffled roar.

Like the beating of a storm wave upon a stern and distant shore.

"Kill 'em. Kill the umpire!" Someone shouted in the stands.

And likely they'd have killed him had not Casey raised his hand.

A smile of Christian charity on great Casey's visage shown.

He stilled the rising tumult and he bade the game go on.

He signaled to the pitcher and once more the spheriod flew.

But Casey still ignored it and the umpire cried "Strike two!"

"Fraud!" Cried the maddened thousands and the echo answered
    "Fraud!"

But one scornful look from Casey and the multitude was awed.

They saw his face grow stern and cold. They saw his muscles strain.

But they knew that Casey wouldn't let that ball go by again.

The sneer is gone from Casey's lips. His teeth are clenched in hate.

He pounds with hideous violence his bat upon the plate.

And now the pitcher holds the ball and now he lets it go.

And now the air is shattered by the force of Casey's blow.

Oh somewhere in this favored land, the sun is shining bright.

The band is playing somewhere and somewhere hearts are light.

And somewhere men are laughing and somewhere children shout.

But there is no joy in Mudville. Mighty Casey has struck out.

1 Feb. 1944
In Port

Dearest Honey:

Well today brings to a close the pleasantest week I've had since I left you in S.F. last Sept. It has been wonderful, so completely divorced from the ship and all ship's routines.

For once I have found an intelligent head of a Red Cross unit. Her name is Miss Parks, she's about 45 and used to be head of a Red Cross unit. Her idea of running a rest camp is to serve good meals, see that the ice-box is full of cold beer, and for the rest of the time to stay out of the way and let you plan your own amusements. None of this organized hilarity that is usually so prevalent in a spot like this.

For four straight afternoons I went off by myself for about 3 hours. I brought a .22 rifle up from the ship. An I took that and a pocketful of shells and had a wonderful time tramping through the country-side. I walked miles every day, it was so wonderful to feel good solid earth beneath your feet. I found a charming little river about five miles from the camp and I used to make that a stop every afternoon, sit in the sand bank for an hour or more and think of you.

It has really been wonderful. And I am so glad I got to come up here. The last three days I have been going to this AA school down the road, but that only lasts from 8:00-12:00, so I had all afternoon and evening to do as I pleased. I can't say I enjoy the idea of going back to the ship this afternoon but we go out tomorrow, so I guess I don't have much choice in the matter.

The only saving factor is that there should be a couple of letters for me to you, and that always saves the day. I hope to know more dope on Evans when you leave etc. Wouldn't it be wonderful if we could have a month together again! It is all I think about right now, and I hope nothing comes up to ruin my chances. As soon as I know definitely that you are coming I will start my campaign to get there too, and I'll bet a buck I make it too! We are only going out for a couple of days for practice in my dept., so I will be a busy little bee for the next couple of days. But by the same token there shouldn't be much of a gap in my letters. I suppose you get the same thrill out of getting mine that I do yours. Although I'm afraid mine are pretty dull and much the same. You write a wonderful letter darling, but then you're wonderful everyway, or have I told you so recently?

Well our friends the Russians are cooking on the front burner south of Leningrad and with big things in the air but here the war looks quite promising.. Not that it won't be a while, but even to be able to begin to see definite progress is encouraging.

Use this ten bucks to buy something nice and useless, but that you want, because if I were with you that's what I'd do with it. Honey I love you so much and miss you so constantly it's hard to believe. You are in my thoughts constantly, and very nice thoughts they are too. I'm afraid if I ever get to see you soon I'll love you to death, but at that it wouldn't be a bad way to die would it? Il write again in a couple of days.

All me love darling — Chas
XXXXXXXXXXXXX

2400 El Contento Drive
Hollywood 28, California
Feb. 2, 1944

Dearest Honey;

You know I have just been thinking that Dearest honey" is the way we both start out letters. I's funny that we should both feel that is the best salutation there is. But it is the best and it is the way I feel like saying helo to you.

I just got back from the Lathams where I spent the evening for the first time in ages. I went up for dinner and to do some sewing.

I am making myself a robe which I think is going to be very pretty if I can ever finish it. It seems as if I have been on it for weeks but that is merely because it is so difficult to get up here to the machine I suppose if I were really smart I would hire one for a couple of weeks and get two or three things done The cab fare to get from the bottom of the hill at Laurel and sunset would almost pay for it for a week and just one trip too. You should see Linda and I pray you will soon darling. She is almost grown up...not that she is talking yet or anything like that but she walks so well and her posture is already that of a little girl instead of a baby. She coordinates her actions so well too. She is feeding herself now and she hardly spills anything. Today...I got there in the late afternoon...Jack called up and I held her up to the phone and told her to say hello. She just jabbered away into the receiver. Of course she didn't say anything intelligible but she knew she was supposed to talk at least. The Lathams are fine. Jim Eagleson and his wife are doing to spend tomorrow with them and I told them to have them call and say hello. Also they have recently seen some character named Bob Green from Washington who asked after you. I didn't know him and I'm afraid I forgot to ask what branch of the service he was in.

Oh honey, the thing I should have said first. The two lovely straw bags that you sent me came today. I was so surprised. I wasn't able to see the date on them because the package was so covered with customs marks and marks that they had been opened buy the censors but I suppose they must have come awfully fast since they were airmail. Honey, there were so very attractive and I was delighted with them. It was such a surprise because I hadn't expected them. If only I had known the date, I might be able to figure out where you bought them...at least to my own satisfaction but without the date, I couldn't...thank you so much darling. I will really have a lot of souvenirs of the South Pacific. And I am so proud of them all and I think that they are so lovely.

Also your missing letter number 47 cam today...the one you said you were atoning for in the next letter. It was quite a letter honey. Of course I'm not mad. There is a foundation in what you say and I realize you would never said it unless you had been a lot lonesome. I think you will find any imperfections that you pointed out are gone when you come home. It was pointed out to me that my physical condition might have had a little bit to do with it and that is all really fixed now so you can love me now even if there is a good roll in the hay involved in the whole thing. I love you with all my heart honey. I can think of something I'd like to do with you at this point...and how!

Mary's little coast guard man...although he isn't little...asked her to marry him. I think that she might think it over very seriously with no harm to herself. After all, after he gets out of officer's school he may be around a while. He wanted her to marry him immediately but she said that she would have to have a chance to know him better and also give him a chance to think it over himself. He was a very nice boy and very good looking. I say was because he left at noon today. She saw him off on the train and then I had lunch with her. She was pretty depressed but still interested in giving me the account of her adventures. The usual ones are pursuing her I don't know how she does it, she meets more people and has more things happen to her in the course of one day than anyone I have ever met. She and her friend Merlaine have pretty well decided to stay down here. Mary says she is going to look for a job tomorrow. I shant give you any news of the boys because I am enclosing their letters.

That is about all that has happened to me in the last two days since I wrote you honey darling. I am getting pretty impatient about my little deal but it is all set and just a matter of waiting now so I suppose I shouldn't be. Bt, under the circumstance, I can't do anything but wait for it and it is beginning to irk me. I finished up the x-ray treatments on my scar yesterday and it looks much better...it had to be done...looks or no looks because so much scar tissue had been formed hat it would have been harmful unless it was caught immediately. The tooth situation is pretty well under control now. I don't have to go to the dentist for a week. I am still continuing with the tap lessons and trying to do my best. I can do a whole routine now and am getting pretty good considering. But I am impatient for action and I Hope it comes soon.

I am crossing my fingers darling for the possibilities involved in what might happen. Even actually pray that it might come true. I love you...insufficient as it may sound, as you say, it is just the right way to say it. See you soon.

All my love,

Jane

The Lord watch between me and thee, when we are absent from one another

XXXX

All my kisses are yours

4 Feb., 1944
In Port

Dearest Honey, I kinda got my numbers mixed up when I went up to the rest camp but I think that 53 is right at any rate I'll go on from there and keep 'em straight.

I got a letter from you yesterday mailed on Jan. 26, that's the fastest I've had them in quite a while. It makes you seem much nearer to me darling when the letters are only a few days old that way. You have been wonderful about writing, don't start sipping will you honey?

Well the big news, Stanley is back out here we had a letter for him yesterday and he is up at the next stop which is where we are heading in a day or two, so I will be getting my Xmas package before you read this! Of course it means also that when he gets back aboard I will be eligible to go to that school! Oh honey if we can pull this off! If I could just see you once for half an hour I would be satisfied. Well maybe not satisfied, but anything over that would be gravy. Just keep your fingers crossed and hold the right thoughts, and it will work out.

Look honey, while I think of it you have any important dope on when you are leaving or such put it in the next few letters. That way if some of our mail keeps coming here after we shove off I will still pick of the info in the next letter or so. They will probably now in time to stop forwarding our mail here, but just in case, repeat briefly the dope — okay?

Maybe we better get on another topic of I for one am apt to bust a gusset in delirious anticipation!

A couple of days ago I had the nicest letter from Woodie-Lou in which she rambled on about her love life (marriages) and her job et al. It was such a very nice letter and I was rather disturbed by it. She is certainly sold on you honey, she just raves about your beauty, wealth position and power! She really likes you a lot, She seemed to think my letter was so charming It beats me as you know the kind of bildge I pump out, but then I too am charming, wealthy, positionful, and simply reeking with power!

[I've just racked my brain for the source of those lines and it's from 'Personal Appearance', where Carol Arden says, "Jealous cats, afraid of my beauty, position, etc."]

So you got down to Laguna, I'm glad for you, 'cause that's a very pleasant spot. Was anyone else there but Izzy and the kids? Is Susie as much as a problem as ever, and is Torie still as cute? I think she is one of the most wonderful children I have ever seen. She may not be too bright, but gad she is cute! If you haven't written your bread'n butter note yet, say hello o them for me will you. Remember the 'throw-ups' in the Cranes back yard, especially when I was full of beer, and damn near dead?

I have disregarded your cautions and told the Skipper and Capt. About you (I swore them to darkest secrecy, however!) and they both think it's wonderful. Capt. Is on my side and is going to try and get me up and the Skipper wants to give me his wife's address for you to look up. It would be a place for her to put her head," he said. I wonder if two could fit Oh honey darling I love you so God damned much!! I'll write again in a couple of days.

All my love, Chas

XXXXXXXXXXXXXXXXXXXXXXXXXXXXXXXXXXXXXXXXX
XXXXXXXXXXX

4 Feb. 1944
In Port

Dearest Honey:

Yipe! I'm in like a rabbit, I leave here in a couple of days for you know were! I think I will probably fly, so Ill e there soon. If I ain't the luckiest guy in this whole war, you tell me who is!

Oh got honey it's all so wonderful I can' believe it but as the old colored gal said, "here t'is". Ill give you an address to use until I send another, or see you!

Ens Chas J. Flynn
c/o Fleet Postmaster
San Francisco
Please Hold!

Be sure and put the 'Please Hold' on each letter, otherwise they will forward it to the Gamble. The way it looks I should be there 6-8 weeks, some fun eh kid! I still can't quite get used to the idea.

Write me honey to that address giving me what dope you have, needless to say I will be an eager beaver!

Honey I hate to make so enormous a missile so short, but I've got eleven million things to do before I leave. Write me quick and let's see some action on your end. This end is doing fine!

Oh my God honey, I'll cross my fingers, and hold my breath, so don't fail me. I love you a hell o a lot darling!

All me love

Chas

XXXXXXXXXXXXXXXXXXXXXXXXXXXXXXXXXXXXXXXXXX
XXXXXXXXXXXXXXXXXXXX

SOON!

2400 El Conento Drive
Hollywood 28 California
Feb. 7, 1944

My Dearest Honey Darling;

I received a wonderful long letter from you u last night. It was the one where you were in the Red Cross place and my question of the last letter was answered. Here I thought it was so terrible and it sounds as if you were having a lovely vacation. It sounds grand darling and I am so glad you had a chance to go up there. It certainly will relieve the strain of everything. Here I was in such a stew about the whole thing and didn't realize how wonderful it was. I told you that I tried to send a cable to you I think but they said that with nothing but the name of the ship, it would be no use because it would just be mailed like a regular letter What do people in the Navy do that have babies…I am always hearing about people getting cables "Son born" and such stuff.

I wanted to answer your letter last night but I was having such a trouble with my darned tooth and had been having it since Sunday that the thought of a type writer almost made my head burst. As evening I tried a codeine tablet that the Lathams had and then that didn't work so I took three straight shots of bourbon and that was no use so then I just gave up and took two sleeping pills and went to bed…all with the result that I had a horrible night. I had the most awful dreams…just like being drugged. I thought I was trying to get up because I was being stifled and thought I was calling to people to help me although I really wasn't. I slept eleven hours and have been absolutely dopey all day. I thought I was having a recurrence of trouble with my gums. I put off going yesterday but I dashed down to the dentist this morning and pleaded with him to do something. I couldn't even eat...I was so miserable. He said it wasn't my gums...that they were now as healthy as even healthier then anyone's...that it was cavities but more likely the darned impacted wisdom tooth. I was inclined to believe it was the wisdom tooth because it constantly throbs back there and I have an earache. He said to be very moderate about what I ate...no fruit juice or anything acid and possibly it wouldn't bother me...but that would involve never even having tomato juice. Well, it might work but I have been in such perfect misery that it is ghastly. I really can't go away with this thing hanging over my head much as I hate to spend the money...what money? I went p after I went to the dentist to meet Mary for lunch and I was in agony. She and Merlaine, her friend, persuaded me to call the dentist so I finally did. They said if I would come right down they would take care of it as they already had an x-ray but when I got there, they said they would do it in the morning. I am still in the throes of indecision because it cost so much and I haven't gone to the dentist the Uncle Milt recommended to me but he is way downtown in the Paramount building and I would have to go back for treatments and to get down there especially with a tooth like this is a major effort. I know that this Olson is the best man and three dentists have told me to go to him because he is the best man and have said that it was a major tooth operation and he wasn't charging too much. I just don't know what to do but I think that I can't go way with this hanging over my head and I really am going. So maybe I ought to just go and have it done and then worry about it. The time is getting short and it is just ruining my disposition and making me unhappy and moody and cross because it hurts so all the time.

Yes, honey, I really am going and I am getting a little impatient for it to start but there are millions of details to be arranged and I suppose one must learn the virtue of patience. But all is still fine and it won't be long now. I'll let you know as soon as I hear anything and how we will cross our fingers. Don't be in too much of a hurry though because I understand we spend two weeks in San Francisco after we leave here. So you know what I mean...don't be in too much of a hurry.

I talked to Hazel Sunday.. she called and what do you think...
she is coming down for a week. She wanted to see me before I go
and this is here best chance. She will be here Friday and leave
the next Friday. Mary and I have been looking madly for a place
for her to stay but haven't found anything yet. But Mary says
she will tomorrow. Your family is certainly out on a limb when
you don't have a place to live. I feel so guilty about it but there is
nothing I can do.

Gosh honey, I'm glad you liked the pictures. I thought they were
fair but not super. I guess you were right when you saw what I was
thinking about but that is a private matter between us.

Since I wrote that last paragraph I have been asleep. I have been
so darned dopey all day. I just couldn't stand it a minute longer so
I thought I would go over on the studio couch and lie down for a
minute, now it is two hours later...In fact, it is past midnight and
I am still dopey but have had two hours sleep I am ashamed to say
What woke me up was that Nina and Don and Lee Gale came in.
They had been out someplace...in fact, I think Nina and Don had
been over to Pats for dinner and had stopped down to see Lee at
Sardi's and brought him up when it closed. I have been too sleepy
to get any further information out of them. I haven't seen Don for
a week I guess. He is working pretty hard on his picture and it is
coming along very well. They haven't started shooting yet thought
and it seems to me it is pretty slow.

Honey baby I haven't been a very good letter writer this last
few days but it is because of my tooth. I will do better after this,
I promise. Don't think it is because I don't love you or anything.
Starting tomorrow I will do a lot better. You said my letters were
always filled with a lot of dirt and excitement and what I had been
doing and with a lot of love. I guess this one is only filled with love
because every word holds a lot of it for you and added together, the
sum total is amazing...in fact, it is terrific...and enormous. I am
going to stop writing now but tomorrow after the tooth is taken
care of, you will have a dilly. I love you honey with all of my heart.
Take care of yourself and come back to me soon.

All my love,
Jane

2400 El Contento Drive
Hollywood 28, California
February 10 1944

My Dearest Honey Darling;

It seems to me that I remember very distinctly writing you day before yesterday that I would write the next day which was yesterday but you will have to forgive me honey. I had the tooth out and was definitely dazed the whole day and far into the night. The only thing I wanted to do was sleep and moan...not that it was so bad. It wasn't half as bad actually as I had expected it to be and it has hardly any swelling...it was a pretty big thing too...complete with abscess...and stitches...quite a deal. Then this morning I felt better and who should call but hazel...yes, I men Hazel Patten and she was down on Wiltshire boulevard So I threw on some clothes and was at the door to welcome her. I think I told you that she was coming down for the week but I expected her a day later. Daddy had led us astray by saying in his letter that she was starting Tuesday instead of Monday. We spent the day sitting out in the back yard talking and then this evening we came home. Don came along too so he furnished the transportation. Also paid for the dinner...I hadn't wanted him to do that but when the bill came it was little more than I had thought it would be and I didn't have that much money so I had to let him. (By the way, honey, did you realize that this month is the last uniform payment, thank god!!!)

We have been in a definite stew about Nina for a couple of hours but she just called to report that all our worries were groundless. It was really a very silly thing. She left us in front of Musso's saying she was going straight up to Glen and Lou's to spend the night because Glen was in a play and Lou was lonesome. Mother is staying here tonight because she got here a day earlier than we expected and we didn't have a place for her. Anyway when we got home Lou called and wanted to know were Nina was. Well, with that we began to wonder because a couple of hours had elapsed. We checked everyplace without seeming too obnoxious and not a trace of her. Lee Gale said to call the police but I said they would call us if anything had happened. Well, by midnight we were all getting pretty worried because it is not particularly safe nowadays for a girl to be around Hollywood all by herself. The upshot of it all was that she had gone to a movie and had thought of calling Lou about it but had neglected to do it. So all is fine and she is not a white slave. It seems a little funny in retrospect now but subject as she is to moods, the way she completely disappeared had us all a little bothered. Besides that there was somebody that she is just crazy about in Musso's tonight with another girl and we thought that might have affected here. It is Lou Langlan who thinks she is so temperamental though. Personally I don't agree with her.

It is simply grand to have Mother here. I know she had a fine time tonight and I also know she needed a vacation. But one day can't pass without that clash of will between her and Mary. Mary worries here and it seems that she glories in it...Mary I mean. Merlaine, Mary's friend went home because she was sick to her stomach. Bill Bowles who had a tentative date with Mary and joined us for a drink instead of having the date since Mother came took her. He came back and said he didn't think she was really sick. Well, it appears that perhaps she wasn't but she likes to be alone and was just using this as an excuse. I don't really know but Mother thought she was really sick. Well, Mary announced that she was going out with Lee Gale after twelve when he finished work if she could arrange it with Bill. Mother said she should go home and take care of Merlaine and I did too only more tactfully. Mary said Merlaine wasn't really sick and it led to quite a scene with Mother getting awfully disturbed. I overstepped my bounds a little and gave them both a little lecture... Mary on being inconsiderate and Mother on getting disturbed about inconsequential things. I pointed out that if I allowed myself to get disturbed about the things that were really important...Meaning you being away and my worrying about you, I wouldn't be able to stand it and she ought to be ashamed of herself and get herself actually sick about such a little thing as Mary's staying out too late. I suppose I shouldn't have said it but I think they all do far too much worrying about Mary. It isn't wrong that she is mainly occupied in going out. She is looking for a man to fall in love with...the last generation, that was the natural and right thing for a woman. I still don't see that it is necessary that she should have some consuming ambition to make something of herself. She will settle down when she finds what she is looking for. Well, those are just my ideas. It is too bad though that it had to happen on Mother's first night here. But it is both their darned faults. I have found that nobody can enjoy and appreciate life until they find the main requisite of it is to learn to be calm about things It takes a lot of discipline sometimes and nobody knows that better than I do because I am inclined to be excitable and unbalanced but you have to do it and people should learn it. Why honey, if I didn't have pretty good control over myself, I would simple go crazy with the passing of each day thinking about where you are and what you are doing.

I have had four talks in the last two days with the people about my little project. It is definitely all set and I think two weeks is the deadline...but we must allow for mistakes and delays. So about your little project, delay it a bit if you can so there will be no possibility of a slip-up. I'm so terribly happy and excited about it and I will really be glad to shake the dust of this town off my feet for a while. There is something to this make-believe business that doesn't sit well with me especially at this time. So cross your fingers darling and save a big kiss for me. I will let you know my address as soon as I know. But remember, darkest secrecy. I think it would be best to communicate through that Scoop Richardson or the captain's wife is in case we were uncertain of the other's whereabouts. What are the addresses? When I get here I'll call them immediately and you can do the same...

Oh honey, I love you.

I got a wonderful letter from you yesterday darling. It made of lapse of three though...maybe you got mixed up on the numbers though and maybe something will come tomorrow. In the meantime be good and take care of yourself and I'll see you soon. An soon the war will be over.

Al my love to you honey darling,
Jane
XXXXXXXXXXXXXXXXXXXXXXXXXXXXXXXXXXXXXXX
XXXXXXXXXXXXX

Hollywood , California
February 11, 1944

Dearest honey;
I have just finished re-reading your letter 51 which as missing. It was day before yesterday that I got the number 5. This was written on the first of February and you were just about to leave little paradise. How I wish I could have been with you honey when you

went for the walks in the afternoon and sat by the river. To think that when I first heard of it I was so worried about you. Now I know how marvelous it was for you.

We have just returned from dinner at the Adamses. Mother has gone over to stay with Mary and Merlaine in their little room. I'm afraid it is going to be pretty close quarters but I think that Nina is planning to come home and bring Pat and I haven't seen her all day...she stayed up at Glen and Lou's last night and mother stayed here. I have the feeling now that I have imposed on Nina terribly... not that I have because she likes to have me but the thing is that I couldn't ask Mother to stay without asking her and I might embarrass Nina. I feel just horrible about it but didn't know what else to do. I have just been going crazy all evening thinking about it but I couldn't find Nina so what else could I do. I daresay she will be alright though.

I have the most beautiful new coat and am so terrible delighted with it. I needed it badly to take with me to wear in the evening because they said to come well equipped. It is really an evening coat but can be worn with short dresses too. I is bright green and is a mandarin type of thing with braid down the front and with slits at the side...with black braid also along the slits. It is the most exotic thing I have ever owned. We were riding up the elevator in The Broadway today and I spied it. We came down to look at it just as a matter of curiosity...it was just what I needed and Mother said the Ma Wee had said to give me a present of the thing I needed and wanted most so this might as well be t. So I have it...and honey I can hardly wait until you see it...it is so gorgeous. It definitely does things for me if I say so myself.

By this time, Dave has probably rejoined you and you have the long missing Christmas presents...I am afraid that they won't really be p o all the expectations. When you can probably start working on your deal. The only thing which I keep repeating I know in case you didn't get the last letter, don't hurry because the longer you wait...I know it is hard to stand, but the longer the wait, the better established I will be and have some time off. When I first get there, I will be rehearsing all the time and they probably won't give me a minute but as soon as one play is on, than I am pretty well set...and will know them better so I can get more privileges like getting out for the night...I will be in the army so I have to figure about regulations. I don't want to wait but it is worth it if we can have more time together. Oh honey, it is so wonderful that I barely dare think about it. As soon as I know anything definitely I will let you know.

Our letters are beginning to come more regularly again now and it is such a relief. There were about three weeks there when I only got two letters from you and I was a pretty miserable chick. But there have been three already this week and I consider myself pretty luchy. I don't know the thrill you get from getting mail but I can tell you that mine is enormous.

Honey thank you for the ten dollars. I can really use it. I can especially use it in the next couple of weeks and believe me, it came in handy. I think I might buy some material for an evening dress with it although I am afraid I couldn't make it well enough. But I am trying to economize and I will see if I can try. I saw some gorgeous stuff today. That is probably whit it will go for. Thank you so very much darling.

That is about all that has happened to me since I saw you last night...How can I say that I saw...I was talking to you and looking at your picture...each letter I write I imagine that I am seeing you... unfortunately it isn't true but it helps a lot to think so...so since I saw you this is the expression I will use. A good good night to you my darling. You will be in my dreams.

All my love,

Jane

XX

XX

I saw Mary Davenport and her husband last night as Musso frank's... also Helen and Al Leavitt who used to live with Tom and Marge. They said that Tom had just this week gone overseas and that Marge had been back here for quite some time but had been quite ill...flu that turned into pneumonia. She is fine now and I must call her up. I think I will tomorrow. Mary looked just wonderful. Jack Latham, unknown to Marg, wrote his draft board and asked them not to give him another deferment. They haven't answered yet but just after he did it Pat Bishop the newscaster found that he was to be drafted and they are planning to give jack his place...the best announcing job in the station and really an executive position also. It's really too bad that that had to happen. I will go to bed now so I can get up early in the morning and hear Chet talk about you. All my love.

15 Feb. 1944

Dearest honey:

Just time for a note before dinner. I am a little behind so won't be able to write you a real letter for a couple of days.

I got air transport up again. Pretty lucky huh? I have been here a couple of days trying to get squared away, but it looks like I am in the clear now, or almost.

What's with you? If things are on schedule you will probably never receive this letter anyhow, t such is my husbandly devotion that I'll continue to write. Naturally I am eager to hear from you, honey I've done my par, now be sure to handle your end, and quickly!

I had dinner with Bob and Katie Richardson last night, very nice and peaceful evening, a few good drinks and a lovely chow. I fair and made me homesick.

If things do work out with Camp shows Inc. call them as soon as you get here, and I'll keep in touch with them, the number is 69384, no prefix.

I am sitting on a hot tack until I hear from you so don't make it too long. When you answer use the new address on the envelope. That will be until I tell you differently.

I met a couple of characters on the plane coming up so they may call you to tell you I'm well, be nice to them they've had a long stretch out in them parts.

Well darling, that's about all for now, I'll write again in a couple of days. Hurry an answer back.

All me love

Chas

Ens C J Flynn

1 March 1944

Dearest honey;

Well, Pal, get set for a blast. I got two letters from you today, one full of love and stuff and (repeat, and) the other full of vile statements, recriminations, etc.

Look, darling, whatever acts I may have committed, or whatever things I may have done, I did for only one reason, to try and establish contact with you. (May I interpose a mild statement? I have now had a few drinks, yes, they permit that, and I have been trying to make less the feeling I had when I read your last letter. Nothing drastic darling, but I think you went a little overboard).

Suppose you were a guy that loved a wife with all his heart and one day he heard that she was going to a [MISSING] intent, no matter how definite it seemed to you. You were so cruel and self-centered in your last letter that I can't help feeling that whatever I say is just a little like a small voice being stilled in the wilderness...

Darling the fact that my life is going on only because of you, and that my attempt to do, shall we say "my part", is for you doesn't seem to make much difference.

Because I'd had two letters, one telling me of the job, and the other saying you were leaving Feb. 15, I've suddenly become a bastard who is trying to thwart your war effort. I'd had only those two letters before I got here, and what would you have done?

I suppose I must say that I was selfish and thoughtless, but why don't you know the facts before you so vigorously condemn?

I've just read over what I have written. I'm very hurt, and awfully mad and by now a little drunk. (The last happened only when a kindly soul invited me in for a share of a bottle after the movie. I didn't trust myself to write before.)

Darling, secrets and such are only when they give comfort and aid to the enemy, or so I have been taught. I didn't regard myself as an enemy, and I know damn well that there was no comfort in those lines..

Forgive me if I sound bitter, but that last letter did more to make me feel like a fool and unnecessary than anything yet in my life.

I'm sorry as hell honey —

Chas

Ens C J Flynn

2 March 1944

Dearest honey;

I was an awful stinker to write such a letter as I did last night. I won't apologize for my feelings because they were justified, but I am ashamed of myself for giving vent to them without more thought.

Today brought me a packet of mail from the ship, all of your missing letters and mom's too. I realized when I read them that you must really love me, and that you were just a little aroused when you wrote that stinging epistle I received yester eve.

Actually, I don't think I did or said anything to louse up your chances. As I said the guy I talked to sounded as if he might spread his wings and fly right over the phone to me. His sentimentality was touched by my story of love's young dream and I think it did there, If anything develops at least let me know before I go back to the ship as I would love to push is cap down his throat!

After thinking it over today I have come to the conclusion not to contact him again. If damage has been done it's done, but if I talk to him or go and see him his frustrated little soul might see a way to gain a little publicity for himself and really make a hash out of things.

Well enough of that. I'm sorry I was so vehement last night and that I sound so tough. I just happen to love you darling — that's why I was hurt. I see by and old letter of yours that I got today that you finally got the big box, also the knit shopping bags. I'm so glad you like td them, and that they got there. The small shell (brass) incidentally is not for candles, but for kitchen matches. You know, a set on a coffee table with the ashtrays! Also I noticed another letter that you were to spend two weeks in Pat's home town. Well give my love to her and the commander, but as long as the green light hasn't flashed as yet it looks pretty grim form this ed. Time marches on and stuff. But at any rate we we'll see.

I am still being a hermit and virgin a hell, although I did have dinner tonight with Ed Griese's wife (and mother and father). You know, the guy with the lecherous eyes we ran into coming back up on the Daylight? Well she was very swell, and so were the old folks and it was a nice family evening, not that I objected but she might have been a siren! Or is that what cops have? At any rate darling I'm still good and loving with you with all me heart. Please forgive yesterdays unhappy letter.

All me love

Chas

Ens. C. J. Flynn

1738 North Palmas Ave
Hollywood 28, California
May 2, 1944
Letter 90

Hello darling,

Well, my mind is relieved for the present about you anyway. IT has been nearly three weeks since I've had a letter from you but one came from your Mother today saying that she had received one from you last Thursday and that you had just finished writing to me. I would give my eyeteeth to know when the letter was written as mine hasn't come yet. Things like that happen though I know and it has just been delayed someplace. One better come before Friday though because I am leaving here then an after that, I won't be hearing from you for a while. So I am praying that it will find me by that time. I will send you the address as soon as I know what it is but in the meantime a letter addressed to Jane Patten or Jane Patten Flynn, care of the USO in the city where I am going would reach e just fine. So until you hear from me, write here. Gosh I'm pretty happy and excited that all this waiting is just about over...I can hardly believe it is true. I get a little sick to my stomach from excitement but I'll have to stop that in a hurry.

That's about all the news I have of any note. The rest is just waiting and reading and seeing the same people once in a while. I read "A Tree Grows in Brooklyn"...it is really grand...I had been afraid to read it because of the possibility of its being over rated but definitely isn't. It's beautiful. Also today I read two books about the war which was very interesting. "Joe Foss, Flying Marine" and "Bridge of Victory" which was about the Aleutians. Honey I would send you more books only the trouble is that I don't know how now whether the three that I have already sent have ever arrived. If you would let me know, then I would know whether it was a good idea to keep on sending them. I can send them from where I will be too if you want them.

I want owing last night with Nina and Pat and did very badly. In two whole games, I only made one strike. The first was not as good as the second though which gave me some satisfaction. I am constantly ashamed of my ineptness at any form of organized athletics. I guess it's a combination of having been raised in the woods and not having the old will to win and be an expert. I really should have gone in for some thing though while I had the time but all sports are so darned expensive. Then too it was just for the last couple of months I was capable of it. But I should have done something about it then. I got our badminton rackets out and never played so put them in storage. Maybe I'm lazy when it comes to physical exertion...not my idea of pleasure. I've had several opportunities to play golf but haven't gone. Of course those were lately when I was afraid of leaving the phone.

Someone admired my little turquoise ring the other night and I remembered the time we went in to buy it after just getting engaged while riding down Hollywood Boulevard. Remember, we only had fifty cents. And remember buying the wedding ring. Just think honey, that was over six years ago. We were certainly a couple of kids then weren't we...and or little honeymoon cottage. It was almost like playing house. But thank goodness we've never lost the capacity for fun that some people have only when they were kids. We've got an awful lot of time to make up for when you come home.

Be safe darling. All my love to you...

All our letters will be censored after this.
Jane XXXXXX

Hollywood 28, California
March 13, 1944
Letter 78

Dearest Honey Darling;

I just killed a black widow spider and burned up the toilet. Here is how it happened. It seems that under the basin in the far bathroom, the one off the living room I saw one the other night when I was alone...Saturday to be exact...I didn't have the courage to deal with it individually so I left a note for Nina and Pat but they didn't get in until about seven in the morning and that was too late to wake me up...rather too early and so they didn't and I forgot bout it. Nina reminded me of it a little while ago so I made a torch and smoked it down and turned it over and there was the red hour glass so Nina stepped on it while I put the torch in the toilet...only the torch blazed up and caught the paint of the toilet seat on fire and so now I have to paint it again tomorrow. It is nice to have such a menace to nudity and safety out of the bathroom though.

That was the next to the most outstanding event of my day. The first most outstanding was the fact that I talked to "the people" today and they told me to hold myself in readiness for any minute now...I don't hold hope for much less than a week frankly but it is drawing close and if it is within a week, that may be time enough. I hope so, darling...I am just praying so much that I can hardly think about anything else. I just do hope that this is it and that it will be in time.

I have been working awfully hard the last few days trying to get the final organization on things. There is still an awful lot to do of course, but it is so hard to do it unless you know definitely when it should be finished. I've got all our boxes packed and now the only question is where to put them. I'll probably delay so long that I'll leave them here...that is the best solution anyway. There is method in my madness. There is one evening dress on which I have to put the final touch and there are some things I have to buy but I am trying to wait to do that because of the financial resources. I got myself a little behind because I mixed up and overdrew and last month was a bad month what with the wisdom tooth and the pyorrhea and the x-ray treatments and the permanent to get ready and all. But I think I have everything as well under control as can be expected. Honey...you didn't say you were sorry about the wisdom tooth...I think you would be sorry about the price of having it out...definitely.

I went down about the income tax today. I had been told that I had to file some sort of a return for you even if you were overseas. Well, I got up bright and early and went down to the Federal building and you have never seen such a mob in your life. I think there were at least a thousand people in that floor that enters on Main street. Luckily I didn't have to go there...the section for the military was comparatively uncrowded. I only had to wait about half an hour. Well, as it turned out, I had been told wrong and you don't have to file one until three months after you are out of the service and then has to be filed in Syracuse New York because they group last year's and this year's together. So it was all for nothing. I made out all kinds of information and have thousands of cancelled checks to prove it <u>etc. so</u> I will save them for future reference. I even went armed with a Power of Attorney because I had been told I would need it.

I cooked a lamb stew for dinner tonight and lettuce with thousand island dressing and baked squash and biscuits. It was just like one of the dinners we used to have and it made me terribly homesick. We will have it again when you get home.

Honey you still haven't really told me anything about what you are doing...can't you. You tell me about the weekends with the Captain's wife etc. and it sounds wonderful and I envy you the steaks although I would rather you had them and I really don't do so badly on them if we want to be perfectly truthful but you don't tell me what you do in the daytime or anything about where you live or anything. Please do honey if you can.

The Captain's wife sounds very nice and I'm just as glad Mrs. G. wasn't a siren. Maybe if she were, he wouldn't have had such an eye out for them...that was very funny.

Gosh, I really had a big workday yesterday...from noon until three in the morning...did everything...packed, sewed, cleaned, fixed myself some dinner and started all over again. I ended up with a straight hour of practicing tap dancing...the same Saturday. I feel very virtuous in the fact that I am getting well-prepared. Honey darling, take care of yourself and write me and I love you with all my heart. Nina is going down the hill now and she will mail this. I love you, I love you, I love you.

All me love, Jane Pray honey and I think we'll h [ENDS]

2400 El Contento Drive
Hollywood 28, California
March 19, 1944 Letter 79

Dearest Honey;

Hold on to your hat...I am hoping like mad that it is in time. I am leaving here the twenty-seventh of March which is a week from tomorrow and is a Monday. I go to San Francisco to await transportation and from there on to you know where! The staying in San Francisco is distressing but I figure that with a definite date set by them for leaving here, they must have considered when we would go and we will probably leave San Francisco almost immediately. So by the sixth of April I figure I should be there. Pray God that it is in time. I found out about this yesterday and I should have written you immediately but Buddy was here...he left at six this morning. I have been in a flurry of excitement ever since dashing around trying to figure out the last minute things to do and believe me there are a million and one of them. This week is really going to be hectic. Besides getting my things ready I have to put the final touches on those sketches I have been memorizing. Tomorrow I have to be out at the Victory Committee at two-thirty to sign my contract and get all information about shots and uniforms. I imagine you will go to your own doctor for shots, rather, I will and they will pay for it. The information about the rate of remuneration is this. Originally I understood it was all expenses and seventy-five dollars a week but it has been changed to all expenses and ten dollars a day — which makes it seventy — but it is far better that way because it is completely tax exempt...imagine that, it saves about fourteen dollars a week that way. *That* starts the night you leave Los Angeles. Also the Mark Hopkins is the place we stay in San Francisco. *That* wouldn't be hard to take if I weren't in *such* a hurry but I won't be enjoying it this time. I'll be too impatient. If you are just there for three weeks more honey... please be...please. I'll write again tomorrow after I've seen them and know more details.

Well, Mary got off to New London alright...Friday morning on the El Captain. Right now she is on her way between Chicago and New York and should be in New York early in the morning and in New London tomorrow afternoon. I told her the name of that wonderful train that we took and told her to get that if she could. She only had a reservation as far as Chicago...after that she was on her own. Buddy got here Thursday night and we had dinner and she saw him and he stayed all night with her and Merlaine that night. Then Don said that he would drive us down to the station. She had no reservation...just a ticket. She was determined to catch the El Capitan because it is only forty hours to Chicago. They had told her to be down there ahead of time and she could probably get a cancellation. Well, she had seven people ahead of her. She told us to go away so she could get the man's sympathy so we went and ate breakfast. When we came back we just had to stand back and wonder whether she was going to be successful. She was... ten minutes before the train left, she got her ticket. She told the man that she had to get there because she was going to be married on next Tuesday. When he gave her the ticket, he said, "I'll be thinking of you Tuesday." "Tuesday?" she says, "Tuesday?"..."Oh, yes, Tuesday!!!" Thank heaven she already had the ticket before she made that break. It was too late to check her bags...in fact there was just time for her to run through the gate. Don and Buddy were carrying *the* bags and they ran through with her and I started to and he wouldn't let me go because only one visitor was allowed and she already had two. I begged him but he was adamant. She couldn't come back so I just screamed goodbye. They got her on the train, threw the bags up, the porters closed the doors and she was off without a second to spare. The Patten family is becoming quite a legend around here. People just look at us and shake their heads in wonderment. The funny part about it is that they insisted on calling Mary Flynn...they say "Oh, you Flynns. You're crazy."... Then of course with Mother having been here and Buddy showing up on his furlough, they think we all never stay in one place long enough to unpack our bags...then I give them a few of the stories about you and they are really amazed.

I think that Buddy had a fine time. Gosh, honey that is one person that I wish you knew better and when you get home, we must make an opportunity for it. He is so darned nice it is just unbelievable and not in a stuffy way. He certainly made a great hit with everybody here. I was pretty touched by the fact that he came all the way down here just to see me. There is a new rule that you can't hop a plane except for cross-country flights because students are flying them up and down the coast and they think that is dangerous for passengers. The train service between here and Sacramento isn't at all satisfactory so he hitch-hiked.

He started to hitch-hike back at six this morning. I drove him out to the monkey farm and he caught a ride in the first five minutes. He's the easiest person to entertain...he always wants to help you instead of you doing things for him. Thursday night he got here about eight-thirty. We had been waiting for him and so had Don and Mary and Merlaine and her Bill. Merlaine, who is Mary's friend, and Buddy and I went to Musso's for dinner and then to Bradley's. Then Friday morning we went to the station and took Buddy to Olvera street. It was very interesting because when we went in that old house...remember...the oldest one in Los Angeles that is down there — well, we met the woman who owns the place and who owns and developed Olvera Street. We talked to her for about half an hour and she told us how she had first bought this house when the city had condemned it and then developed the whole street. It was mixed in with a goodly smattering of the history of Los Angeles and terribly interesting. She loves the Mexican people and is sort of a Mother to them. She gives them those little stands they have down there free of rent. She has even engaged a doctor who is the official Olvera street medico and he checks every one of them over once a month. She did that when the blacksmith in the street died unexpectedly and the coroner said that he needn't have died if he had had proper medical care. She even gives them all vitamin tablets. A month ago the Mexicans in the street had had a war bond rally which she really organized and they had put on this stunt of trying Tojo...they had the darnedest life-size model of him that you have ever seen. Well, they had raised forth-three thousand dollars in war bonds and she was pretty proud of them. It was really an interesting experience to talk to her. She took us into the rooms in the house that are chained off to the general public. After that, Buddy and I went home and sat in the sun and drank some beer. Then Don had really taken a terrific fancy to Buddy...he thought he was the nicest kid he had ever met so he asked if he could take us to dinner so we went to Mike Lymans...it was pretty late when we finished dinner and we were all terribly tired from getting Mary ready and off so we went home then. Buddy stayed here. The Saturday morning I got my news and Buddy and I went down on the boulevard and bought me some shoes and did a few other things I had to do to get ready and then he had a haircut and we looked at the Chinese theatre and had a beer in the Brown Derby and went into Sardi's and had a drink and then we had dinner with Nina and Pat and Manon. Then Buddy and I came home and talked until about eleven thirty. The doorbell rang and I opened it and there was Don again. He was supposed to have gone to Big Pines with a date and two other friends but the plans had been changed so he said he had come up to have a drink to bid Buddy goodbye. He had a fifth of bourbon with him so we drank most of that and swapped stories about our childhoods then he went and we went to bed and got up at six and I took Nina's car and drove Buddy down. He's really a wonderful kid.

Monday Jack Finch came up with that friend of his, Grant Miaben and a Marine who is going to officer's school or something at USC. We talked a couple of hours and then they went and I have been trying to do something constructive ever since. Unfortunately I had to clean the house first because it was filthy. But that's the last housework I do this week. There are more important things to be accomplished. It is difficult to believe that a week from tomorrow morning, I will be on my way. It is too wonderful to be true. Oh gosh, if it is only in time. Did you ever get the anniversary card I sent you. In one day...tomorrow, you will have been gone six *months*. That's way too long honey.

Buckley *is in* town for several days on his way back to the Pacific Northwest where they are going to shoot a picture. He wants me to have lunch with him tomorrow but I don't see how I can. But something can be worked out.

Oh honey darling, cross your fingers and pray. I'll write you again tomorrow. I love you and by the way, I have only had one letter from you all week...why honey? Don't you love me any more... just when it is all so close? Be god darling...I love you, I love you. I LOVE YOU

Jane XXXXX Anticipation!!

2400 El Contento Drive Hollywood 28,Calif.
March 27, 1944

My Dearest Honey;

I had fully expected that tonight I would be on the Lark, listening to the clacking of the wheels rolling merrily northward but such was not to be. Maybe tomorrow night. I, myself, strongly suspect Wednesday. I suppose I shouldn't fuss because I am getting paid for whatever I do, starting today, but I'm in a hurry and you know why. We were supposed to leave tonight...as a consequence I stayed up until five o'clock last night getting things all packed so I could do any last minute thing that was to be done today. This morning at ten they called. I had planned to sleep until they did but that wasn't enough sleep. The good word was that we wouldn't leave tonight but that we were to get right out to Sak's in Beverly Hills and get our uniforms anyway. I got up and threw on my clothes... skipped my shower for the first time in I don't know when and dashed out there. They had made a mistake...the coats and caps and accessories were there but not the uniforms proper. I sat there three hours in company with various others but they didn't come in so now we have to go out tomorrow and get them. There really isn't much excuse for such inefficiency...on the part of Saks. But what I did get was awfully pretty honey...I look real military. Here I am sitting...did I tell you that I had yellow fever in one arm, typhoid in the other and smallpox in my hip...today I had a typhus shot in the yellow fever arm, and of course, there are more to come. The typhoid was really terrible. I put in a bad two and a half days. They gave that to us Thursday afternoon, and that evening here I was running around, trying to pack with a temperature of a hundred and two. My arm was so big I could hardly get it into my clothes and hurt! Yipe! The typhus bids fair to be just as bad. Lovely lovely. I have been trying all week to buy stuff I need and to get the rest of our stuff packed and into storage and to pack some clothes to send back to Seattle and the rest to take with me and having these damnable shots at the same time. It's been great! So if I seem to have neglected you, honey, please forgive me. It's been really mad and hectic and awful but fun in a certain way. When I think of the money I've spent I just quail. I think I've written a hundred dollars worth of postdated checks, but I had to because I suddenly discovered that you don't wear your uniforms after you get there and you are expected to have a complete wardrobe. Well, you know me, just the minimum of this and that. I really had to get busy... and spend a lot of money. Of course, the returns are worth the initial investment, but I just haven't dared think about the money I've spent. It's awful. I have three new pair of shoes among other things. I really should have five but I figure I can take care of the rest later. Little did I realize it would entail all this. It's like you and your uniforms. They give us the uniforms, however. They come from Saks and are gorgeous. They not only have skirts but slacks too and I can see myself in those as much as possible. Oh honey darling, I'm crossing my fingers and holding my breath. I had two of the most wonderful letters from you last week, and if only they could soon be a little more intimate, I would die of bliss.

There isn't much of anything else that happened to me last week except this constant running back and forth. When I even speak of it, it makes me think of it, and then I get dead tired. I'm so sleepy now I'm dying, but I have to stay up a little longer and see if I can get my second wind. I didn't. Just after I wrote that, I thought to myself, I will lie down a few minutes, and then I will feel better. That was ten o'clock. It is now one, and I just woke up. Fine fine. And I had a million things to do tonight. But since I have had three hours sleep, I think I will do a couple of them and go to bed again. I just poured myself a glass of beer. That should help. I feel so ashamed of myself. If they had stopped the war since yesterday, I wouldn't know it. There is some big fuss between Dies and Winchell that everyone is talking about, and I haven't had time to read it, and I don't know what Churchill said Sunday. I am really badly informed the last couple of days, but it is because I have just driven myself every minute with not a bit of time out.

I'm pretty worried about Ma Wee. Mother called Saturday night. They didn't have an address for Mary. I didn't either, but Merlaine had given me it, so I told Mother, and they were vastly relieved. But the reason they wanted to know mainly was to let her know in case anything happened to Ma Wee. They said that she was just all worn out and to be prepared. It is all very well to say she has had a long full life and that you should be prepared. You really miss somebody as nice as that, and I have a feeling too that it isn't going to be much longer. I hate to think that she can't go on living much longer. People who are so young in heart should always be young in body too.

I had lots of fun today trying on my uniform...what I have of it...they gave me the trench coat and the overseas cap and the purse that goes over the shoulder and the shirts and ties today. I am so military, and it is so much fun to enjoy the sensation. Nina wants to take some pictures tomorrow, and I think we should too so I will be able to say to our children...this is how your mamma looked when she entertained the soldiers in the last war. I know it's awful getting fun out of anything like that, but it does give you so a sense of satisfaction to be a part of the world, no matter how bad it is, instead of sitting in some backwash until it is back to fairly normal again.

Golly darn, honey, I guess that is about all the news. Cross your fingers and be good, and I'll see you soon. I love you like the dickens. I do so hope another letter comes from you before I go. Keep mum about this now honey...take care of yourself. I love you so terribly much...

Millions and millions of love, Jane

2400 El Contento Drive
Hollywood 28, California
4/4/44
Letter 83 [?so new number]

My dearest Dearest Honey Darling;

Gosh honey, I am still here...I guess that won't seem very astonishing to you because you will probably get this letter before you get the letters mailed to the old address saying that I was going. I am still on this two-hour notice deal and every time I leave the house before eight in the evening I have to check back. Every day I have a premonition that this particular one will be it but I guess it is just wishful thinking. I will have earned ninety dollars by midnight now though just for waiting and tomorrow night it will be a hundred so that is one good thing. The trouble is that I don't have it...I mean I had them send it back to the bank but then I suppose if I don't have it, I can't spend it and that is the purpose f not having it. I intend to get bills paid so don't want my hands on it. I must say that it is getting nerve wracking not knowing from day to day...it is like us in San Francisco the first time but with each day that you didn't have to go was such exquisite relief that the whole day was bright and happy. When you are anxious to go and don't you feel awfully thwarted.

Still not a letter from you honey since your note...that is the only reason I want to stay. When one doesn't come in the mail, then I pray to be here for tomorrow's mail so one will come then. Honestly, honey darling, I am beginning to get worried about you...I suppose that is foolish of me and that I would get all the way there before I would have a letter from you...and with all the activity going on down there now...You could be right in the thick of it...they don't make dates clear in the papers...in fact they don't give you any dates. Today Knox announced the victory at Pau but we are still completely unenlightened as to when it was. A recent letter from you would be welcome honey. I know there is nothing you can do about it but I think and think and think about you. The prospect of not getting one before I leave absolutely petrifies me. But I don't suppose you like to hear me stewing about you too much. I try to keep it to yourself as much as possible but once in a while, it just bursts out.

What news of or friends. Dan and Cassie were here yesterday evening. They came about six and left about eight thirty. I got some rum to give them and I'm so glad I did because they seemed to enjoy it so. Poor Dan has a terrible case of poison oak all over his body. He was being a Spartan about it but he was suffering. His arms looked like yours did and one hand was swollen so that it was absolutely bloated He had been working right through it too. The worst is over though. Park got his commission and he got his Flight officer. He is going someplace back east to some sort of instrument school for a while. They didn't have much more news of anyone and kept asking me for the latest. I told them as much as I could about you and about hearing from Dave Oswald. Nina was quite enchanted with them and they are making arrangements for Dan to talk to Sophie and Arthur and then they will all come here some evening in the next week. They wanted me to come out and spend the night with them but I really was afraid to get so far away from home. It would have been fun though. I can't rely on anyone around here to answer the phone though.

I had a long talk with Mel tonight. Nina called him to get Wilbur's address so he could give it to bob Skiles. I said hello and we really went into a conversation. In the first place, Tom is in Tucson. I told you remember that he got a J.G. commission. Mel said that the course had been terribly hard but he had got through it alright and that it was easing p a bit now. In addition to complicated mathematics, they have been having five hours a day of assorted exercises... wrestling even judo and all such. Tom likes it very much however.

Mel had a great piece of news which he cautioned me not to tell anyone until the first thing came out...he is actually writing at the studio now...I don't understand the reason for secrecy but evidently they want to keep it quiet for a while because they gave him a special deal and they are afraid there might be jealousy among the other readers etc...Not only that but he has been doing some radio writing. He ghost wrote on thirteen weeks series and then told them he was finished. His point was that he was earning less at the studio but he wanted to have plenty of time to devote to it anyway because he is more interested in movie than radio writing. They offered him $250 per week to do another thirteen-week series...I guess it doesn't take thirteen weeks to write them but he turned it down. Also he was offered the job of plot man for the Amos and Andy program, which he also turned down because he says he is no good at plots. But now it looks as if he were going to e offered a job writing for the Charlie McCarthy program and he is seriously considering that. Mel said he saw a play last night...one of the people in it was so similar to you in appearance and mannerisms although he said, not as good looking that four people remarked it to him. Mrs. Crutchfield form Samuel French, Bob Brown from Seattle and Mrs. Kutler and somebody else. He said it was quite amazing then of course you were brought up in conversation and everyone wanted to know all about you and what you were doing. I wish I could see the place but it is way out at the Ben Bard playhouse, which is now called the Geller workshop so I don't imagine I will have a chance to.

Well. Honey, it is now eleven thirty. I think I will fix my hair and climb in my little bed. These shots sort of knock me for a loop as far as reserve energy is concerned so maybe it is a good thing that I don't have a lot of pressing engagements or scads of work to do this week.

Honey darling, I love you with all my heart. I hope you get this letter soon. Take care of yourself...very good care honey. I'll be seeing you soon.

All my love to you darling which is an enormous lot...
love, love, love

Did I tell you that I got a letter from Bob Marinaro's mother the other day asking me if I was the Mrs. Flynn whose husband was Chuck and that Bob used to live with. If so, would I answer and tell her because she had a question she wanted to ask me. I answered and am now waiting with great curiosity for her reply.

All my love darling,

Jane

XXXXXXX

Letter 85
2400 El Contento Drive
Hollywood 28, Calif.
April 7, 1944

Dearest Honey Darling;

Oh honey, what bliss. After all the worrying and stewing and fretting I have done...came a letter from you yesterday and another day...I didn't expect any ore because you said there probably wouldn't be for a few days. I was getting absolutely desperate...I didn't know whether you got there alright or where you were and I was imagining all sort of wild thing. I was really getting the jitters because I hadn't heard from you and then come two such wonderful letters.

I see that I can now address you by your new title...I am so used to addressing the envelopes the other way that I will probably slip up and have to re-do them. That is wonderful honey...I am very proud of you and I am so proud of what you said about getting back on the ship...it doesn't sound egotistical...that is grand honey.

So you finally met up with Dave. That must have been quite a time. I've owed him a letter for ages. I must answer it come he morning. The reason I didn't send you a card from Carroll's was that I figured the competition was a little heavy for me...the picture I mean and I didn't want you to see it but I did think it would be funny to send him one...the way he is always talking about women in his letters. Evidently it had quite an effect but not just what I had anticipated.

Well, as you can see I am still here...wild rumors are floating around about time of leaving and reason etc. But I won't repeat them in a letter. In any case, I do think now that I'll be here until after Easter which is day after tomorrow. I hope not. The thing that would make a day really happy for me would be to leave. I suppose I can't fuss when I am being paid. If you were still there, I would be going crazy though. I am as it is because I will be rank to say, I'm pretty anxious to get away from Hollywood and to get started doing something useful. I don't particularly like or approve of the atmosphere around here. I think I have a soul mate in Johnny Harmon. He is going to sell his car and his radio and his Electrolux and raise in total about fifteen hundred dollars and go to New York in a couple of weeks. He says he is sick and tired of sitting around this town waiting for jobs and as each day goes by, you get lazier and lazier and aren't doing anything worth letting you live for. He says if he really wants to act, he has to do something about it and right away. Of course I am not getting lazier because I won't let myself. I drive myself crazy with all the projects but it is so darned true that people shouldn't live suck a life as they do around here when there is a war going on. It's a sin. Soon now though.

I bought myself a dress today...nothing very great...just a cotton one but I needed it terrible badly seeing as we spent last summer in san Francisco and there wasn't much se for them there and I will need a few to get started on. It is brown and white striped seersucker...it has no back and no sleeves...then it has a brown bolero jacket...which makes it useful for all kinds of occasions and weather. It is very good-looking and remarkably cheap — only nine dollars...it was really a bargain. I got it at Dorothy Beal's where I got that beige suit. The only other cotton dress that I had seen that I would have was at Nancy's for 17.95 and that was out of the question for a cotton dress. I need some sort of print silk dress for better wear but I'll just have to wait for that because I definitely can't afford it. I had to let all our bills go last month as it was and the money I make this month will have to go on them, most of it. It's always money, money, money...it drives me crazy each month figuring out where I can put it to keep everybody happy. Anyway it's a pretty dress.

That is about all the news from here, honey darling...nothing happens to me except the waiting. I went to dinner with Nina and Pat last night. We had planned that I should cook it up here but Nina, when we went down to pick up Pat, wanted to stop in at Sardis for a drink and to say hello to Lee. Well, we were there so long that there wasn't time to cook for them and get to a show. We dropped in to Tip's...hone it has fallen. This is the first time I have been there since I have back and their hamburgers are the littlest tiniest things you have ever seen and not well cooked any more and the waitresses aren't nice any more. The pea soup was still good though. I guess we'll just have to wait until after the war to have our wonderful hamburger steaks there again.

Honey, I'm not your child-bride anymore even if you do still think I'm pretty and like the pictures. I'll be twenty-six next June...the years are passing...remember when we went and had a drink on my twenty-first birthday in that bar over in highland. I remember that Dave Web was with us and that we me Sophie and Wilbur walking up the street and you asked them to come in and celebrate the fact that I could have a drink legally. Life is passing by. Now don't start moaning about being thirty-two because as a man, you're getting into your most attractive age.

Look honey, I don't know why I didn't think of it while you were up there but if you ever get into any place where you can have your picture taken, would you please do me a favor and have one taken for me. I don't really have any good pictures of you and I would certainly love one...please honey try to do it if there is a possibility any place.

I hope that this will be the lat letter I will write you from here darling. Be good honey...I'll see you soon and all the love there is to you my darling...

All my love,
Jane

LEGAL NAME
Dorothy Fay Ritter
Jane Patten Flynn
Martha Wilson Shaw
Nancy Lee Worth

STAGE NAME
Dorothy Fay
Jane Patten
Martha Wilson
Shaw Nancy Lee

EXTRACT
WAR DEPARTMENT
The Adjutant General's Office Washington 25, D.C.
AG 230.42 (7 Apr 44)OB-S-SPSPS MN/map-2B-939 Pentagon 8 April 1944

SUBJECT: Invitational Travel Orders, Shipment IJ-161-BP
TO: San Francisco Port Of Embarkation
The Chief of Transportation, Army Service Forces
The Director, Special Service Division, Army Service Forces

1: 'Upon call of the port commander, the following named theatrical troupe members are authorized and invited to proceed by rail from Los Angeles, California to the San Francisco Port of Embarkation, for further movement by water transportation to an overseas destination under Shipment IJ-161-BP, and to such other places within that theater as may be directed by the Commander, United States Army Forces there for the purpose of entertaining troops and at the end of this mission to return to Los Angeles, California.

3. *Travel directed is necessary in the public service for the accomplishment of an emergency war mission and is chargeable to Allotment Serial No. 1-5000 P 431-02 A -425-24.*

4. *The Chief of Transportation, Army Service Forces, will furnish the necessary transportation and coordinate with all concerned.*

5. *By order of the Secretary of War: Lr' COPY*

2400 El Contento Drive Hollywood 28, Calif.
April 9, 1944
Letter 86

Dearest Honey Darling;

Well, it is just a few minutes past Easter day, and I thought before I went to bed, I would sit down and write you a letter. For the first time in my life, I actually went to church on Easter and to a Catholic mass at that. Five in the morning, only we got there a little late thinking we were getting there early for the six o'clock one, only it was at five instead. I was sitting here memorizing last night when Don called about midnight and said he had some bourbon and would I like a drink...so he came up, and then Nina and Pat came home, and then we all talked a while, and then Don left...then I talked to Pat a while, and then I got to thinking that last Easter at this time we walked down fifth avenue after we went to the Grand Central station...remember the light streaming in the windows...how beautiful it was. Then we went on the statue of liberty boat...remember. Well, I got this sudden desire to go to church-why I wanted to go to a Catholic one I don't know, but I did. Pat is sort of a backsliding Catholic so I started playing on his better nature...it took me an hour and a half, but I finally persuaded him to go. I guess I could have gone by myself but didn't like to while it was dark. Then Pat persuaded Nina to go. It was very beautiful, and it made me feel good...like I had done what I should have on Easter Sunday. I just felt like I had to go. I rather wished after we got started though that I hadn't been so insistent or had gone by myself...it wasn't the question of the car because Nina couldn't even be driving it without the gas I have gotten for her, so that couldn't be objected to, but she was in sort of a bad mood and resented going so that you could just feel the vibrations. Why she went, I don't know because she didn't have to, and it kind of spoiled the whole thing. Then it was kind of embarrassing because she wouldn't put anything on her head, and that seems awfully disrespectful, and she knew that she should. It was light by the time we got home, and I went to bed immediately and then got up about one o'clock. I'm pretty tired now, needless to say. Nina and Pat slept until after six. Pat when he came downstairs said that she had been perfectly furious over the whole thing...so I wish I hadn't insisted, even-if I do think that it was childish of her, but Nina is subject to the most violent and distressing moods...it is perfectly amazing.

Well, yipe, the phone rang and it was Nina. It seems she had just had a wire which came up to Lou and Glen's about somebody that she used to go with that is coming tomorrow and will be here for the next five days. She wants to be alone in the house with him, so she asked me if I could go up and stay at the Lathams. I haven't yet decided whether I will go there or to the Padre hotel. Laurel Canyon is so darned far when I have to be downtown so much. I'm afraid I'll have to stay down here. Not that I am particularly unhappy about it, aside from the inconvenience just before leaving, because I have been pretty miserable here recently as you may have been able to detect from my letters. I haven't been able to quite cope with Nina's moods and have been working terribly hard trying to keep the house clean to be doing my part, etc...I have wanted to go, but to move down to the Padre or something just before I went would have looked like I had an argument with her, and it seemed a shame to make anything look like an issue when it could be sat out a few days longer. I wish I had now though because it would have made me make the first move. Lee is not here, although he has been staying here. I called him. He gave me the number but said not to tell anyone else what it was...I told him about it and said that would give him a chance to tell her first that he was leaving. They had had sort of an argument, and Nina was in the wrong about it. He had been planning to leave anyway but hadn't picked up his clothes, so I thought he might as well know so he could say it first. I'll have to come up here every day to pick up my mail of course. Frankly, I think I will be quite relieved. Nina has been asking me to stay all this time, but the news is beginning to trickle in to me that she has been saying just opposite things behind my back, and I don't like to be put in a situation where there is any room for question. It's all the fault of my damnable penchant to accept things at their face value and believe what people say to me. It has been a very trying situation for me...I've tried to sit it out gracefully but am almost relieved that I don't have to any more. I have just suffered from day to day wishing that they would call, and when they haven't, I have thought I just couldn't stand another one. But I couldn't just say I'm going because then I would have to give a reason, and that might hurt somebody's feelings, and that seemed unnecessary at this late date. I'm very grateful to Nina...she has been a true friend, but she would have been a better friend if she hadn't said one thing to me and another behind my back. Well, that is that. Fortunately I have everything so well organized that it won't take me more than half an hour or so to pack.

Woodie came up this afternoon, and I spent the evening with her. She had to drive out to the Lockheed air terminal, and so I drove out with her...then we went up to the apartment of a friend of hers who works also in the Hills-U-Drive and had cold roast chicken and vegetable salad and some other stuff and some scotch for dinner. It was a very nice evening...I like her an awful lot. She said that she had a letter from you...evidently you wrote it on the same day that you wrote me last-she said that it was quite frank but awfully cute...guard your words a little dearie...I can't help feeling a slight twinge of jealousy when you write to girls you don't even know, even if she is a good letter writer...I can tell you to be discreetly bad, but when you write to my friends, I get a wifely reaction, and am not particularly happy about it. That is awful isn't it honey. I guess it's because she makes so much over it...or that I'm in a sensitive mood right now.

Honey, did you ever get the Christmas presents I sent you? If you didn't, they are probably moldy by now anyway, but I would sort of like to know whether Dave Stanley ever got there with them. Also, if you haven't written Hazel and Jack thanking them for the books, I do wish you would. She has asked and asked if you received them, and I have had to say no. Please do this honey for me...right away...please.

Wherever you are tonight, darling, I am thinking of you and loving you with all my heart. I hope that there will be a letter tomorrow to tell me that all is going along well with you. Soon we will see each other again…I just feel it in my bones. Keep the letters coming honey, and I'll do the same. It isn't as good as seeing you, but it's second best, and that will have to do for just a little while longer.

I guess I'll go to bed now so I can get up real early in the morning and get to work and move and have another typhus shot. I'm awfully proud of you honey…

All my love to you darling, Jane

#38
13 April 1944
In Port —

Dear Mom:

Well we got back in late yesterday, and I had some mail; it was wonderful, although the last letter was dated March 31st from both you and Jane. That's only 12 days at that, so I guess I shouldn't complain. It is a long time though when you are anxious for news. I presume that Jane is in Honolulu by this time and starting on her new job. You don't seem very keen on it mom, I wonder why? The pay is good, she gets all her expenses plus ten bucks a day clear. We are going to have a nice nest egg after the war if things keep on like this. Well you never were too keen on the theater but then that's what makes horse racing.

I was so happy to hear that the Anaconda stock came back and that winds up the whole deal. Just think, almost a year getting everything settles up. That's awful long time to handle everything as straight forward and clear as I am sure Dad's will must have been. Well at least all of us hope that is over now honey and you can forget all the trouble you had with the red tape. I know the next few days are going to be hard for you, especially the 26th, but remember mom that my thoughts will be with you on that day, and we must remember dad, not with sadness, but in a loving and grateful way for all the fine things he stood for. And the unselfishness way he loved us both. Words don't help much in times like these, but you know what I am trying to say, don't you honey?

Well we are back in port again. Got in late last night and as I say got some mail. Fry's boat was in the harbor, and he came over for dinner and stayed for the movies. He is the boy that lived right across the hall from me at Cornell, and he and his wife spent a lot of time with Jane and I in San Francisco just about a year ago. Gosh honey does it seem possible that it hasn't been even a year since I left San Francisco the first time. June 12th. It sure seems a lot longer ago than that. Just a little over ten months. Well the time does pass, but it is pretty slow, however, they say things are moving out here the last few months, maybe the war will be over quicker than a lot of people think. I still say that August 1945 should see peace everywhere, and that's only about fifteen months, so we can hold out that long, yeah, and if necessary another fifteen after that! It's not pleasant, but we will <u>finish</u> this job, but good, and you can quote me!

Well I was delighted to hear that you were proud of me making j.g. I was pretty delighted myself. By the way, should be in little letters, and in (jg). I haven't any letters from you addressed that way as yet, but I bet the next one is. I'm not sure how long we will be here, but we haven't any orders to do anything yet, so maybe a few days. Now that it is fall down here the heat isn't so bad. Of course it's still hot, but bearable. Our duty is still a long way behind the front line, so you don't have anything to worry about in my case. I'll tell you the truth about that I promise you, so when I say don't worry, don't!! If we ever get up in it, then I'll tell you that too, and you can say a little prayer for me everyday. I know you do, and I think you are the most wonderful mom in the whole world.

Well sugar, lunch is about to be served, and the body needs nourishment. I'll sign off this time, but will write again in a few days, at least before we leave here. Chin up Honey!!

All my love —
XXXXXXXX CHAS

1738 North Las Palmas Ave
Hollywood 28, California
April 16, 1944

Dearest Honey Darling;

Well here it is Sunday afternoon and I am still here. As you can see, I am established down at the Las Palmas hotel now. I stayed up at the Lathams from Monday to Thursday and then I didn't want to impose on them any longer and it was rather unhandy place for me to be and I was able to get a room down here — so here I am. It is really a very nice little hotel...pretty and clean and in a perfect location...it's just half a block above the boulevard. It's very inexpensive too as rooms go...only two dollars a day which really isn't all bad. I have pretty good reason to believe that tomorrow or the next day will bring the zero hour so I shant be here much longer I guess. The mail is going up to the Lathams now...then they will forward it to me from there. I figured Margaret would probably be more reliable than Nina on something like that.

In a little while I am going down to the house of Martha Shaw, one of the girls who is going and I am going to wash a shirt and some stuff and do a little sewing and then stay at her house for dinner. I haven't an iron because I let Mary take ours to New York...I figured I wouldn't need it because the other girls were taking theirs and Mary really did. This Martha is awfully nice and we have become very good friends. She knows a lot of people we know...she was at Pasadena when Will was and knows all of that Donde Fore and Johnny James Crowd. She says she knows who you are but she has never met you. She lives with her mother and her grandmother so I shall have a very relaxing and family afternoon. Last night we had dinner together at Musso's. That wasn't quite so relaxing because I have a terrible case of the shakes this morning caused by Martinis. I guess drinking is just not for me. Every once in a while I get impatient and have about ten...it provides a good emotional release for the moment...you just don't care for an hour or so but oh the next day. It isn't worth it. I had beer and martinis and bourbon and it serves me right that I feel awful. That's all. I won't be able to have them anyway when I get going.

Oh honey, I loved all your big plans for the money. I hope that we can do it but we'll certainly have to watch to be able to. I shall write the bank a note as soon as I finish this instructing them that you shall be depositing money there too and we'll both do our best. As soon as I get going, I'll be able to salt plenty away. The initial outlay has been pretty big for me but I'm finished now. You know clothes are part of my stock in trade and I've had to have some new ones. I hadn't realized how far down my wardrobe was...it was all right for winter but I just didn't have a thing for summer. I needed some kind of silk dress awfully badly. I had just searched the town for one but couldn't find one I liked. I saw one in Saks the first day I looked...when I was out there about the uniforms. That one I was just wild about but thought that the price they wanted...thirty-five dollars...was a little high so I said I wouldn't take it...well, I looked and looked and looked and couldn't find anything else that I liked...all the dresses are so fussy and frilly this year that it's positively disgusting. Well, yesterday I saw the same dress in Myer Siegels...I had gone down to Wilshire to see what I could find...I just threw up my hands and said it was fate and went in and bought it. I know that I shouldn't have but it was true that if I want to be good I have to make an outlay and this thing is so darned becoming on me that nothing else could equal it.

I've been reduced to wearing my uniform around town because the three suits that I left out to wear are all filthy dirty. It's really very good looking and it is kind of fun to wear it because it causes such a sensation...everyone wonders what it is...people knock themselves out trying to be friendly so it appeals to my sense of the theatre.

Honey, I don't suppose it's a god idea to comment on it specifically but I'm awfully proud of you for why you left so soon. I near burst. I think you're absolutely wonderful and I love you with all my heart.

I hope I'll be writing you next form the train...

All my love — to you, Jane

Don't address any letters to here. The Lathams would be best until you get another address.

LOVE — LOVE — LOVE XXXX

Palmas Hollywood 28, California
April 18, 1944
Letter 87

Hello Honey Darling;

Well, it has been quite a day...at times trying but highly amusing. Today is William Shakespeare's birthday...figure it out for yourself which one...he was born the twenty-third of April (the celebration was a little premature wasn't it) 1564. I attended a birthday party for him, believe it or not. Here is how it was…this Munro Manning who was with Evans was asked to give a lecture on Shakespeare to the soldiers…rather how the soldiers liked Shakespeare for the women at the Wilshire-Ebell club. He asked if we girls wanted to go…(pardon the phrase, we girls…it's the clubwoman atmosphere of today) Well, he is an interesting talker, and he has been so nice and helpful to us that this Martha Shaw and I figured it was the least we could do. We got down there at ten-thirty this morning, figuring that he would give the lecture and then we would leave, but such was not to be…we were there until three this afternoon. I have never seen such an unadulterated striving for culture among clubwomen in my life. Fist we had a speech from the president of the club-of course she was shaking in her boots…then the minutes were read You know how women are-they enunciate everything so very clearly and precisely. Then we were treated with a reading over the microphone by an older pupil of the Meglin Kiddies studio of Queen Titania's speech to the fairies, then some of the kiddies came out and did a ballet…oh honey, how awful it was. Then Munro Manning gave his speech, and it was really very good and very interesting. It just set all the ladies a flutter because he is so good looking…he was just their naughty boy. After the speech we were invited to attend the luncheon. We tried to get off, but they really nailed us. When we got up there, the poor disorganized things didn't have places for us, but every time we would try to leave with the plea that we were causing inconvenience, another one would get us. Finally they set us right in the middle of the speakers table. It was rather embarrassing because each one wanted to know what we did, and we couldn't tell them. They'd say…oh you can just tell me. I won't tell anybody — ha ha! Well, we had chicken patties and tomato aspic salad, and then the president gave a long intro-duction of everybody who had ever been an officer in that or any other club. Then they introduced the honor guests. They insisted on introducing us, so we said that they could say that we were with USO Camp Shows…that would have been alright, but the poor thing introduced us as USO Camp Followers…that was too much. I tried to keep from having hysterics. while we were making our little bow but dissolved into quakings and shakings of silent laughter as soon as we sat down. Remember William Farnum…he gave a reading of Cassius' speech to Brutus about Caesar being mortal the same as everybody else. It was full of the old ham, but it was really wonderful. Then some very old man of at least ninety gave a beautiful reading-the one about the seven stages of man's life. Then Gilmor Brown spoke, and he wasn't very good. Then we were treated to the worst book review by one of the lady members that I have ever had the horror to hear-it was of Good Night Sweet Prince. You know, the life of John Barrymore by Gene Fowler. I sent you a copy of it. Let me know when you get it. Then the meeting dissolved, but we had a terrible time getting out of there. They were all convinced that we were going someplace, and they would say...I have a son in Italy. You must look him up. Oh! Then they were fluttering so over Munro Manning that we had to wait for all that because he was driving us up to the boulevard. The President even gave him a lei that she had made herself. Martha and I headed straight for Sardi's and had a beer.

Next day honey...Wednesday noon now. I had just written that much last night when the phone rang, and they told me that Jack Finch and a friend of his were out in the lobby. So they came in. Jack is being transferred up north of Santa Barbara someplace-no more evenings in Hollywood. Incidentally that rumor about Ken Anenson was entirely false. It merely started with the old thing about his not being able to stay in the Naval Air Corps because his eyes weren't good enough. I gave them a glass of sherry, and we were sitting talking when the phone rang again, and it was Jim Hill. I was certainly surprised. I had talked to him that afternoon but don't think I had seen him for at least two months. He was more like his old self than I have seen him in ages. We all went out and had a drink and then a cup of coffee, and then by that time, it was after midnight, so I went to bed without finishing this letter. This morning I got up and took a uniform shirt up to the little cleaners up here to be ironed. I have to keep them clean, and they had told me that if I washed it, they would iron it. Then I dropped off my moccasins to be shined and had breakfast. Then I came back here, and I have just finished memorizing the Shooting of Dan McGrew. I have been having an awful time finding enough material for sketches and stuff and have had a lot of time to memorize. So the other day I asked some sailors...made a point of it...what they would like to hear, and they said Dan McGrew and the Cremation of Sam McGee...so I picked up a little book for a quarter, and I have been having more fun with them. They are so darned corny and should be said so seriously and tragically. I am getting back my old ability to memorize again. When I first started, it was terribly difficult for me, but the training is reasserting itself. Thank heaven.

Honey, I wrote the bank as you asked me to and said that you would be sending money in from time to time. It isn't a joint account. It couldn't very well be because your signature wasn't available at the time it was established. All you have to do is to say to deposit it to the checking account of Jane P. Flynn. The Bank is the Seattle-First National bank, Seaboard Branch, Fourth at Pike Streets, Seattle 1, Washington. Remember honey that we have a lot of bills and some personal debts I have to pay before we can really start saving money. I haven't even dared add them up for fear it would be too discouraging.

You know, it's really kind of fun living here so close to the boulevard. It reminds me of how we used to love to walk along and look at the people and the things in the windows. So now I do it and think of you and how much you would enjoy it. Of course there are more servicemen now and not so many peculiar characters, but it is still fascinating. You know, Hollywood boulevard is one of the dingiest looking streets I have ever seen. Every day it bears more resemblance to a midway.

Little Mary Hull is back from New York and dying to go back there again. If a job that she thinks she has back there comes through, she will leave immediately. But it seems that Adele is trying to have another baby...she lost the first two...and she has been pretty sick. Then it looks as if John, who is really and truly in the army, would be going over the water soon so she came back here to see them both. I think she spent most of her money on this trip, so if she doesn't get that job she will have to go to work for a while to get back. She didn't see Mary there. In fact, she really didn't see anyone that we knew. I think she was pretty well occupied with Cliff. She said that he wanted her to marry him, but she just couldn't bring herself to do it. You know, Mary's hair is getting so darned grey that she's going to have to do something about it. It makes me feel old because I am two months older than she is. I congratulate myself though that I still don't look twenty-six, which is what I will be in June...imagine that. It seems such a short time ago too that we were celebrating my twenty-first birthday. We went into that bar over on Highland to get a drink legally, remember, with Dave Webb and we met Sophie and Wilbur walking up the street.

I think I recalled that same incident to you the other day. That is a sure sign of age when you start repeating yourself.

I had a phone call from Nina last night after I was asleep. You know, I am over having my feelings a little hurt by her. I am so much happier down here anyway that it all worked out fine. But the poor thing, I do feel so sorry for her. She is so lost. She is seriously trying to get into this Red Cross thing and I have been helping her fill out her applications. But she has sort of turned to me for help...even to asking me to see that Lee doesn't take the cat away because he left the house and threatens to take it with him.

Honey darling, it must sound to you as if I led an awfully idle life, and it is true that I really do, but it is not from choice. It is just like our waiting in San Francisco...you just can't do anything else but sort of stick by the phone and read and memorize stuff. I will soon be working awfully hard though and really doing some very useful work. I think it has been well worth waiting for.

Honey darling, I love you with all my heart...keep writing as much as you can...I'm saving up an awful lot of love for you when you get back — all my love,

Honey, I forgot to mention that it would be better not to mention by name your ideas of where you think I am.

Loads and loads and loads of love, Jane

Hollywood 28, California
April 22, 1944

Dearest Chuck;

I decided to write this letter today by hand because it seems to me that lately, when I type them, they give the impression that I have just sort of banged them out...I guess I'm just of the old-fashioned school that doesn't compose well on a machine. After all, the letters we write are our greatest means of keeping together in such a long separation. Of course I know no matter what that I love you and I'm sure you love me but the purpose of a letter is to send a little part of yourself to the person you love. I know it gets awfully difficult after all these months to keep the correspondence up to the high standard it was at first. After all nobody loves to write letters and then too your lives run in different channels for so long that after a while you find yourself just saying-I love you without giving any real part of you-just using the words. Heaven knows you mean them but from writing it so long, you stop trying to write them really expressively. For example, do you realize it has been at least three months since I've had one of those wonderful letters from you that you used to write when you were on the mid-watch. In fact the last month I have had an average of not much better than one letter a week from you and those written in haste. It's not that I think you don't love me and I know you are busy but we are so inclined to forget to sit down and try to write something really valuable to the person we love the most. We expect them to understand it anyway — and they do but at the same time, it's wrong to stop the effort. Of course we could never grow apart or strange to each other, no matter how long the separation because we have done so many wonderful things and have had so much time, trials and triumphs together. But I think that the lack of effort at communication with people who don't know each other as well is responsible for the sense of strangeness and the lack of adjustment that come when they are together again. To think that the fact that I am writing this letter by hand started me out on this! The point is honey, let's be very careful never to lose even the slightest bit of the intimacy and understanding which we have always had. You will be different in many ways when you come back and undoubtedly I will be too. Experiences change everyone and we haven't shared them and won't be for a little while. But we can keep pace with each other through our letters so there won't be a single miss-step when we are together again. Do I sound awfully solemn-well Mr. Flynn it's just because I love you (what a prosaic way of speaking-there should be a new expression like — el moola wa —) I tell you — I wrote you three pages-single spaced last night. When I had finished it, I Looked it over and I said "This letter is not worthy of being sent to the person who means more to me than anyone in the world" So I chucked it out-tore it in little pieces and this epistle is my effort to send you something that truly belongs to both of us.

There are various pieces of news about people which I'm sure you'll find most interesting — some good, some bad. Good first. Last evening I went to dinner at Musso's with Nina and Lee. I was sitting there eating my bouillabase (Which incidentally, I didn't like — it's my first and last time at that. But maybe it's better in Marseille. I'll try again when we get there.) when I looked up and there was Levis standing at the bar. (Incidentally I was wearing my uniform for two reasons, first I have practically nothing else that is clean to wear without unpacking and second I had worn it out to the doctors that afternoon because he, being a thwarted actor at heart, wanted to see it) Well who do you think was with Levis — Pred Vinmont no less — back a week from India — a Captain in the Air Corps and fairly covered with ribbons. He had a Presidential Citation and the Air Medal among other things. A couple of stars on his Asiatic-Pacific ribbon and a couple on the one for European theatre. It seems he was in North Africa too — In India he was flying between someplace there and Kunming. He was sent home because he was ill but is well now and informed me he has been trying to imbibe all the Scotch he missed while he was gone. I hurriedly finished that darn fish chowder and had a drink with them — skipped going to a movie with Nina and Pat and sat with them while they ate their dinner. There was much good talk — remember the whip cream machine! And Levis went through the whole story of our buying the Packard from Johnny Meeham. How he wouldn't speak to Johnny for a week and Johnny finally told Levis that he should feel grateful to him as he had barely been able to restrain us from buying that Rolls-Royce that belonged to King Alphonso. They wanted to know all about you and of course I told them as much as I could with not a little boasting about my wonderful husband. Of course Levis nearly fainted at the uniform (He was surprised enough to see me, not having known I was in town) you know what a fuss he makes about such things. It was a very pleasurable time and it struck me as so amazing that with all the time that we all spent together, we are on such different roads now. Who would have believed it a few years ago. Pred said he would give anything to get back to those days. They were wonderful but what I want are the new ones when you come home.

Margaret Latham called this morning with some astonishing news. When I heard her voice I hoped it was a letter from you but no such luck. Darn. It seems that Jack had just phoned home to say he had read in the Citizen News (I have been trying to get a clipping all day to send to you but can't find one) that Marge was suing Tom Potts for a divorce because of Mother-in-law trouble. Tom is in North Carolina I believe. Do you suppose that Mrs. Potts has been back there all that time? I strongly suspect it. I know that Margery went back there last winter and shortly returned. Maybe

that marriage wasn't especially good from the start but it seems
a darned shame. It seems ironical that two people who think they
have the world so well figured out should have such confusion in
their personal lives.

More bad stuff — Did I tell you what Jim Hill told me the other
night about Truman? I don't believe I did. About the court martial.
The results we don't know yet — I'll call Jim sometime during the
next couple of days and fine out. Well you know he had his own
destroyer — I don't suppose it would be best to mention it here
if you don't know. Well they were up north and had been out for
a long time with the men not being on shore. He got a three day
authorization to stop in a certain harbor to let the men go ashore.
Unfortunately he couldn't refuel there and they were too low to let
the steam go up for three days and get to their next destination for
refueling. He decided that the men had to go ashore so they turned
off the steam. But then bad weather came up and they couldn't get
the stram up in time and the ship went on the beach. That, according to Jim, is the gist of the story. I understand they were towed
back. There was an investigation and T. thought it was cleared up
to his credit. He gets married and then they bring it up and start
proceedings. Heaven knows what will happen. I do so hope it turns
out right for him. Never take a risk like that honey. That may not
be the true version but it's just what Jim told me.

Yes, darling I am still here. Incidentally after I leave, our letters
will be censored so don't even mention where you think I might be.
The delay is getting very irksome and I find myself spending too
much money. There are so many things I need but I could probably get along as well if I didn't get them. Today they told me it
might very possibly be the first week in May before we leave here.
I nearly died at that, but after all that is only a little over a week.
Eventually though, I know I'll go.

Poor Mary. She's in New York. She didn't marry Sam. He was
ordered to a transport and he's gone — and she got the bad ki9nd
of measles and had to quit her job and didn't have any money and
didn't want to tell anyone about it — well poor thing — it has been
pretty grim for her. On top of that she's just heartbroken over Sam.
I feel responsible but I know she would have gone anyway. I've
taken care of everything as much as I can and informed Daddy of
part of it so I guess she'll be alright now. Guess it's just taking her
a little longer to test her wings.

Daddy sold a piece of timber which he bought for $1800 and sold it for $20,000 — he'll have it all inside of two years I understand. He's so happy about it because it will help him get back into the lumber business which he has been longing to do. I wish he wouldn't but it would make him happy.

Good heavens darling, I'm afraid you'll be awed when you see this hunk of paper come out of the envelope. I better stop before I scare you to death. But I just get talking to you and keep on.

Be good my darling. Be safe and I love you so — what a happy day it will be when you come home — What jubilation. I couldn't talk straight the last time. You'll think your wife is a jibbering idiot the next.

All my love,
Jane

April 25 1944
1738 North Las Palmas
Hollywood 28, California
Letter 89

Dearest Honey Darling;
I guess that today I can write you a very good letter by typewriter...it is like coming back to it refreshed after a vacation. Very little has happened to me since I wrote you a couple of days ago. Life had gone on in this darned enforced idleness that is just about to drive me crazy but which is unavoidable and at which I shouldn't chafe. I should be thankful for the opportunity to improve my time and to memorize more stuff but I just can't seem to keep my mind on it. I'm afraid I only do good work under pressure like in "Sailor Beware". But I have definite word now that the idleness will come to an end the first of the next week so try to content myself in counting the days. The fact that I haven't had a letter from you for ten days adds not a little to my uneasiness. I suppose you are thinking that I am gone and so there is no use in writing but honey, that is a fallacy. Keep writing. The letters will always get to me... not ten but eleven days and tomorrow will make twelve. Two more days and that would be two more weeks which is about the longest stretch of not hearing from you that I have had yet.

When I finish this I shall write a not to your mother as tomorrow is the twenty-sixth of April and I know she would appreciate hearing from me. I am disappointed that things didn't work out for her to take her trip east but perhaps she will later.

I had rather an interesting if unsatisfactory evening last night... unsatisfactory because all the talk was so pointless if well informed. I was supposed to meet Manon for dinner and Nina and Pat came along too. It was rather fun because everyone was in a good and happy frame of mind. I wasn't particularly when I got there but Manon was so bubbling over with happiness because she had just received a telephone call from Jimmy Manion to whom she is engaged...you remember him, the tall handsome boy with the white hair...he would be here on Saturday. She hasn't seen him for nearly seven months. She was so excited and joyful that she communicated it to me and I started to bubble over too. We were at the perpetual Musso's again. You have to eat someplace when you live in a hotel room and that is close and had the best food in Hollywood and is not expensive. The night before when Nina had dropped in to see me, we had been exclaiming about the number of people you meet there. I had said that I wouldn't even be surprised if Chuck Flynn came walking in. Looking at her so happy, I got to thinking about the thing which would make me happiest and started to play around the idea that you might walk in. My eyes lit on the sleeve of a J. G. and I imagined it was you and I broke into a big welcoming smile...just letting my imagination runaway with me. The poor startled young man thought I was a pretty bold flirt I am afraid. I had to jerk myself out of it in a hurry and quickly turn my head. After dinner we went out on the street...I was bound on my way home but Lee walked up and wanted Nina to go see somebody with him and Pat asked me if I would go with him to visit this woman who is sort of flirting with T.B. and has to stay in bed most of the time. He said she was an old friend of his and truly one of the few intellectuals he knew. I thought it would be interesting and besides it seemed like a good idea to go visit her so I said I would. She was only up the street a few feet from the hotel. Therein the evening was disappointing. She was very well informed but very dogmatic and her approach to everything was completely emotional and illogical. It was almost annoying to talk to her because she was so positive. The conversation was stimulating in one way and stifling in another. I was rather anxious to leave after the first hour but since she was a friend of Pat's I couldn't say anything...s we stayed there. After that we went down and discussed it over a cup of coffee. God save me from positive people. When I disagreed with her she dragged out a notebook filled with quotations from books she had read and said them as if they were the gospel truth. That was supposed to end the argument. When I had temerity to disagree with Edington...tish tish.

That was my last evening. Sunday was rather a solitary one although it was rater interesting in the morning. Martha Shaw came in to get her check. I was dressing to go out to eat so she waited for me. Then Lee Gale called and said that he would be right over and we would all go together. SHE had his current flame with him... some girl who sings in a night club on La Brea. I warned Martha that she was about to meet a couple of characters and not to be surprised by anything. Tat Lee is so amazing he never fails to amuse me except when I am in a cynical mood. The other night he came in popping in here with two decks of marked cards. I expressed curiosity of how it was done and I got a liberal education. Nobody could put anything over on me. But we all started walking down the street and some character said Hello Galey to him.. I asked who the afore said was and Lee answered, "Oh that's Frank the Burglar"..."Is he a real burglar? I gasped. "Certainly" Lee answered. "What kind of burglaries does he do? "Ohh the specializes in house burglaries:,, he said. I give up. I guess he as a real burglar too. I hope you aren't shocked by all this honey. It used to bother me but now I am just amused. I'll soon be gone. Well, of course I didn't have much room for talk when Bill Bowles, the one from Seattle came literally floating up to me in the sweetest way possible and greeted me with the ecstatic little cries. Martha went four years to Pasadena so she didn't think anyone was such a character. We heard Gilmore Brown speak the other day...I told you I believe about going to William Shakespeare's Birthday party. I remarked that he swished when he spoke publicly and that got her started about him. She is intimately acquainted with Vic Mature and told me just how he got all those leads in Pasadena. It is the traditional thing it seems...the way in which all young men over there get a succession of leads. She said he had never been able to respect him since. I must say that I was amazed and I thought how terribly surprised your would be. Enough of the dirt.

Remember about getting that ballot darling...That is unless you want Hoover to be Secretary of State under Dewey...I am enclosing a clipping from Frey Pearson today that may interest you. Elections at a time like this do seem a waste of national energy but since they can't be suspended, it is the job of everyone of us to do his bit to see that they don't turn out wrong. I understand that they have made it quite simple for servicemen from California to get the ballot. Imagine that...Earl Warren keynoting the Republican convention. From district attorney to possible vice-president in a leap and a half. The Republicans are nuts...especially since they threw Willkie out.

I receive the most unsatisfactory letters from Mother lately.. She writes with carbon, devoting one section to each of us...I must complain that mine seems invariable to be the fourth carbon and that I wish she would get some onions skin paper so I could read it. Buddy is now in Tempe, Arizona and Bobby in Merced. I get a letter from Daddy practically every day. He has really been enjoying arranging his bank account business. I think he just likes the correspondence.

Well darling, this is about thirty for tonight. I am going to mail this right away so it will go out to San Francisco tonight.

All my love to you honey darling...keep writing

Jane

XXXX

From: Lt. (jg) Charles Flynn
To: Mrs. E. M. Flynn
U.S.S. Gamble
1321 Grand Ave
c/o Postmaster
Everett, Washington.
San Francisco, California
28, April 1944 At Sea

Dear Mom:

Well we get in tomorrow morning early, and I want to have a letter ready to go over to the beach with the first trip. I expect to have some mail from both you and Jane tomorrow, so I hope I am not disappointed. In another envelope I am sending you the last batch of stories that I sent to Chet. They will probably get to you at the same time this does. As you see, we got to someplace a little different this time, and it was very interesting indeed. My room-mate and I went over two different afternoons and looked the place over. Those marines sure lead a rugged life. I am pretty lucky, I realize now, in being in the kind of spot that I am. We've got it all over them in the way of comfort and chances of getting home all in one hunk.

We had some pretty grim weather the last couple of days, but today is lovely, and the sea had died down till it looks like a lake. It never bothers me much, but some of the lads get awfully green looking when she is bouncing around like a cork. The only trouble with that is that you get so tired just standing your watch that there is nothing else you can do except eat and sleep. As a result, you get behind with your letters and all the other work you have to do in running a division on board a ship. I am all caught up now though, so I thought I would bang out a few lines to you.

I thought about you a lot two days ago honey, and I know you got through the day in good shape. It's a tough anniversary to remember, but one that we can never forget. He was an awful good guy pop was. Do you remember the cocky Irish way he would put his hat on when he was waiting for us to go down town? He sure had a wonderful face. So expressive and so full of understanding for the human race. Many a mid-watch I spend remembering him and little things he said and did. You have an awful lot of time to think in the middle of the night, when the whole ship is blacked out and you are steaming through the night.

I wonder if you know that. No matter how many ships we are with or whether there is a moon or not, even if it's raining cats and dogs, there is never a light showing on any of the ships at night. Yet we keep from running into each other, make turns and keep going at our normal speed all night. So you can see that the officer of the deck has something to do even though it is nighttime.

I don't know for sure, but I don't think we will stay in tomorrow, however we will be back at one of our old stamping grounds in four or five days, and I'll get another letter off to you from there. We are supposed to spend a few days in port, so I'll have time to get off a couple of really good letters. Those letters to Chet tell you the most interesting things I have been doing lately. That spear fishing is really very much fun. Of course I am not too good at it yet, but I've speared four or five already, and I'm getting better all the time.

Well honey I've got about five or ten minutes to go put on a shirt, have a cup of coffee and go up on watch. If we stay in tomorrow night I will answer any mail I may get in the morning. If we don't, I will drop you another letter in about five days. Keep the old chin up honey, and always remember that I love you very much!

All me love — Chas XXXXXXXX

Commodore Hotel
San Francisco, California May 7, 1944
Letter 91

Hello Honey Darling;

Well, I had to go away without hearing from you, but maybe there will be a letter waiting for me when I get there. I am holding thought. I just sent the Lathams my forwarding address and I'll give it to you now too darling. It is Jane Patten Flynn, APO 5265, Care of Army Postmaster, San Francisco, California.

Honey, everything has been so rushed and exciting that I find it kind of hard to settle down and write a letter and make it sound sensible. I think I was in a virtual daze all day Friday getting the final things packed. Then I got that awful jittering about missing the train that used to drive you so crazy last year...I nearly died of relief when we finally got on and finally got on and got all that luggage on. Honestly honey you have never seen so many bags in your life. I counted thirty-five. The Lark is the most gorgeous train I have ever been on. It definitely did not put me in mind of the Lehigh Valley Special. We had compartments. Yesterday the army met us at the train and then took us to this hotel. It isn't so hot, and they apologized...you remember darling. We stayed here the second time we were here for the first two nights. If I had only known then that you could have your breakfast sent up. Last night I went up to see Pat Zemmer and we had dinner at the Iron Pot. It was just as good as ever and just as cheap. Then we saw Megan and Harry who just got in. I wasn't so impressed with him, frankly. You should have seen Ollie, He nearly fainted when I walked in in my uniform. It was good to be back and see all those people. I dropped up to see Pat and Jerry Strauss. They have the most adorable little baby girl that you have ever seen. She is just ten weeks old. She has long black hair and the prettiest little round face. I changed her diaper. They were quite surprised that I was an expert at it. They wouldn't let me in the Black Cat because it was out of bounds. They said that actually they had no jurisdiction over me, but they would prefer I didn't go in. So we didn't.

This morning we slept until eleven and then had our breakfast sent up, and then I typed out a script and phoned-Mother, and she phoned Daddy in Portland, and he phoned me. I wrote the Lathams a letter with my address in it, and then I decided I would write a letter to my honey darling.

It is pretty hard to believe, darling, that I am actually on the way, and it is turning out so wonderfully. All the girls are simply grand, and we get along beautifully.

It makes me pretty lonesome for you to be up here where we had such a good time together darling. Maybe before too long again we can be here together. When I was sitting up at Pat's, I caught myself running to the window whenever a cable car came up...I just couldn't believe that you wouldn't be getting off one. But not you darling. It was an awfully disappointing feeling.

San Francisco looks just as good as ever, and I still love it. Maybe you identify a city with the happy times you have had in it, and I really think that ours here was just about the happiest time of our marriage — in spite of the suspense and the not knowing every day if you would be here the next. Ollie said that he had to give me some Rainier to commemorate you, and I said I would pick it up on Monday.

Honey darling, I love you so much and miss you so. I know I shouldn't keep talking about it, but being up here just brings you back to me a little too vividly for my own peace of mind...not that it isn't wonderful to remember, but you keep wishing that it could be repeated right this very minute.

Pat said that she hadn't had a letter from Fry in a long time and that she used to get one about every ten days. She was a little worried about him, but I suppose he is fine. I haven't the vaguest idea how to get in touch with Truman. T. B. Hinkle. I don't know whether that is his middle initial though. But this party doesn't answer the phone. I'll keep trying and inform you if there are any results.

Well, honey, I guess I will get to re-organizing my bags a little bit because they are picking up the luggage the first thing in the morning. Be good and be safe honey.

All my love to you darling, Jane

Commodore Hotel San Francisco May 9, 1944
Letter 92

Hello Sweetheart,

This time I'm afraid I've really lost my fountain pen. It's been missing for two days, but I'm still sure it's in this darned hotel room — Feeling in a handwriting mood tonight though; I am compelled to use a pencil.

As you can see, darling, I'm still here & probably will be for a few days longer. San Francisco is pretty nice though, and I am quite enjoying it. The only trouble is, darling, and that trouble looms large in my life — that Friday will make four weeks since I have heard from you. Tonight I called the Lathams, but there was no one home — just the girl next door who was over taking care of the baby. I called to tell them that I would be here a little longer and that if there was a letter from you to wire me and then to forward it. Even if I didn't get it, to know that there was one would be a great happiness. I know I will probably seem like a silly idiot to you darling, but after that, I phoned Mother & Daddy and asked them to call your mother and to tell her the news of me and to inquire tactfully, without worrying her, when she had last heard from you & to let me know. They said they would wire me back when they got in touch with her. I know that your letters are probably going someplace else darling, but the thought of going away without hearing from you just gives me cold chills.

Since I wrote you yesterday — what has happened to me — well, we have been trying to change our hotel because these quarters are pretty grim, and we are really entitled to better, but there isn't a single darned thing in the city — the army has invited us to stay in the guest house at Fort Mason, but it is so darned far out that we really didn't want to. Besides, we felt that we would just be besieged and while our job is entertaining, it is not in a purely social way, and we didn't think it was a good idea. We may have to come to it though.

I'm awfully happy with this group of girls, darling. I haven't known any that I liked more — besides they wear well and are grand to live with. Such a variety of types, too — everyone different and everyone so darned pretty and nice and intelligent. I am just delighted with them.

I had an awfully nice time last nite. I met that Jack Hanover on the street — remember him. He was waiting for orders. I went out to dinner with him and with three of the other girls who were with army lieutenants. We never did get dinner until after midnight, as we went up to his room at the Mark Hopkins and had a drink, then two, then three. Then we went to the Officers Club at the Fairmont & danced & then — it was midnight so we finally ate at Neijas. He asked me to go to dinner tonite, but he got his orders and had to leave. It was just as well as far as I was concerned because I was tired and I've had a lovely evening in the hotel room just lolling around & washing my hair and my clothes and writing to my honey — meaning you, pal.

I wore my uniform today. I can't get over the darned thing it still amazes me. It is fun to wear in the daytime but at nite you feel a little gaudy.

Honey darling, I'm so sleepy I can't stay awake, so I guess I better hit the downey. So much love to you my darling. Perhaps tomorrow will bring a letter. (Remember Honey, J.P.F., APO #5265, Care of A.P.M., S.F., Caly.) All my love, Jane

May 10, 1944
Letter 92
Fairmont Hotel,
San Francisco, California

Hello Sweetheart;

This is going to be a letter written in haste. I was downtown looking over the stores this afternoon with the plan in mind of coming home and taking the typewriter out on the balcony and writing a letter to you, and when I got home, there were the orders to leave waiting for us. So I have been dashing around like mad ever since. It is now one in the morning, and the last thing to do is to write to my honey.

I am pretty worried about leaving without having a letter from you, but the worry has been relieved in the last day because I had a letter from your Mother this morning, and she told me all about what you said to her, so I feel almost as if I had received your letters. I am almost wondering what they are like, darling, aside from the fact that they are wonderful because it has been so long. But I know that there will probably be some waiting for me and that everything is alright.

Gee, honey, I am getting like you. There isn't much that I can tell about what I have been doing because it would give something away. One thing I can tell you though is that we moved up here to the Fairmont and have been living in the lap of luxury. I am convinced that this is my favorite hotel in San Francisco and that we have to stay here for at least a little while when you come home. We have a suite...in fact, two with three girls apiece in them. We have a living room complete with radio and more than all the comforts of home. I kind of hate to leave it because it has such a beautiful balcony. It isn't as good as the Top of the Mark, but it almost is. I've been missing a lot of *sleep* lately because I so love to go out on the balcony at night and look at it, and in the morning, I think it's an awful waste of time to be sleeping when you could look at the view.

Tonight I went out with Pat Zemmen and a friend of hers who flies overseas for Consolidated. We went to the Cirque room and then over to the neighborhood of the Iron Pot. We went up to see Ann Parkhill and Johnny Wrognt in Johnny's apartment, and Annie looks just wonderful. She has gained a little weight, but it is very becoming.

Darling, this letter is written in sort of code. I hope that you can read it. Tomorrow I shall start writing you a very long one that will go over days and days and days. In the meantime, remember that I love you and that my address is Jane Patten Flynn, C.S.O., O.S.U. # 237, APO # 5265, San Francisco, California.

All my love to you honey,
Jane

May 12, 1944
Jane Patten Flynn U.S.O...O.S.U. #237 A.P.O. 5265
San Francisco, California
Note new address on envelope

Hello Honey;

I'm afraid that was a heck of a letter that I wrote you last night, but I had been in such a hurry, and I was so tired, and then going out with Pat Zemmer made me later too, and I was so dead that I am afraid that you will think the darned thing was in code, the typing was so bad. I took one look at it this morning before I mailed it and threw up my hands in holy horror, but there wasn't time to redo it, so I just mailed it and trusted that you could read it.

I'm afraid I sound like a phonograph record, but today it is four weeks since I have heard from you, and heaven knows how long it will be now. I trust that there will be something waiting for me when I get there. It would be a big disappointment if there weren't. Now I know how you feel when you don't get your mail for a long time.

You know honey, I have been reading the censorship regulations, and there is absolutely nothing that I can say about what I have been doing or what I am doing now. It is just amazing. I understand that this is even more strict than others, too, so there is just nothing that I can say except that I am just fine, and this is terribly interesting. In fact, it's fascinating, and I feel so darned lucky to have an experience like this during war time. It certainly makes you understand a lot more. I am beginning to realize how absolutely one-side was my view of the war and the people in it. Mine was simply concerned with people coming home on leave and with the highlights of their experiences. Interesting as this is to me, it is so evident that there is so much that is boring and monotonous and inconvenient. But that gives you more understanding of the whole thing. Of course, I am looking at it from the standpoint of a person who doesn't have a set routine and isn't busy enough. That situation will soon be remedied however. The schedule for this evening was to have been for me to type up some scripts, but Dorothy has disappeared with the material, so that is impossible. We have to give some sort of variety show. We all have our separate acts, but they have to be coordinated. Since we weren't hired primarily for that, we were given no help on its organization, so we just have to worm it up for ourselves. We will have to do it within a few days, so tomorrow we will have to get busy. Personally, I am not very worried about my own repertoire, aside from the fact that I haven't had much chance to try it out in front of an audience...but getting them all together is the thing.

Do you know what honey, it was just a year ago today that we arrived in San Francisco. Remember those days of suspense, but what a wonderful time we managed to have in between the times of your reporting...Number one August Alley and Ollie and the beer and our trips on the cable car down to Fisherman's wharf and peeling the shrimp and throwing the remains from the side of the cable car...then the whole pound of shrimp would be gone by the time we got home, and we'd get some beer and start in on the crab. And remember the afternoons with Viv and Fry in the Manx hotel and the Commander and his Sue. Someday I'll tell you something funny about that and where I am right now. It was a wonderful time darling, and I'll never forget it.

Well, honey, this is about all there is to say for tonight. Now that my letters to you are censored, they will probably become more and more personal, but I guess you won't mind that. It gives me an awful nostalgia though. All my love to you honey, Jane

Jane Patten Flynn
USO — OSU #237
APO #5265
San Francisco, Calif.

Dearest Honey,

I'm afraid I haven't been a very good correspondent on this little trip, but the truth of the matter is there hasn't been anything I could say — so <u>what</u> to write. I can't mention where I am — the people here or what I'm doing. Except I'm not doing much but sitting in a deck chair getting a suntan and generally enjoying myself most of the time. Honestly honey, this has been the most amazing experience. I never cease to wonder that such a thing should happen to me even though our life hasn't been exactly prosaic at all times. I don't suppose you would find anything unusual about it, but gosh, I've certainly learned a lot. The living conditions are pretty grim — in fact worst than you would expect, due to the type of conveyance — but you soon get adjusted to that. The five other girls are all awfully nice. There isn't a "bitch" among them. We get along beautifully. You know Dorothy Southworth, and I've mentioned Martha Shaw — the girl in whose company I used to neutralize my shots with beer.

Tomorrow nite we have to put on a show. I'm not looking forward to that but it's our bound duty and part of what we're being paid for — but the problem of six "actresses" getting together a variety show is a little difficult. Three — no, four of the girls are singing — they all have different styles, and we had no accompanist. Then when one was found, the problem of finding a place to rehearse was really something. By hook or by crook, we'll get it on though. I'm going to do "Casey" & "The Waltz" — they are the only two sketches in the whole thing. The second I just don't see how I'm going to do *with a P.A. System.*

Oh, honey, it just seems perfectly amazing to me that not even two weeks ago I was in Hollywood. I'm so glad to be gone — everything is so different here — it's like getting back into a real world again — a little grim at times but real.

Oh yes, honey — remember in San Francisco I said I lost my pen — well, I really did — I searched and searched, but I can't imagine what happened to it. Well, I have a new one — I tried to duplicate the one that you gave me but had to take one a little different — this is a Parker 51, and it is grey and silver — I'm sick about the other, but it may possibly turn up yet because I have left messages at both hotels.

My goodness, honey — it's getting near eight in the evening now, and it's still middle of the day warmth — I do love this, although I wouldn't like it to get too hot — this though is wonderful — I could bask in it forever. I completely broke out of uniform today because of the heat — it is not against regulations and is much too hot for flannel —

Honey, this is the next morning — We are just starting rehearsal in a minute, and I imagine we will be at it all day, so I'll finish this up in a hurry — because in the morning we'll be someplace else, if you get me. There is a general air of elation and excitement which is much fun.

So until tomorrow nite, my darling, I'll bid you au revoir. I love you, honey — (Martha just spilled a coca cola all over a green billiard cloth — we were invited for refreshments before rehearsal. She said "That's my pet trick. I just wanted you all to see it before the trip was ended.")

Be good, darling, and be safe — I love you with all my heart.

All my love, Jane

I'm praying like the dickens that there will be a letter waiting for me.

TENTATIVE ITINERARY FOR MAINLAND GIRLS

Saturday, May 21.
9:30 am Arrive on Oahu. Go to quarters at DeRussy.
1:00 pm Leave DeRussy to attend matinee "Free For All"
Schofield Little Theatre, 5:00 pm Dinner at Kemee Farms
7:00 pm Attend performance "Love Rides the Rails" at Pali Area
10:30 pm Return to DeRussy

Sunday, May 22
Morning free
Afternoon for publicity photographs
6:00 pm Leave DeRussy to attend performance "Out World" at
*   Bloch Recreation Center*
10:00 Return to DeRussy

Monday, May 23
Morning free. Identification to be arranged.
1:30 pm Leave DeRussy to give reading of "Personal Appearance"
*   in Band Room at 1:45*
6:00 Leave DeRussy to attend performance "Out of the Frying
*   Pan" at Schofield Little Theatre*
10:00 pm Return to DeRussy
Tuesday, May 23
9:30 am Leave DeRussy for song and dance audition on stage at
*   Farrington Hall.*

May 21, 1944 U.S.O.-O.S.U. #237 A.P.O. #963
San Francisco, Calif.

Dearest Honey Darling;

What a wonderful surprise awaited me yesterday. All your missing letters in one bunch...I nearly died of excitement. I read the last one first to see what you were doing recently...just think, it was only written last Sunday...that is a week ago today...then I arranged them in order (One was missing) and sat down and lit a cigarette and had a cup of coffee and had a thoroughly happy time getting caught up with you. The things to Chet were very fine pieces of writing, dear, and I was awfully proud of you. The thing that broke my heart was that yesterday they met us and didn't even give us a chance to get cleaned up...started out on this schedule right away...I didn't get to read any but the first one, and then we had to dash off, and I had to wait until after ten at night to read the rest of them. I nearly died of suspense.

I haven't been able to figure out whether the reason we started off with such a routine was that they were trying to test us to see if we could take it or whether it was that they had been waiting so long for us to come that they just had to get started right away. At any rate, there were a bunch of tired little girls all day long. I just struggled to keep my head up and cheerful. A good drink would have helped matters, but that wasn't on the list of activities. About eight last night we did have one that was thrown down standing up and then on to more activities. Finally though, I got my second wind, and I really enjoyed the evening, thank heaven. I'll tell you about it later.

From what I have seen of this place, honey, I am perfectly delighted, enchanted, and in love with it. The weather is so perfect and the scenery so beautiful, and believe me, I have seen a lot of it in this short time...practically the whole thing as far as distance is concerned. Everyone has just knocked themselves out to be nice to us. We even have a whole house to ourselves...three bedrooms, and tomorrow we start having a Korean woman for a maid. We really need her because with the schedule that is laid out for us, there is no time for housework. They presented us with a typed itinerary for the week when we arrived. There was one evening off. That was tonight. But tonight was ruined as far as getting any unpacking or laundry done because we are reading

Personal Appearance tomorrow, and we spent the evening reading aloud. I noticed in your letters that you were a little worried
about my social life. You needn't be darling because there just
isn't any time for it. As far as I can see, there won't be any except
that which is official and supervised. The program is much too
filled already. Tuesday we read "Blithe Spirit" and Wednesday,
"Twelfth Night"...so the next evenings late will be spent brushing
up on those.

So many things have happened since yesterday that I just skip
around in trying to explain them all. Yesterday we went to two plays
and to lunch and to dinner with various way stops to see different
theatres and various points of interest...and all this without even
a chance to brush the uniform that we had been wearing for so
long. It was darned interesting though. Captain Evans is perfectly
charming and so very nice to us. The rest of the people in the Special Service are also wonderful and just knock themselves out with
welcome. I only hope that I will be able to read well tomorrow...I
mean be in a good mood for it...so that all their welcome will be
vindicated. From what I have seen of their work, it is very fine,
and the audiences are something that you just dream about...the
most responsive and appreciative that I have ever seen. I got as
much kick out of looking at their faces as out of looking at the play.
When you see all those poor kids and how hungry they are for
something outside their routine, it just makes you want to work
all the time to do your best for them. Movies are wonderful, but
there is really something that they get out of seeing actual flesh
and blood people up there on the stage that can't be duplicated by
the movies. Yesterday afternoon we went to Schofield Barracks
(I think it is alright to mention it) and saw a musical which was
simply grand. All the music was written by two boys here, and
they did a fine job. Then, after we had dinner, we started driving,
and believe me, it was a long ride, to a place where they were doing
a melodrama on the caravan stage that they have. They tow it
from place to place. It was on the way there that we had a drink
at some Officer's club. The costumes and the scenery were simply
amazing, they were so good. The person who designs the scenery
is that friend of Will's named Freddie Stover...he used to come
up to the house with Will when we were living together on North
Sycamore...remember he was tall and thin and was from Pasadena.
After that, we stopped by at the Hams Club, which is a place they

have fixed up on the campus for themselves, and had coffee and hamburgers. I was really afraid that some of the girls would be sick, they were so tired, but we all managed to get a good night's sleep. We had the morning free today, but in the afternoon we did publicity photographs on the beach. Then we went to dinner, and then Eloise and I took a walking tour with the lieutenant who is the censor and who is very nice, and then we came home and read the play, and now I am writing to you. We went to the Willard Inn where we were to have stayed. It was very lovely, but we liked our own quarters better. Then we went to the Halekulani...if that's the way you spell it. It's a hotel where most of the Navy seems to stay. It was perfectly lovely...I was almost awed. You probably have been there.

We are close to the water and have a place to go swimming if there is any time. I forgot to mention that I went swimming today after the publicity pictures. Imagine going swimming on Waikiki beach! (I think that's alright to mention too...although these are really censored.) (We find out the censorship rules in the morning.) The water was so warm and lovely that I wasn't very energetic. I just lay on my back and floated and looked at the sky. As a matter of fact, I almost went to sleep.

Honey, it was so wonderful to get caught up with you. Reading all those letters almost made me believe that you were really here with me instead of so far away. Oh, honey darling, I'm so tired that I can hardly hold my head up. I'm afraid I'll have to stop writing. Just remember that I love you, and tomorrow night, I'll write you another letter and try to make it better. I love you with all my heart.

Millions and millions of love to you honey, Jane

[V-Mail letterhead:
To: Lt. (JG) Charles. J. Flynn
From: Jane P. Flynn, civilian
U.S.S. Gamble
Entertainment Sect. — S.S.O.
Care of Fleet P.O.
APO #963 c/o P.M.
San Francisco
San Francisco]
May 25, 1944

Hello Darling;

I know you don't like V-Mail, but the truth of the matter is I'm out of stationery and haven't had a minute or an opportunity to go get any — that busy and I'm not kidding. Well, honey, your little Janie has really grown up I guess — I am actually going to play Carole Arden in P.A. — I find it amazing, too, and I'm also going to have to find a blonde wig. I knew I'd changed since you left but not enough to do that part. It's a big responsibility, and I do hope I'll be able to do it well. There is so little time though, as we are doing a variety show at the same time. I learned a whole routine today — complete with picks & bumps — I'm stiff. I'll do "Spring" among other things in that. I brought a copy. Doesn't that bring back old memories! I talked to Mrs. Armstrong today. She called because she had seen my picture in the paper. I'll send you one but have to check the censorship regulations first. Gee they've been all over here for three days — practically noteriety. She was so nice to me. She said the Skipper would have a message for you shortly — as soon as she saw me. I'll try to meet her soon, but with this schedule, I don't know when. Every minute of tomorrow is taken — I'll only have 6 hrs. sleep tonite, and I haven't even started to memorize my lines. Don't *worry*, no social life for Janie. But the work is certainly fun. I love it, and Evans is wonderful. Goodnight, my darling. I love you an awful lot — Take care of yourself — All my love, Jane

[V-Mail letterhead:
To: Lt. (JG) Charles. J. Flynn
From: Jane P. Flynn, civilian
U.S.S. Gamble
Entertainment Sect. — S.S.O.
Care of Fleet P.O.
APO #963
San Francisco
Care of Postmaster
San Francisco]
May 29, 1944

Hello Sweetheart;

   I know this is a dirty trick — writing another letter to you on V-Mail, but I'm at rehearsal, and it's so much easier to carry the blanks and write you between scenes. This way I should be able to write you one or two every day and then a long letter every few days when I get time — Time has become the essence of my life lately — not a spare minute. We are not going to the Marshalls as soon as we thought we were because of the time not being auspicious. I guess I never told you that we were because I thought I couldn't, but I since found out that I could if I didn't mention any specific locations — we are going to take Personal Appearance and a Variety Show and then do PA the first nite and a Variety Show the second — they have marvelous material for the V. show — original music & lyrics and all written by a couple of boys here — It is running here now and approximately the same show will go — minus the production numbers of course and with us in the cast. The others do the singing and I do sketches. We are opening P.A. here the 14th, so that doesn't give much time — it's especially difficult for me with a part so foreign to me, but I think by that time, I'll be OK. Honey darling, you'll die when you hear this, but I have to bleach my hair — not platinum but a darker blonde. You put a red rinse in it for the performance and wash it out for regular life. They'll take a sample and die it back when I'm finished, of course. I quailed at first, but now I'm kind of looking forward to it. I'm so tan, I think I'd make a good-looking blonde.

   I'll continue this on another blank, darling. In the meantime, I love you so very very much — Jane

[V-Mail letterhead:
To: Lt. (JG) Charles. J. Flynn
From: Jane P. Flynn, civilian
U.S.S. Gamble
Entertainment Sect. — S.S.O.
Care of Fleet P.O.
APO #963
San Francisco
Care of Postmaster
San Francisco]
May 29, 1944

Hello, darling; this is the second half of the letter — Although I guess you could read it first if you want to.

Life has been definitely on the strenuous side since we got here — you have to have good health to keep it up, especially with the change in weather — but I'm doing pretty well. I've gone through a couple of days in a haze of tiredness but always get my second wind. Of course, we are besieged by all kinds of men, as you will know, but I sort of walk blindly through — speaking politely and impersonally to all of them — so you don't need to worry about me, honey. We've only had one evening off so far — As far as being out, all I've done is go to dinner twice — once on the evening off and yesterday in the two hours between rehearsals — with a lieutenant from the ship. He's the first lieutenant. I enjoyed talking to him because he looks very much like you and your lives were almost an exact parallel. He bicycled around Europe at the same time you did and went just about all the same places. So I can talk all about you. That's the extent of my social activities — now there won't be any, as we don't have any free time. But this is terribly exciting work, and I want to spend all my time at it. The trip will be one of the greatest things that has ever happened to me — Just think of the pleasure it will be in our power to bring all those poor characters. Gosh — it's a big thing.

Write me, darling — I love you so darned much, Be good I'll write again tomorrow — All my love to you—Jane

2 June 1944 In Port

Dear Jack and Hazel;

I suppose, by this time, you have branded your son-in-law as not only an ingrate, but also an illiterate who is unable to put pen to paper. Not that I could blame you much, but there is one mitigating factor in defense. Last Feb., shortly after I received the two books that you so thoughtfully sent me for Xmas (which not only I, but the entire Wardroom enjoyed thoroughly), I wrote you a very nice, long letter. The same day I wrote Parker Williams, Jane, and a boy from Cornell. It must have been one of those unfortunate shipments of mail, for no one got those letters. I have had a howl from Parker and also from the boy from Cornell. Jane told me, in one of her last letters, that you have never heard from me, so that's why it was. I'm sorry as the dickens, and I'll try and cover all the ground in this one to make up for it.

To get back to the books, it was so damn nice of you to think of me and that very lovely card that you sent me. I guess I am just lucky as all get out. So many of the lads seem to have in-law trouble (and a lot of them just plain marital troubles), that it is wonderful to have people like you to be related to, even if it is only by marriage to Janie. What I'm trying to say is that I love the whole family very much, individually and collectively.

Well, that's enough of that. Why is it, when you are trying to say something that it is so simple and easy to think and feel, that it becomes such a problem to get it on paper without feeling like "orphan Annie" in the Sunday comic strip? C'est la vie. Speaking of books. Our reading problems have been solved recently. An organization called "Council on Books in Wartime, Inc." has been doing a grand job. Available to us now are all the current best-sellers, as well as the top books in the last ten years, plus the standard works. They are printed very much on the order of the popular twenty-five cent paper books, and are free to the armed forces. They are not condensations but the entire book, and they are available in such numbers as to relieve any and all reading problems. Also, they make available cloth-covered books, up to a certain number, depending on the size of your ship. Then, above all that, they will exchange any cloth books you are through with for an equal number of new books. When we got the word about two weeks ago, several of us, including the Captain, who is a terrific reader, took off our shirts and went to work on the wardroom library. It was stacked to the eyes with such goodies as "The Brand Stealer," "Riders of the Purple Sage," and the "Mystery of Lady Whoosie Drawers." The best we put aside to give to the crew, and then we got about six hundred of the new books. About a hundred were cloth-bound and the balance paper.

We retained the more worthwhile books until we have all read them, and the balance, largely detective and western stories, we used to start a crew's library. I don't mean we slighted them, but their tastes in lit. are, on the average, are pretty low. Their favorites seem to be comic books, when they get them through the mail, so you see. Also, anyone can have any book from our library simply by asking permission, so all is well aboard the Gamble along literary lines.

Of course, reading helps pass the time, but what this ship needs more than anything else right now is a few days in a big liberty port. Eight and a half months now since we left S.F., and there are some men who have never left the ship. The extent of excitement for those who do is a couple of beers and a softball game on some hot, steaming little island's so-called "recreation center." A rather poor excuse for "Wine, women and song." At least the officers have a few clubs scattered through this area now, but with the amount of stuff that is out here now, even those lose much of their charm. It is possible for us to go over and get good and boiled once in a while though, and that helps. At least, it does in my case. Not that it takes much in this climate, a very in-expensive spree, I must say, but I find that about once every three weeks, keeps the tension from building up inside me. I guess it's a rather weak-kneed arrangement, but you have no idea just how grim this life can be out here. I'm not complaining, rather just stating a fact. How men in their right minds can choose the sea as a profession beats me. It's big, it's lonely, and worst of all you are so damn far away from your wife! Gets rough, too!

But about this liberty port. We are underway this afternoon (by the way, we are swinging on the hook now, and it is 0130 in the morning. I have the mid-watch, but in port it's pretty relaxed), for a port that might very easily be the last stop before the so-called liberty port. I think the chances are about fifty-fifty that we will make it. For the sake of the ship's morale, I hope we make it. Of course, I have the edge on everybody because of my five weeks in Pearl a while back. At least I saw lights in houses and cars on the streets and observed that girls still wear tight skirts and jiggle in places when they walk, but most of the lads on here have almost forgotten. I was censoring a letter the other day, and one seaman said, among other things, "Thank God for the movies we have when we are in port. They are the only thing we have to tell us that women are still built different from men."

Another officer and myself have found something to do though that takes some of the curse off this duty. That's spear-fishing. Our equipment consists of 1/4 inch steel rods 6-8 feet long, notched like an arrow on one end and with a collapsible barb on the other. We fire them with a sling-shot arrangement made out of inner-tube rubbers and a six-inch, hollowed-out section of broom handle. The spear is put through the hole in the handle; the sting is fitted to the notch; and when a fish swims within range, 3-15 feet, you just pull back and try and hit him. We are also equipped with underwater glasses. This boy's wife sent him some pairs from Honolulu, and he gave me a set. They fit very tightly around the eyes and prevent any water from leaking in. This gives us just as good vision under water as the fish. This morning was our biggest day so far. Ed got a 17 1/2 pound rock bass all by himself, and the two of us together, both spears in it, landed a 20 pound rock bass. We also got six others from one to three pounds. All this in an hour and a half! As I say, this was our biggest day, but we never come back without any fish anymore.

We work in and around coral heads and go down up to thirty-five feet. That's about as deep as I care to go. You see, we don't have any helmet or air hose or anything, just us holding our breath. It is the most beautiful place in the world. The coral is all colors of the rainbow, as are the fish, and the formations are simply fantastic. The nicest part of it is we can fish anywhere we happen to be. If we are way up in some forward area, the others are unhappy because there is no club, no recreational facilities, but it just makes us happier. The fishing is better and the water clearer. Not that it every gets very dirty, even in the crowdedest harbors. This morning I could see bottom at well over a hundred feet! I hope this doesn't sound silly to be so hipped on a sport, but in this area there is so little, that even a thing like this is nice to have to enjoy and preserve your sanity.

As we don't have the mess boys stand a watch in the pantry when we are in port, I just went up to the galley and got a cup of "joe." As you probably guess, that's Navy for coffee. But Navy coffee!! Wow, is that something. The men insist that they, the cooks, put some boiler compound in each batch. I wouldn't know, but I've dragged myself, half awake, up to the bridge to stand a mid-watch of a night and had one cup of coffee snap me right wide awake; as a matter of fact, almost snap me out of my skin. Is it strong! Of course, the cups hold just under a pint, which is quite a shot. Also, I drink it black, that is, no cream and only one teaspoon full of sugar. When I think of back in civilian life (wonderful phrase) how I used to put 1 1/2 teaspoons full into a small cup, my, my, how we change.

Our duty right now is pretty much on the dull side. No excitement for quite a spell now, but maybe things will pick up again. We were really having a time when we first came out last fall, but it's very tame now. The war seems to progress, as the French would say. Down here, things are moving along at a great clip, with bigger and better deals always in the offing. I wish to God that "second front" would open up, give the Russians a hand with the job and wind that phase of it up. The sooner that happens, the sooner we get everything out here, and the sooner I'll be marching down Tojo Blvd in Tokyo, tripping over my sword in the victory parade.

Well, I've covered the ground pretty thoroughly in an hour and a quarter. I slipped a carbon behind this, so I'll send that to Jane, but this is really to the whole family. So, when you finish, will you send it on to Mary and Buddy and Bobby? I'd write them all, but I'd have the same things to say to them all. But if you will all write and give me an address to answer, I promise that I will answer the day I get the letter. How about it, kids? Remember, I am your only brother-in-law to date, so how about telling me what goes on with each of you and building up my ebb tide morale? It's not really that bad, but I would love to hear from you all. Mary is or was in New York the last I heard. Buddy is in either California or Utah; I think California 'cause Jane said she saw you, and as to Bobby, I am completely in the dark.

Won't it be wonderful, Hazel, when this whole stinking mess is cleaned up for good and all to see all the component parts of your family together again around a wassail bowl! I hope when the time comes there will still be some wassail juice available. And Jack, Jane tells me that you did a neat trick on a piece of timber. What does that mean? Are you fixing to go back into the lumber business?

Seems like it might be a very right time, with about two-thirds of the world to be rebuilt. You should see the profitable outfits they have down here, and the docks and staging they make out of Philippine Mahogany yet. When I think what that stuff used to cost at home, even a veneer of it.

Well, people, I am about used up, but for me this is a pretty long letter. I would like to hear from all of you, and, as I say, I will be a good correspondent. What shows did you see in New York, Mary, and what kind of planes are you flying now, Buddy, and are you still in that college Marine Corps Reserve, Bobby, or are you going to active duty? See, look at all the things I don't know.

How is Ma Wee? Is she staying with you now, Hazel? If she is, give her a big hug and a kiss for me, and tell her that I will be around to handle it personally before very much longer. My personal opinion is if the Gods are good, we might get back for another overhaul sometime around the end of the year. Hold the thought!

All me love to all — Chas XXXXXXXXXX

P.S. Haven't heard from Jane since she left S.F. Thought I'd get a letter today, but no luck. Maybe tomorrow. Hope she didn't get sea sick! Chas

Jane P. Flynn, civilian
Entertainment Section, SSO APO #963
Care of Postmaster
San Francisco, California June 4, 1944

Hello My Darling;

I am enclosing in this a V-Mail blank that I started the other day when I was in the beauty shop and never finished. I'm sorry, honey, but just then they started in to work on me, and then I had to go back to rehearsal, and I have been literally running ever since then.

I have been phoning the Willard Inn every day for letters, but since the last two the other day, no more have come. It is wonderful to have them from you so quickly, darling. I don't suppose you will get mine any faster though. There is certainly a great bunch waiting for you somewhere, if you haven't received them by this time. It will be a happy day when a letter comes to the correct address and we are really in touch again.

I am finally a little happier about rehearsals — the part is beginning to come to me. It just goes to show you that you can do practically anything if you set your mind to it. Today Captain Evans told me that it was coming along very nicely...he volunteered the information. Such praise from him amounts to a eulogy from anyone else, so I was quite set up about it. The blonde hair really helps a lot. It is really gorgeous honey, and I do think it is a definite improvement on nature, as I may have said before.

Jeeps, what a busy time this has been. Here is a typical day... yesterday. In the morning we went out to Fort Shafter to help with the war bond thing they were having out there. That was really quite unusual, but they begged so that Captain Evans gave in in spite of rehearsal. That was fun and terribly interesting but definitely on the strenuous side, and of course, when we finished that, they insisted that we have lunch at the Officer's club and that they show us around the place. It was terribly interesting. I just wish that I could talk about it. Then, after that, we went to rehearsal. That wasn't quite so strenuous because I think they saw that we were looking a little tired, so they let us off early. Still, we had to all go to the formal dinner dance the Officers here were giving, so we had to dress for that. That was really very nice...I wore my new print formal which is very swish and had a lovely time dancing. It was fun to relax for a little while...besides, the bourbon was flowing freely, and that was fun too. That will be the last evening like that for quite a while though because we really work after this because we are opening a week from Wednesday. And don't worry, darling, your wife's head is not being turned. She is still too much worried about Carole Arden and wants to see a certain big blonde character very much.

I talked to Mrs. Armstrong once, but I just haven't been able to see her because they haven't given us a moment. She was very nice and terribly friendly. I haven't called Scoop Richardson yet because what is the use? I suppose I should though to be courteous. I will tomorrow. I told you that ??? said the other day that he would take a note to Valerie for me. He'll come over and get it the first night I'm free...Heaven knows when that will be...maybe next Sunday night.

Oh, honey darling, I wish I could see you tonight or any other night in the near future...or any day or just see you...that's the point. But I guess it's no use fussing. Did I mention to you the other day the coincidence that, on my birthday, you will have been gone exactly nine months. Think what could have happened. That reminds me, it is getting awfully close to the coming of the Price baby...perhaps I should write them a little note tonight of congratulation. If you'd like to, the address is 1435 Stone Canyon Road, West Los Angeles. Goodnight, honey, I love you with all my heart...I'll see you soon, I hope...All my love to you,

Jane I can't make marks for kisses any more, the censor tells me — So, kiss, kiss, KISS

Entertainment Section, S.S.O. A.P.O, #963
Care of Postmaster
San Francisco, California
June 1944

Dearest Honey Darlin;

I have been haunting the Willard Inn for the last few days but nothing from my honey. It may be possible that by this time you have received my correct address and that the next letters will come here, but then it is also very possible that you haven't been any place where you could mail letters for a while. At first they used to come singly but lately I have been used to having them come in batches. It will be quite a day when I know that you have received all the mail from me...it will be from so many different points that it will be like a travelogue. I will be quite relieved when I know you know where I am, honey, because to me it's a great help when I think I have even figured out where you are. Of course, I am probably completely wrong, but it's still a comfort.

You know, darling, when I was in Hollywood, I had more to tell you about what I was doing...here, it is really the same thing day after day. This is a typical one which is today. I set my alarm for eight o'clock because I had a ten o'clock appointment this morning to have some more bleaching done on these blonde tresses. Unfortunately, when I got home last night, I was pretty sleepy, so I set the clock an hour slow, so I didn't wake up until nine and had forty-five minutes to get <u>there.</u> it isn't very far and some kind characters gave me a ride in a jeep up to the Willard Inn to see if there was any mail from you...then I walked up to the beauty shop, stopping on the way to pick up a dress I had bought the other day...which had been altered. I wasn't particularly happy with it, but if you can even find an old sack to buy around here, you are lucky. Then I had the hair done. I had a sandwich under the dryer, and then they picked me up to go to rehearsal. We rehearsed until nearly five and then came back here. I had a quick swim...I swear I wasn't in the water more than fifteen minutes...the primary purpose was to put a-little life back in the old body. I came home and mixed myself a drink which I ate while dressing, went over to dinner, came back, and they picked us up for rehearsal. We rehearsed until nearly midnight and then came home. So now I am writing you, and I still have a little washin to do...I do not have anything to do until one tomorrow though, so I figure that I am rolling in the luxury of time. Every day since I last wrote you has been like that...oh yes, we had Wednesday night off. We got home about six, and I went to dinner and dancing at someplace called the Kewalo Inn with some of the girls and several officers on the Post...a very sane and quiet evening, and we were home by ten, naturally...not having a blackout pass. So, honey, that is my life...don't think I am complaining because I think it is wonderful. It is fun to be rehearsing so hard...especially on a thing for which you are not fitted. I have been terribly worried about it for several days now...it has been hard for me to think about anything else. But last night I think, with Captain Evans' help, I began to get it, and today I really think I am making a lot of progress. It's a work challenge, and I want to be able to do it well. So I think about it even when I'm supposed to be thinking about other things...I'm terribly absent-minded lately. But there is such a short time. Honey, I wish you could see me with the blonde hair and the silver lame dress that is just absolutely pinned to me...and some of the other things too — you wouldn't know your shy little character, although I am happy to report she isn't terribly shy any more...a definite character who will probably give you trouble — but I think you'll like it. I really don't mean that. I guess I'm troublesome enough as it is.

You know, honey, I don't think I have told you about my companions on this little venture. I know you don't know them and might not be interested, but I think you would be, besides if you should happen to meet up with them unexpectedly some day, I wouldn't want you to be completely unacquainted. First there is Eloise Hardt, my roommate. I thought, when I first met her, that she was a rather peculiar girl in certain ways, but now I think that she is definitely the most kindred soul, at least she's the easiest for me to get along with absolutely no annoyance...which should prove something about me. She has had definitely a different background... she's been a Power's model and knows thousands of people and definitely glamour and all that, but she has a fine carelessness about her appearance in spite of it all, which I definitely admire...there is nothing persnickety or snobbish about her in the smallest way. She is perfectly sincere and a grand person...not in a hypocritical or naive way...just because she knows what everything is about and goes her own freeway according to her own lights. Still, she is unhappy about a lot of things and thinks a lot and has a fine intelligence. Then there is Martha Shaw...the one I used to neutralize my shoes with...she is a little tiny brunette, very neat and precise with a well organized and well informed mind and a temper that flares up like a firecracker...thank heaven, she doesn't take it seriously, and you can make her laugh with some remark like "Martha has a very even temper. She's always angry." She's a little spoiled due to the fact that she has always lived at home, and she has been the breadwinner for her mother and grandmother, who did everything to make things easier for her at home, but she's coming out of that. She didn't know how to iron, for example, but she's learning. She went four years to the Pasadena playhouse, and that, combined with a definite flair, makes her a darned good actress. Actually, she's the one person who seems to know what makes me tick, and she has enough interest to try to work on me the right way. Of course I know what she's doing, but it makes me feel good anyway. She has taken upon herself the little task...which really isn't little, of making me believe that I can walk out on the stage as Carole Arden and not make a fool of myself...due to a different physical equipment than Betty Kennedy. We have sat in the kitchen far into the night with some coffee spiced with bourbon while we discussed this and that but mainly to persuade me out of my inferiority complex. She's little, cute, quick, and intelligent. Right now Martha is out in the kitchen talking to Margo...Margo Guilford is a redhead with the color of hair that looks as if it couldn't be true but is. She, I think, is a little more sophisticated and theatrical than the general run of us. She is engaged to Antonio Moreno...the actor, you know. She is the type that does the rumba and sings Spanish songs and has as sexy voice and a terrific sense of humor. Actually, I really can't understand why she isn't playing the part I am...she may not have enough acting experience...I don't know. Primarily she is an entertainer and is already working as the leading lady in a variety show called "Free for All"...it had been running for a while when we got here. They wanted to replace the current leading lady with one of us, so we went to the show and all of us immediately said that Margo was the one. She is the kind that says "My dear, you just don't realize..." on the surface and is a good sport and a terrific person underneath. Then there is little Nancy Worth...when you first look at Nancy, you think she is a glamour girl, with dark hair drawn straight back and usually a snood and very simple clothes, but she is really very little with a very wistful face, and after you have known her a while, the thing you think of is the girl in the Song of Bernadette, Bernadette, to be exact. She lives in a dream world of her own...she is twenty-three years old and seems to be absolutely untouched by life...I don't think she has ever had a bad thought. She is a terrific actress emotionally but not at all finished technically. She is a little psysic — she reads your fortunes with cards and the things she tells are perfectly remarkable. You know Dorothy Southworth...she is a lovely, fragile looking strawberry blonde, as you remember. Dorothy amazes me...of course she was saddled with the job of managing the accounts and being the unpleasant thing if she had been an unpleasant person. Personally, I dodged out of it, not because I thought it was unpleasant but because I was afraid of the responsibility...my addition has always been so faulty, but she has done a beautiful job and without antagonizing anyone... she also amazes me because I had had the impression that she was just perfect, and she really has a fine sense of things and a great enjoyment of all the things that happen to us.

Well, honey, that's that...I hope you've been able to read it through. Each person I have been with, including myself, has grown so obviously and so much, and it has only been a month since we have started.

Darling, it's terribly late, and I guess maybe I should go to bed because I have a full schedule tomorrow. I love you, honey...write often and take good care of yourself. I'll be seeing you, honey. All my love, Jane

From Jane P.Flynn, civilian
Entertainment. Section, SSO APO #963
Care of Postmaster
San Francisco, California

Dearest family.

You would have laughed if you could have seen me a few minutes ago…sitting over a pan filled with tincture of benzene inhaling like mad, for laryngitis and when you rehearse every day, that isn't good. However there is a very fine doctor right here who takes care of every little ailment and I have all the medicines available and him hovering about me to see if I am regaining my voice, The only part I like about it is that one of the cures 1s a cough medicine which is mixed with equal parts of whiskey.

All things are coming along beautifully. The main thing I have been doing and thinking about lately is that part of Carole Arden in Personal Appearance. It is so completely foreign to anything I have ever done that it has been really starting from the bottom. I am so happy about it the last couple of days though because I am beginning to get it…talk about a new personality. It is a complete metamorphosis. Today Captain. Evans went out of his way to tell me that it was coming along very nicely…that much praise coming from him is comparative to a eulogy from anyone else. It goes to show you that if you are expected to do something, you can always do it. I don't think I have ever had such good experience in my life…I do think though that the fact that we had my hair fixed has helped a lot. Did I tell you that I am now a blonde. Well‚ I am since last Thursday. Personally I think it is a definite improvement on nature. If I say so myself I look pretty darned good. I had some pictures taken the other day so I'll send you some as soon as I get them. I had rather looked forward to the change but didn't expect that it would turn out so well. Mary would die of envy because my hair is just a little bit lighter than hers and I have a tan. It was quite a tedious process. It took a whole afternoon. But it can be dyed right back the same color it was before. I am inclined to keep it this way for a while, maybe even long enough for you to see it. I am used to being fairly good looking but I have not been used to having people turn their heads every place I go and it is a pleasant sensation.

Our new radio is playing…very lovely music. One of the girls is ironing, one is washing, and the others are writing letters. It is quite different from last night. One of the girls opened in a musical review, she was replacing the lead...she had only had a little over a week rehearsal but she turned out to be just fine. The rest of us went to the dance at the Officer's Club here as we had the evening off...It was so much fun. It seems they have a formal dance once a month. I wore that print with the blonde hair on top of my head and rhinestone earrings, it did look lovely. The dancing. Was outdoors right on the ocean. The other girls went with officers here on the post but I went with that Ivy lieutenant that I said I had been out to dinner with. The boys here had had him over and so they asked him to come along. It all worked out beautifully. It was simply wonderful.

[V-Mail letterhead:
To: Lt. (jg) Charles. J. Flynn
From: Jane P. Flynn, civ.
U.S.S. Gamble
Entertainment Sect. S.S.O.
Care of Fleet Post office
APO #963 c/o P.M.
San Francisco
San Francisco
June 5, 1944

My darling — We were at rehearsal tonight when the news of the invasion of Europe came over the radio — it was pretty hard trying to be Carole for the rest of the time. I was thinking that it had been all of four years since Dunkirk, and I was thinking of all those poor boys on the beach in France tonight — but not unmixed with that was the hope that if all goes well, that will bring you back that much sooner — then we can concentrate on Your end of affairs. It has been a pretty stupendous day in the history of the world. What amazes me is that I don't feel it more. I don't feel as if something big had happened — it's just like being here after waiting around so long — you get used to it so quickly. Jeeps, it's so dramatic that on the day they take Rome, they start the invasion. I can't help feeling that something will be coming up here — in the Pacific. The psychological impact is terrific. I hope not though, darling, because that's where you are. I love you so much, honey.

What is there of me — nothing — I have gorgeous costumes for the play — one dress if of silver lame, and there is a negligee of black chiffon underneath. It is coming along well. You wouldn't believe it. I keep imagining the time when I will see you again, darling.

Heaven hope it will be soon— All my love, Janie

V-Mail letterhead
To: Lt. (jg) Charles. J. Flynn
From: Jane P. Flynn, civ.
U.S.S. Gamble
Entertainment Sect. S.S.O.
Care of Fleet Post office
APO #963 c/o P.M.
San Francisco
San Francisco]
June 11, 1944

Hello, honey darling — You have really been neglected the last few days, but as a matter of fact, so have I. I know there are letters from you someplace en-route, but evidently they have been delayed. Oh, darling, I have been so darned busy — from eight in the morning until midnight — two hours off for dinner and freshening up. The rehearsals have only been in the afternoon & evening but the mornings have been taken up by fittings, hair and going shopping for shoes & stuff for the play. They get it all, naturally, but I have to go along. This is such a difficult thing for me to do and I have to be good — that I just have my mind on it all the time — it's awful — I wish we had more rehearsal time, but at the same time I catch myself wishing that Wednesday nite would come so the suspense would be over with. Remember honey how Skip used to get up & do things for you. Well, Evans does the same thing, and I just stand there enthralled — Good God, what a talent that man has.

Let me see, my only social life has been going to dinner last nite — we had a little more time — didn't have to be back at rehearsal until eight. Remember that Jack Hanover — well he's on some kind of staff here — just got here — so he called to ask me for dinner. It was very nice — and fun to see somebody from home. He had been in San Francisco after I was and had seen a lot of Pat Zimmer — Evidently she's a good friend of his sister's. He said he had been down to No 1 and I said we used to live there. Megan has a Capehart in there and about a thousand records so you can imagine how crowded it must be. I haven't seen or met anyone else because there hasn't been time. I'm really practically a recluse — not really because I'm never home — always working.

I had a long letter from Mary yesterday — She is really planning to marry her Sam but not immediately. She's rather concerned over the Catholic problem because he is one. Personally, I'm not in favor of it, but only time will tell. Sam is a nice boy, but I don't think he's my ideal of a brother-in-law. But that's her business — I just found out that my cousin, Robert Patten who is a J.G. — is in the hospital at Pearl Harbor with rheumatic fever. He's in radar. I must find him.

Darling, in case I *didn't* tell you before — but I think I recollect saying something about it — I love you and miss you very much. It will soon be nine months. That's a long time — honey — but it will probably be lots longer so we just have to take it.

Darling, this is just about six months late but did you ever get the Christmas presents from me or the books I sent—

Honey, here comes my cue — I'm at rehearsal. All my love, Jane

Entertainment Section, SSO
APO #963, Care of Postmaster
June 18 1944
San Francisco, California

Hello, Honey Darling;

I am dressed and waiting to be picked up for the performance tonight. We are going over to the Pali to the other side of the island, so it is a pretty long trip. We usually start about four-thirty in the afternoon, have dinner there and then give the performance. If last night is any example, they invite us in for a drink afterwards. That is rather nice, as you can't have one before, and after all that ranting and raving I do all over the stage, a drink is just what is needed.

Well, as you may have gathered, the play opened night before last, and it was a great surprise to me...it was good. That old thing came through...that thing that you never get before you do a performance. I have never liked to rely on it, and this time I was sure that I wasn't going to have it for some reason or other, but it was there. It was really a great success which makes me very happy. I still find it amazing that I could be a convincing blonde hussy, but the reaction shows that I am. In fact, it is rather funny because, after seeing the play, people that I meet expect me to be like that in real life. My whole life is beginning to be like a masquerade...I just keep on playing Carole after the performance to satisfy them. But it has worked off by morning, thank heaven. Night before last, the audience was composed of special service officers from all over the island. Last night was our first GI audience...and quite an experience it was. They screamed and whistled and commented. In fact, they lived right along with the thing. They almost broke me up once...there is a line where I turn my back to the audience, put my hand on my hip, make a little movement and say "I couldn't draw a straight line myself"...their reaction was so violent that I almost broke into laughter...also the entrance where I come in with this silver lame dress with nine orchids over the shoulder...you just have to stand there and wait for a few minutes. They are the most satisfactory audience in certain ways that I have ever played to though...it is thrilling that they are so enthusiastic. Of course, the more subtle things they just don't get at all...remember how Carole is always getting her words mixed up...they don't laugh on those a bit. I have developed for the character a sort of swaying walk that I fondly imagine is sinuous and sexy and that just kills them every time I cross he stage. It's an awful lot of fun.

Oh, honey, it was last Friday that I started that letter and now it is Monday afternoon. I just don't know what has happened to the time. Still no letter from you though...I think it has been over two weeks now since I have had one...now I am beginning to worry again, although I suppose I am being silly. I do know that you couldn't be in on the Saipan thing, but I am wondering if it is just due to natural delay that there has been no word from you. I suppose so. Just as I wrote that last sentence, they came to pick us up. That was quite a performance that night...it is known as the most riotous place on the island, and it certainly is...I was hoarse the whole next *day*. Then Saturday night we went someplace where you couldn't smoke cigarettes...it was pretty lonesome for those poor boys out there. They were a wonderful audience and we gave the best performance so far. Saturday afternoon before we went to the play we went over here on the post to a party which a captain that we know was giving for his men. It was awfully nice...they had it in a sort of arbor and we drank beer with them and went around and talked and had our pictures taken with them. All those poor kids are so lonesome and most of them have been out here for so darned long...*just* boredom mostly *has* got them. After the performance Friday night too we went to a beer party that the men were having...we stayed half an hour I think. Such a fuss as they made — poor kids. That's part of the job we think we should be doing...talking to the men. We hadn't had much of a chance to do it before the play opened so we are happy for the opportunity now. Of course here where we live it is entirely restricted to officers which is better socially but part of the reason we are here is to talk to the boys after we do a play or before and so on.

Yesterday was the first day off that we have had since we have been here...a complete one. It was perfect bliss. I slept until about eleven in the morning and then made myself some breakfast and then a bunch of us went swimming...we swam for four hours straight and I mean real exercise, not just lying in the sun. First we swam all around here and then we walked down the beach about three quarters of a mile to get some boards. I didn't go on them but decided to try my hand at body surfing. I swam out about a quarter of a mile I think but the waves are no good for that. I tried and tried but they wouldn't carry me...then we came in and walked back home and went swimming again. Then we dressed and went over here to dinner, and then Jack Hanover called had the evening off and a jeep and would I like to go over to see Mare and Bob Cooke...I said I would so we did. We talked over old friends and they said to say hello to you. I just got back in the gates before ten o'clock. It was such a nice day with no rushing and no bustle and so healthy. Now I am ready to go back to work. I went swimming again today right after lunch. I try to go every day because it zips you up in a climate like this where lethargy is apt to get you.

Tomorrow is my birthday...good heaven, getting old...and I have to spend the day having my hair bleached again. Mother writes that it sounded lovely, but she was so afraid that it would look artificial... well, it doesn't, it looks perfectly natural...but it is an awful bother because it grows so fast that the roots are always having to be done.

Just think, honey darling, tomorrow it will be nine months that you have been gone. Our year is three-quarters up. It's been a long time, but it's amazing to me that that much of it has passed. I keep imagining the time when we will see each other again...I have a feeling that it will be by surprise...that I will just sort of bump into you...gosh, what a thrill that would be...if I didn't fall over in a faint...you too...just think of it...wouldn't that be fun...good heavens, I just stopped typing for five minutes and thought about it...oh, honey, it's not good to think about such things — it would be just too wonderful...I wonder if you are thinner or fatter or blonder and tanner now or what. My goodness, it will be the greatest day of my life when I see you again, honey.

You know darling, if you ever get to a liberty port, you could call me up. I can't give you my telephone number, naturally, but you can reach me at the address on the letter...The only time I am surely not here is between four in the afternoon and possibly eleven in the evening. I don't know the difference in time exactly, but you could figure that out. If you ever get anyplace where you can do it, why don't you call me.

Well, darling, I have to get ready to go again. I love you, honey...
Jane

V-Mail letterhead:
To: Lt. (jg) Charles. J. Flynn
From: Jane P. Flynn, Civ.
U.S.S. Gamble
Entertainment Section S.S.O.
Care of Fleet Postoffice
APO #963 c/o P.M.
San Francisco
San Francisco
June 22, 1944

Hello, honey darling; The reason I am using V-Mail this time is that I understand that practically no mail is getting through, and I thought that it is, while it might not be faster, would be more apt to get there because of its size. I haven't heard from you for three weeks now, and every day I just get up hoping that something will come. Of course, it is what I could expect because I know the mail is not coming. I keep having a lurking fear that things might have been reorganized, and it would be possible for you to be up where the fireworks are going on. I suppose that is borrowing trouble, so I shall try to cast the idea aside. Tomorrow I know a letter will come.

Now for something cheerful. The play is going fine. We are playing out at Schofield Barracks now, and I guess we will be there for three weeks. It is really nice because they do everything they can to make us comfortable. They send a lovely station wagon complete with springs and cushions to pick us up, and we have dinner in a nice restaurant...then they send cokes and sandwiches and stuff after and during the performance...you really appreciate those things after the inconvenience of some of the places we were last week.

Tuesday was my birthday, and I was so touched by the party that they gave for me. Eloise first had the idea that she was going to bake me a cake, and then she and the captain, who is the dentist here, got together and planned a party. They got special permission to hold it after ten when we got home. They had steaks and sparkling burgundy and a big salad and bourbon and brandy and everything. The sweetest part about it was the following...Just as Eloise finished the cake, it was almost time for us to leave for Schofield. I was out in the kitchen helping organize things. We didn't have time to leave it to cool long enough, as she wanted to get it iced before we left. She put the layers together, and it was still too warm, so it fell. She was so disappointed, as she had been planning to have a regular monument, and it was just half the size it should have been. Just then, some of the officers on the post came in and saw her distress...when we got home that night, they were all here, and they had just finished baking a beautiful cake. It was all of their first experience, and they had killed a bottle of bourbon in the attempt, but the result was marvelous to behold and even better to taste. They had happy birthday Jane on it and everything. They were like a bunch of kids because it had been so long since they had been in anything like a home that they wanted to help with everything. Well, we cooked the steaks and made the salad and had a drink, and then we ate, and I cut the cake, and I blew out all the candles...and you can just guess what the wish was...anyway I blew them all out, so I know it is going to come true soon. Another little project that had been taken care of while we were gone was the present...they had about twenty gag presents each one complete with a little verse — all written on this typewriter. Then we played the game which put me in mind of you. It was a wonderful party. The Major who is the C.O. of the post and the Major in the special service who sort of has charge of us were both here. I was so touched. If only you had been here,...it would have been perfect...All my love, Jane

V-Mail letterhead:
To: Lt. (J.G.) Charles J. Flynn
U.S.S. Gamble

San Francisco
22 June 1944

Hello, darling [second part of letter]. I guess that's all about the birthday party. Everybody enjoyed it so. Today has been a very busy one. I got up early and decided to do all our washing. It seems that there was a general inspecting the post today, and I was afraid he'd come in here, so I got up to do the dishes from last night before the maid came. She is pretty careless, and the kitchen is never really clean, so I made a big project of it and really got things spick and span. The only thing I didn't do was scrub the floor, so when she came, I gave her strict orders to do that, which she did. There is a little difficulty in making her understand what she is to do. It was days before we could get the idea over to her that she should wash the dishes. We finally pantomimed. Now she is speaking English pretty well though, and we can almost understand her. Her favorite expression is Okie-Dokie, which of course we taught her...After that project was finished, I made starch in return for which Martha did most of my washing...1 starched her clothes because she didn't know how — then I did an ironing, and then it was time to go to lunch. After lunch Eloise and I put up an enormous map of the pacific that was given us... it is about five feet long and four high...we have little flags so we stuck them in all the islands that we were sure about. Then I did some more washing, and now I am writing you, and in about ten minutes I have to iron a dress and have another shower and get ready to go out to Schofield. And I haven't done my knee chest exercises or gone swimming, both of which I have strict orders from the doctor to do every day...as of yesterday...so I will start that tomorrow. If we could only get somebody to do our laundry it would be wonderful because with all the other stuff we have to do, and starting next week, we have to take dancing lessons every day, there just isn't time.

Well, honey, this has really been a domestic letter hasn't it. There isn't any more time so I guess I will have to stop. Dorothy just went up for the mail, and I am praying that she will come back carrying a little epistle from you, but probably I will have to wait a little while longer. I love you, darling, and I am living for the day when we see each other again.

All my love to you, honey,
Jane

Entertainment Section, SSO A.F.O. #963, Care of F.M.
San Francisco, California
June 25 1944

My Dearest Honey Darling;

I just finished writing a long letter to the family, and when I finished, I realized that I had an extra carbon because I didn't know Bobby's address and that I had told them all the same things that I would be telling you, so I thought that I would send you a copy of it, and then I could write you about the more personal things. I hope you will pardon this method of procedure, honey, but with the limited time that I have...of course I wasted the whole day yesterday with people...but I thought you wouldn't mind.

It may seem to you, darling, that I am meeting a lot of people, and I can see you skipping from there to the fact that my head might be turned or that you might be jealous or something, but if such things should start going through your mind, stop it because it ain't true. Of course, I find this all very interesting, but one hour with you would be worth months of it. It also may seem to you that I have mentioned Jack Hanover quite a bit, but it is because it is nice to know somebody that you knew before and who knows you and with whom you can discuss mutual friends. Besides, the other girls and myself are the only people he knows. So don't think there is anything there. Just remember that no matter how many dozens of people get around this place, there is one person in my mind all the time, and that one person is you. Besides, I have only one day off a week, and there is no time for play on the others.

In the letter to the family, I said that I had been rereading your old letters...I read them all in bed last night...and, honey, they are really beautiful...not only are they interesting but so loving and, honey, they are beautifully written...they are all saved...you really have a gift for expression, darling. They're not just the brief note type of thing but something you can read over and over.

Remember how much we used to like maps...well, we have the wall of the living room practically lined with them now...great enormous things. I bought a set of little flags...about two hundred of them, and I check with the paper every day and move them around in accordance with military actions...it is very interesting. Unfortunately it is much harder to get the news here because the papers don't have as complete a coverage. A boy who has a subscription gives me his copy of Time magazine every week, so that sort of helps me to keep up. It takes him one day to read it, and then he sends it to me. I wonder if you would like me to send them to you. I suggested to your Mother that she send you the baseball clippings, and I understand that she has been doing it. I am enclosing a note from Maureen and one from Mary V that I thought you might like to read...also a couple from Margaret Latham. This letter is really going to be a volume.

I've been doing an awful lot of swimming lately, and I simply adore it. I've been working hard trying to improve my form on the crawl... now I don't get half as tired dong it as I used to. They have some feet flippers over where we swim. You have to keep your legs stiff when you use them, so it improves your kicking. The only trouble is that they give me cramps in the feet. Anyway, it's awfully good for the figure, and the doctor told me to go swimming every day. It seems that darned suspension is slipping a little bit, so I have to swim and do those knee chest exercises every day...otherwise everything is fine. There is an ideal place for swimming here. I want to go spear fishing or at least put on goggles and go down and look at the reef as soon as I can because you have said in your letters about how wonderful it was...of course, it won't be as interesting here, but it will be something like it, and I will think of you.

You know, every time I write a letter to you, it takes me the longest time because I always stop right in the middle of it and think about seeing you...I think I have imagined it in every way it could possibly happen...I have to jerk myself back to reality, and it's no fun. I don't think I have ever been as happy in my life as I will be that day. I can't decide whether it would be better to have you surprise me or to have you let me know you were coming...either way it would be wonderful. Gosh, I better stop thinking about it because then I get to wondering why I haven't heard from you...I just wait for the mail deliveries every day, and I mustn't think about them too much because there is probably some perfectly natural reason for the delay in the letters. Besides, I <u>know</u> that nothing has happened and that you are alright.

Gee, darling, I better get off that tack and talk about more interesting things to you. I suppose you must get bored to death with me in every letter talking about not hearing from you.

Oh honey, I finally have another Zippo...an officer on the post got me one yesterday. Unfortunately it is the black kind so I can't put your name on it but I think of you when I use it...do you still have mine? And did you ever get the books I sent you let me know and if you didn't, I'll replace them.

Well, darling, it's nearly two o'clock...I think I'll go for a quick swim...do my nails, dress, and then it will be time to leave for the performance. We have an hour's drive out there, an hour for dinner and then another for makeup and we have to start the performance at seven...so that gives me two hours...all my love to you my darling and I'll see you soon...

Love, Love, Love, Love, Love, Jane

June 25, 1944
Entertainment Section, USO A.P.O. # 963, Care of P.M. San Francisco, California

Dearest Mother, Daddy, Ma Wee, Mary, Buddy, and Bobby;

This is a carbon to all, Mother, so you don't need to send it on. Well, the mail this week hasn't been so bad...one from Mother, one from Mary, and a V-Mail from Bud...by the way, I understand that V-Mail from the mainland is censored at times, while other mail isn't. I don't know the truth of this situation exactly, but Dorothy received one which had been censored. I've been writing Chuck on V-Mail lately, because there is so little mail getting down there with the offensive at the present moment, and I thought that, while it takes a little longer, would have had a better chance of getting through.

This last week has been terribly busy but perfectly amazing... yesterday really took the prize. I have been laughing about it ever since, and don't think I will ever think of it without a slight chortle. This little island, as far as people are concerned, runs a close second to New York. Here is how it all started out. It seems that a friend of Eloise called Friday night. He is assistant to Frank Capra, who is a colonel in the army. So, Saturday she and I went to the Outrigger Club for lunch with him and Capra and another man, who is a lieutenant colonel , who used to be at paramount. That is a perfectly beautiful place on the beach and very famous...it seemed funny to me because in Hollywood, where women are so abundant, they wouldn't pay much attention to you, and here they just fall on your necks. I mean, I'd never met Capra before, and there he was, making a terrific fuss over me. Well, we invited them to breakfast Sunday, fully thinking that the other girls would be there, too. Eloise and I woke up Sunday morning to find all the other girls going on various activities and only us two left. The breakfast really expanded — there were twelve people, all men, and us entertaining them all...of course, when we had invited them to breakfast, there wasn't a darn thing to eat in the house, and we hadn't had time to go shopping. So, Saturday evening, when we had dinner with a certain division — it seems that three or four nights a week, we go from place to place eating with the men and talking with them. This group had been on two of the biggest offensives we had had and had borne the brunt of both. I wish I could tell you what it was, but I can't. Anyway, it's very famous. Saturday evening, instead of one to the table, we each had dinner with a certain sergeant... each one, having been picked out for good conduct or something They were a fine looking, nice group of boys. I was so glad that I had read a few books etc., and was acquainted with what they had done. Well, they always give us a pie or so after dinner, so this time we asked if we could have some breakfast stuff, too...they just loaded us down with eggs and bacon and bread and three pies...we use to buy groceries, but now people give them to us every place we go. Well, I nearly died...Capra sliced the bacon — one colonel made a whole dish pan full of scrambled eggs and did them in the broiler pan...there were army officers running all around borrowing silverware and cups and stuff — it was quite a breakfast. Eloise called Captain Evans and asked him to drop over...well, we went swimming after that, and on our way back, whom should we meet walking over to our house but two Dutch and an Australian flyer that we had met the day before at the Outrigger Club. Then, while I was still running around in a wet bathing suit, Captain Evans came in with his assistant. Eloise and I were madly trying to get all this varied group together and happy. I forgot to say that Jack Hanover was here by this time and had gone swimming with us. Then, who should come strolling in but Edgar Rice Burroughs. It seems he lives at the hotel right outside the post, and he came over to see Capra and the others. Imagine a Sunday afternoon out here, having Maurice Evans, Frank Capra, and Edgar Rice Burroughs in the same house...plus all of us and a bunch of American army and navy officers. I just had to sit back and laugh. I didn't get a chance to ask Mr. B. about Tarzan, but I heard him discussing Johnny Weismuller over in the corner Well, after that, they wanted us to go over to Doris Duke's for dinner, but Eloise and I both had previous engagements. Jack and the boy she was going with had been planning all week on taking us swimming and to dinner, and we had been busy most of the day, so we really couldn't break them. One thing you have to do out here, when there are so many men wanting to take you out, is, when you make an engagement, stick to it, come hell or high water, because it is so easy to hurt people. Well, the crowd finally left about four-thirty, and I went over to go swimming again...and tried out some feet flippers that make you go fully three times as fast.

Then, we got dressed, and I went to dinner at the Halekulani hotel with Jack...that is right on the beach and unbelievably beautiful. Then, after dinner, we walked down Waikiki...it is wonderful, whenever you feel the urge around here, you just take off your shoes and nobody thinks anything about it. It was so gorgeous...the sun was just going down, and as the waves went back from the beach, the sand glistened all different colors like a rainbow. He left about nine to get back to Pearl in time, and I walked over to the jeep to tell him and a couple of other people goodbye, and who should be here when I got back but the allies again. We talked to them a while, and we had all arrangements made...I was to go up with one in a Ventura this morning and Eloise with another in a B-25, and we were going to meet over Diamond Head at nine-thirty. Well, they called at the crack of dawn...they had received their orders, and now they are gone. They were highly educated and very intelligent...one had been in Amsterdam before the war and knew of Agnes, although he didn't know her.

Here is something that will really kill you. It seems that there is this boy named Captain Fothergill, who has sort of adopted us and vice versa. He was on the post...last week, he had a beer party for his men, and we went over and talked to them...I told you about that. Well, he is a battery commander. I had heard him refer to Randolph frequently, so I asked him what that was, and he said that was the name of his battery, that it had been established just after the Civil War and was one of the oldest ones in the army. And I'm darned if it wasn't named after Papa Frank's father...isn't that perfectly amazing...it kind of gives you a thrill.

Mother, would you mind being very careful about saving these letters? Since I am not allowed to keep a diary, they are the closest thing I have to recall what I have been doing.

A week or so ago, out on the raft, I met a navy flier and got to talking to him. He said that he would look for Bob Patten for me...so a few days ago, he came back to report no success...he was with a friend whom he introduced as Irving Cummings...I didn't think about it, except for the fact that he was just another navy lt., but he is the son of the famous producer Irving Cummings and was at Fox himself. Eloise knew his father, in fact, she was with him the day her son was having an appendectomy...it's a small world. Then Saturday afternoon they came back with a commander that Eloise had known a few months ago in New York.

The play is coming along quite well...it seems that the boys are crazy about it, and our run has been extended at least until the first of September, so I will spend quite a long time as a blonde. I am glad of it, because this part is such a challenge to me that it gives me that much more time to improve. I spent Saturday evening after the performance working on it with a boy who is an absolute genius at direction — and the same for a couple of hours last night... oh, yes, I did that too yesterday. I was terribly impressed with this character's ability, and I think I have made a lot of progress. The current rumor around here is that there is another prestige play like Macbeth coming up. That makes

the generals happy. They were thinking of doing "Twelfth Night," but now it seems that they may be planning to do Saint Joan and have either Katherine Cornell or Helen Hayes come over to play with Evans...I hope so, because that is my favorite part, and I would like to watch a great actress do it. It looks very much as if we would do a variety show after this one. We are starting dancing lessons this week. I have actually learned to carry a tune when I sing along with other people. I can't do it by myself yet, but with that much progress, I feel as if there were hope.

To get down to fundamentals, though...and something which I try to keep myself from worrying too much about, but which does worry me, it's been nearly four weeks since I had a letter from Chuck. Of course, I realize that very little mail is coming through, but gosh, every day I think there will be one, and then there isn't. Yesterday morning, there arrived a letter from Margaret Latham which was filled with a lot of them, but they were carbons of ones I had received here weeks ago...1 read them all over and it made it seem as if they might have just come, but they were written six weeks ago. This afternoon I am sure something will come, though. The sort of reorganization of the fleet that I have been reading about in the papers worries me because I am afraid that he'll be someplace where I think he isn't.

Daddy, let me know as soon as you can if you have paid those bills and how the bank balance is coming along. If you have paid those, I will send you some more. I have four weeks salary here coming, which I will get in a few days, so I will send quite a bit of it home to you, and you can put that in the bank, too. Chuck has been planning to send some, too, and I wonder if any has arrived.

Also, I still don't have Bobby's address, so maybe, Buddy, you could send this letter on to him...you keep this one, Mother, for me. I was glad to hear, Bud, that you are getting along so well with flying... it is fine that you had it before. I hope Sam is all right by this time, Mary. I had a letter from Mary V. yesterday in the bunch of letters from Margaret Latham...she and Herb are in New York. I don't suppose you have ever got in touch with them. The address is 155 East 38th St. Give them a ring, and tell them hello for Chuck and me. And Mary, what do you think...I had a note from Bob Hinkey, which I am just about to answer. He had left it at the USO office downtown...they had got it a little mixed up and told him I was in Hawaii, which is another island, because one of the other girls, who is in another show, is...I shall write him and make arrangements to see him and then tell you how he is.

That's about all the news for now, and my time is getting rather limited, so loads and loads of love to all of you...Jane

Entertainment Section, SSO APO #963, Care of P.M.
San Francisco, Calif.
June 28, 1944

My Darling;

<u>Finally</u> today arrived a letter from you, the one with the pictures in it telling about your liberty. It had been <u>four</u> weeks honey and I've been a little whacky. In fact I had a nightmare about you the other nite, and I had to get up and smoke a cigeratte and read before I could forget it. Honey, undoubtedly there are letters missing, but evidently for a while there you didn't have time to write — please honey, don't let time go by again like that before writing — especially at a time like this with so much going on — my imagination plays wild tricks. There are probably missing letters but honey, don't under any circumstances forget to write.

So you finally got to a liberty place — honey I'm so happy for you for having such a good wild time. You deserved it after all these months. It was awfully sweet and I loved you honey for going to all the trouble of explaining about your going out. You're marvelous darling — but don't worry, I'm not the kind of person who would begrudge your having a nice time — if I didn't have any more faith than that in you, I might as well not think our marriage was worth anything. I try to have a good time so you should too. I'm so darned happy you found somebody nice to have it with. It sounded perfectly wonderful and as if you had the best of every minute. I'm glad you took care of the boys after the dance. I only wish I had been there but someday soon darling. Maybe it won't be so long honey. Gee darling, I was so happy to hear you had a good time.

Well honey, it is Wednesday nite — we got back from the play a little while ago — a couple of the girls are out in the kitchen eating, a couple more on the front porch and Eloise and I writing letters in the living room. On the way home from the play, we stopped a few minutes up on the campus — there the people in this department have a place called the "Hams (you know, actors) Club" where you get hamburgers & coffee. There was great activity around there — among other things there was a boy up there painting a great big portrait of me for publicity — it was the first I knew of it as he had made a sketch from watching the play — I'm supposed to pose for the face tomorrow — it's going to be gorgeous — of course it doesn't look a thing like me, that's not Jane. It's sort of a body profile view with the head on one shoulder — shows a lot of back. By the way I've ordered some pictures so I should be able to send you some in a few days. We also found out that we were starting dancing lessons in the morning and that, in the future we would be doing those and hospital shows in the morning and performances in the evening. It's a pretty wearing schedule and at times, I feel as if I were going to give out but that's more a thing of the spirit — when I get lonesome for you, than it is of the body. That always bounces out of bed in the morning, ready to go again. Actually I'm so terribly happy to be here and to have something useful to do — I try to do the very best I can all the time — Actually there is little praise in reward as Captain Evans and the people associated with him make almost a fetish of being non-committal. That's a little hard at times but I suppose it's good for the soul — After all, they can't know that I need my ego bolstered. I just have to learn how to do that myself. But the pleasure the boys seem to get out of the performances is a joy — you can't fool a G.I. audience either — you have to be sincere and give your performance straight from the shoulder or they'll know it. You know, darling, I'm afraid I have this acting bug pretty badly again — there were a couple of years there that I thought I'd lost it, but now I realize it's a hopeless case. I'm afraid I'm going to have to keep working on it, because, although it's an awful headache, I'm afraid I have to have it. — More "afraids" in here — Frankly though, I'd never go to work in Hollywood again except on my own terms, and I think if I keep working hard here and later, I might get those terms, not that they particularly interest me — my, what an outburst, but I know you'll understand the feeling. The CBS & the news, etc., is not for me — I want to be darned good at this and I will be.

Thanks for the pictures, honey — They weren't exactly flattering because of the light, but it was so good to see something more recent than last September. You looked nice and slender. You mentioned a bracelet, honey. It didn't come yet, but I daresay it will soon. Thanks so much, darling. Honey, I sent Daddy the most important of the bills and told him to pay them for us and when they were finished,

I'd send him some more. I told him to be rather careful of doing it too fast though because I have no way of knowing how long I'll be here — of course I'd like to stay as long as I possibly can — I did want to have as much money as possible saved though, I sent $50 to him today that I'd saved out of the amount I get here — but I'm trying to get as much in there as possible so there will be freedom of action at a later date. I can't really get along on my allotment without going into debt, so if there were a while later when I wasn't working, if you weren't home, I think I'd go to New York instead of back to Hollywood — as per Connie Root — remember — there's nothing for me in H. without you, and even with you, I wonder if we should live there — this is silly I know, honey, because I'll probably be here a long time hope so — I was just sort of talking things over with you like we used to do. It must be sort of hard for you though to get back into such a conversation after having been "down" there so long. Maybe it's that my 26th birthday sort of impressed me.

Well my honey darling, it's nearly two, and I have to be up early. Remember I love you with all my heart — and I'm writing and hoping that the day we see each other will be very, very soon. All my love, Jane

Entertainment Section, SSO A.P.O. #963, Care of P.M.
San Francisco, California
June 29 1944

Dearest Honey Darling;

I have been just flooded with mail from you lately, and it is perfectly wonderful! Four letters this week and on top of all that arrived the little bear yesterday...the letter telling me about it arrived today, so you can see that the mails are slightly mixed up — either that or packages come as fast as letters. It is the cutest thing, honey...I had been trying to decide on a name for it and thought it was particularly wonderful that you chose Mike. You know, darling, that did an awful lot for my morale — it is a sort of psychological thing — it's been an awful long time since somebody thought of me in that strictly useless and loving way...I mean I've been so independent and so much the master of myself...all that stuff you know and then you send me a little fluffy animal. It's marvelous.

It makes me feel sort of helpless which is a good feeling to have once in a while. Thank you so much, honey — it is now reposing against the pillow of my bed...

It is Thursday night...we just got home from the show. This is our last week at Schofield, and I will sort of hate to move because it is a very nice theatre, and everything is so convenient...of course we have a long ride each way, but it is a very nice car and heaven knows what we'll draw next...not that I don't love the adventurousness of it all, but it has been sort of nice to sort of settle down in a show. I think this show will run until the end of September, and I'm pretty sure I'll be doing something after that...I think a couple of the girls are leaving but think that I will stay...I would like to very much. We will play around here for a while, and then we will go to the other islands for possibly a week at a time...it is possible that we may go down under early next month, but that is still in the rumor stage, and if we do, we will only be gone two or three weeks. If we did though it would be in this area and not in the South Pacific because we are assigned to the Central Pacific. So I don't think I would miss you if you came through...oh, darling, I am living for that day...I do so hope so, honey.

Talk about a schedule...we really have one now...we don't get home until after eleven, and then we start rehearsals at nine-thirty in the morning...we have a couple of hours off, more if we can possibly manage it...I try to get in a swim and wash a few clothes, and then we have to get ready to go to the play...lately we have had to leave early because of eating with different companies of men... then we have the play, and then it starts all over again. Of course, we do have Sundays off, but I usually wear myself out swimming all day — it's a great life. I got awfully tired yesterday but then I got a good night's sleep and was already to start out again this morning. It doesn't leave any time for pleasure or personal life, but that's just as well. The only great problem I have is the laundry one...it seems that we just can't get anyone to do it for us, and so we have to spend most of our spare minutes at it...at this point, I would be willing to pay practically any price to get somebody to do my washing for me.

Tomorrow I am going to make an ardent effort to get a woman to come in two days a week and do it...because it makes life a little too complicated. You have to look nice all the time, and it is so hot that you can't wear a dress more than once, and it has to be washed again. Laundry seems to be so darned tied up with the war...I think it is one of the things people won't forget.

Honey, you got a second sunburn! Darling, won't you ever learn... I had just said that you would have to reconcile yourself to one a year, and then you go out and get another. Honey, please be careful. I know the spear fishing is fun, and I am so glad you are doing it, but don't stay out in the sun so long, honey.

I got a bunch of pictures today, so in the morning, I'll find a big envelope and dispatch them to you...the Carole Arden ones are rather interesting because they show what can be done...they are not good photography or anything, and they were done with stage makeup on, but I think you will be interested in the contrast between those and the one brunette picture.

Honey darling, will you please stop beating your gums about Jack Hanover...I see he made two letters of yours...Of all things for you to start being jealous, that is the silliest...I told you he only came over here because he knew me and didn't know anybody else. So stop it, honey...don't you know I love you and nobody else...so don't fuss like that. Besides, I only see people in bunches anyway... living n a house with six girls, it is never anything but a crowd, and when we have our day off, I am so tired, I never want to go more than a block or so off the post...I have so little curiosity about this island lately that it is amazing...There isn't much local atmosphere at the present anyway, as you well know. Oh say, speaking of people from Seattle...Bob Galer called today...he is just back from the Mainland, and he brought me some bobby pins which is a great event. He asked me before he went if there was anything I wanted, and that was my request...I've never met him...just on the telephone. It is absolutely impossible to get bobby pins over here though. You'd think that out in the middle of the Pacific, in times of war, that I'd be occupied with something else but laundry and bobby pins, but the mere intricacies of living assume a terrific importance. Besides that, things that are really of moment, I can't mention in the letters. I laughed so tonight...thinking about our conversation in the dressing room before the play...we really got into a good one. We were talking about Saipan, and then we got into the war and the reasons for it...well, it seems that Martha and I see eye to eye on the whole thing and are inclined to take the long view, associating it with the history of the world and trends and such things...like you and I do, and Dorothy and Eloise, Eloise especially, strongly objected to that...they seem to have a strong antipathy toward theories and ideas and regard things, as so many women do, purely from the personal standpoint, not necessarily the effect on them personally, but well, I can't quite explain it...it is a rebellion against ideas perhaps...well, it was going hot and heavy, and Eloise was really quite disturbed...that is really because she doesn't have a very good fund of knowledge...I think she was on the defensive more than anything else, and she kept contradicting herself...when who should walk in but one of the men from Mid*Pacifican...he pricked up his ears and finally got involved in the whole thing. He wanted to ride home with us tonight, but we said there wasn't room in the car so he should go with the boys...it was the truth too...but he wanted to go home with us so he could hear us talk some more and write about it...1 hate to be on my guard like that.

Oh, I didn't tell you about my wonderful dinner tonight...I had filets...two of them and rare...they were simply marvelous. It seems that this woman who is the head of the service club out there invited us to have dinner with a group of her friends on the post...colonels and such stuff, and they had steak. It was lots of fun, but frankly, I would rather not have gone because I hate to do all those things before a performance, but you have to be polite...besides, we had only forty-five minutes, and I do so hate to rush. Last night we were eating with the MPs, but I got into the mess hall, and I was so tired that I just couldn't face it, so I went and lay down in the theatre and had them bring me a sandwich. You can see, darling, that you have nothing to be jealous of...I'm too tired and busy to carry on even a slight flirtation...besides the men are so numerous that they are more of a bother than a pleasure...I have just developed a habit of saying no to everyone. Besides, did I ever tell you I love you? I do an awful lot, and that is what counts, so stop it, honey.

Darling do you realize that it will soon be eleven months since we have seen each other...what a great day it will be, honey, I am just praying that it will be soon and everything in regard to your rumor works out. Oh honey!!!!

I talked to Mrs. Armstong the other day, and she told me that Ed Geise was here, but he hasn't called me, as far as I know.

Well, honey, I think I'll hit the hay...remember I love you with all my heart...I'll be seeing you...All my love to you, darling, Jane

Monday
July 3, 1944

Hello Honey Darling;

A wonderful, long letter came from you this morning — no, afternoon...they are still arriving sparsely, so it was cause for a great bit of elation on my part...and then the news that it carried that such a thing as doesn't seem possible, might be...gosh, honey, I just can't believe it. I am trying not to get too excited as you cautioned me, but I just can't help it. I have everything all planned out already. It would really be too much to hope that I would not have a show, but that would be all that I might have to do, and — well, it would be just wonderful, so my fingers are crossed. I do so hope it is right, and I shall be praying for it. Oh, honey, that would really be something to tell your grandchildren. And you are not the only one who is lonesome...I guess it is mental transference or something. It gets pretty bad sometimes when you realize that there isn't a thing you can do about it personally, and you just have to wait your chances as patiently as you can. It's not good for the old morale, but I'm here to improve everybody else's, so I'll start with you and say not to get too downhearted...it won't be long...and think how wonderful it will be when it does happen.

We just got home from the show about half an hour ago...it is eleven-thirty. I thought I would write you and go to bed, as we have a pretty hard day ahead of us tomorrow. It seems that they are having a big fourth of July celebration out at Schofield, and we have to appear — not to do much, but it is a very long day. We were to have left at nine in the morning but we pleaded off until noon — that still makes an eleven hour day. They are having a big aquacade with men swimming through fire and all such stuff — it should be a very interesting. I am always harboring my energies so I can be a vigorous Carole through so I often look at things to do in the daytime a little dubiously. I had better stop that though because after tomorrow, we will be rehearsing a hospital show, and then, when that is done, we will take it around in the daytime and have the performance at night. It takes the constitution of an ox, but I am rapidly becoming convinced that I have it, either that or sheer will power. I had two ballet lessons last week which was the worst time of the month and got through them alright. Of course, the situation isn't half as bad as it used to be.

Honey, you have never told me whether you received the Christmas presents. I am beginning to wonder if something happened to them that you didn't want to tell me about. It is bothering me — not because of the presents but because you seem to studiously avoid the subject...but perhaps that is just imagination on my part.

It looks very much as if our original plans for going down under might materialize in the next month, but it is still very doubtful...we would only be gone a couple of weeks, so I would be back in plenty of time in case our wonderful hope comes through. I would really like to do it darling, but it would have to be at the right time or I'd be pretty worried about missing you.

Yesterday I went to a baseball game that was really something — the 7th Air Force versus the Navy...Joe DiMaggio was on the army team, and there was really a crowd there...the score was nothing to nothing into the twelfth inning...they walked DiMaggio once, and the next time up to bat, he struck out...just like Casey...he did make a sensational catch in the tenth inning that saved the game for them once. But then in the twelfth inning, with the bases loaded, he hit a double, and two men came in, and then the next man up hit a double, and the score was four to nothing. The navy wasn't able to do anything in their half, so that was the end of the game...it was really good tight ball, and it was a pleasure to watch it. I got quite a kick out of being way out here in a war and in the middle of the Pacific and at a baseball game.

What's more, it was probably of better caliber than the people at home see. After that, we came home and bought some vanilla milkshakes on the way and mixed them with rum and had a couple of drinks apiece. Then we went out to dinner at the house of some friends of one of the boys here on the post. It was really so nice to be in somebody's home again. We had the most wonderful Martinis and good conversation and actually steaks for dinner. We were a little over the deadline getting home but nothing untoward happened. In case you are wondering, I went with a lieutenant who is over at Schofield. It seems that he used to be up here with Evans, and they parted company, so now he is in special service someplace else. I was terribly perplexed about my part and he helped me a lot with it. Of course it had to be done on the quiet because that wouldn't be appreciated by the director of our play. But his help was what did the trick for me — he is actually a very fine director and seems to be able to tell me what to do so that I understand it. So it is fun to talk about the theatre and politics...everything very impersonal just talk...so don't worry. That's the extent of my social life...certainly not daring and very impersonal. So stop your screaming about my getting involved with anyone.

So you got a sunburn again...Honey, I guess we'll just have to resign ourselves to the fact that you will forget yourself and get one every once in a while and that you will just have to suffer through it. Such an incautious character as you are — although I will admit I rather admire you for not pampering yourself about it.

I forgot to tell you that I had a cable from Will yesterday morning saying that a baby girl was born Friday, the thirtieth and that Maureen and the baby were fine. They finally made it, thank heaven — I'm so happy about it.

Honey, I'll have some pictures to send you in a few days — in the meantime, I'm enclosing a clipping from the paper MIDPacifican... it isn't terribly *flattering*, and I can't understand why they used that one, but I thought you might be interested in seeing it. I'll keep the pictures coming after this.

It never rains but it pours, or some such trite thing. I now have two Zippo lighters...after all these months...I think I will send one to Mary in New York. I'm afraid that Mary has been having a pretty hard time...she said in a letter that I got from her today that she hadn't been well and hadn't wanted to tell Mother and Daddy about it. I kind of wish that she would go home, and she seems rather doubtful about marrying her Sam. I think instead of that dress I was going to buy downtown that I will send her the money because I am afraid that she could use it. I'll enclose the letter. Maybe you should write her if you have time.

Well, sweetheart, it is getting pretty late, and, as usual, I am darned tired, so I'll call this thirty for tonight. Keep the letters coming now that they have started again and I'll keep my fingers crossed and keep praying. I have the whole thing planned out already.

All my love to you honey, Jane

July 10, 1944
Entertainment Section, S.S.O. A.P.O. #963,
Care of P.M. San Francisco, California

Darlin; I was so thrilled when the bracelet arrived today. It is perfectly beautiful, and I was so touched by your going to all the trouble of making it for me. It fits perfectly around my wrist — thank you so much, honey...I couldn't have had a nicer birthday present...not only is it good but it's darned interesting...innumerable people already have asked me where I got it. It is perfectly beautiful, honey, not only from a "souvenir" but from an aesthetic standpoint. Thank you so much, honey.

The mystery of the missing mail is finally beginning to be solved. I received a letter from you Saturday that had been mailed the twenty-fourth of May...you had received all letters from up to the time I left San Francisco and were commenting on them — also it picked up a few loose ends that I had asked you about and which I thought you hadn't answered. I'm glad to hear that Dave did get back...isn't it awful that all those letters were lost. Maybe I will get a few more of the missing ones now — that is really peculiar that they would have been held up so...I had a couple letters from you last week that were mailed the first of July.

I haven't written you since last Thursday because I had the silliest thing happen to me...it reminded me of your little tussle with Pete Dix only I didn't deserve it. I washed my hair Friday morning...bleached hair is awfully hard to comb when it is wet because the bleaching takes the wax off each hair and it isn't as smooth...well, I was brushing like mad, and all of a sudden I laughed at something Eloise said...it caught me off guard when I was making a hard brush, and it pulled me neck out of joint. We were just about to begin rehearsing a hospital show, so I went out to the kitchen and asked the boy who plays the piano and coaches us on the song if he could put it back in...he snapped it back, but it was too late, the damage was done. It seemed that I had some sort of muscular spasm, and all the muscles in my right side...even down the back just went into knots. Well, I stood it that day, but I woke up screaming Friday night and Saturday was ghastly. I went up to the dispensary and they sent me up to an army hospital, and they gave me a diathermy treatment, which is a heat treatment. That made it worse...by afternoon I could hardly see,...I mean I was trying to walk back to the dispensary, and it would catch me and just blind me and sort of paralyze me...I went back to the hospital for another treatment but it was still worse...by this time, they were debating whether to cancel the show, so they came down to see me and decided I could never do a show that night, so they cancelled it...imagine that...I have never had such a thing done because of me before. Well, Captain Evans insisted that I go downtown to an osteopath of his...I didn't have much faith in them, and by that time I was ready to die anyway...my head was way over on one side, and I couldn't move it, and it hurt all over whenever I moved. I finally went though, and he did me a great deal of good, prejudice or no...I have my days mixed up...it was Friday that this all happened, and Thursday night when I last wrote you, it just hurt a little bit. Saturday it was better — the doctor said no, but I insisted on doing the show with a stiff neck — it was fairly straight by this time — as those things so often are, it was a darned good performance... Captain Evans said you couldn't have told if you hadn't known...I was so glad I did it. It is almost well now, although it still bothers me some. Isn't that the funniest thing to happen to a person — this muscular spasm was so bad that it locked several vertebra and pulled two ribs out of joint — all that had to be put back. I'd start laughing at the situation and nearly kill myself. Of course it made me awfully mad that I couldn't go swimming yesterday...but in a few days it will be well enough so I won't have to worry about it.

We did a show tonight that was really a thrilling and a bit of a harrowing experience. We played in a hospital, and the audience was boys who had just come back from down south. Honestly, honey, when I did the prologue in front of the microphone and I looked out at all those boys, all of them in robes and half of them in wheelchairs, it really wrung my heart...I wanted to make them have a good time watching the play so badly. And they laughed so...they were the most wonderful audience we have ever had...After the play I went out with Eloise down front and we talked to them and signed all their programs and autographed people's casts...those poor kids. There was one boy who had been in the big musical review that they did here a while ago, and he had a shot up leg...all the cast crowded around him. They were all so darned nice and so grateful that you gave a show for them that it was pitiful.

Honey, I think something very thrilling is about to happen next week...it is fairly definite, and this time I think it will really take place. We will be gone about three weeks, so that makes a month from now, and it seems as if that time were perfect. I do so hope that it does. If so, and we are starting rehearsals tomorrow morning on the Variety show, we will have to get it worked up in a little over a week, but Personal Appearance is going to be the big production and the other secondary, so we should be able to do it. I hope so and think it is definite, so cross your fingers, honey — the time is perfect too. I'll let you know in the next few days or tomorrow if I can, but this time I think it will be.

Well, darling, I guess I'll dash off a little note to Mary and hie myself to bed. In case I haven't mentioned it before, I love you with all my heart, and if I could, I would hold my breath until I see you again...as it is, I am waiting and hoping that it will be very very soon.

All my love to you my darling, Jane

Entertainment Section, S.S.O. A.P.O. #963, Care of P.M. San Francisco, Calif.
July 17, 1944

Dearest Honey Darling;

My, I have been so popular lately...I've had practically dozens of letters from you — all the loose ends are being tied up. The carbon of the letter you wrote the family arrived, plus the short letter the day before you had the liberty...the one you apologized about...then a couple of recent ones...and the one telling me about Dave's getting back and your getting the presents and not getting the books and the one that told me what the inscription on the bracelet was and asking if it fit...and by the way, honey, it fits my wrist exactly...I have had it on practically every minute since you sent it except for the performance, and everyone has commented on it and said how beautiful it was. Do you really and truly have some more under way.

That letter you wrote the family was a gem and so darned inter-esting to me...you described so many things that you hadn't to me — in a more impersonal letter, you describe` your life more than your feelings...there were so many things in it that I hadn't known... it was a sort of summing up of what you had been doing all these months — the family is still talking about how enchanted they are with it...they really are — it was so grand of you to write such a long one...that is something that should be preserved...I save your letters, and Mother saves mine, and you save mine — we should really have quite a wealth of material by the time the war is over.

In your last letter, you asked if the army was keeping me busy...a truer question was never put...I have neglected you most woefully the last few days but if you could see this

July 18, 1944...Tuesday...darling, that was a pertinent way to be writing that last sentence because here it is the next evening, and I haven't finished the letter. It seems that just as I was writing that paragraph, I realized that it was time to get ready to go to the performance, in fact it was past time...I had thought that I would be able to get in a quick swim and write you too, and you suffered. So I threw my clothes on and dashed out of the house, planning to continue writing when I got home. But it seems, as happens too often that we had to accept an invitation to stay for a couple of drinks after the show...sometimes we are able to turn them down, but sometimes it is too awkward and hurts people's feelings...they think they are doing you a big favor, and they do offer you their bourbon...we got home about eleven, and I was so terribly tired that I just went straight to bed. We rehearsed until twelve-thirty today and then went to lunch...then this afternoon I had to do some shopping because I didn't have a decent pair of shoes left to wear, and Dorothy and I had to get some groceries for the household, so we had a car sent over and went downtown. By the time we got back, it was time to leave for the play again. We discovered though that no arrangement had been made for us to eat out at Hickam Field where we were playing tonight...they had thought really that they were giving us a rest so we wouldn't be tired before the show. When you eat with the men, you sit one at each table and have to keep the conversational ball rolling...some of them are so shy from being out here so long that it is very difficult to talk to them. Then they always want you to look at the kitchen and meet everyone in the joint, and they want to take pictures and show you around, and you love to do it, but by the time you get to the theatre, you are usually late and exhausted. Well, we had to leave too early to eat at the officer's club so at the last minute, we decided that instead of going to some restaurant where it would take a long time to be served that we would cook up a little something at home, so we did...it was really one of the few times since I have been here that I have been involved in cooking a whole meal...it only took us twenty minutes and was very simple but it was fun for a change — not as a steady diet of course...I find myself perfectly contented with what I get if I don't have to cook it. We were at an outdoor theatre tonight. Those aren't so good because you have to do the first act with the sun in your eyes...the heat, of course, is not so oppressive as it is in some of the theatres. Everything was all sort of messed up, and the theatre was dirty...last night we played in an outdoor theatre too for a company of M.P.'s, and the theatre was perfectly spotless...but I decided tonight that I wasn't going to let it throw me...I don't know why it should have, but you know how you get psychologically before a play once in a while...well, the upshot was that I think I gave a darned good performance...now I am sitting here with some greasy stuff on my hair...when I finish writing to you, I shall wash it and then go to bed...so goes my day...it's usually darned interesting though, and it will be soon terribly interesting.

This time we are really going...I can't tell you the exact date, but it is in the next two weeks...just about exactly that...we will be gone three weeks, so if you come, I won't miss you. We are rehearsing a variety show in the mornings, and starting next week we will take part of the variety show and take it to hospitals in the afternoon... with rehearsing the morning and playing a show in the evening, we will have a pretty full schedule. I just hope we can take it and aren't too tired by the time we go...but it is all in a day's work and I really enjoy every minute of it Honey, you would be simply amazed at the times I am doing now...you never thought that I would be singing a song did you Well I am and it's about the most complicated one in the show — the catch is that I don't sing it, I talk it...But you still have to do it with the rhythm and very tricky rhythm it is too...they say I am doing it well which I find hard to believe...It is a thing called "Publicity Man"...it's a little off color in spots, but the way I do it, it's alright...I'll write it down for you...

You ought to be in pictures.
You're wonderful to see.
Aaaah, you ought to be in pictures. Oh, what a hit you would be.
Why, for weeks and weeks in Hollywood, that's all I ever heard.
From producers and seducers of the movies and their herd.
You're gorgeous. You're colossal. You're gigantic. You're divine!
Let me put you and your home town on the map!
And they all end up with the same old...line.

Now baby, if you'll only treat me right,
Why honey, I could make you...famous overnight.
Your name would blaze in signs of electricity
Baby, if you'd only let me handle...your publicity.
I'll put your picture in the papers.
I'll toss your torso in the news.
Why, I'll pose you in chinchilla While you're lying...on a pillow.
And baby, there's not much that you can lose.
I'll put your photo in the roto You know,
on one of those swell beige Packard cars
Oh, baby, stop acting like a piece of wood.
Act like you should to me. You better be good to me.
Or no publicity.
I'll put your undies in the Sundays.
When you're seen on a cruise.
And if you'll pose without a stitch of clothes,
I'll try to get your picture in the news.
We'll make a test in technicolor.
You'll wear a one piece bathing suit.
And baby, you won't need bright spangles
To bring out those lovely angles.
I'll put your lovely looking figure
Right on the covers of Click and Look.
MGM and Warners too will have their feelers out for you
And baby, you won't even have to cook. End-pause...then...
And soon it's back to Hollywood is the thought I've had in mind,
To those producers and 4-Fers
Of the movies and their kind.
So I'm going to take back with me
A bodyguard of Makin soldiers (fanfare) or whatever island we are
Purer than the driven snow...(fanfare)
A bodyguard of GI's willing to protect the status quo
From producers and seducers of the movies that I know.

It's a little colorful I know but the way it is done, it is cute and it's what the boys like and besides its darned good experience for me to do something like that. Another thing I am doing is a skit called "Visiting Star"...about this French movie actress on a USO show... it is just filled with wonderful cracks and is marvelous slapstick comedy. I had the choice between doing that and Spring, which I

brought over. They said I couldn't do both because they were the two
biggest sketches in the show, and I had the lead in the other play,
so which one did I prefer to do. I chose the Visiting Star although
sentimental memories of you made me want to do the other...but
I knew I could do Spring well, and I wanted to take a crack at the
other because I had never done anything like that. I have a book
of foreign dialects, and I have to go over the whole darned thing
and make a chart of my dialect...I have the idea of it, but it is not
exactly correct, and I want it to be just right. I certainly do have
the bug, don't I, darling.

Darling, I went to the most wonderful place Sunday...it was our
day off, and we went on a picnic...it was a very impromptu thing,
and the food was picked up at the last minute from the mess...but
it was the scenery that was so wonderful. We went over on the
north side of the island and drove through sugar cane fields and
then right up to the edge of the mountains. We had to walk about
an hour...it was a mile and a half up to these falls. It seems that
it is a legendary residence of the Gods, and as you go up the trail,
you offer gifts to them. You pick a pretty leaf and put it on a flat
rock and say a little something to them and then go on your way.
The country was unbelievably beautiful, really tropical...so lush
and green. We went straight up this canyon that wasn't over fifty
feet wide at the bottom and with a stream running down it. We
crossed the stream at least six times on the way up...the walls of
the canyon were hundreds of feet high, and they didn't go straight
up, they hung over, and they were covered with moss and ferns...
when we got up to the end of this canyon, there were the falls about
a hundred feet high and very narrow...just tumbling down — it
was a little dark and terribly lush and green with the black walls
of the cannon. There was a deep pool right under the falls, and we
went swimming in it — we swam under the falls and it tumbled
down on our heads...it was like a Dorothy Lamour picture...the
best way of describing it.

It was the first real Hawaiian thing I have seen since I have
been here, and it was a wonderful experience. When I got home,
Mike was sitting on the bed, and he told me to write a letter to
you right away...but I said I'm sorry, Mike, I'm so darned tired...
goodnight... I'll write in the morning.

I guess I haven't kept you very straight on the news of the family,
darling. You thought that Bobby was in the Marines, and he is an

Air Cadet...pilot. Buddy is at Santa Ana taking the course there, and Bobby is at the University of Denver. Mary went to New York to see this boy that she thought she was in love with, and now she's not in love with him any more — she's working there, but I think that the best thing for her to do is to come home. I've had two pretty depressed letters from her lately. She took an apartment with that darned Anne Lonergan...you remember her — the one she had the apartment with in Hollywood. Then Pat Lonergan, you remember him, came to New York and said that Anne should move because she wasn't getting enough service there and that she simply had to be waited on. So Anne moved without giving Mary any notice, and Mary was stuck with the thing, and the expense was really too much for one person. I think she is having some very unpleasant experiences, and I do wish she would go back to Seattle. I suppose the twenty-five dollars that I told you about sending her came in pretty handy. Poor kid. She's so mixed up. You know Sammy and Larry are both in on the European invasion, and neither of them has been heard of so far. I'm getting pretty worried about them.

Sweetheart I have just rambled on and on about things — but it is because I love to pretend that I am talking to you, so if you are bored reading about things that happen...I mean the little things about where we ate dinner and all, I apologize...but that way I make myself think that I am closer to you...I love you and miss you so darned much, honey, people around here don't say "your husband" to me...they call you Chuck and want to know what you think about things and what you have done and where you are. You will be a very familiar character to them when they meet you. You will have to remember the description of the girls so they will be familiar to you too...some of the descriptions have changed but not enough to make a big difference. Honey, I have met quite a few people who were going down there, and I always tell them to look for you and to say hello, but so far, no one has found you. But maybe someday you will be surprised to have somebody come aboard with greetings from me. Certainly there are plenty of people looking for you.

Well, sweetheart, it is getting pretty late, and the hair is still covered with the oil. It has to be fixed sooner or later, and I guess it might as well be now so I can get up early in the morning and work on my script...remember I love and adore you, darling...and I'll be seeing you...

All my love, Jane

Entertainment Section,
July 1944
SSO A.P.O. #963, Care of P.M. San Francisco, California

My darling; I'm sitting out here in the front yard on a blanket with the typewriter in front of me and the wind blowing the paper all around...the sun is pretty violent, so I expect that by the time I finish this letter, I will have acquired a little more of that native hue. We are having a break this afternoon between shows...the tonight one is at Fort Armstrong, which is fairly close to here, so we don't have to start until a little later than usual. We got back from doing a hospital show about an hour ago — had a post mortem and decided to cut out most of the show and spend the time just talking to the boys. You know, honey, I have never felt since I have been there that I was really doing something concrete until we started the hospital shows. The boys we have gone to see are all back from Saipan, and it just kills you, only of course you mustn't show it. I suppose after we are accustomed to doing it and see them day after day, it will seem to be such a big thing that we won't take it personally. They are awfully keyed up, and it seems that our going in and talking really helps them, they are so glad to see girls that look like the ones they knew at home. The show we are doing they like very much, but some of them are so sick that they can't concentrate on a show. The boys Sunday could because they were further along, but in this ward we were in today, there were some boys who just arrived and some who were still awfully sick from Saipan, and the task of concentrating on the continuity was too much for them... they would lapse into their own thoughts...what they need more than entertainment is to have a chance to talk...so that is what we are going to do most of the time after this. It's really a harrowing experience but I would willingly spend all my time at it.

We played for two Negro audiences last week. The first one didn't seem to get the play, but the one last night was perfect. When you can appeal to a Negro audience it is quite a victory, because you can't rely on the wisecracks to carry you through...the character itself has to be funny. I have been trying to work on Carole from that standpoint, and I think from this it succeeded. A lot came back stage after the play, and they just killed me because they were like Ike in his most formal moments, and more than a few of them were like Emery. They were so formal, effusive, and flowery that it just delighted me...bowing and scraping around like mad and offering practically with bows from the waist, their autograph books to be signed. It was very fun.

They have sort of let up on our rehearsal schedule a little bit. It seems that, in addition to P.A., they were getting together a very elaborate variety show to take down under — there wasn't enough time for rehearsal, so the boy who is directing it told Captain Evans that he would have to cancel some performances and let us rehearse. Well, the upshot of the whole thing was that they decided it was silly to spend so much time on the variety show because we wouldn't have a chance to do it, going from island to island as fast as we will be doing. I must say I was relieved because our schedule for this week was absolutely superhuman anyway and we are leaving the first of next. Oh, honey, I mustn't miss you. I talked with Mrs. Richardson last night, and I will call her again so she will know what to tell you in case anything happens. And if you can't get in touch with her, call Captain Evans in the Entertainment Section on the campus of the University. We'll be back in a little less than three weeks. Oh, honey, how I hope it turns out...what a great day that will be.

I haven't had a letter from her, but I hear through the grapevine that Pat Zemmer is getting a divorce, only it is Hal that is asking for it. I suppose it is because she didn't want to stay in Washington. Maybe it is just as well...I hope that Pat can find some way to be happy. Also I hear that Edith Laumeister...you remember her, is getting a divorce too...I must write Pat immediately if not sooner...I don't know whether to mention that I've heard it or wait until she tells me. I hope it isn't too hard for her without the security of Hal behind her.

My goodness, honey, the sun is getting so hot, I'm positively dripping, although it isn't ladylike. I find it very easy to adapt myself to this Hawaiian summer, luckily...I suppose it's my brunette personality, although you wouldn't believe it to look at me. By the way, honey, I sent you some pictures airmail a few days ago — they should be there soon, so watch out for them.

Well, honey, it is about time to go in and have a shower and sash over to dinner and then to the play again...it's a busy, busy life isn't it. When you get here, I think I won't have anything to do in the daytime, and then you can go to the performances in the evening if you want to, either that or wait for me. I figured we could stay at the Halekulani, which is perfectly beautiful and near here...I think you would like that. Oh, honey, wouldn't that be fun...Well, darling, I will keep crossing my fingers and hoping...

Honey I just got a letter telling me that you had that infection on your back from coral...honey, please be careful...I hope that as you said, it is well by now, but honey, you have to watch out for those things. I get kind of worried about you doing so much spear fishing because there must be sharks around there. Have fun, honey, but do be careful...

So much love to you darling, Jane

Entertainment Section, S.S.O. A.P.O. #963, Care of P.M. San Francisco, California
July 20, 1944

Hello, Sweetheart;

Well, this is our ten months anniversary, darling. It hardly seems possible that this would have happened after our being together almost constantly for so long...the year is almost up — maybe we will see each other before it is.

Darling, I got a letter from you yesterday that was a little worried about whether I was having too good a time and filled with wild statements about socking people, etc. I'm so happy to know that after six years you still love me enough to get excited. And I realize that you have been down there all that time without having much fun...just your liberty and that wasn't long. I know you didn't have a very good time up here, so you are inclined to get disturbed about things. But, honey, remember that you are supposed to respect me as a person as well as your wife...we've had to live separate lives the last year...it has been forced upon us, but the fact is there. I know it hasn't been any fun for you, but it hasn't always been fun for me...some of it has been pretty miserable and lonesome...I've done the best I could...when I was in the hospital, when I had to worry about the doctor bills and couldn't find a place to live, and when people tried to take advantage of me. Believe me that last was legion. This work over here is the only thing that has given me any real happiness since you have been gone. I love it, and I do love to meet interesting people — but, honey, if you don't think that you know me well enough by this time to stop telling me not to have too good a time or to think a lot of things that you seem to infer, what <u>must</u> you think of me? I have the satisfaction now of knowing that I am doing something as best I can in the war, that I'm doing my work fairly well and making progress at it and that I have created some sort of life for myself to fill in the gap. I do find it fascinating... but it is the groups of people and the circumstances that interest me, not specific people. Like that letter to my family, when I told about all those people coming over on that Sunday, and you didn't like it and started talking about socking Colonels...honey, those people weren't interested specifically in me or I in them...it was the combination of them altogether in the house that I thought was so wonderful...I thought it was a very humorous situation, and I thought that you would share vicariously in the humor of it. At the time I thought, if Chuck were only here...how he would enjoy this, and how he would enter into the spirit of it. That's the basis of our relationship, darling, even from a distance...okay, honey. I hope I haven't hurt you, but, darling, you were way off the beam. I hope I haven't hurt you, honey, but I kind of thought that you'd be a little happy because I was happier about things than I was before. And if you wish to be purely practical, certainty there is less danger of "seduction" here than there was on the mainland because even if the desire were present, which it isn't, there would be no opportunity in the closely organized life I lead. So stop beating your gums, honey.

Honey, I am sure that you will enjoy this situation...the phone rang last night...we got home from the play rather early you see... and it was Bob Hope...he and his company wanted to come over and have a drink with us — it seems that they have been working with the Special service here and had wanted to see us. Eloise and Dorothy knew them, but they were out at Schofield...we weren't particularly anxious to have them come but didn't see how we could be rude about it...the four of us had to entertain them. There was Bob Hope and Jerry Colonna and the guitar player, Tony Romano and a comedian called Dean...several people on the post came in, and it was kind of fun...but I did laugh about it. Eloise is rather celebrity conscious...thinks that's the right way to get ahead, and maybe she's right...it just isn't a thing I could bring myself to... the funniest part of the whole thing to me was that she was gone... she has made rather a point of seeing important people, and it has become a little too obvious...isn't that silly...as if that affected the way you do your work. I had expected some real pearls of witticism to drop but no results — they were tired, of course, having done four shows that day...Hope is funny just to look at, of course, but Colonna isn't a bit amusing...in fact, he's absolutely dead pan with nothing behind it. That little Tony Romano told some very interesting stories about their experiences in Africa and England...he seemed to be the most intelligent. I finally gave up and went to bed...they stayed much too late, I guess, and it's really against the rules of the post, and you shouldn't make exceptions, even for movie stars, but it was darned interesting...the situation, I mean.

That is about all that has happened since I wrote you last day before yesterday...but the most important thing in this letter is that I wanted to say that I think I'll be gone a week before your birthday and about nine or ten days after, so don't get that leave then...that is the way the plans stand now, and they seem very definite, so start praying and betting that it is after the middle of the month...it would be utterly tragic if such a marvelous piece of luck shouldn't turn out...there isn't much more I can say about it...but remember you can get hold of me through the Special Service Section of the Campus of the University of Hawaii, through Mrs. Armstrong or through Marie Sullivan Cooke (Mrs. Robert) or through the Richardsons. The censors won't allow me to tell you my address and phone number...but if worse came to worse, you could get it through the APO #963 etc. address.

Well, sweetheart, it is getting pretty near to the deadline for getting ready...well, as a matter of fact, it isn't...I have a couple of hours in which I figure I can go to the post office, go for a swim and lie down for a little while, but it's running a pretty close schedule...so, darling, I'll stop writing now...all my love to you, sweetheart, Jane

Monday, July 31
Entertainment Section, S.S.O. APO #963, Care of P.M. San Francisco, California

Dearest Honey Darling;

When I came home from the beauty shop today...yes, I have to go to them every week now to have my hair bleached and it gets very dull. Not that it isn't pretty...the hair, I mean...it is always a great improvement...but when I came home, there were three letters from you waiting on the bed...I dove and literally devoured them in no time at all. It was so good to have them, honey...I think the mail has been held up lately because it has been at least a week and a half since I have heard from you. By the way, you were talking about the unsteady arrival of my letters...it is because of the current activities, honey, and just can't be helped...the mail has been bad everyplace...I admit that I haven't been quite up to my usual prolific standard, but that is because I have been so busy... but I have still written far more letters than you have received... at least from the way you talk.

Gee, I've been terribly busy the last week...sometimes I wonder how I take it. But in a couple of days, I'll have a chance to relax for at least hours at a time, so I'm just trying to hold out until then. We rehearsed this week in the afternoons and gave a hospital show most every morning and did the performances at night. We did have Saturday night off, but that wasn't much of a vacation because I went to the dance on the post and danced like mad for relief from acting. Last night though we had a performance of Personal Appearance under conditions which were deliberately calculated to be worse than any we would encounter on our trip. We had been rehearsing to play it Penthouse style, and it really was...there were about 1500 to 2000 boys there, some of them sitting in the chairs and most of them on trucks and in trees and everything. It was right out in the middle of a dusty field. They put a canvas down for us to play on, but the entrances were bare dust, two inches thick...we had four spots and [missing] all...then we had a dressing tent [missing] entrance...[missing] to be on our toes to know where [missing] it wasn't blowing dust in your mouth, it was raining like mad...but in spite of it all, it was more fun...Captain Evans came...he is never effusive in his praise, but he let it be known in no uncertain terms that he was simply delighted with the whole thing, so the evening was a success. I got a terrific kick out of stopping the show on a couple of occasions...ah ego, ego ego!!! Awful ain't it. I had planned to write you a letter after that, but I came home and had a glass of milk with rum in it and then talked a little while and then collapsed in bed. It's not exactly easy work. Then yesterday afternoon, I was planning to write too, but instead I thought of your going spear fishing, so I put on my bathing suit and got a pair of goggles down at the swimming pier, and then I swam out to the reef and went under water and looked at the coral and the fish. Of course, the coral isn't colored here like it is down there, and the fish were tiny, but it was so much fun, honey, and when you get here, we can go out together, and you can initiate me into the fine points of the whole thing. Besides that, here you can get feet flippers which you put on, and they make you go twice as fast, and then when you want to go under, you just give yourself a little push, and you are way down there. I am told that on our trip, in our *spare time*, there is some wonderful swimming, and I am really looking forward to it.

You know, honey, up in that last paragraph, just after I had finished talking about the show, the boy who is the stage manager came in to pack our makeup and get the final word on the wardrobe and stuff...also the boy who sings in the variety show and does the chauffeur in the play. I haven't had a thing to eat today except half a malted milk. We offered them a drink, and I had one myself, and I am absolutely looping. It reminds me of one of the letters I got from you today...the one you wrote when you were drunk. By the way, who is Vannsy...and why is he relieving you as gunnery officer, and how did he know who Eloise was. Of course I will be glad to get him a date with her...as a matter of fact, I read that part of the letter to her...and she said she would love to meet him. She is on the cover of the July Coronet if you can get a copy there. Don't count too much on getting dates for everybody more than once or twice if you are in here because most of the girls have their own commitments. Maybe if you were all here for a couple of days we could arrange a party though with all the girls. Would that be fun.

Honey, as you may be able to detect, I am leaving in the next few days. I can't tell you when, naturally, but don't count on my being back until the final week in August. I was so happy when I read in your third letter today that you would be delayed a little while. That is perfect...then I will be able to see you and not miss you. I think things will be a little eased up when we get back. Honey, it is absolutely impossible to get a beach house, and besides that would be impossible for me because I have to be close to the center of operations, so I thought that either the Halekaluni or the Niu alu which are both close and within short walking distance would be wonderful...besides, they are both beautiful places, and I would love to spend some time there with you. Besides there would be no complications of life or eating. We could get a bungalow there... then we could have a wonderful time. I have surveyed the situation, and that seems best to me.

Darling, it will be your birthday in a few days, and I want to wish you a very happy one...we will celebrate it when you get here. But the thing is that if I were to send your present, heaven knows when you would get it, so I will just hold on to it for a little while until I see you...besides what it is, you would need to see first. I will see you shortly after your birthday, and then we will have a birthday party for you, and I will give it to you then — is that alright honey... the mails are so bad now that I thought that would be better.

Darling, I have to stop writing now and go and get ready for dinner...I love you, and I'll be seeing you in a few weeks.

All my love,
Jane

REVISED ITINERARY — PERSONAL APPEARANCE
3-4-5 Aug KWAJALEIN
6 Aug CARLOS
7-8 Aug ROI
9 Aug ENJIBE
10-11 Aug ENIWETOK
12-13-14 Aug MARJURO
15-16 Aug MAKIN
17 Aug TARAWA
18-19 Aug APAMAMA
20 Aug TARAWA
21 Aug CANTON
22 Aug CHRISTMAS
23 Aug CANTON

Entertainment Sect: SSO APO #963
c/o P.M., San Francisco Aug 3-4 — 1944

Hello, Darling;

Well, by this time I suppose you are wondering where I am — I haven't been very clear about everything, but I did the best I could, honey, in view of restriction — I left a message with Mrs. Richardson— Needless to say, honey, I'm pretty thrilled over this whole thing. I've had enough new experiences to last some people years, and there are many more coming — We are already completely off schedule and doing the unexpected, but it makes it more fun that way — yesterday we gave two shows — in quick succession — one thing which can't be repeated because it is too much for my voice, having to project as much as I do — to do that part twice in a row without a breather. Golly darn, honey, I wish I could tell you what we've done and what we're doing now, but I guess I'll just have to store it up in my memory. I'll venture to say though that I have been and soon will be a lot of places you haven't seen and some that you have. I would have loved to have seen Dave H. while I was down here — after you did, but I understand he has moved — who knows, I might [MISSING] my correspondence, honey, the last week or so, but forgive me, honey, please, and remember that there were about three weeks recently when you were going someplace that you weren't very good either. This new method of being en-route as we are during this writing thrilled me immeasurably at first and still does — it's simply marvelous.

I talked to Hazel the other nite — Ma Wee had been ill with jaundice, so I called to see how she was — She was much improved no worries — the connection was grand, and really it's quite inexpensive considering — I think nine dollars. Of course, there's practically nothing one can say — it's just like this letter to you — but just hearing the voices was fine. Ma Wee loved it — Jack was away, but I had to put the call through anyway, so I couldn't call later.

Oh, honey, I just hope that everything turns out right and you get there at the right time — wouldn't that be something — practically historical — I guess speaking of that — historical I mean — I was at a place yesterday where they said & took a picture of it that I was the first white woman ever to dance — Amazing ain't it.

But, darling, I'm sorry this has been such a sketchy letter, but there is such a limited fund of uncensored conversation under the present circumstances. By the way — I think they like the play — you know we're [MISSING] if they will like plays [MISSING] — if so, then it would be possible perhaps to send them down quite frequently — Last night's audience was one which hadn't expected anything — no show, was surprised when it wasn't a variety show and liked it anyway. Of course, we could probably sit on the stage and recite the multiplication tables and they'd clap — poor kids. I was pleasantly surprised at the wonderful living conditions — at least where we were, but where we were, that was to be expected. Nevertheless everything was so much less primitive than I had expected — But you know all about that.

Well, darling, cross your fingers, I hope everything there is fine with you and that things aren't too tight for comfort. Let's hope for the best, sweetheart, and second best but darned good in any case that I'll have a pile of mail waiting when I get back.

All my love, darling, Jane

U. S. NAVAL AIR BASE
HARBOR DEPARTMENT
NAVY 3234
6 August 1944.
Miss Jane Flynn

Dear Jane;

Just a note to express our deep appreciation for the grand performance that you and the rest of the cast have just presented. All hands at the Harbor department join me in congratulating you.

I am very happy to say that I am the envy of every officer in this department, in that I was the one fortunate enough to be chosen to act as your host at dinner on Friday evening. In a very few weeks, I hope to have that pleasure repeated, only next time, shall we have one of "Trader Vic's". famous steaks? The first thing that I plan on doing after arriving at Honolulu is to call the Special Service Department at Fort De *Russy* — *I* hope that you will be there and that your answer will be yes.

You were grand —
Jim Borgen
James E. Borgen, Lt. (j.g.) USNR.

Entertainment Section, SSO APO #963, Care of P.M.
San Francisco, California August 8, 1944

Hello Darling;

Well, honey, happy birthday. If I were writing you from Honolulu, your birthday would be tomorrow, but I have missed out on a day someplace, so it is my honey's thirty-second (that I shouldn't have said) birthday. Your present is sitting up in the closet of the place I now call home, waiting for you to come and collect it personally. I would have liked to have found a nicer one, but it was the best I could do under wartime conditions, and I know you will be able to use it. But I can't send it, so you better come and get it.

I'm trying to think where it was I wrote you from last, honey... you are the only person who has been favored with a letter because I have been so darned busy working and trying to absorb everything interesting that there hasn't been time for letter-writing. Needless to say, I am in a constant state of wonder and interest. I wish I were sure how much I would be permitted to say. But we no sooner started on our trip than the people who were flying us decided we should go someplace else, so we dropped out of the sky completely unexpected... that upset the whole schedule of course, but it has worked out very nicely just the same. We spent three days at an island paradise...the veritable garden spot of the Pacific...we were royally entertained when we weren't doing shows...but we did two shows a day...the afternoon ones were more than a little uncomfortable, and as a result, we have decided that one a day would be the quota after this and that we would go to hospitals and visit the men in the afternoon. I know that to the people who were stationed there, this place was pretty dull, but I can't imagine a lovelier spot to spend a honeymoon after the war. Now though, we are up on an island which is the greatest example of devastation that I have ever seen in my life...I mean I didn't dream that war could so completely destroy...the conditions, of course, are rather primitive, but the fact that they are as good as they are after such a short time and the horrible job that they had to do is completely amazing. Sometime I will be able to tell you the terribly interesting parts of this thing, but now I can't...we are certainly in a position to get a bird's eye view of the whole thing. I was talking after the play last night to two people who had just come in from Saipan...I asked questions, and they were answered for two hours...if only I could remember all these things.

Darling, I absolutely give up. This is three days later, and I haven't had a minute in which to write. This is interesting, but it certainly is the busy life. Between the shows and going to hospitals and to the men's messes and the officers' clubs and the trips from place to place — there isn't a second. Where we were when I started writing you, it was really rugged — and I mean really — but [MISSING] the lap of [MISSING] is probably about the most luxurious place in the Pacific — Navy of course. I can say that we in the [WHITED OUT] We have seen places where there has been a lot of fighting. I *can't* tell any more.

Darling, I am doing my hair now and the bleaching stuff is beginning to burn, so I'll stop writing. Just remember, honey, that I love you — and I'll be seeing you.

    All my love, Jane

U.S.S. GAMBLE (DM 15)
8 August 1944
From: Lt. (jg) C.J. Flynn, U.S.N.R.
To: The Commanding Officer, U.S.S. Gamble
Subject: Leave- request for

1. It is requested that I be granted ten (10) days leave of absence commencing 9 August 1944 to visit with my wife who is a member of an Entertaining Section (U.S.O.) in this area.

2. I am not a member of any court.

3. If this request is granted, my address will be:

9-11 August — ENGEBI
12-14 — MAJURO
15-16 — MAKIN
17 — TARAWA
18 — APAMAMA

4. I have had no days leave this calendar year.

C. J. Flynn, Lt (jg) U.S.N.R.
U.S.S. GAMBLE
DM15/P18/00 9 August 1944
Serial 72-44
1st ENDORSEMENT
From: The Commanding Officer
To: Lt.(jg) C. J. FLYNN, U.S.N.R.

1. Returned, leave granted.

2. Upon the expiration of this leave you will report to the Commanding Officer NAVY 145 for transportation to the port in which this vessel may be.

3. Priority for air transportation is authorized in execution of these leave orders.

D. N. CLAY
Aug 16, 1944

Dearest Family;
    You would just die of amazement if you could see me now, but unfortunately there isn't anything I can tell you about it. Suffice to say that I am well and fine and having a group of more thrilling experiences than I ever believed could happen to me. There is so little that I can say — not where you've been, where you're going, how you travel or what you've seen — so there's not much left. Frankly, out here where I am, you can well understand the need for censorship. The not so long ago forward areas have an awful lot of Japanese firmly entrenched in back of them. I can say though that we've been in the Marshalls and are going to the Gilberts. Some of the places have been perfectly gorgeous — south seas, beautiful moon, palm trees waving in the breeze, and others have been so shot up that you wonder there is even the ground left, no living vegetation on them except the stubs of a few palms which have been left in the hope that they'll take new life — such devastation I never imagined — where it's been cleaned, it's barren and where it hasn't been, it's a tangled mess — some places there

are so many Japanese buried, that you can't even wash your teeth in the water. I've developed a great respect for the men who live there month after month. Through it all, we've managed to remain in fairly good condition because if we get a rugged place, the next would probably be one with fine living conditions, and we could get cleaned up and ready to go again. The Navy usually afforded opportunities to improve appearance.

We're about — or a little over half way through now — and when I get back to Honolulu, it's going to be days before they can get me out of the bathtub — and from the front of a typewriter. I'll write as much as I can.

I see that the news of Roosevelt's visit has come out in the papers. I saw him. He reviewed a very famous division at Schofield Barracks, and Martha and Dorothy and I were the only three guests on the whole post, which I understand is the largest we have. If they release the newsreels, you may see us.

The play is going beautifully. It's in the nature of an experiment because if they — the boys, like plays, they can alternate them with variety shows and send a show a month down it would be wonderful if they could.

Well, darlings, we are about at our destination, so I'll stop and write again soon.

So much love to you all, Jane

August 24 1944
Enroute from someplace to someplace

Hello, Darling,

I know I've been the darndest letter writer these last three weeks that ever there was, but honestly, honey — it is just that there hasn't been a moment, and when I get someplace like I am now, I have all good intentions, but I look at the view a while and then fall asleep in the wonderful soft chairs and don't wake up until we are almost there, and then the routine starts all over again. Honestly darling I don't know how many thousand people I have met and talked to or how many hundreds and hundreds of times I have had my picture taken — If half the people send them to me that say they will — it will be enough to fill a whole album — and the men we have played to — some audiences have had as many as six thousand, — night after nite, that mounts up.

My God, honey, I was sick the other day — heartbroken would be the word — we arrived at a place, and I found that you had been there just two weeks before — as it happened we weren't so terribly far away from there — one of the closest places we could be, but we had gone up the line. If only it had worked out a little differently. I couldn't get it quite straightened out where you were bound for, but I'll soon find out, as we are headed for our last stop & by tomorrow nite, we will be back where we started from. This has been the most fascinating thing that has ever happened to me — I'll be glad to settle down in one place for a while though, and then I'd like to come out again. If only I hadn't been late the other day but soon, honey — Of course, I'm really expecting to see you in the next few days — I suppose I'm due for an awful let down, but for now I'll keep hoping. At least until tomorrow when I should find out.

Honey, I met a friend of yours the other day with his establishment — where we did a show. I should have known him myself, but I didn't — he's a fraternity brother of yours from Wash — a boy I think his name is Bob Broussard — a j.g. he said he had been planning to have dinner with you and Tom Harmon last spring at Pearl but that he had to leave unexpectedly. I could have seen Tom Harmon too, if I could have got over there — but we didn't go there. It's funny — this Bob asked me if I were really from Seattle and we got to comparing notes — When he said he was a Figi, I said "Why you must know my husband" — and he definitely did. I also met another boy in a different place who used to play football at Washington he was a Psi U & his name was Don Thomas he was quite famous that year that Anna Lee & Jim and I went to see the Stanford game — in fact I remember his being badly hurt in that particular game — he knew Sammy & Patty besides all the other people that I know. It's funny how things can lead to things because I got to talking to this navy lieutenant, and I told him about it, and Anna Lee was the first girl he ever took out at Stanford and what's more he knew Don McKean. The reason we were talking was that I was over at your & Dave Hill's old stomping grounds and what a beautiful place it is too — and I asked him if he knew Dave. He was a very good friend of his — we won't be stopping where he is, so this Navy lt. who is going up there is taking up a message for me. It's really fascinating, the number of tee-ups and coincidences.

There is so much about this trip that I couldn't bear to forget. I am always anxious to get on to something new, but when we get back, I hope I can live in the past long enough to write it down — Viewed as a panorama, life has always been pretty interesting, and I hope it will continue to be.

I am sorry as the dickens, honey, that your new situation is not so happy as the old — I hope, honey, that it won't be too long — maybe it won't be —

You know, honey, it's so darned hard to write where you know that everything you say besides the personal things — will all be taken out — the personal thing that I feel like saying over & over again is that I'm hoping and praying I'll see you soon — I violently, not just passively want to see you, honey — I know what must be, must be, but I keep so hoping.

I loved the part you wrote about the blonde picture — I've read it to everyone as an example of what a clever fellow my husband is — If you say so, I think I will keep it awhile. I think it's pretty striking myself, but it certainly requires a lot of care.

Well, darling, were almost there, so I'll stop writing — one more performance and then a vacation — I'll really write a volume in the next day or so. In the meantime, honey, I'll keep hoping that the person I want to see more than anything else in the world — I will see.

All my love, honey, Jane

Entertainment Section, SSO APO #963,
Care of P.M. San Francisco, California
August 26, 1944

Dearest Honey Darling;

Life, the last few days, has definitely been a succession of blows as far as you and I are concerned. The night I got home, there was the carbon letter to the family telling of the little deal that didn't go through…honey, I was sick, and then I started to boil. That sweet man — that was what we thought he was…we stayed in his house, and we were there for three days, and he never said a word to me about it…I guess he's just nice when he feels like it. It makes me so darn mad I can hardly stand it. Two or three other things happened about like that-well, not the same but in the matter of controlling us...the claw in the velvet hand, as it were. Tell me, darling, in case I'm not blaming anyone in the wrong, was his name Jones?

Oh, honey, this is probably going to be a heck of a letter...I've been writing the darndest ones lately to you, but when things keep happening so fast and are as confusing as they have been for me in the last few weeks, all literary talent...even the small one of writing letters completely deserts me. I only wish, darling, that you were here-and that was the second blow...to find that you wouldn't be for a while. When we came in yesterday, I almost expected to find you waiting for me...wishful thinking and all that...but no such luck. I really had visualized you standing there. But soon, darling. I honestly don't know how long I will be here. I would like to stay, and Captain Evans has asked Dorothy and Martha and me to stay after the first six months is up near the end of September, but it looks as if there may be some political difficulty...with the local USO or something and that, fight as he may, he may not be able to keep us-that is because they are jealous of the army. However, I think it will turn out alright...and I'll know in a few days...I'll see you someplace. I am very anxious to continue with this work, no matter where I am though. My goodness, I do sound confused, don't I. I'll give you the straight of it in a few days, honey, and in the meantime, there is nothing to get disturbed about. Well, our trip was a great success...a few little things went wrong here and there, but the thing is that it all came off better than anyone could ever have expected I don't think I will ever forget it my whole life... it was the most thrilling and interesting experience I ever hope to have. To think of being a girl and seeing as much of the war as I have — it's a thing that is granted very few people...in fact, I would say that I have really seen more than most any of the people who went out — we tried to circulate and see the men as well as the officers and got a wonderful cross section of the whole thing. Another thing that made it interesting was the fact that we didn't have our own special means of transportation and had to pick up rides as we went along...it was remarkably simple and so much fun to be sort of hitch-hiking around the Pacific. Of course, the larger impressions I will never forget, things that were so impossibly grim that I don't see how men could stand them and the impression of the terrific power of this country and the wonderful natives, and the tension and people being killed — the things I just can't tell about in a letter. Anyway, honey, I feel terribly privileged to have seen what I have, and I do feel a little bit proud of bringing a certain amount of enjoyment and a little lift to a lot of people, and I mean a lot...

Well, sweetheart, time is passing.._I have to get ready to go to dinner soon or I won't get any...we are back on our little place and we have to get over to dinner on the hour or it is not forthcoming. I have been to the hairdressers today and done my ironing and been shopping because I wore all my shoes out on the coral...in fact, it has been too full a day. We start the play again tomorrow night. Darling, the thing is that if I stop writing now, I can mail this tonight, and if I continue it, it will be later, so I will try to write another one tomorrow.

Honey, you remember my cousin, Bob Patten...the J.G. who was in radar...Uncle Bob's boy...well, he was killed down there last month. I haven't seen him for years, but I did grow up with him. He was such a very brilliant boy too. I hope he will be the only one in the family. It's a pretty bad feeling to have even one. I can't imagine what happened, but I can't tell you about it...it was in action.

Honey, just remember that I love you with all my heart and that I am dying to see you, and, darling, it will be soon, I know it...

All my love to you, Jane

[Aug 1944]

THIS IS A RESTRICTED PUBLICATION AND CANNOT BE MAILED! Page three (Aug. 11.)

AJAs COMMENDED ON ITALIAN CAMPAIGN RECORD

Washington, Aug. 1_ —The War Department today issued a special commendation to the 100 Infantry Btn., composed of Americans of Japanese ancestry, for their part in the battle of Italy.

According to the announcement, the unit went all through its campaign without a single case of desertion or AWOL. The closest thing to being absent without leave in the unit, the Department said, was the case of two wounded men who left the hospital without permission and hitch-hiked to the front to join their comrades.

The Department said the AJAs had an "impressive record" in action, held 1,000 Purple hearts, and several hundred Silver Stars and Distinguished Service Medals — Fifteen of the men were commissioned from the ranks since the unit went into action.

MEDICAL ASSOCIATION DON'T LIKE DRAFTING OF MED STUDENTS.

New York, Aug. 10. — The American Medical Association today said that if the army continued drafting medical students before they had completed their courses, the number of doctors in the United States would be reduced by 15,000 by 1948.

The statement was contained in an article in the Association's Journal. Particular target for the attack was a statement alleged to have been made by Maj. Gen. Lewis B. Hershey.

"There is undue concern over the supply of doctors in the United States," Hershey was quoted as saying when approached on the proposition of deferring Med Students.

"PERSONAL APPEARANCE" PLAYS TO RECORD HOUSE

Personal Appearance, a USO show featuring the five ladies scheduled to visit here today, opened on the big island before a record all-male audience last night. Another showing is scheduled for this evening.

"All the world's a stage" but it's better when women are with the actors.

"Personal Appearance" would have been a great success simply as personal appearance of the five lovelies who filled 5,000 pairs of eyes with more than theatrical techniques and deep dashing thespianism.

Ably stated by an unknown. critic from the back row was the clear cut, simple cat call: "We don't care what they say. Just bring them out!"

Jane Flynn as Carole Lerden lent a charm of her own, a credit to her parents and a treat to the audience in a silver evening gown. The play could have stopped right there. The photographers hoped Jane would stop long enough for appropriate pin-up art.

Nancy North's too brief appearance was a high point of the play, and Eloise Hardt did not reveal, but ably suggested. The critic assures that a relocation would have resulted in rebellion to the rigors of morals, discipline and worship of drama.

It was a pity that characterization cancelled true physical identity of Martha Shaw as Aunt Kate and Dorothy Kay as Mrs. Struthers. Ennubirr addicts will find today that a play called "Personal Appearance" can be one thing — personal appearance in the truly identified personages of the five femmes is another and better phase and no discredit to the nice job of emotion either.

Some men did some good acting. To Hell with them.

THIS IS A RESTRICTED PUBLICATION AND CANNOT BE MAILED! *Page two (Aug. 11.)*

At the western end of the Peninsula, the German garrison declined an offer to surrender and the city was last reported under heavy assault by British and Canadian forces. Other forces were said to be converging on Lorient.

Supreme headquarters also disclosed that 300 WACs were already on duty in France.

ALLIES HAVE SUNK 500 NAZI SUBS SINCE WAR STARTED

Washington, Aug. 10. — A joint statement issued simultaneously by President Roosevelt and prime minister Winston Churchill disclosed today that the Allies had sunk 500 German submarines since the war in Europe started in 1939. The statement, while warning that the German underseas fleet still was great, commented that the sub "now was the hunted rather than the hunter."

Seventeen submarines were destroyed in the English channel while attempting to halt Allied shipping bound for the French coast.

RUSSIANS DRIVING ACROSS LATVIA; WARSAW OFFENSIVE RESUMED

Moscow, Aug. 10. — Two powerful Soviet armies stabbed across Latvia today toward the port of Liepaja and Riga, capital of the Baltic nation. Meanwhile, according to the Soviet communique, "the offensive east of Warsaw has resumed and is making progress."

The Russians reported gains on many sectors of their long front despite heavy German counterattacks, especially in Poland, where Soviet columns seriously threaten East Prussian.

WE'RE SORRY AS HELL, BUT MISTAKES HAPPEN

THE EDITORS of THE ALLEN ISLAND ECHO regret a serious error which appeared in yesterday's edition. We erroneously stated that the Russian armies were 822 miles from Berlin. Actually they were 228 miles. This apology is printed in the hope that it will lift the morale which we so ruthlessly crushed to earth by our thoughtlessness yesterday.

GUAM VIRTUALLY SECURED, NAVY ANNOUNCES

Pearl Harbor, Aug. 10. — Admiral Chester Nimitz today announced that the island of Guam was virtually secured by American marines and soldiers and that the last remaining organized Japanese resistance was being eliminated.

Only one small pocket of enemy troops remained on the northeast tip of the island. They were completely surrounded and cut off from escape — either by land or sea. American forces were cutting into the pocket.

Nimitz said the Japanese forces were under constant bombardment from land and air.

WASHINGTON, Aug. 10. — The War Department today banned the motion pictures "Wilson" and "Heavenly Days" on grounds that they violated provisions of the soldier-vote bill.

The bill provides that no controversial political stuff be allowed to influence the soldier vote. Wilson is a picture about America's last wartime president, while Heavenly Days, starring two widely known comedians, allegedly criticizes Washington conditions.

Meanwhile, Democratic leaders in the Senate began working on an amendment to the controversial law which would grant the soldiers all forms of political news now available to civilians.

HEADQUARTERS CENTRAL PACIFIC BASE COMMAND
OFFICE OF THE COMMANDING GENERAL
APO 958

SUBJECT: Travel Orders.

1. The following female members of the cast "Personal Appearance"
will proceed from APO 963 I accordance with the itinerary outlined
below, and return to APO 963 upon completion of this tour. This is
for the purpose of entertaining military personnel.

Jane Patten Flynn, Nancy Lee Worth, Eloise Hardt,
Dorothy Fay Ritter, Martha Shaw

Leave	On or About (date)
APO 963 for APO 241	3 August 1944
APO 241 for FPO 825	7 August 1944
FPO 825 for APO 243	9 August 1944
APO 243 for FPO 3234	12 August 1944
FPO 3234 for APO 459	15 August 1944
APO 459 for APO 240	17 August 1944
APO 240 for APO 242	18 August 1944
APO 242 for APO 240	20 August 1944
APO 240 for APO 914	20 August 1944
APO 914 for APO 915	21 August 1944
APO 915 for APO 914	22 August 1944
APO 914 for APO 963	23 August 1944.

2. Each member of the troupe will be allowed fifty-five (55) pounds
of personal and professional baggage.

3. Travel by government air and motor transportation is authorized.
Travel directed is necessary in the military service.

By command of Major General Burgin:

H.S. Thatcher Signature
H. S. THATCHER,
Lt Colonel A.G.D.,
Adjutant General.

Sept 3rd 1944
Entertainment Section, SSO APO #963, Care of P.m.
San Francisco, California

Dearest Honey Darling;

Well, finally I get down to this typewriter to beat out a letter. What has been the matter with me the last week, I don't know...I have written one letter to the family, and it was the first one since I have been back. Really I think it was because I was pretty tired, and after the fundamental business of living and working was finished, I just didn't do anything. I am beginning to get caught up on my energy now though, and my desire to communicate has come back...not that I didn't have the desire all the time, I just didn't do it. Please try to forgive me, honey. You know I was thinking that there are times lately when I haven't been as considerate of you as I should and want to be...in the way of writing and telling you what has happened to me...I've sort of fallen down on my end of the deal — but it's because I've spent so much energy trying to be considerate of thousands of other people who are in the same position that you are. Then there are so many things I can't tell you, but. you understand I am sure that it was because of censorship regulations...there is so darned little, for example, that I can write to you about the trip...aside from the fact that we went to the Gilberts and Marshalls and Phoenix islands and that it was terribly exciting and that the reception was terrific...and that the whole thing was a great success. I'll talk more about that later... now I'll tell you what I have been doing lately.

We were supposed to have a hospital show today, but I woke up pretty late this morning to find that had been cancelled because some of the girls were pretty tired. Poor things, I don't blame them. It's perfectly amazing though. I seem to be able to take it better because I really do more things, but I think that my old habit of falling asleep at any given moment is coming in handy now because I can refresh myself. Really, our schedule hasn't been at all bad since we got back. We had two nights vacation, and then we started the play, but we were so used by this time to doing it under rugged conditions, that it seems nothing to me...except for the fact that my particular part takes a terrific amount of energy, I'm scared to death that you won't get up here before the play closes...I would have so loved to have had you amazed by the whole thing. Plans are in a very indefinite stage now though. It may run another month, and then it may run another three months. This play has been a terrific success...the only reason they would take it off is because they want to give us something else to do. Of course, I get tired of playing the part — it has been three months now, but I would like to play it long enough for you to be here. I won't have the lead in the next play, naturally...I think they're going to do "Over 21" and that Martha will do the Ruth Gordon part. Of course, there isn't the distinction when you don't have the lead but then there is the lack of responsibility that you feel...with that part it's a big responsibility. This week we are playing at Schofield Barracks. They have a very nice theatre, and it is a pleasure to be in one place for a whole week instead of every night a different place, some good, some grim. Of course, when we are up here, we take the set with us, but some of the dressing rooms last week were worse than any we had ever had down under. Of course it is an hour's ride out and back, but the rewards of a good theatre and a very intelligent audience are worth it. Honey, what I haven't learned about how to handle an audience...it is wonderful. This experience is something invaluable...that you would never have a chance to duplicate in your life. Professionally, it is one of the finest things that has ever happened to me. We are due for another change next week. We are going to one of the other islands, Kauai, and play for a week. It should be very nice and relaxing because I hear that is a very quiet island. When we get back, we will probably go to the other islands. When we get back however, we start rehearsals on this play because Nancy and Eloise are going home, and Martha and Dorothy are changing parts...from playing Aunt Kate and the mother, they are going into Joyce and Gladys, and then we are getting some other women...older for the other two parts. Margo is either going home or going over to the USO, so that will leave Martha and Dorothy and me here. We still don't have specific permission from the USO, but we are proceeding on the assumption that we are going to stay. I went to lunch when I finished that last paragraph, and on the way back, Dorothy and I saw Captain Evans. He says he still hasn't had any word, but he assumes that it is alright.

Oh, darling, it is such a rat race around here...I start writing to you, and then the phone rings or somebody comes in, and I completely lose my train of thought. With six girls in the same house, things do get a little confused. Then girls are inclined to get upset about little things, and sometimes like today, things are in a turmoil...and all over the silly little fact of whether we will stay at Schofield Thursday night or come home in the morning. It seems that a very famous character is giving a party for us that night, and the question is should we stay there with the hostess or come home later. Personally I don't care.

Oh, darling, I do rave on about things in which you probably don't have the slightest interest, don't I. But I am trying to let you know what I am doing as much as possible. Tomorrow we start on the hospital shows again in the afternoon. That is kind of wearing but you feel privileged to have the opportunity to do them.

Darling, I am so worried to hear that you are not as happy as you were in the former situation. I am sure that your sense of humor will hold firm and that you will be able to take the whole thing in your stride, but I am sorry to hear that you are not happy about it. I was wondering if, with a promotion coming up before too terribly long, you couldn't apply to do something else. I don't know the procedure on such things, but I think if you apply for something specific, it is usually given consideration. However it is, honey, I hope it works out alright. Keep your chin up, honey, and preserve that old Flynn sense of humor...I remember that old twinkle in the eye.

Well, darling, it is getting on in time again, and I have to have a shower and dress to go to the play. When we have to go a long way, the days seem to go so fast. I don't know where they disappear. Just remember, darling, that I love you, and I am crossing my fingers and not giving up hope that we will meet before the end of the year — you better hurry though...thirteen days.

All my love to you darling, Jane

According to information available at this time, the five girls, members of a USO show, will arrive at the pier shortly after 14.30. Lt. J. R, David will meet the visitors and give than the key to the island — The five girls will be the first civilian white women to set foot on this island. Only other woman seen within miles of the place by the personnel was a pregnant native woman who came over to see the little world series between the Radio Station and the native baseball teams several months ago.

In announcing the visit of the charming ambassadors of good will, Lt. David issued a few cautions to his peons. "Let's take it easy, men," Lt, David said, "Just stare at them as if you hadn't seen a women in five or six months.

"Perhaps it might be better to greet them with closed eyes, then open the right eye just a little, then the left just a little, then both eyes a little, and then, after wholly prepared,, LOOK. If this procedure is not followed., Casey =7 have some shock caws,

Described by Am. troup as "the greatest thing since the invention of Ration I supper unit," and toted by radio room personnel as "better than a good dinner of Span and C Ration," the event is more important than an announcement that the President, Winston Churchill and Josef Stalin had chosen this island for another conference.

It was generally believed that most men would not start out on a shell hunt, or sail boats in the lagoon, or go over to the other island for a haircut while the visitors were here. However, there was no confirmation of this fact.

Largely responsible for the appearance of real (pinch yourself) white women on this island was Correspondent Norman Paige, veteran radio and Newspaperman, currently stationed on the island in connection with federal government work. Mr. Paige met the ladies through Gen. Limey (Hereafter referred to as "Kin" by Mr. Paige) while at Kwajalein yesterday.

Although no definite program has' been announced as yet, it was believed that the visitors would participate in the dedication of Loews...

4-AuKs m MJL FRC FRECH CAPITAL

Entertainment Section, SSO APO #963, Care of P.M.
San Francisco, California
September 19 1944

Dearest Honey;

I know. I know. You are about ready to haul me into the divorce courts for my long silence. I have been so bad about writing to everyone lately that I almost dread the mail coming because of all of the letters I haven't answered. But I'll make this a good long one, darling, and after this, there will be a reform. It isn't that I haven't been thinking of you, but it has just been one of those times...I just got back last Saturday from a week in Kauai with two performances a day, and since our return, we have been so upset about our future plans that I just didn't have the stomach to write anyone...I couldn't have told you what I was going to do, and I kept waiting for fear that I would just confuse you. As a matter of fact, I still don't know, but I can't wait any longer to write. But more of that later.

I was little mixed up for a day or so because I got the letter telling me that the splint was off your hand before I got the one telling me about what happened to it. Darling, you were so lucky that it wasn't worse, but it was bad enough as it was. It must have hurt terribly...I hope, honey, that it is well by now.

My gosh, speaking of now, do you realize that this very moment... the twentieth of September is dawning, and it is exactly one year since I [bid?/bade?] you goodbye in San Francisco. I never really thought it would be possible that I wouldn't see you for that long. I always kept thinking that something was going to happen. As a matter of fact, there were a few hours there that I was hoping you had missed the boat, but that was because they didn't give me the message up at the Navy dispensary. It's been a long time, and a lot of things have happened to both of us in it, honey. Think of all the things we will have to tell each other before too long. It's a year that I can't say I'm sorry to have seen pass, and I hope that the next time that we have to talk about will just be a tiny fraction of that. That's quite an anniversary, isn't it, honey.

I was horribly shocked to hear of Max's death. I remember meeting him on the ship one day in San Francisco and hearing of your dinner table conversations. I know how it must be for you, honey... living so closely for so long, it seems as if a part of yourself were gone. A thing like that will strike you more sharply than someone's being killed in the war. I'm terribly sorry, darling.

The week on Kauai, in spite of the two performances a day, was pretty refreshing. I had never quite recovered from the tiredness of our down-under trip and the feeling of not being able to sit down and relax and stop rushing. It was a perfectly beautiful island — the way you would imagine this one to be if you hadn't been here. We stayed in practically the only hotel in the place, a lovely group of bungalows surrounded by all manner of fruit and flowering trees. It was very quiet and a little old fashioned, and the food was good. As a matter of fact, we did have an afternoon off, and we took a long ride up into the hills to see a canyon which is supposed to be more beautiful than the Grand Canyon. Those who had seen both told me it wasn't, but it was certainly an awe-inspiring sight. The end of the canyon went right off into the level and before that was the ocean. It was so lovely. We had a car at our disposal all the time... we could walk a few blocks to a little village...then too, the play was in one theatre, only five minutes ride away all the time, and that made it a lot easier. When you sometimes have to ride over an hour each way, that makes the whole thing pretty long. The only extra curricular thing we did was visit the hospital, and that wasn't very large, so I came home really refreshed, only to plunge into a pack of complications that have had us stumped for days. It seems that two of the girls want to go home at the end of the month, and Margo wants to transfer to the local USO, and Martha and Dorothy and I want to stay on. Captain Evans asked us if we would and we said yes...then it seems that he got a wire from the war department saying we all had to be home by the twenty-seventh of September which is the date our six months expires. So he sent a cable back requesting that they extend the contracts of the three of us and transfer Margo. All that came back was a cable asking for further clarification...after several such exchanges, he got a cable — rather the heads of special service got one saying that an answer to the request would arrive shortly...then they got a really big shot to work, and he signed a request to which there has, as yet, been no answer. In the meantime, he asked Dorothy if she would send a personal wire to Laurence Phillips, the head of the USO, asking him...because she knows him. When we got back from Kauai, there was a personal cable waiting for Dorothy saying that he regretted that he could not extend our overseas engagement...Well, that isn't official...just personal, and they can't act on that and send us home, so in the meantime they are interpreting the last wire saying that there would be an answer to the request as meaning that they should keep us here until they get an answer...that gives us a little more time, and we have put everyone we know to work on it. Last night we had a big talk with a man from the USO called a "trouble shooter" who is over here and he is seeing Captain Evans in the morning.

He may very probably do something to help out the situation. In the meantime, of course it is very difficult to get transportation, so we will just keep on running the show. Perhaps they will send the other two girls home. The whole thing seems so utterly ridiculous because Captain Evans and the whole Special service are terribly anxious to have us stay, and they need us so badly. It is a terrible waste of government money and transportation to send us home when more than likely we could come right back out again. I am so anxious to stay because we haven't even scratched the surface of the work to be done here, and it seems a waste. Besides I want to be doing something to help the war along, and this seems to be about the best thing I can do. Well, we have been working like little beavers on the whole thing and thinking and talking of nothing else for the last few days. Evidently there is some mix-up someplace. Perhaps the USO in New York just doesn't realize what we are doing out here. It is customary for people to go home at the end of six months, and maybe they just can't understand why we should stay. This man tomorrow may be able to take care of that.

So you see, honey, I just don't know if I'm coming or going, and if I do go, when it will be. Now if I do go, and there is a chance of seeing you on the coast, I shall see you in San Francisco, and we shall have your time together, and then I will go to New York with Martha and Dorothy. We figure that if we go home, this is the best time of all to go to New York, when we have this fresh behind us and have been working as we have. We work together beautifully... far better than one person could...we combine our forces and really go to town — if we do stay, it will be simply because we have put our heads together and worked out every angle that we could think of...a regular campaign. I hope you don't mind if I do that after I see you, honey, but if I am going to get anyplace and I have to go back to the Mainland, this is the time for me to get started. I want us to have something solid when the war is over.

Well, darling, that is as much as I know of where I will be in the next little while. I'll write you the minute I know anything more, but if I don't in time, I guess you'll just have to stop and find out. All you have to do is to get in touch with the special-service section on the campus of the University of Hawaii and ask for Evans, and he'll tell you. Oh, honey, I'm sorry it is so confusing, but there isn't anything I can do, and I hope to Heaven I'll see you someplace soon.

(I changed to red because the black is really worn out) I'll try to get a new ribbon tomorrow.)

I thought the letter from Park was very cute, although I must confess, I had a little difficulty reading it. I was surprised that he could say where he was, although I suppose it is such a big place that that much is allowable. I have met a couple of ATC pilots who know him in Long Beach. By the way, I had a letter from Dave Hill yesterday. When I was on Canton, I sent a message up to Palmyra because I couldn't get there. That was too bad because I had been looking forward to seeing him and completing the circle. I tried to find your name on the register of that hotel, but they had put last year's away. It was later that it occurred to me that you might have been there this year too. Wasn't that an amazing place to be right out in the middle of nowhere...and with hot water too. That was what I found so completely amazing. We had had it on one other place, our first stop, and since then it had been all brackish and cold, either or both. Dave said to send his best regards to you when I wrote. He should be up here the middle of next month. I hope to heaven that I am here. He asked me to write and tell him if I thought I would be.

About that airplane business, honey, I can't do anything about it until I know, and besides it has to be in the orders or you can't get it, so take care of that if necessary. Without the orders for that type of transportation, it is, I think, impossible.

Well, darling, the night is drawing on, and I have to get up fairly early in the morning...it is now well into our year's anniversary. I shall drink my bottle of beer that is sitting beside me as a toast to you and a toast to the hope that we will see each other soon. It's been too long...so in the meantime, millions and millions of love to you, darling...

All my love, Jane

Entertainment Section, SSO PO #963, Care of P.M.
San Francisco, California September 26, 1944

Dearest Honey Darling;

I have put off writing you for the last few days because I frankly have been on tenterhooks about where I would be. I still don't know...I may be here this weekend even, and then again I may not be. I may be here for the next six months, and then I may be home inside of two weeks. So whatever you do, if you don't hear from me in time, leave yourself a loophole until you find out. If you do not find out in time, call the Special Service headquarters or the entertainment section on the campus of the University of Hawaii and ask for Major Maurice Evans and tell who you are and you can find out where I am. Oh, honey, I'll see you one place or the other, but for heaven's sake, don't let's get too mixed up...I pray for that. It seems that a reply to the army's request to keep us is still pending. Our first six months is up tomorrow, and that cable better come in a hurry because they feel that if it doesn't come, they will have to send us home sooner or later. Of course, the whole thing is perfectly absurd... it is just one of those damnable mix-ups caused by red tape, but we are sitting right in the middle of it. Who knows what will happen. We close the play tomorrow night, and then if we stay, we will recast it with navy personnel and run it for the navy for a couple of months.

I just got your letter in which you said you hoped you would see Park. I guess from that that all our business will probably be settled, and you will hear from me in time. If I am not here, get in touch with Pat Zemmer.

I had some very bad news from Mother yesterday...this time it is true...Tom Potts was killed in Normandy in the early days of the invasion. It was pretty much of shock to realize that someone who had been such a big part of the old life was gone. I suppose it was foolish of me, but I had always kind of hoped that possibly he and Mary might get together since the divorce was so final. It was just a little over a year ago that we were so worried about the rumor of his being killed. She, Hazel, also wrote that Uncle Bob had seen some of the companions of Cousin Bob Patten and that he was definitely gone...there was no question about it.

I was just coming in from dinner Sunday night when I heard the phone ringing. I dove for it, which is sometimes unusual for me because we aren't so enthusiastic about answering that phone...it is always ringing, and who do you suppose it was, Kenny Price. He had arrived just a little while ago. I haven't seen him yet because he hasn't had any time off that I have, but with the days at the end of this week off, perhaps we can have dinner. He said that the baby, whose name is Bronwyn incidentally, is perfectly beautiful. Will is still at Pendleton but is expecting to get away in a month or so-but then he always is. He asked after you, and I told him the tragedy of missing you by six days. It was so amazing because he sounded exactly like Will...it didn't make me homesick because I don't think anything could, but it did seem a little like old times..,

Oh, honey, you will laugh when you hear this, knowing me-and how I am always trying to take care of somebody. I spent the day trying to win a baseball game for the army in the little world series tomorrow. It seems that the army players, Joe DiMaggio and Bill Leonard and Johnny Beasley, have been coming over to the house quite a bit. They know some people in the entertainment section, and we met them there. Well, this Johnny Beasley showed up today a wreck-he lost the first game, and I guess he was pretty discouraged-he has to pitch again tomorrow, and the army has to win this one or the series is over. The other two were along too, but DiMaggio isn't playing, and Bill Leonard, as a catcher, doesn't have to do so much. They all get discouraged because so much is expected of them, and it is so hard for them to keep in shape, being in the army and having other duties and all...the other two were sort of egging Beasley on-he's a lieutenant incidentally so I decided that something had to be done about it or he would definitely lose tomorrow. They had a party planned for tonight and all. So I insisted that he go swimming and made him stay out on the raft all afternoon and then took him to the play with us...the whole cast had dinner and all out at the Marine Air Station at Ewa...then dropped him off at Hickam where he lives after the play. It was just ten, and it was early enough to get a good night's sleep but too late to go anyplace or to have a drink. So if he wins tomorrow, I will congratulate myself. I would love to go to the game, but it is about fifty miles away from the play, and I don't think we could make it. I went to one out at Hickam the other day. Gee, honey, it was a thrill for me to see all those wonderful ball players that we had listened to on the radio for so long. It was a pretty good game. The navy won in the ninth inning. I remember now when the Cardinals won the series in 1942, and we were rooting for them, and that Johnny Beasley pitched two winning games. It is funny...he is just a kid... only 25...and a little spoiled in certain ways but fundamentally a very sweet character. DiMaggio is very nice too, but he is more the typical baseball player type. It worries Johnny B. because he is afraid the others will think he's trying to be somebody because he's a lieutenant...but I guess he made a good record in OCS, I thought you would think it was kind of funny though, my working so hard to win a game for the army...and believe me, it was work...I thought of all the persuasion I had used on. you...psychologically I mean...on certain occasions, and I put it all to work. This time I was successful though...not one single drink...and I have a pretty good sunburn.

Oh, darling, I hope that by the next letter, things will be straightened out. I haven't been much good to anyone as long as this thing has been hanging in the balance like this. I want to stay so badly. It would make everything work out perfectly, both for us and in a professional way...but all I can do now is cross my fingers and hope. I just had Nancy read the cards, and she sees a change of residence and a document arriving, but the change of residence, which, incidentally is for business reasons, doesn't involve an ocean voyage...it would be here because if we stayed, we would probably move...she saw no voyage...! Guess I haven't told you that Nancy is really quite remarkable with the cards...she's guessed too many things for everyone to have it just be luck. It's amazing. The night Bob Hope was here, just before he went down under, she told him that his trip was going to be cut short, and he would have an accident during the course of it. Both things happened. She told me though that I was going to have a wonderful business deal within the course of three months, so I'm waiting. She has told me twice that something was wrong with Mary, and it was true. She told a boy who was here the other day who thought he was going to be transferred that he was definitely not going, and he didn't go. I wish she had been a little more specific with this though. We have all come to the point that if we are worried about what is going to happen, we go and ask Nancy to read the cards for us.

Well, sweetheart, I think I had better stop now...cross your fingers, and in any case, I'll see you soon. In case you haven't heard it before, I adore you.

All my love to you, Jane

Entertainment Section, SSO APO #963,
Care of P.M. San Francisco, California
October 2, 1944

Dearest Honey;

I received a short note from you today...written the 29th of September, only four days ago. Still you hadn't had any word of your future plans or if you had, you couldn't tell me. In case you get this, I just want to tell you not to plan on my being here or there. Eloise and Nancy left yesterday. They forced the issue because Ellie was very anxious to get back. Of course that stopped the play until it can be reorganized but they can't start reorganizing it until they get a notice from the War department that we can stay and the answer still hasn't come. We are visiting the hospitals this week which is very worthwhile work and something I am terribly glad to be doing...but I don't know how long that will last. I sorted all my papers this evening and I think I will just start to pack in case of eventualities. The others flew out since it means quite a difference in the bankroll to the three of us, I think we will take the other method — not that it costs anything. We just earn more that way. If that should happen, I should be seeing Hazel and Jack first and then Pat Zemmer. But I do have to go to Hollywood for a week or so after I get back. But who knows what will happen.

Mrs. Armstrong called me to tell me that a great event would probably take place about two months after your birthday...a couple of days less. That is the end of the week so I think I will see you then. But in any case, call her for my number because Katie Richardson is seldom home and Mrs. A seems to always be. Or act according to previous instructions.

We spent about four days today at a naval hospital going around talking to the boys. Those poor kids. I guess there isn't much I can tell you about it but it is terrible — just horrible...boys eighteen years old totally blind for life. Maybe I am made if too stern stuff or have seen too much by this time...because in one of the wards the whole thing practically was devoted to those boys...Spencer Tracy who was here last week couldn't stand to stay there. I carried on with great aplomb and laughed and joked with them. I guess you can get used to anything. I had a letter from the ship we came over on...I can tell you now that it was a hospital head... it said that the last load off the beach was the worst yet. Some of the boys up there were intimately acquainted with that ship. Some had seen our show down under...Good God. What a war! I am almost afraid to go home for fear I'll be objectionable and start telling a few people off. Actually I don't want to go back there. I dread it. I've seen too much of an overall picture of this whole thing. I'm not going to like the contrast.. Especially some of our dear friends in Hollywood. But enough of that darling...we'll trade a lot of talk when we see each other again and if the fates are with us, it won't be long.

Dotty is asking me to come help her bleach her hair so I think I will stop writing. The house is so quiet — there are only three of us left now and we are fairly rattling. Here is a picture of the five of us that I thought I would send. I'll put the names on the back... see if you can guess before you look.

I love you darling Jane

I have another birthday present waiting for you & I don't know what to do with either of them — I've just been waiting — Much love darling —

Special Service Office ENTERTAINMENT SECTION
Central Pacific Base Command
APO 963
3 October 1944
Miss Jane Patten Flynn
U.S.O. Camp Shows O.S.U. #237 Hollywood, California

Dear Jane:

It is a sad parting and we hate to have you leave, as you know. You have done a wonderful job for us, and it is certain that wherever you continue this valuable work you will leave after you the same story of success.

The record-breaking four-month run of "Personal Appearance", the variety show, and your many visits to the men in hospitals throughout the Central Pacific have actually been a greater experience for the troops than even we had dreamed.

It has been a distinct pleasure to work with actresses of your sincerity and energy. Until we meet again, Jane, the best of luck and my best wishes always.

MAURICE EVANS Major, AUS Officer-in-Charge

Oct 4 — 1944

Darling—

A quick note to let you know you won't find me here. Call me at Mother's or at Pat Zemmer's and I'll come a runnin' — Have to leave honey.

All me love Jane

Oct 5, 1944 En-route

Darling—

Well as you were able to gather by yesterday's note, the worst has happened — I know it won't seem so bad to you but I was pretty unhappy to leave — but it seems the answer from the War Dept to the army's request that we stay, never came and they couldn't legally wait any longer. — of course if an affirmative answer does come there is a slight possibility they may send for us again but that is very slight — difficulties are too great — I shall wait until I see what you do and where you are and then made plans. I love this work so — in fact I love to work as hard as I have been. I imagine I could go to the European theatre without half trying. I have to go to Hollywood as soon as I get back with the other girls, Martha & Dorothy but I shall leave word as to where I am with Pat Zemmer and you can call me and I'll come a flying. Martha and Dorothy and I are going to try to stick pretty much together because we are a combination that seems to get places.

Maybe it is better for us honey that I should be where I am going but it would have been so much less complicated the other way — a wonderful place for a leave. I guess there's no use crying — just start slugging when I get back but I really am sick about it. It seemed to be doing so much good —

I called Mrs. Armstrong and Scoop Richardson — they just had a baby. All the time I was there I never saw them. That's something you will just have to understand though honey — I didn't have time — one day a week I sometimes had off, and I want swimming or something. I should have, I know, but I lived in sort of a different world — the service world entirely really.

Well, sweetheart — I'll see you soon — As we went out I saw one just like yours — I nearly had heart failure — then I noticed there were four instead of three you know whats — so it was alright.

Whom do you suppose I met here — a friend of yours from Everett & Washington — a crew man called Dutch Shoat. — He's a Navy Lt. & has been at Haneohi — it was so funny — we were just talking along, and suddenly all this came up—

I love you honey— Jane

9, Dec. 1944 [sic?] in Port

Dear Chet:

Just as we were coming in here I heard a wonderful story about this place back in the earlier days of the war. He got it from an officer in the New Zealand Artillery, and he claims to have been here on the beach when the thing happened. It's entirely possible that you have heard it before, in that case stop me, but it might very well be entitled a "Comedy of Errors" with apologies to the Bard.

It seems that one rather cloudy night an Allied cruiser was laying an anchor sitting in the harbor. A Japanese sub closed in on her and lined up the misty bulk in her periscope and let fly with a torpedo. Whether she was in too great a hurry or her aim was bad no one knows. At any rate the torpedo missed the cruiser and hit a reef about half a mile beyond and exploded.

On the cruiser the lookouts saw the explosion and felt the concussion and the ship was sent to. General Quarters. Not unnaturally they manned the anti-aircraft batteries and prepared to stand off a high altitude bombing attack.

The sub, in the meantime, seeing no pronounced activity aboard the ship, reasoned that she was a big and relatively unarmed transport or merchant ship and decided to surface and sink her with surface fire and save her valuable torpedoes.

She surfaced and was about, to knock off what she thought would be a sitting duck, when the cruiser saw her and everyone shifted to the main batteries. The sub saw this and, realizing her mistake, crash-dived and made good her escape before the cruiser could get her big guns trained on her. So with the exception of the one torpedo that hit the reef, not a shot was fired in this rather bewildering engagement.

If I were a sports writer, I would be tempted to score this one, no runs, no hits, several errors! Sounds incredible doesn't it, but they claim it actually happened. Well that's all for now Chet, I have to go on watch. I'll write soon again Regards.

22 Dec. 1944 In Port —

Dear Chet:

I suppose that at one time or another every average American has walked out of a theater having just seen Dottie Lamour slink through the better part of ten reels fetchingly clad in a sarong and made a firm resolve to himself that sometime soon he is going to chuck up his job and take a fling for himself on one of those South Pacific Isles. Lest you accuse me of a feeling of superiority, or a patronizing attitude, let me hasten to add that a short while ago I was well up in the front ranks of such thinkers. Now I hate to say this, fellows, but it ain't so. I have yet to see one damsel that remotely resembles Dottie. There doesn't even seem to be a young woman around, they are either six or sixty.

As a matter of fact, there is only one department that lives up to advance notices. That is the marine life, and brother, it's got everything. The other day we were in the whale boat going over for some mail. We took a short cut and passed over a shallow reef. The water is very clear, and as we were going slow we really had a treat. The most incredible formations of coral. Some in branches like a leafless tree, others looking like great mushrooms, and still others like squatty round cacti. In, around and among these formations, swam fish like you have never seen before. Bright Indigo blue, flaming red, yellow-green, purple, blue, you name it and it was there. They varied in size from the kind we keep in fish bowls back home to two and three feet long. Of all the ones we saw though, the one that impressed me most was only about six inches long. The body was sort of an iridescent yellow-green and evenly spaced along its sides were red dots about a quarter of an inch across. If this wasn't enough, the fish had a bill or sword about two inches long, and so help me it was bright red. I'm glad I'm not a drinking man or I wouldn't have believed my eyes.

Well, there you have it, Chet. If its piscatorial pleasures you are after, by all means come to the South Seas. But if, on the other hand, you had in mind chasing glamorous golden hoydens through the palms…u-uh. Dig for your wallet, and stick to Paramount and Dottie, you'll be a lot happier!!

Regards

Chas

★1945★

U.S. Grant Hotel stationery — San Diego, California
January 7, 1945 Number one — 1

My Darling;

It is now about ten in the evening, and I am sitting here in this wonderful bed of many memories with the covers drawn up around me and the bed lamps on — writing to my honey. It's darned hard to think that this is the first of so many — letters that will have to be written in place of seeing you, but, all of a sudden — just since I have been writing, I have a sense of something concrete, something that I can feel and say — replacing that horrible blank feeling of utter misery that has been locking my heart ever since I waved goodbye to the Mighty G. and to one of its officers — standing on the after deck house waving his hat back and forth in profile against the sun's light.

It is hard to describe the feeling of complete desolation that I have had — it is as if someone had bodily lifted all of your feelings except the one which made you feel as if there were no feeling left. Remember when I used to keep saying that there was no adequate way to describe my love for you. Well, it's true — there isn't — it's as if I feel a complete person when if and don't dare think of the sort of shell I am when you're gone. If, in the past, you have felt I've replaced my love for you, honey, it isn't that, it's (and this I really think is true) it's that I've felt that I must <u>make</u> myself think of other things — perhaps I did too much but never again — I know now that we have a secure and understanding basis on which our marriage will endure, and I'll think of you and what our life will be with a great and fine anticipation of what will come to us. In short, my darling, I love you with all my heart and I'll never forget it. Oh, my darling, if only you were here for a few more minutes so I could look at you and talk to you and tell you I adore you. There have been many bad times in our last three months but there has never been a time when I haven't loved you and wanted you with me every minute. You're for me honey and that's all there is to it.

After I almost watched you out of sight — I felt my presence was becoming a bit embarrassing to the little Marine on guard. He asked me — "Your husband, ma'am?" — I said "Yes" and then he came running up to tell me that in case I couldn't see, you were waving — I hadn't been quite sure that was you — your hat was going so slowly — then I waved — oh honey, it was such an irrevocable feeling of parting — but darling, it won't be for long — the ship became sort of a blot on the horizon, so I went and picked up Chief Lang who had been waiting all that time. As delighted as he was to get his transfer, I guess it was pretty hard for him to see her go out without him — Bouncing on that darned clutch, I drove him back into town — I <u>finally</u> found an open gas station — by the time I did, the discomfort was excruciating. When I got back to the hotel, Hazel wasn't — here yet — I heard band music — it sounded as if it were coming from the Plaza. At the end of the Hall, there is a balcony over the street, so I opened the door and went out — Sure enough, there was a band in the Plaza — with all the people clustered around — was almost dark, and in between the clattering of the streetcars, the music rose above the people — I stood there and watched until I became unbearably lonesome for you — then came in and went to dinner with Hazel —

Gee, honey — I was writing that at ten last nite — when I fell asleep. I woke up about two, got up and fixed my hair and I then didn't wake up until after ten — in a minute, I have to pack to go — Oh, sweetheart — I miss you so very much — I'll have to start remembering things too — even the last few days have a host of wonderful ones —

Keep safe, my darling — I love you. Jane

P.S. I'll get your pins before I leave here

#1 in new series
January 8 1945 364 days to go
At sea

Gosh, honey, it even comes hard to put the paper in the machine and get ready to talk to you. It would seem so much more natural to be able to lean over and take your hand, or you in my arms. But there is no use crying, I guess; the die has been cast, and we are on our way. The only thing to do now is hold on to all the wonderful memories and relive them until the time comes when we can make more memories together.

I think the hardest thing I have ever done in my life was to climb out of "passionless" yesterday and walk aboard that ship. I guess you saw me run up to the bridge for a pair of glasses, and with them I watched you standing by the car long after I knew you couldn't see me. Despite the fact it touched the hell out of me, I couldn't help wishing you would get in the car and get going, because I knew you would be dying to go to the bathroom with all that beer in you. So you see, darling, you kept me smiling through the tears. I'll have to admit a couple of dry hot stinging ones rolled down my cheeks as we went steaming out.

Last night I had the eight to twelve watch, and it was interminable. I kept remembering little things I should have said to you, thoughts I should have left with you. I even should have kissed you again, but hell, baby, no matter how thoroughly I did all that, I would still think of other things I should have done. I've got the mid-watch tonight, so I imagine you will be with me for another four hour stretch in an unbroken chain of thought.

By now you are ensconced at the Lido. (I just took a few minutes out to see the movie, that is about two reels of it, Ann Corio in "Sarong Girl" — Brother!!!) I suppose you had a good trip up from Dago. I hope you got checked out all right and had enough money to swing it.

Honey, I'm just writing words. What I am thinking and feeling is such a God-damned empty hole in the pit of my stomach that it is hard to describe. I knew it would be bad, but I'm sitting here missing you more than I thought would ever be possible. I feel like someone just took the living part of me away and left the shell of the body behind. I looked through that scrap book just a minute ago, and it makes me feel that even now you are growing away from me. Don't let it happen, honey; if we both try real hard and don't let anything ever make us forget each other, then we won't. And if it's going to be a long time, well hell, we can take it, but we've got to work at keeping the other person right near us. And in our hearts.

Please forgive me for sounding off like this, but the old man is a little low tonight. I guess the initial shock will wear off, and life will go on. But, baby, it's damn hard to see the forest for the trees at this writing.

We had a wonderful break getting so much time together, the fact that it got us back into the habit of loving and being loved is just one of those things. You gave me minutes and days of being the happiest guy in the world. I realize that we also gave each other some of the worst, but those fade very easily into the background in retrospect, and only the wonderful and the nice will remain. I don't think we will ever have that kind of readjustment problem again. As you said yesterday, we are a little older now, and also a hell of a lot more matured emotionally. So the next time, when I come back for good, we will know how to handle it darling, more and better than I ever have. I always will too, darling, hang onto that thought and know and believe that I'll come a steaming back some day just as surely as you saw me steam out the other day.

I'd better turn in tonight and call a halt to this, but I'll make a lot fatter package out of it before I get a chance to mail this. Remember I love you, honey. All me love Chas

Jan 8 — 1945 6500 Yucca St. Hollywood—Number 2

Hello, Honey Darling;
Well here it is nearly midnite, and we just arrived at the Lido — not that I care — I have no place I care whether I get to in a hurry — when you're gone — of course I'm tired because, as you know, driving that car is no picnic — When I went down to get it this morning, the battery was dead — so that took an hour to fix — then you know how the clutch is — then they had a prize fog all day — Honey, what I could see of the ocean looked so rough — I thought of you with sympathy — well, all in all it took simply hours to get here, and I have to go down to Whittier in the morning to return it — I still believe in that sign "Next time, take the train." I decided to stop and see Izzie at Laguna — stayed about an hour — she is fine — the kids are enormous — we had a fine Martini and then and then were on our way again — I wired here to make sure they held the reservation — which they did.

The most horrible tragedy took place a little while ago. I could and would cry about it if I felt that it wouldn't be hurting Hazel's feelings — you know how she is always breaking things — she gets excited and doesn't think — well I had my little duffel bag with the perfume in it nicely braced upright behind the seat — I pointed out time and again that it must remain so. We get here, and I get out to get the bags out — she jumps out, grabs the duffel bag, drops it on its side and leaves it there, which I didn't know. After I got the bags out, I discovered it lying there with all the perfume spilled! Well I wanted to scream, but I couldn't — it's the only really lovely perfume I've ever had, and it's all gone! And I'd been so darned careful with it too — I'd carried it all over without spilling a drop — and I love it so much because you gave it to me. Hazel is awfully intelligent, but she's so flighty she makes me terribly nervous if I don't control myself all the time — and if I tell her to calm down, then it hurts her feelings — so I just grit my teeth and smile and am ashamed of myself for being bothered.

Darling, if there were only words to describe how terribly blank this day without you has been. I just want to scream at people — "Don't you realize — my husband is gone!" — so I smile and try to act casual when all the time I'm dying inside. I know I have to find something to do right away to fill up this void because I think I'll go crazy missing you if I don't — A year of days like this is unthinkable — I know so well you are gone because I saw you go — it's too definite, honey — not to have any hope that there will be a few more days. I'm glad I don't see people who remind me of you because it would be so disappointing when they weren't. Remember, darling, I love you — I keep thinking of all the things you do that I like so much — like being nice to people and over tipping them because you like them all — and laughing at silly things and telling me you love me — and bringing home champagne for Christmas and going to the lingerie department for a pantie girdle — oh, honey, there are so many wonderful things to remember.

Baby, I got your pins — three dollars actually! It seems they are handmade. You can send me things airmail but it seems the rules state that I can't return the favor so I had to send them First Class. I hope they catch you before too long — Mrs. Cass had a chicken cooked — she had thought I would be there in time to eat it — I was terribly sorry but had no way of knowing — it was sweet of her —

Give my best to Smiley —

All my love to you darling — Jane

Jan 9, 1944 [1945] Lido Apts 6500 Yucca Number three

Hello, sweet Darling;

It is pretty late — I just got home from having quite an evening — it seems that Martha told me that she and Margo & Nancy were all having dinner together at Perinos so would I come — so after a wild day, I put on my clean black dress and hied myself down there. After that, we went over to Mrs. White's — her son is over with Evans, and she had the parents of some others who are — then Jack Merton came because he had been in the army over there — such talk and garble! Jack Merton took Martha and Nancy and me up to his apartment for a drink — he is really awfully nice — wanted to know all about you — of course that's all I want to talk about, so that really started something — then we had the most wonderful political discussion — He agrees with everything we do and knows whereof he speaks, having really made a study of it — I forgot to tell you that the reason Mrs. White had the gathering was in honor of Frank Rooney who was in P.A. — who was having a leave. All in all, I really enjoyed the evening muchly — a lot of good talk and a couple of Martinis.

Darling, did you know you had completely captivated Martha's family — I was indulging in a long monologue for her — all to the effect of how wonderful you were, and she said that there was no doubt about it — you were all I said — and her family still hasn't stopped talking about you.

Darling, with all due respect to Cisco, I finally got rid of his car and breathed a great sigh of relief — I never did master the intricacies of that clutch — I got up at eight this morning, drove down to the Union station to get Hazel's bag — then to the Mayfair to get mine, but the car was too small to get the baggage in, so Hazel took it in a cab, and I drove down to Whittier — Yipe-! fog as thick as soup! I stayed for lunch — the rest of the fried chicken with the Cass's — they are really so sweet — we talked about the ship and everybody on it — then I took the bus trip back — two hours! — to find that we were being moved to this room on the first floor — what a divine place — Yellow wallpaper with maple furniture and such pretty lamps and curtains — and only $8.50 a day for two people! Hazel is delighted with it and enjoys being by herself here, so I can follow my own pursuits without worrying about her —

Oh, sweetheart if only you were here instead of way out there — I miss you so darned much, honey two days have passed now, and it seems like weeks and months —

I am going to call today — tomorrow — it is after midnite here today — to see what Jack Latham decided to do — also Jim McHechney in the morning —

Mother called the Adams — they said the pictures taken Xmas were wonderful, so I'll seen you one as soon as I get it —

All my love to you, darling, Jane

#2
Jan 10 1945 At Sea—
362 days to go.

Dearest Honey:

Hiyah punkin! What's the good word with you today? Have you landed your job, are you on your way, is your way my way, or N.Y. CentPac for the CBI theater? Answer this right away, even if you don't know.

Do you detect a hysterical note of false gaiety in my missive so far? Don't be too deceived, darling, although to be actually factual that first awful nail-knashing and head-against-the-wall-head-beating, etc., has lessened up some. You ain't being forgot though, baby, sometimes I go as long as two-three minutes without even thinking of you. The way I feel now though is I am absolutely on my way, no last minute reprieves, no more extra days or forty-eights, so the best thing is to get interested in it all over again and to get the hell and gone out there where it is going on and start doing my personal bit to clear it up that much sooner. And the — I'll be coming home again Kathleen!!

I broke out my banjo for a few minutes today and actually got it in tune and started playing a few practice scales. Not much, you understand, but at least a start. Won't I be handy to have at parties when this is all over to sit around strumming me old banjo whilst all and sundry make the welkin ring? I'm just busting with little red-hot tidbits. I actually got for myself today a ZIPPO!! No kidding, they had one left in the ship's store, and I nailed it. War time variety and all that but at least I'm back zipping again instead of bumming (matches).

I find this so delightful to sit in my room of an evening and reach for the old Royal (works like a charm) and start off a letter to my honey. It just fits into a little space in the desk, and I've got the cover off it and cover it with a wool cloth with a very little bit of light oil in it to keep that old devil rust away. It's so damn convenient that I will not have an excuse in the world for not writing to you a lot. And by the same token, when we finally get caught up on our back work for not spending a lot of time on the old creative side. You'll see, baby, I'll be the big money man in this family yet, so you hold the thought and maybe you will be able to play parts you like someday not parts that pay the best dough.

We had a bunch of porpoises stay with us for a couple of days, and I remember telling you about them, and you said "But, honey, isn't that supposed to be good luck?" They were and are, darling, but they damn near scared the hell out of me the other night. Seems the water was very phosphorescent, and two of them made a run at our bow, now mind you, I've never seen a torpedo wake close by, but if they could look any more like one than those damn fish did I hope to live to tell you about it. Damn near scared the lonesomeness out of me. (not quite though) Now on top of that the old Pacific has decided that she is misnamed. The mighty G is bouncing around like a six weeks old colt, and the seas are running might high. So high that it is causing the score machine to make errors. When it rolls against the tension on the roller it will often sit in one place and put two or three letters right on top of one another. Luckily, the bourbon didn't seem to affect my "sea legs," and so I am still up and about. More than I can say for several officers and about half the crew. Say, we did have our share of bourbon at that, didn't we? I hope I didn't build up a craving in you for the stuff, because that kind of drinking over a period of time does no one any good. Yah, Yah! I can hear you saying, Look whose talking, and where he is sitting!!! I know I don't have to worry about you on that though, darling, or any other for that matter.

Gosh, I just remembered I haven't said I adore you yet today. I adore you, darling! As I say it I am looking at three eight x tens and some little snaps that are looking right back at me. You are so darn beautiful, baby, and I love you such a hell of a lot. Stick around for another 362 days, and I'll prove to you that I really mean it.

I hate to say it, but I have to get some sleep. Think of me a little, honey, and love me all you can scrape up. Course I've got millions to spare for both of us as far as that's concerned. Goodnight baby, kiss kiss.

All me love, Chas X <u>red</u> <u>hot</u>!

Jan 11, 1945 6500 Yucca St. Hollywood Letter #5

Hello, my Darling;

You would laugh if you could see me now — sitting here in bed with one of those benzene inhalers going full blast — you know that stuff that gives out with the steam — I guess I was sort of tired and depressed — my firm theory is that you don't get things if you are excited and happy. I caught a germ someplace, so it lodged in the bronchial tubes, poor rusty things — Last night for cold chills and aching bones I would have been sure I had bengae if I hadn't know it was not possible. So I took a bunch of aspirin and decided to stay in bed today, and Hazel got me this inhaler, and now I feel better & which is good because I <u>have</u> to get busy. Right now I am stewing over the question of whether to ask the USO to give me a man to improvise something or to go ahead and get one myself — the second course costs money, so I'll probably do the first — This Detroit thing seems to resolve down to whether or not Clarence will go — they should know more about it by five this afternoon.

Whom do you suppose called me just now. Pat Manning! She had Martha's number from the Xmas card. She is out at the scenario dept at M.G.M and wants me to have lunch with her tomorrow — whether I can or not depends on my state of health in the morning.

Just as I finished the last sentence, darling, Martha and Lee Gale dropped in — they shot the breeze a few minutes — then I read Hazel's composition to Martha — the consensus of opinion was that it was too long, so I cut about a quarter of it after they left, and now it is better. I think I will call the Victory Committee in the morning and ask for a pianist. I also called Jim, and he is going to see Clarence late tonite, so he wants me to call him in the morning.

A letter was just received from Mary saying that Sam had given her an engagement ring with three big diamonds which "fascinates" her. I think the ring is all that does because she would marry this "Doe she has been seeing if he weren't an Italian "although he doesn't look it" and if she thought he could earn a living after the war so that Mother and Daddy wouldn't be disappointed. It is really unbelievable — the girl is mad and why she doesn't go in the Red Cross, I don't know! Darling, her address is 38 west 70th st. — New York — Maybe you could write her and tell her what a fine thing <u>you</u> think it is — I think, darling, that you are the only one who could convince her, and everyone would consider it a great favor if you did. So why don't you just write a note about what fine work they do and why doesn't she follow up their interest, etc. —

Hazel just came in — she has been at the symphony — matinee — with Gladys — I was going to get dressed for dinner, but she asked the coffee shop, and they said they'd send it in. This is the first time I've spent the whole day in bed since my operation. When I had the flu last year, my temperature was high so I seemed to lose my sense, and I went around doing the housework. It seems silly to stay in bed, but my bones have begun to ache again, so I'll just play safe until tomorrow. Besides in case that show in Detroit <u>did</u> work out and I should decide to go, I wouldn't want to have a cold — I guess.

Nancy called a little while ago to see if I wanted to go out to the Actor's Lab Monday to see about doing a play to go overseas. I might as well see what they have to say.

Yipe — this Luzan thing has really broken loose hasn't it — the Naval battle and all — I am so thankful, darling, that at least you aren't there for that. I guess my strategy about the offensive was wrong — only time will tell — only guesses, and we can all guess — we can all wish too, and guess what mine is — that the war were over — ? <u>Yes</u> Oh, darling — if it could only be soon that you'll be coming home — we'll know how to get a right start and won't have to work into it — it was surely nice though —

All my love, baby, Jane

#3
12 Jan 1945 360 to go.

Dearest Honey:

Good evening, my sweet. I adore you. There, I remembered right off the bat tonight. See, I'm getting better already aren't I? I don't know who first dropped that pearl "Absence makes the heart grow fonder," but just that much of it is so damn true. We will forget the last of the line, match! Darlin, you just can't imagine how completely you are always in my consciousness. It's like I have a second blonde elfin self constantly at my side, more than at my side, sort of in and around and part of me. I suppose in the long and varied course of events that this battered old world has experienced, somewhere, sometime there <u>must</u> have been a man that loved a woman more than I do you. But by the same token I'll bet my new face-plate. that it would take the research powers of the Rockefeller institute to uncover him. Gad, woman, do you

realize what Putty I am in your hands? To realize how completely
and with what free abandon I give myself up to the sole purpose
of loving just you? No, I guess you don't, and p-raps it's just as
well. I'd look awfully silly on a leash, now wouldn't I? Old hellfire
charlie brought to a heel by a blonde bombshell of half his weight —
well — 1 1/4 his weight!!!! Zounds what copy!! Stop the presses!!!!
Chas give in — like Flynn!!!

Stuff and nonsense, like what little girls are made of. I'm rambling and babbling, but I do love you, baby, but then that you already
knew. The anesthesia is taking a long time to set in, you are still
with me and alongside me. But even after only six days there is
a physical me that says "the hell she is!" six days!!! Ma God in
six months what will I be doing? Either tackling Tojo&Co single
handed or back seeing you on a thirty day survivor leave — there
just ain't no middle course!!!!

It's getting rougher by the minute (to get back to less thought
disturbing ground) and I don't quite know how I am managing
to sit here and bat this out. I suddenly skate half way across the
room, but I keep right on typing (small rooms you know!) and the
next roll skates me right back into position. Amazing! A lot of the
lads are feeling the weather, but you know old salty Charley, let
her roll says I.

We went through an enormous school of porpoises today, literally
hundreds of them, and they all seemed to be running races with
each other and kicking up their heels and in general having a hell
of a large time. They would pop out of the top of a big wave and
leap with a grace and distance that beggars description. Must be
nice to have so little on your mind. That's where they have it over
their human cousins: they don't have to think.

Looks like I'll be in the land you love come manana. I have to
control myself and not walk around with clenched fists and leering
into every male's face on the island. That would take a lot of leering
wouldn't it? No, I'll be good, honey. After all you said you loved me.
That's good enough for this kid. I hope I'll be here long enough to
get mail from you and some kind of an address.

I guess I will send these to the Lido, but if I have to shove I will
mail all else to Martha until I hear from you. Cisco just poked
his head in the door and said as follows: "Ask her if she got home
without becoming a nervous wreck or a casualty." That you did, I
trust. Got home safe I mean.

So far, so damn far from you already, and just think how much further there is to go. Well, baby, if I'm not right at your side it doesn't matter a hell of a lot if it's eight or eight thousand miles, but I'll tell you one thing, you had better make up your mind to have sort of a constant companion with you when this mess is over, cause sis, I'll be your shadow.

Have to go on watch now, darling, I love you with all my heart. I wonder how the letter-a-day plan is progressing — natch! I kiss you goodnight —

all me love — Chas xxxxxxxx

12 Jan 1845 At Sea

Dear Mom:

Well here I go starting off another new series of letters to you. Doesn't seem three months ago that I last wrote "at Sea" at the head of a letter, but that's the way life goes. I have no complaints on that score though, we got just about a month more than I thought we would.

Well this being my year for the typewriter, at least you will be able to read my scrawls without so much effort. It is pretty tough to write tonight though as I have to stop typing every few words and grab ahold of the desk. The old lady is trying her best to turn inside out tonight. Rolling like a thing possessed she is, and we have [a lot] of seasick and unhappy kids aboard. Old Charley goes right along as usual though, for which I continue to be grateful.

Jane and I had a wonderful time in San Diego, and even the ten spot was wonderful. Pretty

hard to be really gay though when parting is so imminent. One of the officers who lives practically in L.A. drove his car down, and Jane was to drive it back for him. So the last day after I came back in the morning I got to go back into town and see Jane. As a matter of fact, I got permission for her to come to the dock we were to sail from. So we sat in the car and talked until the very last minute. Then she stood and waved us goodbye, the only woman on the dock. Boy, I had a lump in my throat as big as a base ball, but it gives me a nice going away picture.

Say, speaking of pictures, those we had made for you for Xmas should be done about the time you get this, so you can be looking forward to getting them in a couple of days. There will be one of me alone, and one of the two of us together. They looked pretty good in the prints, and I hope you like them. I just looked over beside my bed, and there are the three of us standing in the side yard. You know the last thing I do every night just before I go to sleep is to say "Goodnight Mom, goodnight Jane" So you see you are pretty much in my heart too!!

Seems very funny to be alone and back at sea again. Each time I leave the old US it gets a little tougher. I really hope that when I get back the next time it will be for good. The news today looked wonderful on all fronts. Who knows, with a little break I may spend next Xmas at home without the thought of going back out hanging over me. We will all do our best to make that come true, believe me.

The weather has been beautiful so far, but the seas have been enormous. That's funny because usually when it is nice and sun-shiny the seas seem to respond and stay flattened out, but not this time. Ran through a tremendous school of porpoises today, and they did seem to be having the best time running races (looked like) and leaping high out of the water to kick up their heels. They seem such a happy fish, not bothered with thinking like that poor fish the human.

Well, baby, I guess this hasn't been much of a letter, and I'm afraid I sound a little unhappy. Well I'm sorry, Mom, but the truth of it is I guess I am a little. Well the first few days are always the hardest, and I'll take her in my stride just as I always have. I promise the next will be more like the old Charlie. I'll always have a letter to go when I hit a port, and when we are in I will write about twice a week, so I'll keep my end of the. correspondence up, and I know you will too.

Forgive me if I sounded dreary, honey, I am not so bad really, and I do love my mom very much indeed!!!!! All me love — Chas XXXXX

Lido Apts
6500 Yucca St. Hollywood Jan. 13, 1945
No. #6

Chuck, my Darling;

Well, time does pass — I sometimes wonder how — here it is Saturday, and it has been just about a week since you left — After the first day, I've managed to remain cheerful and not too much of a burden on my fellow man, but it's a feeling that having a drink makes worse, where you tear napkins in twice as many little pieces, and if you stop an animated conversation with people for even a minute, a feeling of utter desolation — a desperate loneliness comes over you — a void that can be filled only by you — and that will be there until you get home. In other words, darling, I miss you so much that it is almost unendurable — but it has to be endured, "so chin up — eyes front and away! — Nellie, pull your belly in — it's for the U.S.A." and all that — and stuff — but it's still awful.

I seem to have recovered pretty well from my one-day bout with the flu — I went out today and met Dorothy and Martha for lunch. This was the first time I'd seen Dorothy since that day she took us to the train. She looked a little tired but otherwise fine. Frank Rooney came in and brought with him a friend whom Martha knew — named Warren Lewis — a sergeant. It seems this character was pretty good in radio and stuff and now is one of the producers of the army hour — he suggested that we get together a short — 3 act play about our trip overseas — using the characters from life but just talking about the men — something on the order of "the women" but not so extreme and take it overseas — it seems if we could get a script they would do it. He offered to write an outline of a plot — then he said we could fit in the gags — Well, it's true the dialogue would sort of write itself if the whole thing was constructed mechanically. I could get Mel to help. It sounds like fun, but I don't know if I'll have time to do it because Jim wants to talk with me <u>definitely</u> tomorrow about this Detroit thing — if it's good enough, I think I'll take it because I can't afford to wait around for the Victory Committee, and I could go overseas with more alacrity when this show is finished. I'll decide after I talk to him tomorrow. All I know is that I want something to do and in a hurry — because I'm lonesome!

Darling, you may as well write me here because it looks as if I could stay here as long as I am in town, and they are wonderful about messages and letters — there wouldn't be any chance of missing any. I have been wondering and hoping that you would have the opportunity to call — it would be so fine to talk to you for just three minutes, but I don't suppose you will — it's just an idle dream, I know. I should be having some mail in a few days.

All my love, my darling,
Jane

6500 Yucca St. Hollywood
Jan. 13, 1945
No. #7

Hello, Honey Darling;

Well, here it is Sunday nite one week since you left — as last time, I don't start out counting on 52 — now there are 51 left — God willing, there will be less — it would be beautiful to wake up in. the morning and find that they had all gone by during the nite. I have been in a bit of a stew all afternoon — it seems that they want me to do this show in Detroit — In the first place, I object to some of the material, and, in the second, the money isn't enough. After thinking it over, I have decided that the material I am being silly about, and I think before I sign the contract in the morning, if I do, I will be able to get more money. The only reason I have for taking it is — one, I want to work — two; I could save a little money — 3; when I finished, I would be near New York and could maybe do a show for the American Theatre Wing. I don't dare sit around here waiting for the Victory Committee because it may be months. After I left there today, I went to have a drink with Clarence — I told him I hadn't decided what to do because I needed more money — a hundred is what they want to pay — he said I was perfectly right, and he would speak to Jim. He did, and I think it will turn out alright. I'll let you know tomorrow. In the meantime, darling, keep writing me here — be sure to number your letters so I'll be sure to know if I get them all.

I guess I really need an agent, as you told me — When I get up on the stage, I know what I'm doing, but I'm absolutely incapable of talking for myself — Isn't it funny to think that this nice aggressive character which you said I am, isn't at all. I would really hate show business if it weren't so much fun to actually get up there and do the show. Hazel, of course, is still here — I imagine she'll go home in the next few days. I know she would kind of love to go to Detroit and then to New York to see Mary, but I don't imagine she will — it would be kind of complicated — It's really been simply swell, and we've had some fine talks.

I've hardly seen anybody we know, darling — I just haven't wanted to call — I would like to talk to Mel about that play idea, and I would like to talk to any friends we have that might have friends in the American Theatre Wing — that may sound awful, but it's all for a good end. As far as pure conviviality is concerned — I don't feel like it.

I did go to dinner tonite at that Villa Nova with Clarence and a Captain in the Signal Corps named Lou Appleton who used to be a producer at Columbia — he made that picture of the Battle of New Britain — Also that Jean Barry and some girl he was going with named Helen Talbot. He is the former husband of that Peggy Barry out at Jim Heils that nite — I was home by nine and glad to get there. It isn't fun without you, honey. Of course I realize I can't spend all my time in a hotel room and must get out, but there's no joy in it. A character by the name of Flynn adds all the zip

Well, sweet darling, that's about the summation of my activities for the day — since I wrote you last nite — I love and adore you and miss you with every little bit of me —

All my love, my darling, Jane

The pictures should arrive in a few days and I'll airmail them to you.

I love you honey —

Cartoon I heard about; Doctor examining woman's chest — said woman disrobed to waist. This is what the doctor saw on woman

[DRAWING OF SHIRTLESS WOMAN]

Doctor's remark — "I suggest you see an oculist."

Lido Apts
6500 Yucca St. Hollywood, Calif. Jan 15, 1945 Letter #8.

Hello, Honey Darling;

Well, another day — a lot happened today,. but I find myself chiefly wondering whether I will hear from you tomorrow. (Hazel is — she found it — she thought she had lost her railroad ticket and was going through the agonies of the damned. She gets so upset that I wonder she doesn't have indigestion and then experiences such a delicious relief when it is right where it should be that maybe it is worth it. I think the great difference between this generation of ours and the one before, is their unalterable conviction that Life is real, Life is earnest and all that. Something slightly bad is immediately regarded as of tragic proportions — our generation shrugs its shoulders and decides that it could be worse — so what. It isn't such a strain on the nervous system and I really think it makes stronger people.) But to get back to the first sentence — perhaps I will hear from you tomorrow, but I suppose it will be later in the week. I will feel as if we had sort of re-established contact.

What a day this has been — First I got all mixed up in this Detroit deal — they were angry because Clarence said a hundred a week wasn't enough and kept saying they knew a girl in Detroit who would be happy to do it for that. I pointed out that I hadn't asked Clarence to say that — although I had been going to say it myself — besides I didn't want to do that courtroom scene — one of the parts is where you wriggle your hips and bump until the judge said — "Get back in gear girlie" — and if they could get a girl to do it for that, to get her, I wasn't very interested anyway. So I just left — it was courageous, but I was kicking myself. But I guess I didn't need the money that badly. Then I remember they said — this woman is on trial because she slew her husband on the nite of January 17th — and I jump up and say — "That's a lie!" — I don't like the word 'slew' " — (giving it a grind) — Why not? — "I like (big one) bumped off!" Cripes, I don't like that stuff — Well after I left there, I went over to see that agent Max Shagrin that Sally told me was so good — he seemed so nice and wanted me to come back at five to meet his associate. Psychologically I put it as asking his advice because I just didn't know what to do — but, then I met Nancy and Margo to go to the Actor's Lab to see about doing a play. Things are really pretty quiet there because the transportation is tied up until after the offensives — but we knew that if we had some good ideas — so we talked over three — the main one being the idea for the play which I had worked but pretty well in my mind. Well, who do you suppose was in charge, Helen Leavitt — you remember she and Al used to live with Tom and Marge. She knew about the January 16th thing, and I guess I had sort of proved myself in her eyes because she was most overboardly cordial — and she was crazy about the play idea and is getting a writer for it — it's supposed to be almost a farce — and the specialty numbers in the middle as if we were rehearsing them...All the ideas are mostly mine — Martha's jitterbug thing I see as a chance for audience participation right in the middle of the play — so I arranged that tomorrow all — the girls should get together to make a list of the gags and funny things for material for the author. I'll have to make a list of requirements of when we meet him like: Don't everybody talk at once, and don't push yourselves too much, and don't object to having your character burlesqued, and no extraneous material. From my association with Nancy today, I respect her reasoning processes and she certainly talks in an organized manner, but Martha talks too much — she gets way ahead of herself and then gets bogged down, and it ends up in nothing but talk —

Well then I went back to the agent's at five o'clock, and he fell on my neck and said he was so glad to see me because just after I left — a big deal came up about a good play going to San Francisco and Chicago and would I be there at one tomorrow because he thought there was a good part in it for me — Honestly! Then I went to have dinner with the Adamses, and when I came home, there was a note in the box to call Eddie Ryan at RKO in the morning. I found out from Martha that it was about something that Jack Merton thought of — what I don't know.

Needles to say, this is all very confusing, and I hope to Heaven it amounts to something — If kept under control, it might.

Oh, honey darling — I love you — in the little social life I have had since you left, there is no zest, and I don't give a darn for it — so I will work hard, and that is all I want to do until you are home – I don't like to think of where you may be on your way to, but I know we will be together again soon. I love you my darling, Jane

#4
15 Jan 1945 In Port 357 to go.

Dearest Honey:

Well, Darling, here starts another mid-watch letter, the first of I'm almost afraid to think how many. Before I go any farther though, let me tell you how happy I was yesterday to get not one, but two letters from you! They were numbered one and three, but I guess you counted that part you wrote the next morning in Dago as #2. At any rate, very little mail came aboard, a couple of other officers got one, but there was old Charley with two! I just can't tell you what they meant to my old sagging spirits. A shot in the arm, doc. That's what they were.

Wasn't it funny how our first letters almost paralleled each other in thought? We even used some of the same descriptive style in trying to express that awful lost sort of feeling. I could mentally picture you writing in that bed (oh that wonderful bed!), and then as those beautiful orbs of yours began to give in to sleep I could see it in the writing. It almost trailed off into illegibility there at the end. So far I've read those letters four times. Silly, I know, but it is the most concrete link I have with you, and I find myself reaching for anything that can preserve the allusion that I am still with you, at least in spirit. It's strange how I sit here trying my damnedest to find words that will give you a clear picture of my feelings and fail to find them. I love you, I miss you, I want you, I feel lost without you — those are the bare feelings, but there is a nice subtlety; a gradation and shading of meaning that is roughed over when I say it like that.

Maybe there are some sort of physical wave lengths that people in love set up. Because when I am in the same room or even the same house with you there is a feeling of inner rightness, an almost complacency of well being, a sense of — well, I guess completeness is about the best word. Conversely, as I sit here writing to you, I know that our love is secure and understood and completely rounded, but there is that physical lack (and I use it in the higher sense of the word, though God knows the other is there too!) that keeps the picture from being fully complete. To carry the illusion further, it is as though one were studying a picture of great depth and fine line, and another person kept jiggling it ever so slightly. The sweep and scope would be apparent, the color and the focal point would be clear enough, but try as you will you lose the blossoms on the bushes, the birds in the sky and all the host of tiny, but important details that make it a full, again, a complete picture. Just so it is when I'm not actually with you. The picture is still great, will win prizes and be hung in all the best galleries, but just misses that really greatness that is immortality. I don't say we are any Dante and Beatrice or Romeo and Juliet, but I will always maintain that when we are together we could give them a hell of a run for their money!!

By this time you are probably convinced that the old man is roaring drunk again. Far from it, baby, the last drink I had was with the prettiest blonde in the world, and it wasn't in this island paradise either. It was just that it was late, and I was alone, and I wanted to try and tell you a little of how I feel, and how much I love you and what your letters did for me yesterday. If the story is a little garbled and cloudy, believe that it is not due to lack of clarity in my mind, rather to my inability to capture winged emotions and reduce them to black and white words.

Well enough of that. I've probably lulled you to sleep by now. We had great excitement aboard the day we came in. Dolly had her pups+!! Gads teeth it was funny, you would have thought we had just single-handed sunk a Gongo class BB the way everyone sort of took personal pride in the whole affair. She had a litter of four, which is pretty big for her size dog on her first accouchement. One is all white with a black face, one is mostly black with some white, and the other two are the godawfulest mixtures of shades of brown that these old eyes have ever seen. I suppose it all goes to bear out Mendel's law, but they are weird and wonderful to behold. Of course, the poor little dog is about out of her mind. 150 officers and men have to make a personal check on her and the pups' condition at least two or three times a day, and she is about ready to snap anyone's hand off. Not that I blame her, either, but then you can't blame the kids, after all she represents everybody's dog back home, and we all feel a proprietary interest in her well being.

What is really funny is to see loud-mouthed bos'n mates and rough tough Gunners mates down on their hands and knees worrying if the pups are getting enough to eat and whether she is sitting on them, and are they all right, etc. No matter how loud they talk, and how salty they become, when you boil it down they are still just kids that should be home playing with their own dogs and not out here perfecting themselves in the art of knocking off other human beings.

I had to go over to the Sub base today and tried to pick up a La Holla bag for you, but all they had were those that are all gooped up with <u>that</u> word, so being as we will be here for a few days I will try again in about a week, they expect to have some more in. I hate to say this about this place, knowing how you feel about it, but, honey, it's worse than ever. It's growing so damn fast it reminds you of a Metro movie where money is no object, but just stun the hell out of them with sets and people and color. Well it's doing just that, and on top of that the reaction of shore-based people here gets more and more rear area minded every day. Bah! I know the reason you liked it so well was because, although your work took you into the seamy side of the war, the wounded, etc., still your spare time was on the dreamy island romantic side, cavaliers fighting for your favors, good swimming, and charming people. I think you got a somewhat distorted view of the place. You'll probably go through the rest of your life swooning at the mention of the name at the same time I'll be being quietly sick to my stomach behind a potted palm!

It's not quite that bad, honey, I won't <u>really</u> get sick, so get those hackles back down, and don't take pen in hand to blast me!

I had the duty today, natch, so I didn't even have a glass of beer. I called Katie Richardson this morning, and I guess I'll go in there for dinner tomorrow night. I'm still sorry you didn't get to meet them, such nice people. I'm going to call Armstrong tomorrow too, there is a chance he may still be here. If so, Smiley and I will go over and see them, if not I'll just skip it. After I see the Richardsons, I think I'll confine my activities to going over to this little club near here and having a couple of drinks before dinner on the days I don't have the duty and make that my social life. I think Pritch's father is here, he was trying to find him today. If he succeeds, I will take his duties so he can spend some time with him. He sure was nice to me when I had somebody special to see.

I don't know quite what's come over me, but the boys were talking tonight about "lining them up" it just left me cold. Old monastic Charley, that's me. It's not that I'm denying myself, darling, it's just that having you in my mind is better than an island cutie in my arms. God, it's hard to believe, isn't it?

In regard to our activities, it looks like I'm going to get my wish. Things are going to be far from dull, and I'm not going to have much time to sit around mooning over my absent wife. That's the way I wanted it, and brother am I going to get it!! Time will go by like a shot however, and practically before you know it I'll be back cracking your ribs with a tremendous bear hug! God speed the day, darling.

I remember those last few days together but good! It was so perfect and such a perfect union of love that I will never forget it. I think when the war is over I will make a pilgrimage to Dago and place a plaque over the starboard bed in old 209 — you be thinking of an inscription — I've already got mine figured out!!! Wow!

Well, my baby, the watch is drawing to a close, so I guess I'd better secure this for tonight. Give Hazel all my love, and say hello to Martha and her family for me. I guess I'll use Martha's address from now on, send me a permanent one as soon as you can.

Keep up the good work on the letters, if I know I'm really going to keep getting mail from you I think I can hack it. It's not as good as being with you by a hell of a long ways, but it's the best we can do under the circumstances. Don't forget I love you with all my heart — and you know why? LS-MFT That means, "so round, so firm, so beautifully stacked!!!!" all me love — Chas

P.S. Don't forget to send those pictures you had copied in S.F. also the ones of us, also the ones from Xmas. Also the one Mary is going to make for me when you get to N.Y. — YIPE!!! one for the road! X

Lido Apts
6500 Yucca Hollywood, Calif.
Jan 16, 1945
Letter #9

Dearest Honey Darling

The jackpot! Three letters from you arrived today — all full of the wonderful Charley talks that I love to read — Now I have you placed in one place, I shall start thinking about the next I have been following you in my mind all the way to your first destination — may the porpoises always be with you, darling.

You may tell Cisco that I didn't quite have a nervous breakdown — I told you how close I came to it. You were so right, darling, when you worried about all that beer in me — I suffered more acutely than I thought was possible until I found a gas station — the one where we stopped on the way out was closed so I had to go on. I was very, perhaps too frank in confessing my suffering to the chief — I think he might have been shocked.

Well I had a great day today. Hair fixed at nine — then three appointments. Time has mellowed all the girls, so when we met today we were able to get together quite inspiringly for the ideas on the play. I am beginning to have a sneaking hope that it may amount to something because this morning the Actors Lab called me — and they already have a writer — we are meeting him in the morning — by the end of that I should be able to tell a little better whether it will really work out — I am beginning to think it might.

Also at RKO today I saw Eddie Phine and Dick Stockton — they wanted to know all about you, and Dick was insulted when he thought you hadn't looked him up — I told him you'd be in San Francisco all the time. This thing today didn't amount to anything, as I wasn't the type the director wanted — they both volunteered to keep me working however — which was very sweet and might be handy if worse came to worse — although it's _not_ what I want to do — they both made a great fuss over my hair.

This show in San Francisco is a kind of nebulous deal — I don't know what it will mean — I'm seeing the people again tomorrow. Frankly I'm a little discouraged about doing what I want to do immediately — the moment has sort of passed I'm afraid — If these things don't turn out, I could do better than I've done before, but — well maybe I'm impatient — if the overseas thing comes out, wonderful — if it doesn't, I wish to Heaven I had the money to go to New York and just start plugging. I realize you can't expect things to materialize in a week, but I did have every reason to believe things were pretty good, and now they sort of fold up around me. Something good better happen soon or my carefully built up "ego" might collapse. Silly, isn't it. But true. Elloise has been reading for Sophie and may get some sort of contract — I got indignant because I can act circles around Ellie — still if I did see her — that is pictures again — I want to be a good actress if I can afford it — Forgive the grouching — but when you long to work so badly, you are impatient and unhappy when it looks as if things were going wrong.

You were worried as to whether I would develop a craving for bourbon — with the high consumption of it — I must confess — it has been something of a problem — I recognized it as such and determined it had to be licked — it was really something. I'm doing pretty well — it's a darned bad habit to get into over a period of time though — it made me kind of nervous for a day or so.

I'm so glad you got a Zippo, darling —

Keep your sea legs through the rough weather — Keep typing to me and keep loving.

And much — the mostest love in reply, Jane

[My letter to Major Oswald was returned undelivered. Dave Oswald died, I'm not sure when.]

17 Jan 1945 In Port

Dear Oz:

All right, so I am a double dyed shiftless skunk what never answers letters and is all the time running home to Uncle Sugar. But bad as it is on your morale, brother, it's mighty good on mine! Don't get me wrong, Dave, I'm not gloating, as a matter of fact I think it's a God damned shame that you are still sweating it out, but after all, while 13 months doesn't sound like much time compared to what you've got racked up, it's still a hell of long time away from home and the little wifling. And although we have only been gone ten days this time, I am ready and willing to go right back, and for keeps too!

I'm sure your mother wrote about having your birthday party for you, and I just missed it, however we got in on the other side of the bird the next night. They are swell people, Oz, and they sure love you a hell of a lot. Sandra was there, and I liked her very much. She looked swell and seems to be still in love with you, why I'll never know. When I left that night, I kissed her goodbye for you (very chaste and proper believe me) and told her I'd deliver it to you. So that should make quite a sight in the Army-Navy club bar in Manila P.I. to see a Navy Lt(jg), hanging a buss on an Army Major — don't you think? All your family looked just fine your Dad seems to be all over his illness, guess he had a bad bout with the flu, and Liz and Nellie looked just wonderful.

Only people I saw up there outside of your family was Gracie and Marge and Kramer the barber in the Medical-Dental building. We talked quite a lot about you and Parkie. I imagine you could really go for getting a hair cut from him again huh?

We had a really wonderful time back there. Lots of loving and bourbon and good food. Brother, wait till you get there, and you'll know what I mean. We were very lucky and got an apt in S.F. for the six weeks we were there when I came back from Leave. It wasn't quite like a house of your own, but a little of the feeling was there. Had a fireplace and such stuff. You know, the most amazing thing was Jane only got back two days ahead of me! She had a chance to go out with a couple of other shows while I was there, but she told them as soon as I left she would be glad to go. Well now she has a deal to do a show, legitimate, in Detroit, and the dough is pretty good, on top of that there doesn't seem to be much in the air on this Camp Shows Inc right now, so she may go to Detroit. An address where they will forward her mail is 5416 1/4 Harold Way, Hollywood 28, Cal. c/o Martha Shaw.

I wonder where you are now, probably up in the Philippines would be my guess. Things look like they are going to be hot and heavy for us for a while, so much the better, the damn time goes a lot quicker. Must remember to duck on time though.

Well, Dave, not much of a letter, but answer and I'll do better on the next.

lovin' kisses — Chas

6500 Yucca St. Lido Apts Hollywood 28
Jan 20, 1945
Letter # 12

Hello, Honey Darling;

Before I start the letter part, I got yesterday's date mixed up and put January 21 on the letter when it was really the 19th, so don't be confused.

Well tomorrow is another Sunday — our two weeks anniversary, one twenty-sixth of a year — 351 days to go — honey, time does act as if the machine age hasn't come when you want it to realize it's the twentieth century and things had speeded up —

Prize story for today! Sit down — Remember Norman Harrington! Enough said — I have just learned that he's in New Guinea and that he is a Lieutenant Colonel!

Well I sort of arrived at or was forced into a decision today about my course in the next little while. The Victory Committee called to offer me a job as the M.C. on a show which will tour all the hospitals in the country — Salary one hundred dollars a week with no income tax and expenses paid. That amounts to quite a bit. I didn't know what to do. I knew that if I turned it down and this play thing that the man is writing didn't go through, then I'd kick myself. Besides, the other day when they had mentioned the hospital shows, and we said we'd rather stick together and go overseas, they said they'd have to decide where we were most needed at the moment. So I don't know. I didn't want to make them mad. What I figured I'd do is this — I'll be around town about three weeks — in the meantime the author will be working on the play — if it looks like it is really going to amount to something, I'll give my notice. If it doesn't, I will have saved enough money to go to New York — or perhaps I will do another show for the Victory Committee and go overseas from here and then go to New York. You know that right now this Victory Committee is really the biggest thing in show business. I'm a little worried about that M.C. business — but they have all the material, so I guess I can do it. I wish I were quicker with the wisecracks though. The whole thing will be good for me — more & more poise, you know.

We met with this Jack Elliott, the writer, again today — and all is going well. It seems that now he wants to make a production out of the deal and write a play that will be commercial as well as for the G.I.' s. That's why I don't want to miss out on it. I'll find out absolutely definitely from him on Tuesday though exactly what he is going to do. The thing seems to have fallen in my lap to manage, and I don't know that I like it. I have to manage everything and do most of the talking, and I'm afraid I'll make a mistake.

I also met this man about the talking songs today — For a price, I'll find out what it is on Monday, he'll write some numbers for me and teach me how to do three next week — then if I can do them well enough, he'll arrange to break them in at the Hollywood Canteen — me doing them — next Sunday — It would be good because I could tell what I did wrong. The whole thing is very confusing. I only wish, darling, that you were here to tell me what to do and to give me the old shot in the arm — It's quite obvious that these people take me for a much more clever character than I am and that they are going to find out.

You know the only thing darling is that I keep worrying that you are going to get bored with this detailed account of my activities.

Baby, can you see the pen beginning to trail off? — I sleepy, my darling — so goodnite — sleep tight — keep safe — I love you — come home to me soon — oh, darling honey — I'm so lonesome for you —

All my love,

Jane

The pictures came from San Francisco today. I'll airmail them "I adore you"

#7
21 Jan. 1945 351 to go

Dearest Honey: You talk about jack-pots! Yesterday afternoon I got four letters from you, the last dated the 17th. That was the one where you had just gotten three from me. As you say we have reestablished contact. Honey, you are so wonderful about writing, and you don't know what it means to me. Yesterday I was high man on the ship with four, but more than that it just made my insides roll over and come up nice and warm and happy. I don't suppose your letters sound like much to you, but they are so interesting to me. You are so lucky, every day you have lunch with someone or an appointment or something that makes a little talk-talk. The most important thing is that by writing me a little very day I get a better picture of what you are doing, if you save it up for three or four days at a time, you forget a lot of little things. Of course, baby, I'm not fatuous enough to believe that this will go on ad infinitum, but just for these first few weeks it's really lovely. Two days in a row I didn't get any mail, and my little heart she about break. Silly as hell, but I so look forward to a letter every day. Not many more days of this fast delivery service either, I might just get an answer to this one, and then off we go. I imagine mail will be largely b' guess and b' gosh for some time to come. You're going to be proud of your old pappy afore much longer. About calling you, I am going to try and do it, but there is a hell of a lot of red tape for a service man. Still we will see.

I'm still looking for a bag and some nice daytime perfume for you, but so far the results have been nill. You know old Charley though, persistent cuss so you may still be surprised. Pete and I had a wonderful time yesterday. When the supply officer came aboard he took over ship's service. We closed out our stock, and when the dust had settled we had about three thousand dollars to do with as we will. We bought about three or four hundred bucks worth of athletic equipment, but that only dented the surface. Yesterday Pete and I bought a phono-radio combination. A good Philco with a Capeheart record part. $450.00 can you imagine? It goes in the wardroom, but it is hooked up to all the speakers in the men's compartments, so they will hear it all. Then the part I figured in so prominently. I bought about a hundred and fifty bucks worth of classical music. I was lucky and got all pre-war recordings. It was such fun just to go down the line and pull out album after album without a thought of the cost. I remember how we used to listen to them and weigh the price before we would buy one!! Fun, fun!! I got Sibelius 2nd and 7th; Beethoven's 3rd, 5th, and 7th; Tschaiskowsky's 5th and 6th; Dvorak's 5th; Shubert's Unfinished; Offenback's Gaite Parisien; Tschaiskowsky Romeo and Juliet Overture; Nutcracker Suite; Strauss Waltzes; Smetana's The Moldau; Ballad for Americans and so on and so on. Of course, we also got about 400 popular records for the jive minded crew and officers. All in all we spent almost $800.00 bucks in one morning. I hope the hell we don't lose the old bucket before we get to play at least a few of them!

Honey, I had a lot of fun just now, I came on watch at 0400, and it's now 0530. I reread all the letters I've gotten so far. It made you seem awfully close for a few minutes. So much has happened to you, and you have so many irons in the fire. Almost like me when we were married almost seven years ago, God! I hate people who make statements like this, but I can't help having a feeling that something good is going to work out for you, and it will be the right one. It must be fun to be watching them all and wondering which it's going to be.

Here I go sticking my neck out again. Honey, I notice Lee Gale's name a few times in the letters. I'm not trying to dictate friends or tell you how to run your life, that after all is up to you. But, darling, he is somewhat on the shady side, I know he is a nice enough guy, but his activities, his ways of making a living aren't exactly top drawer. Not for God's sake that I am a prude or speak only to

Cabots, but Lee is a little too earthy and frankly animalistic for me. Okay I've said it, now watch the fireworks!!!

Two weeks today! Two down and fifty to go. I don't know about you, but they are about the longest two weeks of my life. This "Nelly pull you belly in, it's for the USA" is pretty good in a song, but it kinda sticks in my throat when I try and sing it. Except for the fact that the fast mail service will be out, I'll be glad to get the hell out of here. Swinging on the hook makes the time go twice as slow. I want to get going and start swinging. From the looks of things, early summer might see me back on your favorite island, while it's not good, in fact I hate it, it has a lot more to offer than some places I can think of. Might even run into a USO outfit there, with a sensational blonde doing the honors. Boy, I am sure giving that arm a workout with the needles aren't I? Well, darling, that's about the extent of our thinking. How soon will it be over so we can pick up where we left off. The four freedoms, Dumbarton Oaks, International airlines and South American policy seem to be pretty small potatoes compared to holding you in my arms again. Doesn't seem possible that one guy could love you so much. I am so lonesome and want you so much that I am a kind of a nice big overall ache.

I've got to get over thinking about you all the time. I've only been in town that once when I had dinner with the Richardsons. In fact, there is a club about six hundred yards from here, and day before yesterday, when I got no mail from you, I didn't even go over and have a drink. Just stayed aboard and saw the movie and hit the old sack early. I know that is a little hard to believe coming from me, but it's the truth so help me.

Don't go getting perturbed about me though baby, I'm not going to die of it, or anything else for that matter! By God, that's not right either. I just plain old love the finest wife in the world completely and with all my heart, and if I miss her so much it makes me unhappy, there is nothing to be ashamed of. Maybe some guys don't love their wives as much, in fact I know they don't, but what the hell, that doesn't make me wrong or a freak now does it?

You keep plugging away at the old career and loving me a bit on the side, and I'll shortly start slugging away and loving you a hell of a lot on the side, and pretty soon we will be together and knocking the hell out of the show business in the finest little old combo that ever hit that screwball town!! Yessir Jackson.

I love you ducky, completely, always, and with every part of me — there will be no false starts on the next one, so cross your fingers, keep loving, keep hoping, and stay sweet for pappy! all me love — Chas

So round! So Firm! So beautifully stacked!!

God love a duck! XXXXXXXXX [BIG ONES HANDWRITTEN] Great little pen!

#8
22 Jan 1945 In Port —
350 to go.

Dearest Honey:

Well I got a wonderful long letter today, although I got none yesterday. Hell, baby, I know there will be days when you just have to miss writing, that's okay with me, just so they don't happen too often. I did get the pins yesterday, and it was such perfect timing — I got a new map of Germany and the immediate surrounding countries yesterday morning it's a Navy news-map and I mounted it on a board and drew with a compass red circles 100, 200, and three hundred miles from Berlin. When I came back to the ship from the club there were the pins, so I've had a field day today trying to get my line in. Having a hell of a time staying up with the Russians incidentally, but that's the kind of problems I like to face. I wonder just how long they are going to continue at this rate? They are averaging over thirty miles a day. If they can do that for five more days they will be in the town. Here's hoping.

Say, I got a wonderful souvenir for you today that I will mail off tomorrow. It's a Japanese fragmentation hand grenade that has been unarmed. We've got an underwater demolition expert, a jg, attached to us for temporary duty, and he brought back some little gadgets like that for some of us for presents home. He is taking us over tomorrow morning to see the museum of Japanese weapons they have here. I guess they have just about everything they throw at us, land, sea or air. Should be very interesting.

Darling, the pictures were wonderful, thanks so much. Did you get them from Martha, or did one of those wolves out here send them back to you? Grr I hate em!!! You know, darling, I catch myself looking at people in the 0 club and wondering if you sat under the apple tree with them when you were here? Isn't that the damnedest thing? It's just awful how much I miss you, baby, and the hell of it I think it's getting worser instead of better. You don't suppose I will wither and die like a lonely untended wild flower do you? Ain't I elfin though? Oh, darling, I'd give my right hand to be with you for just an hour tonight, extravagant talk, but I mean it. Say, do you remember when you were doing your swing with the show and you thought you might go on out to another place, but they decided it was too hot for you? I'll give you the straight dope on it soon. When I shove off there will be quite a few days without letters, as I think that will be the first mailing drop available. From there into the wild blue yonder. You said you were worried, don't baby as I told Smiley today, "Hell Smile," says I, "There ain't been the bullet made with my name on it." "Oh no," says Smiley, real sarcastic like. "No," I retorts, "Didn't you know that it will take a silver bullet to get me?" "Yeah," says Smiley, still sarcastic. "Then I'll bet they're pouring one right now!!!" How about that guy? They aren't going to get me though, baby, I've got too damn much unfinished business with a blonde I know. And I do mean monkey business Woo-woo! I love that girl!

Say doc, starting with March you'll get $200.00 potatoes a month, changed the allotment today. I figured you are much, better at getting it to a bank than I am, and if you need it well, you just need it that's all. So don't go buying slinky evening gowns to knock some jerk's eyes out when he is squiring my tomato around — get it? Anything else, okay. I love you.

I was a real good boy today, went over to the club at four thirty, had four drinks, and came back to the ship at quarter to six for dinner, saw the movie and now am writing to my sweetie pie. It's the first time n the 18 months I've been on this old bucket that I ever came back for dinner before the drinking shut down. How about that. Do you realize what a sterling character you have got talking to himself? Do you know I adore you? Do you realize it's only fifteen days since I saw you and that already the physical me is about to go through the overhead? And how's with you? Hell ain't it? Still fifteen days is 1/24th of our year, and the fraction gets bigger by the day.

I am getting brown again, and my hair is <u>definitely</u> blond again, so there. At least I'm sleeping with a blond again, but damn it, there is only one of us! Well, honey, my love, I've got the first watch in the morning, so I better get my beauty sleep. Maybe you'll come see me in my dreams. What a nice thought. And so with the farewells of the happy islanders coming across the waters to us we slowly steam away into the sunset, leaving behind us the beautiful island of Lack-of-nookie with its peaceful childlike people

    I kiss you goodnight, my darling. All me love Chas

6500 Yucca St. Lido Apts. Hollywood
28 Jan. 22, 1945 Letter #14

Hello Honey;

    Yipe, darling — that wonderful D'Arsay perfume arrived today — what a wonderfully lovely, I started to say fragrant, but that's trite — it's better than that — Martha brought the package up, and she nearly swooned with envy informing me that it was a hard to get as gold. Thank you, baby — What more could a girl ask than to have such a thoughtful husband — I don't know — Really I don't.

    This has been a rather social afternoon — I didn't go out to dinner because the grocer gave me some liverwurst, and it killed my appetite — The Vandraegens came in, but first came the Lathams and-before that Lee and Martha — Martha with the perfume and Lee with news. It seems he knows this man who was going to give me the material — I met the man today and found it was going to cost me two hundred dollars! Well, that was out of the question — Lee said he would try to get it lowered, so he came up to tell me he couldn't — I don't really need the stuff any way — it's just to have additional thing. Jack Latham is going to contact somebody he knows who'll do it for me. The Lathams were fine — the Vandraegens were too. Jim Hill, they tell me, has had pneumonia again but is alright now. They all sent their love to you. Luckily I had a bottle of "Privelege" on hand, so a nice conversation was had by all. Dan was on Jimmie Fidler — some silly thing — he was joking about it.

    When I finish writing you — I'm going out and mail it and buy a newspaper. Honey, things are going so fast. I'm almost afraid to believe the Russians are doing so well. Marg said she hoped the Russians wouldn't get all the credit, and I said I didn't care who got it, just so they stopped shooting. If only the Pacific looked as if it might be over so soon — if only only.

Goodnite, my darling — I love you so very much — completely — come home soon, baby — Keep safe, my darling — please please. That's the closest I can come to saying I'm worried, so I won't worry you —

All my love, darling, Jane

I didn't hear from you today (Monday) I pray I'll have another letter before you leave there — I love you —

6500 Yucca St. Lido Apts Hollywood, Calif.
January 23, 1945 Letter #15

Dearest Darling honey;

Here it is, the end of another day — in fact it's really the beginning of a new one — I am sitting here at the little desk — dressing table in those wonderful pajamas that you gave me — Hazel is in bed reading the papers — very peaceful.

Honey, you wouldn't know me — I went to two movies tonite — First the newsreel and then that thing with Edward G. Robinson and Joan Bennet called "Woman in the Window." It was really awfully good, and it took much will power to restrain me from biting off my new manicure. Hazel and I went to dinner with Lee. She was slightly disapproving of it because she doesn't approve of him, but his invitation was so sincere that we did — we met Pat Gleason who was alone and he came along — it was really a remarkably pleasant evening with a fine dinner conversation.

I went to the first rehearsal today of the hospital show, and it should be fun — I have to take more responsibility than I thought I did though, so I'll have to be on my toes. In the meantime, I'm sort of between the devil and the deep because the author told me today that provided all goes well, he would have that play ready soon. He wants me to go out with him to the Actors Lab to see about arrangements. So I'll string along another couple of days and see what happens.

I am beginning to have a lurking fear, darling, that I won't hear from you for a while — I haven't had a letter since last Friday, so the gap is getting pretty long. I knew it had to come, but still it gives me a funny feeling when I realize it has. There is so very much of my joy in the business of living that goes when you go — even when I seem to be enjoying myself, it's on the surface — there isn't that fine deep feeling of happiness underneath because there is nothing to fill it —

I am sitting here looking at that lovely perfume — Such luxury, darling — thank you, baby.

I love you, honey — Keep safe, darling — please — be careful — for me —

All my love, sweet, Jane

#9
25 Jan 1945
347 to go In Port

Dearest Honey:

Two days in a row and no mail. Ah well, I guess I am the forgotten man. Funny what a rock bottom ebb my innards hit yesterday when everyone got some but me. Don't I feel sorry for myself though? Aw well, today will bring a packet I have no doubt. I did get a couple from Mom yesterday, so I didn't quite draw a blank.

I imagine you are busy as a bird with all the irons in the fire, I wonder which will come out first. I find myself hoping that it will be something in the states. I know that's selfish because the boys do need entertainment out in the broad Pacific, but I need a wife too, and I can't help feeling I'm liable to lose you all over again if you come back to this land of no women. Honey, I know it's silly, but I make myself miserable around here. Yesterday Van and I went into town to see a young married couple he knows. We sat around and had a few drinks, and then he took them to dinner at the Moana. I caught myself looking at several nice girls dining with Majs and Cols and such like, and I wondered how many times a certain blonde had been there causing sparkle to come to some jerk's eyes. It just made me unhappy as hell. I know I'm being ridiculous, but it's so hard to tell your insides that. They don't seem to hook up at all well with the rational part of the mind. As a matter of fact, I hate this town worse than ever because every place I go I can picture you with some devoted swain hanging on your words, and I get a panicky feeling. You say you love only me now, and I suppose it's true enough, but when I think how close it was it scares hell out of me. I'll bet if you'd stayed another six months and I hadn't come back in that time I would be getting a "Dear John" letter.

Oh hell, baby, don't take me too seriously. I'm just unhappy and missing you acutely and wondering when and if I'll ever see you again. I hate letters like this, but I had to write or say it to someone, and you was elected. We will be out of here afore long, and then time will start skipping by. I guess the phone call is out. When you are on the beach here it is pretty easy, but on a ship there is a lot of red tape connected with it and plenty of time, which I now don't have enough of, to cut it. I'll call you from Manila P.I. afore many moons go by.

[MISSING]

That's really going pretty well isn't it? By the way, I saw that the 25th was in on it in the paper the other day, so old Oswald is again sweating it out I guess a lot of your new friends are in it too, hope they all come through all right, and I mean it. I still hate 'em though!!!

Honey, honey, I adore you with every ounce of my jealous twisted little mind. I don't know what's come over me today, I'm through with it now, and the next letter tomorrow will be all sweetness and light and love. I got that package mailed off to you today. It will go first class, so should take a little time. There is a story on page one that's wrapped around the knife that I thought you might be interested in. Top of the story right next to the girl's picture be sure and remember to look at it when it comes. Left hand top corner.

Baby, I don't know if a guy can die of a lonesome heart, but I'd hate to say one couldn't because I am sure in awful pain missing you. Think of me a little, and love me a lot, and get ready for the post-war world. Brother, am I ready right now!!!!

Ran into Charley Meyers for a minute yesterday and am going to see him again this aft, I hope. He has just been home on thirty days leave and is on his way out to set up a spare parts outfit on Guam. What a life he will lead. Having had leave like that, he will probably be there till it's all over. Not too happy about the whole thing. Hasn't heard from Abie for quite a while and neither have I. Hope he is still all right, but then he will be. Horne is having stateside duty now, Gee that means Fry is the only guy who hasn't gotten back yet. I'll be afraid to run into him. I bet he is plenty unhappy about the whole deal.

Well, darling, chow is going to go down in a minute, and I want to get this in the mail. I'll write again tomorrow night, and I won't be this gloomy and stupid again, believe me. I love you with all my heart, darling — all my love, all my life. That's pretty inclusive, isn't it?

KISS KISS !!!!!!

All me love, Chas

P.S. Saw Martha O'Driscoll at the Moana last night in a U.S.O. overseas outfit. So I guess she is heading out.

6500 Yucca St. Hollywood 28, Calif.
Jan. 25, 1945 Letter #16

Hello, honey;

I just came in from rehearsal — its about six o'clock — almost — Hazel is still out, so I thought I'd start a note to you — Honey, when I came in, there was a letter from you — tomorrow it would have been a week — I was so happy — don't you <u>dare</u> wait five days again (I've been checking dates) when you're in port. I spent an hour last nite just silently with the tears dripping because I hadn't heard from you.

Darling, what a thrill it must have been to buy all those records! — and a Capehart — my gosh.

Well I spent a little money today — I bought a pair of green lizard shoes that are a dream — pumps, and there was a bag on sale to match — my one pair of black suede was beginning to sort of get a little feeble — they are now in for rejuvenation. Then I got a makeup case — it's like a small suitcase with a handle on the top — no perfume spilling dangers any more — Actually, I did very well getting the whole kit & kaboodle for thirty dollars, but I'll have to hurry and get to work.

I feel a little better about this hospital show today — I suppose it's good for my morale to know I'm getting paid more than anyone else. I also found out that Ray Mack is having this wonderful gag writer write the material for me. I talked to him about this Jack Elliot who is writing the other script for us — just to get the thing straightened out in case I should want to make a change, and he (Ray Mack — he's the new head of the Victory Committee) said that in his opinion I couldn't sit around waiting for a man to write a play. He has a point there. There is a rumor that this show may go to New York and then overseas instead of coming back here — I can't believe it, but it <u>might</u> be.

Oh, honey — just then Hazel came in. She wanted to go to Musso's for dinner because they had shrimp curry there, so we did. We met Pat Gleason, and he ate with us, then he came back here for a coffee royale. Gladys gave us an electric plate the other day. He told me a whole list of little known facts about baseball including the time that Bill Wamsgans made a triple play unassisted, which I thought I could work into that baseball quiz — In the meantime, Hazel was packing because she is going to Las Vegas for the weekend to see Bobby — He leaves next week for Texas or Louisiana — I think this is his last course before he gets his commission. If so, I'm firmly convinced we'll have a marriage in the family — because Pat — is staying with Mary in New York now — Daddy called Mother and said he had had a letter from Pat telling him about it. She's going to become a member of the family or bust, and I must say, I certainly like her for it. Anyway, Hazel is leaving about seven in the morning. She's all ready now and getting to bed.

Honey darling, this is a horrible letter. By the way, it is definitely <u>not</u> fun to sit around and see which job is going to work out — it's ghastly and utter misery. You know, after all these years, I have no faith in irons in the fire, and I want to work so badly at the best thing that not being definite about it is nearly enough to drive me mad. It's fun to read about it, but the experience isn't. Besides, I don't lead such a busy social life as one might think — I've really been someplace with somebody besides Hazel one nite this week, and that was the nite we went to the movies with Lee and Pat.

Honey, I received your little, shall we say, "lecture" about Lee Gale today. I realize as well as you what you are aiming at. It is a little silly for me to say that all that talk hides an idealistic and sensitive soul, although it is true. I realize, as Hazel tells me, that it is not good for me to be seen with him too much — as a matter of fact, I've been to dinner with him three times — I've tried to avoid it as much as possible. But he is so fundamentally kind that it is hard for me to hurt him by chopping him off, and I would think the less of myself if I did it — I would feel like a perfect snob and never forgive myself — as his conduct toward me has always been exemplary. However, I realize the impression he makes on others, and I will be very careful not to see too much of him or be seen — I promise you. Okay?

Sweet darling — it is late — I will say goodnite — Remember I love you, my darling, with all me heart — Come home <u>soon</u> All my love, Jane

Continue to write me here — I love, love, <u>love</u> you.

6500 Yucca St.
Hollywood 28,
Feb. 1, 1945
Letter 24

Hello honey darling;

This, I am afraid will be a tiny note because I am about to drop in my tracks — with rehearsals and all — eleven hours today and still nothing really done. I thought this thing was opening on Monday and now they want to do it Saturday so I will have to get up very early in the morning and start memorizing it. I'm too tired to do it tonite.

Darling, sometimes we don't mention the thing we are thinking of most. I say that because I forgot to tell you that yesterday I was trying to find some Macadamia nuts to send you — then I come home and there is the package from you with some for me in it. Thank you darling.

Baby the pen is slipping into illegibility. Will you forgive me if I just say that I love you with all my heart — and go to bed —

Goodnite my darling. I love you

Jane

6500 Yucca St.
Hollywood 28
February 2, 1945
Letter 325

Dearest honey darling;

Again tonite a short letter — it's because I rehearsed ten hours today — then Buddy was here when I got home at nine — so now it is after midnite and I've been trying to memorize my script with very little success. They have a dress rehearsal tomorrow and a show Sunday and the only way I'll be able to remember it is by consulting the darned thing between each act — with 17 acts, it's a little difficult to remember just what you are doing — I hope the pictures will help make up for the short letter — I know you have them but thought you might like to have them in this size.

Buddy just came down from Bakersfield for the evening — it was awfully sweet of him considering the fact that he has to be back by noon tomorrow — meaning that he has to start about five in the morning.

Sweet darling, I won't know until tomorrow just where to write me but I do know that from about the 16th to the 23rd of February, I'll be in San Francisco so why not write me at Patsy's and I'll keep in touch with her. Tomorrow's letter will have exact directions.

Darling I've just been sitting here thinking while I'm writing this letter — how very much I love you — I have been dashing around worrying about rehearsals and script and about how I am going to get my clothes packed — but all the time I can't get over that empty, vacant feeling that my honey isn't here and without that, nothing can be completely fun or absorbing. You don't need to worry about my getting too occupied because there is nothing that could take the place of you — I love you immeasurably and inexpressibly and I miss you every minute of the time you are away. Keep safe my darling — keep loving — I shall see you soon —

All my love darling,
Jane

#13
3 Feb. 1945
In Port
338 to go.

Dearest Honey:

Well baby I wish I could tell you how overwhelmed I was when the mail came back the day before yesterday. I had six letters from you! As I told you in my letter I didn't expect any as I thought it had gone on ahead. Well I was so overcome by the unexpected windfall that I disciplined myself. I made myself go up to the movie, course I didn't stay for the whole show but then I came down got into adjusted the pillow stacked up the cigarettes and ash tray by the bed and then proceeded to fall in love with my wife all over again. Honey it was so much fun just to be able to kind of relive your life with you day by day. Don't ever worry about my getting bored with "your day" darling if they come from you your letters could say nothing but schdrdlu, schrudlu, copasetic, schrudlu and I would still love to get them! Actually though darling they are extremely interesting. I see you gradually shaping up for one thing and another and it's fun to watch it develop from letter to letter.

Before I forget it there are some things I would like to comment on. I'm so glad you liked the perfume baby, I've been trying to find some more I thought you might like, but no luck. It's pretty scarce even out here. I'll tell you what, I'll post off a quart or so when I hit Manilla, P.I.!! Okay? Second. You mentioned a feminine trouble. That was on the 26th and I've had two more letters the 27th and the 28th and you made no m ore mention of it. By the time you get this its probable came and went, as us illerates say, but how about letting me know if all is well? You mention Dr. Stevens. I was going to ask you to see him again before you left the states on a show of any kind. I know as you do, that all is well, still I'd feel a lot better if you would have a check-up again. How are those lovely things doing by the way, are they still keeping SR-SF since the old man went away? Honey if you only know how much I miss holding on to you, it just kind of makes me weak in the knees to even think about it. This God damned war anyhow! Romantic daydream over for a moment, back to the letters. You also said that you would send a list and dates in the next, I guess you didn't get them because they weren't in it. Maybe there is a chance we might pick up some last mail this morning, if not I will to have to address all of it to Martha's until I hear from you again which will be quite a spell. I guess her Mom will know where you are so she will just have to forward the letters. I'm so glad Martha is going with you, you get along so well, but just don't let her little romantic and impetuous nature lead you into any romantic entanglements!! I guess the last thing I wanted to comment on specifically was Bob Deming. Damn that's a shame, do you know any more details or just that he is missing? This Goddamned war, hits anyone anywhere doesn't it?

Well baby so much for your letters, only don't get the idea that I am casually dismissing them. If you only knew what a feeling of happiness and being loved they brought to me you wouldn't begrudge the time you spend each day. I know I'm a romantic goop for being so in love, but it's something I have no longer any check rein on so you'll either have to humor me and keep writing or break my wittle heart as Red Skelton would say. I love you awful good baby, but then I guess you know that. I spent all afternoon today remodeling one of those bracelets for you. It is now all silver, knowing your weakness, and it looks pretty good. It's perhaps nothing that would cause Benvenuto Cellini to roll over in his 15th century tomb, but there is a lot of lovin effort in it anyhow. I hope I didn't make it too small, right now would you take a ruler or tape and measure your wrist note down how far around it is and send it in the next letter., this guess work is driving me crazy. The bracelet and a little pamphlet I am mailing this morning are to be considered a happy valentine present. Speaking of valentines, I got that cute one from you darling, also the other card about missing, ain't it the truth. That's one of the things I like so much about you baby you can see the fun and humor in little things like that that most people our age would consider very silly. Thank God we are still basically childlike enough to enjoy small things in life along with the biggest ones. You know darling give us a little time to work at it again and I think you and I can have just about the closest relationship ever achieved by two people. Of course loving you so much that my insides do a half gaynor with a pike every time I think about you helps too, but there is more to the story than that. Do you happen to know I adore you? Yup, so help me! Well to get on, also in the box with the bracelet is your anniversary present, the seventh God help us. I was going to wait and mail them when it would get to you at about the right time, but the way things look now I'm not going to take the chance. In the first place I won't be able to mail anything for nearly two weeks if then, and I know the mail will be in very bad shape for a time why, you know only too damned well. As a matter of fact don't count on any mail from me for about three weeks, then you won't be disappointed (you do love me don't you darling, I don't sound like a fatuous ass when I say things like that assuming that you will be looking for letters do I?) Of course I will write every two or three days when we are underway, I can't help myself darling, but I'm afraid that they will all come in one fell swoope. Well to get back to the anniversary present. It's a set of earrings and they are real, they didn't quite break me, but they cost enough so I know they're real! Either that or I got royally taken, but being as I got them though a ship's service I don't think so. (They really did break me darling, Smiley owns me body and soul and my pay for weeks to come, but what the hell, where I'm going you can't spend it anyway!) That's one of the reasons I'm also mailing them off now, if the Mighty G should come a cropper I don't want to have to whistle down to my room to pick up odds and ends, not this kid, over the side and away!!!! Pretty talk, but with a note of truth. Well baby I'll send it airmail so you can start admiring them and using them. I can just see you done up in black for the evening (with some knuckle-headed colonel no doubt) and wearing them. Honey just know that I love you and want you to look pretty, I don't give a damn if you go out with the whole bloody U.S. Army singly or collectively if just once during the evening you will touch them with your finger and say quietly to yourself, "there is a guy named Chas who loves me so much more than any of these characters that it's just silly to talk about" just say that and I'll be happy!!!

Well that handles the situation pretty well I guess, except to say that with the present goes all my love to the sweetest wifling in the entire world! I had myself a time yesterday. Remember those extra guns that I was so concerned about for the admiral's inspection at Dago? Well I went over and tried to draw some mounts for them. Of course I was turned down as we really don't rate them. Well then the old Flynn do or die spirit came to the fore and what with wheedling cajoling and a little outright lifting I managed to get almost what I wanted without any chits at all! I found two oldtimers whose idea was that they were on the beach to serve the forces afloat which is the case, but try and cram that idea into some of the knot heads that are getting their bottoms spread behind a desk for the duration. At any rate it was a most enjoyable day, I love to thwart knot-heads!

The night before Smiley and I took off for town with a jug and all set to raise hell. It was our last night on the beach as we had the duty yesterday, (this is on the 4-8 in the morning) so we decided to howl. We found a little hotel and got a room and then wandered around town. Our hell-raising was of a most innocent variety however, but it was a lot of fun. We found a shooting gallery and amazed the proprietor, with some of those milk bottle affairs which caused us to nearly throw our arms out of joint. Then we found a couple of souvenir shops, where we picked up the pamphlet I am mailing to you, and also supplemented our collection of feelthy pictures. I did show you that collection one day when you were aboard didn't I? At any rate we now have about thirty different nudes and we put up a different one each week as the "pin up girl of the week" Then all the officers and the mess boys and any of the men who can figure out a reason to get down there take a gander at it. Aren't men the silliest things? I'm enclosing one of the milder ones in the front of the little book, but don't go getting any ideas! For you I mean. I bought the book as a gag, but on thinking it over maybe you could use it in your work, but as I say don't get any ideas from the picture! Well as I say it was quiet, but kinda fun to wander around lighted streets with people and stuff, God knows when we will see that again. We got back to the little hotel about a quarter of ten and hit the sack after a couple of drinks. Gay night life in the Paris of the Pacific! Bah!

By the way honey Berk wanted me to give you Alice's address in Dayton. He would love to have you see her and his dad and her family if you get back there. Also he says his dad goes to Detroit every week and would love to take you to dinner if you get up there. Mrs. H.C. Berkeley Jr. 2325 Ridgeway Rd., Dayton, 9 Ohio. Wan4891. Also Alice has a sister, Mary, who nearly went out of her mind when Alice told her about you and what you have done. She would give her eye teeth for a picture of you with an inscription to her from you, I gather she is about 16 or17, and bats about people in this business. If you have anything you could send her I wish you would. Her address is Mary Wiltshire, Westover School, Middlebury, Connecticut. She would probably go out of this world. Thanks honey.

Well, doll, the people are getting up and I must be about my business, it's mighty hard to say goodbye to you for so long but such is the way of a world at war. Remember I adore you darling, and stay true to me please. Not much more I can say except that you have all my love, all my life —

All me love Chas

P.S. Honey would you find me a good basic instruction book on the Standard or Plectrum banjo and send it on out. I couldn't find one here. Be sure and not get one for Tenor, that's no good. Thanks baby. Love love, kiss, kiss, kiss!!!!

1500 Yucca St.
Hollywood 28, Calif.
Feb 4, 1945
Letter #26

Hello honey darling;

Oh honey I missed last nite because when I came in I was just dragging — I didn't get out of rehearsal until after midnight and then I had a whole new script to memorize. Mr. Lowery didn't like Jack Elliot's material so he gave me a lot more! I rehearsed all day today and when I got home, I had to pack and bleach my hair — I hadn't had time to go to the beauty shop — it is now about two in the morning and I have to go to Santa Ana to do a show tomorrow — Then come back tomorrow nite — and leave for San Diego Tuesday morning at 7:45 — and I get through that — all is OK because only one show a day for awhile, I'll be in San Diego through the 10th, Santa Barbara until the 14th, Salinas (Fort Ord) the 15th and 16th and San Francisco at the Manx from the 16th to the 25th — So darling — write me at Patsy's and she will forward it — that's just about the schedule for February — By the time I leave Pat's, I'll have the schedule for March. If you are uncertain address letters to me in care of Daddy 3700 Main St., Vancouver Wash.

Darling, there is a delivery Sunday here so I got your 11 and 312 letters. I couldn't imagine until I read the second how they got mailed — I'm sorry I was cross about the Honolulu associations baby and you didn't need to apologize. Oh honey wherever you are going — keep safe — I love you awfully much — even if I am dense about beards and birthday presents — I won't say any more — except that I love you with all my heart — be careful my darling and soon we'll have a whole life as happy as San Diego.

Goodnite sweet. I love you,

#14
5 Feb. 1945
At Sea —
336 to go.

Dearest Honey:

Well darling here we are on our way again. Only this time it looks like we will keep right on going. Although it has only been two days since I wrote you, it already seems that we have been at sea weeks. The only nice thing about going was that the mail orderly brought back three letters one from Mom and a card and a letter from you. It made it easier to sail away. That was the cute card about "When the duck says cluck" etc. Very very cute darling. It's kinda fun to find silly little things isn't it?

Speaking of that, yesterday being Sunday (4 weeks!!!) we had holiday routine so Smiley and I spent the day fixing up our little nest. One of the first things I did was to put up that cartoon of the pink elephant right at the head of my bed and then right above it I secured the little one you bought for me. It looks quite like a girls room at school except for the fact that all the pictures surrounding it are of a girl. I took that big picture of you at the sea-shore (quaint, ain't I?) page and all out of the album and put it right alongside my pillow. Now which ever way I turn to go to sleep I see a picture of you. That one I put on the end of the desk you know where I showed you where I had them before. On the other side are the two folders with numbers of pictures. You know darling an outsider looking into this room might conceivably get the idea that I was enamored of a certain gal. Might be something to it at that! Enamored! Gad that is a prize understatement. We certainly had ourselves a time last night though, you and me I mean. Course it was all in a dream world that involved San Diego, the U.S. Grant, no clothes, big beds, oh honey, it was sensational. Dream world or no, it was out of this world let me assure you of that. Wonder if by some mental telepathy you got in on it too? Sure missed a wonderful evening if you didn't!! Am I depraved darling? Well, maybe a little, but mostly just missing you like billy-be-damned.

You know one of the things I think I miss more than anything is not being able to kiss you when I want to. It used to be such fun to just kiss you whenever the mood moved me. Course I know at times it drove you out of your mind, but then there were times when you seemed to like it too. That one spot on the back of your neck, especially when you were up to your elbows mixing biscuits or something — ummmmm!!

Well baby we are making it all on one jump to the place you almost went to. Gosh that means that it will be the 13th before I can even mail this, course you will know that because it will be on the front of the letter. Say darling when this operation is over I will be able to tell you where I was at least. The Capt called the crew together yesterday and told them our first destination. He didn't mention the ultimate goal, but he did say when it was wound up we would be able to say we had been in it. Course knowing my smart little cookie I doubt if you don't know where I am the minute it hits the headlines back home. But then you already have your whole was strategy mapped out anyway don't you? Wasn't that exciting about Manilla yesterday? I wonder is Doug managed to enter on a white horse "God and I have returned" I suppose this will be pretty dull reading when you eventually get it, but hell darling, its just kind of a way of talking to you over all these bounding miles of ocean. One of the men had a very cute line in his letter the other day. He had been writing to a friend about the progress of the European war and concluded his remarks by saying "But one thing's for sure, they will be selling Vodka in Berlin before they do hot dogs" aptly put I thought. I wonder if as you read this whether the Rusk's will be in Berlin. Here's hoping.

Well my darling, I have just time to have a cup of coffee and a cig before I go up to take the 20-24. Lots of time for thinking of you on that one. And I will!! I notice you keep signing your letters "keep safe" don't worry darling I'll do just that, Why? Cause I have something so special I'm going back to when this is over! I kiss you goodnight baby.

All me love —

Chas

P.S. Signed with my new Parker 51 pen; I also got a matching pencil — how about that?

XXXXXXXXX

Makes good kisses too!

U.S. Grant Hotel
San Diego, Calif.
Feb. 7, 1945
Letter #27

Honey darling;

Sackcloth and ashes. I missed two days — I know — I know — but oh darling, if you had been through those two days with me you would wonder that I am among the living — really. Monday four shows at Santa Ana — then home to Hollywood at eleven at nite — finished packing — up at five Tuesday morning and down to the train at 7:30 — off the train at Oceanside and then up to Camp Pendleton where we did six shows! — then back to the train — arrive in San Diego at eleven — and that darned manager hadn't verified our hotel reservations and they'd cancelled them — actually there wasn't a place in the town to be had — it seems that the USO in your contract that guaranties reservations at good hotels but the man who is managing this one is mad — (crazy) at least he was until he got a good dressing down today — now he's better — well, it was an awful mix-up and we had to sit in the lobby for four hours — finally at three they got the [ILLEGIBLE] to put up some cots — we had to be up and out of there by nine-thirty this morning — then a show this afternoon — honestly honey — I was through — if it hadn't been for the money and the fact that I would have felt like a shirker, I would have given my notice — not because of the reservations but because of the unplesantness of working with the man — he is being very nice today so I could be wrong — but I don't think so. However I have every confidence that they will soon change managers.

Honey darling — I love you — write me at Pat Zimmers and then in care of Daddy at 2700 Main St. Vancouver — I think we are in Seattle several days from about the 5th of March. Then we bounce around Washington for a while — Spokane 5 days. Is there anyone you want me to get in touch with?

Darling, whom do you suppose I ran into today. Martha and I were having a drink in the Rendezvous room — and who was there but John Haman from Ithaca. He is on an APA — and was so delighted to see me — Time had mellowed him a bit — we had dinner — he sent his best to you —

Baby I'm so darned sleepy — Remember darling — I love you — with every bit of me and miss you very very much.

All my love darling, Jane

Feb. 8, 1945

Dearest honey darling;

As you can see by this letter — I love you — with all my heart — I know I keep saying it in these very same words all the time — but I do — It is utterly inconcievable — to think that another person, no matter whom — could have such a hold on me — I love you so much that I can't think of anything else and the only thing I desire is for you to come home. I am so God damned (pardon) lonesome without you that I think sometimes I am losing my sanity — like tonite — I stood out on the balcony of the U.S. Grant tonite and heard the band playing in the patio across the street — It was the same band that I listened to after you left and it made me ill with missing you — oh darling — I love you and I'll write you a nice long letter tomorrow

All my love my sweet

Jane

#15
9 Feb. 1945
At Sea —
331 to go.

Dearest Honey:

I know that you are going to think that I am a very unloving guy to let this many days go by without writing, even though I can't mail it for a few days. Well darling it really has only been three days since the last one, despite what the date is on top of the letter. You see I am now one day ahead of you again, all of which makes it a little confusing as to what you are doing now and what day it is. Lets see it's now 0200 in the morning where you are, which I guess is San Diego. I suppose you are snug in the downy by now and mayhap dreaming of your old man, I hope!! As I said in the last letter I haven't gotten the list from you so all I can do is mail them to Martha's mom and try and imagine where you are.

You never did tell me if this show is going clear across the country or just the coast or what. I suppose a letter with all the details is no doubt on it's way to me, but incase it isn't please give me the dope. Just think a month age yesterday I was saying goodbye to you in San Diego and here you are probably back down there. Does it arouse any nostalgia darling? Or am I just an incurable old romantic? Probably it. At least one month is gone that's 1/12 of what we have to go. I love to write those fractions down as they get smaller, just imagine soon they will be over the half way mark. I don't mind saying though that this has been the longest month I have ever existed through in my life. They ought to go faster now, for a while at least.

We are very much back into the old routine. G.Q. every morning, watches, paper work and with luck about five hours sleep a night. Doesn't seem to bother me though, and the weather has been wonderful, very calm and nice. For that at least we can be grateful. I did get a lapse this afternoon. I had the 0400 to 0800 this morning and then tonight that gave me the short dog from after dinner about 1830 until 1945. Just a little over an hour and the nothing until the 0800 to 1200 tomorrow morning, except G.Q. about 0600 of course. Well I have finished the short dog, and so I have a chance to write to you, see. To get back to this afternoon. I spent from three until five listening to the new record machine. I heard Sibelius' 2nd symphony, Tskaiskowsky sixth symphony, and the Carnival of the Animals by Saent-Saens. It was the first time I had heard the second in a long time. I found myself remembering one time we sat on that old davenport of ours with your head on my shoulder and my arm around you. Outside it was raining like hell and our little gas fire was burning in the fireplace. I recaptured that feeling perfectly this afternoon. and that's strange because the water was running off me and there was nothing that resembled your lovely face in the wardroom, but strangely I could almost imagine that you were alongside me listening to it. You know darling, we had some wonderful times together even in those days you know it? I'll admit that there was a lot that could have been a lot better, and I think most of it was my fault, but even at that there were times when we hit something pretty fine. Like that night listening to that symphony. well just think darling, think what a wonderful life it will be when it all good and the way we occasionally hit it! And it will be, because if nothing else this war has straightened me out on a lot of things and thinking and I guess you too. So we should be sensational.

Honey, please don't think that this is a cringing little man desperately fighting to hold onto your love. I've always been able to take it as well as the next and usually a hell of a lot better when the chips are down. But the way I have been writing you lately you might get the idea that my backbone has suddenly turned to a bright yellow jelly. When I say that I think some of the bad parts of our marriage were my fault I am making a statement of fact, not pleading with you. Hell, you had plenty of faults too, only mine overshadowed yours and I'm beginning to realize that. All I'm trying to say is that with a new understanding and a fresh approach we will have not just a fairly happy marriage, but one of those marriages that even after twenty years has sort of a golden glow around it for everyone who comes in contact with it. Not just a successful marriage, but one where the love gets better and deeper as the years go by. You know what I mean. But about the above out-burst I am still a fairly complete person without you and should you ever give me the old heave-o I will not wither and die like and unwatered desert flower, although I'll be the first to admit that it would take a hell of a lot of bloom off me. And I know you've never said I wasn't a complete person, but I just wanted you to understand why I write so much and such tripe and mush. Love you hell yes. Miss you? You're damn right! Homesick? unbeliveably. But a clinging vine? Nuh-uh, not for me. I hope some of this gets a little of the ways to you, it doesn't read too plainly to me. I guess it boils down to the fact I love you very much and I want that love returned as it was offered, not mixed up with pity of protective feelings or duty or any such stuff. Just a good old fashioned love being returned in kind and with nothing else attached. Maybe that makes it a little better.

Sorry darling that I got so far afield, but then there is so little to put into letters except your thoughts out here that I guess it doesn't hurt to ramble on for a bit about them. I said that I also played Tskaiskowsky's 6th this afternoon. You know the first time I really remember hearing that in a concert hall, was in Munich in1935, nearly ten years ago. I'd heard it before of course, but this was the time I really associated it with things, and it is the first time I remember hearing it played. I remember I had gone alone to the concert that night, Pete was tied up and it was the only night they would be there. It was the Berliner Philharmonic. The sixth was the first number after the intermission, and I left right after it was over and went to a very quiet little beer garden, sort of family style and sat there reliving the music over a few glasses of beer. I felt very warm and loving life and continental and in a vague sort of way, romantic. I mean being conscious of the romance of the setting. American alone in a German beer hall being buoyed up by memories of beautiful symphony by an elegant Russian and played by one of the worlds most outstanding orchestras. Youth and romance and R6 cigarettes. (they tasted like dry horse droppings in those days, wonder what they are like now) All in all it was a wonderful afternoon. Today I mean. When we build our house we are going to have a really good speaker and a fine collection of records that we will add to every month, think of the fun of going down and buying a new symphony, together.

Oh honey I guess I'm a dope but I miss you so much it's truly awful. All I can think about is getting this damn thing over with and getting home to you. Despite any amount of protestations on my part I really am kind of counting on you being around when I get back. Let's give it a whirl, Jackson, it should be pretty nice.

Well darling this is my one chance to get a whole seven hours straight in a row, so I think I'll turn in. I'd better my eyes are beginning to drop closed over this. Not that I don't love you baby, just that the old frame is crying for a little sack time. Keep writing and loving. I adore you darling.

All me love —

Chas

XXXXX

Between san Diego
and Los Angles
Feb. 10 — 1945
#29

Hello sweet darling —

Well I left the old U.S. Grant at seven this morning — it gave me a great deal of nostalgia — oh honey when I think of the lovely time we've had there — it almost seems like home — I kept hoping that you would come walking across the lobby — this ache of missing you — gets worse, not better —

I hope you were able to read my last letter — I was awfully tired when I got home from the show — I had a bite to eat — went to sleep a while — had a couple of drinks and they really hit me — it was disgraceful — haven't had one since — not that I did anything except sit down and write a letter to you telling you how much I loved you — but it was sort of unintelligible —

Love

Jane

Carillo Hotel
Santa Barbara, California
Letter #30

Honey darling;

I gave that effort of writing this morning — the train was jiggling so that it was practically impossible to form the letters — we soon got into Los Angles — had a two hour layover and then took the one o'clock train to Santa Barbara — shades of the Leigh Valley honey-I swear it was straight from there — it was half an hour late starting and an hour late getting into Santa Barbara — hot, dirty and stinking — it is the same train which takes seventeen hours to get to San Francisco — I have now seen everything in the way of trains on the coast.

Honey when I got here today — I had better explain all this — hazel was at the station — only she didn't come to meet me because she didn't know what train I was coming in on — she was walking down toward the beach to Patty's when the train came in — she looked to see if I might be on it and there I was.

Well it seems that the day after I left, the pictures from the City of Paris came — so now I am sitting here looking at your face. Darling — in that double picture, I'm not so hot I think — but the picture of you is absolutely wonderful — it is the best possible picture I could ever have of you — I have just realized since I put it up this evening how very much it means to me to have it — I will never tire of looking at your face in that. The single one I'm not quite as pleased with — but only because they retouched it too much and took the highlights and the character lines out of your face — it's still nice though honey. I have decided that when I get to San Francisco, I'll have those of that other proof that we liked made up — you know — the one the one in which you are looking at me with an amused expression. I like that one of you with the tipsy expression on your face too — even if you don't —

Well to get back to "My Day" — we had a horrible time getting our bags off and cabs at the station — we finally got to the hotel — it's a horrible dump really but I've discovered the personnel is very nice — you know honey, no matter how rushed people are, if you are decent to them, they'll bend over backwards to help you — besides I seem to have developed some air about me of naturally expecting things — not exactly that but sort of that — "sure" shall we say — so while other people are bumbling around, I usually get what I need. Silly huh! Well, Martha and I had a shower and then went over to Patty's — we had an old fashioned and thick steaks — actually as tender as Tony and Marias — really — they had been well hung and blood red — broiled. After dinner we had southern Comfort — we had a fine evening of talk — and I feel like a normal human being again — much more settled and sincere — This last week has been pretty hard on my nerves — I now know I have them.

Speaking of the last week — that will be my worst writing record for the year — I was upset, unhappy and tired — Tuesday morning we left on the 7:45 train for Camp Pendleton — well of course that is a 12 mile drive from Oceanside — we did 6 ward shows there and one stage show. The ones in the ward are without benefit of mike and pretty hard on the voice — by the time for the stage show I was just about through — it always goes back on me when I'm tired anyway. Well, I told you about the trouble with the manager and how our reservations were gone when we got to San Diego at eleven that nite and how we sat in the lobby for nearly three hours and how we finally got a dormitory at the Y and had to be out by nine — thirty in the morning. We went and gave the show regardless of hours of sleep — *this was at the big naval hospital there — as a matter of fact, it was the best show I had done yet. That over with, we heard we had reservations at the Hospitality House — well we thought that was something for visiting dignitaries and were delighted. I was so looking forward to a shower. It turned out to be a dormitory — filled with very crummy looking people — the U.S.O. Hospitality house off all places — I took one look at it and said, "I will not stay here. Come on, Martha."* I went up to the Grant and gave them a line of dialogue with the result that one hour later I had a lovely double room. That was the nite I met John Harmon. He and some Marine friends of Martha's got all our luggage and brought it to the hotel and I finally had a bath. Don't think that this goes on everyplace because the U.S.O. doesn't allow it and it is a violation of the terms of our contract. It was a result of the manager's inefficiency. He was trying to direct the show when he should have been worrying about his job — reservations. Well the cast reported him to the Victory committee and he's pretty well straightened out now — he's still repulsive though — I still have the feeling it's the calm before the storm and it's going to end up someplace with my trying to control myself at all times. It will probably end with my quitting or getting fired — not really — I'm just kidding — I have a hunch they'll replace him — if they can find somebody — we had a long talk today and he was very prais-ing — he's a funny man but he's still repulsive.

Thursday we played the Naval hospital again but in a different place — and Friday — yesterday we went 60 miles out of San Diego just over the border from Tecate — (remember the try with the Dobrins) to a re-habilitation hospital. We did two shows — arrived home at one, washed my hair and up again at 7:45 — up at 5:45 — none too much time.

Darling, that lack of sleep is getting acute-so goodnite my honey — I'll get your plectrum book for the banjo-playing. I received the letter about it today — Martha's mother came down to the station. Honey I'm a little worried about the registered package you sent — it arrived at Martha's but she was gone and her mother couldn't sign for it so she forwarded it to Pat Zemmers — I wrote her just now and told her to get it if she could and hold it. Your letter today told about the earrings — I assume that was the package and don't like to have it bouncing around — About the earrings — darling — I have never been so touched in my life but you shouldn't have done it. Still it was awful nice of you and I love you so very much. I just hope it won't be too great a hardship on you. Honey, let me know if you need some money. Honey, in case I never told you, I LOVE you.

About where to write me darling — I'll be in San Francisco almost until the end of February and then in Oregon, Washington and Idaho. I really think that if you figure I have left San F. — you should write to me in care of John P. Patten, 3700 Main St. — Van-couver Washington — He is a regular whiz at forwarding — That's the safest.

Darling, my love, I'm so sleepy I can hardly see —
All my love,
Jane
I'll send the pictures Monday when the post office opens again.

Carillo Hotel
Santa Barbara, Calif.
February 12, 1945
Letter #31

Dearest honey darling;

I started this letter last nite but didn't finish it because I went to sleep and the sentences sort of trailed off into illegibility — I am becoming the darndest correspondent lately because I'm so tired — now tonite all the fatigue has changed into a sort of flu that isn't too nice but I'm drinking a hot toddy now; I have on my red wool jersey ski pant pajamas that I bought for cold weather — so I'm going to bed and hope. It's been quite a day — I wanted to get down to Patty's early because Hazel is leaving tomorrow so I decided to do my hair down there. One of the girls introduced me — "Charles of Taylor" would be interested in this — a new kind of oil bleach. It is very easy to apply and doesn't hurt the hair and is wonderful — that, plus some washing and ironing done, I went back and got ready for the play — then we did a show — then went back to Patty's — Hazel and Patty went to the show tonite and were delightfully surprised — they thought it was good.

This hasn't been a very good day — due to the fact that Martha got her notice — I am simply sick that she won't be going along with me — they say it is because there is no room for gags in a hospital show — that they want to put her in a Victory Unit which plays the camps. She's pretty upset about it although they have made it plain that it isn't her ability they are questioning but the fact that they have a more suitable place for her. The truth of the matter is though — although in loyalty, I shouldn't say it — she hasn't been working well with me — why, I don't know — perhaps it's my fault — but little things like not using the mike and killing her own lines because she insisted they could hear her anyway — and standing backstage not because she meant to but because she forgot — it's funny because I know she's good and she can do it. I think it's a question of adapting yourself quickly to a different medium — nevertheless, the whole thing is heartbreaking — it certainly will be much less pleasant for me — She leaves when we leave San Francisco.

Yesterday was our day off — I spent most of it with Hazel — went to a wonderful place out on the pier for dinner — seafood and all that — when I got home was when I went to sleep over the letter.

Darling, I was utterly fascinated with the hula book — I shall study the motions as soon as I get time — then when I get those down pat — maybe I'll study the technique — this is just an idle dream of course — I loved your pin-up girl.

She looked like Hedy La Marr in the face — the rest I don't know about —

Baby darling — keep safe — I think of you every minute — with all the love in the world. Tomorrow I'll get the banjo book and send the pictures —

I love you. I love you. I love you.

Jane

Write me at Pat's and then c/o Daddy, 3700 Main St. — Vancouver, Wash.

#26
12 Feb. 1945
At Sea —
329 to go

Hi, Darling:

Of course I should know better and get myself in my old sack as I have the 04-08 in the morning, but the temptation to give up the time and write you proved too much for me. Here goes, I only hope I can whip up something deathless now after that build up.

Honey, it looks like he days of smooth sailing are over, the mighty "G" is beginning to commence to give it that old dipsy-do. Just as I wrote that line I slid about two feet in my chair. Kind of makes a game out of trying to type though. One minute here you is, and the next minute you're up against the bulkhead. Well we had nine straight days of the nicest weather I have ever seen in these parts (that's old salty Flynn talking), so we actually have very little to complain of. You know though, darling, I am definitely not cut out to be a man of the sea. There is something too much of the earthy city dweller to go for these long extended whiffs of fresh sea air and sunshine. (Though I must admit I'm getting quite blonde and handsome. I really am very brown in the face, and the body is coming along.) The Captain lets us stand our underway watches on the flying bridge and take off our shirts, so get set for a brown baby when the time comes for me to come home. But getting back to that earthy city dweller — perchance it is the lack of certain feminine companionship that causes this life to wear so thin so quick! I'll bet you that's it! S' pose? Well one consolation it's not going to be boring very shortly. I suppose I should be scared pea-green, but lout-like I'm beginning to get that old-college-try feeling. I'm actually looking forward to one thing and another! What the hell, I've got me a red-hot bunch of boys, and watch us go to town!

Speaking of the kids, with the captain's permission I have instigated a daily news commentary. Boake Flynn the call me in these waters. Actually, what I do is sometime in the afternoon I listen to a couple of newscasts and take notes and figures down and then go up and give it to the kids in a sort of Flynn-reviews-the-news sort of style. I guess it's pretty good, because practically everyone has commented to me about it, and most of the crew thank me for taking the time to give it to them. See, our new radio is pretty good, and I get it direct from the states. Of course, as there is no script, I sort of dish it off the cuff so to speak, and some pretty funny things come out of me if I say so myself. The best to date was this afternoon. I had just finished comment on some German propagandist's plea to fight to the end even if it meant death, because the other alternative was allied military occupation for twelve years and supervision of the country until the year 2000. (Remember our plans for the year 2000? Drinking champagne like water and getting boiled as lobsters, me a racing 88 and you a sparkling 82?) Well, back to the story. When I finished the squib I asked in a very solemn voice, "Now ain't you guys glad you're not dog-faces?" My God it looks corny when I write it, but believe me, baby, it brought down the house. They love me on the Gamble! Well that's about all about that, except you see we don't have a morning press any more, so I give them the word. It makes a little work for me, but what the hell if they get a kick out of it that's good enough for Chas.

Fell onto an old copy of DeMaupassant's short stories the other day and have been re-reading them. My God but that man had beautiful succinct style. Not a word that didn't have a direct forwarding of the story. He put as much plot and character delineation in a thousand word short story as you find in 95% of popular novels. To be sure, his subject matter is a little earthy, but then hell, aren't we, the subject of his writings, pretty earthy when you come right down to it? He seemed to take a peculiar pleasure in making the husband the cuckold in many of them. I wonder if it reflected personal troubles with a nymph tending spouse? Quin Sabe? I remember one of them was called "Ball-of-fat" read it if you run across it, truly a little gem itself. Quite long for him, but still only a short story, and yet you finish with a perfect picture of several people and incidentally very little use for the stuffiness of the majority. The prostitute is the only honest character in the yarn, a beautifully done story.

Well, my pet, again the old sack calls. Seems like time has a grudge against me. It goes so slowly in the grand total, but still I have so little time each day to devote to Chas and what he would like to do. I think until this little deal is over I will have very little time to try my creative efforts on anything but my letters to you, however in a couple of weeks I should be able to get started.

Don't forget to remember there is a guy out in the Pacific that adores you, honey, yes damn it, I do mean me, too! I kiss you good-night, baby.

All me love — Chas

X one for you!

#17
13 Feb. 1945
At Sea —
328 to go.

Dearest honey:

Hello you lovely thing, I hope the world goes well this morning, that you miss your husband, and that the war news pleases you! If you can answer affirmative to all those, then you are set for a happy day. And I am sure you can.

I guess I am getting a little too sentimental writing you so much, but then hell it's a small form of indulgence and if it just happens that you like to get even a few of these deathless lines then it doesn't hurt anyone does it? After all I get the pleasure of writing them, and if it's too much to read I don't even have to know that , so there you are, everybody happy. Believe me darling, were I where things were happening or I could talk about what I would like to , then there would be no apology forthcoming for the tone of these letters. However when the whole thing must of necessity become a matter of saying "I adore you" in a variety of ways, then is when I feel that your interest might be slipping just the least bit.

Smiley and I indulged ourselves in a bit of a dream world yesterday. The Captain was talking to him about who would be Exec when Pete left, and he said he expected that would come very soon. Stewart he said, is ready for exec so that takes care of that, and Van Metre can take over gunnery when Chuck leaves so that takes care of that, but who is going to replace you as navigator? You'll probably leave the same time Chuck does, or shortly thereafter. "Better start breaking Cass in a navigator" well there was more in the same vein, but on talking it over with Smiley we agreed that he expected us to both be gone sometime within the next six months. Honey, just think what that means! In six months we will have had over two years continuous sea duty and the war will be pretty well along. I think there is a good chance for some duty ashore in Uncle Sugar. I not, then at least new construction and that means thirty days leave and then a couple of months fitting her out and stuff like that before we go to sea!

I hadn't thought too much about it before, but it is true that about two years is a normal tour of duty aboard one of these. That varies from twenty months to thirty, but Smiley and I start out twentieth in exactly one week. I will be the first of the two of us off the ship as I will make Lt. before more than a few months. In fact about three I think. So how about that baby? Maybe it won't be the whole 365 days between looks at you. Speaking of that, 37 days have now passed, that is over 1/10 of the whole year gone! I know I have to be patient, but darling the desire to see you and talk to you and hold on to you grows day by day with leaps and bounds. (how's that for no punctuation?) Well, one way or another I will see you soon, but its kinda nice to know that there is only one man who will be transferred ahead of me. Do you know Pete is the only guy aboard who has been here longer than Smiley and I? The other possibility is that if I am on here longer than six months I will be exec. Not for this kid.

I really don't want the job, but if is put on me I am damn sure I can do a better job than Pete is doing. He doesn't have the temperament for an exec., he is too petulant and thinks he is picked on too much. I don't think I am being over-confident when I make the above statement. Well darling, time alone will tell when I see you again, but the thought that it may not be a year is like a shot in the arm. As a matter of fact it has been pepping me up ever since I talked to Smiley and I'm going to keep on feeling that way and looking forward to seeing that lovely blonde thing!

Bare possibility that there may be mail tomorrow. Hoping might help, in which case I will have positively stacks! Speaking of that this will be the last for a spell, but I'll keep writing faithfully and when I get the chance again will post off a batch. Don't worry, but cross your fingers and don't throw any hats on the bed. And stay away from beds!! Don't I have a horrible mind? God love a duck, darling I sure miss you.

Well baby the mails are supposed to be closed by now, but Chefu is standing by to initial this when I finish it so I'd better sign off. God know I hate loin-girders, but there is always a chance one will come up silver, it's pretty damn slim actually, but there none the less. If the Flynn luck should run out weep not for me. I have had a good full share of the nice things in life and I won't even be resentful if that's the way its to be. I'm no Pollyanna darling, as well you know, and I really mean this. I've had more life and love and good things with you in our seven years than most mortals crowd into fifty, and then never experience what we have. It is very important to me that you believe me darling, I'm not just murmuring a formula. I don't suppose I can ever tell you how much I do love you, how much you are an integral part of me but I daresay you have a rough idea. So if it does come up silver darling, let there be no moaning at the bar, no donning of the black. Better wait a suitable interval and don the hunting clothes and a new face-do and start stalking a new bloke. That's the way I would really like it. I guess that about winds up the grim and solemn. My God, who can be hammy-er than an ex actor? The answer to that is no-one. By the same token though, we must allow him an exit line to the swan song, so here it is — I adore you.

All me love —
Chas
XXXXXXX
Hell darling, I'll be mailing you another batch of letters soon, and kissing them lovely lips in the flesh afore many moons. Chin up Jackson! It's going to be a short war!
Chas

#8
13 Feb. 1945
At Sea —

Dear Mom:
Well here is your boy again as scheduled. This bouncing over the ocean waves is not very productive of good material for letter writing, but I will do the best I can.

And speaking of bouncing! I guess I told you in that letter a couple of days ago that the sailing was smooth, well if only to make a liar out of me the Gamble is now kicking her heals in the air and rolling like a thing demented. As a matter of fact it's pretty tough to stay in front of the machine as I keep sliding across the deck in my chair. Doesn't bother me in the least, except that it makes your sleep a little disturbed and you don't seem so rested in the morning after you fight to stay in your sack all night. However you know your son, if its sleep that's at stake I can sleep anywhere, anytime. You know when this is over I don't think I'll ever go back to eight hours a night. If I can get six I feel fine and I can get along indefinitely with five. So why waste all that time sleeping?

This new radio of ours is wonderful. We are still getting news directly from the states anytime during the day or night. The old one we had used to pick up a couple of stations at night once in a while. I now have the choice of ten or twelve any time. As a result I have been sort of appointed as ship's commentator. I listen to a couple of news casts and make some notes and then go up and give it to the crew over our new announcing system that goes over the entire ship. In censoring the mens mail this morning I noticed most everyone commented on it and said how much they liked it and how good I was. It made me feel very happy about the whole thing, I like to do it for them and I'm glad they think it is pretty good. Of course nobody has anything to say about my copy, as a matter of fact all I have is a few notes, so I sort of retell it in my own way and through what humorous remarks happen to come to me as I go along. I guess it's going over pretty well.

Might possibly get some mail tomorrow, but its pretty doubtful. Still we will be able to get some mail off the ship so here this comes. Might be quite a wile again before I can drop more, but I'll keep writing every few days and when I get the chance I'll mail them all off together. I'm sorry they will come in bunches at intervals, but there is not much I can do about it. At least we are winning the war and pretty soon there will be no need for mail, so we will plan on that great day coming soon.

Well honey, the4re is not much more to say, except that I am looking forward to getting home again when this is over and that the prospects of that get better every day. Won't that be some day! Well mommy keep writing to the guy who thinks that you are the best mom in this whole world, and who loves you with all his heart!

All me love — Chas XXXXXX

Letter #32

Dearest honey darling;

What a ghastly evening. We got home from the play around seven-we had eaten at the army hospital around four so Martha and I did our packing because we are leaving for ford Ord tomor-row-Hazel left this morning — so Patty came up and brought me some stuff of mine that was at her house — Martha had lost her identification bracelet at the El Paseo when she had dinner there the other nite — so we walked down to get it — knowing that it was really the nicest place in town, I said to Patty that I would buy her a drink of Southern Comfort which she dearly loves — in partial return for her hospitality. So three strong, we go into the bar and sit down. There was a middle aged army warrant officer sitting next to me who said he had seen the show last nite and had enjoyed it — I thanked him and turned to Patty and saw this look of utter horror on her face — it seems I had spoken to a stranger. She pointed out that we could go into a bar unescorted if we wanted to but she had to live here and it was discracing her — you know how Patty can get — well — the upshot of it was that from an innocent little drink I was made so miserable so we very precipetaly left there, went and had a hamburger and came back to the hotel — called a cab for Patty to get home — well we had to wait — two enlisted men who were harmlessly drunk came up — they'd seen the play — I was so upset by this time that instead of brushing them off politely as I know well how to do, I did it brusquely and then Martha jumped on me with both feet for being rude. Then Patty said she'd had enough of being bad — this evening would do it for six months. what she had done that was bad, I'm at a loss to know — but it certainly was ghastly. Gosh there was nothing done. But Patty always has been a fusser.

I guess I haven't spoken much about my work. About half of it is in wards and the other half on the stage of hospitals. Today we went to a place which is greatly devoted to deaf cases — all of them wearing their little ear sets — but they turn them off when you are close so they can read your lips — poor kids — we did four shows, three in the wards and one on the stage. I feel it's really a shame that we don't get to talk to the boys more — but here they never seem to have the same ideas that they did overseas — all they want is a show.

I am so hoping darling that when we arrive in San Francisco there will be at least a couple more letters from you — Oh honey — I hope so because if there aren't I'll start worrying like a crazy woman.

I love you my darling — I miss you immesurably —

All the love there is,

Jane

Oh honey — I know how very much now a fine big picture means — I talk to you literally — oh darling I do love you so very much

No plictrum books in Santa Barbara — only tenor — maybe tomorrow though — one store had some on order.

I had my teeth cleaned today and learned that the cavity situation was hopeless — I have to do something about it in San Francisco —

I shall write to Alice and her sister —

All me love darling

Jane

Feb. 16, 1945
Letter #32
Monterey, Calif.

Hello my darling;

Here I am sitting in Betty and Mike's house in Monterey — right in the room where we slept when we were here a year ago last August — with the addition and detraction of a couple of pieces of furniture if is still the same. But that little tiny Gay whom Betty was so worried about the last time we were here is as large as Mickey was then — and Mickey still has the same bright red hair but he is taller and thinning out. Betty brought them both out tonight — Gay was sleepy and confused — Mickey too but he still had his ready smile.

Should I tell you darling the reason I didn't write last nite — told you in the letter before that we were leaving Santa Barbra for Salinas and Fort Ord — well we caught a train at 9:50 last nite. We were in from our show at 7:30 so Martha and I went down to Patty's and had a couple drinks of bourbon. Just as we were leaving Beth and Al called — They had just arrived in town complete with moving van — as I told you, Mrs. Woodill is moving to Santa Barbara. they dashed down to the station to say goodbye — when we got on the train, my only idea was to go to bed — but they didn't have the berths made up until eleven — so we fooled around moving from place to place — when all was arranged — I went to sleep — we arrived in Salinas at five this morning, went to the hotel and then back to sleep — then we did four shows at Fort Ord today — two complete stage and two ward shows — They went over beautifully. As we get further away from Hollywood, the boys appreciate entertainment more. As a matter of fact, I'm beginning to be a pretty good M.C. — it's definitely an art — If it weren't for this awful man, everything in spite of the constant travelling, would be fine. He is utterly obnoxious — I haven't spoken of him since San Diego but the feeling is there just the same. If I hadn't let other things go by to do this and didn't feel as if it were my duty to 'the boys' I'd give my notice. As it is, I want to make the best of it until we get to New York — if we don't have an argument first. Of course I figure that he can hang himself and I shall see if I can manage it. Perhaps so. You know that I am comparatively easy going as far as people are concerned — well someday I'm going to see this man squirm and laugh —

After the show tonite I wanted to catch the 8:10 bus from Fort Ord instead of going back with the troupe. It was a pretty narrow squeak. It seemed the pianist had a rehearsal in the morning for a new finale so I asked our esteemed manager what time the rehearsal would be. He refused to tell me until the whole cast was gathered — I pointed out I would miss the bus — he said he didn't care — I didn't want to make a scene so concurred and missed the bus — had to wait an hour ,I was so happy I came anyway though because it's been such a pleasant evening.

I'm sorry if my sensitiveness to a character seems to blot out my other impressions.

Honey, I heard a lot of news over the radio tonite which disturbed me no end. Darling keep safe please — you are the postwar plan. Darling, I love you with all my heart —

And now goodnite —

All me love,

Jane

Santa Lucia Inn
Salinas, Calif.
Feb. 16, 1945
Letter #34 [Letter #33 was labeled as 2nd #32]

My dearest darling;

Tomorrow I will be in san Francisco. I am praying that there will be some mail waiting there from you — but I am so darned scared that there won't be — and now with all the papers today filled with the bombing of Tokyo and the fleet gathered off Iwo Jima and the projected invasion — needless to say — until another letter from you does come — life will be a bit of a hazard. Oh darling, no matter where you are — remember I love you. When I realize it's possible you could be doing something 'disasgreeable' right this minute — honey it ain't good. Well darling, enough of that — I guess I'd better not worry you. Just remember I love you very very much.

After I wrote you last nite — I had a fine sleep in that lovely bed — then the drive over here this morning was perfectly beautiful — sp bright and lovely — the show tonite was cancelled — I intended to stay home and do my nails and hair but I got involved in a group that Martha and the others were going out with — well I have never been so inordinately bored in all my life. I nearly died of sheer eennui — oh honey, you don't need to worry about me — sometimes I think I am lonesome and would like some social life but I just don't take to it — I know Martha doesn't think I am a good companion but I can't help that. If I go out and am bored and unhappy, it just makes me twice as unhappy because I think what a lovely time I could be having with you —

With that my darling — finis for tonite —

I love you — I love you — I love you —

Jane

Broadmoor Hotel
San Francisco, Calif.
Feb 17, 1945
Letter #35

My dearest Darling honey;

Such horribly disquieting news in the paper today — <u>full</u> of it — of an attack on Iwo Jima itself that was supposed to have started yesterday and of one warship — category unidentified being damaged — honey, I'm sure that is where you are, and I am living in a state of suspended animation. If I let myself think about it, I can't even get tight — I get sick — darling, everything will be alright — it will. Oh, honey darling, please do keep safe. I love you so very very much. The paper says that the Japanese say two landings were repulsed and there is heavy bombardment continuing. Oh, honey, that's so darned close. I pray that my guess is wrong, but I'm so afraid it isn't.

Things on this end aren't too pleasant. We arrived in San Francisco this morning — It still looks like a nice place, but without my darling, it doesn't have its zip and sparkle — it's a has-been town. On top of everything else though, the mere living of life has become practically unendurable because the character of our manager becomes more obnoxious every day — everyone in the cast is united in the determination that either he goes or we do — and it won't be long now — if it weren't for the fact that I want to go overseas again, and I sort of burnt my other bridges when I took this job, I wouldn't have stood it this long. The man is the most cruel, gross, inconsiderate, inconsistent, blustering, lying, inefficient person I have ever dreamed of. I hate him worse than I hate Hitler — perhaps because he personally typifies to me every despicable trait — I think if I saw him meet sudden death, I'd chortle with glee. Actually, I think he's a little mad more than anything else. However, the heads of the USO are coming up Thursday, and then we'll get rid of him. They have to find out what he's like because he was sent out from New York — they don't know him.

We went out to the hospital at Hamilton Field tonite to do a show — we went over the Golden Gate Bridge — oh, honey, I thought about the pennies — how many are there now. I hope to Heaven there'll be another one soon — yours.

I am just getting through a most frightening experience. We arrived home from the show — having had no dinner — he expects us to eat about four in the afternoon & get home at 10:30 — any good manager would make arrangements for us to eat at the base — well I went out to dinner with two of the girls — had a fine steak — then decided to do my hair tonite, as I didn't want to spend all day tomorrow on it — I had bought-another-bottle of that fine oil bleach I told you about — but I bought it in the drug store instead of the beauty shop, so the bottle was a little different. I put it on, and, darling — one swab full spread all over the top of my head and it was dark brown dye! I was in a panic. I ran over to Pat Walker's room and asked her what to do — she said to wash it immediately — it took part of it out and set the rest. I was frantic. She had some peroxide & I had some ammonia, so I started bleaching — the hair will probably fall out of my head but it's almost blonde again. Oh, darling, I was frantic. Believe me there is going to be a stink raised about that come Monday morning. I owed Pat a bottle from the other day, and I had bought her some of the same — ! It seems to me the whole thing has something to do with pure food & drug laws, and the least they can do is give me some new stuff and repair the damage over a period of time to my hair for having all that stuff thrown on it to get the color out. If I were the wrong type of person — I could really fix them. It's so strong, I still don't have it off my fingers. In a minute now I can go wash it.

Martha just came in — and I fell on her with the story of my hair. Then she told me the story of her evening — honestly she is the darndest girl — in Santa Barbara with the family I tried to include her in everything — to my slight inconvenience at times, but when she has a date — you'd think she could lord it over you. Not that I have any reason to be envious — it just annoys me slightly that she assumes that I have — I must be in a bad mood I am — but what I said still goes —

It's been a long day — we got up at six this morning — took a bus to Castroville — caught the train for Monterey there and then San Francisco. We discovered we had reservations at a prize dump on Market Street called the Federal Hotel. They put four of us in a room (due to another mistake in reservations) in a room without double bed and a pull down bed — but the room was too small to pull down the bed. So we walked out and by a little wire pulling, got reservations here — this is really a very fine place — we even have a living room — Martha & I for three dollars a day apiece — it's more than I'd want to pay all month, but on Saturday afternoon it was really something.

Darling, I've been saving the best — the good — for the last — honey, the perfectly beautiful earrings arrived today — darling — I nearly cried — real pearls and so perfectly exquisite — oh, honey, it was so terribly wonderful of you — Really, darling, they are exquisite they add such a fine quality — I put them on today with that black suit, and it made all the difference in the world — honey darling, thank you so very much — the next seven years will be fine ones too.

Darling, the bracelet is perfect — it fits my wrist exactly it really is as nice as the much lamented first one. I know it must have been a lot of work. I shall wear it constantly.

Darling, write me in care of Daddy — 3700 Main St — Vancouver —

Be careful, my darling — I hope you're not where I think you are, but if you are, be doubly careful —

I love you, honey — Jane

Broadmoor Hotel
San Francisco, Calif
February 19, 1945 Letter #36,

Dearest Honey Darling;

Oh sweetheart — more violent stuff is happening in the paper today — and I am so very [SPLOTCH] worried about where you are and what you are doing. I cut out a picture of battleships off Iwo

Jima and I thought I saw your ship in it. I am probably mad, but I derive some comfort out of the fact that the ship I think is yours is sitting there nicely. Oh, honey, I know you're a lucky Irishman and that nothing will happen to you, but just the same — I'll be so awfully happy to get a letter from you.

Today we went out to Dibble Hospital in Menlo Park — four ward and one stage show. I found — or had found out that the boy Roger Rooney that I told you about who was blinded on Saipan -that we helped give a birthday, party in the hospital for, was out there — so I found him — and you'd think it was an old class reunion. He was so darned glad to "see" us. He had with him a friend of his who had been totally blinded and whose face had evidently been almost shot away — he had had eighteen operations — plastic surgery — it was still pretty bad, but it was coming along — you could still see where they were constructing new features, but you could see where it eventually would grow together. Martha and I talked to him for an hour with the result that on our first free evening after tomorrow, they are going to come in town, and we are going to meet them at the bus station, and we'll go someplace. It's my first "date" since I started on this trip, and I have a feeling that you would highly approve of this.

This hospital is the closest thing I have yet seen to overseas. We played one blind ward — one of psycho-neurotic patients — the windows were barred and the whole place completely fortified — however, they seemed happier (if a little weird) — at least happier than the other boys.

One of the Special Service sergeants out there used to be a big radio writer and he gave me a lot of gags — plus a few tips on how to get rid of our manager —

Darling, the paper says the 4th Marines landed on Iwo Jima — if so, honey, Will Price is there.

Baby darling — honey — keep safe — I pray, I'll have a letter soon — All my love, Jane Write in care of Daddy — 3700 Main St, Vancouver

February 21, 1945 Letter # 37
Broadmoor Hotel San Francisco —

Oh, darling — when I came home tonite I called Pat, and there were four letters from you — so I ran up and got them — oh, honey — they were so fine to read — the last one was no. 17 — since you wrote it, an awful lot of headlines have come out in the newspapers — darling, I know there isn't any such thing as a silver one, but, baby, I'll be so darned happy when the next letter comes from you — the number of casualties in two days at Iwo Jima came out in the paper tonite 3650 — it is unbelievably immense — oh, honey — soon a letter will come, I know, and then won't worry — It hardly seems possible to me that life could be going on while I am waiting every day for a letter from you. You can't oppress other people with your worries — they have troubles enough of their own — but all the time when I am smiling and talking, there is that thought in the back of my mind.

I really had quite a day today — we went to Napa Calif — to the Napa State Hospital — it's for psycho-neurotics — Oh, honey, those poor kids — they make the best audience as far as receptiveness is concerned — (Jeeps, I just had to take time off to cough up my dinner again — I am getting worried " it happens far too often — practically every nite — I have this bad cough like we had the first time we were here — and have to get rid of it some way — but I'm afraid my stomach will get a reflex action when I eat if it doesn't stop.) to continue — they wouldn't have cracked if they weren't sensitive. We were a great success, so they even brought out patients in solitary confinement — and they were fine. From there we went to Mare island where there are mostly amputations — oh, darling — the show itself was terrific — they loved it — which made you feel as if you were doing a little — not much but a little —

Baby darling, remember I love you with all my heart — Write to Martha's still. You wanted to know about this show — it is supposed to tour across to New York and then go overseas, but who knows for sure now?

Honey, keep safe — I <u>love</u> you,
Jane

#18
23 Feb. 1945
At Sea —
318 to go

Dearest Honey:

Well, darling, I can imagine that you have been more or less looking for this letter. No more than I have been looking forward to writing it. Honey, I never thought I would go ten days without writing you, but then on the other hand I never thought I would ever go through ten days like the last. Rugged is the word for it.

All I am allowed to say is that "We have been in action, we have suffered battle damage." Of course, on top of that I can assure you that I am all right. By that I mean really all right too, darling. My only casualty was a scratch on one knee, and so superficial too! We would of course like to tell you all about it (the plural is because Berk is sitting next to me trying to say the same thing to Alice), but you know how God and the Navy Censorship Dept. is about such things. Rightly too, don't think that I am complaining. However I have a wonderful story written in my mind about the whole deal, and it will be pretty good.

It was pretty rough, and although a good many of them weren't made of silver they were a close enough approximation to give one the old whistle down the spine. I am happy to report, without violating any confidences, that we got in some damn good licks at them before they finally connected. The whole damn ship was wonderful, the men, the officers and the discipline. More than that, I guess I can't say for now, except when the chips were down and it was touch and go, everyone came through like a trouper. A very inspiring performance, if I may linger in the jargon of the theater.

Speaking of that, the theater I mean, I felt a little silly about the speech I gave the character in my last letter, that is, I felt silly for a while. No more. It was the luck of the Irish combined with the Flynn propensity for such that enabled the author to hear the whish instead of the slash of the old gentleman's scythe.

I am sure that you are agog with curiosity at this point, and believe me, darling, I'd love to tell you all, but there are things we don't do at certain times, so until later restrain yourself.

In my last letter I said that I expected, rather hoped, to get some mail; well, darling, we didn't, however manana may be another day, at least we hope so. I haven't set foot on solid ground since I left your favorite island, and you know how long ago that was. I hope to get ashore and have a drink on one you almost, but didn't quite see, tomorrow.

How are the shows going?-I suppose you are half-way across the. U.S. by this time, but I'll bet the kids love you even in the hinterlands. Is Marty knocking their eyes out? I'll bet six, two, and even that she is, give her my love.

Berk just leaned over my shoulder and said "Have you given her my best yet?" As I haven't, I enclose it herewith. Minnie, this is such a scrambled up letter that I don't see how you are making sense out of it. In situations like these it's pretty tough to write a normal bantering sort of letter, the kind which I love to write and which must be much easier reading. As a matter of fact, I have made an effort to keep this rather light and airy, cause god knows I don't feel that way.

My God, there is a lot of ham in your husband! Guess I'd better knock it off and try and do better tomorrow when I get all that long awaited mail from you. I'll say just once again, so you are absolutely sure, that I am definitely all right. Sorry this couldn't have been better, but I guess you can understand. I adore you

all me love — Chas

P.S. Honey, just as I was about to seal this, rather send it in for censorship, I realized that I hadn't made any protestations of love. Believe me, darling, such is not the case. I love you more than ever, if such a thing is possible. As a matter of fact, when caught a couple of hours sleep the other night, my first in two days, guess who I dreamed about? That's right, you. As for that unfortunate six-bit word above, that's just my college education coming out. I didn't want to protest my love for you, rather I wanted to sing it from the housetops!! Honey, I love you so much —

Broadmoor Hotel
San Francisco, Calif.
February 24, 1945
Letter #38

My dearest darling;

I have missed two days writing to you — but honey it isn't because I haven't been thinking of you and loving you so very very much — oh honey it seems so hopeless — I watch the papers every day — devoureach item and read that Iwo is worse than Tarawa and I can't find anything that says you are alright — oh darling I should hear from you soon — I know I should — I caught myself talking to your picture today —

I have had an awfully busy bunch of days lately — and I'm still way behind on what I should have done — dentist — today at nine in the morning — I was so tired that the novacaine knocked me out — I had four cavities filled — twenty dollars cash — then on to the hairdressers — then the show takes more than a little time —

I think we are beginning to see progress on our campaign to get rid of Mr. Evans. We played at Treasure Island day before yesterday — oh what a place and what a gorgeous theatre. well anyway, there is a Navy lieutenant there named Paul Moss who is sort of the laison man on the coast between the Navy and the U.S.O. — and I think he's doing something. He knew several of the girls and he asked me if I'd like to meet Elia Kazan — you know the one who was with the group theatre and directed plays on Broadway and just finished directing "A Tree Grew in Brooklyn" so of course I said I'd love to. It seems he is here awaiting transportation to the South Pacific — he's working for the Secretary of War on some sort of re-organization of entertainment and news presentation for the troops. He's a little tiny guy — a Greek — very very homely but really charming and so darned human — more like a character out of Saroyon than anything else. We all went eating to an Italian place called Luppa's which was the best food I've tasted in San Francisco. Then tonite after the show I went with several of the other girls and them to a place called Jacks. I met the owner of the El Marraco in New York — and his sort of companion — or court jester. Actually they're like retired gangsters — you know that monogrammed overdone elegance — they probably were at one time. It was really very interesting. They evidently knew a lot about jewelry and they certainly admired my earrings darling — I very proudly said they were my anniversary present from you.

The man who owns the bar downstairs — it's called the Cuban room — his name is Alto and he is from Washington — he's a very good friend of Truman Hinkles — grew up with him — they spent most of their honeymoon at Alta's ranch.

Honey when we did the show at Oak Knoll, I saw Doctor Stevens and everything he says is fine — no need to worry.

Oh darling, I keep thinking if only you were here — we could have another enchanted time in San Francisco — I think we've spent the best times of our life together here — of course the U.S. Grant was really a topper of all time. But soon darling you will be off the Mighty G. — and before many moons have passed we will be together again — I know we will — I love you every minute my darling —

　　All my love,
　　Jane
　　Remember c/o J.P. Patten, 3700 Main St. Vancouver, Wash —

#19
26 Feb. 1945
In Port —
315 to go.

Dearest Honey:

Well, darling, I have been delaying writing for a couple of days in hopes that I would be able to give you some dope on me and the ship and what is up, but the way things progress out here nothing is settled yet. I still have hopes of seeing you before too long, but the chances don't look as good as they did a couple of days ago. Still nothing is settled as yet and so while there is life there is hope. Oh what I said.

By the way honey, the enclosed picture was taken after our trouble and as you can plainly see I am cocky and rugged as ever. Of course I never can just stand and let somebody take my picture, not old Charlie, I've got to be muggin'. Well once a ham always a ham.

We had a little mail waiting for us, three letters from you and the pictures. None very recent 31 Jan and 3 and 5 of Feb. However

I loved getting them and I know they sent a lot up the line to us, so they should be coming back down within a few days. You gave me your itinerary until the 25th but that doesn't do me much good today so I'll send them to your pop until I get a better arrangement.

Say, this tour is not going to take you out of the country is it? Because if it is don't let it. I mean if I should catch a thirty dayer I don't care where you are just so it's someplace in Uncle Sugar. Things should get a little more organized around here in the next few days and I'll let you know just as fast as possible.

The war in Europe seems to moving satisfactorily and the one out here is going forward. However, not as smoothly as we would like to see it by a damn sight. Those bastards are plenty tough and they take a lot of blasting.

Honey just the thought that I might get home to see you just makes me jump in anticipation. Wouldn't it be wonderful??? Oh honey, you can't possibly imagine how much I love and miss you. It gets more and worse by the day, if you follow me. I am strictly a family man and I don't mean perhaps.

Well darling this is another stinking letter, but when I've got so much I could tell you and can tell you none, it makes it damn difficult to write. Also my old eyes are about to drop shut. Also I have to get up really early because smiley and I are going for a hop in a big bomber early in the morning and we have to leave here about six o'clock. I'll have the days duty tomorrow, and I'll get off a nice long letter tomorrow. Until then darling I'll kiss you goodnight.

All me love —

Chas

#20
27 Feb. 1945
In Port
314 to go —

Dearest Honey:

Hi darling, how goes the road show kid this morning? I got some mail from you yesterday, but the last one was the 13th and there seems to be some missing somewhere along the line. In one from Santa Barbara you referred to the letter of the night before, only there ain't one, but it's undoubtably coming somewhere. Say baby there is only one I would like to question you about. Who did you get so drunkie with in San Diego the night of the 9th? Brother!! That usually rounded schoolgirl hand of yours ran all over the sheet and some of it was pretty scrably. The address looks like my work in one of my better moments. It was an awfully nice letter though darling, especially because you sounded like you really missed the old man. I hope you do and keep on missing him, because you are sure the number one for this lad and always will be. Honey you say you don't see how one person could have such a hold on the other, well it's just because we happen to be in love I guess. God knows, our thinking is certainly attuned to each other. Little things like the Macedamia nut for example. I am glad that box got through all right and you like the knife. I picked it up in the Solomons last year and it turned p aboard after we left. You may not be good on beards and birthday presents, but you can read. I thought that was pretty cute little story didn't you. The locale was especially dynamic and simply loaded with potentialities which later proved to be more than justified, in fact quite horrible in retrospect. Well so much for the story review, I'll fill in what details you overlooked later.

Honey my darling, I hope the little box with the bracelet and the earrings got through to you allright. It was registered and the thought just occurs to me that it might have been held up at Martha's, but I am sure by this time you have them and probably a letter is en-route somewhere over the vast watery distances. God, sheer poetry that!

I still don't know where you go from Washington. On east I have no doubt. Well I will catch up with you wherever you are. The possibilities of such took a sharp upswing today, so cross your fingers. I was so sorry to hear about Martha, personally I always thought she had Martha very much at heart, but I don't mean that in a catty way at all. Just some people give that extra little push at all times regardless of whom they are shoving. I like her very much though honey, so don't misunderstand. I can easily forgive you for missing a few letters when you give me your days schedule, it sounds pretty damn rugged. Honey don't let it get you down and above all don't let it run you down. You are the only wife I have, or ever want, so keep up your strength!!

I don't remember if I mentioned getting the pictures the other day. The one at the plane and the other one!! Woo-woo! What a beautiful wife I am married to! Honey I love you so god-damned much I am just about to bust a gusset. Don't ever forget that honey, even for a minute will you baby?

In that little picture I sent you yesterday take a good look at it. See where I am standing and what should be alongside me, also out in front of me. And a long gray beard and a birthday present to you too darling.

I guess this will about get to you by the 8th of March so honey even though I can't send a present, know that my love and thoughts are with you and about us on our seventh anniversary. I hope to god the next one will enable us to be together for balance of those we can look forward to. I don't think any man ever loved his wife the way I do you darling, so hold onto that thought and lets look forward to a lot of them together.

Ran across a beautiful quotation the other day. It appears on the Scottish war memorial at Edinburgh and they are by a man named Laurence Binyon.

"They shall not grow old as we
that are left grow old.
Age shall not weary them nor
the years condemn.
At the going down of the sun
and in the morning
We will remember them."

Don't you think that is lovely? If you have to write any letters to people who have lost someone, as I do, I think it's a beautiful thing to remember to enclose. I know it's tough to bring any comfort to people berieved by this war, but some things do help a little.

Well my darling, the mail man is about to hoist his sack and away to the fleet P.O., so if this is to be on its way to you I guess I'd better chop it off.

Looks like I will be in one spot and have plenty of time to write for quite a spell, by the same token I should start getting pretty regular mail for you know who, so try and get em out baby, even if they are just notes. Just keep telling me you love me and miss me, and I'll keep smiling. I adore you darling —

All me love —

Chas

X down payment!

XXXX intrest!

Fresno Hotel
Fresno, Calif.
February 28, 1945
Letter #39

My dearest darling;

Here I am in Fresno and it has been three whole days since I have written to my darling. In the meantime — I have been watching the papers like mad but all I can read about is what is happening on the island of Iwo Jima — not off it. It gives me such a horribly unsettled worried feeling — something I can't live without and I have a horrible time living with. I told Martha when she left yesterday morning to wire me as soon as a letter came from you-it should be the end of the week — oh honey darling I hope so. I hate to think of your being involved in that horrible thing day after day. Honey, I will be so happy when the letter comes.

Honey, it is two in the morning and we just arrived at Fresno. Yesterday morning very early, we left san Francisco — we came across the bay on the Ferry just as it was getting really light — I shall never cross that bay without thinking of you — it seems to be so irrevocably associated with us — we did only one evening show last night — we were all so dead tired it was a good thing — five ward shows today and then we caught the train at ten tonite. Darling, I haven't said much about the hospitals this time and I am kind of worried about myself because I haven't. I'm afraid I'm getting almost like a nurse — no disrespect meant — but I've seen so much, I almost don't notice it anymore. I know you are no good for the patients unless you are casual and I know I am not getting callous but nevertheless, I still worry about it. Mr. Evans, the manager, asked me the other day if I wanted to go overseas with this show. I said yes and he said fine — fine, it was all set — I don't know whether he is handing out a lot of malarkey — he said I would have my shots in March — the boosters — I still don't believe him though — I don't see what they'll do with a girl M.C. — people who have seen me are now saying I'm the best girl M.C. they've ever seen but I know I have a long way to go — more gags, an easier manner, better ad libs, faster — better technique. I'm really not very interested but I suppose I should be good at everything I try — and I'm kicking myself because in San Francisco, I didn't go to one theatre — it was always so late and I was so tired but I should have made the effort. I'm kicking myself for it — after this I'll be all business.

Martha left yesterday morning — I had already done the day before's shows without her — I do miss her a lot — there is really no one else here with whom I am very congenial so I'll sort of have to be by myself from now on.

I told you that Martha and I were going out with the two boys who were blinded on Sunday-well we met them at the bus and went up to our living room at the hotel — drinks and dinner and back to the hotel, then put them on the bus back. It was a pretty strenuous day — the simple problems involved in going any place with people who are newly blind — every door, step, and street is an obstacle course — and the simple act of eating you feel for them is an ordeal. But it certainly was worth it — they were such fine boys and so happy to be away form the hospital. Mac, who used to be a newspaper reporter had evidently had the whole side of his face blown off — perhaps it's a good thing he can't see himself right now — it will be alright but the plastic surgery is still far from complete. He will always be totally blind — but such a cheerful, joking fellow — so alert and interested — always asking what everything looks like. Roger, the other one, is the boy I told you about — in the radio station in Saipan — we went to his birthday party at the hospital in Honolulu — he cann sometimes see light and dark — he was a very fine young actor. When the day was over, I was dead tired — but they were so darned wonderful —

Monday nite darling, I received the news of Dave's death. Although my knowing him couldn't have been compared with yours, from the fact that you grew up with him and from our correspondence, it almost seemed as if a part of us were gone — this horrible war — if only it would stop before we have lost everything. I know it must make you very happy to have seen him and had such a fine time together — well I know I shouldn't dwell on it but it's a damned shame. If they had been fair about the whole thing, he would have been home by this time — From what you said, he wasn't fit to be in combat — and if he even got wounded slightly, no wonder he died. They had no business having him there — even in war, there are some things which aren't fair.

At last news Mary had been accepted for the overseas Red Cross — I imagine she will be leaving for Washington soon —

Poor Buddy — his eyes — he can't be a pilot and has to study navigation. I am so darned sorry because he wanted to fly so very badly. It also means a delay in his commission.

Darling honey — I've got to get to bed before I die of fatigue. This definitely the most hetic trip I've ever taken.

Just remember that I love you and am thinking of you every minute.

All my love to you my darlng,

Jane

Darling — write me in care of Daddy — this month I'll be in Yosemite, Auburn (Calif), Klamath Falls, Portland, Tacoma, Seattle, Spokane, Farragut, Walla Walla, Sun Valley and Brigham (Utah) — it would be a little hard for you ton estimate the arrival time from way out there and he'll know exactly —

Yosemite Lodge

Yosemite National Park

California

Feb

Fresno, Calif
March 1, 1945 Letter #40

My dearest Darling;

By the time you receive this, it will probably be past our seventh wedding anniversary — I remember last year I wrote that you would surely be home by the next one — well, darling, you aren't — but we had some time in between so I guess we shouldn't fuss — oh, honey — maybe by the time the eighth one comes around we'll be together permanently.

Oh, darling, I could tell you again and again how beautiful the earrings are — everyone admires them so, and I am so darned proud every time I wear them I could practically bust — It was wonderful of you, honey darling.

I had intended to get to bed early tonite, but the schedule I laid out for myself was too much — wash hair — fix nails, etc. I was going to do it here right after dinner, but I ate with the girl who is the pianist in the show (she is older) and a friend of hers — a former baseball player, a man of about 52 named Dutch Leonard — he has a -very beautiful place outside of town and he invited me out there to do my hair. He had a little house all complete with steam bath, sun lamps, a special needle shower and a hair dryer. I had the time of my life. I missed the musical part of the evening though — most of it — his whole house is fitted with built in loudspeakers, and he has a collection of thousands of records — everything — darling, you would have gone mad over them —

I nearly had heart failure tonite — it shows what a state I am getting into — I was listening to Chet's ten o'clock news — doing my hair — he said — "the Navy announces the loss of three ships" — I nearly died — I really was scared — especially for some reason because I was listening to Chet — well, of course I was imagining things, but golly, I was so relieved, my whole evening was made happy —

Happy next seven years, my darling — The last I have loved —

All my love to you, Jane

#21
3 March 1945 In Port

Dearest Honey:

Golly, here I've let three days go by again without writing. It's not that I don't think of you, but it's really because I've been trying to find out something definite about what's to be done to us. Still it's all up in the air, so to hell with it. I'll write all the time from now on, and if there is no news, I'll just say I love you a couple of hundred times.

Still looks as though we might get that thirty day leave, more than that I can't say for sure, but it looks better than the last time I wrote. God, I hope we get it, what I wouldn't give to see you just once more. I suppose I am a hopeless dope, but I do love you so much that sometimes it hardly seems worth while to go on living without you. Well!! that's pretty talk, I must say. Sorry, but I sure as hell do miss you like the very devil.

Well Smiley and I finally got our ride in the bombers. It was only a practice mission, assembling at a point that sort of stuff. Although we did bomb an island that still has Japanese on it. It was really pretty spectacular especially when you realize how big they are, and we flew tight formation flying for nearly all the way. Wing tips practically overlapping. We were up just under seven hours and flew about 1400 miles. We saw all the islands in this particular group I am in. I've always had a tremendous amount of admiration for these boys, but after seeing how they live, what lousy chow they get and the cramped hours they spend on a strike, well nothing I can say in the way of tribute to them would be too grandiose. They are really fighting this war, brother!!

I got a letter from you three days ago which was dated Feb. 20, came very fast. You said you had cut a picture out of the S.F. paper. Well hang on to it, darling, as you were absolutely right. We were moving in pretty hot company, eh? The mail situation is still snafu as hell. I got some yesterday from you dated 1 Feb and 13 Feb., but there are still lots missing. There was also a sweet letter from Hazel. One of the nicest I've ever received from anyone. It's a wonderful feeling to have your mother-in-law say "Keep safe, Honey, I'll be praying for you and thinking of you" or words to that effect. Isn't it awful, honey, how much I love you and everything about you including all your family? Awful, hell, it's wonderful!

A boy I met at Pearl about a year ago came by yesterday, and he is sending a boat to take me to lunch in about ten minutes, so I'd better chop this off. I also ran into Scarpa at the club yesterday. Remember him at Cornell? He ran around with Davy Crockett a lot. Very good looking in a sort of an Italian way. He said to be sure and give you his love and also to Giddy. I told him we were gold star parents in that respect, and he was awfully sorry. He had an officer off his ship with him, and he raved about you and your beauty. I'm terribly afraid I just sat there with a look of happy complacency while he raved about you. It does make me feel awfully good somebody who knows you is describing you to someone who doesn't and uses expressions like "The most beautiful thing you ever saw" or "how a lug like this ever married the most lovely gal in the country is beyond me."

Well I'd better knock that stuff off or there will be no living with you. I guess you get the idea pretty well that I adore you though, don't you?

Honey, I'd better close this for now, but I'll write again tomorrow. I'll try and get one off at least every other day, but you don't have to worry anymore about me, at least until I get out of this spot. Hell, this is safer. than Market St. any day in the week, but I'd still like to take my chances on Market!!!!

Goodbye for now, darling, all my love and a million kisses. I'd certainly love to hold you tight in my arms right this minute. All me love, Chas XXXXXXXX

Auburn, California
March 3, 1945 Letter #45

My dearest Honey Darling;

I know you will say — darn Jane — she won't write on papers which will fit my files — but, darling — I'm out of stationery, and I haven't had a chance to get any more, and I thought that you might kind of enjoy seeing the pictures of the different places I am — Believe me, this is a very idealized picture of this place — it could look like this I suppose, but as it is, it's pretty grim — but it's interesting enough, and there is so much of historical interest here that it is worth it — just think, it was only nine miles away from here that gold was discovered at Sutter's mill — the hotel was built right then, so you can imagine what scenes must have taken place. By the way, I'm a little vague about just where I have been in California, but I know this is about 35 miles northeast of Sacramento — it's in the middle of the Bret Harte, Joaquin Miller, Mark Twain country.

We played four shows in the hospital wards today, one psycho-neurotic, one paralysis and two convalescents. It's mostly composed of boys who were on Saipan and Palau — and then the poor things who've been here for a long time. People always warn you against psycho-neurotic wards, but they are the ones I like best to play because they are so sensitive — it's really the intelligent people who mentally break under a strain, not the dullards. Now I am spending this evening in this ancient place washing my hair and doing my ironing — and I seem to be so slow about it — I had planned to get so much done, and I haven't.

Oh, honey — it seems like I am just bouncing from place to place so fast that I don't have any continuity in my letters to you — I feel as if I weren't giving you enough of myself — but, honey, I feel when writing that there is so darned little to give — I go to the hospitals and do the wards — and try to have a couple of drinks when I get home and keep my clothes in order it seems as if there weren't any great thing in me to write to you about — it is a wonder to me that I keep my "freshness" of approach as much as I do — I find myself wondering if, when this is all over — I will be content to settle down (unpacking suitcases does seem awfully good) or will still want to go bouncing around.

Honey, I am sitting here in this old room — the girl I seem to be rooming with now — her name is Pattie Ray — she's a very fine pianist — is writing letters — we have an adjoining room with two girls who are singers — they are really very nice, and they keep bouncing in and out — it's sort of like a sorority — Its amazing, darling, how much living I've done with women since I've been married.

Darling, I know I'm busy and all, but that isn't really what counts — What is important is the fact that I miss you so terribly much all the time — Keep safe, my darling — we'll be together soon again. In the meantime, I know we have to do the best we can and not fuss, but I certainly do <u>wish</u> with all my heart that we were together tonight — and every nite —

I send you all my love, darling.

Jane

Hotel Tioga
Merced California
The Gateway to Yosemite
Letter #42
March 5, 1945

Dearest honey darling —

Gosh — my letters can't keep up with the stationary I steal — I picked this up at Merced before we left today and now here we are about 35 miles above Sacramento at a place called Auburn living in the oldest hotel I've ever been in (they haven't bothered with the modern conveniences) but it's very interesting — it's all tied up with the discovery of gold and Mark Twain etc.

The Saturday at Merced proved to be very successful — the hotel was really lovely and a fine time was had — sort of a back in civilization deal. We left there at seven this evening — the train was two hours late because of a wreck on the line — then we had to take sort of a local cattle car to Sacramento — then the army brought us up here — around about one in the morning.

My little altercation with Mr. Evans has been all straightened out amicably and he is now sweet as sugar candy.

I talked to Martha today and she said a letter from you with a very recent postmark had arrived — darling. I was so excited — and now I have to wait until I get to Klamath Falls Wednesday nite to get it — but my mind is so relieved — thank goodness.

Darling it is two in the morning and nine comes so quickly-so honey I'll close and send you all me love — Jane

#22
5 March 1945 In Port 308 to go.

Dearest Honey:

Hello, honey, my darling, how goes the cutest chick to leave the sticks? I was grievously disappointed today. Mail came, but none from you. Alas and alack. I got a letter from you about a week ago dated the 20th, and these today were dated the 21, but none as I say. I know this operation has screwed up the mail deal, but boy it's tough not to get them when I know they are on the way somewhere. I had another nice letter from your mom and one from mine. That's me, the pride of the mothers but the bane of the wife. I'm really kidding honey, and not complaining about the mail. Because you have been more than wonderful about writing. It's just that I feel so very close to you when I get letters every day, and these long pauses in between drive me a little nuts. Your mom said in her letter that you were worrying about me, I hope you got that letter-I mailed the twenty-fourth in good time cause you hadn't had a letter from me for over ten days when I mailed that. In one of a batch of older mail I got a few days ago you told me that you knew I was a lucky Irishman, but to be careful. I'll never dispute that title again as long as I live. I had God right in my pocket that night, that's all I can figure. Lucky Charley, that's me, kid!

No more dope on coming home, but everyone seems to think we will. Everyone except us, we hate to let ourselves begin to think about it, although I must admit I have, I do and I am!! Next to having the word that the whole thing was over, I can't imagine any dispatch I would like to read better than that one. If it does come *through*, honey, we won't have that long trying getting adjusted deal to do again, because believe me, we will be adjusted!!!

Gosh, honey, since I wrote the last line six hours have passed. I went over for dinner, had to take the watch, saw two movies, and it's now nearly midnight.

In Hazel's letter (which went to Bud, Bobby and myself), she told about seeing the show at the hotel in Santa Barbara and about how super you were. I really think you've got what it takes, sugar. You've grown up, and you've got poise and personality, and above all you aren't afraid to stand up and sing your own song when the occasion demands it. That's all it takes. Then when you throw in that body and that face!!! That did it, Jackson! By the way, how is that lovely body coming along. Lonesome at all at times? Oh, honey, I would cheerfully give up my chances at a front seat in heaven for a couple of hours with you tonight. I miss you so much it's just a big empty hunk of nothing where my heart is. If I sound a little overboard don't disbelieve me, I swear it's all true, only I'm afraid, badly put.

Say honey, did you ever get any of those pictures we took on Xmas day? I'm sure if you would drop Gladys a note she would get some to you, and you could send them on to me. I'm really not interested in how my classic beauty turned out, but I would like to see the rest of you, and especially you!!

Honey, remember sitting on that dock in San Diego just as we sailed the G out to sea. And how we sat there sipping at that jug and holding hands now and then. You know, darling, I don't know how it would be possible for the human mind to feel a greater .or more complete emotion for another person than I did for you right then. I know you didn't approve of the drinking right then, and neither did I, but I promise you you would have had a big bawling character on your hands without it. It may be false courage that whisky gives one, but with me it does give an aplomb and savoir-faire that I would have been sadly lacking without it. Just sitting here remembering the look of you and the feel and even the smell almost makes me think you are with me. I am so close to having you as a tangible thing, but there is just that fine line that makes it only my imagination. Darling, stay good, and remember and miss a little the guy who happens to adore you.

I kiss you goodnight, Chas X here T'is !

#23
8 March 1945
In Port

Dearest honey:

Well still sitting on our rusty dustys awaiting some kind of something to happen to us. It's beginning to be pretty monotonous, but after some of the things we saw maybe it isn't too tough duty after all. The first few days were mighty pleasant, but now it's beginning to wear a little thin. Still we will have some kind action taken on us in a few days at the outside, so until then we will sweat it out. Still looks like a little leave might be very possible, here's hoping.

As soon as I finish this I am going to clean up my spear fishing gear and tomorrow start fishing again. I haven't shot at one since we left the Solomons last summer, so I'll not be worrying our little finny friends for the first few times. All that time I spent fixing them up for us to use when we went back. Ah nostalgic memories of the last time I saw you. Honey, honey!

The last time I saw you reminds me I am just starting "Life and death of a Spanish town" by Elliot Paul who also wrote "The last time I saw Paris" which is what reminded me of him. He has a peculiarly gutless style for my money. Sort of an emasculated Hemingway. Nice color and clear characters but they never do anything. The town he writes of though I found particularly interesting as it is on the island of Ibiza and his little town is only nine miles from the town of Ibiza where I spent a few happy hours. I wouldn't recommend the book however for the average reader. A lot of beautiful guff. Well I have deprecated Mr. Paul enough for one day.

I am starting tomorrow to devote most of my time to this little machine and to the gentle art of spear fishing. I've had enough of the club to last me awhile. Although I do admit you can pick up some amazing stories over there. Wish to God I could write them, but of course that is impossible. We have become pretty well acquainted with the leading navigator for this whole wing of big bombers, and he has some amazing and wonderful experiences. On top of that he is about as nice a guy as I ever have met. Quiet and modest and withal an excellent navigator. I'll tell you more about him when I see you again. We've been doing a little much drinking though, that I am frank to admit, but the first few days that was about the only way you could get a good night's sleep was to get good and blind and then you didn't even remember anything.

Baby I sure miss the hell out of you. Wouldn't it be wonderful if we could get together for awhile? I've about given up the idea of getting any mail, as they are holding it up somewhere back along the line. Maybe they know something we don't, I wish they would let us in on it. At any rate, it's tough to keep writing and never get no mail back. I know they are somewhere though, and what a field day I'll have when I finally do catch up with them, or they catch up to me. I have no idea of how far east you are going, how long the tour is going to last or anything. I suppose you have written and given me all the dope, but I still am in the dark. I was kinda hoping we would screw around long enough getting home, that is if we get home, so that the tour would be over and before the next one, or you go to New York of whatever, that maybe you could hang around with me wherever I have to wait or what they do with me. Just think in June I'll have two years sea duty, might be a chance to get on the beach back home for awhile, oh well, just wait and see, and do a little praying.

Honey the mail is about ready to go so I'll close this. Remember this day seven years ago in Tijuana darling? It's very clear to me and even clearer that I love you a million times more today than I did then. As I said last year I hoped the seventh would see us together again. Well let's hope the eighth will be the lucky one and the whole deal over with. I am thinking a lot about you today darling, wonder if you are too?

Well goodbye for a couple of days libeling, keep well keep missing me, and never forget I adore you!

All me love.

Chas

XXXX 2 mos yesterday. 1/6 of the year gone!

9 March 1945 In Port—

Dear Jack:

I realize I am a stinker for not having written you before, but with that stream of letters going on to Jane you probably realize that I am still up and about. I'm afraid I'll have to continue to send them through you, as our mail is being held up somewhere, and we haven't had any for about a week. I don't know Jane's schedule, so if it's ok I will continue to send them to you, and you can forward them.

If Jane came through Portland I suppose you know about our little trouble. The rules allow us to say "we have been in action, the ship suffered battle damage, but I am alright." I'd love to elaborate on that for you, as it's quite a story, but no point in bucking regulations. One thing I can say though, is that before we got ours I had the satisfaction of knowing that I sent several of the enemy on their way to their honorable ancestors. I say several because those I actually saw, I think and hope there were a hell of a lot more that I didn't see! I was very proud of my kids, they came through like troupers, and as a matter of fact we got a very nice commendation and a "Well Done" from our admiral. So the old lady did a good job as long as she was able.

We are now back down the line a ways more or less sitting around waiting to see what they are going to do about us. The way it looks, we have a pretty good chance of getting some leave back in good old Uncle Sugar. I realize we just left there, but it is a nice place to go back to and the oftener the better.

We have gotten acquainted with some bomber pilots here and the other day were fortunate enough to latch on to a flight in a practice mission. We were up about seven hours and actually bombed an island that still has Japaneese on it. I got a tremendous thrill out of it, especially the formation flying. Wing-tips almost overlapping and they stay that way for hours, in and out of overcast. Brother!! They are so damn big it's like a flight of apartment houses going by. I have all the admiration and respect in the world for those kids. They are really fighting the war, and in a very big way. Much as it would break their hearts, I hope Buddy and Bobby never get an overseas assignment. Even in the little time we have been here, there are several boys who don't join us for a drink any more. They sure play for keeps up there in that "Wild blue yonder," and it ain't for marbles either!

I've had several nice letters from Hazel, and she gives me all the dope on the family. I see where Mary is going through another emotional crisis. Trouble with that gal is her heart is just too big. She hates to hurt anyone, and as a result she is always involved. I'd like to see some lad marry her who was big and tough enough to browbeat her a little. Though I'm forced to admit it would take quite a guy. She would be a wonderful wife, and with her intelligence and enthusiasm would make a great companion. She's a great kid.

Well, Jack, I've been rambling on here for quite a spell, so I guess I'd better knock it off and get some lunch. Would love to get a letter giving me all the hot dope from the city of roses, and how Janie was when she came through. Don't worry about me. Where I am sitting now, the only thing that could kill me would be boredom. But sometimes that's not too hard to take in comparison! Funny thing, I was so damn sure we were going to get it on that last one that I started a letter to you and was going to enclose a note to the kid with it, in case I got it. It seemed a pretty corny gesture, so I tore it up. Glad now I didn't send it. Not going in for mock heroics but I do think I've used up all the Irish luck that was allotted me on that one night.

Well enough of that stuff, I came out without a scratch not even a Purple heart, which I hope is always the case!! Drop me a line when you get the time. love — Chas

March 9, 1945
Letter #44
Hotel Nartonia, Portland

Hello my Darling—

Oh, honey — yesterday afternoon in Klamath Falls, I received the first letter I had had from you in so <u>darned</u> long — and what a <u>relief</u> it was — not that my worst fears of where you were weren't justified but just to know that there had been no silver ones was the best anniversary present I could <u>ever</u> have hoped for. Then today when I got here — Daddy had two more from you — including the one with the picture — oh, darling, it was so darned <u>good</u> to hear from you — I'm afraid there were too many things in your letters that must for the present be left unsaid — I'm worrying about what they may be. As a matter of fact, I'm pretty worried about Cass, so I pray that you will feel free to write and tell me that he says hello.

Whatever it was that took place, my darling, you will tell me sometime — it must have been pretty darned grim — my love was with you all the time. As a matter of fact, my love was with the mighty G — After seeing her pull out that day — it seems to me as if she were a part of you — I hope she is going to be in good shape soon.

Oh, honey, there's not much I can say except that I'm so darned happy to have heard from you and so very very thankful that you only have a superficial scratch on the knee — oh, darling — it is so good — I guess everything will be fine for me after this. I was so worried about you —

Well, darling — to get to "my day" — I haven't been very good about writing you the last couple of days — In the first place, I was nearly going wild, and I couldn't write — now I can write and tell you what has been happening to me — Let me see — it's been pretty darned strenuous the last few days — trips like mad — we left Auburn at light Wednesday morning and arrived at Klamath Falls at eleven at nite — then Thursday — yesterday — we did two shows at the Marine Barracks there — that's the closest to an overseas audience I've seen yet — they all are back recently, and they all have that non-coveted decoration — the purple heart. That Paul was there — he looked much better, having lost that horribly yellow hue and had gained about 30 pounds — I had a couple of drinks with him at the Officer's Club, and that was that. Then we caught the train at eleven last nite and arrived in Portland at ten this morning. At the last minute, they gave our reservation to a bunch of military patients. We had to get up, and it wasn't much fun — only the seats in the ancient cars were left. However, you know me — I can sleep any place, so I didn't mind — this morning Hazel & Jack met me at the station. They went out to the show at the Barnes Hospital in Vancouver — I was a little worried about Daddy's seeing it because the conditions were kind of rough, but he liked it — which amazed me. We went to dinner tonite to that Blue Diamond where we all went — listened to that crazy woman. She asked after you — I really had a very fine time. I was so happy at having heard from you, and Daddy was in fine fettle — we had a bottle that he brought — of Waterfill and Frazier.

By the way, Mary is getting in tomorrow. She has turned down the Red Cross and is going to marry Sam! Honestly, I am a little indignant with her, but I guess there is nothing I can do about it — but I don't approve of Sam, and I do approve of the Red Cross.

Oh, honey darling — I do love you so very much. I've tried to understand about your "long beard," and I think I do — Really though — what I do understand is that I know you are alright; I miss you so darned much, honey — if only you were here tonite —

I love you, honey, and my happiness at hearing from you is so great I can hardly describe it. I only.hope that other things aren't as bad as I imagine them.

All my love to you, honey, Jane

3700 Main street
Vancouver, Washington
March 10, 1945
Letter #46

Dearest honey darling;

Here it is the end of another day and I am dead tired again and it is too darned late again...but I wouldn't pass up the chance to write to my honey on this wonderful typewriter...not that I can use it anymore because I barely can.

Mary got into Seattle this morning so Hazel called her and asked her to come down here. We met her at the train in Vancouver at nine tonite...since then there has been much talk. They wanted me to stay over here tonite so I did although I would have almost rather stayed at the hotel. If it hadn't been for seeing Mary, I wouldn't have wanted to gather up my stff and come over. We get so little opportunity to settle down in a place for a couple or three days that it seemed a shame to leave it right away. Well, there was much talk. I just don't know what Mary is planning to do and frankly, I don't think she does either. She has a sort of delay deal from the Red Cross — her Sam is much against it he has said he would cancel all relations if she joined — if anybody said that to me, I'd join I think — Well she sort of has to chose. Mary's a sentimental person and she wanted to come home before she made her decision — why I don't know because Hazel and Daddy really can't cope with her problems — I suppose she wants to get back to her roots or something.

We had to go see the Petermans after the train came in tonite — I really can hardly bear that — not that they aren't sweet there are so many things you can't say and have to conceal. I'm afraid I'm an incurable rebel and the best thing for me to do is to stay away from my family so I won't break any images.

I'm kind of disappointed. I'd been so proud of her for going in the Red Cross and now she probably won't do it — it's like talking to a blank wall telling her how much good it would do — someone has filled her full of false tales about it and I think it's a darned shame.

We played four wards today — some hospitals have a feeling about them; bright and cheery and it makes even the worst patients feel better but this was one of those old army posts — olive drab wooden buildings — so darned gloomy with a cemetery straight in view of the windows. I understand they are doing some fine work there but as far as the morale building effects of the atmosphere as concerned, they are strictly nil.

You will be wondering darling what goes with this letter. Well, first I started on a large typewriter...I just couldn't handle it so I tried one pen and then I tried my own...then I found this portable typewriter aqt another desk and now I am highly satisfied. No I'm not...Daddy just came in and said that the man whose typewriter this is...at least it is on his desk, can't stand the smell of smoke... so I had to move the machine into the bedroom.

I had been kind of expecting that there might be another letter nfromnyou yesterday...I know. I know. I am never satisfied. But I waited so long that each letter is like manna from heaven.

My two days in Portland and Vancouver only served to confirm my impression that Oregon and Washington are at the ends of the earth...it is green but that is all...sort of an grey green...even when it doesn't rain, it is dark and forbidding. There seems to be absolutely no joy of living likw there is in California and you can definitely feel it everyplace.

Honey, I can't send you any more schedule for a few days because I don't have one...I should have it soon though. One thing you don't have is the schedule after the twenty-fifth. We are going to Walla Walla and then to Sun Valley and then to Brigham Utah. That takes us through the third of April. We are going to the Marcus Whitman Hotel in Walla Walla and I am so hoping that we will be there long enough to go out to Wailatp and sort of dedicate the trip to you.

Well, my darling, I love you with all my heart...I miss you every minute nad I know that it won't be so very long before we see each other. I haven't quite b een able to make head nor tail of the business of thirty days...off and on again...I am so hoping that it will come through...and if it does, it would work out very nicely...you see you could fly to where I was and then we could sort of go together... even if I do go, I'll be in this country until July so we don't need to cross any bridges right now. You see, it would be fine...then that way we wouldn't have any difficulty with families or apartments... we would be someplace new together.

I received the little picture of you honey...you ham...I did see what would have been in front and to the side of you and it gave me cold chills...and where you stand is usually right above there I know. I nearly had heart failure...but the picture of you standing up there so cocky it was like a tonic to me.

Well, darling I guess it better be thirty for tonite...I am definitely on the tired side.

Goodnite honey. I love you.

Jane

#24
10 March 1945
In Port —
303 to go —

Dearest Honey:

Well yesterday we got a puny batch of old mail. Two from you and two from Mom. Much as I like to get the ones from you, I almost wish I hadn't received any because in Mom's first letter she had to give me the news that Dave Oswald had been killed on Luzon. He was injured on the 19th of January and died in a hospital the following day. Mother said they were taking it very well. I guess I didn't take it so well. I did all right all yesterday afternoon after I heard until I started to write Mrs. O a note of condolence. Seems so damn unfair, the length of time he had been away, that little girl waiting for him back there and all. Makes me God-damned mad, too, I'm really itching for another crack at those bastards now. It's a personal war from now on as far as I'm concerned.

In your letters, written in San Francisco, you were so worried about me and where you thought I was. Must be something to this thought transference or whatever it's called, because that was the night we got it. Allowing for the day's difference and the time difference, I figure you were writing it just about an hour before we got hit. That was the night you put the brown dye in your hair, if you remember, and I guess you will. How did that come out, by the way? If I do get home I'm not going to be met by a zanie with a bald spot and a fringe of blonde hair am I?

Honey, I hope you didn't get too distraught with waiting to hear from me. There was just no way I could get a letter off to you until I did. I know it's tough not to hear and to worry. I just said today, much as we like to get mail, it's far more important for it to go the other way, especially during an operation, as people back home get so worried.

Cheefo just stuck his nose in and said to say hello for him. Hello! You mentioned a while ago that Will is with the fourth. In that case, he is really getting a large chunk for his bite. I sure hope he is all right, but I wouldn't bet any money on it. That is really rugged. Talked to a couple of people and they say it's unbelievable. Maybe we are lucky we got it so quick. Might have been much worse later. Can't quite see how though at that.

Well enough of that. Honey darling, I would love to see you tonight for a moment, all night! If I am wishing, I might as well make it good! Baby, I miss and love you so damn much. I'm praying we get that leave and I get to see you. If you will forgive me, I'll chop this off here. I'm not much in the mood tonight, but I'll be better tomorrow and will get off a good one. Forgive me honey, it's not lack of love, but I'm still a little shocked about Dave.

All me love,
Chas
XXXXX

#25
12 March 1945
In Port

Dearest Honey;

Damn it, still no mail. It's getting pretty discouraging. We sent a dispatch to where they are holding it for us over a week ago, surely we should get some in a day or so. I really should have a batch from you, that is if you've been keeping up the good work the way you started.

I'm sorry about that last letter, I guess I shouldn't even have tried to write when I felt the way I did about Dave. I'm better now, after all this is was and death is pretty commonplace in it. But it is mighty strange how someone as close to you as that hits you.

Honey I had the most God-awful dream about you last night. Somehow I'd gotten mixed up with a B-29 outfit as Naval Liason officer or some such, and I had made several Toyio Nagoya raids with them. Well I was decorated and brought home the other way around and I had two days to spend with you before I left for Russia on a diplomatic mission of some kind. I found you in a hotel in Cleveland. I had already registered at another hotel. You were in the lobby waiting for a date, a Colonel no less. When I went to kiss you, you turned a lovely cheek to me. Then you said, "Why Chuck, how nice." Something inside of me just froze into a large hard lump and then splintered into a jillion pieces. I guess that was my heart. I tried to talk to you and you keep the whole conversation on a light plane and just then your date showed up. You introduced me as an old friend and then toddled off with the Col. As you went off with him I asked if I couldn't see you later at my hotel and you said airly "I'll try to look in on you tomorrow" I then dazedly groped my way to the bar and tried to get stiff but liquor didn't do any good , so I went up to my room and laid there all night staring at the ceiling and thinking about us.

Well you did come in just as I was finishing breakfast about ten the next morning. "I only have a moment Chuck" you said, "What was it you wanted to see me about" "Well" says I "I guess I just wanted to see you and hold you in my arms mostly" "Don't be ridiculous" says you. Well we talked in nice stilted conversation for a few minutes and then you said "How long will you be in Cleveland?" So I said I was leaving for Russia in a couple of hours. "Well, have a nice trip and let me know when you get back" says you. "Honey," I said in desperation, "This is Chuck, your husband, don't you remember?" "Oh let's not get dramatic" says you "and now I really have to fly, take care of yourself" and out you go through the door. Well thank God I woke up then.

When I first woke up for a minute it wasn't clear it was only a dream and I lay there for a moment very sick at heart indeed. Suddenly I realized it had been a dream. I leaped out of bed and suddenly the world was a thing of great beauty. I was so damn happy I'm afraid Smiley thought I had lost my mind. Baby, baby, don't ever let me dream like that again. It was if you had stuck a long thin knife into me and then slowly twisted it. It was so damn vivid and real that I was in a cold sweat when I awakened!

Honey, what wouldn't I give to by lying in bed with you right this minute. Just lying there next to each other our whole lengths with my arms around you. I think there could be nothing more soul-satisfying in this whole world. I don't think I'd even go to sleep. Just lie there and savor the beautiful wonderfulness of it all night.

Golly, I sound like an adolescent jerk don't I? I am enclosing a couple of little things I picked up on the beach the other day. One is a silk powder bag I took out of an unexploded mortar shell, there was no danger because I knew what I was doing. I cut the back out and took the powder out. The other thing is the label off a box of rifle ammunition. I am going to send a box of trinkets to you today. Open them up and look at them if you don't want to keep them with you, which you won't, send them on in a box to mom to keep for us until after the war. There is a cute little blue bottle with Japanese characters on the side that I thought you might find a cork for and carry aspirin or something in your bag. This little silk bag I thought you might be able to fill with face powder and sew up the little slit and use it as a powder puff. Maybe I'm nuts, but that's what I thought.

Among other things in the box is a Japanese book, seems to be a child school book, a reader of something of the sort. It's pretty well illustrated and not in too bad shape. I thought it was quite interesting.

Well ducky. If this is ever going to get to you I'd better close it off and get it going.

We still don't know what disposition they are going to make of the old G but we are sitting and waiting. Not a bad place to sit at all this hell going on everywhere.

At least we won't get any more bombs thrown into us sitting down here. I the mail would just start coming I could reconcile myself to a long sit.

How goes the tour? Do they love you in Denver? Honey, honey, I miss you so. Please lets have this war end soon and let us get back together again! I adore you darling, now later and forever. Keep true and keep loving me.

All me love,

Chas

X because I don't believe in dreams!!

Hotel Winthrop
Tacoma Washington
March 13 1945

Dearest honey;

It seems as if every nite when I start to write you, I am sleepy. But I guess we might as well resign ourselves to that fact — I like best to write you when I am sitting here in my nightgown and robe — almost ready for bed — with just you to think about. Unfortunately that has usually been at the end of a pretty long day. This morning, for example, we arose at five, caught a six-thirty bus — why not the train — I don't know — do things the hard way — although perhaps the bus is just as good — certainly it's cleaner, we arrived here about twelve-thirty, dashed up and changed our clothes and went out to Fort Lewis to Madigan Hospital — we did a show on one stage — then dashed over and did one on another stage. The audience was something you dream of — they were just back from parts unknown and this was the first show they had had. We ate out there and arrived home about seven. Hazel and Mary had driven up from Portland and were at Gerald and Margaret Patten's so I changed my clothes and went out there — talked far into the evening — then on the way back, Mary wanted a glass of beer so we stopped and had one — she and Gerald and I — then I came up here and fixed my hair — on top of everything, Mary wanted to talk tonite about her future plans — well, I just couldn't make it — families are wonderful and they do so darned much for you but at times they certainly are demanding...I'm afraid the three days in Seattle are going to be pretty hard on me.

Darling I'm so darned excited over the possibility of your coming home — I hate to think about it for fear I will get my hopes up too high and then they won't be realized . Wouldn't that be wonderful!

Baby darling — I'm so sleepy — when I get past Seattle — expect a succession of fine letters — All my love, Jane

3854 42nd Ave. N.E.
Seattle 5, Wash.
March 14 1945

My honey darling;

Well, honey, here I am back in Seattle — it's a wonder to me I'm here though — Hazel came over from Tacoma this morning with a friend of hers — and Mary kept the car for us to ride over in tonite instead of going on the bus — I invited three of the girls to ride with us as the rest were leaving later — they were thrilled, so about eight we started — well we weren't out of Tacoma when the light fuse blew — I finally found a station — the man finally put the car up on the hoist after he'd put in a new fuse and it blew- he thought he found an exposed wire under the fender. Well, we went about three miles and that blew — so I finally found another garage after driving through pitch blackness — it seemed that some sort of coils that were supposed to absorb the shocks had burned out and I couldn't have them replaced tonite. There I was with all those girls and I had to get the car to Seattle. On top of everything else, I noticed the car had no gas, so I asked Mary for the book and Hazel had taken it to Seattle with her! Well, there was a man at the same garage having his tire fixed and he offered to let us follow him into Seattle — well Mary insisted on driving and she nearly killed us. She can't see at night. She couldn't keep up with the car-when he got way ahead — I told her to toot so he would stop, as pre-arranged. She did. He did, and with that, she loses sight of him and turned out in the middle of the road — right across the highway in the path of oncoming traffic — well I scream at her to get back — it was a very narrow escape. With that, I insisted I should drive because I could see him perfectly plainly. I had quite an argument about that — I finally had to say that she had the responsibility of four people on her hands, and she was endangering them because she couldn't see. Well, the rest was easy — I kept about 15 feet behind him all the way and well over on the right, and we made it fine — of course it was raining, and the swipe broke, and we had to stop and fix that — what a nite — well we got the girls to the Benjamin Franklin, and then Mary said she wanted to drive again — a policeman stopped us for no lites — then she let me drive because, although he was very nice, if he'd asked her for her license, she didn't have any —

We <u>finally</u> got here — then much confusion and I'd been so worried — calmly but really worried with the responsibility of the girls that my disposition got bad — I was convinced that everybody but me was inefficient, and I'm still not sure I don't have a point there.

(I decided to try the typewriter) I'm afraid I've been banging around too long and have learned to take all things into consideration...I mean, be more efficient.

Previously to the horrible experiences of the evening, we had done one theater and two ward shows out at the Madigan hospital at Fort Lewis. They were really awfully good today, and it was a lot of fun to play them. We played one of the wards for officers. It was the first time we had done it and probably the last for a long time. They were a much more subtle audience. I just caught on at the last minute that they were officers and changed my talk accordingly... it was more interesting to play to them.

When I have been at Fort Lewis the last two days, I keep thinking about that place when it was just a little army post...now it is the third largest we have...I think of you going down for National Guard in the summer when you were in high school...and of Dave Oswald...and I keep being so glad you didn't continue it as seriously as he did because if you had been in the army you might be where he was right now...the Navy is bad enough, but I'm still thankful it's not the infantry. I keep thinking of all the life you lived in that same place before I even knew you and wondering if someplace I happen to be is where you might have been. Of course you would have been walking in the woods because the hospital is all newly built, but you might have been there.

The Madigan hospital is going to be the army's largest...7500 (seventy-five hundred) beds...they have 5300 now. It will be taken over by the veterans after the war. It is a beautiful place as hospitals go, but I can't understand why they have it in that rainy place.

I wonder where this letter will reach you...I haven't heard from you for a few days...wouldn't it be wonderful if you read it while we were together. I know that's too much to hope for, but a person can't help dreaming...can they.

All is going pretty well with me aside from missing my honey... I'm tired but getting used to the schedule and taking it in my stride. The show, such as it is, is pretty good, and I'm doing alright. Mr. Evans and I are the best of friends...so all is quiet on the USO front.

Well, darling, again I am about to faint from fatigue, so I will say goodnight and send you all my love...Let me hear from you very, very often or I will begin to worry again, and that ain't good. I have had a glow of happiness since the letters from you last week. All my love, darling, Jane

#13 (I think)
15 March 1945
In Port —

Dear Mom —

Well we did get a few letters a couple of days ago, pretty old mail, and I almost wish I had gotten none. It was the letter telling me about Dave. I guess you can understand how it knocked the pins out from under me. I made myself sit right down and write them a note, but I'm afraid it wasn't much good. As a matter of fact I haven't felt like writing to anyone since then. I tried to write to you and Jane a couple of days ago and even that was no good.

I suppose it's the unfairness of it all that's as bad as anything. God knows Dave had done his share and more without going into the Philippines. Then he had been all that time overseas with no leave or anything. I bet the Oswalds feel terrible about it, but I know they will stick out their chin, as so many people I know have to do in these awful times. It does seem that that's asking a lot of people who had already seen their boy gone for almost four years.

Well it made me unhappy and then it made me damn mad. After our trouble I thought I could welcome some duty back in the States, but now the quicker they put me on a new Destroyer with a lot of guns to shoot up those...the happier I'll be! It's a personal war from now on as far as I'm concerned.

Well there is not much more to say about Dave except he was a grand lad and I'll miss him very much and do my damndest to settle the score for him at a ratio of about a hundred to one. Hundred to one hell, there aren't a million combined who would be worth one boy like Dave.

We are still just sitting here waiting for somebody to make up their minds about us. It's all right of a life, except that it gets pretty dull day after day with nothing to do. One nice thing about it though, it's nice and safe, and nobody shooting at you. That's one very good phase of it. The weather after being perfect ever since we got here suddenly has been blowing 30 to 40 knots and we have to keep on out tows to see that we don't break away from the ship we are tied up to. Seems to be dying down now, so maybe the blow is over.

I went over on the beach the other day and scouted around some old Japanese positions for souvenirs. These two I am enclosing. One is the label on a box of rifle ammunition. The little silk bag is what they pack their powder in their mortar shells. I slit the back of the bag and removed the powder, so it's just a piece of silk now.

Well our mail is still as fouled up as ever, the last letter was the 20 of Feb. Although I understand you get ours in less than a week. They sent another message on ours a couple of days ago, so we should be getting a big batch here in a day or so. Well honey, this is not much of a letter, but I'll try and do better on the next one. Keep writing, I'll get them eventually!

All me love — Chas

#25
15 March 1945
In Port—298 to go

Dearest Honey:
Well at last I can start writing 2 hundred and some days instead of 3. It still seems like an incredibly long time, but at least it's going in the right direction. Still no mail. It seems rather stupid in the face of everything to be so concerned about a little thing like that, but it still remains an unpleasant fact. Every day the mail man comes back, and everyday his answer is a shrug of the shoulders. If I thought it was just because of the operation I could forgive them, but the damnable thing is all the other ships here are getting theirs. I daresay it will be along in a day or so, how many times have I said that I wonder? At any rate, when it does come we will have a field day.

You know, darling, it's so strange that with you the little incidents of the day make up a very cute and interesting letter. But with me, there is so little I can say that it's mostly just guff and stuff and I love you. I say it's strange because I feel so full of it, my recent experience I mean. I can think of a hundred little things, human

interest, courage, even heroism and tragedy, but I'm absolutely tied
down. This period would have been a golden opportunity to write,
but that one experience so completely overshadows anything in my
life that it even stultifies my imagination. I've made several valiant
attempts to write, but my mind is always doing flash-backs. I am
toying with the idea of trying to write about it, but how I could ever
get it cleared is something else again. I had in mind a descriptive
article of the kind Colliers seems to be partial to. Guess the best
thing is to try and write it and then try and get permission to submit
it. The hell of it is to get it cleared I should be a correspondent,
rather than trying to ask, to get something cleared so that it can
become eligible for a rejection slip. Well I think I will have at it at
any rate, beginning in the morning. The title I have already in my
mind "The Mite-y G," or is that corn? I thought of a quick resume of
her work up to this time in the war, her duties and areas and then
about three-fourths of the yarn about this last go-round. What do
you think? And if I can get it by, any suggestions on submission?

 Wonder where you are and what you are doing right now? Answering my own question, if you're still on the coast you should be asleep
because it's four in the morning there now! Hope you are alone too!!
Only kidding, honey, believe me. Last I knew you would be in S.F.
until the 25th, god that was nearly three weeks ago, how far have
you gone by now. How is the work, darling, is it terribly hard and
wearing? I know it's damn satisfying, those poor kids need something
so desperately. I have spent a little time in a big hospital here, but
there is no reason to go up there anymore. I tried to see everyone I
could when I did go though. The one thing that strikes you is their
utter disregard for themselves. They always want to know how so-
and-so is making it, and will he pull through. They never complain
and just lie there and take it. Wonderful. And some of them are
such babies too. I really hope that if I have to get it it comes in one
big bang and none of this days and days stuff. I guess Dave didn't
suffer much, only living one day. Thank God for that at any rate.
Have you heard anything about Will? I have made queries here but
so far have had no results, thank God again. I almost hope to find
him slightly wounded, as I think that would be the best you could
possibly expect. I hate to sound pessimistic, but when a spade is a
spade there is no ducking the implications. Rugged.

 I catch myself looking over at pictures of you as I finish a paragraph. Strange, darling, how I want to turn myself inside out and

lay bare my innermost thought so that you, in some kind of a far-reached way, can feel closer and I can get a feeling of unity. For no relevant reason at all do you remember how many times during an evening I would kiss you? I always was afraid that you were a little annoyed after the fifth or sixth hundredth time, but you bore up well. You know, right now if I could be sitting beside you in front of a fire with something like Tchaikovsky's fifth or sixth playing and your head on my shoulder and your hand in mine — if that could only be, I don't think life could hold a hell of a lot more. I'm sorry if I get sort of sticky sentimental, baby, but I've really seen just how slight the margin between never hearing any music again or knowing the touch of a loving hand and a nice full life in the post-war world can be. It's razor sharp and of cobweb strength. Either you is or you ain't. And I do mean period.

Hell, darling, I didn't mean for this to be a morbid letter, all I'm really trying to say is that I adore you and realize what a wonderful wife I've got and would like to come home to for good.

I wrote to Hazel today, for all I know you may still be around those parts, but at any rate I did. I've been a lousy correspondent with everyone except you, and I suppose I could do better and will on that score, still I've averaged one every 2 1/2 days, and considering that a lot of days I couldn't mail them that isn't so bad. I sent her one of those little powder bags and the Japanese label as I did you. What she will do with them, I don't know, but at least they are of momentary interest. I'm glad you got the earrings and like them. Also that the bracelet fit. I have a feeling I've said this before, but I just re-read all your letters this afternoon, and. you did seem to like them. You know how I would love to give you the whole damn world tied up with a blue ribbon, don't you, darling? We've got a little cleaning up on it to do before it would be a fit present, however. That, however, is now in the process of being done, so that all that will remain for me to do is latch onto the world and get a sufficiently large blue ribbon!!

Remember the day back in November 1942 when you came down to see your old man sworn into the Navy and spent about nine hours sitting on your rusty-dusty? Damned if I'm not full of stray thoughts tonight!!! Remember the U.S. Grant and the last four days? Jackson!! Damn it all, honey, I love you!

Just finished a book by Maugham called "Ashenden," a story of a British secret agent in the First World War. Not too great a book but there is one memorable passage where the very precise and proper Ambassador of Britain to a country where the hero is espionaging has him to dinner and over their brandy tells the story of a man, a foreign office clerk just starting on his career. He calls the character "Brown," but by the time the story has only well started we know that it is his own youth that he is talking about. At any rate, after trials and tribulations he has quite an affair with a very low woman, a female acrobat, if you please! (Which certainly conjures up some weird mental bedroom scenes!) She accepts him, but he of course falls madly in love with her and chases her all over the continent. Virtue of course triumphs, and he marries the daughter of the important family who can further his career. She turns out to be a complete frigid frost, and in a moment of desperation in their early years he tells her about the acrobat. She never forgives or forgets. As he finishes the story, his wife comes in to the embassy from a concert and steps into the study to pass the time of night with them. As she enters, he gives her a look of intense dislike but then immediately becomes the suave ambassador again.

I've very briefly roughed it in, but it is a wonderfully done scene of a man who found no happiness in life as a successful member of society (in the eyes of the world) but who would have at least known the joy of living, as he realized too late, had he continued on with the slut of an acrobat. Maugham wrote it in about '27 I believe, and parts are excellent. His characters really breathe, which is more than can be said for a hell of a lot of so-called successful authors.

How did I get started on this? I've really got to turn in, honey, it's pretty late, and the old eyes are drooping. It was a nice little visit with you though, baby, even in proxy. [END MISSING]

March 16, 1945
3854 42nd Ave. N.E.
Seattle 5, Wash.
Letter #48

Dearest Honey Darling;

It is God awful hour of two-thirty in the morning, and I am just starting my letter to you...thank heaven, I don't have to go to work until four tomorrow afternoon...but then...yipe...we have to go over to Bremerton, do an evening show there come back here...we won't arrive until late and then leave for Spokane at eight in the morning. It has been quite a day. I got home a little after ten last night from the show at the Naval hospital...it would have been earlier but Mary stopped to see a friend and was late picking me up...it was perfectly alright with me though...except your Mother was here... she came down last evening...we really had a perfectly lovely time... you know, I'm really terribly fond of her...she is so darned sweet and tries to do so very much for you. She was just going to stay last night...but this morning...but more of that later...it seemed that I had promised last night to put some of this wonderful oil bleach on Mary's hair...well, by the time I had finished that and my own... it was three o'clock, and I had to get up before seven for an eight o'clock dentist's appointment. The dentist was so darned slow that I just had time to go home and grab a bite to eat and get downtown again...change my clothes too, of course, and then out to the Naval hospital...we played five wards today...some of them were

pretty depressing...especially the two T.B. ones...(Negative) it kind of broke me up when I saw one boy dying of it and in the next ten minutes too. Well, we came back to town...Daddy was coming in on the five-thirty train, and Mother left the car downtown for me...she had to go to Tacoma for a meeting. The train was late, and by the time we got home, it was seven. Your Mother was still here...she stayed to help because it seems that Mary got her neck out of joint this morning, and she was in terrible pain, and we had to take her to the osteopath...Mother had to leave, and I was gone, so she held down the fort. Mary was better although still looking pretty grim...she had had the same sort of muscular spasm that I did. Then your Aunt Genevieve Flynn came, and then we had dinner and did the dishes, and then we talked, and your Mother fixed some new slacks I got to wear on dirty trains for me, and I pressed them. Then Daddy took Gen downtown and picked up Mother, and I reorganized all my worldly goods...with the whole household helping...it has been quite a day for only three hours sleep...the trip to Spokane I understand is beautiful, but I'm afraid I'm going to miss a lot of it.

Honey darling, I had three letters from you today...maybe that's what makes me feel so good. The last one was mailed the eleventh... that would be six days ago...you still hadn't had any word of your future, but I feel assured that for the present the fact that you have dragged out the spear fishing equipment will make the waiting go by a little faster. I am thinking of you with the new feet flippers on... hurtling through that turquoise water, and I wish so that I were with you, terrified as I am of the more vicious denizens of the deep. I know so well how you might have been a constant patron; maybe the getting out and the swimming will help a little too.

Daddy had a very wonderful letter from you which he was kind enough to let me read. It told me a little more than mine had. Honey, you don't need to be afraid and pull your punches with me. Darling, I threw away that picture I cut out of the paper the fateful night I dyed my hair dark brown. I thought I was being ridiculous...but I saw the same thing in Life a couple of weeks ago, and I'll get it again. I was sure at the time, but then I thought I was probably imagining things. I knew that something was happening that was affecting me that night...I really felt very strongly. I guess you could tell that by my letter.

Honey, I am enclosing the pictures taken on Christmas. I would have sent them sooner, but we just got the negatives and had them made. I am also enclosing an article that was in the Times today about me...the picture is utterly awful...in fact, I am even considering cutting that out...as a matter of fact, I think I will. It's the worst that has ever been taken of me. A lot of it is a lot of baloney, and I didn't mean for them to put that part in about that blind boy...they overdid it, and I would never want him to see it. All in all, though, it was a much more constructive article than the last one...oh yes, that was one of my yesterday's activities. I had to meet the reporters at the Olympic. I'm afraid that Mr. Evans was greatly annoyed because they didn't include him...I hinted around that they should, but they evidently thought he wasn't of much local interest.

Oh, sweetheart darling, I just want to tell you again and again how terribly happy I am that you are fine...it is the greatest thing that has ever happened to me, knowing that you are alright. I will say goodnight, my darling, and pray that I will see you soon.

All me love, Jane

Mary is still in the throes of decision. I think your Mother veered her toward the Red Cross. She received a letter from them yesterday saying that she could join from here any time she wanted to...so I think she may do it...

All my love again. Jane

#26
18 March 1945 In Port

Dearest Honey:

Another day and no mail. We are really beginning to get just a little unhappy about the whole thing. As a result, we now have a new complaint. It's not very pretty but very true "What a life we lead — no sail, no mail and no tail!" The old rumor factories are grinding again, we are going home on transports, we are going to be towed back, we are staying here, etc., etc. You pay your moneys, and you take your choice.

Things have come to a pretty pass. The other night Cheefu and I played 65 hands apiece of solitaire banking each other with the deck costing fifty cents and five cents for every card up. At the end of 65 games we both owed each other $8.70, so we called the whole thing off. The funny thing was that neither of us ever completely won a game in all that time. As I write, this Van Metre and Cass are sitting at the other end of the table going out of their minds playing slap-Jack!! Honestly, the things you do when you are bored. Though I will admit that I am far happier today than I was on the same day last month. What a day!

Yesterday being St. Patrick's Day I should have gone ashore and celebrated with the rest of the Irish, but it was pretty miserable, raining and blowing, so I stayed aboard. Today however is a beautiful sunshiny day, and a Sunday to boot which means there will be a band at the club. I think I will go in with Smiley and Vansy and meet some of the boys from the fly-fly branch of the war. We know a good many of them up there now, and it's wonderful to get the straight dope on their activities. They haven't been doing badly here this last week either. If you follow me.

They like to meet us at the club, as the Army has to have the rank of Major before they can get in unless they go as guests. So we are most happy to take them as guests. The stories they can and do tell are wonderful. I could certainly tell you some wonderful ones, but of course that is impossible.

There seems to be some indications that we might get some mail this afternoon, if not maybe tomorrow. Of course that is what we keep telling ourselves, but this time there is a little basis for it, as we got quite a bit of mail for the ship yesterday, when that happens, our air mail is usually not very far behind.

Darling, I know this is a stinking letter, but the last one was a nice long one wasn't it? If there is some comes in this afternoon I will get off a big long one tonight. The mail man is just getting ready to go to into the beach, and that is my ride too, so I'll say goodbye for this time. Remember always how much I love and adore you, and keep good darling!

All me love,
Chas

Yosemite Lodge
Yosemite National Park California
March 18, 1945

Dearest honey;

No darling I'm not back in Yosemite — I'm still out of stationery — I found this in one of the compartments of my file. I'm sitting here in this horrible train to Spokane — the only virtue it has is that the Great Northern roadbeds are a little more smooth than in the Southern Pacific's — then too, the cars, though just as antiquated are a little cleaner — we are going through some very familiar, nostalgia provoking countryside north of Snohomish — the sun, in all the time I have been here hasn't deigned to raise its head and Mt. Rainier has remained hidden. However, I am still looking forward to seeing the snow and the mist in Stevens pass. You know I have always screamed against Seattle but this time, rain and all, I've decided it's a pretty nice place.

We took the ferry over to Bremerton yesterday evening — played at the Naval hospital there — just as we were about to make that return trip I discovered that Kenny Price's ship was in — honestly, I was furious that it was too late to get in touch with him-I'm going to write him a note right after I finish this and ask him to reply in Spokane. We can find out about Will in that way. I'll let you know — it's been in over a month too!

It seems that they have been having the high school basketball conference at...Yipe what crags! Covered with snow and with clouds drifting about them — perhaps I am getting older and beginning to look for some roots — there is an indefinable something about all this that draws me — it doesn't seem to appeal to other people — perhaps it is only because I know this kind of country first — I think Thomas Wolfe could describe my feeling about it far better than I —

I just bought a box of applets — I was seriously considering sending one to you but I know darned well they'd melt before they got there — maybe I'll take a chance anyway;

As I started to say — they were having a high school basketball tournament at the pavilion and the Spokane team is returning on the train — they are pretty obnoxious but, poor kids, they won't have a chance to be for long so they might as well enjoy it — one of the boys looks so darned much like Vanney that it is perfectly amazing — those big brown eyes.

Darling, I am glad you were thrilled by going up in the bomber and I would have done the same thing myself — as a matter of fact, I tried and I certainly appreciate what you mean about the cramped quarters, long hours, the cold and the general stinking inconvenience of the whole thing. Not to mention the danger — but honey what are you trying to do — thumb your nose at Lady Luck — she's been pretty good to you so far — don't work a good thing to death — huh.

Darling, it is my considered opinion that you are now on Saipan. If so, would do me and the Patten family a favor that will never be forgotten. I was up at Mother Patten's yesterday and she asked me to ask you if you were ever there — Bobby Patten is buried on Saipan and they wondered if you would go look at his grave and tell them about it. If there isn't a Naval Cemetery there, he's buried in the Marine Cemetery — it's Lt.(jg) Robert Patten — [I think the middle initial is A. but I'm not sure] He was on the Colorado. I know this may be a little difficult but if you'll do your best on it, I'd appreciate it. If you do find it, perhaps you could take a picture of the grave. If you are able to do this — their address is 1242 15th Ave. N.E. — Seattle, Washington — Mother Patten, Frankie and Bob — And if you do write them a letter, would you send me a copy of it.

We just went over a curved trestle where a whole freight train went over a couple of weeks ago — they've got donkey engines down in the canyon pulling it out. What a mangled mess.

I should write more letters to you from trains — a regular play by play travelogue.

We are now going through the Cascades — Stevens pass — the road is way below us — everything is covered with snow —

I know the family really hated to see me go this time — conceited as it may sound — but they don't know where I'm going or when I'll be back and I guess Mother kind of wanted me around to advise Mary. Ma Wee looks pretty good but she is getting older all the time. Last night she called me in the bedroom and said I mustn't forget to give her love to you and she wanted to know if I thought you liked her — she likes to have a lot of fuss made over her because she's always feeling she's bothering someone. So I assured her that you talked about her all the time and thought she was wonderful and that pleased her so much. It would be awfully nice if you had time to drop her a line.

Keep the letters coming to Daddy darling. That is the best way — As a point of interest I'll send you my next month's schedule in a day or so — I'll get it tomorrow —

We are now going through the Cascade tunnel — eight miles under the mountain.

Well sweetheart I think I will not write anymore and try to go to sleep. I have my fingers crossed for thirty days!

All my love,
Jane

#27
20 March, 1945
In Port —

Dearest Honey:

Hi ho my darling! How goes the battle on the home front? If it's half as boring and exasperating as this life out here I can sympathize with you one hundred percent. As you probably have gathered I still have received no mail. There were a few letters two days ago, but only one days mail and neither you nor mom happened to mail one that day, so I didn't get anything. Moan, moan! I would certainly love to see about ten bags come aboard this afternoon. Wonder if I am just dreaming. Probably.

Little bad news the other day. One of these bomber boys that we have gotten to know pretty well caught a chunk of flak and they don't know if he is going to make it or not. A single bullet but it was a 12.7. That's a bullet about half again as big as our fifty

Caliber machine gun bullet. Hit him in the hip and ricocheted up to his insides. Had to take out some of his intestines and one thing and another. He was supposed to pass his crisis at midnight last night. Hope to hell he pulls through, he is a very nice boy. He is the bombardier and just stood up to take a picture of his pattern when it hit him. If he had been sitting it would have killed him outright. I have a feeling he is going to pull through. He is nice and rugged.

That's the hell about this war. People are getting killed all the time. It may be that we are definitely on the road to both here and Europe, but there are going to be a hell of a lot of nice young lads catch it before that final day.

I wrote you a while ago that I was going to start doing a lot of spear fishing. I have had to give up the idea as they are constantly working on deepening the harbor and underwater blasting goes on all the time. It is not permitted to swim under those conditions. That's the stilted navy way of saying very possible getting bottom shooted off. I finally got my little tool box cut open the other day. I had lost my keys and it was a pretty tough lock. Now I will be able to start indulging in a little handicraft for my honey. Have to see if I can't whip up something nice and tasty to decorate the prettiest girl in the world.

Saw the most amazing picture the other day. It's a big enlargement about 24" X 36". Seems that a Marine captain who is a camera bug talked his wife into posing on the bed. The way the picture looks they had other things in mind than photography but it the cutest thing you have ever seen. She is a cute gal and she is laying on the bed with the most wonderful expression on her face and she is crooking her finger at him. Wow! Seems that the negative got away from him and now the bomber strip is plastered with these pictures. Don't get the idea that it is just a dirty picture because it isn't, it's really cuter than hell and you know just what she was saying when he took it. "Put down that silly camera and come to bed honey." I'm certainly glad I don't live in that hut as seeing that thing more than once would drive me out of my mind. Guess who my thoughts flashed back to when I saw it? I'm sure I'm not abnormal sexually, but it's been a mighty long time since I left you! Only ten weeks and it feels like ten years. I hope your work is strenuous enough to keep you busy. Too much inactivity as I am now going through is bad for thinking. I've been chasing you around in my dreams about three times a week! I guess I am pretty awful huh?

One more story and I'll be through with sex. One of those bomber boys used to be with ATC and he tells the following. He was flying a big Marine home about a year ago. He confidently told Noel that his wife would be waiting for him in S.F. "WELL," said Noel, "you know transportation is a problem in the states, maybe she won't get there in time." "Don't worry," says the Marine, "She'll be there." "But how can you be so positive?" Asks Noel. "Well, I wrote her see and says as follows. 'Coming home, if you want to be first — meet me!' She met him!

I hope you don't think I am degenerating honey, I just thought it was cute. Remember that I adore you darling and keep on loving and writing. Maybe we will have some mail tomorrow in which case I will have another letter off to you post haste in the meantime honey —

All me love
Chas
XXXXXX

Spokane, Wash.
March 20, 1945
Letter #45

My dearest darling;

I am sitting out here in the Red Cross building of the Baxter hospital (army) waiting for our first ward show — so I thought I would write you a letter to tell you I love you so very much and miss you terribly.

Thought perhaps today our record of rain every day since we've been in Washington but the sun was very shy — a brief entrance and then it faded —

I haven't called anyone at all in Spokane-n I know I must call Cay Beets eventually but I didn't want to get involved — our schedule is pretty difficult — afternoon and evenings and after the Seattle stay I'm pretty darned tired — Had a letter from Martha this morning and it seems that after she left the show, she was terribly sick-delirious with flu and on the verge of pneumonia — I'm convinced I must be an Amazon-The little I've seen of Spokane has convinced me I don't want to see a great deal more of it-of course the lakes may be nice in the summer but right now it's pretty dismal and dead looking — our stay at this hospital though has been very nice — this is the third day — tomorrow we're going to Farragut Idaho to play for the Navy.

Well, after all my screaming about Mr. Evans — all the things he has done have redounded and the grapevine has it that he's been fired — he told me yesterday that he was leaving — we've been getting along so well lately though that I kind of hate to see him leave.

Honey we have just now finished three ward shows and are waiting in the Red Cross recreation room. Gee I've certainly learned to wait with equanimity. Even a cigarette line fails to impress me any more — and life has become a constant succession of hospital wards — it's perfectly appalling.

Last nite I went to the newsreel and saw the pictures of Iwo Jima — they were the most complete pictures that have ever been taken of a battle and I came away speechless — appalled — my God honey, when I think of you there — there was a great many Naval action pictures — you could see many of the ship numbers very distinctly — I strained my eyes looking for DM 15 but didn't see it — it changed today and it was the 9:00 o'clock newsreel last nite — the last one — but I thought I might be able to catch it again in Walla Walla Sunday nite — I might just catch a glimpse of the Gamble. If Willy had anything to do with that photography, he can be proud — that's the kind of thing that will make people at home realize — Oh, honey, I'm so glad you are safely away from there. When I think of you in that, it gives me nightmares.

I haven't had any letters from you darling for several days — (I'm at the hotel now) and I keep wondering and hoping and hoping that it might be an indication that you were on your way home — Oh honey — I shouldn't even say it — how perfectly unbelievably marvelous that would — with that happy thought darling, I'll say goodbye for now.

All me love

Jane

#28
22 March, 1945
In Port —

Dearest Honey:

Today was the day!!!!!!Nearly all of our back mail caught up with us finally!! Oh Honey I suppose it sounds silly for a grown-up man, but I was so damn happy I just about cried. Then I was so excited reading them that I was trembling all over. Honey if you love me half or even a jillionth as much as I love you, than I can really imagine the agony you went through waiting for word from me. It was only 23 days for me, but honest to God it seemed like a lifetime. You made me feel very ashamed, for as time went by my letters got more and more irritable and not very amusing. While yours went on in that wonderful way you have, even though you were beside yourself with worry.

I don't mean to sound fatuous when I say something like that. I really believe that you do have a love for me so in order to speak the same language I sometimes say things that could be misconstrued. I mean by all this that I'll never take you for granted. You have a zest for living that sort of cries out against anyone having too firm a hold on either your heart or your head, but of one thing I'm damn sure if anyone is going to do it I'll be that gent!!

Honey, I got 13 letters from you!! Can't you just imagine what a field day I had with them. I arranged them all as to date and then turned to on them. One was a beautiful long one from Santa Barbara that had been addressed only to c/o Fleet P.O. and no ships name. I don't know if you or Patsy readdressed it, but it filled in one gap. Then of course all this wonderful stuff about Mr. Evans the moronic manager and how you finally put him in his place. And Yosemite, and hospitals and Paul and blind boys and Mary and her problems and Hazel and Jack and the bottle at the Blue Diamond. Honey, it was like taking a pull on an oxygen bottle at high altitude. I could see you and imagine you in all those situations, the funniest thing, I loved you in every one of them.

I'm probably being melodramatic and silly but when I say that I literally mean it. I'm not going to be a clinging on you darling, (that in itself is a very funny thought, what a trellis for what a vine!!) but you must know, or at least I'd like to tell you that my life is pretty damn well wrapped up in yours, and that anything that happens to you vicariously, happens to me. When after a long time, I get a peek into the life you are leading, it suddenly supplements mine and gives me a reason for being here, for doing what I am doing.

If I were creating a new world, Huxley-like, I think I would make one of the prerequisites that no-one ever loves anyone the way I do you. That would lead to a clearer brand of thinking, and probably a finer sense of eugenics and certainly a less snafued world. But Gad, think of the wonderful feelings they would miss!!!! Think of never missing someone so much that you get a physical pain in your insides, or think of never knowing anyone that just to hold on to them would make you cast aside all future shots at cloud sitting and ambrosia sipping! In short, think of never being able to love anyone the way I do you! Unthinkable!

Next Day —

Honey, sorry as hell I couldn't go on with this but Cheefu was a little drunkie and had just gotten the word that he had lost an old friend. He was pretty cut up about it and had to tell me a long involved tale about them. I kept trying to chop him off but on he went. He was wonderful when I got the news about Dave so in all fairness I had to stand by him. By the way Cass said to say hello. I don't know what I said that made you think when you did it but it ain't so. By the way his Mom is taken with you but completely. He had three letters from her in a row that mentioned "Janie" Might be nice if you had time to drop her a note. Nell Cass, 117 North Friends, Whittier, Calif. she would be pleased.

You will be glad to hear that Mac, our bombardier friend is past his crisis and should make it all the way. Damn glad to hear it. He only had nine missions, but those are really missions out in these parts! We were all pulling for him. In a way he is lucky, the war is over as far as combat is concerned. Nice thought.

I thought we were going to get 30 day survivor leave when we first got here, but the picture has slowly darkened and now it looks like re-assignment here. I wouldn't mention this to anyone as yet, although now that over thirty days have passed the veil of secrecy can properly be lifted a little. We were so bad that repair was a waste of money so therefore we will probably go to something else right here. God keep me out of the amphibs! But there is very little chance for that what with all the work Minepac has lined up for themselves. Well, we will see.

About Mary, I confess I am too far away and too unfamiliar to be of any help. I would be careful not to be too intolerant about the whole thing though, maybe it is real love, in which case you can forgive just about anything. Mary is a wonderful gal and I have every confidence in her. I only hope she does the right thing and isn't made unhappy.

You know the most wonderful thing about your letters was that you loved and missed me just like I keep telling you to do. That one you wrote after you got my first letter telling you I was all right. I imagine that was pretty good getting the word. Of all the stilted and silly sounding letters, this is it. You keep telling me I can express myself, hell darling when I read aver some of this stuff I write I wonder that you hold down your supper at any time. Say about that, has it cleared up? And are you sure it isn't breakfast you lose? And did things work out, periodically speaking, after I left? But to get back for a moment. I will never be able to tell you how much I love you, you see it's all mixed up with me; my insides, how I think, what I read, the music I hear, the stories I hear and tell, the clouds, the roll of the ship and the sight of a line of ambulances from here to there waiting to take off wounded marines. You see what I mean, it's so positive and solid a thing that's it's like an arm or a leg yet when you reach for it, it dissolves in your hand. A paradox, I guess that's what I am groping for. It's a real thing without substance, a tangible something without physical properties.

My God! How far back did I lose you? all this stuff is just a complicated way to tell you that I adore you, but it's kinda fun trying.

Well my little cup-cake, the mail man is beginning to make preparations, so if this is to be speeding on its way to you I'd better post-haste. That's not too bad, now is it?

Had a letter from Hazel yesterday giving me your schedule but afraid this won't quite catch anywhere so will send it to Jackson. How was the land of Marcus and Narcissa, wonder if the damn thing will ever sell? Wonderful thought, but strictly in-the-arm thinking.

I loved your letters baby, and anytime you can spare a moment, just drop old Chas a line, they are my only connection with you you know. Say, can't you borrow a camera and shoot a roll of film and send to me. All of you, naturally, I'm dying to see how you look and see if I see any lonesomeness in those big eyes. How about it ducky — thanks a million.

Don't forget LS — MFT!!! SR,SF,SBS!!! I love you sugar so I'll
close by sending —
   All me love.
   Chas
   Say, if in your travels you should run into Bollier or McAdams
or Cook, (I forget, but I guess you never met him) give them a great
big hello, will you? They'd be glad to see you. Pritchard's gone.
Goodbye for now again —

A.E. Houghton, jr.
780 Gower street
Los Angles 38, Calif.
RKO Radio

Dear Charlie —
   I write on this formal letter-head to indicate to you at a glance
just who it is who is helping me pay the Houghton board bill now. I
went to work for these fine people about two months ago; there has
been no sharp rise in our corporate profits hereabouts as a result,
but the nail bench talk has it that such will not be long in coming. I
am classified as Assistant to a party named Jack Gross; he is probably a newcomer to you; he came from the exhibition company about
three years ago, and is now one of three Executive Producers on the
lot with six producers (and an Assistant) in his unit. My function
is apparently to grab anything I like the looks of (not things under
contract, mind you) and do what I can with it. As a result, I have
tagged onto a couple of stories which are being prepared without
Producer assignment, have helped two producers with cost problems
they had on prepared scripts, etc. etc. All very interesting.
   To be really good as a correspondent, I should try to tell you
something of mutual friends I have seen. There's Mary Salt, nee
Vickery; one of my first jobs here was with Waldo, her husband, with
the result that we all had dinner together one evening; I even saw
the baby, who is very cute and small. Mary looks very well, and is
at present preparing to go to New York; Waldo has taken a job with
the same OWI outfit of which I finally despaired and they are leaving next week. Waldo has just finished a fine job for us — a musical
around the Sleepy Hollow legend, by way of Washington Irving.

I have not seen much of Hill because of the gas situation; he shares a ride from the Valley to MGM, and I have just about enough to get from home, which is now 620 So. St. Andrews Pl, down near Wiltshire and Westin and RKO. But we gas on the phone from time to time; Jim is still on that story that he started on a year and a half ago, and getting fairly tired of it; his love life is a shoddy and scattered as ever.

Bill Bowers, whom you will remember as author of your tour-de-force Where Do We Go From Here, is here at RKO after a few years in the Air Force as a flying instructor; they finally decided that he was overage to be a glider pilot which was all they could use him for when they started curtailing their pilot program. He is doing very well; as you know he's an exceptional writer with light, fluffy material, mostly dialogue. Bill Dean, who appeared in that play too, is around now too; he has just returned from three years in the Persian Gulf theatre as Theatrical Technician — which means he put on shows of his own devising.

I got a card from Janey in Seattle about a week ago; I had an idea that she'd be further on her way to NY than that by now, but I guess they are taking it the slow way. I can't get over my first reaction to Janey's [REST MISSING]

George Wright Hospital
Spokane, Wash.
Letter #50

Dearest honey;

Another letter between shows — I am sitting here in the Red Cross recreation hall of the hospital — The rest of the girls have gone over to the PX but that one pack of cigarettes didn't mean enough to me today — my feet are tired — perhaps it will mean a lot soon but I still have quite a few —

Tomorrow morning ends our stay in Spokane — it has been a pretty strenuous 6 days — the last two out to Farragut Idaho — to the Naval hospital there — fifty miles each way — yesterday — seven shows — six wards and a theatre one. Tomorrow afternoon we'll be in Walla Walla — staying at the Marcus Whitman hotel — I'll be thinking of you honey — and of you and Buck writing nite after nite — and Mrs. Sunday's cabin — and Buck insisting that cream soup be brought to a boil — oh honey — that was a few years ago — wasn't it — it was so much fun —

Honey they came back and we went to dinner and I met that Ed Bailey — he was a friend of Fran Andersons and Bill Oakies — he was always talking to me about Huxley — he was at the parties at the Beachwood — remember and remember the nite we went out to the party at Fran's — out at Westwood — he was there. We had a big talk — Did you know that Fran is married and she has a baby and that Bill Oakie is a lieutenant in the army and he's in Australia.

It has really been a pleasure staying in this hotel — it's perfectly lovely — for a change — after some of the places — and towns — we've been — now until we get to

Denver though — it will be a succession of out of the way places — this is kind of a grind but I enjoy it —

Darling tomorrow I will have my next month's itinerary and I'll send it to you —

The mail has been arriving regularly from you honey — thank heaven for that — I only hope that by this time, yours from me will have reached you — there should really be a stack of it — Honey I haven't been as faithful about writing as I was at first but I am thinking of you every minute — the spirit it there but the body is weak sometimes when I'm awfully sleepy —

Darling, I have to get dressed and made up now — so I'll say goodbye. I'll write again either tonite or tomorrow —

My fingers are still as always crossed — 30 days —

All me love —

Jane

#29
In Port
27 March
286 to go—

Dearest Honey;

Hiya babe! What's cookin on the back burner? I know nothing is on the front one cause I ain't had no mail since that one big haul about five days ago. Guess you have gone and forgot me huh? Out of sight, out of mind, that's me! Oh well, there are other pebbles on the beach, that's all. Seriously the only mail that has come through has been inter-island and you know what that generally means. And by now you know anyhow don't you ducky. Smarty-pants!! I love you so damn much cookie, I wonder that they don't send me home just as a Christian act. I think it would make wonderful publicity for the Navy. Most-in-love-sailor-in-the-whole-damn-United-States-Navy-all-oceans, gets sent back to his one and only on account of he can't took it no more without her!! Hope this needle full won't leave any bad after affects when it wears off!!! Better have your fun now honey, after they turn me loose I am going to be within touching distance of you at all times, and that's for damn sure.

Still no dope on what's to be done, I am powerful afraid though, that it ain't going to mean going home. Nothing concrete to back up that statement, just how I have a feeling, but I'm afraid honey, that's all. Only thing to do now would be to get a break and get assigned to do something that has been out here for quite a while and is due to go home soon. There is a pretty good chance to gain some months that way, as no-one could have been and out here less! So maybe even if the worst comes to the worst we will still make it within the year. If you should go overseas say in July, how long do you think you would be gone, would you be back by Xmas do you suppose. Oh honey if I got back and you were in Europe I would die. I really would get a flight to N.Y. and try and talk my way into an overseas hop just to see you. How's that for love? From the Pacific to across the Atlantic just to see you. Hell it would be shorter to go the other way come to think of it.

One thing is for sure, if you do go in July I doubt very much if there will be any shooting still going on. The wonderful news these last couple of days. Hell, I think that thing might well fold up within a month. I believe that the Ruskys will really crack through on the eastern front., as a matter of fact a big push is starting for Wein right now so maybe that V-E that's supposed to be v-e day will come before much longer. Wherever you are when it happens, raise up a glass of the best champagne you can get and then pour out another one and drink it for me. Would to God I could be there to drink it with you. But someday we will honey, god and the Irish luck willing.

You asked me if I needed money in one of your letters. No I don't honey, but thanks for the thought. My places to spend money here are pretty limited, and I am doing very well. Speaking of dough the old bank balance should be getting pretty healthy again. Just as a guess I bet about four hundred a month goes into it, is that about right? Gee that is really putting it away, isn't it? We won't be so foolish and spend so much the next time we get home, will we. That's going to be used to put you in a good show in New York and what's left, if any is going to buy El Rancho Fleen, God again willing.

Honey darling, I would love so much to be with you tonight and talk and plan, and then just hold you in my arms. Saw a movie "Two girls and a Sailor" and there were a lot of cute chicks in it, but none as cute as you. Still you begin to get ideas seeing all these lovely female women. Oh! Jackson. Remember the U.S. Grant? Honey, honey.

Our bombardier friend is still coming along, but he has a fixation that he is going to die in his sleep, so he won't sleep and that is pulling him down. He has a pretty good chance if he will only snap out of the mental quirk. If he doesn't he is a gone gosling. Hope to hell he makes it. Berk and I were going out to the strip today, but a little too much rain, can't make it tomorrow, have the duty, but probably will go the next day. Sure is interesting around those lads. As I said before, what stories they tell. Vansy just brought in a letter to be censored and said to give you a big hello and a healthy chomp. Chomp!! That goes double for me.

Well honey my lonely sack is beckoning to me with open arms. It's not very wide, but I know two people you could fit it like nine million potatoes!! Guess who? All my love honey to the purtiest wifeling in the whole world. I adore you.

All me love.

Chas

XXXXX

Letter #51
March 27, 1945
Enroute between
Pendleton and Shashane

Chuck darling; what a negligent wife you have had the last few days — a very bad writer — but darling, it will stop right now and the letters will start flowing in like wine.

Honey this road bed is like something left over from the Oregon trail so when you receive this — don't ask me whom I've been drinking with because I haven't — this is the most jiggle train I have ever been on.

Tomorrow morning at 6:25 we shall be in Shoshane and I won't have to do a show all day — so I shall write you a letter that will really be a dilly — with a complete account of what I've been doing — how much I miss you — everything darling.

This trip is definitely on the strenuous side and some days — like yesterday are pretty spiritually enervating. We played seven shows yesterday-six wards — they were all paralysis cases — it is pretty darned disturbing to see all those young, outwardly healthy kids, lying in beds helpless, paralyzed from the waist down — to know that the majority of them will end up in the Veterans hospital and be in that condition the rest of their lives. Of course I shouldn't be telling you the tragedies of this war — your realization of it would make mine pale — I know that it isn't a subject you should discuss with a man overseas — so I apologize. Nevertheless I am terrifically in awe of the spiritual caliber of all these boys — the ones I see and the ones you write me about — like all your flyers you have met lately.

Honey you do have the darndest dreams about me! Honestly, why don't you dream something true that is nice instead of all this stuff about Lieutenant Colonels and hotels — what a sub-conscious alarmist you are my darling.

Honey, I've said it before and again — don't go on any unsafe airplane rides. It's such a relief to know that you are alright and for the time being, even if it is boring to you, sort of out of danger. I don't like to be a fussy wife but have you considered lately the real thrills of spear fishing. But stay away from the sharks. And, by the way, how are your feet flippers working.

Chuck I heard something the other day which I don't think you know and which, as far as writing is concerned — would help you a lot — it seems that the bureau (Navy of course) has a magazine article department which devotes itself to placing articles written by its personnel. That's how so many stories get in magazines like the Post. Why don't you make inquiries and I'll make further ones and you could get in touch with them. It's really a good deal I understand. I was most enthusiastic about your idea of an article about the "Mighty G," — it's a natural — and if you could just write it as you feel it — as it comes out of you — honey I really think it would be used immediately. I'd be awfully happy too if you tried not to neglect the fine resolutions about writing. I know that what you've been through is awfully close to you and it feels best to forget about it — but if only you could convey even a small bit of that on paper — it would be a very fine work — something to be proud of — just as were those pictures of Iwo Jima that I told you about seeing. You have a talent for expression darling and its that talent which is needed now. Well enough of that darling — but honey I wish you would write the article about the Gamble.

Honey, the train stopped for a few minutes but now it is worse than ever so I'll have to stop —

I send you all my love

Jane

Didn't get to see a darned thing in Walla Walla that would mean anything to us. They didn't even have any interesting postcards. It's a hole — Marcus and Narcissa would be ashamed.

I adore you

Jane

Here's my next month's itinerary — as a matter of interest. But I suppose it would still be best, due to the uncertainty of mails to have Daddy forward them. My love, Jane

Mc Fa hotel
Shoshane, Idaho
March 28 1945
Letter #51

Dearest honey;

I am sitting here in this little town in the middle of nowhere. It is about ten in the evening. I have the bleach on my hair — In the morning at 9:30 we are leaving for Sun Valley to do two shows at the Naval hospital — our afternoon is free and is supposed to be devoted to winter sports but since I don't have any clothes with me for that sort of thing — I don't imagine I'll do much skiing. We return here tomorrow nite — then we leave at 6:30 the next morning for Brigham, Utah — the first of next week (this is Wednesday) we will be in Denver. I am planning to get in touch with Bob's mother and find out the news on him. I'm afraid that when I wrote last nite I forgot to enclose the itinerary so here it is really — so you will know where I am. You have been to all those places and can visualize them. For me this will be new territory and will make the travel part of it more interesting.

Since all my trouble with Mr. Evans has stopped — all has been delightfully amicable. I even had dinner with him and his wife tonite — so personally all is very pleasant now.

I haven't had a letter from you for several days now — I've just been reading over the last ones and wishing for more news of you — I don't suppose there will be any until I get to Brigham or Salt Lake City — honey I don't see how they could keep you waiting around there much longer. One consultation, and a great one to me — though — is that you are going to miss what comes next.

Darling, the bleach has worked — I must go wash the hair — then the stockings, then pluck my eyebrows — the whole darned routine that you know so well — so for tonite honey — goodnite — the thought of you will make these boring tasks only an interlude —

I pray we shall be together soon.

All my love,

Jane

#30
29 March
In Port

Dearest Honey:

Hi darlin' What gives? Damn double damn, another day and not a scrap of mail. I am beginning to get very unhappy with this off again, on again sort of delivery. Guess I'd better write to my congressman. Well, maybe I'd better wait and see what tomorrow brings.

Berk and I are going out to the bomber strip this afternoon, and probably will stay the night. I wanted to get off just a little note to you today even though there is not much to say.

As a matter of fact no mail, coupled with the fact that I spent most of the morning writing some letters of condolence for the dear

Captain (Peterson) sort of took me out of the letter writing mood. Believe it or not, I have written every one of those letters for him. I grant you he isn't too good making with the words, but if I were in his place that is one thing I would do myself, even though it were badly done, and hard to do. I am officially the "War Records" officer, but believe me, under this set-up that is a pretty elastic phrase. It covers just about everything that Peterson ducks doing. I never did like the guy, but since this new change he is absolutely insufferable. Loud, illogical and stupid. Well, enough of that.

I can only guess at your activities these days, but according to my list you must be about in Utah somewhere. You are certainly turning into a traveler since this thing haven't you? I can remember not so long ago when we went into Arizona and it was the farthest east you had ever been, or was it only Nevada? Never mind you you gone a good many miles and states since then, haven't you darling? Please don't go finding one of those super-attractive men in all this wandering, God knows I was never very pretty and as the years are creeping up on me I get less and less, so I would hard put to compete with a glamour boy. Except in one thing, I happen to adore you. After all I've been in love with you for seven years, and that should give me somewhat of an edge!

Stuff and nonsense isn't it darling, still I do love you, so don't you go forgetting it! This afternoon I know where there is a wing off a Japanese plane and I am going to get some of the skin. Maybe I'll be able to whip up some nice bracelets for a little cutie I know. Might even include you in a couple, how about that? They are all screaming for me to "bear a hand" so I guess I'd better run or I'll miss the boat to the beach. I'll really write a better letter tomorrow after I get all that wonderful mail from you. What a pleasant thought to close on. I loff you, bud good!

all me love —

Chas

XXXXXX

#31
29 March
In Port
284 to go—

Dearest Honey:

Hi punkin! Here I am again to spend an hour with you. Not much to say other than chit-chat but then I don't know whom I rather spend the time with than you, even if it is by proxy, and pretty proxy at that.

Again today no mail, getting might tough to keep smiling especially when other ships still seem to get gobs of it. Only hope mine is coming through to you allright. Still it really doesn't make much difference other than hearing from me, I mean that with this sitting here there is nothing to worry about in the way of silver ones for example.

Had a fine time out at the strip. Had a tremendous party. we took out some lighting fixtures to several of our friends, you know those little bed lights that we had put in back in the yard. They sure do live in pretty crude quarters, at least six of them will be able to read in their sacks from now on. We also took a quart of whiskey and a quart of alky (torpedo milk) Well it started quietly enough. They told us that Mac (the bombardier I told you about) had died the day before. That sobered everybody up for a bit, but soon all the liquor began to take affect. Much singing and jollification ensued. As we ran out of liquor one by one somebody would disappear and show up with another quart. Even the Col. of the outfit a pretty stuffy guy broke out one of his and proceeded to get drunk along with us.

He is very publicity conscious having been pilot of the Famous Fort, "The Memphis Belle" which was the first Fort to complete her twenty-five missions over Germany. They brought the whole crew home and there was much to-do, bond tours and the like.

Well towards the end of the evening who do I end up with but an Irishman named Mahoney who had a real Irish tenor voice and who knows all the come-ye-alls and wonderful old Irish songs. we were all so boiled by this time we just sat and listened to him sing. Those of us who were Irish with big tears in our eyes. He really had the best amateur voice I've ever heard, I think. I was a little boiled. At any rate about three o'clock everyone turned in. As no one was out on a mission last night there were no empty sacks as there always have been before. So we slept on the wooden benches in their little club. We were all so paralyzed that we could have slept hanging on a hook. Well Chefu got Cass and myself up about seven-thirty by dint of much heaving and hauling and then we couldn't find Berk. We looked all over hell for him and didn't think he had gone back to the ship because his hat was still with us. After about half an hour we decided that we had to leave and started out. Just then we ran into a pilot, one who hadn't been in on the party. After a good laugh at how we looked he said, "Isn't that one of your lads asleep down there on the coral?" We walked down and there was Berk looking like something dead. HE was asleep on top of actual chunks of coral. When we asked him how come he said the benches were too hard!!!! We are still ribbing him about that one.

(I have Fred Waring on the radio, they just played "Stardust" "Smoke gets in your eyes" and now they are into "Begin The Beguine" Oh honey, how I miss you!!)

Well that is all about the party, except that it was a very elegant drunk. Say honey, do you remember the picture I told you about, the gal on the bed with the come-hither look in her eyes? Well since I last saw it someone has printed above it "So Round — So Firm — So Beautifully Stacked" I really got a bang out of that, I was under the impression that that was our private little joke! Noel told us another good gag. Seems he had a party the night before, with some of his old crew. (these guys fight hard and play hard believe me) Well the hut they had the brawl in had a whole wall of pin-ups. Some very choice ones too. Seems this one gut special-izes in them. For a gag they put the head of a gorilla, a picture of course, right in the middle of the collection. He didn't notice it until about midnight when he was good and boiled. When he saw it he put his head in his hands and said in a loud voice "My God, how did she get in there?"

This Noel is a guy (whole name, Noel Alton) the lead navigator for the squadron who has more missions than anyone up there, to be exact. He is going home the fifteenth of next month, at least for 30 days and maybe for good. He will be the first one back. If I have a schedule of where you will be I will have him call you. At any rate he got pretty drunk last night and started talking to me. He wondered how long we had been out when we went home. I told him 13 months. He has been gone about 8. I could see that something was bothering him so I told him to spill it. Well, he said, I don't want you to think I am being crude or anything, but something has been bothering me about seeing my wife again. Yes, I said, just what is it? Well, he says real embarrassed, how is your sex life when you first get home? Quick I said, brother it's quick. Well he says, that's what's bothering me. I know all she will have to do is touch me and boom, that will be that. Well, I said, I know that's true but there is nothing you can do but keep working at it. Finally, if you can stay home long enough, it gets back pretty much to normal, but never quite. God he says, that's terrible, I'm going to be so embarrassed. But as you say, I'll keep trying!

I hope I didn't shock you honey, but that was a very funny conversation at the time. I guess it doesn't bear up in print but at least there it is. I know I would damn well be embarrassed if *could see you again tonight, right this minute. But how I would love to be. Darling I adore every little hunk of you and it gets worse all the time. By worse I mean better if you know what I mean.*

Still no news about our disposition, so here we sit. In the meantime the Yanks in Germany are running wild, more power to them. I hope they wind it up within a month. Honey, it's now one o'clock, and I'd better get some sack time in. Keep missing me a little love and remember as usual, I send on to you

All me love —
Chas
XXXXXX

Mc Fall Hotel
Shashone, Idaho
March 30, 1945
Letter #52

Dearest honey,

In the half hour before the train leaves, I thought I would start a letter to you and then finish it on the train — I intended to write last nite but it was so darned late when we got back from Sun Valley — oh honey — there is a divine place — I would certainly it to be a part of post-war plans — Pocatello — Idaho

It was almost time for the train to leave darling — well the darned thing jiggled so much that writing was impossible. It is six in the evening now — it was about two when I started writing you — we are sitting on a little local deal that goes to Brigham — waiting for them to put the engine on it so we can get started. Rollie who is the pianist, and I have as usual sort of detached ourselves from the rest of the group and they are carrying on the inevitable loud jabber-wacking. Honestly, I'll form no lasting friendships here except for Rollie. Most of these girls draw attention to themselves and are so silly. Well, I suppose it gives me more time to devote to the "worthwhile things!"

I started to tell you about Sun Valley — really a dream — I went skiing all yesterday afternoon — powder snow — and amazingly enough found myself doing better than you have ever seen me — I'm complete with sunburn now. We arriver up there a little before noon yesterday — spent the whole afternoon on Uollar Mountain — what a joy that lift is — you can spend all your time going downhill — the lodge is absolutely gorgeous — all the Navy's of course — Darling, you should have duty there — what a deal. Yesterday afternoon I had just skied back to the bottom of the lift when an elderly man came up to me and introduced himself to me — he said his name was Bill [ILLEGIBLE] and that he had been in show business up until 35 years ago and he wrote the song "I want a girl just like the girl that father used to know" and a lot of others — and that the Naval director officer had thought it would be nice if he were in the show. I said that was fine, referred him to Mr. Evans and started talking — he explained that his son was the ski instructor. Just then up skied his son whom he introduced as Bud [ILLEGIBLE] I gasped and said "where is your home?" — Ithaca, New York he said — and it was that Bud [ILLEGIBLE] remember he was a civilian and we saw him at the Fiji house and you went skiing with him — and we went to their house. Well he wanted to know all about you and about Gideon — he brought his wife around later — they came to the show. When he wasn't in ski clothes, I saw that he was an enlisted man and that's his job — talk about a deal — she's there and the children. They both wanted to be remembered to you.

I took the ski lift to the top of [ILLEGIBLE] mountain yesterday — I hadn't intended to go straight down — just sort of work my way down the side — well Mr. Evans saw me and was afraid I would break something and sent one of the instructors up — so I had to start from halfway down. It was a little embarrassing but there wasn't much I could do — probably was being a little foolhardy anyway.

Oh honey — I kept thinking how much you would have enjoyed it — I've never seen you look happier than when you were skiing — I could just visualize you jumping around and going down like mad. We'll go up there some time. It's unbelievably beautiful and they make it so much simpler than other places.

This day definitely wasn't as memorable except in the opposite extreme. We have priorities on the railroads but you'd never know it — they've cancelled or forgotten our reservations so many times it's become the rule rather than the exception — it's so bad that I guess the New York office is going to make a big fuss about it. This morning for example we were supposed to leave at 6:30 and they didn't remember the reservations so we had to wait until 2;30 — then we were supposed to have first class seats and they put us on the coach — and the worst car was the only one with any seats left — and the train wasn't even filled with service men — with civilians going heaven knows where. The railroads really aren't at all cooperative. Civilians, I can see, still get preferential treatment over servicemen. Well, my nice clean hair is filthy, hands grimy, and I feel as if I've been eating dust. I don't think they ever clean these cars.

I'm hoping that Daddy will have forwarded some mail from you- and that it will be waiting for me at Brigham. It's been days since I've heard and pretty soon now honey, they will have had to make up their minds about what to do with you. I hope so when I open up each letter that it will have good news in it. Perhaps I will get one tonite that will.

In case I haven't told you I miss you and I love you

All my love,

Jane

April 1, 1945 7th 2nd wedding anniversary
Harvard Hotel Brigham, Utah
letter 356

Dearest honey;

If there seems some slight discrepancy in numbers, it isn't that there are any letters missing — it's that I forgot to keep my chart and I got mixed up — The last letter I wrote you was night before last, March 30 — and it was numbered #52 — let's start out from here now — I notice you are mixed up too — the last two letters I received from you were both numbered #25 —

Well darling here it is our 7th wedding anniversary. Remember two years ago today we were in New York and what a divine time we had-last year I was hoping you would be home by this one — now I am hoping for the next. I bought you two slight remembrances — unfortunately I wasn't able to find them before last night and today I found the second by a stroke of luck in the restraint where we ate — they'll be a month or two late and they may even reach you here — God willing — but that's what they're for.

I had every intention of going to church this morning. Unfortunately this is almost a completely Mormon settlement and the only other services were being held at the hospital. Like a fool, I loaned my alarm to Pat and told the clerk to buzz me — which he forgot to do — when I didn't appear, Pat decided the body must have been stronger than the spirit — so they went on. I woke up about noon — feeling wonderful. Perhaps I'll go next Sunday — this once a year business is kind of hypocritical — it would perhaps be better to pay my respects in an everyday sort of fashion. I got up and took one look at the swirling snow outside — yes snow — but it was the wet kind that dissolved as soon as it hit the street — no fun at all — and decided this was the day for domestic activities — so I re-organized everything, washed, ironed, did my hair and now I am pretty well caught up with myself and have a sense of inner satisfaction about the whole deal.

This is definitely a very dead town — actually it's quite a pretty little place — At the end of the Great Salt Lake and three sides ringed with snow covered mountains — but it certainly is quiet and most inconvenient. The maid was telling me today that last Christmas not even one café was open and the people in the hotel nearly starved to death — they finally went out to the army hospital and succeeded in getting a hamburger at the P.X. — can you imagine. I can't help feeling there would be a mint of money in establishing at least decent looking eating places in some of these little towns — there is enough to support them — and certainly a crying need.

The hospital yesterday was pretty grim — we played five wards — all amputations. Although it is far from the worst of casualties there seems to be something so much more concrete as a result of the war in an amputation to me — than anything else. Most all of the boys on the street are without a limb — and those who have their new ones are so proud — showing them off to their friends — it's heart rending. I encountered a group of 15 Brazilians yesterday — Most of them without both legs — who had been fighting in Italy. The sign language we talked back and forth brought them some pleasure. I also met a boy who had lost a leg who was one of the most inspiring people I have ever met. We got talking and he followed from ward to ward. He actually sparked every show. He had set out from the time he was hurt to give as much pleasure to everyone else as he could and not think about himself. To me, he was almost sanctified.

I had a letter from Daddy yesterday — it said he was enclosing a letter from you — well it wasn't there so I wired him to ask what had happened to it — so far I've received no answer.

Tomorrow is Hazel's birthday. I wasn't able to get anything where we've been lately so I wired her some flowers and I'll get her something for us in Denver.

Honey, write often — it's been over a week — much over — since I've heard from you — as a matter of fact, I've only had two letters in the last two weeks — of course that may mean something good —

All my love, darling, Jane

#32 2 April 1945
In Port 282 to go —

Dearest Honey:

Lo, honey! How are you receiving my mail? Must say that this end stinks! Course I guess the explanation is the invasion what's a' going on. But I still fail to see why that should hold ours up — well, mine is not to reason why, merely to do and die — of longing for you. Hardly a warrior-like speech is it? Still, as long as we just have to sit here there is not a hell of a lot else I could do. Being even more un-warrior like, I'm not too disappointed that I'm missing this one. Must be a hell of a lot of excitement, but you know my heart and how I must avoid repetitious things that provoke it.

I guess I'm only kidding myself. I would really love to be up there right this minute. Naturally I want to live through this war and try and make a fine life with you after it is all over. I also know the fewer of these deals I go in on the better chance I have of realizing that dream. Still, I just don't feel right sitting here when a hell of a lot of people I know are busting a gusset maybe worse up there right now. Don't get me wrong, darling, it isn't dramatics or mock heroics, as a matter of fact I would probably be scared silly right about now, but I would still be able to do my job, which largely consists of shooting a lot of the enemy in the bottom. I wouldn't have time to worry about my mail but rather how to cream that bunch of jerks that just put that six incher by our bow!!

It's such a funny sort of a contradictory life I am leading, darling, sort of now I am and then you isn't, kind of a deal. God knows nothing could happen to us here (lessen the tired old bloody world givers up completely), but it's that very sense of comparative safety that makes it so damnable.

I didn't want to leave you when I did the last time. I still want to come home and spend the rest of my life looking at you and busting my arse to make you happy. But then there's that other thing. I guess it's what the Rotarians try to say when they urge everyone to "put your shoulder to the wheel." Might be it's the pioneer idea of pulling your own weight. (remember Marcus? he damn well could, and did!) Probably it's only that thing that figures so much in politicians' speeches and little in the consciousness of the people — love of country.

Whatever you choose to call it, it's there. Might be that it was brought on by our recent trouble; might be it was watching those incredible Marines hit that bloody beach at Iwo; might be it was getting the news of Dave's getting it — Whatever it was, it's now there and good and done.

The funniest thing of all though, remains to be told. Whether I do or I don't, whether I get a new DD or a new DM or whether I come home to Uncle Sugar for 30 days, whatever happens, I don't have one damn thing to say about it!! I paid my money, and I took my choice, now BUPERS does all my deciding. I still think I would have made a hell of a good Marine!

Okay, honey, sorry I let you in for all this. Guess I was thinking out loud. Tell you one thing though, no matter which way the ball drops I won't squawk. Somebody a hell of a lot smarter than I am is figuring out my next assignment, I'll leave it up to him. If it means home and seeing you, well, I suppose I'd go out of my mind. If it means reassignment here and something going to go poke one at the enemy, I'll miss seeing you, but I'd sure welcome the chance to poke!

Yippety-yipetty, yipetty!! How I do run on. Again, forgive me. Can't ask you much about yourself 'cause I haven't heard anything about you for ten days or more. Still, I'll make a guess — You're still lovely as a Renoir picnic miss, you are still working hard as hell and you are still making a lot of kids a little bit happier than they were before! Right? Right! You are such a wonderful guy, sympathy for those who need it and a prod for those who need that. Try and remember through all this kaleidoscopic change of scenery that there happens to be a gent in the Pacific who adores you, and that with his adoration he also sends you — all his love Chas

Letter #50
Newhouse Hotel Salt Lake City, Utah
April 3 1945

Dearest honey darling;

Another day, another city and another hotel and still no letter from you and at this point I'm getting a little frantic and all sorts of wild ideas are going through my head — like for instance you went on another ship and went up to Okinawa — I suppose that is silly but with so long not hearing from you — I begin to put two and two together and five or six out of it — maybe you are even on your way home but my fears are such now that I imagine the bad things first — probably you are still in the same place and the mails have been delayed —

We left Brigham at 6:30 this morning and arrived in Salt Lake City before nine — it was a beautiful ride — the purple mist of morning over the valley — and the snow capped mountains rising straight out of the Great Salt Lake —

This hotel is really very luxurious and after the very cramped accommodations which Brigham had to offer — my desire for sight-seeing is definitely exceeded by my desire to be in the luxury of this room. Evidently the natives here live on beauty alone because as far as I am able to see, it is otherwise a very dull place. You even have to have a permit to buy wine — I haven't had a drink for ages — I'm kind of happy to know it doesn't bother me — Rollie and I are planning to have a Martini before dinner the first night we are in Colorado though — that will be Thursday — Probably we will have an evening show and eat at the hospital — and it will have been a beautiful idea.

We played three shows at the Regional hospital at Camp Kearns today. It was the first time I had ever felt that at least two of the shows were definitely failures — and it really wasn't our fault — it was actually the result of an attitude, a depression, lethargy — almost a bitterness that you find so often in army and never in Navy hospitals. I think it's because the places themselves are so darned ugly, drab — with no life to them — eventually it would stifle anyone. I felt rather badly at not being able to really do something about it. It was explained to me that probably no one could — but at the same time it was rather depressing. The fact that these were all local casualties or just boys with a stomach-ache probably had something to do with it.

When we got back into town, Rollie and I wanted a beer — we were informed by the clerk that we could only have it in our room because there was probably no place "ladies" could go without escorts. That made me so indignant that we found a place a block away — had two beers, went to dinner — now she is asleep on the bed and I'm almost dropping off just sitting here — I'll probably be found in the morning with my head cradled in my arms — seated at the desk.

To prevent that honey, I think I'd better go to sleep just about now — the situation is getting desperate —

Just remember honey — I love you — I miss you — and I'm praying to see you soon —

All my love, Jane

Letter #59
Train between Salt Lake City and Greenwood Springs, Colorado
April 4, 1945

Dearest honey darling;

Had to leave Salt Lake City tonight with still no word from you — so I'm practically holding my breath until we reach Denver Friday morning — if there is nothing then — I will begin to be slightly frantic to say the least. Heaven knows where I will imagine you. Who would have thought that when the typewriter went on the Gamble that I would go through so much green ink and that I would actually begin to enjoy writing by hand — I almost do.

Today was a fine day — I slept until eleven — ordered breakfast in the room — devoured pots of coffee-then went shopping — the air was tangy and the sun was bright — the only thing that marred the picture was that at some time during the night the mountains had lost their coverings of snow and there they were — clean and bare — looking almost shockingly naked.

To get back to the prosaic — I went through an awful chunk of cash today — sixty dollars including tax to be exact — business of course — after a stint at the war field and nearly a hundred wearings in this — that flowered dress was about to stand up by itself — I had and to have a new one — the other isn't worn it's just dirty — so I found one I really loved and bought it-I'm going to wear it long enough to have my first dress cleaned and then save it until we get near New York — I'll wear it when the people from there start coming to see the shows — I'll see if I can draw a picture...

It really has to been seen to be appreciated. I'm afraid I'm going to have to have some pictures taken in Denver as the New York office wants them for publicity — so I'll wear it and then you can see it.

Mr. Evans told me that as far as the New York office which is the final criterion is concerned — I could definitely go oversees and plan on it if I wanted to. So I will see what happens.

I know it seems kind of silly to be drawing pictures of dresses with a war going on — but after all this dress was bought with just one purpose in mind — to make the wounded boys who have been in the was feel better — that is not losing sight of things. I guess there's not much danger of my doing that anyway. — in fact none — not with what I see every day. I was talking yesterday with a boy who had been in Burma two and a half years. I'd really like to go there.

Oh honey, I hardly dare hope you may be on your way home — I know it's a wild dream but dreams come first — don't they. I wonder if I could will it into being. Sometimes I just sit and imagine that the phone rings and it is you — oh honey — I guess I shouldn't even imagine such things — I'm too disappointed when I come back to this earth and they aren't true. But they will be someday and in the meantime it is fun to imagine. If only I felt that I knew where you were. I haven't heard from you for so long that I'm sure you must not be in the same place — and I can't visualize you anyplace.

Darling I am going to have to stop writing before I fall asleep —
I love you my darling and we will meet soon again.

All my love, Jane

#33

5 April '45

In Port —

Dearest honey:

Cheerio ducky. Wonder where you are and what you are doing
at this minute. Wonder if you are missing me at all and if you are
still writing to me. As you probably gather the mail situation still
stinks, but good. Do you realize that in the last two months since
we left Pearl I have had mail from you exactly twice? Not very good
for keeping up morale would you say? Heard on the news today
the lads at Okinawa were already getting mail. I'm glad for them
and they rate it, but it does burn me up a little not to get any here.

Well to hell with the weeps. I'm getting awfully ashamed of
myself starting off every letter with a bitch. Since I wrote a couple
of days ago nothing of note has happened. We still sit without any
word and wonder if we are due to fight the rest of the war here.
Since we have been here now nearly six weeks it begins to look like
it might be possible at that. I guess I got a little wound up in that
last letter to you, sorry, but you begin to feel pretty ornamental
after a certain length of time.

Berk and I keep our war maps up to date, I may say up to the
hour, as we get several stations with our little daisy as well as the
local boys. We can be seen almost every hour on the hour moving our
pins. It's just unbelievable the way the laddies are doing in Europe.
Can't last much longer over there. And this Okinawa thing is going
so damn well; when are the bastards going to read the handwriting on the wall? Went to the club yesterday with Berk and Cheefu
and ran into one of our pilot friends who had just gotten back from
taking a correspondent and a radio man over the island. Maybe
you heard the broadcast. Said he circled at 7,000 feet and the only
thing that threw any flak at him at all was on his dawn approach
when our own Navy opened up on him. He retired, but quick, and
waited until it was fully light before he ran back in so they wouldn't

fail to recognize him! Quite a tale he told and quite a guy. Told us a story about some Atlantic duty he had earlier in the war. He was flying from Africa to Ascension island, you know the one midway between Brazil and Africa. One day he was to rendezvous with a convoy east bound. As he made his run-in, right on time by the way, the can that was our escort opened up on him. Rather than running he put his nose down and being as he mounted a 75 mm cannon he put five round right in a line across the can's bow. As he tells the story, "I didn't have a bit more trouble with that boy, we got along fine" I can imagine! He is quite a guy, name of Pickerill, you may read something about him one of these days. He joined the RCAF long ways back and then transferred to out AAF when we came in. He has completed a tour of duty in N. Africa another over the continent and was one of the first four pilots here and will complete his third tour before very long. He lied about his age to get in, cripes he is older than I am, really about 36 or 7 but still quite a lad. We have had several pretty good drinks together, both at the Navy club and at their little squadron hut up on the hill. (I just re-read that last paragraph, from the number of "quites" in it I read like a bloody Limey!)

Last night we had "The Song of Bernadette" as a picture. I must say I was very impressed by it. I thought that gal really did a first class job. Of course it was the dream part of all time, all the sympathy and the most wonderful situations in the world. Still not to detract because it does take a damn talented your lady to handle as meaty a role as that was. I thought the casting of Charles Bickford as the village curate was wonderful. I thought he turned in a most outstanding job. That was really a job, well done. Salty as hell, ain't I? I'll bet you are getting better by the day, aren't you darling? All you ever needed was self-assurance and I bet you have that by the nth degree by now. Suppose I'll have to resign myself to being known as "You know, Jane Flynn's husband." That's fine with me, darling, but give me a couple of years to catch up when it's over and I'll try to make old C.J. a name in itself.

I don't know how it is with you, darling, but I am missing you so much it's almost unbelievable. You are in all of my waking thoughts and in most of my dreams. I can think of nothing that would be finer than to be in Carolina or any other damn place in the world, providing that I had you to look at and talk to and dream of our future and start living again. I nearly wrote loving right there, and that would be all right too! My sex life, rather lack of it, is getting pretty acute. Nothing I can do about it here, course there are some nurses on the beach but the idea leaves me a little cold. Also there are so damn Amour boys with oak leaves and eagles and stars and such that they largely corner the market. I haven't even made an attempt to meet one though baby, and that's the truth. I imagine you must have your own problems, but damn it you are surrounded by eligible outlets by the thousands. I try not to think about it, but I can't help it. Well if it gets too bad, pick out a nice lad and make with the fun in the hay. Only one condition, make damn sure you've just met him and don't keep up the acquaintanceship when the roll is over. Sort of an emotional blood-letting as it were — okay?

In two days it will be three months, one quarter of the year gone. I still think that I am going to beat that time limit, one way or another. Right Now I would give my shot at heaven for one hour with you. I love you awfully good and a hellufa much darling, remember that. Someday we will again have a regular "Flynn Saturday night" with a lot of nice people. Then when they all go home there will be that big oversized bed, not the old one, a newer and more oversized one! And then you'll go to sleep in my arms and I will know what I spent this time out here for — Until that day comes though honey I guess all I can do is send you —

   All me love
   Chas
   XXXXXX

Cosmopolitan Hotel
Denver, Colorado
April 6, 1945
Letter #60

Hello my darling — Yipe — I got here today and all my fears proved unfounded — you aren't reassigned — you aren't anyplace bad and you are still there — bored as I know you are — I'm darned happy about it — there were five letters from you — including #31 — *I arranged them in sequence and sat down and read them through over and over again — they were happy for me to read darling but I know an awful lot of things in them must have been pretty sad for you — I was pretty sick about the bombardier as I had followed his progress through four letters and I was so hoping for him-Gosh honey, the mental attitude has an awful lot to do with the whole thing — from the sublime to much much lower-that's one reason why hospitals shows are important. If you can take a boys mind off himself for even a little while, psychologically, it helps in their recovery.*

Oh honey, before I forget — would you tell Berk that I shall be in Ohio next month and I'd like to see Alice — but I've lost their address it seems — so send it to me post haste. We'll be in Dayton so I'll see Viv Freihofer too. What of Frei — is he alright — have you any word of him?

I don't suppose now that I am so far inland that I will see Ballier or Mac Adams or Cook — More than likely they would be at [ILLEGIBLE] or someplace nearer the coast — if you have any word of their whereabouts, I would love to see them. I'm deeply sorry that I won't be able to se Pretchard on this particular tour — I now see the significance of your poem — it may be true but the whole thing still strikes me pretty darned deeply.

Honey, Rollie, my room-mate, the pianist — who is incidentally an exceedingly fine person has a friend on Saipan — if you are ever there you might look him up — he is a very fine writer and political analyst — his name is Staff Sergeant Lou Houston, Hq &I&q. — 7th Air Force APO #244 San Francisco —

When I got to Denver today — I called Bob Marinaro's mother. Truthfully, darling I was almost afraid to call but I could hardly wait to get it over with. Well, leave it to Bobby — he's alright. He's still flying the Hump and has received the Air Medal and is about to get the Distinguished Flying Cross — You might drop him a line, darling. His address is Lt. R.L. Marinaro, 1337-AAFBU, ICP,ATC, APO#467, Area 5 c/o P.M., New York. I may see Mrs. Marinaro for awhile on Sunday. Bob's sister's husband — remember the wedding pictures — is in the Philippines.

Everything came out periodically alright months ago, darling. I should have told you about it — but I forgot —

Charles of Taylor should have been functioning tonite darling — I did my hair — I have a new oil bleach which can't hurt it so the job is comparatively simple but it would have been fun instead of drudgery if you had been here — Gosh, I have so darned many things to do in what spare time I have that it doesn't leave time to do any sight-seeing.

Honey, I still think you should be recording on paper — all the things you can say — and that you are thinking and feeling and I wish you would — I know it's hard but it's one of those things which should be done.

Congratulate Pete on his new position for me — and just stick it out darling and everything will be alright. What I didn't understand is where is Commander Clay?!!

Oh honey I was awfully disappointed to have all my imaginations and dreams come to pass — and to really know now that I won't see you for awhile. I know how this waiting and uncertainty and lack of hope must be for you too honey — in the meantime, visit the flyer — he'll make it even if it isn't fun —

Darling — I just now fell asleep over the paper so I'll say "30" for tonite.

All my love, darling,

Jane

#34
In Port
9 April 1945

Dearest honey,

Might as well as get my chipping over with now, yep, that is, still no mail.

We sent Cass down by plane the other day to check at the main base around here and sure enough they found out that one dispatch hadn't gone on through and as a result mail was being held at Pearl. Well another dispatch went out and either tomorrow or the next day we should hear, I mean we should get all our back mail! So with that pleasant thought I will get on to something else.

Our situation is largely unchanged, the only thing we had a board of three officers come aboard to make their report on what should be done about us. Knowing the navy red-tape I won't even venture to predict how long it will take to go through all the channels, but I bet we are soon going to be the longest people on the island in the point of time. We are getting to be so well established that all the shore personnel know us and speak and at the bomber base there is one squadron that I swear we know a good ninety percent of the officers.

Next Morning —

Sorry honey but things happened. There is a hole in the galley deck house that we pulled some equipment out through and what should happen but one of the lads fell through it. Seems he is having wife trouble, she wants a divorce and he was sort of waking in a dream and stepped into the hole. He fell into the galley and knocked himself out. Then when we got him out he complained of his leg and from the angle of it it looked like either a dislocated hip or a break way up on the leg. By the time we'd gotten a traction splint on him and put him in a stretcher and started him on his way to a repair ship for x-ray pictures the evening was gone and it was time to hit the sack. Luckily the pictures showed no breaks. All he has are badly pulled ligaments severe sprains. He was certainly a fortunate kid.

Just about the time I got back down in the wardroom from that little episode, Pete, Stu, Van and Cass arrived back from the bomber strip. They had intended to stay all night but they came back home about midnight. Well of course they had to tell Berk and me about the pictures of the last strike and such stuff. Also all the sex talk that had gone on and the feelthy pictures they had seen. Both Berk and I had to give up on our letters, just too much competition. It looks for sure like this Noel is going home in a week. Poor guy he is so darned happy about it and still he thinks he will catch another mission before he goes. Naturally he is a little worried, he had been so lucky so far and only one more to go and then home to mama. That will make 23 for him if he catches another and sugar, that's a heap of missions! Sure hope I get some mail from you before he goes so he can give you a growl. Sure will be nice when the mail starts coming regularly again. This way I feel so damn lost and out of touch with you. But when it starts coming it will be fine because it's coming through for other ships in less than a week. Matter of fact a guy next to us got a letter from San Pedro that took exactly four days to get here. That's really service.

Well how are you honey? Is the work awfully tough and are you standing up to it alright? I think it's wonderful but you know I catch myself hoping you don't go across the Atlantic, I just have the feeling that I might be back about the time you said you would leave. Nothing definite you know, but just a feeling like one gets sometimes. Oh well, it will all work out one way or another. Do you realize that over 1/4th of that year is gone? I won't say already, because it seems years ago I left you in San Diego, but at least time is passing. The way the war situation looks right now it may be over before even the more optimistic of us had imagined. Just think if Russia comes in and starts across China from the back door while we go in the front. That would lop months off the schedule right there.

Well baby pray for the best and we will make out. This is a stinking letter without any coherence, but try and forgive me and I'll do better when we get some from you. I adore you —

All me love —
LS-MFT Chas
SR-SF-SBS!!
XXXXX

April 9, 1945
Letter #61
Plains Hotel
Cheyenne, Wyoming

Dearest honey darling;

This is a fine time to start writing a letter — it's two in the morning and we just got into Cheyenne — I thought that while Rollie was having her bath, I could make up in some way for neglecting you the last two days — which I have darling — but it wasn't because I wasn't thinking about you I just got sick of writing by hand — if I could carry a typewriter around, I think I'd get one but I couldn't carry it anyway but it seems to me I write so long and say so little —

I haven't heard from you since the wonderful group of letters of Friday — but I daresay when I get back to Denver Thursday, there will be some waiting for me — my hopes are high and my fingers crossed — The last few days have been kind of hectic — the shows were hard — lots of them and we had to do so much walking in between — today for example we started at ten this morning — did shows until four — then you see I have to work the whole show — except for Rollie, the pianist, the other girls do their stint and leave — we then left for Cheyenne at eight in the evening — just now arrived — it's been a long day and I haven't started getting ready for bed. When we get back to Denver though, the schedule is beautifully simple — I'll be able to really get a rest. With a lot of spare time though I have to keep myself from shopping because I've been going over the amount I've planned to spend lately and I have to sort of curb it — Rancho Fleen you know.

You'll never guess where I spent the day yesterday — out at the Marinaro's — not strictly it was at the Lombardi's — Bob's sister's husband's parents — she lives with them with her baby and Mrs. Marinaro comes over there. Lillian is really a beautiful girl and her baby is adorable — her husband is in the Philippines.

They overdid themselves to make me welcome — I was so touched — they knew all about you and me and everything I could think of about Bob — they were hungry to hear — I don't know when I've had so much food and drink — I'm not going to tell you because it will make you unhappy — then they took me all about — well a ride to see the view of Denver from the mountains — it was gorgeous and they must have used all their gas — well I sent them some flowers today — it was the least I could do.

Darling it approaches three — I'd better get to bed pronto — I love you my honey and I miss you every minute —

All me love

Jane

Remember the time honey we got off the train to get the pint and you had to tell MP it was for medicinal purposes only.

I still owe you $26 (and that's all!) for gin rummy — Love — Jane

Plains Hotel
Cheyenne, Wyoming
April 10 1945
Letter #63

Hello my darling; Honey I know this won't fit in your files but it's delightfully western — so Cheyenne-ish that I couldn't resist writing to you on it —

Did I tell you that last night when we arrived here there had been some misunderstanding about our reservations and they were expecting us today! Well, we finally got rooms — I was rather annoyed about the whole thing because they have the most comfortable chairs in the lobby — well ours was fairly decent except for the fact it had no sanitary facilities and to get them, or into them — or out to them — you had to call the desk and have them send up the key — well there were luckily no emergencies before they fixed us up this morning with a fine room with —

The decorative theme is Navajo as is the whole hotel — and I kind of like it — it's in the middle of the country that you found the vest —

Honey darling I love you and I want to keep on writing — but my penmanship is getting a little blurred from fatigue — so just know honey that even if it is only a note — my love is with you all the same —

Goodnite for now my darling

Jane

Plains Hotel Cheyenne, Wyoming
April 11, 1945 Letter #63

My dearest Honey Darling Chuck;

That was quite a salutation wasn't it — well it was because one or two words wouldn't have been enough — I felt all of them, and I could add a lot more ad infinitum — And do you realize, honey, that four days ago — five to you — our third months anniversary rolled around a quarter of that year we looked forward to so unhappily — I was thinking so much of it that day, but I missed saying it to you — but not for lack of love —

It is nine in the evening, and I'm in bed — the truth of the matter is I'm having a bout with what promises to be a fine case of the flu if I don't lick it first — now that I'm in bed, I feel better, but getting through the ward shows today was a miserable struggle — aching bones, cold chills, hot face and waves of nausea — the only thing that really bothered me though was that the last ward we played was composed of a group of boys who, half an hour before — had come in on the plane from Europe — all amputations — they hadn't been fixed up very well as yet and seemed a little conscious of it. I was in holy terror for fear I would lose all the food that wasn't there and the poor boys would think they had caused it — it might really have bothered them — absurd as the thought is to me — well all was fine and I think they felt as if they'd had a happy welcome — I hope so.

I daresay I'll feel better in the morning. I better as we have to catch a train at eight and do several shows in Denver tomorrow.

Honey, your letter about staying out there was very fine and very beautifully written. I shall always treasure it. It worries me because it makes it more dangerous for you when the chips are down — still, honey — if everyone had that same attitude, it would make it a lot better world for the boys now and for them to come home to — it leads to a sort of feeling of oneness with your fellow man — which could be a lot worse feeling — but, darling, do be careful, and don't try to create too much empathy.

The Evans stopped in a few minutes ago and offered to bring me a cup of tea — which I accepted with thanks. Since we've established friendly relations — there's not enough that they can do — it makes life much less nerve-wracking.

Honey, remember the time we stopped on the train — well today I found the liquor store where we got the pint and right across the street — was the Mayflower Bar — it has an apple green front — remember we went in for a beer at the bar, and there was a man who insisted on getting them for us — then we went back to the station, and I went into the ladies room and the M.P. — accosted you about the bottle, and he let you keep it because you said it was medicinally for me — Oh, honey, what memories I'll have in Chicago & New York —

Honey, Bob's address is 1337 AAF,
BO-ICD, ATC APO 467 AREA 5
c/o P.M., New York

Honey darling — I think I'll not wait for the tea & go to sleep before the old tummy does more nip-ups,so goodnite, my darling. All my love, Jane

April 12, 1945
Cosmopolitan Hotel Denver, Colorado
Letter #64

My Darling Chuck;

I am sitting here tonite in my hotel room listening to the broadcasts of Roosevelt's death — I can imagine how you must be feeling tonite — personally I think it is about the greatest shock I have

ever had in my life — to think that after all these years of fighting — that just at the brink of victory — this should have happened
to the people of the world — I realize now how very much a part of
the consciousness of all the people and the sort of leader I looked
to to guide us — he had become. It was as if he were a member
of my family and a part of my life — he's irreplaceable. I find my
sympathy for his family far overshadowed by my sympathy for the
world. If only we could hope that Truman would be able to stand
in even a small bit for what Roosevelt stood for — God — honey —
it's awful. The radio has been trying like mad all evening to build
him up — and that is as it should be because unless we all stand
behind him as he tries to carry out the President's plans — we will
have so much internal dissension that all will have been useless.

We were out at the Fort Logan today — I was in the PX standing at the counter when one of the men came in and said that the
President was dead — no one believed him — they keep saying it
isn't true — it's a rumor — are you sure — some people giggled
like the time I giggled when we saw that horrible accident by the
Hollywood bowl — people stood around the radio listening as if it
were a bad dream — of course our show was cancelled — thank
Heaven —

They have just told us of the church bells ringing in Denver
where we are — and now Governor Warren is speaking — what
must it have been like where you are — do the boys there feel as
lost as the people do here?

Well the way I look at it is that we've been sitting back and
letting all the work be done for us — now everyone has to put his
shoulder to the wheel and see if they can't do a little too but — not
only now but when we make the peace and later — we could have
a revolution but if we do it right — we could have a better country
for it — and I just have enough faith in us to kind of think we will.

One reaction that amazed me by its prevalence today was people's — especially soldiers saying — if only Wallace had been Vice
President! — over and over.

Oh, honey, I probably shouldn't keep raving on like this — it
won't make you feel any better — but by the time you get this the
news will be past. I thought you might like to see the front page of
the first extra — I'm putting it in another envelope.

Write me, darling —

All my love, Jane

#35
12 April '45
In Port 270 to go!

Dearest Honey:

Oh, love, guess what? That's right, we got some mail in today!! Such a happy ship it turned into in about five minutes! Course it was just the first installment and was only one week's worth. 12 March to 19 March. I also got one from you dated 15 Feb. the night that you were at Betty and Mike's. Can't understand just <u>what</u> happened to that one. At any rate, I read it along with the others and got a big kick out of them all.

That's expressed so inadequately. Big kick indeed! Honey, I really started <u>living</u> again when I began to read those letters. It's been so long, and it seemed as if you were growing away from me. I know it's silly, but doing nothing but waiting as we are your old mind gets to working overtime and has a bad effect on one. But when you would say things like you loved me and missed me and I was your post war plan, honey, I just expanded. The world suddenly seemed such a wonderful place to be in, and it seemed so damn nice to be alive and have a charming wife and somebody to come back to. From what I could gather, my mail seems to be coming through to you pretty regularly, at least that's good. I think we will get the rest of our back mail in a day or two, and then if it keeps coming I will feel more in touch with you. After all, if you can read a letter and know that the other person wrote it just a few days before, it makes you feel pretty close and not so terribly separated.

From yours and Mom's letters about the Seattle visit, it sounds pretty successful. I'm glad Mom could be down there. with you. She wrote a letter that was full of you. How lovely you were and pretty, and that you seemed to like her, too, and all in all it was mighty nice. Mom's a great old scout, nothing in the world wrong but a little too much possessive love, and, after all, all of us have it to some degree. I'm really happy you two got along so well. The she got to see Jack and Aunt Gen got out, too. Quite a clambake darling. The Patten menage doesn't seem to have changed much. Everyone making trains and coming in or going out of town. I know a disorganized life like that is a little above Mom's power to cope with, but as with me, honey, I like to have things bustlin' and ahustlin', if you know what I mean. Mostly I would like to be huggin' and alovin' you!! Get me, ain't I the forward thing, though?

I guess I gave you the idea in the letters you were getting about that time that I was pretty sure of getting home. Well, at that time it did look like that was the way it was going to be. Now however, the picture is a little darker. The sky hasn't completely blacked over however, and I might still manage to make part of that tour with you.

The one thing you asked me to do in regard to Bob Patten. I will certainly make a trip out there tomorrow and take Cass's camera with me and try and get some pictures. I also thought I might try and get a bronze plaque made like we did for some of our people. The only trouble the ship that did them for us has moved on to another port, but I may be able to get someone else to make me one. I know his family would like that, and I certainly will make every effort to get it done.

You will notice the enclosed junk. What there are follows: first is a label off a beer bottle, second is a wrapper off a can of crab meat, third is a page out of what appeared to be a field manual, and the last looks like a page out of a personal dairy or expense account. Now how we came by them. Cass, Berkeley and myself went on a hunt for some Japanese belly tanks the other day. We were going to make little sail boats out of them. Well we found them alright but they were so badly shot up that to fix them would be more trouble than they were worth. We noticed a big block house right behind them, and so we investigated that. Then we began looking over the caves and hills right behind the block hose. I am Not exaggerating honey, but I'll bet we saw five hundred bodies on that one hill. Most of them lay where they fell, of course they are mostly bones now, but they are still in uniform, and most of their gear is scattered around them. I tried in vain to find a pistol or a rifle but no luck. They all seemed to have gas masks around them, I don't get it. I know damn well we didn't use gas on them. Well, anyway, no one seemed to have ever been up there since the fighting passed by them. In these little caves they had all their rations spread around plus literally hundreds of empty sake bottles. I'm beginning to believe that a lot of these Banzai! charges of theirs are made when they are just plain stinkin'. At any rate, it was very interesting. We all had a stick and we poked around trying to find something that would be interesting. I brought back three little mess plates with

Japanese characters on the bottom. I thought we could use them for ash trays at El Rancho Fleen comes V day. Another little bottle, a wooden dog tag. Odds and ends like that. Remember a long time ago I said I was mailing a package, well I didn't do it, as I was trying to get the primer shot out of a shell I picked up. I couldn't get it done, so I'll make up a little batch of stuff I have including the Japanese book with the pictures and send it on to you tomorrow. After you look at it if you want to re-wrap it and send it up to mom to hold for us until that great day comes along. Okay?

Now for the hair raising part of the story. We had been on this hill all afternoon yelling Banzai! and whatever that cry was of Danny Kaye's in that picture where he captured all those enemy soldiers, something like Hoi Denizai!! Well, about five-thirty we went down to the road and thumbed a ride from a chief in a jeep. When we got in the car he said, "Say you guys aren't afraid of much are you?" Well of course we said, "Hell yes, why?" Well, he says, "A chief friend of mine was shot fifty yards up that hill just two weeks ago!!!!!" Brother! I'll give you my word, darling, that's my last trip for souvenirs on this island. I can think of better places to stop a Japanese bullet than on an island we have held for months. Not that they got any silver ones here either, but as you said about the bombing run we went on, no sense in crowding our luck. At that, I am glad we went up there, especially as no one shot at us. We found one big concrete pill box that was built between two great chunks of rock. It was about 1/2 the size of a Quonset hut and a big shell, I'd guess about 16 incher, had hit it right smack on one end. The result inside was a perfect shambles. Berk and I guessed there must be about thirty Japanese just blown to bits scattered around that room. Talk about a mess!! I like to think I might have done some of the same at Iwo, bet I did too! I am not really callous or blood thirsty, honey, only when it comes to the enemy, that's all. I'd like to cook hell out of 'em all.

Well, that was one afternoon on this island. Tomorrow promises to be another shambles, but of a different kind. Noel leaves for Uncle Sugar on Sunday the fifteenth, and the best day for his farewell party fell on Friday the 13th! So natch that's when it will be. I have a feeling it will be pretty liquid, I think the only people I have met yet who can keep up with the Navy in the drink dept is the fly-fly boys. Especially those out here, but then they have a perfect reason for doing it. They have a rather grim gag up there, every time someone takes off on a mission somebody always says, "Say Bart, where do you hide your whiskey, just in case!" They of course think it's funny as hell, but the sad part is the whiskey does get drunk up. We helped them drink up one boy's the other day who won't need it any more. Lost over the target — uggh! Tell those kid bros of yours to stay the hell to home, I never want to see either one of them out here! That's for sure. Well, honey, I won't get too drunk tomorrow, but I'll have fun. You said in the last letter that you were going to give me your next month's schedule, hope I get it before Noel takes off so I can give him where you will be on certain days. He is a 4.0 gem and no doubt about it. His wife and two year baby boy are waiting for him in S.F., what a reunion that will be. Only one that could surpass it would be the meeting of the Flynns!! Right?

Thanks for those pictures of Xmas day. I must say we all looked like real nice people. I already have them safely pasted into the scrap book. Course I showed them to everyone in the wardroom, and they all barked and made wolf growls in no uncertain terms. They also said to send you their love. They all feel I am too old and ugly to rate a beauty like you well, maybe they are right, but it's going to take a mighty husky gent to get you away from me!

Honey me darlin, it's now 0130, and I have to get up early to censor the flood of mail that will hit us, so I guess I'd better say goodnight for now. Wonder if you know just how much I love you? Still, it doesn't take any reading through the lines to see that I adore you. God speed the day that we can be together again, for good! all me love — Chas

Letter #64
Friday — April 13
Cosmopolitan Hotel Denver, Colorado

Dearest honey;

It is about five-thirty in the afternoon, and I am sitting here — with really a blizzard outside — listening to the radio — man-on-the-street broadcast on the President's death — we just came home from Fort Logan where we did an afternoon show for the Air Corps — convalescents — you know those boys seem to be pitched on a different key than the others — you do admire them so much but sometimes I get mad at them for being a little too "smartie-pants" — You know, it's amazing how terribly intelligent all these people on the radio sound — they are all inclined to be optimistic about "carrying-on" in the future — I hope they are right — I want to be, but I'm still a little scared about Truman — the paper today spoke of possible cabinet changes — we'll all have to just keep checking.

What an ordeal this morning was — Mr. Evans went off the beam today and how — Jackie Lee who is the best singer in the show was annoying to him over a period of time — she was slightly obstreperous but not as much as he thought — he finally got to blaming everything on her — I don't know what he said to the New York office about her, but whatever it was, it must have been very unjust because the New York office sent her her notice in definite and almost insulting terms. So he had the cast together this morning and launched into a disgraceful tirade against her — I was shocked — you couldn't reason with him at all — it was horrible. Really the man horrifies me — I'm almost afraid of him, even though I know that I can handle him alright — my psychology on his is good — but all I want to do is to get to New York and then be able to thumb my nose at him. Jackie can get along alright — she has too good a voice — she'll have a job tomorrow if she wants it but that any man should talk like that, horrifies me.

Your #33 letter was waiting for me this afternoon, darling written April 5 — That's not bad — poor darling — I know you're getting tired of sitting there — waiting and not knowing — but at least darling, it makes me feel nice to know you're safe. I'd be going crazy if I thought you were up at Okinawa — with those ships being sunk like mad — Oh, honey, I hope so that something good for you — for us — will come. Each letter that comes, I think it will have some news in it, and I get so excited — thinking you might get a leave — but still no news is good news — and you are safe there — which is definitely something —

I have just decided to eat up here tonite — then I can get some work — accounts and washing done that has been haunting me for days — perhaps go down with one of the girls later and have a drink — perhaps not — but to bed early and look out at the snow can you feature it there darling — snow —

I'm having my hair darkened a bit in the morning — it's almost platinum now, and I don't like it — it won't be yellow — just darker —

Honey — in case I haven't mentioned it, I love you — with all my heart —

So very much LOVE, Jane

15 April '45
In Port — 267 to go —

Honey me darlin':

I have a feeling that this will probably end up as a very snafued letter. Lots of things on my mind and all scrambled up. First though, let's get one thing straight — I sure love you like the dickens!! Now then, our mail is finally starting to come. I got two letters today of the 5 and 7 of April. Course there still are eight missing between Walla-Walla and Denver, but I daresay they will be along tomorrow. While we will have to admit that you have fallen off the letter-a-day schedule, you are still doing damn well. The one on the 6th of April was #60, so when I get the missing ones I'll have sixty letters in eighty-six days. Darling, I'll never complain about that, in fact I think that busy as you are its damn wonderful. You said you had my letter #31, so you see you are just twice as good as me when it comes to writing. But just because I am not so good please don't stop writing me honey. If you're tired, just a note is wonderful. You see, you do see new things and places and stuff so just a commentary on your activities and something about missing me would keep me very contented indeed. Well, I qualify that statement, as contented as I can ever be this far away from you.

But here I ramble on about letters and being separated when the most awful and important fact is before us that we have been separated by death with the greatest President that ever ruled these United States. The news reached us first on an early morning broadcast on Friday the 13th. Naturally it was the twelfth back there. Berk woke me up to tell me, and darling, I was floored. Seemed absolutely unbelievable somehow. He had so much of the future destiny of this tired old globe resting on his shoulders; he had such universal respect and such a fine reputation and knowledge with and of the little people of this world. I really feel, as do most of the others aboard, that it was a personal loss, like one of the family.

Strangely enough though, I don't feel that this will slow down the war effort, or the speed with which we will take our objectives. Rather I believe that everyone is going to do his damnedest to "Put one across for Rock." I know we went out to the bomber strip that day, and most of our friends were taking off on a strike. Most of them said just before they hauled "This one's for Roosevelt," or, "Watch me burn those bastards tonight." They did just that, and I think that is the reaction all around the world. A lot of people really loved that guy, and they know how much he wanted peace to come back to this old earth and a fair shot at the four freedoms, and I'm damn sure that he won't be let down now. I'd like to make one thing clear to you though, honey, great as our loss is, it's not irreparable. Any man with the foresight and vision of Roosevelt would have laid plans for just such an emergency. He was a capable man, and as such surrounded himself with the best brains that the country could produce. Just as a ship suffers a loss when its captain is killed, so have we. But by the same token when a ship is unfortunate to lose its Captain then another man steps forward. The engines turn up just as many knots, the guns shoot just as hard and as fast. The ship can still do battle and still come out victorious, because it's a unit, not a personal vehicle. Just so, the country can override the loss of a great leader and still come on punching. The only place an experienced captain's loss will be felt is when the water gets shallow and knowledge of ship-handling is the only saving factor. The next in line probably will do the right thing, but only the situation presenting itself will prove it.

Personally, I feel sorry for President Truman, he has grabbed a wild-cat by the tail, and he has got to kill it. If he lets it go, it will claw him. I do think though, that if everyone in the country realizes that it is up to all of us to give him a fair shot at this job, help him take in the slack, and above all don't feel that we are backing a lost cause, then, and only then, will things work out the way Roosevelt wanted them and would have had them.

Well, that concludes Bro. Flynn's sermon for tonight. I meant everything I said, but I seemed to be getting wound up! Your last letter was from Denver, and you had called Bobby's mother and found out he was all right. I'm so damn glad to hear that. You know, that letter I wrote him in S.F. I never got an answer to. Naturally in times like these when you don't hear for a while you begin to wonder if one came up silver. I'll get a letter off to him tomorrow

at the address you gave me and see if we can't re-establish contact.
Sounds as if he is doing a damn fine job, what with the air medal
and coming up for the DFC. Just was remembering today, after I
got your letter, how devoted he was to you and how I always said to
him that it was all right for him to love you — but from a distance!
He was a great boy, think of the lovely times we will all have shooting the breeze over a stein when this is over!

You also said that you would be in Ohio and what was Allie's
address, (by the way I asked Berk about the address and he said
to be sure and call her Allie and not Alice, as she loathes it!) well,
here it is

Mrs. H. C. Berkeley Jr. c/o V. H. Wilshire 2325 Ridgeway Road
Dayton, 9, Ohio.

Also, I'll bet a plugged nickel that you didn't send an autographed
picture to his sister-in-law. Now did you? It would really be nice if
you could, so try for pappy will you, honey?

Mary Wilshire
Westover School
Middlebury, Conn.

I'm enclosing a letter I had from Allie in answer to a page I
enclosed with one of Smiley's letters right after we got down here.
I just reassured her that Smiley was all right and had done a
damn fine job when things got a little sticky. Her reference to the
"Bloomin' hero" was the fact that he was ably pitching ammunition
over the side from a burning ready locker. Couldn't tell her at the
time, of course, but it's so long ago now that no harm can be done,
so I'll drop her a line.

He really is a great lad. The horrible proximity in which we
have lived the better part of two years would put most people at
each other's throats. Sure we occasionally snap at each other, but
all in all we get along beautifully. If the only thing I get out of this
war is the knowing of Smiley, then I can truthfully say that the
time wasn't wasted.

Well that's enough of the roomie and his wife and family. Now,
how are you? Bearing up? I was relieved to hear that my days of
prospective father-hood are still in the future. Not that I wouldn't

like a couple, but not right now, thank you. Say, honey, there may
be something in that day system at that. I'd love to give it another
try, sometime soon preferably!! I miss you like hell, honey, not
complaining, just stating.

You also said that it was all set if you wanted to go across with
the show. Baby, that is one thing you are going to decide for yourself.
Course, if I got home before and got to see you would be one thing,
but if I was in the process of coming and you wasn't there — not so
good. Still, if you want to do it, my hat's off to you and more power
to you. I know how important your works is and what a hell of a
lot of good you are doing. This whole damn war is a little bigger
than for us to figure it around to our own advantage. The only one
other thing though to be considered is this. When you hit N.Y. and
should somebody like you, (who could help it?) that's when the new
fall shows are going into production. God knows, darling, that this
is the Golden Era of the theater in New York. Every theater has
a show, and nearly all are clicking, if I can believe Smiley's New
Yorker. Might be that it would be the best time in the world to give
it a good whirl if that is what you want. As I say though, punkin,
it's up to you. Do what you think is the right thing and I'm with
you up to a jillion percent. Still, you won't be in N.Y. for a spell yet,
and undoubtedly I will know what I am to do by that time. You
managed to stave them off for a while once before, should I be lucky
enough to get a thirty-dayer we might be able to whip something
up. Wouldn't it be fun to spend it in the east together? Dear God,
don't even let me dream of it.

Speaking of that, what with a bad dream the other night and
a day of no mail, I managed to give myself a bad time for a few
minutes. I could see you still getting mail from those people from
last summer out there and you answering, but nothing and no time
for Charley. I remembered the little cross and the ring, and, baby,
I was miserable for a while. Then my better sense came to the fore.
I said to myself, either Jane loves you, or she doesn't. Either you
trust her, or you don't. And either she loves you, judging by our
last few days together, or she is the best actress in the world. And
we both know damn well that ain't so — yet! So then I snapped
out of it, and life became a nice place to be in again. Still, darling,
I'm not all dope, and I do know that the ice we were skating on
when I first came home was very thin indeed. Still, one can forget
a lot about a person in a year and more than that can remember

what they want to recall. We didn't really get back to a Jane and Chuck relationship until about ten days before it was time for the ship to leave S.F. From there on out it was beautiful, and I think you caught the being in harmony feeling that we had. I don't know whether that feeling has dimmed or was only a thing that built itself up without a real foundation as far as you were concerned. But as for me, each day away from you strengthens it and makes it a lot more durable and workable than anything we have ever known before in our lives.

I'm not trying to reopen old wounds, darling, neither am I going to be an ostrich about this life we lead. I am so much in love with you that I would do anything you say that would make you happy, including giving you up, if that was what you wanted. I know that doing the sort of thing you are now you meet a lot of nice guys. And I mean just that. The memory of old Chas doesn't get any clearer as the months go by and not that I'm not egoist enough to believe that it does. On top of that, Old Chas is a pretty applicable term. By the time this is over it's going to be a little late in life to try and make a big name for myself in any of the Horatio Alger formulas. I'm going to have to play the field and try and hit the daily double. Now, I'm not selling myself short, I still believe very strongly in me, and personally I think that I will do all right. But the incontestable fact remains. I probably will be reassigned here; you probably will go to Europe on your deal. Both things being so, it might be the end of the war before I see you gain. A bad, horrible thought, but nevertheless, pretty possible. Now, the point is this: should you, in the next year or so, meet some gent who had more concrete possibilities than I do of being the kind of guy you would like to spend the rest of our life with, not forgetting that there might be a silver one somewhere in that pile they have; should you find such a guy and really mean it and believe it, then, darling, I hope you will grab the shot.

See, punk, you married me when you were hardly dry behind the ears. I've given you some very bad times, and with the state of the world when this is over, perhaps a good many more. The only thing I can really hold out to you can be summed up in two little points. You'll never lead a dull life; you'll always be adored.

Sorry I got onto this, but it was troubling me when I started to write this letter. Facts are sometimes bad and the truth when unvarnished is sometimes not too palatable, but it's a lot better to think them out, either out loud or on paper, than let them ferment inside of one. As for me, I've thought it out. You are my girl the rest of my life, win, lose or draw. I also understand that a few years can make a lot of difference in people, and if, when this is over, we don't see eye to eye then the only honest thing to do is to admit it.

I'll have to admit though, darling, that should we get back together ever again and there seemed to be a rift in the marital skies, I'd do my damnedest to stitch them up before I ever let you go. Should you decide before then, I'd have no recourse but to wish you all the luck in the world, and mean it! Times, viewpoints and people's philosophies change, and nothing exists that can be done about it.

Again, sorry, honey, this was pretty somber talk. I only know I wanted to talk about it to you and with you. You see, my kind of love can understand just about everything except playing second fiddle or being patronized. Left out? Yes. Scrapped? Yes. But never a cold deal off the bottom of the deck.

Darling I've been writing this for two hours and a half. It's now 0200, being as I have to get up at 0600 I guess I'd better knock it off. I could say that I don't expect you to understand all I have written, or why, but the truth is that I know you'll understand not only everything I have written and the reason therefore, but also the things that I haven't said.

Mommy, I love you. Complete, without reservations, without logic or rhyme or reason. Just all of me for you today and tomorrow and the rest of my life. I hope that sounds dramatic — I meant it to be. Not for effect, but because I mean it. Keep writing, darling, you are my only normal life communication channel. Please miss the guy who always sends you —

all me love, Chas

American Red Cross
Bickley Field Denver, Colorado
April 16, 1945Letter #66?

Dearest honey darling Chuck

Well, what do you think; I got hold of a typewriter. That is one good thing about being in this Red Cross Lounge. I spied it sitting over here and found out on inquiry that it was for anyone's use. It doesn't work very well but it's a pleasure to use it anyway. I keep wondering as I write each letter to you when you are going to receive it. You get mail so seldom that it is getting almost as discouraging to me as it is to you. I keep wondering how many dozens of letters behind me you are...in receiving them I mean/ But I'll just keep writing honey and someday they'll catch up with you. AND then everything will be alright.

I have sort of slipped up the last couple days on writing you. I think it's just because I get so darned sick of writing by hand. I am not fussing. I couldn't carry the typewriter around with me anyway but after all these years of being used to it, my communicative nature can't adjust itself to the slower medium.

Can you believe it darling...there is actually a foot of snow here and it is still coming down. AND I lost my galoshes on the train to Spokane and have never bothered to replace them. I didn't even go out of the hotel all day

Saturday but there is plenty inside so I didn't suffer. Saturday was the day of the President's funeral and also the day of my terrible hair experience. It was so white, remember I told you that I was going to have it darkened a little...well the stuff they put on it turned it a sort of dirty color of brown and they had to bleach it all out again. When they got to what I thought was a golden blonde, I told them to stop but the funniest thing happened. When it was washed and dried, it had darkened again and it was about the color of your hair. It was a pretty shade but it definitely looked terrible on me. Well, by that time I had spent six hours in the beauty parlor and I went upstairs and found Pat Walker and we got out the Roux bleach of our own and started all over again. And we did it...it is now just the shade I wanted but it took a whole day and a lot of bad moments.

Hello again darling...there was a short pause there to go to dinner and now I have half an hour before I have to start getting made up for the evening show and I can employ the time very well writing to my honey.

I went to dinner again yesterday with Bob's family; they are really very fine and they lean over backwards but they literally kill you with too much kindness...The first time I was there it took me days to recover and it is going to be the same this time. I spent the day yesterday doing the little domestic things, washing and ironing and listening to the radio...they were to pick me up about six. They wanted to take me to their club for dinner. Well,

I thought I would probably get away early but no...the club was one of Italian American businessmen and it was a dinner dance. I never expect to see so many Italians together again outside of Italy. They are certainly lusty eaters, drinkers and laughers and dancers. It was a great bunch of families? All relatives to the others I swear...all of them seemingly very prosperous. I will be frank to say though that I nearly died of boredom and I could hardly relax because they were really showing me off all the time (I was the only blonde there.) Well, of course they stayed until the last...and I started to go to sleep like the horrible time at the Cirque room when you got so mad at me...remember. I held out and at twelve, silently thanking God for the curfew, I thought...now I'll be able to go to my lovely room and GO TO BED. But no. They drove me out to their house and started pouring Southern Comfort in me. Now there is nothing bad about that but I was tired. Well I finally got home at a quarter after one and I had to be up at the crack of dawn this morning. Not only that, but I was the center of a fully hatched set of plans to go to a nightclub tonite///It just grew and before I knew it, I was involved. BUT the fact that we found when we got out here tonite that we had an evening show gave me a reason to call and cancel it. I really adore them and they've been nice to me beyond all reasoning...they seem to just adore me too...they sort of hang on my every word and Mrs. Marinaro is really grand...loads of fun and a very good looking woman...but it's just too much for me/ I can't take it when I have to keep up a schedule like I do...Our day today will have been nearly twelve hours long and it ain't easy work/ Tomorrow is a day I wish I could sleep through. We leave for Colorado Springs at eight in the morning, do our shows, leave there at nine in the evening, go to Pueblo and at midnight catch the sleeper for Salina, Kansas and arrive Wednesday...by Sunday we will have gone to Abilene and Topeka and be in Lincoln...then the next few days aren't so bad. But no social activities definitely...I shall investigate the town within the range of time and then get to bed. Kansas is a dry state anyway.

Darling, you must write Bob a letter, and be sure to tell him how much I enjoyed seeing his family. I still haven't seen the shopping district of Denver and I guess I won't now.

By the way, honey, did you receive my letter asking what Alice's address was? We will be there pretty soon. On second thought, it's in one of your letters and all I have to do is go through the files.

Well, sweet darling it is just about time to get dressed. I wonder where you are tonite...I mean exactly what you are doing and if you have had any news of your future. I keep hoping against hope that I will have some word on it from you when I get back to the hotel. If not, I'll have to wait for Wednesday for mail so I'm crossing my fingers.

Before too long darling, the war will be over and we will be together again...it seems like ages but it has to come and until it does, I am loving you.

Goodbye for now my honey. I'll see you soon.

All my love

Jane

I'm wearing my Navy pin.

#37

18 April 1945

In Port —

Dearest honey;

Gad zooks, when we get our mail, we really get it. I guess all those dispatches we sent blasting hell out of the coordinator really resulted in someone saying "Now see here lads, anything for the GAMBLE put it right on through" What this all builds up to is that I got a letter from you at ten o'clock this morning that was mailed in Cheyenne Wyoming at ten o'clock in the morning exactly five days before!!!! I don't know if that sounds so terrific to you, but to me it's wonderful. Don't you see darling, I can now write you letters and ask a question and within a couple of weeks get an answer. Makes me feel that we aren't so immeasurably far apart at all! I think one got skipped on me, but it will show up tomorrow, I hope. Also there are still eight missing from the last of last month and the first of this, however I have a feeling they are coming surface, probably from Pearl. Ah, well, life is wonderful. Just keep writing cookie, and that's all I ask.

I finally got your package off yesterday, was going to send it airmail, but it was a mere $3.87 so I sent it first class for $.98. Viva El Rancho Fleen. Besides I gotta be economical. We play a little modest poker around here once in a while, and I have been tucking a little away. The other night out at the B-29 boys house though someone brought out the galloping ivories and ZIP — there went all my winnings. What the hell, I ain't going anywhere, and I still have a few bucks. I only draw about a hundred a month now, and what with a few mess bills, laundry, cigs and a few chit cooks at the club now and then I don't have much left with which to gambol or gamble either. And besides there ain't any oOf the former anyhow! And I can't do any of the latter until I get some more pay, and that ain't for a while, so don't worry about me going to hell in a bucket!! Whew!!

You said you were worried about spending so much on clothes, hell honey, shoot the works. Just don't strap yourself if you decide to take a crack at New York, but then you would need the clothes anyway, so what the hell. The dress you sketched for me the other night looked awful cut indeed, but the funniest thing. You forgot to tell me what color it was! Minor detail anyhow. But just for fun, what color is it?

I was so happy you remembered Bobby's family lived in Denver and got to see them. If I'm not too sleepy when I finish this I'll drop him a line. Sounds like you had a very nice day, I hope you had fun. That's good news that he is still going strong and I'm glad he got the Air Medal and is up for the DFC. I'd better get going on that Navy Cross or I won't even be able to compete for my own wife's hand. Which reminds me of Commander Clay. He moved his flag to another ship right after we got here and he is now in this current little go-round and very warm for May it is too. That was a good one to miss.

I am also glad you finally remembered to tell me that fatherhood ain't for me, leastwise not at the present time. Would have been a bit awkward to say the least wouldn't it darling? Not nearly so awkward as another pregnancy though at this time huh? I'm just kidding pudding, joke, joke! You wrote that letter from bed with a case of incipient flu, baby I pray that you knocked it out that night, please keep me posted. I'll say a little prayer for you and I'll bet you will be all over it very soon. Don't overdo again, sugar, You are the only wife I've got, at the present time, at any rate, and I don't want you to get sick on me 'Cause it's a hell of a long swim back to you!

Your reminiscing about Cheyenne and the little bar and then saying Chicago and New York and Samsom — Ithaca!! I got to remembering our little apt in that house and the stewed chickens and the steaks and the fireplace with the logs, millions of em for three bucks!!! And wonderful Sundays and taking Giddy up to the cemetery and sitting listening to that little radio with my arm around you and the late Sat night dinners and how cold that God-amned bed could be to crawl into! Honey, honey, I can think back on so many fine things and experiences we have shared.

I have been wondering just what your reaction to that last long letter was. I'll bet you said I was either nuts or roaring drunk. Actually I was neither, but I sure missed the hell out of you and loved you so much it was a physical pain. Everything I said I meant though, so if thou would'st take me up on it —

Last night one of the Bombardiers from the '29s came down to spend the evening with us. Nice big lad name of Clark. His wife is sweating it out in Hollywood on Ogden drive somewhere and he about next high in missions after Noel. Clark should finish his missions within the next month or six weeks. Well we had dinner and then saw the show and then sat around and talked. Everyone finally went to bed but Cheefu and myself and then he said he would like to see the pictures that all the other boys had been raving about. (the others who had been down to the ship) Well I hauled out the big album and he was a wonderful audience. He sighed and moaned and whistled at just the right places. As for me, I was about one just ahead of a sheer bursting of pride. You are so damn pretty, and such a wonderful gal — well, I just looked over at that big picture of you sitting on the table and you seemed to say in a mocking sort of way "Not really all that, darling" — so I kinda haulted in midstride, so to speak.

Well anyway we thoroughly discussed you and then his wife and little boy and then Cheefu turned in so we sat until about two-thirty and finished up the war, the political situation, sex, lack of it, post-war plans etc etc. Very good guy to talk to. About thirty, 6'3" but pretty thin, about 150. Hell of a guy though. Hope he makes it all right.

I don't know if I told you before but Cass got a "Dear John" letter the other day. He apparently always thought that he would marry this little gal when it was all over and she writes him one of these nice trite things, "Hope we can still be friends, and I will think of you a lot etc" Well poor old Cassso took it pretty big. Insisted I read it, I didn't want to, but he made me. Well today he screws his courage to beyond the sticking point and whips off the acknowledgment of the new status-quo. Poor little Cisco. He is really such a baby. I had to read the reply, too, he insisted on that. Well it was all right but the old trite corn was there too "Let's just forget about being friends now, but if the time ever comes when you need a real friend, old Bill will be right on hand" etc. It's really tragic-comic because Cisco takes it so big. I guess he really did like her a lot, but I dare say the shock won't be fatal, he is pretty rugged.

Today, as everyday, I had a sun bath and then a good long swim off the forecastle. I'm really turning into a bronzed thing of beauty, honey, except I'm going to have to start working my old tum down again. This indolent life is hard on my figure, especially when there is all that liquor on the beach just waiting to be drunk up. I only go over about every third day actually, but ever since we got hit we have had beer on board and I consume a few bottles of that a day. I'm not exactly obese though darling, just plumped up a little. Before you ever see me again I will be the slim smiling youth you knew of old.

Hey Mommy how about a couple of snapshots of you and your troupe and such stuff. Migad, someone must have a camera of sorts. Please send a few little ones out. I thought those at Christmas were very good, but I've about worn them out just looking at them. Concentrate mostly on you too, will you darling?

Oh honey, the awfulest thing. I just looked in my drawer for a pack of camels and I saw the best little bottle of all three had been left out of the package I mailed yesterday. Well, I have a little bauble I have been making for you so when I send that I will enclose the little blue bottle. It's really quite cute and if we ever settle down again could have a little stopper fitted and used as a perfume bottle on your dressing table.

Honey do you suppose the day will ever come again when I can lay in bed and watch you getting ready for bed I suppose that is merely wishful thinking, but I would dearly love to watch you tonight. Being as I can't do that I'll just tell you that I adore you and send you a big smacker along with
all me love.
Chas
X Here 'tis!
P.S. Wrote the Lathams a note this aft and gave them Jack's address — do you ever write them?

LS MFT-SR-SF-SBS!!!
Vancouver, Wash. 3700 Main St.
Wednesday, April 18, 1945

Ol' Man Chuck;

I can still see you going round the corner in the hallway of the Mayflower hotel in L.A. having goodbye with a big smile and a foreboding heart, and me too damn sick with a cold and flu to realize that you might be disappearing forever. But it didn't turn out that way, and it is not going to do so either, so just keep your chin up and in, and I'll put the cow in the barn every night so that when you get back we can have a couple of glasses of fresh milk, and maybe a little buttermilk too.

I showed your letter to a couple of friends of mine, and each of them, after reading it, said, "That son-in-law of yours must be quite a guy, I'd like to meet him." So I have a couple of dates for you already.

Your letter #34 passed through here yesterday. I forwarded it to Jane at Topeka, Kansas. She will be there Saturday, the 21st. Just keep the letters coming to this address, and I will see that they are promptly sent on the way to Jane.

Everybody seems to be pretty well around these parts. Mary is still at home with Mother (Hazel) and is still undecided as to what she will do. One day it's Red Cross appointment, and the next day she is about ready to marry Sam. By the way, did you ever meet him? I never had, and I wonder what he is like. Maybe you can tell me. Jane has met him, says he is a nice enough fellow but does not recommend him for Mary. So if you have met him, let me know what you think of him.

I suppose that Jane has told you that Buddy got bumped on pilot training and is now in Florida taking special training as a radar navigator on a night fighter which he volunteered for after getting bumped out of pilot training. He expects to finish training in July and then will become a guinea pig in the new type of service. I don't know much about it, it is something new, so the guinea pig element will be ever present. Bobby will also finish about July, I think, so they will both be ready for active service about the same time, and I expect to see them get plenty of it too, as the Japanese angle may last quite awhile. We have been whaling hell out of them, but there still are a lot of them left, and there still is a long way to go. Uncle Joe and his boys could shorten the affair a lot, and I fully expect to see them jump in as soon as they get ready. The Russians want some warm water ports on the Pacific, and the best way to insure themselves of getting them is to move in and take them from Japan, and then stay on indefinitely in the taken areas. Just squat there, and nobody will be very anxious to go in and move them out. So o o o o, I think Uncle Joe will get busy when he gets all set. Imagine anyone in the US, three years ago, referring to "Uncle Joe." Now the newspapers regularly refer to him in the editorial columns as Uncle Joe, and everyone knows who is meant by that one. But they haven't done so far yet as to call him G.I. Joe.

We have lost our President. A lot of people have been jubilating over his death, people that would not know there was a war on if they could get all the gasoline, meat and butter they want. That is all that the war means to a lot of them, they can't get this, and they can't get that. They have no kin in active service, they don't know what it is all about, but nevertheless they rant and rail at a man who did and who moved in time to preserve their property and wealth for them and to preserve the American way of life which we would have lost if Hitler and Mussi had been allowed to continue to grind out the little fellows. I expect to see Truman recede somewhat from some of Roosevelt's advanced positions, and there will be great rejoicing among the economic royalists UNTIL they find that he will back the Unions just as strongly as FDR did, then the axe will be unsheathed for him too. Well, I guess I can't win the war by moralizing so had better get at something else. Take good care of yourself, Chuck, remember the promised fresh milk! Drop me a line when you can, and tell me about Sam too, if you have met him, that is, when you were in Calikkyfornikky where the Native Sons are not taught to "shake it" as California "liquid" sunshine is "good to the last drop." Dominus Vobis cum, Chuck. Dad

Abilene, Kansas
April 19, 1945 Letter #67

Hello Chuck Darling;

Here we are in Eisenhower's home town — and it's a very lovely little place — I had expected Kansas to be grim — but I'm seeing it in the spring, and it's really beautiful — so green — and yesterday when we got to Salina — there were the first leaves of spring — I was so thrilled because we'd seen nothing but barren branches and snow until yesterday — the flowering shrubs are coming into bloom, and the air is heavy with their scent — there's a new feeling in the atmosphere — and just as I had my wardrobe all organized, I have to start thinking about spring clothes again —

I have spent the last half hour trying to copy out this darned itinerary for you and the family — Now I'll have to make another one for your mother. I'm sending the carbon to you because you won't really be using it as the family will — but I thought that when you thought of me — this next month — you could now place me.

We played at Fort Reilly today — it's ages away from Abilene — but that is really an army post — with gorgeous grounds and houses. It's like a small city. I kept thinking — wouldn't it be nice if Chuck were stationed someplace like this and we had a house!

Darling, I've been a bad writer — I've missed two days, but our schedule has really been <u>bad</u> and will be for a few more days Tuesday morning our train left Denver at 8:30 for Colorado Springs. We arrived there about ten, and we had to wait in the station two hours for the army! It seems the special service lieutenant had been committed to the psycho ward that very morning — when they finally got that straightened out the driver they sent for us was in such a hurry that he took a shortcut and got stuck in the mud — When we finally did get there, we played six ward shows, and believe me, they were hard ones — The boys there were suffering from that "trench rot" in their feet — most of them had lost their toes and those who hadn't were barely hobbling around or had them black and rotting. Then we came back to the station, caught the train to Pueblo — due to the floods they've been having here — the train to Salina was late — so I didn't get to bed until after midnite — at Salina we had two hours at the hotel to get cleaned up — did three wards and a theatre show — Poor Rollie — they had no piano in the wards, and poor Rollie can hardly walk today from pumping — and I had to hold the thing while she was playing so it wouldn't slide across the floor — this morning we left for here. We had an hour to clean up and went the 30 miles to Fort Reilly — where we did two theatre shows — and what a wonderful audience they were! Now we're back at the hotel in Abilene — and, darling — just writing about this has been too much for me — I'm so tired I'm about to drop — so I'll say goodnite, darling — I love you — please write as often as you can — The letters haven't been so frequent lately —

All my love, my darling — Jane

#38
In Port —
21 April 1945
261 to go—.

Dearest honey:

Oh honey, God love a duck to say that yesterday was a big day for me would be putting it mildly! I got nine letters from you, plus the page one of the Post and a Postcard from the Marcus Whitman hotel. Honey I guess you know by this time that am very much in love with the little wifling, but I don't know any time when I really loved you quite as much or as deeply as I did when I came back from the club and found all that mail. Berk and I had gone over early and borrowed a jeep to take some pictures of Bob Patten's grave. We could only find one R.A. Patten, 200-444. He is in the 4th Marine cemetery grave 1040. The sgt. In charge of the records said he must have been interred somewhere else and moved later as this is a very late grave. It wasn't marked as Lt. J.g. but it did have a navy insignia painted on the marker. I wish you would write to your mom or dad and have them contact Bob Patten Sr. and check to see if that is his file no. 200-444. I don't think I will be able to get prints made here but I do think I will be able to get the film developed and then I can send the negatives to either you or Hazel and have them made up. It's really a nice place, right near the beach and an arch over the entrance and a large flag-pole and flowers in the center of it. Be sure and let me know about the number though honey as I'd hate to send the wrong pictures. If this isn't his grave though, then he isn't here and must have been buried at sea. I'm pretty sure this is his grave though.

Well after we got the pictures we took the jeep back and then dropped into the O club. We were so filled with coral dust that a drink was absolutely in order. We had a few and then who walks in but Berk's Fraternity President that he hadn't seen for years. A Lt. Comd'r and exec on a D.E. they had quite a clambake and then

I found a friend of mine that I first met when we came in here. A Navy Doc. And a great friend of Parks. He is attached to the Marines however. Well he left here a little while ago for a deal and I heard rumors that his outfit hadn't been used. So I took a tour around the club and damned if I didn't find him. He was so glad to see us and we had a lot to talk about. He had been getting mail from his wife right along but hadn't been able to write since the seventh of March. He said he last couple of letters were nearly frantic. Poor kid going out of her mind. I dropped her a note this morning and said Hi and that I had run into our old friend "Tex" at the club yesterday and he had promised to write soon. So at least her mind will be somewhat quieted down. I shudder to think of those other people. You know how you get when the mail is a little held up.

At any rate both he and Berk's friend spent the night with us. They both went to the movie with the others while Smile and I read our mail. When they came back down the Doc said "Why the beautiful smile Charley" and so I told him what a great batch of mail I'd just had from the most wonderful wife in the whole world. Everyone got a great laugh, but baby, you will never know just how happy and thrilled I was to get those letters. I fully realize just how damn busy you are, and how tired you get with all those shows but honey you would feel well repaid for the time spent if you could have seen the happy daze you had me wandering around in today. You have also made me realize that I am a stinker averaging only about one letter over three days while you have done two every three days. I am going to try and write every other day from now on. They may not be long masterpieces, but at least I'll try and keep them from being dull. For a while I was concerned about giving Jack trouble forwarding them, but then I thought that probably some gal does it and even if not he probably is only too happy to do it. Maybe he even thinks it's nice of a husband to write so many letters to his wife. I finally found your schedule for April and think I could get this to you at Springfield, Mo, but I guess it's best not to take chances on the vagaries of over-Pacific mail and to send it to him.

Matter of fact we are due for a blow sometime in a day or so. Looks like it might be a pretty good one, at least enough so that the mail schedule might be thrown off, so I'll take no chances and send this to Jack too.

Besides your letters I had four from Mom, one from Hazel, two Fraternity newsletters and one from J. Buckley Fairweather. It was awful cute. When I answer it tomorrow I will send it on to you. The newsletters were not so good, besides Dave they announced two others killed in action, bringing the toll for that one chapter to 12. That seems like a hell of a lot for one house, doesn't it? Major Frank Garretson got the Legion of Merit for his work on Saipan, he had already gotten the Navy cross for Tarawa. Also Dave Kellogg got the Legion of Merit and he has already received the Bronze Star. Looks like I'd better get off my arse and catch a new can. I'm awfully undecorated, darling. Do you suppose you could stand to be seen with me. I won't even make Lt. for a couple of months yet. Gosh, I guess I'm goofing off! Speaking of being seen with me I guess that there still is a pretty good chance of that thirty days after all. Seems that some new dope has been put out by the bureau and I am sure we qualify under it. That is if they don't hold on to the emergency clause and reassign us here. Matter of fact I think it looks better now for us than at any time so far. I don't want you to get to needling yourself, but a lot of stranger things have happened. So say a prayer and hold the thought.

Radio from the States just announced that Nimitz has released the dope on the sinking at Okinawa. Pretty damn bad. I knew several fellows on those ships. I've also talked to some that have come back down from there. Strictly rugged, guess that was one we were well out of, they had to clip us to stop us though. Must be quite a go-round up there.

You will notice the enclosed ballad. Berk got it from his pop yesterday and I thought it was pretty cute Then I tried it out loud this morning to myself, and I says to myself as follows, "Hell, charley, that would make a wonderful talking song for the kid," to be done in certain circles only, of course. It is a bit on the salty side, but I don't think offensively so. The only line I think might be softened a bit is in the third stanza,

"To earn her board lying in bed" I think it could be changed to something like "Much easier for getting ahead" The rest of it I think is not too bad and it's a very catchy thing. I thought you might be able to use it for small groups as in wards. Course I'm not trying to tell you what kind of material to use, but I thought you might like it.

Honey, I was going to make this such a nice long and interesting letter but I find that my eyes are drooping and I have to get up at six because I have the early duty in the morning. It is now approaching 1:00 so I'll only get five hours at the best. Tell you what. I'll knock off now and write again tomorrow.

Let me just end by saying that nothing made me happier than all those wonderful letters from you. I love you so damn much darling. Might even be safe to say I adore you. Okay, I'll say it. I adore you! Keep missing me punkin and maybe I'll see you soon.

All me love —

Chas

Dear honey, These are some of the best cartoons I've seen in "Yank" Love, Chas

XXXXXX

American Red Cross
Topeka, Kansas
Winter General Hospital
April 21, 1945
Letter #68

Dearest honey darling beloved Chuck;

Sweet — you are going to murder me for writing on this paper so much but in the places where I find myself and I have time to write-it is pretty hard to be consistent about the size of the sheets. Right now we have an hour and twenty minutes before the show so I thought I would take advantage of it as I have a pretty definite feeling that when I get back to the hotel tonite, all I'll be capable of is collapse. We arouse at the bright and happy hour of five this morning — took the bus for Topeka at six — we've now done four ward shows, eaten and will do a full show at 7:30-all I am pointing toward is that bed in the hotel. You know I have really come to something when I can't wait to get to bed — just to sleep — I can hear you saying that — by the way darling — the subject of what I made the crack about — there have been several dissertations from you — on the problem and my dealing with it — don't worry honey — I'm pure as the driven snow and I intend to stay that way —

This trip is really an exhausting grind — definitely no fun aside from the interest of seeing the country — and I'm beginning to abhor Mr. Evans again more and more day by day — but if I plan carefully

I can do my job well and get enough sleep — but I'm determined to stay with it until we get to Florida — then willy-nilly I either go overseas or quit. I'm going to have to start saving more money though. It's so much more expensive than I thought it would be —

I received your #34 letter today — this is #68 which — a coincidence — is the double mark — it was the letter written before and after the boy fell down the hatch. Poor kid — that's a darn mean thing of his wife to do a thing like that to him — I hope to heaven they have sent down your mail by this time — you should have dozens of letters from me if the last one you had was written from Portland — Gosh honey, that was about seven weeks ago — it makes us seem so out of touch. Probably you will get my later ones first. Fortunately the numbers are pretty accurate as I keep a chart in my Day Book — Did I tell you about that little project — it's a diary and it has big pages — and I've been very faithful to it — the whole trip will be accounted for — then if you wish, when you come home I'll have a record for you of what I've been doing.

Honey, just as I finished that last paragraph I asked solider reading across the table if he knew the time — he told me and then he asked me — if I had ever read The Prophet — (Kahil Gibran) I hadn't so he started showing it to me — I was amazed because he was the Joe Blake type and it seems that he reads a bit of it every day — it's a short book and he can cover it in half an hour — which he has done many times. I copied down two quotations which reminded me of us — They do say so much.

"Let today embrace the past with remembrance and the future with longing."

"How often you have sailed in my dreams and now you come in my awakening which is a deeper dream."

Could anyone say it more simply and beautifully —

There was a boy at the show tonite in the front row — 16 years old and he'd been overseas in the army two and a half years! It seems that when his father went into the army and went overseas — this thirteen year old kid stowed away and he wasn't found until they reached England. Evidently the boy was irreconcilable to leaving his father so his father got him in the army — the father was killed in Germany and the boy wounded — now he's an ambulatory patient in the hospital. Tonite after the show he was sitting at the at the piano playing some very weird boogie and from that, with marvelous technique he launched into the classic — and from that into a burlesque of concert pianists that was wonderful — and fascinating — I nearly burst with laughter he was really fine. The art of pantomime fully developed —

After the show tonite I had to spend an awful hour with the Evans having a beer — I hate that man so and yet, at times he seems to be so fond of Rollie and me — they just hound us to have beer with them — It is a constant struggle with myself to keep from blowing up — but I will stick it out — and I really feel as if I'd like to have revenge on him — but I have to bide my own good time. My gosh darling — here it is Sunday morning — I had on my night-gown and robe and I lay down on the bed — just for five minutes and I woke up at seven this morning — then I crawled under the covers and went back to sleep — I've had eleven hours but that still isn't enough — However I think I'll stay up now and go out and look at the Capitol — it's a beautiful Sunday morning and I feel as if I should go out — and see something — Pat and I are planning to start sunlamp treatments and wanted to have one this morning but there's no place in Topeka to do it — we'll have to start tomor-row in Lincoln — I want to get a tan because pretty soon it's going to be too hot to wear stockings in the day time.

Now darling we are sitting on the train waiting for it to start-and it looks as if it were going to be really late — it's one of those little locals that are made up here and are always late — we have a change at St. Jo — Missouri — if we're too late, we'll miss our connection-Some of the tracks are out because of the floods and we just have to creep along when we do get started. I understand — If we do make the connection, I don't know where we'll have dinner because probably the diner on the next train will be shut — this trip is a wee bit rugged from now on I'm afraid —

Oh — we're going to cross the Missouri river today — I got a map in the station just now — my geography on the middle part of the country is a bit vague. Well, I just found out what's holding us up — the cattle car hasn't arrived yet. It goes on the back actually!

Well my honey darling — I'll stop writing now and then write you again on the second train — that will make two letters —

I love you honey —

Jane

Hey honey Pat Walker just said she knew somebody on the Gamble — she says he's a wonderful character — she gave him a ride back from Dallas and invited him to her house — he didn't

know anybody — and he was enchanted and took care of her baby —
and she's been hearing from him ever since — His name is Le Roy
Burke. She thinks he's a boatswains mate 2nd class — You must
let me know and say hello for her!

Honey, they just put the cattle car on — they really did and it's
filled with cows! I went back on the observation platform and looked
through the slats —

The odor is terrific —

My love,

Jane

#39
22 April 1945
In Port —

Dearest honey: Hi darling, here I am again just like I said I
would be. So eager to get started that I can't even space right, see
above! Well I suppose you will get all my mail in a packet again
but I hope there are more letters in this batch than the last one.
As for you no mail for two whole days now, ain't it dreadful? Boy
after the last few days haul I won't even have a legitimate beef
coming for days and days.

The wind I spoke of seems to be unable to make up its mind
about whether it's coming in or not. Course there is a nice little
breeze blowing about now, but it is a zephyr compared to what
might show up. Still quite a ways away though and might poop
out before it gets here. Here's hoping as besides everything else it
would screw up the mail again.

I didn't even leave the ship today. What with the wind coming
and all, but more important the news from Europe. Berk and I have
been hugging the radio every hour waiting for the news that the
Russians and the Yanks have tied up together. (Just as I write this
I hear the 11:00 news start) But imagine the Russians in Berlin!

Well I had to go out and listen. They are coming into the main
streets of Berlin and a momentary link-up with the Americans
near Dresden is expected. Darling I'll bet you never dreamed how
much pleasure you would give a couple of guys when you sent those
pins out to me. Berk and I keep it corrected up to the hour. Green

for the Yanks, (western front) Yellow (Italian Yanks) and brown for the Russians. [PAGE TWO MISSING]

Cheerier and less morbid subjects. I spent the whole afternoon fashioning another bracelet for you. I don't think it will turn out quite as well as the one you have now, because the little Japanese inscription is not so good, but we will see. By the way, do you ever wear that one or is costume jewelry out in the east. I say east because it sure as hell ain't west of L.A. but Neb. is still the hinterland as far as Gothamites are concerned. Whether you can wear them or no or whether they are even attractive is not too important. I like to work on them because you might get a small kick out of them and I enjoy making them for you. I got a nice batch of sun today too, as I was working on a bench aft. If I get this one done fairly early in the morning I am going to attempt to mount those three cats-eyes on another. If I can only figure out a way to hold them on I think it would make a really nice piece.

You told me not to have any more of those bad dreams about you but I did. I woke up this morning in a tizzy. Seems I got home all right, but you just couldn't stand me around didn't like to kiss me or anything. It was eight o'clock in the morning and as one's mind is not at the best at that time I suddenly wondered if perhaps mommy was playing fast and loose at right that minute with some Col. Or such and my telepathic powers were attuned and bringing you in. As I took a shower though sober thought showed me that you would be having an awfully peculiar time of it. After all, three o'clock in the afternoon is hardly the time for l'amour, now is it? Don't get mad at me darling, I only tell you this because I think it's rather funny. As a matter of fact I had another dream the night before and the cast was the same, you and me, but the script for this would have jolted Hayes right out of this world!! Honey, honey!!

I never think bad thought about you when I am awake, but I certainly do think of you a great deal.

As a matter of fact I sometimes think you must be awfully bored with these protestations of devotion. Every letter seems to be pretty sticky with sentiment, but really honey that's the way I feel. Maybe I should work on a savior-faire, a certain casualness in my relations with you. On the other hand I like being completely in love with you and knocking myself out trying to find new ways to tell you so. I'll guess you'll just have to bear with me darling and get used to having me tell you I adore you.

Still no word about us. No nuthin'. Big news of the day was we managed to draw a month's ration of coke for everyone. 12 bottles per month per man so we brought fifty cases aboard. (36 to the case) seeing as only about fifty of us live on the ship and the rest live on the beach it looks like we won't thirst for coke for a while. One of the warrant officers on the dry-dock made ensign yesterday and he invited us all to his wetting-down party at the club tomorrow. Might join the lads and tip a few. Why not indeed? Honey my darling I'm about run out of chatter for this time so will sign off. Write when you can and don't forget that your old man loves you very good indeed —

All me love — Chas

#40
24 April 1945
In Port —
258 to go

Dearest honey:

Hi sugar-foot how goes it with the cheer-up girl? My chart tells me you are about in Lincoln Neb. tonight and with luck you might get this in Springfield. Some of the lads got some mail today, but none for me. Ah well, tomorrow is another day.

Our big storm that we were all set for to the extent of anchoring down Quonsets on the beach with ducks and tanks has dissipated itself at sea some two hundred miles from here. It apparently was a dilly of a storm but it didn't seem to be able to get anywhere. Just fretted around in a area of a couple of hundred miles in radius and then just died a natural death. Can't say that I am sorry it won't be heckling us. With the ship in the shape she is in I am pretty sure she would have gone down. Of course we would have all been aboard the floating dry-dock and not on her, but still I'm glad it didn't hit.

Speaking of going down I had some sad news yesterday.

The plane I flew in on that practice bombing ditched yesterday and only three got out. Only missed making Iwo by about thirty-five miles. There were only two new men in the crew that I didn't know out of the eleven and both of them got out. When eight guys you know pretty darn well get it all at once like that it sort of makes you think. Several of them were married and all were planning to get married first shot at Uncle Sugar. Like everyone else they were full of Post-War plans and things they were going to do after the war. We are sure enough winning this God-damned thing, but there are a lot of fine lads that aren't going to be around to enjoy it when it's all over. I'm putting in a chit right now for about thirty years when this is all done. Right now I'd settle for a lot less but that is what I'm going to hold out for.

Time is certainly skipping by. Yesterday night someone said well tomorrow we will have been here for two months. That made it the twenty-third yesterday. Suddenly I remembered that nine years ago yesterday I arrived in Paris for the first time. Looking back it doesn't seem possible that it was that long ago. Details are still so crystal clear in my mind. The places I went, what I drank and where, the people I met and the looks of the streets and the smells and the sounds of those funny taxi horns. Honey, honey, I'm getting old! If you were with me, rather if I was with you and we were doing things together it wouldn't seem so bad, but right now it just seems that years are being snatched away from me and they can never be replaced. I'm not complaining, darling because I realize that I am but one of many millions all over the world, but what a stupid solution to any problem no matter how great is man destroying man. Our little tour of duty on this old globe is short enough anyhow for all the things we would like to do, but to force millions of people to waste three or five or six years in the bloody business of killing one another is inexcusable.

Well, philosopher Flynn has done for the nonce. On to [missing]

April 25, 1945
Train — en-route from
Lincoln to Kansas City Missouri
(streamliner too!)
Letter #69

Hello honey darling;

We're finally in a good train but it started so darned early that I'm not enjoying it much — it left at 7:30 this morning but that fool Mr. Evans had us down to the station so darned early — one hour in advance. I just don't seem to be able to get to bed by ten so I'm sort of sick to my stomach from sleepiness — and twice so from irritation which is becoming almost a constant habit with me — of course I let myself in for it because I go up and talk with the character — but it's the only way I can get anything out of him or see that he doesn't put anything over on me — but that anyone should be so damned dumb and so malicious and think he's so smart at the same time-it makes me sick — literally ill. I must try and develop a more oriental calm and just wait patiently until he hangs himself but it's kind of hard sometimes when you'd like to be pulling the rope — But enough of that — I'll keep a weather eye out and see what plans I can make. A guest star joined us for two weeks — he's a character actor in pictures and his name is Raymond Walbern — you'd know him if you saw him — He's really very nice-Mr. Evans said some awful things before he came but is now busily engaging him in what he thinks is cordial conversation. I just had a run-in with Evans with Walbern on my side about what he was going to do in the show — But just about two days and he'll cook his goose — the trouble is that the Hollywood office sent him out so he can't do much.

Lincoln was kind of a nice town — big stores — the hotel was lovely — and everyone very friendly. They have the darndest looking state capitol though — like the Empire State building with a gold top — I don't approve of it at all —

Yesterday Pat and I started our sunlamp treatment project — since we have no chance to go to the beach, we thought it would be the only way to get a tan. Besides, it's good for that very persistent cough that I've had for months. I got a little too much on my stomach though and I feel as if every rib were exposed. It's also a little sore where I sit down — there is nothing like an even tan all over. We have a six hour layover in Kansas City today before we catch the train for Joplin and we thought we'd have another — but perhaps I'll skip it until tomorrow —

Honey — I received your letters Monday nite — and — written when you'd finally received my mail-that I was so happy about — I too feel as if we were back in touch again — I certainly could tell by the pieces of paper you sent me — the labels and the page from the notebook — that they came from a rather unsavory place-they smelled like Kwajalein — those things will be awfully interesting for us after the war.

One of those letters also had that long discussion in it about our "marital status" — While I appreciate your consideration and love, darling — it really wasn't necessary — but I can't disregard it because then you would think I was avoiding the subject. But to be blunt, if you think I am considering looking around for someone who could support me in the style to which I would like to be accustomed after the war, you, my darling, are nuts! I am perfectly conscious of the fact that it may not be too easy to really get going and that there have been a few years lost. I am hoping that before that, I will able to gain something which will ease the pressure a little — All I require for happiness is that we don't return to the "laissez-faire" policy that we were so assiduously practicing before the war — with that I can't be happy but I don't think you want that either so that's no problem. If Don's proffered job turns out-then there is something interesting and constructive. I had hoped that you would be using the typewriter other than writing letters to me, because honey, you really are such a darned good writer — I hate to see the gift wasted — I know you've been under a strain but it doesn't sound as if you had so much to do now — so I wish you wouldn't keep putting it off — and just sit down at the typewriter and look at it if need be until something comes out.

Yes darling I know too that we were skating on thin ice — I don't want that to ever happen again — we do have certain differences but we're grown up now and a little adjusting here and there should take care of that. And I'm not giving you reasons for getting so upset. We've had a lot of fun and love and prosperity and even hardships together — what better foundation is there for a fine relationship? Honey I trust that's your answer — I think maybe the best answer is "I love you — you big lug" — So there.

For heavens sake honey, if you ever go poking around Japanese ruins and bodies and exposing yourself to getting shot again, when it's unnecessary — I'll start proceedings on grounds of insanity. Honestly darling — the way you stretch your luck — inveterate tourist — look what happened to Ernie Pyle. Honey, sit down and write about what you've already done — Don't go sticking your neck out so far — please darling —

Well, I straightened my seat up and I'm beginning to feel a little better — I'll change my clothes in a few minutes — then I'll sleep from Kansas City to Joplin —

Honey take care of yourself — you're for me and I love you — with all my heart,

Jane

#41
26 April '45
In Port —

Dearest Honey:

Well, honey, I had a letter and a post card from you yesterday. Now I'm sorry I blew my top so about not getting mail for so long because I felt that you were discouraged about my not getting the letters and it sort of took the interest out of writing them for you. I figure though that just about the next time you get mail from me it should be some that told you I had mail, so maybe the old interest will come back. I feel that I have been doing very well lately. This is the fourth letter in six days, and all of them have been big long fat ones. I sometimes marvel that I can fill up so many pages with such little drivel as goes now to make up my life. However, dull as it is, it's "my day" so you'll have to bear with me. When it gets too dull just stop or skip lightly over, but please don't stop writing to me!

Yesterday, as per plan, I got the bracelet finished and polished it all up. Then I coated the little name plate with nail polish so it wouldn't tarnish. You don't need to worry about the bracelet itself as it's stainless. If the plate does start to tarnish, polish it with any silver polish or some such, and give it another coat of nail polish. Please don't think your old man has gone gay darling, but I had this bottle that Pete gave me a long time ago when I made that first bracelet that got lost in Hawaii. He originally bought it, so he says, to coat his buttons on his blues!! I don't think it is too good as far as costume jewelry goes, but as I said the other day, it was a lot of fun to make it for you. The "C" right under the writing stand for centigrade, natch. Thought you might like to know. Also enclosed is the forgotten little blue bottle that I thought might do for perfume. I cleaned all of them out as well as I could, but I would suggest that you boil it well and get the rest of the stuff out of it. I assure you though that there is nothing harmful left in the bottle, as, among other things, I soaked it overnight in a strong solution of caustic soda. Believe me, that would kill anything. That's what pitted up the aluminum mess kits. After it happened I looked over the can that had contained the caustic soda very carefully, and in very small print down at the bottom of the label it said, "Do not use with aluminum!" Well we live and learn.

I got the package off this morning, and as it was air mail it should get to you before this. Honey, once more, will you take a tape measure and send me the number of inches you are around the wrist, do it now!! This, by guess and by gosh, is all right as long as they fit, but it's hell when they don't, as witness last year. Oh, that awful night. Funny strain and tension in the room and then about your first remark was, "Honey, but you are so fat!" and then the Goddamned bracelets didn't fit!! That's one of the nights I'll be willing to forget, but don't get me wrong, baby, there were a lot more later on that I will always remember.

We had a very busy day, that is for us. After two months I got tired of taking my showers out of a bucket that had holes punched in the bottom, so I decided to do something about it. After lunch, Berk and Van and I got busy. First we got hold of a fifty gallon gas drum, and then we cut a hole through the deck to the shower. By dint of much hard work and good honest sweat we got it hooked up to the spray nozzle in the shower and then tested it with salt water. Worked like a million. Then we ran a hose up from the fresh water tank aft, started up a little gas pump and filled her up. Worked beautifully. About this time a couple of chiefs began to see the possibilities, and they got one going. Then we began to investigate the piping to our little sinks, after much blanking off of loose pipes and jury rigging lines here and there we finally ended up with fresh water in every room, both the chiefs and officers shower going and fresh water to two sinks in the chiefs' quarters. We were all might proud of ourselves. Here it has been nine weeks since we could turn on our tap and get water to brush our teeth. Everything we used had to be carried down in buckets. Also, now we can have all the showers we want, naturally we have to take pretty easy and not go to sleep under it as I have known some characters to do. May sound silly, but at last this is one day that we really accomplished something, even if it was only getting a shower running. Tough war!

A D.E. came alongside us this afternoon, and some guy yells "Flynn." Well, at this moment I am actually dripping water and engaged in cutting a hole in the top of the drum with a fire axe. Mighty energetic work. Turned out to be a guy who was at school with me in Pearl last year. I had only seen him once since and that was for a minute in Pearl the last time through. Hell of a nice guy, he lived right next to me, and we had a couple of pleasant drunks together. He was, really astonished today because he said they had a picture aboard last night, "Seven Days Leave" I think it was, anyway I remember I had some business in it as a guard when Vic was in the brig and a few lines. He said that when he saw the picture he turned to the guy next to him and said, "Geez if I didn't know better, I'd swear that is a guy I know named Flynn." When he met me he told me about it and then said do you know who it was by any chance, and so I said sure, me! He was really amazed. One of those nice Hinterland people who Love the movies. It was really very funny, acting seems so damn far away from this life we are leading now.

He came on down to the wardroom with us when we had finished the shower deal and joined us in a coke. He told a very wonderful story. There was another guy at school with us who is attached to another squadron of D.E.'s. This guy is a radar and sound specialist, and he goes from one to another of the ships in his division keeping all their gear of that sort in tip-top shape. Well this first guy, named Besch by the way, was on one of his ships up in the Aleutians right after we both left school at Pearl. They had a sub contact and managed to sink her. Naturally he was elated, and when the dope came out in a monthly bulletin giving all the data on it he sat down and wrote a very patronizing letter to this other lad, named Blake, suggesting that he look on such and page and read all about what red-hot kids they are. Well about three weeks later he gets an answer back that really brushes him off. Blake in turn suggests that he read page such and such of the current bulletin and see how things are really done. Seems the ship he was on set up a record for this war by sinking several subs in days. It was damn good, in fact the ship got the Presidential Citation and the skipper the Navy Cross! His only fear is now that he might run into the guy in person. "If only I hadn't rubbed it into him so much in my letter!" Well that's life.

The war news continues to look better and better. We are moving pins at all hours of the day and night now, and still I know we aren't keeping up with some of the lads. Patten went 97 miles in the last three days on the road to Munich. There is one town I hope they don't completely destroy, the main thing I want left is the Opera and the Hofbrauhaus. Someday you and I are going to drink Dunkel bier in those old stone mugs in the cellar of the Hofbrauhaus and then see a Wagnerian opera that night in the old Opera haus. And that's a promise.

Lots of the other things we were going to see in Germany, in fact all over Europe, are not going to be there to see, but there will be other countries and other things. Someday, my darling, we will make our "Grand Tour" and that too is a promise. Maybe we can spend a few months on the island of Ibiza in the Balearic group off the east coast of Spain. Nothing but love, and fishing, and vin du pays and finishing up our new play. Dream on, Chas, it doesn't cost anything to dream. Speaking of writing, I am making inquiries about that service you suggested that the Navy handles. I am going to take a shot at a short story, and I'll let you know how I come out on it. These two months, though dull, have gotten us back into a pretty normal frame of mind. We still flinch when they blast coral on the beach in the quarries and duck when a plane zooms us, but we are a lot better than when we got here. So even if we go to another ship out here we will all make out all right. Just so, I think I can really start pounding this old baby again. I'll send you the first draft for criticism. Okay?

I'm filled with an awful chunk of love for you tonight, ducky, I'd love to see you and talk a lot of things over. I'd love to hold you in my arms and kiss you a couple of million times. Being as that is impossible. Know then that I adore you and send you

all me love, Chas

Letter #70
Cunnar hotel Joplin, Missouri
April 27, 1945

Dearest honey —

Your letter #37 came today and over the chicken salad I was eating for lunch — I devoured it — it was much finer than the chicken salad-when you start to getting your mail it really comes — it is a comfort to know that my letters aren't languishing in some forgotten corner in Pearl Harbor — and it's really nice not to have the first of every one of your letters unwittingly but slightly reproachful when I have written-so now we're all squared away.

I did, as you know now, recover from the case of incipient flu with which I was doing battle in Cheyenne — Although since that time I've been so tired that I finally went to the doctor today to ask him what was making me feel so awful — the answer was obvious — I am tired. However now that I know for sure that it's just a question of certain hours spent in the downy, I can cope with it — Just force myself to go to bed — that's all there is to it — which I shall. I've become a discouragingly quiet character already. Wouldn't you love to be staying at the Fairmont now or even over on Taylor street — a gathering of the nations is perfectly suited to San Francisco's atmosphere — and I'd like to be there and observe a little of it. I do wish the proceedings so far had been as sanguine as the meeting of the Russian and American troops yesterday.

Champagne out of beer glasses!

Darling, you won't be the only one in the family who's black — and what's more I won't have a stomach. Don't you dare come home fat — and me expecting to see a handsome, thin character.

I had my second sun lamp treatment last evening and the brown is gathering. The red is done already gathered. Incidentally two treatments have wonders for my cough — which is a comfort.

This grind still goes on — we're leaving in the morning for Springfield where we'll be for four days — ah blessed four days — all in one place. I'll really feel quite settled which in my mind is coming to be almost a desirable state. It worries me that any satisfaction of my tourist curiosity is well nigh impossible in view of our schedule. Here we are in the Ozarks and I haven't seen a single barefoot boy in overalls. What's more, instead of looking at the scenery today on my way to Camp Crawder, I read Time magazine. That's really bad —

Darling, my sweet, forgive me. I have to do some packing and go to bed — I shall dream of you —

My love darling —

Jane

Colonial Hotel
Springfield, Missouri
April 29, 1945
Letter #71

My darling;

It is a quarter past ten and I have half an hour in which I can say hello to my honey. I had intended that it should be hours yesterday but I made the mistake of trying to fill in my Day Book for the first month we were on this tour and that's bad business — I get fascinated by it and write too much. It's remarkable if you just have one or two clues, what you can remember about every day if you concentrate on it.

When I arrived here Saturday darling (this is Monday morning) there was that fine long letter from you — the one where you told about finding Bob Patten's grave — I wrote the family asking them to find out about the serial number but those are his initials and I think you may be fairly sure that is the right place because he is buried in the Marine cemetery there — That's awfully sweet of you honey and you may be sure that it will be most appreciated.

This town of Springfield Missouri is hardly very remarkable — what I've seen of it and I won't leave here tomorrow night wishing I could stay longer — I think Denver was the last place I had that feeling about anyway — of course all these places are home to somebody and as such are alright. I did love Kansas City, Missouri too that seemed more like San Francisco even in the rain — than any town so far. Pat and I agreed yesterday that actually we lead a very dull life — a constant succession, almost a routine of trains, busses, hospitals, and hotel rooms — it's really a rather solitary life because you never have time to really get to know anyone. On the surface of it, it looks exciting but actually it's kind of a grind.

I suppose Saturday will go down in history as the day of the false peace rumor — actually though it is true — it seems that there was a broadcast from Germany picked up in New York and remarkably enough re-broadcast from there in German. It's not a matter of common knowledge and I think it was a mistake — but from this broadcast it is to be judged that Germany is willing to surrender to the three big powers alright but she has to surrender formally to everyone of the forty-six members of the United Nations — simultaneously — and it is taking a couple of days to arrange the mechanics of it. Then it seems there was a revolution in Munich-the people fighting the storm troopers and the people called for the American troops to come in and rescue them from the Nazis. But the Americans weren't close enough and by evening the Nazis by superior weapons had the whole thing under control.

Nobody here was terribly excited and happy-it seems a little late to be happy — and then too it is really the beginning of the concentrated was against Japan. It was just sort of like breathing a big sigh of relief — then pulling your belt a little tighter and then getting to work again.

Well honey darling, it is time for me to get dressed so I'll say goodbye for now —

All my love to you honey,

Jane

"Aunt Clara" was wonderful, honey — It's a little spicy for the USO but I'm learning it anyway — And the cartoons were priceless — Thanks darling.

29 April 1945
In Port
#42

Dearest Jane:

Hi honey, how goes the struggle? I'm sorry that I missed my every-other-day schedule so soon, but when I tell you what happened to me yesterday I am sure that you will not only forgive, but condone.

I got a letter from you tonight when I came back to the ship. I was so damn glad to get it. They seem to be stretching out more and more between writings. 13th, 16th, 19th, 23rd. Honey whatever happen3d to that one a day deal? Look darling, I'm not complaining and I know that you are busier than seven hundred dollars, but you know when even a few days go by and I don't hear from you, that is, now that mail is coming through on a schedule of about five or six days, I begin to wonder what has happened to my little wifling. Has romance been dulled by distance again? Has the spirit we caught only too briefly in Dago suffered an untimely demise? Then in answer to all my questions comes another letter and all my fears are dispelled.

Of course being a rational being, I understand you haven't yet gotten a letter telling you that the mail is once again coming through. Without that reassurance and as you say, seven weeks of good conscientious letter writing behind you, I can't find it in my heart to condemn a few lapses. (I only hope this doesn't transpose to your mind as stuffy as it reads!) I guess what I am trying to say is don't let the memory get so dim that some time together in the future can't put a nice shine back on it. I once asked you for six months when the war was over without any prejudices whatsoever just to see if we could pull our personalities enough back into a common groove to make a success of our marriage. I guess that's all that I still ask and want, I only hope we get the chance to take a crack at it.

Honey, I don't quite know how I got off on this vein. I'll try and keep it on a much higher from here on out. I got another letter from you three days age just after I mailed my last effort to you. That was the one that you enclosed the two pictures of the girls in. Well I couldn't have picked a worse, or should I say better, time to open it. I got it just before we went over to lunch when Cass, who was sitting next to me saw them, he hollered "Pictures!!!" They, of course, passed them all around the table. If you have any young gals who are suffering from an inferiority complex a two minute recording of the remarks made about all of you would restore in thirty seconds any of their sagging egos. Everyone of course picked out "their Girl" believe me, if the show ever hits a port where the Gamble officers are they will be immediately snowed under. And I do mean a snow job! Naturally the best looking gal of all was Janie-pants, but then I might be prejudiced! I really enjoyed getting them though darling, you didn't tell me where they were taken, but I judge that it was somewhere around Yosemite because I think the license plates were Californian. I have them in the big album along with all the other nostalgic mementoes of the life that used to be. Darling, anytime you find any snaps or newspaper shots of you, hustle them on out will you? I really enjoy them, Painful as it is to be reminded of you too closely.

Well now for about yesterday and why I missed writing. I went over to the club with Cass and Stewart. We were starting to drink seriously, on account of this was the day that Cass's girl was getting married to some stateside Johnnie. We were sitting out in the sort of garden adjoining the club at a picnic table when a character comes up to us. "I beg your pardon" he says, "But is your name Flynn?" I admitted it and then he says, "I don't suppose you remember me do you?" I said no, I didn't. Well," he says, "my name is Pete — and I met you and Jane on the Lark going down to L.A. last fall." I imagine you remember him. A Lt. in the Marines and he was more or less with Dot that night. At any rate I remembered him then and we exchanged banalities for a moment and then he pulls up the guy that had walked up with him and said "But here is someone who really knows Jane well. This is Lt. Losch (or Tosh or some such)

who was Provost Marshall Fort Derussy when the girls lived there"
I expressed my delight at meeting him and asked "Were the gals
much trouble?" "Not too much" he said.

Well, we talked about you and Dottie and Martha and I told them
what you were doing now, but Losch seemed to know, especially
about Martha, where she left and all. Tell me, sugar, was there
anything between them? At any rate I tried to get them to sit down
and have a drink but Tosch [or Losh] had to run and Pete — was
with some other characters. So they shoved off.

A little later I went by the table where Pete was sitting on my way
for some more drinks and he said, "When do you think Jane will
be out here?" I said I thought you would go to Europe if anywhere
out of the U.S. and he said "Oh no, Losh tells me they are coming
out this way and soon, too" Who has been giving who bum dope?
Are you planning on surprising me or has Martha hooked up with
another deal or what? I'm confused! At any rate I told them I would
send you their love and remembrances so here they are.

Well next event (it was a busy afternoon) up comes a J.G. carrying about nine drinks. I took one look at him and hollered "Barney"
and sure enough it was Barney Killion. Well he joined us and we
talked and talked. I ended up by going out to his ship and spending the night. He had a quart of rum in his locker that he had
been saving for an occasion and he insisted that this was it. So
we locked the door and sat in the heat and dripped and smoked
and drank the rum and caught up on over two years since I had
last seen him.

It turns out that he has had state-side duty up until late last
Nov. and the last three months they lived at the Hotel Coronado in
Dago. The room was ten slugs a day and he was drawing about $285
a month. Finally had to sell his car to eke out the last few weeks.
They must have had a grand time though. He couldn't talk about
it without sighing. At any rate their baby is now four months old
and Rita is in Milton, Mass., just about ten miles outside Boston.
I told him that I imagined that you would hit Boston, so I am
enclosing her address. Try and call her and have a drink with her
for auld lang syne.

I came back into the ship this morning and just before lunch
we got the flash "Germany surrenders, unconditionally!!!" So right
after lunch we again took off for the club to get really drunk and
celebrate V-E Day.

After we got there we heard President Truman's denial so to curb our disappointment we got drunk anyway. Not real drunk, just a little. You know though honey, when something comes out as well authenticated as that there must be something behind all the smoke.

Well it turned out to be a very nice afternoon. One of the officers off the D.E. that is tied up alongside us had been up taking pictures with two enlisted men from the B-29 strip. They run the head photo lab up there. Seems thus Lt. and one of the sgts. Had been kids together in the same little town. Sort of like Dave and me, at any rate they were parked in this army munitions carrier about a hundred feet from where we were standing. Naturally we managed to get several good slugs of bourbon out to them as well as all the beer they could drink. It ended up with them coming over and taking a couple pictures of us all at a table, another of just the five Gamble officers that were there, one of me alone and a few others. They are going to print them up for us and we should get them in a few days. If they are any good at all I will send some prints on to you. They also going to develop Cass's role that had Bob Patten's pictures on it and I think they will print some up for me for his family. I hope those of me look half way decent. I'd like to have you see how brown I am. In your letter you talked about getting some sun lamp treatments. I wish you could do an hour with us every day on the flying bridge. Especially if you were in one of those cute bra and shorts outfits. Woooof! Damn me eyes, there goes that sex to the fore again! Honestly darling it is so hot up there that you can stand to lay down for over ten minutes without standing up to get a breath of breeze. I was up there yesterday with Smiley before I had my swim and shower before going to the club and it was so hot you couldn't stand to put your barefoot on the metal deck even where it was in the shade of the director. That's no kidding!

Well it looks now like reassignment out here is about the way it will turn out. Still not definite but it looks a lot like that. I am going to put a chit in tomorrow for advanced Gunnery and Fire Control School at Washington D.C. I think with my background and Pete's recommendation (Which he has already promised) that I should not have much trouble getting it. If I do, it will mean 18 weeks in Washington. If the European thing doesn't look too good to you or you have any desire to see our Capital at work in wartime, this might be the golden opportunity. However your life right now is your pigeon and you are to flu it the way it looks best to you.

I'd like to make it clear too that I am not requesting this school merely to get back to Uncle Sugar, though that would be very nice, but rather because I don't think I know enough about five inch guns to go to a new DD or DM which is what I hope to get. I've still got a lot of enemies to blast before I can settle down again. If things should work out though and I get back, and things could be worked out for you without ruining your chances, four and a half months together in Washington would practically be a lifetime to live, the way things are now.

Well punkin, it's nothing to get hot up about and I'll know one way or another long before you finish your stateside tour, but it does sound pretty intriguing, at least to me. With our luck we could probably even find a red-hot apt right in the teeth of the housing shortage. At least I have no doubt in my mind.

Smiley just leaned down out of his sack and said "My God, is this still to Jane? What in the name of all that's holy do you find to write about?' Oh, I says, just batting it around. "Well," says Smiley, "You are a better man than I am, but be sure and give her my love." Forthwith, Berk's love.

I had a wonderful letter from Jack yesterday. He seemed very glad to hear from me and such. He paid one of the nicest tributes to Roosevelt that I have yet read although I'm afraid it would make some of our Republican friends toss and squirm a bit! He also wanted to know if I knew Mary's Sam. Wanted my opinion on him. The whole letter was so damn nice that it gave me a wonderfully warm feeling inside, to top it all off he signed it "Dad". That really finished me off. I like him so damn much and its so wonderful to know that he likes me too.

Had a letter from Mary too. Ten pages no less! I nearly dropped dead. (yesterday was in-law day!) She also wanted to know about Sam and what did I think. I am going to write her tomorrow. I don't want to put my nose in where it doesn't belong, but since she asked I think I'll give her my honest opinion. It seems to me that if she really loved the guy enough to marry him that she wouldn't even need to think it over. I'll admit he is more than a little stuffy about the Red Cross deal, in fact to my way of thinking, idiotically so, but that has nothing to do with the main issue. To make a good marriage people either have to think and react almost identically to any given situation or else be flexible enough to give and take as the occasion demands. In this case, from my distant view, and in my opinion only, it would be Sam who did all the taking and Mary all the giving. She is such a swell person, I'd hate to have her get anything but the very top drawer in the way of marriage.

My God darling, this has been goin on for well over two hours. Two and a half to be exact. If you are not bored silly by this time I'm sure its only due to my choice of subjects and not my deathless prose. I'd better turn in and try and dream about you. That's not much good, but at least for a while I am with you. I have a feeling that tonight you are not going to spit in my eye! I'll let you know how we came out. Remember that I adore you and that as long as I live you'll always have —

All me love —

Chas

XXX

#43

1 May 1945 In Port —

Dearest Honey:

Hello tovarish! Workers of the world, unite! May day, can you imagine? I remember once in my political youth attending a May Day rally. It was at the old university and immediately caused all the Seattle press to take up the cudgels against the "Red Menace." Seems to me some nice young professor got the bounce on account of it too. Strange how the red monster that was engulfing "Brave little Finland" a few years back has become our most potent ally. War and modern geopolitics makes for strange bedfellows.

Well, darling, now we are really back in touch. I got your first letter that you wrote after you had some of mine telling you that I was getting mail again. (if you can unscramble that sentence you are a wizard) You discussed the problem, or rather the situation, that I raised. I'll kick it around again for a minute, and then we will forget it. You see, sitting around like this one has so damn much time to think that you drive yourself nuts if you let it happen. But to go back a ways. Seems to me that when we were at Cornell we were happy and then in New York and finally at #1 August Alley. Also I thought we were pretty well set when I left the second time. Maybe I was blind, or you were a good actress, but I thought that all was well. If that is so, then all this discord came during the 13 months I was gone the second time. Now, I know that I didn't have anything to do with a change of heart on your side, as I wasn't within thousands of miles, so how could I influence you? On the other hand, you were doing that show and meeting a lot of people. Either I was not quite up to the standard you found in young men, or else time and distance had blurred the good things and left only the bad tastes in your mouth.

Which brings me to the present. The situation is again the same. I am away where I can't bring any influence on you either for good or bad, while you are again in a spot to only remember what you want to remember in any given situation. According to the old proverb, the pen is mightier than the sword, but I'll bet the same can't be said of black words on white paper vs. an ardent male with soulful eyes, a sympathetic nature and a line of chatter.

Okay, honey, I'll knock it off and I won't go back to it again. You said you love me and that you think we will be able to make a go of it after this is all over. Roger. That's good enough for me, but I just wanted to try and logically show you my think process to prove that I am not just all a neurotic case that's fit for a section eight.

I loved the way you are getting your sun tan. I know only too well the feeling of the overdone tum. But the part that really never really has had a tan, and there is quite a bit of it!! I would like to peek in on you and see that rosy bit right now.

You gave me hell again about not writing. Well, darling, I am happy to report that I <u>have</u> clamped my arse in front of this little machine and I have beat a couple of stories around for several days. I don't think either of them will ever resolve into anything worth submitting, but at least I have broken the bonds that chained me, and I can go on from here. I know you really are convinced that it's pure unmitigated laziness, but I assure you that wasn't what I was being held up on. I also have a letter on its way finding out about this bureau the navy has for placing articles. So you see, I really am taking the bull by the horns and getting started.

I also sent in my request for that school in Washington, D.C. Whether I get it or not is in the laps of the Gods, but I got that off. Also, Peterson put a very fine endorsement on it, and it should get me in, I think. Things are finally coming to a head with us here, and I think the most honest appraisal of my future actions would be that I go to Pearl for reassignment to another ship in the mine force. That will probably be a few weeks before all is squared away though, so in the meantime any letters to the Gamble will still find me around and more than happy to get them. I hope that writing won't be such a chore for you now that you get letters of mine that make some sense with regards to your tour and such. In other words, darling, we are back in communication again. Let's hang on to it!

Remember those pictures I told you about that were taken at the club? Well I saw some prints of them, and they came out very well indeed. This boy is coming down to the ship in about four days with several copies of each for us, so I'll send some on to you. I hope you get a chance to pick up some more of yourself somewhere, I've practically worn out those last two with looking already.

Met Barney at the club again yesterday as per plan. He was supposed to stay all night with me out here, but this Exec wouldn't give him permission. What an unhappy ship that is. God keep me from ever getting Amphib duty. It's not for me. Course I don't know why I talk. I guess I am stuck in this mine force as long as I am in the Navy. Speaking of that, I am starting my fifteenth month as a j.g. Should be a Lt. before very much longer. But that's all the rank I ever want out of this deal.

Honey, your warning about exposing myself haven't fallen on deaf ears. I am no bloody hero, although I guess maybe I'm a bit of a damn fool. However, I haven't been back up hunting since I wrote that letter, and what's more I am not going again. So you can set your mind at rest. If anyone is going to try and get to me with a silver one on an island, that island is going to be Honshu and not one we secured months ago!

Well, darling, the old think tank seems to be pretty dry of things to write about. So, if you'll just remember I adore you and try once in a while to recall that tired old puss of mine and that simple guy who likes everyone and really gets a hell of a bang out of life, I'll be content. As far as marital status and inconsistency and such truck, that is a closed chapter. C'est tout finis!

all me love, honey — Chas

Springfield, Missouri
May 1, 1945 Letter #72

Hello Chuck Darling;
    I am sitting here on the mezzanine of the hotel — we just returned from our shows at the hospital, and it is an hour before the bus leaves for Rolla where we are going tonite. I thought I would start a letter to my honey — then go have one beer, and by that time, we'd have to be on our way.
    When I got back to the hotel last nite, honey, there was the package from you with the souvenirs of your very risky afternoon. It's so sweet of you, honey, to collect all those things — and they'll make valuable additions to the den in El Rancho Flynn. I'll keep them for a while so I can look at them for a bit, and then I'll send them on to Laura Gertrude to hold for us. The little bottles, whatever their primary purpose, were really lovely. Cat kept insisting they'd held some form of dope.
    We've had two very difficult days — chiefly due to the fact that they've been so long — nine and a half hours of it yesterday, and now today that we've finished our shows — we still have a three hour bus ride. But I'm still holding up fairly well — and these last three days here have been some satisfaction in view of the fact that the boys here are in pretty bad shape — there were many in the wards who had never had a show before, and you really felt as if you were helping a little.
    Honey, I don't mean to disappoint you about having pictures taken, and I could use one of the girls' cameras, but it is practically impossible to get film. I've been
[INCOMPLETE]

[INCOMPLETE]
5/1 — 8/45]

    The floating dry dock we are tied up to has a big map in the wardroom. (We eat all of our meals over there of course) Well, they have an exec who has no pins but a very fast moving red crayon that he is blocking out our advances with. Every lunch and dinner Berk and I spend arguing with him about some of his claims. I once thought that I was over-optimistic. Hell, if Patten could keep up with him we would be drinking vodka in Moscow. I don't know just how closely you can follow it, not too well I imagine, but out here it is really terrific. Seamen are always stopping me on deck and asking for a breakdown of the latest news, and how does it tie up with what has gone before. I'm so popular! Still, I do get along damn well with the lads, and that makes me very happy.

Well, I'm afraid that the story I told you yesterday about being almost sure of getting home can be laid to scuttlebutt. I took the beer party to the recreation area yesterday, and <u>four</u> of them swore that any ship decommissioned and scrapped in a forward area the men would get the same treatment as survivors of ships that were sunk outright. Well, we got a copy of the publication in question today, and I guess it was wishful thinking, rather reading, because nowhere does it say just that in black and white. I still think the officers, most of them at any rate, and all the higher rates of enlisted men will get at least to Pearl and very likely home for reassignment. So, don't build up hopes, but still don't sell the idea short yet.

Meant to say something last night about your Sun Valley stopover. Honey, it sounded wonderful, and what an amazing thing running into that Bob What's-his-name (I can just hear you on a Sunday morning following a party at say, Nina's, and you start talking about "Hank" who, I say, and then you get mad, "Hank" you scream, "You talked to him for an hour in the kitchen." Oh yeah, says I "Was that his name?" wonderful memories of another life) But the Valley sounded like a lot of fun. I was there once just after it opened, but that was before you were out of high school. Gad, probably grammar school. I would love to spend a couple of weeks up there some spring with you, Mrs. F. Save me a spring around about `47 or `48 okay? I'm so glad you got a little break in the routine though, should help to make it bearable.

I'm enclosing J. Buckley's letter. I thought it pretty cute. He is such a hell of a nice guy, I just wrote him a note before I started this, hope he writes again. I wrote Don about a month ago, but so far there has been no response. Well, I'll wait a week and then shoot him another, there is one deal I am not going to let get cold.

Darling, it's coming up 2400, and I had to get up at 0600 this morning, and I only got five hours sleep last night sitting up so late writing you, so I think I'd better hit the old sack. I think I will try to get off a lot more letters but maybe not quite so long. How do you react? Remember I adore you and spend a hell of a lot of time just thinking about my wifling. Good night kiss, honey — all me love — Chas

#44
3 May 1945 In Port —
249 to go.

Dearest Honey:

Well, darling, another day and no mail from you. Guess I am back on your stunk list or something. Still for all of that it was quite a day.

Truman confirms Hitler's death, Goebbels dead, the whole damn structure coming down around their ears, and on top of that the whole Italian and Western Austrian forces surrendering unconditionally! Looks like the big day can't be far ahead. Probably before this catches up with you. Then we can shoot everything out here and wind this one up in a hurry.

You know, I think I am going to have to change my timetable for this one. I really think that a year after the European thing ends we can finish it out here. That's six months less than what I thought when I was home, but I think it is still a pretty good guess. After all, if they actually get the numbers of B-29's out here that they are talking about, they can go far toward reducing the home islands from the air. Certainly it didn't knock out Germany, but it went a long way toward helping, and Japan is even more concentrated and vulnerable than is Germany. General Le May of the bomber command has gone on record as saying he thinks they can reduce Japan with air power alone. I think that is a little over-optimistic, but they probably can and will raise a lot of hell.

Well, darling, I'm pretty excited. I've at last got a springboard for a story that I think has possibilities. The skipper of this floating dry dock that we are tied up alongside is really a character. His name is Knudson, and he is a big gruff Norwegian. A merchant skipper before the war and has followed the sea man and boy, as the saying goes.

Well, we were at the club yesterday, and he told a wonderful yarn about just prior to the war. Seems he was called to the reserve, but they had no ship for him, and so they lent him to the Army for a while. He took a salvage tug from Louisiana to Dutch New Guinea (n. coast of South America) via Trinidad without any charts, leadlines, chronometers or any of the seemingly necessary appurtenances to navigation. Took her down through a storm and hit it right on the button and brought her back the same way. Then he told an Army Col. to go to hell and hopped a freighter back to N. Orleans and took over all salvage operations and rescue work out of the eighth Naval district.

He is a great believer in getting things done, and if it doesn't agree with the book then it's just too damn bad for the book. One night a combination passenger-freighter was torpedoed in the gulf, and he got word of it. He sent out all his own boats and then commandeered two S.C's that belonged to somebody else. He saved over six hundred people that night, everyone on board except the twenty-six that were killed by the explosion. Instead of a decoration for his work he got well chewed out for taking two boats without proper authority!

A couple of other little things to give you some idea of the man's wonderful flavor. He is very tall and heavy and has tremendous eyebrows. The kind of a gent that can really blast you if the occasion demands. On one occasion he ran across an ensign in charge of a YMS that was in dock having her screws replaced. (The ensign, a former candy salesman, had run her aground by not following the Commander's instructions) When the old boy comes aboard, there is the whole crew sitting on the forecastle gambling and swearing like troupers. (He doesn't hold much with either one in public) He went up to the ensign and suggested that he'd do well to get his crew over the side and put them to work scraping the ship's bottom which was filthy. The ensign looks at him haughtily and says, "May I have that order in writing?" The commander drew a big breath, beetled his eyebrows and roared, "I'll give you five minutes to get them to work!!!!" They were hard at it long before. He is also the kind of a guy that made good friends with a parish priest, a Catholic naturally, and used to play a lot of cribbage with him. The priest called him O'Mahoney and kept trying to convert him. Well, the poor priest had a very broken down car and miles and miles to cover to help all his scattered parishioners. One night, over a cribbage game, the father told him about his car and how he was worried that it was just going to quit and leave him without transportation. The old man didn't say anything, but when he left that night he took the priest's car, stole it in fact. He got it back to the base and turned a bunch of motor macs loose on it. They worked all night on it and had her done in the morning. Of course, the priest called him shortly after he had gotten home and told him that someone had pinched his car. The commander told him not to worry, that he would try and locate it for him in the morning. Well, bright and early, a seaman delivers the priest's car back to him. New motor, new jeep tires in first class shape. As the commander puts it, "I'll tell you, Charley, it vas a God-damned funny looking ting, about half yeep and half his car, but by damn she run good!!!" He paused and scratched his gray whiskers reflectively, "I got some damn fine drinks of Irish whiskey out of that one."

Well, I guess that's enough to give you an idea of the man and what a swell central character he would make in a story. I'm going to try and sketch in a synopsis this morning and then go over and get some background stuff on him this afternoon. He thought it was a wonderful idea when I broached the subject to him, but he said "Maybe we better not use my right name, huh Charley, then ve can give them some much better stuff!!!"

It looks like action is imminent on us, but of course I've said that before too. Naturally I will be among the very last to leave. Van and Cass and Berk, Stu and Pete and myself will be with her to the bitter end.

Honey, don't forget to write, and don't _ever_ forget I adore you. Just scratch out a line between shows or train waits to show me you do think of me now and then. Hope I get a nice fat one today.

Thinking of a tentative title for my effort, "Old Salty," what do you think? I'll have a rough draft in a few days and will send one on for criticism and help. I love you a jillion million, honey, and miss you like the dickens. all me love-Chas

Rolla, MO
May 4, 1945 Letter #73

Hello, my Darling honey;

I am sitting here in the midst of a scene that you would love — I'm literally surrounded by beer bottles — we had the evening off last nite, and Pat and I were doing our hair — so we decided we would have a glass of beer to help the process along — Rollie fell in enthusiastically with the idea, then the three new girls of the trio came in and decided to go get some beer too, so what had been 2 quarts of Pabst Blue Ribbon was expanded to include almost 2 cases of little bottles — it was perfectly delicious, and it certainly helped brighten what would have been a very dull evening of beauty shop operations and washing and ironing in this hole. Earlier in the evening I noticed, when we returned from Ft. Wood, that the Navy picture "Fighting Lady" was at one of the two local theatres — I'd wanted to see it for ages so I dashed up there for an hour — you have no doubt seen it — It <u>was</u> very fine and most impressive — in the pictures of the first battle of the Philippine sea though they sugar-coated it a bit — which they always do.

It is about three in the afternoon, and we're leaving for Louis at four-thirty — it's about a five hour trip — I'd hoped to get some reading done on the bus, but — I had my fourth sun lamp treatment today, and I think I got a little of the light in my eyes — they're watering, and my head kind of aches. I did tell you about the sun treatments, didn't I, honey — artificial tan — I am getting so healthy looking, but I think I'll have to lay off for a while, as I'm beginning to peel like mad, and that's not good. Honey, remember the time you got the horrible sunburn at Laguna and I had to put vinegar packs on you all one day — you screaming like mad — (that was the time you and Will disappeared — I always felt you <u>deserved</u> the sunburn!) We were living in the little red wood honeymoon cottage then — remember — that was a long time ago, wasn't it, honey — <u>seven</u> years. I just stopped at the end of that sentence to regale Pat and Rollie with the <u>wonderful</u> story of that weekend at Laguna, and I had them rolling in the aisles. We <u>have</u> had some riotous experiences, haven't we, honey.

Sunday's the beginning of a horrible ten days of travel that I don't look forward to — I just don't see how we're going to do it, but ten days from now I'll be looking back on it knowing we did it and wondering how — Oh, dear Pat just told me that we're taking the super out of St. Louis tomorrow nite — I thought we were going Sunday morning — that really makes things complicated —

Honey, more letters are coming from you now and I'm enjoying them so much you're still way behind me, but you're catching up —

Oh, honey, I have to stop now and close my suitcase now if I'm going to get anything to eat before we leave —

I love you, darling —

Jane

#45
6 May, 1945
In Port —

Dearest Honey:

Hi darling is spring on the bloom in the great Middle West? It's quite positively getting summery out here not that there is too much difference, just a little hotter that's all. I looked again today for mail, but again in vain. I've been passed up for six days now and I'm beginning to be a bit worried, for the mail is coming through and the dates are way past your last one. I just hope you aren't ill of flu or something, but maybe tomorrow I'll hear from you and then things will be alright again. I know it's silly of me to worry as you are probably perfectly all right, but just so darn busy that you haven't been able to write.

Baby isn't it wonderful? About the European end of it I mean. Everything is now ours but Czechoslovakia and Norway.

Burke and I had the duty today so we stayed pretty close to the radio except for our time in the sun and a swim. It's just so unbelievably wonderful. Things that sort of choke you up too like Copenhagen being freed from a five year domination. Think of it, a whole new little generation who have never known anything but fear and hate and hunger suddenly finding themselves back into a world that is fun to be alive in again. Think of those poor people in Britain, nearly six years of blitz and bombings and lately doodlebugs. After all this time what's left of their families will be able to sit down to a dish of tea without wondering if the next day will find them all there, or indeed the house itself.

I suppose later the full devastation will impinge itself upon our consciousness and the terrible times that lie ahead in the struggle to preserve world peace and the settling of private squabbles in various countries. But now the human element holds precedence over everything else. The little people of that world are at last going to emerge into the light of day and be able to try and reconstruct their lives. For millions of course the only road open is that familiar one of a lost generation. Those who have lost their loved ones and their roots will find it hard to be anything but bitter and disillusioned. But on the other hand there are many millions more who will literally and figuratively pull up their britches and start trying to build a semblance of their lives back. And the cornerstone of each of their structures will be "decency" for that is the one quality that has so long been absent from this old world that all of us will strive to resurrect it.

I seem to have taken off don't I darling? It really is just that that is what seems the important part of the victory to me. Not the valour of arms or the undoubted courage of those who fought and died, but it's the little people of the shattered lives who now have a chance to start rebuilding what is left of them.

Well my darling, tomorrow will mark the fourth month since I said goodbye to you on that dock. It seems without any doubt at least twice as long as all the time I was gone last year, but then it is still 1/3 of the year we had planned on. Speaking of that, I believe that I have at least a one in three chance of getting that Gunnery School in Washington. On top of that, I think I have a one in three of getting to S.F. for re-assignment. In taking the sum total it's a better than even money shot that I will see you long before the year is over. If I do get back and you are still bouncing from show to show I know it will be rather hectic, especially for you. But don't worry about it honey as I will be quite content to see you in the odd moments when they don't demand your presence. The old dream of a mountain cabin and just the two of us fishing and dreaming and making breakfast and pointing out the stars to you still exists, but like everything else in wartime, time and being with each other is rationed by things a lot bigger than a romantic's dream. But I here and now promise you that someday it will come through.

Within a couple of weeks we should know something one way or another. Pete flew down to see some of the big boys yesterday and things could look a lot worse, believe me.

Yesterday Berk and I went over to the club for a bit as it was V-H (Holland) and V-NG (North Germany) day. We ran into some of our friends from the bombers again and they had more wonderful yarns. One of them, this black Irishman name of Mahoney that I have spoken of before is going home! He got the dope the other day and leaves in about two weeks. Well some of the lads have been going back to the land you loved so well for a rest of ten day or two weeks and he has made them haul back a little of the wet goods for him. At any rate he has built up a nice little stock and is throwing a party in a few days to say hail and farewell to this garden spot. As we are not in on any liquor pool we were pretty disturbed about what our contribution should be but we suddenly had a brain wave.

Steaks! They of course eat mostly spam and "c" rations. They really get a lousy break on the chow. At any rate, we broached the idea and it was hailed with shrill cries of delight. So now it appears we will not only get good and drunk, but also eat broiled steaks and French fries. Should be quite a party. As a matter of fact it will probably be our swan song to this rock ourselves so we will throw heart and soul into it. Since we have gotten to know these guys so darn well we have been on the inside of everything. Target for tonight, results, exc. It's all so darn fascinating and so much unable to talk about that it makes me mad. Could I but speak, my love, and I'd write you a really interesting letter. But that, of course, is out.

As I wrote you the other day I spent the afternoon with the Captain, "Old Salty" and got the dope on his background. I have spent a good bit of time kicking the story around but so far I have yet to find the right frame. The love interest is proving a headache of the first water. I thought of having his son appear in the yarn and he could of course pull in the sex. But as yet it hasn't solved itself. It's funny too because I feel I have the whole thing cut and dried and ready to write if I can just unlock the formula. I've got the main theme, the main character, the setting and the time. Now all I need is the dame and a magic spoon to stir the broth and bring out nectar. It will come, of that I'm sure but I am going through the labor pains of the damned trying to give birth to it. One of the things that bothers me as much as anything is that I have such a wealth of material to work with that the tree is obscured by the forest or vice-versa. At any rate, it is fun to try and I think even you would approve of my work. I also think that I am well clear of the slough of despond I was in, and that in itself is very encouraging.

I have no doubt in my mind that if I get through this war I will write a couple of very good plays and maybe a very bad novel or two but right now I would like to get just one mildly acceptable short story accepted and published. Well, time will tell. That and application of the seat of my pants to the chair in the front of this thing.

I wrote Jack yesterday passed the time of day. I don't guess it was such a good letter but I'm sure he will be glad to be able to read one letter from me. He must think I am an awful softie to be such a correspondent but I tried to explain that to him, too. I said that after all there is nothing really wrong with a guy being in love with his wife after seven years, in fact it takes about that long to realize just what love really is. Believe me, honey, I now think I know how to behave so that our future life together will be more than it ever was before. More depth, more understanding and certainly a lot less friction! More love too!!!

Darling, I just re-read the first letter you wrote on the seventh of January. If you were expressing true feelings then, and there is no reason to assume that you weren't then there is no need for us to ever worry about readjustments or such. If we could come that far in three months with a lot of troubles to beset us just think what we could do with a new life in front of us!

You may gather, my sweet, that your nearness is not altogether unattractive to me. I really believe that you could go so far as to assume that it even gives me a modicum of pleasure, yes, you might even go so far as to say I miss you like hell and love and adore you more every day. As a matter of fact, you would be right on the beam!

I was going to send some money to Jack to wire you flowers on Mothers day, but I thought you would probably throw them in the bell-boys face. Maybe when this thing is over and done and we have the time, maybe then I can haul home a whole florist shop to you on mothers day and we could both have something to show for it! On this one though darling, all my love goes to you, not as a "mommy", but rather as my honey.

I guess I am getting awfully sticky and might easily be misunderstood. So rather than that I will curb me love, wish you a bon nuit and end up by telling you that I will always send you —

All me love —

Chas

X for V-E and me!

Hotel Lafayette
Clinton, Iowa
May 6, 1945

My darling Chuck;

It is now about midnite — Sunday — and I've been pointing all evening toward a letter to my honey but it seems that when we got off the train today, there was another train between us and the station so we had to wait for about fifteen minutes with both of them industriously pouring cinders all over us. As a result my hair was black — my formerly clean white sweater gray and grimy — it even seeped into the luggage. All in all I was a mess. So I had to wash my hair — I was just drying it when Pat got the bright idea it might be possible to make it almost a strawberry blonde with some stuff she had in her makeup case — I approved of the idea so we started to work — it is now finished and is a golden blonde with a slight reddish cast. Of course that took about an hour of concentrated effort so that was one more delay. I say one more because this afternoon when we arrived, we were so tired and we had almost a pint of scotch — Mr. Walburn our guest star, gave us a fifth as a going away present — so we had two drinks to recover from the ordeal — then I put on my slacks, took my stationery box and announced my intention of going out in the park and writing you a letter. Only a block away is the Mississippi and on its banks, the "city" of Clinton has a lovely little park as a monument of the last war. So I sat on the grass and watched the river — a muddy blue brown, swollen with floods right now — and quiet — like a pregnant woman. I looked at the river and the grass then I lay back and looked at the sky and that was the end of the letter to you. It was as if I had finally come out of Bedlam and everything was so quiet and peaceful that I went sound asleep with the sun in my face — and your Ray-Bans across my eyes and I didn't wake up until six o'clock. It was what I needed though because, as you may have been able to tell from my letters, the pace and constant living with lots of people was getting me pretty distraught. And there was nothing I could do to cure it — drinking certainly won't — this today is the proper treatment. I feel more at peace with the world already.

Yesterday was really quite a day — we started at noon, played five shows at Scott Field returned to St. Louis — it was over an hour drive — took the sleeper out of there at 11:45 — it was a lovely train-I would have liked to have stayed for days — but no — we reached Chicago at 7:30 this morning, changed stations, had breakfast and took the train for Clinton at ten — it was a miserable ride. We had seats because they always let us in with the military but there were fully as many people standing as sitting — hot, crowded, and dirty. So many people were coming out here to the hospital to see their wounded boys of a Sunday — and they had to stand the whole four hours — I felt guilty for not giving anyone my seat but I knew that I probably needed it, at that point, worse than they did, so I was selfish.

St. Louis impressed as a very fine city — of course I saw very little of it — but I'd like to go back — it has a fine free air about it — like San Francisco. And Chicago looked even dirtier than the time we were there. The station we came into was the one where I fed Gideon the two pounds of hamburger on my way to you in Ithaca.

I've been sort of slacking off on the writing lately darling. I'll try to reform — starting right now.

Darling — last but most important. I've been saving it. When I arrived in St. Louis the other nite, there was a package from you with the bracelet and the little bottle. Darling the bracelet is lovely and the [INCOMPLETE]

Hotel Custer
Gatesburg, Illinois
May 8, 1945 letter #45

Hello sweet,

I had the most wonderful letter from you today — the best for ages — all about fixing the showers and going to Europe — the whole letter was just fun to read.

I meant to write you yesterday which was the day of the unofficial announcement of V-E day — the day the AP got itself into trouble but when yesterday evening came — we got up about four this morning and I knew yesterday evening what was in store for us — I went to bed instead — trouble was I couldn't sleep — my poor body wasn't accustomed to the luxury — I turned and tossed, read — then I finally started reciting everything I had ever committed to memory — that is a fine way to bore yourself to sleep — This morning though, I wasn't sleepy and didn't "suffer" a bit so it was perhaps just as well.

As I started to say — yesterday morning at nine, I was awakened by this horrific screaming of sirens, whistles and horns and real thunder in the distance, all accompanied by a cacophony of rain. I knew this wasn't the usual Monday morning "arise and shine" signal so I went to the phone and ascertained that it indeed was V-E day which announcement later proved to be a little premature. Today however, the confirmation came — I don't believe there is really any general desire to celebrate, too much has been lost and there's a hard job ahead. But at least one part of the job is almost finished.

Great excitement on Mr. Evan's part today — the USO District (that's about 1/3 of the country) supervisor was here — the show went off very well, which made him deliriously happy. Only thorn is that I have to cut a couple of my best gags because one makes fun of M.P.'s and the other of 2nd lieutenants. The army's feelings are getting delicate — I am furiously annoyed about this because one of them was a sure fire roar — a perfect topper. I'm going to have to cut this letter short darling because before I collapse of fatigue I have to study the joke book for something to do tomorrow — I wish I had talent for this sort of thing —

Honey, I adore you —

All my love, Jane

Custer Hotel
[illegible] Illinois
May 9, 1945 letter #76

Hello honey darling Chuck;

Look at this number here — 76 — and today I received #42 from you — almost twice as many — yet at the beginning of almost every letter, you scold me for not writing. You say you haven't much to write about but I haven't received a letter from you yet that wasn't fascinating — and heaven knows now darling it sounds as if you had about twice as much time as I do — also did it ever occur to you that my life of trains hotels and hospitals wasn't exactly fascinating. Of course there's all the driving but you can't look at scenery forever and I fall asleep a lot anyway. Besides that honey, it seems to me you spend an awful lot of time at the club — did you begin that short story you were going to start the day after you finished letter #41 — Huh? Well honey that ends the scolding for today but do you realize that in the four months and two days you have been gone, you haven't sent me one smidgen of all that writing you were going to do — not one paragraph even. Honey I know it's hot and miserable but try to get started on it for my sake, please.

You know you say I don't write enough and the family says I don't — your mother who has been the most neglected is so darned sweet about it — By the way darling — I sent her a Mother's day present airmail today for us — it's a compact — she may not use it much but she'll be so proud of it she'll love to have it to carry. It's sterling silver and it has a lovely floral painting on the top-baked in so it can't chip — it really is lovely — I think she'll like it and she does love floral things.

I was utterly delighted with Daddy and Mary both writing to ask your advice about Sam — incidentally, I think the advice you wrote her was excellent, darling.

What an old home week afternoon you had. I vaguely remember Peth, as he was in a corner with Dottie most of the time and we went down to our compartment but I've heard Dorothy and Martha talk of him a lot. Then of course Dan Tasch I've told you about dozens of times honey. He's the boy that Martha is so much in love with — remember. I believe I told you that he was a Fiji too — as far as being out there soon, honey, I think that's wishful thinking on Martha's part — I had a letter from her the other day and she is doing some radio work and hasn't been near the Victory committee.

You know how Dorothy and Martha are — they blissfully talk themselves into something and then don't do anything about it. Besides, they don't realize as I do now, of how very little importance the Hollywood office is-they're merely a clearing house for New York — besides, unless they were cast in a play, there isn't anything they could do — you have to be a good singer or dancer — you can't just get by — well anyway — I'm having a hard enough time getting good at this M.C. business and I don't deceive myself — up until recently, my appearance was my biggest asset — (it's effective on the stage you see) now I'm learning how to ad-lib and how to keep things rolling-things are better. I still fluff a few once in awhile, but Martha, to be frank, fluffed them all. Acting training is some help in this but a good course of listening to Bob Hope and a disposition which is so good it shines out of you are better — (the latter is what I try to cultivate — I mean sort of a thing that makes people think you're happy — so it makes them feel happy too)Well the point is that if I have a bunch of very fine jokes, I think they'll ask me to go overseas — In the meantime, I'd prefer to be in a play, so I'll see what I can do. But so far as I know or could dream of, there really is no project afoot to be out there — damn it.

At any rate, you'd really like Dan-he's a very fine guy, intelligent, a bit sarcastic, a good drinker and definitely a rebel at heart. He used to remind me a great deal of you — he has no overweening respect for authority but only respect for intelligence and getting things done — didn't hesitate to step on toes of higher ranking people. If you see him again and I hope you do — give him my best and tell him I'll take a good look at Chicago for him — that's his home. (He's with the Special Service)

Did I tell you honey that I'll be ten days in New York and it will be in July — hot — but that's fine because you see that will give me time there to investigate a couple of things and by that time you should know fairly well what the future holds in store for you. I'm making a very determined effort not to be excited about the possibility of your getting to go to Washington to school because I don't want to be disappointed in case it didn't come out — but do you know what honey, if the Gods are with us — it could work out just beautifully — I'm praying darling.

So with that hope I'll close —

All my love,

Jane

Saw a boy today who at first glance looked just like Tom Potts. It's when the shock of resemblance impinges itself on your consciousness that you really realize that your friends are a long time gone —

10 May, 1945

Dearest Honey:

Well, darling, it finally got here! V-E day! Official, complete and all signed sealed and delivered. It still doesn't seem quite possible, but I guess it will gradually grow into a factual thing in time.

I had intended to write last night, but for two reasons I didn't. One was that I must confess to a bit of a hangover as a result of the official celebration, and then I had a tooth pulled yesterday. It was one that I bit in two the night we got hit. Guess I never told you that before, but one of the first things I was conscious of was that I had a mouth full of something, and I began spitting it out. Seems I had chomped down so hard that I had busted a tooth, and my mouth was filled with chunks of enamel and fillings. A very peculiar feeling to say the least. Although it didn't bother me, it was practically no use, being almost not there so I had it yanked, by the way, it was one of the back ones, so don't think I have a spittin' gap or anything like that. I am also going to have a few porcelain fillings put in, and then I am set for eating for a few more years.

All of which seems like a round about way to explain why I didn't write last night, but there it is. That damn procaine or whatever it is they use now doesn't seem to jive too well with residual alcohol, and besides it hurt like hell. I couldn't help thinking of those awful nights in Hollywood where no one slept, and you went through tortures of the damned and me not doing much better. Those grim, ghastly, godawful nights!! Please, darling, the next time I get back, let's don't have any molar trouble hanging around! Honey, I know you didn't want it that way, so don't let your back start arching. Remember that I love you very much and did even then, and greater tests man is not often called upon to go through.

I sent off a batch of pictures air mail to you today, so you might get them before this letter. In which case I hasten to explain that the shots of Bob Patten that I enclosed I sent merely so you could somewhat see the place. I sent Jack a much better set of prints, you see the film was in pretty sad shape, and we had to do the negatives ourselves. Today some friends of ours in the Base photo lab at the strip came down with a Speed graphic and took some more of the grave for me, also the cemetery. They will give me some prints and also the negatives, so I will send those on to Jack.

They took the four pictures of us at the club that I enclosed, so you see they are pretty good, even if the subjects could stand some improvement. The one of the five of us you know everybody. The other people are off two DE's that we know pretty well. They have been tied up alongside us both here and down in the Solomons last year. As you can see, it was really quite a gay afternoon. I think they came out very well though, and they will be nice to keep. I hope you can see a little love light shining in me eyes, because believe me, darling, it's there.

Well, darling, I finally succumbed, and I am now a true Navy man. I have learned to play cribbage! Fact! Berk and I both started learning yesterday, and I have been beating the hell out of him. I get him very mad by asking him if he is sure he understands the principles of the game and that I would be glad to give him a little private instruction at a nominal fee. He really takes off on that!!! Now all that is left to make me a complete old salt is to start playing

Acey-deaucy. I have had a few goes at it, and I fear that is one thing I will never become either proficient at, or excited over.

I am still grinding away on my "Old Salty" idea and still having plot trouble. I am beginning to "Cherchez la femme" in my sleep. I think it's going to straighten out pretty soon though and I hope to have a rough draft on its way to you before too long.

You know, darling, I have been giving quite a bit of thought lately to this "G.I." bill. Anyone can get a year's schooling at any place of their own choosing with all tuition up to five hundred bucks paid, and in my case seventy-five bucks a month. I know that's an awful drop in the bucket, but I was thinking that should you be working either in Hollywood, or New York it might be a very fine idea to take advantage of. What I had in mind was, say, the American Academy, or if in Hollywood maybe U.C.L.A., or if there is a better school for what I want I would take that. What I had in mind was a very concentrated course in play direction, movie technique (if available), short story and play writing and any related or correlated subjects that I could do justice to. You see, you can start this any time within two years after hostilities cease. Which will probably be some time after I am back in civilian life.

Maybe this is very advanced dreaming with a few million Japanese left around these parts, but it does make a certain amount of sense to me. It seems to me now that you are going to be bitten by the acting bug the rest of your life, and if we are going to make it the rest of the way together, I want to be in some phase of the entertainment world. Acting I would like, but you know my limitations, and I get no prettier by the day. Also, what little I ever did know has gotten pretty rusty in almost three years of nothing. Probably be four or more before I could ever start again. Then I really think I could do something along the line of direction.

I included playwriting and short story because, after all, that's the clay that directors work with primarily and actors only secondly. Again, I say that I know for us to live on seventy-five bucks a month is really funny, but on the other hand you seem to be doing very nicely without me now, and there is no reason to think that you will want to quit acting when Johnny comes marching home. Please, dear God, don't get the idea that I want you to support me, darling, and that I intend to bask in the reflected light of my wife's ability. It only strikes me that this might be a very good way to take that readjustment in our stride. After all, a Navy Lt. who's a qualified top watch stander and a red hot gunner has damn little of practical import to offer a man in the entertainment business.

I am pretty sure that that's where we belong and that we can be happy in the doing of it. The fascination and the appeal of it will always exist for me and I think for you too, even though this particular trip seems to lack some of the lustre that your previous one did. I still know you would give your eye teeth to have a fat part in a Broadway hit, and I would give what few snappers I have left to have written and/or directed it for you and with you or both. It may sound, as I said before, a little on the dreamy side, but there is really nothing so fantastic about it. We could do it someday you know.

At any rate, it's an idea, kick it around in that lovely head of yours and let me have your ideas on the subject. Let's not forget that a grown man with an avid interest can learn a hell of a lot faster than a college boy who is interested in "lining them up." I've grown up a lot, darling, and although I'll still think of myself as a beach boy and a two-fisted drinker at sixty, I would like to make a small impression in this little old world we live in. Thirty-three may be a little old to grab the world by the horns and make it say uncle, but hell, look at Joseph Conrad, he not only learned to write, but in another language!!

I guess the old man sounds a little drunk tonight, baby, but it's not so. I had the duty today and not a drop, so help me!

I got a letter and a post card from you today from Rolla Mo. today. I still don't understand why I got no mail for six or seven days whilst others were getting theirs. At any rate, they finally came through, and now letters have shown up for the 27, 29 and now the second. All is forgiven, love, and I know it was silly of me to have you all done up in a drafty hospital room wasting away with peeneumonia!! I'm not really an old fuss budget, honey, just a guy who loves you like the dickens!

Have you any dope on just when you would leave for Europe? You see things are finally starting to move for us and within a few days I should know pretty well what's up for me. All possibilities are still wide open, including the 30er and a shot at that Gunnery School. So you see, me love, I would like to know just how long you intend to be around. Say, just had a thought, will the end of the war there make any difference in your plans, and what did you mean by saying you would stick it out until it hit Florida. I thought you wound up in New York?

Oh well, questions, questions, questions. How wonderful it would be if I could just see you for a while and we could get a hell of a lot of things squared away, couldn't we, honey? Until I do, keep the letters coming and remember I adore you.

all me love — Chas X have one on me !

#47 In Port
12 May, 1945

Darlingest Jane:

Hi, cutie pie, what cooks on the old "on tour" burner tonight? Honey, the most amazing thing, yesterday I got a letter from you (I should say a card) dated May 5th at 11:30. With the aid of a chart Berk and I figured it out. That card came from St. Louis to — in seven hours less than five days!!! If this war produces nothing less than that, I still think it will stand out. Why my golly a guy wrote a whole article about a flight that only took a few hours less and went only a few hundred miles farther and it was emblazoned in a weekly slick for all the world to see. Now in our case, just a plain little postcard that has to be cleared several places and delivered aboard ship arrives in almost the same time!!! Perhaps I am over-emphasizing it but it does really seem remarkable. Especially when I sat in the same place for six weeks without any mail at all!!

Baby, among other things that arrived today were 19 sacks of mail! Of course that included air mail (just a drib) first, second, third or fourth class. We got all the magazines that have due the ship since January. Plus that we got a lot of Xmas presents, packages, etc.

Right now I'd like to make a confession. I'd had the feeling lately that your letters to me were more or less "duty" letters. Not that I didn't think they were amusing and delightful but more or less written with the feeling of "My God, I suppose I should write to Chuck again" I suppose it was really prompted by the fact that ever since I began getting your letters I have filled page after page with bilge but at least a lot of it. Well at any rate when the loot was sorted today there were a set of pictures from you on the S.P., a book from Utah and a jar of candy from God knows where.

Janie you will never know how much those things were appreciated. Not for the things themselves but for the realization that you must have said to yourself "maybe Chas would like that" and you took time out to get it and send it on. I know you are busy and I also know that you have very little time to be writing people, in fact the time you take seems to detract from your sleep which you should be getting more of, but still my darling, my heart took a wonderful leap. Letters, notes, or even postcards would do me very well.

I seem to be fouling this whole thing up. What I really started out to say was that some little unexpected expressions of affection just made me happy as hell! Might be that you love me the way I love you!

Well, enough of that, in fact, quite enough. I've often thought that you must think the guy you happen to be married to is a very peculiar character to whom real love and a sincerity of effort seems to come a bad second try — well, let it lay, let it lay.

About me since I last wrote: I had a letter from Buddy (which I shall answer on the morrow) and a letter from Marg Latham, which was very entertaining. I guess Jack just doesn't believe in dropping a line, as I have never had a letter from him. About us, we are moving, with what's left, for a short haul. From then on it's in the lap, but I don't think it looks too good from here.

I asked you in my last letter for dates and such stuff, well mommy, I really think you can plan whatever you want with a clear conscience. Despite my previous talk and precedent non-withstanding as I see it we aren't going to miss anything from here on out.

C'est the Godamned guerre. "Think of me sometimes, when April comes around again, with its blue skies and sudden showers, think of that — Well doc. Don't forget to think and try to remember that I will always love you —

    Chas

I suppose "YANK" is a part of your diet, but I thought the enclosed was singularly apprapo (don't you sometimes get discouraged with my spelling?)

    Like the dickens —

    Chas

Also got a picture from the "City of Paris" may not be good — but at least we're together!

    Jillions

    Chas

H. L. Hampton
10th Army Troop

Dear Jane;

I suppose you're somewhere in Illinois, or beyond, now. Say hello to the old state for me, will you? All those fine plans I had have gone glimmering out the window, so I haven't even the heart to mention them.

The army, demonstrating to my complete satisfaction that it can manage the impossible without batting an eye, has actually arranged things so I regret the end of the war in Europe. That seems inconceivable, doesn't it? But the whole thing is tied up with the little old readjustment plan.

Now that the war in Europe is over, they've SUSPENDED ROTATION. While two-thirds of the boys in Europe, fighting through wild desolate places like Paris and Rome, with about half my time overseas, are getting furloughs in the States, we're going to be sitting out here for months more, with no chance for rotation or leave, with our only hope of getting home contingent upon being allowed to leave active duty — and you know how much chance there is of that. Isn't that a fine mess of fish!

But that isn't the best of it. We're going to convert the United States into one vast baby farm, we're all going to encourage this with might and main. The point system for discharge has just been announced. For a month in service, a man gets one point. For a month overseas, he gets an extra point. For engaging in a battle, he gets five points.

AND FOR HAVING A KID, HE GETS TWELVE POINTS, TWELVE POINTS, TWELVE POINTS. I tell you, that drives me wild. A guy with two children will be more eligible for discharge than another poor sap who's been in nearly two years, or over-seas for a year. How do you like that? A guy who's been overseas two years, with no chance of raising a family, except through a very nefarious process, takes a back seat to the guy who's been stationed in the states for all that while and swelling the baby crop. Justice is not only blind; justice has now become imbecilic. You should have heard the howls that arouse around here today when that was announced.

So now I miss my brother's wedding, miss my sister's graduation, sit here and stagnate until some guy from Europe, after he's had his furlough a chance to toughen up for what we've been living in for close to four years, condescends to come out here, at which time I may be declared surplus, at the discretion of the commander.

This is as far as I'll trust myself. A parade of profanity most foul parades before my eyes constantly in patterns of red dots, festooned with attractive ribbons of red tape. First stages of paranoia, perhaps. If so, I should soon live in a happier state, and institution.

So the best of everything, always. Buy another war bond to pay for my keep, and a little specially tailored straight Jacket.

My love to you,

Hamp

Post Tavern, Battle Creek, Mich.
May 14, 1945
letter #78

Darling honey;

You would really laugh if you could see me now — with my talent for always doing the right things at the wrong time here I am in my little straw mattressed pallet — writing you by that relic of past illumination, the candle. It seems that I have been washing my hair — foolishly because the bleach was old and never did really work — Rollie and Pat are asleep and this indescribably luxurious room only has overhead lights. Hence the candle — they come with every room.

It's awfully late but I actually slept until eleven this morning so I'm not too worried about tonite the six hours I plan on will be enough.

I received no mail from you today but am so hoping for some tomorrow — I have almost given up the thought, each time I open a letter that it will have news of your coming home but, as I said before I at least know that you're safe — that is when you don't go around sticking your neck out. And you're not any more so that's fine. I was terribly sorry darling to hear about the plane you had been in.

Honey, this was just a note to let you know I'm thinking of you so goodnite my darling — you are always with me —

My love, Jane

#48
15 May, 1945
In Port

Darlingest Janie:

   Look honey, I've had a couple of bad days with myself as a result of that last letter. I guess apologies now would be a little late but at least an explanation might help. You see it had been a bad and trying day in the first place and then we got a dispatch that seemed to really kick in the head all ideas we might have dreamed up about Uncle Sugar. I was more than a little bitter and, as a result I guess I over-sensitized myself and reread your last few letters with a slightly jaundiced eye. Well, in my mood I interpreted them to be nice and casual and slightly impersonal. I realize now, after thinking it over that though they may have been causal they were not meant to be impersonal. Now that you understand slightly the piqued position I was in I hope you will also understand and discount the last effort. I know now that another thing I'm sure of is that I will never have to be the recipient of a "duty" letter. I know you too well and hope that there is more respect between us than to ever allow one to be written.

   What I mean, darling, is that I am sorry. All day today I have had such an overwhelming love for you that you could hardly believe it. When you try and reduce a wonderful felling to the plain word department it becomes pretty trite indeed. But today was something really extraordinary. I know that in your present job things keep you hopping so much that you could have very little time to build mental pictures, but you see with us, time is our mostest thing. As a result I could devote myself completely and without reservation to thinking about you today and still know that I wasn't imparing either myself or the war effort. Splendid thing, this Navy red — tape, gives you so much time to think about your wife! At any rate, I do love you very much indeed, and if that last letter hurt your feelings, I am sorrier than I can say.

   Say you know those prints I sent you of Bob's grave, well I am sorry to say that some of the little ones were only printed once in that small size and in trying to make some more copies we inadvertently destroyed the negatives. I'm sorrier than I can tell but I guess you'd better send the little ones on to his family. I got two fine pictures of his grave from the B-29 photographers and I have the negative of the print I am sending with this letter. That's the one of the grave, I also am enclosing a print of the other shot they made of the arch over the entrance. I have two more prints of that and four more of the grave itself that I will send to Jack with the negative. Maybe after you look at them you will want his family to have them, although they will have plenty without it and can have more made. Maybe you had better keep it for us as I have some shipmates buried in the same cemetery.

I am enclosing some other snaps of the island and some of the boys at the club. Hope you like them and hang onto them for our scrapbook.

The most wonderful story. Yesterday we were censoring mail and Berk said listen to this. Well one of the lads was writing home and says as follows "Well mom, I went to a USO show here last night and it was pretty good. They had some frill named Gertie Lawrence and she did a song called "Jenny" or something like that and boy could she do bumps and grinds! Just like the old burlesque back home!!" Don't you love it? Some frill named Gertie Lawrence!

Well darling there is much hustle and bustle as we are going to move down to another island today and things is about ready. I'll write you a real long letter tomorrow after we get there and tell you what I can. One thing for sure, I will know what happens to me very shortly now so cross your fingers and say a hail Mary for me. Might be that I get to celebrate your birthday with you yet!! Wouldn't that be something!

Take care of yourself darling, and don't get yourself too tired — Cheefu just said the mail is going now so I'll have to close —
I miss you like the dickens!
All me love —
LS MFT!!! Chas
SR SF SBS!!! XXXXX!

Letter #79
Post Tavern Battle Creek, Mich.
May 15, 1945

Hello sweet darling;

I have just finished going over all your letters from #26 to #44 piling them all in chronological order and ironing them flat — of course that necessitated re-reading quite a few of them so it's most horribly late. I've spent the whole evening since we arrived home at eight in general housecleaning activities — it's perfectly amazing what this blonde bag here can find to do with four bags (suitcases to you!) in necessary repacking. I feel as if I had too much stuff but, as I look I don't know how I can manage without all that stuff so I keep carrying it — bother or no bother.

The Percy Jones hospital today is all amputations. You've seen more than your share of seeing them I know but I've never seen so many en masse, and the first time I'd seen boys with all four limbs gone. And their age average seemed to be so much younger than other groups we've seen. That I can't understand but there must be some reason for it.

I have always liked best to write you at the end of the day — when everything has resolved itself and fallen into place but I keep finding myself drifting into the land of nod. Perhaps I'll try writing mornings. It has been a hard day though — eleven shows!

Darling, please try to forgive the brevity of my letters the last few nites. It's not that I don't love you — it's just that life gets a little ahead of me —

I do love you honey — Hurry Home!

All me love, Jane

#49
17 May 1945
In Port 365 to go

Dear Janie-pants:

Honey I wish you could see your old man tonight. You know I've been bragging about my tan and how healthy I looked? Well I had an underway watch this am until noon and I stood it in shorts. As a result I am about the pinkest thing you ever saw! There must be something about being at sea. Truthfully though the only thing that is sore is my forehead and the very tops of my shoulders and already it's starting to turn into a beautiful dark tan, well — maybe a little on the lobster side but definitely going to be ten by tomorrow!

Just found myself wondering where my honey was tonight so I looked up the little list and there you are in Chicago! You are getting around darling. Don't forget to look once at the Lions for me. Last letter I had from you was at Rola and then a card from St. Louis that I told you came so fast. Still it's only been about a week or so and we are in hopes that we may have mail here when the orderly goes over in the morning. We got in too late to check today. But maybe manana!

Honey I'm still contrite about that letter. Every time I eat one of those wonderful chocolates you sent from Ogden I think again what a boor and a goop I must have sounded. Remember to forgive is divine darling so please try. Speaking of those chocolates they came through in the best shape I have ever seen candy arrive out in these parts. Not a one was crushed and they don't seem to melt in the heat. Truly wonderful. Was the can your idea or the stores, and are they a special kind of chocolate made for export? They are so perfect I wondered.

You notice I spoke of the heat, sweet William but it was a scorcher today. We had a wind following us (or a following wind!) that just matched our very slow speed, with the result that there wasn't a breath of air, and that ole sun just glaring down. Mammy I am glad I ain't a sweet as you or I would have melted sure.

Berk just came in and said "Clickety-click, clickety-click. What the hell do you find to write about?" So I told him I had worked over my sunburn and such. So he said "I just don't know. I know damn well I am going to write to Allie tonight, but I have been putting it off because there is nothing to write about" Well darling that's so damnably true. So many things I could say and give you little word pictures of it if it wasn't for that old debbil "security" but its still with us and so —

Just finished listening to "Zero Hour" from Radio Tokio. It's a nightly newscast in English that we generally try to catch. Tonight he gave some especially incredible figures on our Okinawa losses. We had just heard those released on our own Newscast and while they aren't particularly good, in fact very rugged indeed, they certainly are fine to believe after listening to him. He has the most peculiar voice, rather makes me think he is eating a very sticky Baby Ruth bar all the time he broadcasts, but still he is very intelligible. The Navy has not been having a very gay time up there but I am happy to see that their new policy of letting the public in on things quicker (TIME about 25 Feb.) is still going ahead. I noticed in our last TIME (7 May) that they even put out dope on the "Baka". That's quite amazing to me as it was very hush-hush. "Kamakaze"

I suppose has now become a common word at home, but that was kept dark for quite awhile too. Ran into Doc Parks the other day who is just back from there, (he went with Donsy) and he had some incredible yarns to spin. There is one boy who is certainly earning his pay! Honey, I hate to lure you on with statements like that and then chop you off, but that's the way things have to be.

I wrote to Jack yesterday and sent him a very good negative of Bob's grave, also as much as I could describe about its location and relative position etc. Not a hell of a lot you can say to a family to help, but if it's even a little then it becomes worthwhile.

I am wondering if that bracelet and the blue bottle ever got to you. Don't remember just when I mailed it, but should have heard from you by now on it. Hope it got through all right, but maybe if I hear from you tomorrow there will be something about it. If it doesn't come, don't worry, as it has very little intrinsic value. It's just that I did make it for you and a lot of love went into it, even if it doesn't show very much!

Speaking of love, which seems to be my favorite subject of conversation with you; I sure do! Tomorrow will probably give us more dope on our future than anything that has yet happened so unreligious though I may be, I think I'll say a little prayer tonight. I would love to spend a birthday with my honey. After all the last two I have been away from you three in a row is one too many!!! Well darling hold a good thought for me and a little love if it can all be managed. Personally I think you are just about the most adorable thing on this old tired earth but then I may be prejudiced because you know you will always have —

All me love —

Chas X his mark!

Good night sweet darling. I really do love you!

POST CARD
Latin Quarter 23 W. Randolph St. Chicago, Ill.
May 18, 1945

Honey remember the night at the Bal Talbrin and how enchanted we were — So I'm thinking of you tonite — Honey Pat and Rollie want to say hello to you — Dear Chuck: Just a short "hello" Believe

me, I am looking forward to the day I meet such a charming person —
That's what Jane claims-Rolly

Me too, character! Pat (and darling the one gentleman who was
kind enough to bring us) Good Luck Chuck —

My love darling, Jane

19 May 1945 In Port —

Hi, Darling:

How's the prettiest gal in 48 states tonight? Me, I suffered a
grievous disappointment today. Seems that we got mail, that is
some of the boys did, but both Berk and I drew blanks. The letters
were dated the 12th and the last we have had from either of our
gals was the 4th. Now we are both damn sure that all that time
couldn't have gone by without one of us getting a letter, so what
we have deduced is that some mail went to the last port and hasn't
been forwarded down yet. And I'll bet a jillion I'm right! So we are
writing tonight, both knowing that we will get a fat packet in the
morning.

Being as we had the duty today, Smiley, Van, and Stu, and I
went to the beach to explore yesterday. No darling, not for any souvenirs!! This was more in an orientation mood, if you know what I
mean. Well, it's really an amazing spot. I thought I had been places
where the vaunted American industry and the "let's get on with
it boys" attitude had worked miracles, but I must admit they fade
into mediocrity compared to this spot. I'll try and give you a picture
of the most amazing facet of this complex thing. First you have to
imagine a harbor that was never intended by nature to be a fleet
anchorage, and then try and visualize millions of SEEBEES making
nature out a liar. In the first place it wasn't protected enough from
the sea, that's easy they say, we will just build a break-water and
make it a land-locked harbor. Well there are of course break-waters
and break-waters but believe me, this is the granddaddy of them
all. Then they ran into trouble because there were lots of coral
heads, and in places it just plain wasn't deep enough. Cinch, said
the SEEBEES, we will just dig it out a little. Which they proceeded
to do and even now are still doing. I know I am missing the most
important part of this because I am doing nothing about giving

you an impression of the scope of these activities. It's so vast that it takes your breath away. This may help; near the fleet landing they decided they needed more land right on the water. So they bring in mammoth dredges, millions of trucks etc., and the impression I got yesterday was that the dredges are walking out on this land that they have dug up and laid down behind them. Right after them comes the scrapers and graders, and behind them a few thousand Seabees throwing up Quonsets. Actually you could throw a rock from the dredge and hit the side of the first onset, as soon as one is up the paving has already reached it and trucks start packing it with supplies!! It reminds one of a tremendous ant hill that has suddenly been put on a piece work scale and each ant is striving to make the biggest salary that he has ever known.

I hope you caught a little of the feeling; it's really thrilling to know that we are all part of this team that is doing this kind of work. Well, we looked around for a bit and then ended up at the Club. We hoisted a few, but it is not the nice restful spot that the one was where we just left. It's smaller and no garden and full with millions of people. Still the liquor is a little better, when you can get to it! By the time it was closing we had inquired around and found where the BOQ was and the transient officer's mess was. We repaired to that and had a very decent chow. Then Cheefu got on the hook and found a guy he knew from years back. He said he would be glad to come down and pick us up, but they had a stage show starting in about forty-five minutes, and he couldn't get down and back in time. "Hell," says Cheefu, we will hitch-hike. Which we did, well, we got there a little late for the start of the show, but it was just a band, and they leave me a bit on the cold side. This was a very good outfit though, and their finale was very cute. They had a mock-up radio on one side of the stage with a big dial and a bench beside it. One of the lads pretended to be a drunk and kept changing the dial as the spirit moved him. Each time he did it, tuned in a new station I mean, the band would play in the style of another band. They really sounded like a lot of bands. They had a very good trumpet, (Harry James, etc.) and a wonder on a trombone (T. Dorsey etc.) It ran for about fifteen minutes, and the kids loved it. Me too, I must admit. They even had a "Evenin' folks, how y' all" complete with a mortar board and gown.

Well, following the show we went to his quarters and had gin and grapefruit juice and cheddar cheese and crackers. The latter very tasty. This guy, a very senior Lt., seems to have quite a job, I can't go into it, but he did promise us that if we get orders home he can put us on a fast ship that makes it from here to L.A. in about 17 days and has deluxe quarters for 125 officers and a swimming pool!! How about that? Every time I thought about it today I drooled, literally. I kept remembering that remark in "Up in Arms" where one soldier said to another who was looking down at all the nurses (wonks) sunbathing, and sways "Boy, there was nothing like this in the last war" and the other replies "Don't let 'em kid you soldier, there ain't nothing like it in this one either!!"

I don't mean to imply that this dream ship would have women, but a swimming pool!! Well, I just don't know. To get on with our saga. We finally took our departure and he had a driver take us back to the pier. Then we sat around for over an hour trying to bum a ride out to the ship and finally arrived about 0030. Not drunk, but having had quite a large day for our first on the island. I think the thing that impressed us most about this one are the marvelous roads. The last one had pretty good ones and they built a great many more in the time we were there, but this place looks like a freeway between Boston and New York no matter which way you turn. They really have done an amazing job.

Pete just got back a while ago with the nice news that we are now members of the most exclusive club on the island. Can't quite explain the mechanics to you, but suffice to say it opens an hour earlier, closes an hour later and the membership is around 800 rather than the eight or nine million that try to drink at the fleet club every day. Quite a feather in our cap. It's a very nice club, small but with a little garden and chairs and stuff and drinks are only 15 cents!! Imagine! We will have to give it a whirl tomorrow.

Another interesting tid-bit he brought back was that we all now stand a better chance of state-side reassignment than ever before. Of course nothing is certain in this man's Navy, but at least things definitely look on the upgrade at this writing. As the French would put it, Je suis tres excite! If you know what I mean. Of course, darling, I wouldn't worry about any party frocks if I were you, but there is always the chance. Speaking of that, I think it might be a good idea if the bank account would stand it to send me a couple of hundred bucks or so via Postal Money order. Be sure and send it that way as a check might be decorative, but hardly cashable in these parts. Perhaps I am looking too far in the future and jabbing myself in the arm, but I don't think it would do any harm. I am absolutely stony at this writing and if the Gods should take heed of my prayers, I don't want to have to twiddle me thumbs in S.F. or any other spot. Of course I will probably mail them back to you in a few weeks, but just in case you'd better send them on. Okay? Thanks.

We finally got to see "Going My Way" tonight. To say that it was good would only be repetitious, but My God, darling, that Barry FitzGerald was wonderful. What a depth of expression he can achieve by the raising of an eyebrow or a futile or ineffectual movement of his hands. Remember the movie you took me to when I was one jump ahead of a fit in S.F. and he did that beautiful job in "None But the Lonely Heart"? There is a guy I would like to meet. It really was a thrill to see something as fine as that after the epidemic of Universal quicky stinkers that we have been sitting through the past few movies...A picture like this sort of restores your faith in the industry and you suddenly realize that they can tell a beautiful story and really make a contribution to the world if they only spend the time and effort to line up a story and cast.

I think the wonderful thing about "Going My Way" was the manner in which they presented the Catholic faith. It was neither sacrilegious nor scoffing or overboard on the other side. The priests were nice human beings with an understanding of human nature, its foibles and weaknesses. On the other hand, all Catholics were not perfect for that reason, rather there was the nice Irish cop who hadn't been to mass in ten years and Mrs. Quibb or Squid or whatever, the nosey old snoop. All in all, it was a beautiful job of tight-rope walking, in which one misstep in either direction would have spelt ruin to the whole effort.

Well, me darling, I have been running on for a couple of hours, and I'd best hie myself to bed. To say that I miss and love you is but to repeat myself, so I miss you like hell and love you like the dickens!!!

One more thing, darling, and I'm sure you would like to hear it. When, and if, I get back, bourbon is going to be something that we have a couple of for social ability and because that much is enjoyable. It is not going to be a sop or a backstop or a retreat from reality. This time when I get home, there are going to be no differences that we can't solve by just out and out discussion, and a little give and take. Your old man is never going to ostrich-ize himself by trying to bury his neck in the neck of a bottle of bourbon! And that, me darling, is by way of being a promise! The way I love you honey is such that one kiss would intoxicate me more than all the whiskey in Uncle Sugar! (I can almost hear you shout at that one, but it's damn near true!)

At any rate, I thought you would like to know that you will face no liquor problem this go-round, and no half-crocked Irishman who fancied himself unloved, unhonored, and all but unsung. The next time it's going to be mostly sugar and spice and everything nice and lots of love and loving between two grown-ups! How does that sound to you?

I really am going to bed now, but I will probably dream about you. I dare you to entice me into your boudoir, I just dare you! Yipe!!! Remember I adore you, punkin

all me love — Chas

X The shape of things to come?

Letter #82
Train between Oklahoma City and St. Louis May 19, 1945

Hello, Darling;

I know — you will think you are on my forgotten list — such a dearth of mail, but the truth of the matter is that I've had such an experience the last few days that writing was almost out of the question until the thing resolved itself — As you can see, I'm way off my route — I didn't want to tell you about it until I found out the verdict, but now it can be told. It seems that the last few months things have not been entirely regular and I've had a constant pain in my side that at times was excruciating. Well, I went to a very highly recommended doctor in Battle Creek the other day and he told me I had cyst on my left ovary. As you well know, the personal implications of this were not only pretty tragic, but the consequences as far as you and I were concerned were not so good either. I nearly went out of my mind. I decided there was only one thing to do — call Dr. Stevens in San Francisco. So I did — only to discover that he was now the chief surgeon at the Naval Hospital in Norman, Oklahoma. So I called him there — and he said that if that diagnosis were true, it was a matter of such extreme importance to me that I must get a few days off and come down and see him. So I explained the situation to Mr. Evans who said I must go and he wouldn't even tell New York I was sick — which was very fine of him. So I proceeded to get almost in

Chicago the other nite — then I took a plane from there yesterday morning — arrived in Oklahoma City last nite and went out to the Naval Hospital at Norman this morning. Commander Stevens was so perturbed about the whole situation that he'd made arrangements to operate immediately to save what he could of the ovary if the first doctor's diagnosis should prove to be true. Incidentally he's the chief surgeon there, and he brought in for consultation a man who is nationally known as a gynecologist — and they decided that the first analysis or diagnosis had been completely wrong — that the pain was completely functional and that what the doctor had analyzed as a cyst was some sort of structure of my ovary that Doctor Stevens already knew about when he felt it. He told me not to go to another doctor for six months and never to let another doctor touch me as far as an operation was concerned unless he wasn't within reach. He was extremely kind and personally worried about me, which is pretty nice when you're facing something like that by yourself. If true, it would have been just about the worst thing that could have happened to me and he appreciated that. This little trip has cost me quite a bit of money but it has been so well worth it. This pain which has really been horrible has been preying on my mind and there were certainly definite indications of something awry. So now everything is alright and I can raise my head again — I mean I would have felt awfully lacking.

Aside from the suspense, it has been an interesting experience. There was my first plane ride in the United States, which was loads of fun really — I probably could have got another one back tomorrow, but I wouldn't have been positive until morning, so when I was able to get the train reservation, it seemed the best thing to do. I had an upper, but the conductor has not only changed it for me, but let me sit in his compartment so I could write to you — and given me a drink of Old Crow. I just seemed to have no trouble with anything — cashing checks, hotel reservations — everything simple — and in these times, too.

I will say truthfully that I hate to go back — those two days of freedom — of comparative self-determination have been like heady wine — you will know exactly what I mean. The conditions under which I've been living — the personality of Mr. Evans and the complete lack of stimulating companionship, have been rather stifling, and with these two days away, I've already felt my mind doing nip-ups. I've been awfully dull to myself lately and it's been fun to feel the stirring of the buds of spring. I am going to try to keep those buds developing, but it means living so much within oneself that I don't know whether I'll be able to do it.

I have felt a discontent with my work lately — even though I'm doing very well at it — I feel that if I keep on acting — I'm letting something which I might have to offer which _might_ be more important, go to waste. I've been reading and completely absorbed in "Yankee from Olympus," the life of Oliver Wendell Holmes — and heaven knows, my mentality certainly can't hold a candle to his mentality, naturally, nevertheless I have been thinking that the law is a system of rules laid down by man corresponding with the times to govern his relationship with other men — that as such it is the most fascinating and definitely one of the most useful callings this old world has to offer. Don't think, honey, that I am suddenly going to cry "Excelsior" and go bouncing off to study law — but I am going to read some books on the basic principles of law and see whether my theoretical interest is strong enough to apply itself to the grim details. I'll keep you posted on the progress of the experiment.

For the first time today, I met Dr. Stevens' family. His wife was very nice. She drove me back to Oklahoma City and I had lunch with her and a cousin of hers who seems to be very prominent here. We discovered that we had _many_ friends in common — Frei, Vicky Luis and of course, Will and Maureen — I cemented our friendship by giving her a whole raft of stamps from my unused ration book.

They have a little girl and, honey, the loving atmosphere of their home really brought a lump to my throat — well the war just _mustn't_ last _any_ longer.

Sweet darling — I'm in my berth now and I just went to sleep — sitting up — so I'll say goodnite and send you all my love — Jane
Now I'll write _real_ well —

Lincoln Hotel Indianapolis, Indiana
May 20, 1945
Letter #82

Hello honey darling;

When I arrived in Indianapolis at two this afternoon, There were three letters from you and the pictures. Before I forget it honey, did

I ever tell you that you're handsome. I have always thought so but those pictures certainly affirmed it in my mind and to the eyes of all beholders. Honey you really look terrific. Hateful as the tropical climate may be to you, it certainly agrees with your appearance. Rollie and Pat emitted little coos of delight over the five of you. I was reading the first letter then and I told them that more than likely they would have a chance to meet you all soon but then darling I read the third letter, the one where you had just received the candy and the book etc and honey I know you can't say anything but I am in a sense reading between the tones and I don't like it a bit. In fact, I'm nearly frantic. I can't figure it out naturally but darling, I'm worried about you. I know there is nothing either of us can do about that either and I don't suppose it will do any good for you to know you are in my heart all the time and always thought about with love...but do remember it honey. And darling...take care of yourself. I hope to God you won't have to go biting off any more teeth...if you know what I mean. I'm conjuring up all sorts of the damndest ideas. I'm afraid I just lit on the most logical one and I don't like to think about it. I love you honey. That's all I can say.

Back to the little things. I got here about two this afternoon...240 miles and four hours from St. Louis...an average of sixty miles an hour. I changed trains there this morning and the change was almost as fast as the second train. The train wasn't built for speed with the result that instead of the smooth ride I remember on the Daylight or the Lark, it seemed as if we were literally hurling through space with the speed of a rocket and were subject to all the whims of the atmosphere that a plane is in rough weather. When I got here, I discovered that the room I was in with Pat and Rollie was really tiny but had no luck in getting a single. They might have been hurt anyway but I am beginning to have almost a thirst for the uncluttered life...this business of wanting to get alone for a little while is becoming almost a mania and I must get over it, either that or get alone for a little while.

I should have had the psycho-analyst that I was talking to on the train today spirit it out of me. He was an army major and I understand from a doctor that was with him that he is very well known. The conversation ended rather amazingly after we had discussed basic ideas for about an hour with his really begging me to take up medicine and specialize in psycho-analysis...which is really quite funny. He was actually raving about my remarkable perception and logic and my brilliant mind...I don't know what I said that led him to that conclusion...I think I'd been raving about the Holmes book and it was some sort of communicated intelligence that comes and leaves in the course of the book reading.

Darling, in the little time I've had since I read your letter, I've given some serious thought to your idea of attending a school on direction and play writing etc. It's really a very constructive, fine idea but in my mind we have both reached the age when if there isn't in a course a great deal of technical knowledge that you can't acquire anyplace else or a requirement for a degree to practice a profession...I wonder if the best way isn't to learn by doing. For example, if you took this job that Don offered, granted the offer is still open and mastered that and at the same time took advantage of the opportunities around you, of the knowledge of the people who were making a success of actual production, if you wouldn't learn more and faster that way. Of course, if you try and learn that way, you have to be constantly alert and alert on your own, not because you are taking a course...but for a person as intelligent as you are, gaining knowledge through actual production seems to me to be almost more valuable. Of course you have to do some studying on the side so that you can understand the forms that things are taking... that I know...actually it requires more of you if you do it sincerely than going to a school but in the long run, perhaps it leads to more. Actually I don't know...but it is my idea that you learn to write for example by applying the seat of your pants to the chair in front of the typewriter and writing...however I am beginning to see a fallacy in my argument. You should have some sort of schooling on the basic principles of motion picture production...it would be better. Maybe everything I have said is wrong. You think about it and honey, whatever you want to do, your allotment is being put aside every month just to give you that opportunity and a freedom of choice so whatever you do think is right you will have the means to do it. In my mind the world owes you a lot more than that.

I really hated to come back today. I had savored the two days of freedom of choice and found them good. Nevertheless, no matter how I fuss, don't get disturbed about it because no matter how much I object to the regimentation, it's the thing I'm really happiest doing at the present. With you away, life is incomplete at best and I really am doing something useful so even if I do scream, pay very little attention.

Honey it was simply grand of you to take and print so many of the cemetery pictures...you can't know how very much the family will appreciate them and how much they will think of you for it. I know that isn't why you did it, but they will, nevertheless.

I'm enclosing a copy of my schedule for the next month.

It's tiff too.

Honey darling, it's eight in the evening and I'm actually going to bed...I have never been so fatigued.

Darling, be careful and remember that I love you with all my heart...You are my postwar plan...all my love to you honey,
Jane

Hotel Lincoln on National (US40) Highway
Indianapolis
Letter #83
May 21, 1945

My dearest darling;

You have hardly been absent from my thoughts for a second today-the pictures you sent were so wonderful that they tugged at my heart — especially the one of you alone standing there laughing — just the way you were holding your cigarette brought you so sharply to me. When you've known a person so well for so long — just the look of them in a picture is like home — like a part of you that is away for a little while.

Then that coupled with the fact that I have a haunting worry about you — a constant fear that all is not as it should be — well I've been nearly frantic. Nothing else seems to be of any importance. I may be "mad" but I somehow have a feeling you aren't as safe as I have felt you these last two months — and I don't like it. I have never believed I had any powers of intuition but something something is working overtime — something similar. I only hope that I will be proven wrong.

It is my considered opinion that I had a most unpleasant day. After being away from Mr. Evans for two days — it is brought to me with even sharper clarity that he is utterly unbearable. At this point even my hospital crusading instinct is gone — it has struggled too long — and the only reason I stay is financial — plus the hope that if I do stay a little longer and get into better territory, I will be able to get away under conditions advantageous to me — I've spent far too much money lately and I must re-coup before I can think of changing. So actually I'm counting the days — that's a very unhealthy attitude and I must stop-and start counting my change.

We'll be in Dayton three days as you know, so I'll see Allie-also I'll get in touch with Viv Freihofer and see her in Cincinnati. Poor Viv. Just think, in a couple of weeks, it will be two years since Frei's been home — remember in San Francisco that awful evening when the four of you got on the transport — sponsored by the Commander — I was so determined I was going to keep smiling. And I did — although I've never been so desolate in my life. I'm sure I'd find Indianapolis rather inspiring-had I time to look at it — it seems to be replete with awe — inspiring memorials to this and that — but I just can't seem to get out early enough in the morning and when we return in the evening, it's dark. Darling, there is so little I can say — except that I pray — I really do — that you are safe and well — so please be.

So very very much love to you darling,

Jane

[FIRST PAGE MISSING]
May 20-23? 1945
In Port

I hope there is enough of me in them to keep the picture of my ugly puss fresh in your mind. Not just the physical me either, but remember the mental side too, if you can wade through the mass of bilge I pump out!

Well enough of that. I am awfully glad you liked the bracelet and that it came through. The little bottles you speak of mostly held vitamin pills and emergency battle dressing their version of sulphdiozathl and such. When you wear them both you must vaguely look like something out of Salome, but believe me darling, I'm touched. Couple more things in that Madison letter. I didn't see Don Tesch again, and of course where I am now, it's impossible. In the few minutes I talked to him though he seemed like a very nice gent.

I'm awfully sorry I didn't know he was Martha's Don or I would have gone into more detail about her for his benefit. The other thing you chewed me out for not writing. As I told you in the past few letters, I have been writing now for about three weeks, nothing has yet come forth that I am too proud of so that's the reason you haven't seen any of it. When I finish something that doesn't sound like beginning exercises in "How to be a writer" you will be the first to see it. After all it's like trying to start all over again. Not that I ever could write, but at least I was a little more in practice than I am at present. You know darling, proud as a parent is of junior's first steps he still laughs at his awkwardness. I'm beginning to take me first staggering steps, but I'd at least like to be able to walk across the room before I attempt to show off for you. Your confidence in my ability is very gratifying though my darling, and I hope soon to send you something that might in some small way justify your judgment.

I really do want to write, and I think maybe someday I will be able to. Right now I'm planting the seat in front of the machine and doing my intellectual daily dozen. As soon as the muscles loosen up a bit, I will do a fancy bit of mental show-offing for you! Now do you feel a little better about your old man?

Yesterday we went up for a couple of drinks to our new club. It's very exclusive and limited in membership. Thatched room and very fine drinks. All the exoctic ones, too, daqluiries, martinis manhattans, collin's, frappes, and the — special. I stuck to a few bourbon and waters but I think the next time I go I'll have to have a dry martini and think of me honey. Speaking of clubs, you also seem to think I've been spending a good deal of time there. Well I suppose I do drop over pretty often, but after all it's only open from four to six, so it really amounts to a couple of drinks before dinner. Hardly time enough to get rip-roaring, hell-raising drunk. It is a nice time for talk and swaping of stories of which there are wonderful ones flying about these days. Hardly the kind for light reading, but terrifingly interesting. I'm not going dipso on you darling, just convival.

Well yesterday we met Mason, a guy we last saw nearly a year ago at Purvis Bay. He was on a sister ship and I always liked him a lot. We worked with her for months on end, so we have seen quite a bit of each other in that previous year down there. We had a wonderful talk-talk and got caught up on several mutual friends, a hell of a number who are not with us anymore. We were talking of this and that and all of a sudden he said, "Charley I wish I'd had you with me last night" Yeah, I says, why? "Well, I ran into a little trouble with a Major!!" Yes he was one of us mixed up in L'affaire Colonel in Suva so long ago. Well I asked him if he had ever gotten a copy of that letter, and by golly he has! I'm going to get a copy of it and I'll send one on to you. I am aware that you think that the whole episode is a little ridiculous, but it really is

about the funniest and most talked-of thing that has happened to me in this war. You'll see what I mean when you get the copy. Mase is on a ship that is on duty here and he has access to a car when he needs it, so maybe one day this week he is going to take us on a Cooks tour of the island.

Honey Berk just said that in Allie's letter she said that you had written her and there might be some difficulty about getting together and she and her family are going back to see Mary graduate and she may not be back when you come through. I hope you get together, but if she isn't there Berk would like to have you call his Dad. He says at least you might be able to spend a couple of quiet hours in a house with a decent drink and maybe relax a bit. His dad sounds like a hell of a nice guy. His address is H.C. Berkeley, 619 Oakwood Ave, Dayton 9, Ohio. Telephone WALnut 3651. In the daytime better call him at INLAND Manufacturing Division, General Motors. Sales Manager. Be sure and do this honey if you possibly can. At least be sure and call him and if he is out of town they will be able to tell you about it at the plant.

Just looked at the schedule again and you are in Indianapolis tonight. I remember one time I was there and had two weeks and twenty-two dollars to get back to Seattle on and I made it on time via Louisville, Nashville, Texarkana, Dallas, El Paso, Dago, S.F. and home. That was really hitch-hiking. Also that is where a doc took about six stitches out of my head as a result of a wreck about a week before. Charged me a dollar. Can't even remember his name now, but a right guy.

You still haven't told me when this trip terminates but you did mention ten days in N.Y. in July, so I still can get back in time, if the Gods smile on us. Me, especially. We have a cartload of brass coming aboard tomorrow and then things will begin to hum. In a very little while we should know the best, or the worst. At least activity!!! God be thanked for that.

I spect I'd better hit the sack so I will be pretty in the early morn, so goodnight my adorable darling wife. I love you better than the best, moster than the most, and forever and ever and ever!

All me love —

XXX Chas

Hotel Seelbach
Louisville Kentucky
May 25, 1945 Letter #85

Hello my lobster colored darling, and you must be all the time with the amount of sun you're getting — trying to tell me that it turns to tan immediately. Remember me honey — I'm the person who put all those vinegar packs on you year after year. You may be on the other side of the world but things haven't changed that much.

Well, here we are in the land of the Blue Grass and the Kentucky Derby. So far the grass is green and we'll miss the Derby. But we will be here over Sunday and I'd like to see Churchill Downs anyway — knowing me I probably won't — not that I haven't the desire but there is always so much to do just to keep going and this week will be the first Sunday for a month that I haven't been travelling. It does have a certain air about it though. I saw several people in the lobby who distinctly resembled Colonels. As far as mint juleps are concerned, I haven't ordered any yet. I ordered a Martini before dinner and they don't know how to make them.

You know honey I'm seriously considering having my hair put back to its original color because I'm getting tired of being so spectacularly blonde. Of course it's fun sometimes to have people whistle and all and I suppose I am better looking this way but everything I do, everybody thinks I'm so darned sophisticated — it makes me mad. Then too I do look older — which is silly to care about because I'm not ancient yet. Of course it may be better for my work but then again it may not be. In any case, I shan't do anything until I hear your opinion on the subject. The only thing that bothers me is that I might lose my carefully nurtured, confident, blonde personality. What do you think?

Darling, when we arrived today, there were two letters from you. They, thank heaven, allayed those awful fears for you that I'd been having the last few days and gave me so much hope for the near future — oh honey!

But one thing they did do which wasn't necessary. They kept apologizing for the letter before them. Honey I understand that out there with a lot of time to think, you get all sorts of peculiar ideas for a day or so and I don't take them seriously aside from the fact that they make you unhappy. So there's no necessity to apologize my honey. Just remember I love you — that's all I ask — I'm hoping for the birthday present of your presence but I'm not even daring to hope too much.

What a God — awful day this has been — especially after yesterday. We left Indianapolis on the nine o'clock train — the dirtiest yet — debris actually permeating the air. The only seat I could find was over the wheel so I curled up on it and slept for four hours accompanied by the clang, clang, jiggeldy clang of the wheels. The show due to the fact that everyone was tired was slow — not too slow but just enough so I didn't like it. Tell Berk honey that I wrote to Allie telling her when I would be in Dayton and that I so hope to see her. I also wrote to Viv Freihofer and will write to Rita Kellison.

Oh cripes honey — tomorrow I have to go out and spend more money! I need a bag, shoes and hat in the worst way so the only thing to do is go get them.

When I started this job I thought I'd put so much money aside but I haven't been and I just don't seem to be able to. There are such gear demands on it. Of course the allotment goes untouched but the rest just seems to disappear. Hotels, restaurants — cleaning is a major item and the wardrobe demands are something awful. One reason for that is that it's so darned hard to get your cleaning done — and you always have to be dressed up. It's awful, and when I get to New York, I want to be in good shape in case I could put any irons in the fire — and things are so darned expensive now — not to mention my tastes. I curse myself but I don't know what I can do about it.

Honey, I'll send as you asked the grave pictures to the family. The additional ones of you today I loved — but I wish you could send me more just of you and you alone. I never tire of looking at them.

I'm so happy you liked the candy. It was specially packed for overseas. I'll have to write that place and see if I can't get some more. Most candy melts so but this really looks like a deal.

Well, my sweet darling, I think I'll say goodnite now. I love you honey,

All me love,

Jane

#53
26 May, 1945
In Port

I guess I might as well admit that I am more than a little stewed at this writing. Before you go to the extent of acknowledging that your husband is a drunk, may I add one clarifying factor? Today I found out that the good old ship Gamble would be no more. But for sure.

Whatever becomes of the human elements of the situation, one basic fact remains. These kids that I helped grow up from seaman second to Chief Gunners' Mates are going to be dissipated. The associations that have bloomed and fostered for nearly two years, like them or not, officer friends are going to disappear.

Whatever happens to us, the ship is going to be no more. I know that in the midst of your hectic life that doesn't mean a hell of a lot, but when you think of the trouble we went to save what was left of her — I don't know doesn't seem to be a way to explain it. Even while we fought to save her, we all knew that it was impossible. Still the official word that it was a wasted effort sort of stopped us. I guess the best way to put it is that we lost a friend today.

I'll write tomorrow and make a fine fat cheery letter out of it. This stinks, but I have already told you that I am drunk.

You know, darling, right up till now we always thought that she could be fixed. When you find out that she can't be, it comes as a kind of a shock.

Please forgive me for being drunk, and know that I will write you tomorrow. Never forget that I adore you, my darling! All me love — Chas

#54
27 May, 1945
In port

Honey my darling:

Oh brother! I wish I could have seen your face when you got that letter (if it could be called such) that I wrote last night. Believe me darling, I wasn't as drunk as the letter looked. I know I'd had a few, but that was the most horrible example of typing I have ever seen. Well maybe you got a laugh out of it, and that's something. What a character, crying in his beer, ah well, so goes life.

I guess maybe if I explained how come so drunkie it might be interesting. Well yesterday we took some of the officers from the ship next-door up to the little club we belong too. It was very pleasant and we had a few drinks and much interesting talk. Then who shows up but our old Buddy Mason. He had his command car again and when the club shut up he said he could take us on a party if we would like to go. Just Berk and myself. Well we said a party was our dish, so we take off. It was way up at the other end of the island and Mase was a little drunk and his usual unskillful self in the driving, so it was well spiced. There was a wonderful moon so we got a good look at that end of the island.

Well the party was being given by a bunch of Army Artillery-men and what a set-up they have! A great big native-built club. Two large rooms, one with tables and a bar and the other *with* a bandstand and a few little tables around the edge of the dance floor. Yes I said dance floors! Well we were welcomed with open arms and I really mean it. Seems they are so far out that very few of us Navy vultures ever get to one of their shin-digs. They had a wonderful spread of buffet supper and — hold your breath — what seemed to be dozens of female white women! I guess really there was about twenty-five or thirty and only about forty men. That's the best proportion I have ever seen out here anywhere.

We got there about eight and it lasted until eleven. I actually danced with about four different gals and all In all had a nice time. They began flooding us with drinks, and after a terrific battle Burke and Mace and I indulged in several. Also there was the Colonel of the outfit there, but rest easy darling, we got along beautifully. As a matter of fact he bought me several drinks and I guess I spent nearly an hour at the bar with him talking of this and that. Naturally we were the ones to close the place up. Well we got out to the car and I guess I said boy I am really hungry now and the others agreed so we walled back into the club and were trying to make a sandwich by the light of lighters when all of a sudden the light flipped on there stood the Colonel!! "Well boys" he says "hungry?"

It was really funny as hell. I told him that it was such good chow and we had gotten to thinking about all that lovely food just sitting there etc. And darned if he doesn't say "well I'M glad you boys liked it so well, help yourself and turn out the lights when you leave!!!" A regular gent, no fooling. We made a couple of dogwoods and then Smiley found an old pan and we loaded it up with potato salad and coleslaw so all the way back to the ship we spooned in the salad. When I got up this morning and went to the ice box for a drink, the sight of that half empty bowl of cold potato salad almost finished off what was left of me.

Well that's the story of our first "date" out here. Naturally we didn't make much time with the gals, being as their steady boy-friends were always in the immediate background, but it was sort of a breath from another world. Real live women!! Hard to believe. You know, darling, I don't know about you, but my sex life has been, and will continue to be, nil. But it certainly is present. The old urge I mean. Thinking back, it doesn't seem that it ever got this bad last time, and here I've only been gone five months! Maybe it's the memory of those last few out-of-this-world days in the U.S. Grant. Long will those days live in my memory as the highlight of all our somewhat variegated martial relations. Hope I haven't been too outspoken me pet, but that old sex is certainly a wonderful thing!! I think I could give you a bad time for a while, but I guess it wouldn't be long at that!!

Well from my somewhat beery letter you must have an idea about my future. We are still hoping for a reassignment in a more home-like atmosphere, like say, S.F. Some think we will, and a lot say we won't, but I am still hanging on to the thought, and I really believe we may make it at that! You say your prayers and I will be a cinch!

Our movie tonight was "None But the Lonely Heart" I couldn't help but remembering the day we saw that in S.F. Remember that horrible hangover and all the oysters and Olympia beer at the RKO Grill? You were wonderful that day darling. You gave me no sympathy, but neither did you bawl me out. I think maybe you did feel just a little sorry for me at that; how about it? Must say I enjoyed the thing more tonight than I did then. Course the company wasn't half as charming, but I could see the screen and the actors a hell of a lot better! Barry Fitzgerald certainly did a bang-up job in that, remember?

You know, darling, looking back at those three months, even with the bad moments, there were some awfully nice ones and some that were just plain out of this world. Things like "Charles of Taylor" sort of balance out the night you threw the frying pan at me and broke the handle! And coming in that door wheezing with those damn ladders and you would say "Chuck?" and then I would hold you in my arms and kiss you and breathe that wonderful smell about you. Always seemed that you had just stepped out of a shower and into fresh clothes that had been hanging in the sun. Things like that even overbalance the bad minutes like the night in the Fairmount when you said yes, you had enjoyed your illicit love life! That was when my heart went right through my shoes and down eight floors to the arcade in the basement. On the other hand remember the fresh strawberries for breakfast and large pots of coffee, and Charley the old chef keeping it hot in the little pot with the aid of the spirit lamp? Honey, we are so damn lucky having a lot of things to remember. I don't care how happy people are, they all have their bad moments and times when they are at each other's throats, but one thing I'm damn sure of is that when we have our good moments, they are way and beyond other people's! I also know that I have grown up a lot in the three years I have been in the Navy and that I don't think I am ever going to consciously make you unhappy with me or our life again. I may not be the best husband in the world, but if working at it, and at making a success out of myself will help, then I'm going to be well on my way.

Just seeing those girls last night made me really conscious of just how much I miss you, and now I am not talking of the physical side at all. Darling, if I could just hold onto you for a moment it would certainly take the damn old jumps out of me. You are without doubt the best kisser in this world among other things. Do you begin to get the idea, butch?? I'm really crazy in love with my own wife! Ain't it appalling?

Well the war news out here look very good in spots, and not so good in others. The B-29's damn near burned the town down according to Tokyo Rose, but on the other hand those little Banzais crunched into another eleven of our ships yesterday. I'm afraid that means a lot of kids will never make it down Tokyo Blvd. on VJ day. Hope I can keep ducking until that great day. Understand they are getting short of silver anyway, so that's something in my favor.

I had a wonderful letter from you yesterday, well it was pretty short, but as you had been filing all mine that night, but in it you assured me that you still had love in your heart for me, so ipso-facto, it was a wonderful letter! The radio is just playing "Always" "I'll be lovin' you always, with a love that's true, always. Not for just an hour, not for just a day, not for just a year, but always" That certainly says it neatly all tied up in a convenient bundle ready for mailing doesn't it?

In the same mail came that big card from The Latin Quarter. Thanks honey, it was sweet of you to think of it and you are right, it recalled the Bal Tabrin very clearly. Remember we even danced pretty well together that night. Not what you might call first-class, but for us — sensational! Oh memories, damn me eyes, they are really flooding over and around me tonight.

This morning had a sweet letter from Mary, and for her quite a volume. She told me about making some nighties that she might use on her honeymoon, if and when, and she said that Hazel had stopped her from putting a zipper in the side so that she could slip off a brassiere after she hit the sack. Then Haze told her about the bride that lined the bottom of her nighties with fur, to keep her neck warm!! My my, I just happened to think of you in that black Magnin deal. You'd better be saving that one and the short-shirted deal for a guy I know, fellow named Flynn who might be popping in on you one of these fine days.

Well ducky it's midnight, and the old sack calls. I'll dream of you honey cause you're adorable and I love you like the dickens!!!!
all, all me love punkin — Chas
P.S. I am still hitting the typewriter.
P.P.S. I got weighted today — 204 — Exercise best I can.
I L-O-V-E Y-O-U!

Letter # 86
May 27, 1945
Louisville, Kentucky

Dearest honey;

Here I am in a seersucker dress, sitting in the green grass in the city park — Louisville, Kentucky — after a month nothing but rain, summer has suddenly come upon us and it's delightfully hot. I've just been reading the fine long letter I received from you in your new location-where it is I haven't an idea except that it seems to have taken you only a day to get there — so it must be Teman — and if it is there's a Commander Rex Ritter — I believe it's the 107th Seabees — he's in command of. He's Dorothy Fey and Tex's cousin and he was in Honolulu. He was instrumental also in getting us down to the Gilberts and the Marshalls. Then when we were on Kwajallien he came over from Bennet Island part of the atoll and took us over to do a show for his Seabees. You know all those pictures you have of us on that island eating and cleaning mess kits and on the dock and that one of the audience-I'm in that sort of shorts and skirt combination, well he sent them to me — He's really a fine man — about 45 years old — and those Seabees would do anything for him. As a matter of fact I believe there's a picture of him in one of those groups — Well I wish you'd look him up and introduce yourself if that's where you are — you'd really like him — and he's done some fine work — as is attested in the letter you just wrote in your letter. So do please honey.

About the money. I can't get a check of that size cashed very easily so I'll write Hazel today and have her send it to you. We have an arrangement whereby she can write checks so she can pay the storage bills and anything else that comes up. So if you should get back in San Francisco and need money — all you have to do is wire her and she could wire it to you more easily than I could — faster I mean. I regret to say that I haven't built up the bank account to the proportions it was last time — it was down to about $200 when I started working and the demands on me have been much greater but after the next couple of weeks, I should be able to save more. Then I hope to get more money after July. This is of course contingent on your plans — rather the Navy's plans for you.

I hardly dare hope that after all these false alarms, something wonderful like you coming home might be going to happen. I'm just trying to keep calm about it but the prospect of seeing my honey again sends delighted tingles down my spine — and the look of ineffable happiness which comes over my face when I plan such a meeting literally causes people to ask what marvelous thing I am thinking about.

Darling, I did appreciate your telling me the resolution about the bourbon for fun and not for escape business. Under abnormal circumstances it is only natural — but it is inclined to make one exaggerate things and eventually instead of escaping from things, one magnifies them so that one arrives at an impasse. To my mind that can destroy the happiness of any companionship, married or otherwise faster than anything else. To be perfectly honest, I will confess it has bothered me — so it's nice to know it won't any more. And that's enough of that. All will be wonderful.

With that last honey — Pat and Rollie — persuaded me to go to a movie with them — it was the first one I'd seen in months and I thought it might do me good. I find that they still make me slightly restive and it was interesting — "The Affairs of Susan" — it was light and well done — Dan de Fore had one of the leading parts — he shared 3rd billing with Dennis O'Keefe — he was awfully good — sort of harnessed the old charm — brought it under control so to speak. But the most interesting part was an air force picture of the first B-29 raid on Tokyo — it was really fine — and think what it has grown into now — headlines that Tokyo has been demolished — yesterday I kept thinking — these are the men that Chuck went to the parties with — Chuck went up from there — they even had a picture of the Colonel of whom you spoke who had been the Captain of the Memphis Belle.

Then they had the pictures of the Franklin. They were really remarkable — taken right at the time. Gosh, I'm glad you weren't there, honey. I was just thinking honey — I can't find his address. It wasn't the Franklin that Ivan Manning was on — was it?

Well darling — here's hoping for a personal birthday present and a swimming pool on the way —

So darned much love to you, Jane

May 28, 1945
Louisville, Kentucky
Letter # 87

Dearest darling;

Cripes I am disgusted. I just spent the better part of two hours repacking stuff and it's still a horrible mess. I just haven't enough suitcase room for all the junk and most of it can't be worn anyway. I had Hazel send me the clothes from last year and now I'm going to have to send them back because I hadn't realized they were too faded to wear. I guess standards in Honolulu weren't as high because none of them fit very well. There it didn't matter. My gosh there's a white gabardine dress that I wore to a party with seven generals and now I look at it, it isn't fit to wear to a ward. The ravages of time and cleaning and inferior materials I suppose. This clothes problem is rapidly becoming the most irritating thing in my life — it's getting so hot and light clothes get dirty so quickly and the buses are so filthy and if you don't look as if you just stepped out of a band box, they raise the dickens! Damn, damn, damn! I know it's silly to get upset but gosh I had an idea for a story when I was riding home tonite and do you think I had time to put down a word of it — no damn it — there's too much washing and ironing and the bags have to be in the lobby in the morning. Well a person just can't expect to do too much I suppose.

Well enough of this screaming. Allie called tonite. She was so unhappy because she will be gone to her sister's graduation at the time I will be in Dayton. It was awfully sweet of her to call and we'll make arrangements to meet later. Tell Berk I am to call his father.

Well darling the blonde saga is over for about a year. The unsteady bleaching has been just a little too hard on it and it's breaking — the hair I mean — like mad. The hairdressers tell me that the only thing to do is put it back to its own color

And let it grow out — since I'm really afraid to bleach it again — I'll have it done in the morning.

I'm quite confident that I won't lose the new personality it has given me-I'm not so confident that my value as an M.C. will be as great but then it wouldn't be with no hair either. I will just have to compensate for it with good quality work, a feeling that carries over the foots of friendliness with the audience — and a sexy walk. So here's hoping.

I'm going to say goodnite now honey. That old clock creeps around so fast.

All me love, Jane

#55
30 May 1945
In Port

Dearest Jane;

You will no doubt be surprised to get this letter written in pen, but there by hangs a tale.

First though let me get to the letter I got from you this morning. It was the one written when you were coming back from Oklahoma! (not the play, the state.) To say that my heart stopped thumping as I read would be literally true. Then a subconscious of my mind kept trying to tell me that you never would be giving me all the grim results unless they had been proved to be unfounded. However, I will admit that I was awfully relieved when I actually read that all was ok.

Commander Stevens has proved himself to be a real friend. I just can't tell you how happy and grateful and relieved I am all at once. You see I was getting a little perturbed. Last letter I'd had from you was on the 15th, then that card from Chez Paises on the 18th, but other people had mail up through the 21st and the 22nd from the east coast. I remember I said a little prayer that I hoped you were just too busy to write and not that you were ill.

So you liked Mrs. Stevens and their nipper. Maybe I was reading too much between the lines but it sounded like you might like to have another shot at one of our own. Course you know how much I would love that, but on the other hand, first there remains the getting back to a decent life after we finish off the Japanese. I'd be most awfully happy, though, to cooperate fully on any such production scheme! And I do mean happy.

Now about the pen. I tripped over some line coming across the ship alongside in the dark last night and in falling I seem to have badly sprained my little finger and the one next to it. I've been soaking it today per the Doc's instruction but it's still pretty sore. Should be all ok though in a couple of days. Things are moving towards the decision point quickly now. A few days should decide what happens. I'm still praying for Uncle Sugar, but it's still in the lap of the Gods.

Well honey I know this is not much of a letter but my hand is beginning to get pretty sore so I'd better knock off. I'm so damn happy that all is well with the internal Jane for you see darling I happen to be that big lug who loves you!

All me love
Chas
I'll try to write in more detail in the next
One for luck!

Letter #88
Danville, Kentucky
May 30, 1945

Dearest honey darling;

What do you think — I received a letter from Viv today in reply to mine saying I hoped to see her and Frei is home — He arrived in San Pedro in March — she went out — oh heck I'll enclose the letter — The trouble is now I won't be in Cincinnati — If it weren't so complicated I'd go down from Dayton over Sunday and see them but it's about 130 miles round trip and I'm tired and while I'd love to see them it probably would be too complicated.

Well I slept through a hundred and something miles of Kentucky today — if I don't watch out, I'm going to miss the whole state — although today I did follow the Memorial Day parade right to the cemetery and saw the services — It was a very touching bit of Americana — just like in the movies — the band from the army hospital and the young local reverend pronouncing the invocation and the President of the local college making the address. Not to mention the veterans of other wars marching firmly along behind the solders. And the old houses along the way — mellow and worn — and trees forming a canopy over them. Sometimes I rather enjoy staying in the small towns.

My goodness the days do pass somehow. Before I know it, I am three or four days behind in my Day Book — then soon I have to sit down and spend hours catching up on a whole week. So far I've been very faithful though and it's going to be a pretty good record. I wish I had always kept one — the years go and there is only a vague memory.

Incidentally darling — you are no longer married to a blonde — but a very dark brunette and darned if it doesn't look just fine. I'm going to keep it a little darker than my hair was before. It's really just fine. I'd been so worried about it — so now I'm happy.

I'll say goodnite now my sweet —

All me love,

Jane

Danville, Ky Letter #88
June 1, 1945

Well, Darling — the beginning of another month and in six days it will be our five months anniversary — (not to be vulgar, but I truly have been a very nice girl, too) That is nearly half of the year we were counting on and who knows — perhaps before another month we shall have a very pleasant surprise — a happy, happy homecoming — oh, darling, I do hope so.

What do you think, honey — I talked to Frei and Viv last nite. They were in Dayton, which is perfect, as I am not going to Cincinnati but am going to Dayton tomorrow so they'll call and I'll see them there. If I see them tomorrow nite, my darling, we'll have about five big drinks for you — and hope that you'll be able to do it in person soon. Frei said that they heard about the Gamble just as they were coming into Pearl, and he was nearly frantic until he found out that you were alright — he said he understood your trouble was someplace in the engineering department. Perhaps he will be able to tell me more about it when I see them. I forgot to enclose the letter, so here it is in this one.

We've had a delightfully easy schedule these two days — only theatre shows — but so depressing. This hospital is all psychoneurotic cases — some of them really bad ones — These poor kids are just lost in the fog of utter confusion and helplessness. It's tragic. You struggle to find some way to make them smile — to bring them out of it, even for a few seconds, and when you do, the reaction is more often than not, an hysterical thing that flashes for a moment and is gone. Perhaps this is almost the worst result of war.

Last nite, honey — we went to a carnival at the edge of town. Pat and Rollie and I — we strolled through the straw covered grounds and listened to the barkers — pitched pennies — shot at packs of cigarettes saw the "Mean Mad Mystic" sitting in the midst of snakes — rattlers and adders — and for once in my life — I rode everything — It's a wonder I'm here to tell the tale — They gave us passes to everything because we were in a USO show — Made the rides especially long — it was a child's dream of fairyland and I had a good time, too.

Sweet darling — it's eleven thirty and I have to get up at six so I'll say goodnite, my honey —

So very much love, Jane

1 June 1945

Dearest Honey:

Hold onto your hat! I just got orders back to the states for reassignment! Yippee!!

Looks almost for sure like I will be coming surface, so it will be a few weeks yet. I hope there is some way you could postpone the Europe deal for a bit. At any rate, one recent letter said you would have ten days in N.Y. in July. At least we can have that together.

I don't know if I'll be able to get off another letter or not. I might leave very soon, in fact it looks like right away, so if there is a long pause without letters it means I am a 'comin'!

Look, honey, be sure Jack knows where you are and I'll contact him when I get in and then fly to you — and I mean fly!!

Honey, honey, I love you like the dickens and I'll see you right soon — Gad, what a wonderful thought!

All me love —

Chas

Western Union
NA17 NL PD=PORTLAND ORG 3
JANE FLYNN=
MIAMI HOTEL DATN=

WIRE RECEIVED TODAY FROM CHUCK SAYS ARRIVING
PACIFIC COAST COUPLE WEEKS CAN YOU POSTPONE OR
CANCEL EUROPEAN TOUR SEE YOU SOON LOVE CHAS=
   J P PATTEN.
   6/4/45

★ PHOTOGRAPHS ★

O'Neil Girven Logging Camp in Washington State, where Gentie and Ed first lived after they were married.

Chuck and Gertie (1918).

"Personal Appearance" at the U.W. Penthouse theatre (1935).

Chuck's photos from Germany (November 9, 1935).

Charles Flynn (wearing his "nifty German leiderhosen") with Phillip Durr in Seville, Spain (1936).

Bicycles Through Europe and Africa, But Charles Flynn Finds Nw. 'Swell'

By FERN BAGLEY

He skied in the Bavarian Alps, studied German in Munich, hitch-hiked in the Emerald Isles, toured museums in S p a i n, traveled in northern Africa—and now Charles Flynn is back in town and thinks that after all, the Northwest is a pretty good place.

But the amazing thing about it all is the gypsy journey in which young Flynn bicycled 3,500 miles about Europe and northern Africa.

Not at all the weary traveler who "comes home to these hills," Charles, better known as "Chuck," gives an enthusiastic account of his trip, which is one of those things so many people dream of doing, but so few actually do.

Charles Flynn, who is the son of Mr. and Mrs. E. M. Flynn, 1321 Grand avenue, is a student at the University of Washington, where he will return next fall to complete his senior year. He is a member of Phi Gamma Delta fraternity.

This young gentleman, who forsook the ranks of amateur traveler to become a globe trotter of no mean degree, and Peter Dix of Seattle, a University of Washington graduate, flew to San Francisco last August and embarked on the Norwegian fruit freighter Berganger.

Their first stop was LaHavre, France, and then Antwerp, Belgium, w h e r e they disembarked, boarding a train for Munich. Here the boys entered the University of Munich, where they studied German. Late fall and w i n t e r in Munich found them jaunting about the country on week-end hikes and ski trips.

In Munich y o u n g Flynn met Phillip Durr, a Harvard graduate, and who next year will be assistant professor of history at Harvard. The two left Munich the day before the Olympic games started, and as the thousands of visitors were crowding the city.

They traveled by train to Italy,

stopping at Florence and Venice. From there they went to Sicily, bicycling around the western end of the island. A steamer took the travelers to Tunis, Africa, where they began a 700-mile b i c y c l e jaunt across to Algiers, Algeria, Africa. Here the inns and hotels were few and far between, and Flynn tells an intersting story of a 16-hour ride which took them until 10 p. m. to find a place to stay.

By steamer F l y n n and Durr went to the Balearic Islands, off the East coast of Spain, and then to Alicante. Here the rolling stones turned east, and then south to Gibralter. Then they crossed the country lengthwise, taking a train across the Pyranese to France from San Sebastian. O v e r the French border, they bicycled into Paris—500 miles in six and one-half days. One day they traveled 115 miles.

Two weeks in Paris and then

(Continued on Page Two)

From the Everett Herald (1936).

Hazel and Jane at two months, at Patten Lumber Mill, Elbe (August 14, 1918).

John, Mary, and Jane in Seattle, Washington (1924).

Rotogravure SECTION   **The Seattle Sunday Times**   SEATTLE, Washington   *November 27, 1938*

U. of W. Co-Eds Graduate to Hollywood

AMONG the score or more former University of Washington drama students who are storming (with a high average of success) the cinema citadels of Hollywood, are the four girls pictured here

THE SKILLFUL hands of Bill Madsen, Hal Roach make-up expert, prepare the face of Roseanne Coyle, daughter of Mr. and Mrs. William J. Coyle of Seattle, for the camera, while the three other girls wait their turns.

Jane Patten Gets RKO Role

Jane Patten, former University of Washington coed, and a daughter of the Patten lumber family of Seattle, had never been a bridesmaid—until she became a screen "find."

For the newest addition to the RKO Radio contract roster makes her film debut in that role in "Cross Country Romance," featuring Gene Raymond and Wendy Barrie, according to word received here yesterday.

When she was assigned the role, the pretty brunette confided to studio officials that she had never been a bridesmaid in real life for at least two reasons.

One, she said, was because she accompanied her father on most of his extensive travels in managing her grandfather's lumber interests. Another was because of the tendency of the society girls of today to forego elaborate formal weddings in favor of small private ceremonies attended only by immediate families of the couples.

The Seattle girl won a scholarship in high school to the Cornish School of drama, specialized in literature and dramatics at the Uni-

FILM BRIDESMAID—Jane Patten, pretty Seattle brunette and latest R.-K.-O.-Radio Pictures "find," who makes her film debut as a bridesmaid in the Gene Raymond-Wendy Barrie costarring feature, "Cross Country Romance."

Seattle Sunday Times (November 27, 1938).

Chuck and Jane admiring a playbill for "Personal Appearance,"
Hollywood (1938).

Jane and Darryl F. Zanuck (in the background).

Chuck, in Hollywood, working at the typewriter that he later brought to the Pacific Honeymoon cottage (1938).

Chet Huntley in Hollywood (1938).

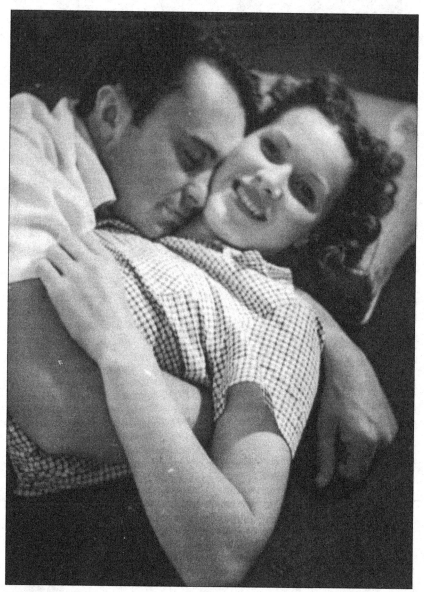

Will Price and Maureen O'Sullivan, Honeymoon cottage (1938).

Jane and Chuck in a Beachwood studio production (late 1930s).

Chuck in the movie Ski Patrol *(Universal, 1940).*

Jane at RKO (early 1940s).

Chuck in A Girl, A Guy and A Gob *(RKO, 1941)*

To the Flynns
With all my Irish Love
from
Maureen
Xmas '39.

22630-16

Maureen O'Sullivan.

Jane (top right) in Cross Country Romance *(RKO, 1940).*

Jane in a publicity photo (1940).

*Chuck on the Cornell campus with some new friends. Left to right:
John Martin, Charles, Sears Madson and Bob Lebner. (Winter, 1943).*

*Jane and Gideon with Chuck's commanding officer, Officers Training
School, Cornell (Winter, 1943).*

Jane's picture (which explains why all the men are smiling. Chuck is half-left of center, slightly ahead of the second group.

Jane, Chuck in uniform, and Gertie after Ed's funeral, Everett, Washington (Spring, 1943). He died from pneumonia incurred after falling in the water during a log rolling competition.

Jane, Chuck, and friends looking at Chuck's orders in San Francisco (September, 1943).

Jane at Nina's, Hollywood Hills (1943).

Jane, in costume.

Eloise Hardt and Jane in the chow line on Makin Island (Summer, 1944).

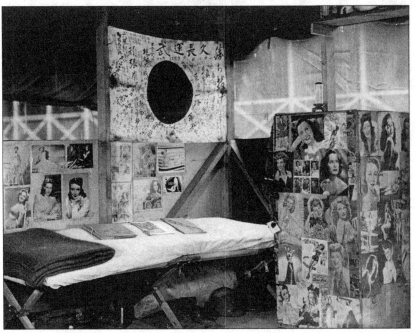

Someone's bunk, Fort Derussey, Oahau (Summer, 1944).

Kwajalein Island (Summer, 1944).

Jane and Martha on Kwajalein Island (Summer, 1944).

Dorothy and Jane tour Island X.

"Island X." The men are mixing concrete to make imprints of the girls'
hands. Jane is helping while smoking a Camel and wearing one of
Chuck's bracelets.

The canvas-covered stage on on Bennet Island. They performed in the middle of a rain storm, and had to change the couch three times (Summer, 1944).

"To Jane from Maurice Evans..." Pictured with Eloise Hardt. (Fall, 1944).

Officers of the Gamble.

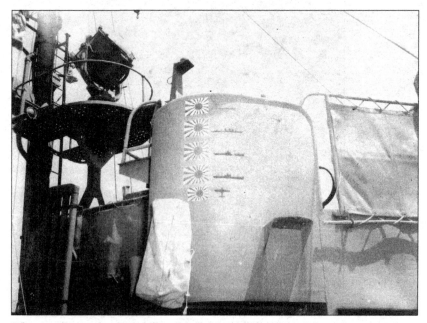

The smokestack of The Gamble, showing a tally of four Japanese ships and one plane.

The Gamble leaving San Francisco (December, 1944). It would be the last time.

The Gamble in Saipan, having suffered bomb damage (1945).

The USO Troupe in front of a bomber (Summer, 1944).

Chuck with fellow officers at the Officer's Club in Saipan (Spring, 1945).

Chuck and fellow officers at the Saipan Officers Club (1945).

Chuck's friends, the "fly-fly boys" in Saipan (Spring, 1945).

The tour company with their awful manager, Mr. Evans (not to be confused with Captain Maurice Evans of the Pacific Tour). Left to right: Janie, Jacque Lee, Pat Walker, Barbara Rockland, Donna Rockland, Soo Linn, Gibouti, Penny Carolle, Lynn Carlisle, Joyce Oliver, and Rollie Wray.

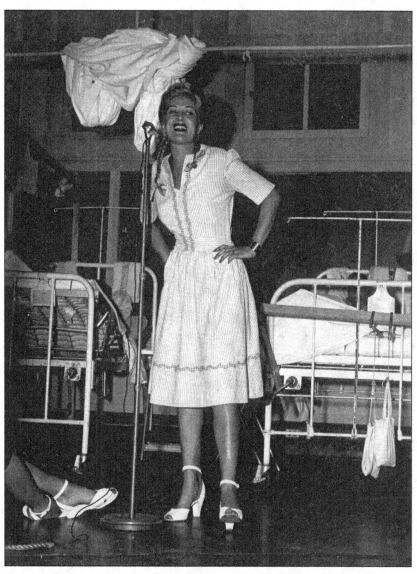

Jane as the emcee on the Hospital Tour (1945).

A portrait of Jane and Chuck after both had returned seperately from the Pacific (Winter, 1944).

★INDEX★

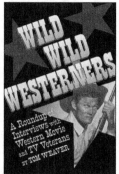

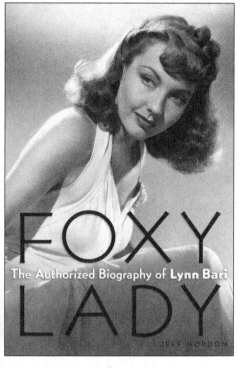
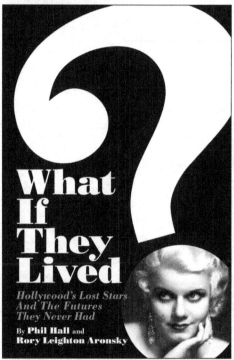

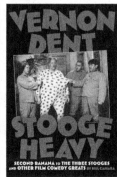

CPSIA information can be obtained
at www.ICGtesting.com
Printed in the USA
FSOW04n1118080117
29247FS